HISTORY OF GAGE COUNTY, NEBRASKA

A NARRATIVE OF THE PAST, WITH SPECIAL EMPHASIS
UPON THE PIONEER PERIOD OF THE COUNTY'S HISTORY,
ITS SOCIAL, COMMERCIAL, EDUCATIONAL, RELIGIOUS,
AND CIVIC DEVELOPMENT FROM THE EARLY DAYS TO
THE PRESENT TIME

VOLUME I OF II

HUGH J. DOBBS

Published by Left of Brain Books

Copyright © 2021 Left of Brain Books

ISBN 978-1-396-31973-0

First Edition

All rights reserved. No part of this publication may be reproduced, distributed, or transmitted in any form or by any means, including photocopying, recording, or other electronic or mechanical methods, without the prior written permission of the publisher, except in the case of brief quotations embodied in critical reviews and certain other noncommercial uses permitted by copyright law. Left of Brain Books is a division of Left of Brain Onboarding Pty Ltd.

Table of Contents

PREFACE	1
CHAPTER I The Discoverers	3
CHAPTER II Territory of Louisiana	14
CHAPTER III Nebraska Up to 1866	27
CHAPTER IV Gage County	39
CHAPTER V Old Clay County	47
CHAPTER VI Topography of Gage County	53
CHAPTER VII Flora and Fauna	63
CHAPTER VIII The Public Domain	73
CHAPTER IX The Pioneers	83
CHAPTER X	96
CHAPTER XI First Actual Settlers	119
CHAPTER XII Narrative of Major Albert Lamborn Green	127
CHAPTER XIII First White Settlers	165
CHAPTER XIV Founding of Beatrice	175
CHAPTER XV Narrative of Mrs. Julia Beatrice (Kinney) Metcalf	186
CHAPTER XVI Founders of Beatrice	196
CHAPTER XVII A Roll of Honor	230
CHAPTER XVIII Narrative of George Gale, with Biographical Sketch	260
CHAPTER XIX Growth of Beatrice from Beginning to 1870	286
CHAPTER XX Beatrice Continued	301
CHAPTER XXI Beatrice Continued	331
CHAPTER XXII Beatrice Concluded	362

CHAPTER XXIII BLUE SPRINGS	392
CHAPTER XXIV WYMORE	409
CHAPTER XXV INCORPORATED VILLAGES	427
CHAPTER XXVI UNINCORPORATED VILLAGES	458
CHAPTER XXVII COUNTY OFFICES AND OFFICIALS	465
CHAPTER XXVIII HOSPITALS	480
CHAPTER XXIX MILITARY HISTORY OF GAGE COUNTY	489
CHAPTER XXX THE BENCH AND THE BAR	505
CHAPTER XXXI PEOPLE WHO HAVE DONE THEIR PART IN MAKING GAGE COUNTY (PART I)	539

Very Truly Yours,
Hugh J. Dobbs

DEDICATED

This volume is affectionately dedicated to the memory of my parents and to the memory of the other pioneers of Gage county, living and dead, whose heroism called the county into existence and advanced upon its rolling prairie wastes the lines of civilized life.

PREFACE

This volume is divided into historical and biographical matter. For the former I am wholly responsible, but for the latter my responsibility is limited to a few biographical sketches—less than a dozen out of hundreds—the remainder having been prepared under the supervision of the Western Publishing and Engraving Company of Lincoln, Nebraska.

The chief value of the historical part of this book lies in its fidelity to facts. It is not claimed, however, that all has been set down that should have been written for a work of this character nor that the narrative is as complete in every instance as could be desired. Time and the limitations as to volume, imposed by my contract with the publishers, have both combined to set bounds to my work. Whatever faults the critical may discover in the following pages, this much can at least be truthfully said of this History—it constitutes an earnest effort to give both to the subscribers and the public, a readable and reliable history of Gage county, something that has not hitherto been attempted.

I am under personal obligations to many for assistance in the preparation of this history. Particularly do I wish to acknowledge my indebtedness to A. E. Sheldon, secretary, and Mrs. Clarence S. Paine, librarian of the State Historical Society, Lincoln, Nebraska; William Elsey Connelley, secretary of the State Historical Society of Kansas; Hon. Charles H. Sloan, congressman of the Fourth congressional district of Nebraska; Major A. L. Green, Mrs. Charles F. Gale, Earl Marvin of the Beatrice *Daily Sun*, Mrs. Anna R. Mumford, William R. Jones, and Mrs. Oliver Townsend, Beatrice; John A. Weaver and J. B. High, of the register of deeds office; Mrs. Mabel Penrod, county clerk, and F. E. Lenhart, clerk of the district court of Gage county; Mrs. Minnie Prey Knotts, Lincoln, Nebraska; Mentor A. Brown, Kearney; Mrs. Maud Bell, Tecumseh; A. D. McCandless and Charles M. Murdock, Mrs. Elizabeth Porter, Wilber; Mr. and Mrs. F. M. Graham,

William Craig, and Robert A. Wilson, Blue Springs; Homer J. Merrick, Adams; Miss Evelyn Brinton, Pickrell; Theodore Coleman, Pasadena, and Miss Benetta Pike, Los Angeles, California; Mrs. Lilian P. Scoville, San Juan, Porto Rico; Dr. James P. Baker, St. Louis, Missouri; Mrs. Julia Beatrice Metcalf, Portland, Oregon; Joel Thomas Mattingley, Condon, Oregon; Louis Laflin, Crab Orchard; Hon. Peter Jansen, Andrew S. Wadsworth, Leonard A. Emmert, Clarence W. Gale, Beatrice; Robert H. Baker, Chicago; W. H. Brodhead, McKay, Idaho; and James H. H. Hewitt, Alliance, Nebraska.

I desire to express my sincere appreciation to the many subscribers to this volume who by letter or otherwise have shown a kindly interest in the work.

Very respectfully,

HUGH J. DOBBS

Beatrice, Nebraska, August 7, 1918

CHAPTER I

THE DISCOVERERS

CHRISTOPHER COLUMBUS — ENGLAND AND FRANCE — FRENCH EXPLORERS AND MISSIONARIES — ROBERT CAVALIER DE LA SALLE — THE NEW WORLD — LOUISIANA

Nothing in human history exceeds in romantic interest the discovery and settlement of the New World. The first voyage of Columbus from the shores of Spain across the unknown waters of the Atlantic ocean, which the superstition of the times invested with every sort of mystery and danger, must always appeal to the imagination as an act of superlative daring—an event of first importance in the progress and happiness of mankind—for he, by adventuring where others dared not venture, by a single act revealed to the astonished gaze of Europe the existence of new lands of wonderful beauty and promise, where none were believed to exist; and, at a blow, dispelled forever the ignorance and fear which hitherto had enslaved the mind and paralyzed the endeavor of the most favored and most intelligent portion of the globe.

Columbus set sail from the port of Palos on the 3d day of August, 1492, with a fleet of three small vessels, the Pinta, the Santa Maria, and the Nina. He was accompanied by the tears and lamentations of the entire population of that small port, most of whom had relatives abroad the ships, and who, as the winding of the shore hid the little fleet from sight, abandoned all hope of ever again seeing the adventurous mariners alive. On board those small caravels the crews themselves, as the distance from the shores of Spain daily increased, were seized with fear and unrest, which greatly endangered the success of the expedition. But the confident Admiral held firmly to his course and pointed the prow of his flag ship steadily toward the west. The sea was smooth, the air soft and refreshing, nature herself seemed unusually propitious toward this momentous and daring enterprise. Soon the frail vessels came within the course of the trade winds and, with a constant and favoring breeze, the little squadron made rapid headway. Occasionally the crews sighted floating weeds and other objects which seemed to indicate the near presence of land and which served to cheer their spirits and invigorate their flagging zeal. On, on, on they sailed, day and night, always toward the west. Uneventful weeks passed without sight of land, but on the night of October 11, 1492, Columbus, who was stationed on the high cabin of the Santa Maria, saw at a distance across the water a faintly gleaming, uncertain light. Few of his crew were encouraged by this sign, though Columbus himself regarded it as a certain proof of the vicinity of land. At two o'clock on the morning of the 12th day of October, 1492, the little Pinta, which from her superior sailing ability was leading the other vessels, fired a gun, the agreed signal in case any of the ships should in the night time discover certain indications of land. The little squadron instantly lay to, eagerly awaiting the dawn. At last daylight slowly broke, and at a short distance the voyagers beheld a green and marvelously beautiful island, lying in a sapphire sea. It was San Salvador, the outpost of a newly discovered world. To their intense surprise, the Spaniards found this island densely populated by perfectly naked savages, so kindly disposed and unsuspicious as to regard the newcomers as gods whom they were inclined to worship. Accompanied by the principal persons of his expedition, Columbus, richly attired, was rowed to the shore. Falling upon their faces, the party kissed the earth and gave thanks to Almighty God. Then unfurling the banner of Spain over this patch of land, Columbus took possession in the name of his sovereigns, Ferdinand and Isabella. A few days were spent in sailing the waters about this island, and having gathered from the natives that, toward the southwest, gold was to be found in lands of yet more surpassing beauty, Columbus, on the 24th day of October, 1492, turned his prows in that direction. On the fourth day of his voyage he beheld the noble shores of Hispaniola, now Cuba, rising out of the ocean before him. Charmed to ecstacy by the mildness of the climate, the beauty of the scenery, the gorgeous plumage of birds, the docility and intelligence of the natives, and the sunlit sea in which Cuba rests, queen of the waves, the soul of the great Admiral glowed with pride and satisfied ambition. He gave up his days to the luxury of his surroundings and to exploring the northern coast of the island, and on the 5th day of December, 1492, having passed the eastern extremity of Cuba, he saw toward the southeast, looming out of the ocean, a new island—high and mountainous, Hayti, the most beautiful and most unfortunate of all the West Indian islands. Here, freed by the softness of the climate and the wonderful fertility of the soil, from toilsome labor, he found a native population that passed its days in indolence and repose. Having lost the Santa Maria by an accident of the sea and being deserted by the Pinta, commanded by Pinzon, Columbus now resolved to begin his homeward voyage. Departing from Hayti January 4, 1493, after a most perilous voyage, guided by the hand of Providence, on the 15th day of March following, he again cast anchor in the little harbor of Palos. He left Spain poor and unknown, he returned rich with honors, having gained the right to have his name forever first on the roll of discoverers, as well as that of those who by greatly daring, greatly achieve.

Columbus carried with him to Spain several natives of the islands, together with products of the soils of these new lands, notably tobacco, coffee, and potatoes, with fruits and spices, as evidence of his discoveries. The great and unusual honors bestowed upon him by the proudest and most powerful court of the world, with the graphic report which he was able to make to his sovereigns of his wonderful voyage and the marvelous possibilities suggested by his discoveries, electrified every portion of the globe where civilization had obtained the slightest foothold. Fired partly by religious zeal, partly by love of adventure and thirst for fame, and partly by the commercial incentive to discover and open an all-water route for trade between Europe and the East Indies, the maritime nations of western Europe joined enthusiastically in voyages of discovery to the western hemisphere.

Columbus himself continued in the great work of discovery till he had added to the memorable voyage of 1492 three others to the New World. Island after island rose out of the depths of the ocean before him. But in none of his voyages did the great discoverer touch either of the

American continents. Ignorant of the vast extent of the ocean, he imagined that he had reached only the threshold of India and that he was upon the point of realizing his lifelong dream of an open, all-water route to Cathay—land of jewels and spices. With feverish energy he sought the one factor which alone, as he supposed, could give value to his priceless discoveries. But gold was rare in those islands, fanned by the great trade winds, and yielding only bloom and fruitage, heaped as by magic upon the bosom of the Atlantic.

On his third voyage, in 1498, Columbus came upon the large island of Trinidad, which lies off the coast of South America, near the mouth of the Orinoco river. Cruising about this island, he found to his surprise that the waters of the narrow strait that separates it from the main land were sweet and fresh, and gazing westward he beheld what he conceived to be the low-lying lands of a yet larger island extending twenty leagues or more along the coast. Never dreaming that these fresh, sweet waters were those of a mighty river that drained a continent and the low-lying lands the eastern edge of that continent, he sailed away to Hayti to visit a colony which he had founded there on his second voyage, in 1496. From this visit he was sent to Spain a prisoner in chains, and he died at Valladolid, May 20, 1516, poor and neglected, old and broken, at sixty years of age, already robbed by Americus Vespucci, an obscure adventurer, of the honor due to his memory, of bestowing his own name on the great New World which his genius and faith had disclosed to mankind.

In a material sense, the net result of his four voyages of discovery was to add to the known portions of the earth those groups of archipelagoes in the western Atlantic which are collectively known as the West Indies, and which, sweeping in a wide curve from Florida to the mouth of the Orinoco, screen the Caribbean sea from the gulf of Mexico and the Atlantic ocean—islands of ravishing beauty, marvelous fertility, delightful climate, teeming with the products of nature.

But who shall ever be able rightly to weigh the tremendous influence of this simple-hearted man upon the physical and mental horizon of the world? The people of all western Europe by the middle of the fifteenth century had so far emerged from the "Dark Ages" as to be measurably free from the forms of government which had characterized the feudal system, and for the first time since modern Europe had arisen from the fragments of the Roman empire its governments were in the hands of able rulers, while national policies had displaced government by individual whim or caprice. It was the age of the Renaissance and the revival of learning. The world was undergoing the process of a new birth. The foolish superstitions and practices which had prevailed for centuries under the forms and guise of religion were rapidly passing away. A universal activity and zeal for the cause of learning had aroused mankind to a sense of its needs. France, England, Spain, Portugal, were rapidly assuming the dignity and self-importance of empire. In the very midst of this tremendous activity and of these vague longings and dreams of national aggrandizement, came Columbus home from the voyage into the unknown, with almost incredible tales of golden islands beyond the furthest rim of the western sea. The vast evolution which was rapidly bringing freedom to mankind throughout western Europe had already prepared maritime nations to a large extent for the discovery of a new world, and, as if by the intervention of Providence itself, this great event was made to serve as an outlet for their highest ambitions.

It is foreign to the aim and purpose of this history to narrate in detail the great work of discovery, exploration, and colonization of America which followed its discovery by Columbus. We know that for years Spain led the other nations in the number, extent, and value of her enterprises. In less than forty years after the death of the great Admiral, she had established her hold on the West Indies by right of discovery, and had grasped by the bloody hand of conquest Mexico, Central America, the isthmus of Panama, the isthmus of Darien, and the continent of South America—a domain which in natural resources rivalled continental Europe, and which for unbroken centuries poured a golden stream into her national treasury. In addition to all this, she claimed Florida by right of its discovery, on Easter Day, 1512, by the aged cavalier, Juan Ponce de Leon, sailing in search of the fountain of perpetual youth, and she laid claim also to the basin of the Mississippi, on account of the discovery of that historic stream by Hernando de Soto, in 1541, and its exploration in part by him and the wandering remnant of his followers after he had sunk to rest in its mighty flood. With more or less definiteness, Spain asserted for centuries proprietary rights in the whole of North America, on account of the achievements of Columbus and those Spanish navigators who followed him.

But her rivals, and particularly England and France, were quick to perceive the tremendous possibilities involved in the possession of lands in the western hemisphere, where at almost a single bound and at a trifling cost in money and life, national wealth, national resources, and territorial dominion might be immeasurably increased.

Thus it came about that in 1498, when Columbus, looking westward from the island of Trinidad, saw the shores of South America, Sebastian Cabot, sailing under a commission from Henry VII of England, discovered and explored the eastern portion of North America from Labrador to Cape Hatteras, thereby affording ground for England's claim to all portions of the continent of North America from the middle shore of the Atlantic ocean to the crest of the Alleghany mountains.

Francis I, King of France, early in the sixteenth century, turned his attention to discovery, exploration, and colonization in the New World. In 1524 John Varrazani, a Florentine in the service of France, sailed from the shores of Europe with four vessels, in search of an all-water route to Asia. Directing his course nearly to the west, on the 7th of March he discovered the main land of the continent, in the latitude of Wilmington, North Carolina. He explored this coast from one hundred and fifty miles south of Wilmington to the remotest point of New England, reaching Newfoundland in the latter part of May. In July he returned to France and published an account of his wonderful voyage, which attracted wide attention, but ten years were suffered to elapse before another effort was made to repeat his experiment. Beginning with 1534, French navigators, aided by their government, flocked across the Atlantic, explored the eastern coast of the great northern continent, circumnavigated Newfoundland, entered the gulf of St. Lawrence and ascended the noble St. Lawrence river. They founded scores of towns, including Port Royal (now Annapolis, Nova Scotia), Quebec, and Montreal. French adventurers, trappers, hunters, penetrated the wilderness to the Great Lakes; black-robed French missionaries preached the gospel over wide areas to savage tribes by lake and stream far into the interior. No fairer pages of history can be found than those which record the exploration and settlement of New France, as the French possessions in North America came to be known. From the early part of the sixteenth century to the latter part of the seventeenth century, this work went continually forward. It was closed by the rediscovery of the Mississippi river by Joliet and his companian, the heroic Jesuit missionary, Father Marqette, in 1673, and by the exploration of that mighty stream from the Illinois to its mouth by La Salle, in 1682.

The name of Robert Cavalier de La Salle will be forever spoken with respect by every man who is at all conversant with his daring and adventurous achievements. No more conspicuous name adorns the annals of colonial history in North America. Amidst the vacillating and shifting policy of Louis XIV and his ministers with respect to the French possessions in the New World, where much was promised and little done, La Salle, with the prevision of genius and great statesmanship, saw more clearly than any other man of his race that the road to empire for France lay in the lakes, rivers, savannahs, and wildernesses of North America. Not only was the prevision of empire his but he possessed also the imagination to conceive and the power and will to put into execution the plans which should have been the colonial policy of France from the first. La Salle was a Norman, born at Rouen in 1643; he was educated by the Jesuits, with whom he spent ten years as a student and from whom he acquired a habit of rigorous abstraction. Abnormally reticent about himself and his work, he made few close friends and many bitter enemies. He was persistent, active, determined, and brave to a fault. In 1660 he left France for Canada. By that time the French possessions in North America had become known to the world as New France and comprised the entire basin of the St. Lawrence river, the Great Lakes region, Labrador, Nova Scotia, New Brunswick, and that part of Maine lying in the basin of the St. Lawrence. To the vain and licentious Louis XIV New France offered but a small and unpromising field for the display of his glory and power and the gratification of his ambitions. It cost money to colonize, defend, and develop the distant province, and Louis was wasting his resources and exhausting the nation in desolating wars with England and the Holy Alliance. He had at last been prevailed upon to send to New France, in 1672, the ablest and most disinterestedly patriotic of all French governors, Count Louis de Frontenac, who, like La Salle, foresaw the approaching struggle for the continent between Protestant England and Catholic France, and was, like him, gifted with the prevision of empire in the New World.

On arriving in Canada, La Salle settled on an estate nine miles below Montreal, on the St. Lawrence. Here he came in contact with roving bands of Iroquois, who told him of a mighty river, far to the west, which rose in their country, flowed westward and he who followed its course for nine months, entered a wide sea. They called this river Ohio, meaning probably to include with it the Mississippi from the mouth of the Ohio to the gulf. La Salle pondered this important information. Like other explorers, he was imbued with the idea of discovering an all-water route to India; and he argued that the discovery of this stream might enable him to reach the Pacific, whose waves he knew in their far course broke on the distant shores of Cathay. With a few Franciscan monks, known as seminary priests, and some men at arms, with the aid of Frontenac, he organized an expedition to explore the region of country west of the Alleghanies, drained, as he believed, by the river described by the Iroquois. Little is known of this venture into the wilderness beyond the fact that the expedition reached the Ohio and descended its course as far at least as Louisville, Kentucky. In 1670 we hear of La Salle again wandering amongst the forests that border the Illinois and exploring the region drained by that stream, but again he stopped short of the great river.

Fort Frontenac had been erected near the outlet of Lake Ontario, on its northern shore, and here in 1678, La Salle was in command of this, the most advanced military outpost of New France. In this environment this remarkably grave, solitary, thoughtful man ruled with absolute authority over a wide region of country. His days were spent amongst the Indians, half-breeds, traders, trappers, voyageurs, and couriers de bois (rangers of the woods), harkening to their strange tales of the wilderness and prairies, of river and lakes, Indian tribes, and the wild life of the woods and plains. Slowly, slowly, he matured the great design of uniting by a bold stroke these unknown and unexplored wildernesses to New France, thereby laying the foundation for a French empire in the New World. La Salle knew that Joliet and the black-robed priest Marquette had in 1673 rediscovered the Mississippi river under Indian guidance, by following the course of the Wisconsin, and had paddled down the great river as far as the mouth of the Arkansas, leaving the question of its ultimate termination still in doubt. By some of his associates it was thought that the Mississippi flowed into the Pacific ocean, others that it discharged its waters into the Atlantic, and some that the gulf of Mexico received its mighty flood. The determination of this vital question was in La Salle's mind the first step toward empire. Resigning his command at Fort Frontenac, he applied for a commission from the king to explore the vast unknown region lying south and west of Canada and the Great Lakes, but such were the difficulties and hardships which he encountered that four years expired after receipt of his commission before he was able to undertake the great adventure. In February, 1682, with a small fleet of canoes, and accompanied by about thirty Frenchmen and a band of Indians from western Canada. La Salle descended the tranquil Illinois. His course was impeded at first by floating ice, but at Peoria lake he struck clear water, and on the 6th day of February, 1682, the small flotilla of canoes issued upon the bosom of the mighty Mississippi.

Without a moment's hesitation, the canoes were pointed with the swift current and the momentous voyage which was to determine the course of the Mississippi was begun. The party floated and paddled rapidly down its current, traveling only by daylight. Day by day they drifted swiftly, almost silently, toward unknown destinies. Slowly the mysteries of the New World unrolled before them like a scroll. The winter passed into spring, and in the bright sunlight and drowsy atmosphere they saw the tender foliage clothe again the wilderness. They passed numerous Indian villages, some of which they visited, and where they occasionally spent the night. Not infrequently they encountered Indians in huge war canoes, but, avoiding all hostile encounters, they drifted on and on toward their objective—the month of the Mississippi. They noted the steady trend of the river, through dense forests, swampy cane-brakes, wild-rice fields that lay along the shore, ever toward the south. Doubt finally dissolved into certainty: they knew that it led on through semi-tropical lands to the heaving billows of the gulf of Mexico. On the 6th day of April, 1682, exactly two calendar months since they had embarked on the river, they reached its delta, where its mighty flood divides into three channels. Directing D'Autray to follow the east-most channel with some of the canoes, the Count Heury Tonty the middle channel. La Salle himself descended the western passage. Slowly paddling down these waterways, they noted soon the odor of brine in the freshening breeze and suddenly before these keen-eyed voyageurs the tumbling billows of the gulf of Mexico came into view.

Proceeding along the marshy shore, La Salle picked up one after another the canoes of his party and, assembling his followers on a dry spot of land a short distance above the mouth of the river, he caused a column of wood to be made on which he inscribed the following:

"Louis the Great, King of France and of Navarre, King.
April 9th, 1682."

Then marshaling his men at arms, amidst the fire of musketry, the shouts of "Vive le Roy" and the chanting of the Te Deum by the priests, while the Indian braves and their squaws looked wonderingly on, La Salle planted the column in its place. Standing near it he then in a loud voice delivered a proclamation, of which the following is part:

In the name of the most high, mighty, invincible and victorious prince, Louis the Great, by the grace of God king of France and of Navarre, Fourteenth of that name, I this ninth day of April, one thousand six hundred eighty-two, in virtue of the commission of his majesty which I hold in my hand and which may be seen by all whom it may concern, have taken and do now take, in the name of his majesty and of his successors to the crown, possession of this country of LOUISIANA, the seas, harbors, bays, ports, adjacent straits and all the nations, peoples, provinces, cities, towns, villages, mines, minerals, fisheries, streams and rivers within the extent of the said LOUISIANA.

Thus the great basin of the Mississippi river came under the scepter of Louis XIV, the most dissolute monarch of Europe, and thus at the word of a single daring explorer, standing on the lonely delta of that great river, the territory of Louisiana, out of which came Nebraska, was called into existence, a territory which comprised vast and unknown regions of dense forests, rich savannahs, sunbaked plains, apparently limitless prairie, watered by a thousand streams, peopled only by savage Indian tribes, the abode of buffalo and other wild denizens of the forest and plain; a territory which stretched from the pure springs of the far north whose confluent streams form the source of the mighty Father of Waters, to the hot marshy borders of the gulf of Mexico, and from the low-wooded crests of the Alleghanies on the east to the river of palms, the bold, naked peaks of the Rocky mountains and the sources of the Missouri of the west.

The New France of Robert Cavalier de La Salle and of Frontenac, comprising Canada, Nova Scotia, New Brunswick, the region of the Great Lakes and the territory of Louisiana, has long since been lost to its founders, but the memory of that glorious empire planted in the wilderness of North America, with incredible hardships and labors which only men of heroic mo'd could have endured, still survives to animate the souls of the thoughtful and the hearts of the daring.

CHAPTER II

Territory of Louisiana

As Part of New France — Attempted Settlement by La Salle — His Assassination — Effect of Extension of New France to Mississippi Basin — France Loses Her Colonial Possessions in North America — Retrocession by Charles V — American Opposition — Jefferson and the Treaty of Ildefonso — Jefferson's Aims Concerning Louisiana and the Mississippi — Threat of Alliance with England — Alarm of Napoleon by Threat of War — Livingston Admonishes Talleyrand — Arrival of Monroe — Cession to the United States — Price — Population — Ignorance of America Concerning New Purchase — Explorations of Lewis and Clark

The history of Nebraska may properly be said to begin with the voyage of the heroic La Salle in 1682. An historical sequence of events leads the mind steadily forward from his discoveries till, by well defined processes of differentiation and elimination, a point is reached where the commonwealth of Nebraska stands forth clearly defined in the mighty sisterhood of states which comprise the North American republic.

In a comparatively short time after its discovery the vast territory of Louisiana became linked to Canada and the other French possessions in North America as an integral part of New France. This process was begun and carried forward by men animated by the desire to realize the ideal of its discoverer, which aimed at nothing less than a great interior French empire, composed of the most fertile lands in the world. The New France, as fashioned by the vision of La Salle, was to be yet fairer than the old, as the daughter will sometimes be fairer than the mother. The work of reclaiming the wilderness was first carried on by French traders, trappers, hunters, and wood rangers, who extended their activities over the greater portion of the Mississippi basin, extending south to the gulf of Mexico and west to and including Texas. Where these went the Jesuit and Franciscan monks followed, preaching the pure and gentle religion of the lowly Nazarene to the savage tribes who inhabited these wildernesses and plains.

The earliest effort to establish settlements in the new territory was made by La Salle, himself, in 1684. Shortly after his return from the long voyage to the mouth of the Mississippi he repaired to France, and was supplied with three vessels, including a ship of the line, and a body of troops and emigrants, for the purpose of establishing a colony and erecting fortifications to guard the great river from English and Spanish aggression. But he missed the mouth of the Mississippi and sailed westward to Mata Gorda bay, Texas. Dissension arose between him and the commander of the war vessel that accompanied him, and La Salle, leaving the ships with a few of the emigrants and men at arms, temporarily established his headquarters at that point and began a search for the Mississippi. Failing in his quest, he, in 1686, undertook to penetrate the wilderness to the Illinois, where Tonty had been directed to remain with supplies and men. While prosecuting this venture this remarkable man fell by the hand of an assassin. Others took up the work of settling New France and occupying at least the lower basin of the Mississippi river; as a result of which New Orleans was founded in 1723, by Jean Baptiste Lemoine, sieur de Bienville. Settlements were made also in the Ohio valley and elsewhere in the wilderness west of the Alleghanies, so that by the middle of the eighteenth century a chain of forts and military posts had been planted by the French from Quebec along the St. Lawrence, the Niagara, the Detroit, the Illinois rivers, and the Mississippi river and some of its tributaries, to the bay of Biloxi, on the gulf of Mexico, while the region of the Great Lakes was guarded by similar outposts of defense. Such settlements were accompanied by the orderly forms of government, supported by the military forces of Canada and France, in the hope of guarding and defending from English aggression on the east and Spanish aggression on the south and west, the most valuable and extensive colonial territory ever possessed by a single European power in North America.

The extension of New France to the basin of the Mississippi river from source to mouth and westward from the heights of the Alleghanies, had the effect of setting metes and bounds to British possessions in the New World. Bitter and implacable rivalry arose between the English and French colonists, and bloody attacks and reprisals blur the annals of both Saxon and Gaul. Britain's claim of all North America from ocean to ocean by right of Cabot's discovery, and the stout resistance by the French to this claim, were the main causes of that series of sanguinary conflicts known in English colonial history as the French and Indian wars, which, beginning in 1690, with what is known as King William's war, raged with great fury and finally terminated at the close of the Seven Years' European war, in 1763, thirteen years before the commencement of the American Revolution. By treaties which marked the closing of these wars, striking changes were effected in North America. By the treaty of Utrecht, in 1713, which marked the close of that colonial disturbance sometimes designated as Queen Anne's war, England made her first great inroad into French territory. By this treaty she obtained control of the valuable fisheries of Newfoundland, together with possession of Hudson bay, Labrador, Nova Scotia, and minor French possessions; and at the close of King George's war, in 1763, under the treaty of Paris, Canada itself and Cape Breton were ceded by France to England, with their territorial appendages, and the western boundaries of the English colonies were pushed beyond the Alleghanies to the eastern shores of the Mississippi river. Thus fell, as by a single blow, the dream of empire which had animated the soul of the courageous La Salle, and of which Count de Frontenac also had dreamed, and thus was laid the foundation of the vast colonial possessions of England in the New World.

Nothing remained to France of her proud colonial empire in North America except that portion of La Salle's discoveries which lay west of the Father of Waters and which had come to be designated in France as the province of Louisiana; all else had been swallowed up by her ancient rival, England. Even Louisiana passed immediately from her control, for on the very day of the execution of the treaty of Paris by which she was shorn of Canada and Cape Breton, she entered into a secret treaty with

Spain, under which the last fragment of the empire of Frontenac and La Salle passed to that country. Thus by the acts of a weak and licentious sovereign, the land of Clovis and Charlemagne was stripped of every vestige of her rich colonial possessions in the New World, and thus ended the struggle for a continent between the two most enlightened nations in western Europe.

But the tragedy of Louisiana was not yet played to the end, nor indeed could be until its destiny was fulfilled. Its cession to Spain increased her colonial possessions in North America, till, with Mexico, they covered nearly half the continent. Whatever secret understanding may have existed between her and the court of Louis XV as to the retrocession of Louisiana in the future, Spain entered into possession of her new province shortly after the treaty of Paris in 1763, hoisted her national emblem at New Orleans, city of Bienville, and, amidst the tears, protestations, and lamentations of the French inhabitants, established her authority over the province, which was to continue to the opening year of the nineteenth Christian century. During these forty-five years of Spanish rule in Louisiana province, most marked changes had taken place in France itself. The monarchy had fallen, the French Revolution had terminated, and an effort had been made to establish a republic, which ended in what is known in French history as the "Consular Government," with Napoleon Bonaparte as First Consul and as such the chief officer of state.

On October 1, 1800, a treaty was entered into between Charles IV of Spain and the consular government, whereby Louisiana was retroceded to France, entire, as respected its former boundaries. Peace had temporarily settled over Europe and Napoleon looked forward to a period of continued national prosperity, wherein he conceived it possible to realize, at least in part, the dream of the unfortunate La Salle. But the ink on the parchment whereon was written the treaty of Ildefonso was scarcely dry when a portentous war cloud suddenly obscured the rising sun of peace, wherein England, aiming at empire, threatened to involve France in another terrible conflict. Actual transfer of possession of the province to France was necessarily delayed and before it could be accomplished the news of the retrocession had reached the United States. The Spanish governor had rendered himself obnoxious to this country on account of certain trade restrictions affecting navigation on the Mississippi and by refusing at New Orleans what was known as the right of deposit.

It had become apparent that the expansion and growth of the United States demanded free access to the gulf of Mexico through the Mississippi. In this country it was understood too that by the treaty of Ildefonso France had obtained also what was then known as the Floridas, thus gaining control of the entire course of the great river to the gulf. Agitation was at once started having for its object the cession by France to the United States, of New Orleans, the Floridas, and that portion of the lower Mississippi basin which reached from the city to the Floridas. The settlers of the western states and territories bordering on the river, particularly those of Kentucky and Tennessee, which had suffered most from the unjust restrictions of the Spanish governor of New Orleans, were greatly excited and were angry to the point of desperation over the proposed extension of a single European power to the entire length of the great river. Resistance was urged to the point of seizing the lower Mississippi, with New Orleans, before the transfer of territory could be effected. In their petitions to congress the settlers declared: "The Mississippi is ours by the laws of nature, it belongs to us by our numbers and the labor we have bestowed on those spots which before our arrival were barren and desert. Our innumerable rivers swell it and flow with it to the Gulf of Mexico. Its mouth is the only issue which nature has given to our waters and we wish to use it for our vessels. No power in the world can deprive us of this right."

On February 13, 1803, Ross, a senator from the state of Pennsylvania, introduced a resolution in the United States senate directing the government to seize the port of New Orleans. It was seconded by Gouverneur Morris, of Revolutionary fame, then representing the state of New York in the senate. It was announced that volunteers from the Mississippi valley were ready at a word to carry this resolution into effect if sanctioned by congress. But the President, the able and prudent Jefferson, restrained this movement as dangerous to the peace of the country, and, preferring to achieve results by diplomacy rather than arms, he set before himself the task of acquiring the lower Mississippi basin by peaceful rather than by violent means. He first aimed to prevent if possible the cession of Louisiana to France and to exact from Spain recognition of the right of the United States to the unrestricted navigation of the Mississippi. As an alternative, in case of failure, he proposed to form an immediate alliance with Great Britain. Writing to Robert Livingston, our minister in France, the President says:

There is on the globe one single spot the possessor of which is our natural and habitual enemy,—the day that France takes possession of New Orleans fixes the sentence which is to restrain her forever within her low-water mark. It seals the union of two nations who in conjunction can maintain exclusive possession of the ocean. From that moment we must marry ourselves to the British fleet and nation.

This threat had been most effectively dangled by our minister to France before the eyes of the First Consul and from the moment of receiving these instructions Mr. Livingston was able to speak in a tone that arrested Napoleon's attention, and aroused in him a sense of a new power beyond the seas. A year had gone by since the secret treaty of Ildefonso had come to the knowledge of our government, and Mr. Livingston had apparently made but little progress. In the Spring of 1803, at Jefferson's instance, James Monroe was dispatched to France as special envoy and minister extraordinary to assist him in adjusting the irritating questions with respect to Louisiana and the Mississippi— questions which had sprung so suddenly into prominence and which were hourly becoming more menacing to the peaceful relations between France and the United States. Even yet the instructions to both ministers did not contemplate the acquirement of the whole of the territory of Louisiana. The most that was hoped for apparently was free navigation of that river for American commerce. To secure this, however, it was proposed that we purchase New Orleans and the Floridas from France, under the erroneous assumption that she had acquired the latter from Spain; and, by proper treaty stipulations, secure to both nations the right to free transportation. Not knowing the full terms of the treaty of Ildefonso. Mr. Jefferson instinctively felt that whatever they were they deeply concerned the United States, and he considered the moment had come to settle forever every question of policy or territory which might in the future occasion dissension with France. With clearer vision than any man of his day, Jefferson foresaw the tremendous advantages of removing every obstacle to the expansion of our country beyond the Mississippi. Guided by an instinctive prevision, he purposed to seize the moment to acquire control of that great stream and secure forever an unobstructed passage to the gulf. Failing to achieve this result by peaceful means, he determined to accomplish it by force, and when Monroe set out for France he carried instructions to demand the cession of New Orleans and the Floridas to the United States, and consequently the establishment of the Mississippi as a boundary between the United States and Louisiana. Mr. Livingston had already apprised Napoleon that such a demand would be made and the First Consul had considered it of sufficient weight to detain the armed expedition which was about to sail for Louisiana.

But the rapid march of events was working more powerfully in the interests of the American republic than any influence the government itself was able to exert. At almost the very moment the existence of the treaty of Ildefonso became known, came the portentous threat of war with England; and Napoleon feared that because of her superior naval power and the defenseless position of Louisiana, England was bound to deprive France of that province and yet further augment her power and prestige in the western hemisphere. There were other considerations which impelled the consular government of France to hearken favorably to the representations of Mr. Livingston. On the retrocession of the great province to Spain, and while the terms of the treaty were still a secret, in order to be in a position to defend Louisiana from a convenient base against aggression from whatsoever source, Napoleon had dispatched an army, under General LeClerc, to San Domingo in 1802. This was partly for the purpose of crushing the negro rebellion then at its height in that island and partly to have an army within striking distance of Louisiana.

But LeClerc was defeated by Toussaint l'Ouverture, and his army had been so decimated by war and disease that it had become ineffective as a military force. Besides these considerations, the increasing expense and difficulty of maintaining the power of France in Louisiana became every day more apparent to Napoleon and his advisers, while like a nightmare the haunting threat of Jefferson of an English alliance loomed before his vision.

By a strategic diplomatic movement as distinctive of his genius as any on the field of battle, the First Consul determined to defeat the arch enemy of France in its aggressive policy and at the same time with bands of steel bind to France the rising young republic of North America, whose ultimate destiny he foresaw was to dominate the western hemisphere.

The existence of the treaty of Ildefonso became known to Livingston in 1802, and in November of that year, learning that Napoleon had planned to send an expedition, under General Victor to take possession of Louisiana, on behalf of the United States he submitted a definite offer to purchase New Orleans and the Floridas, leaving to France all the great territory lying west of the Mississippi. The reticence of both Napoleon and his chief minister of state, Talleyrand, with respect to the representations of our government, and the secrecy with which the terms of the treaty was guarded, led our minister to suspect designs against the United States itself. He warned Jefferson of his fears and advised the prompt strengthening of the military forces of the country in the lower basin of the Mississippi. A winter had passed without action on Livingston's offer of purchase, but Napoleon still delayed taking possession of Louisiana. Spring approached. Mr. Monroe was known to be on the high seas, hastening to the assistance of Livingston. His arrival was momentarily expected. But Napoleon, having reached a final conclusion, acted with the celerity that characterized all his movements. Returning to his palace at St. Cloud from the religious services on Easter Sunday, April 10, 1803, he called into consultation Decrés and Marbois, two of his most trusted advisers, and asked their opinion on the subject of the province of Louisiana. In the discussion which followed, he said:

I know the full value of Louisiana and have been most desirous of repairing the injuries to their country of the French negotiators of 1763. It has been restored to us by a few lines of a treaty. Now we face the danger of losing it. No doubt the English will seize it as one of their first acts of war. Already they have twenty ships of the line in the Gulf of Mexico. Its conquest will be easy. There is not a moment to lose in placing it beyond their reach. They have successively taken from France the Canadas, Cape Breton, Newfoundland, Nova Scotia and the richest portions of Asia. They shall not have Louisiana. While nothing can compensate us for its loss, it may be disposed of in such manner as ultimately to redound to our advantage.

The patriotic Decrés eloquently opposed the proposal. "France," he said, "needed colonies, and what colony could be more desirable than Louisiana? The navigation to the Indies by doubling the Cape of Good Hope had changed the course of European trade and ruined Venice and Genoa." And then, with prophetic vision, he asked, "What will be its direction if at the Isthmus of Panama a simple canal should be opened to connect one ocean with the other?" "The revolution which navigation will then experience" he declared, "will be still more considerable and the circumnavigation of the globe will become easier than the long voyages that are now made in going to and from India. Louisiana will then be on the new route and it will be acknowledged that this possession is of inestimable value.

. . There does not exist on the globe a single port, a single city susceptible of becoming as important as New Orleans."

Marbois admitted the gravity of the situation but supported the view of Napoleon. No conclusion was arrived at, but at daybreak the following morning Marbois was summoned to read the dispatches from the French minister at London. These indicated that war was imminent and rapidly approaching. After considering the purport of this intelligence, turning to Marbois, Napoleon said:

I renounce Louisiana. It is not alone New Orleans that we will cede, but the whole colony, without reservation. I know its value and I abandon it with the greatest regret. But to obstinately endeavor to retain it would be the height of folly. I direct you to negotiate this matter at once with the envoy of the United States. Do not wait for the arrival of Mr. Monroe. Have an interview this very day with Mr. Livingston. I shall require a great deal of money for the approaching war, but will be moderate. I want fifty million francs for Louisiana.

Pending the arrival of Mr. Monroe, Livingston, despairing of success and weary of delay, on April 12th admonished Talleyrand that when Monroe arrived, he intended to advise his government to abandon the negotiations and seize New Orleans by force. On that very day came Mr. Monroe, and on the 13th day of April, while at dinner with a company of friends, the two ministers observed Marbois walking in the embassy garden. On being invited to enter, he stated that he had important information to communicate, but would delay doing so until he could see the representatives of the United States alone. Mr. Livingston sought him out at the first opportunity and was startled upon being informed that the entire territory of Louisiana was at the disposal of his government. In the negotiations which ensued, the demand of Napoleon's ministers for one hundred million francs as a consideration for Louisiana, was gradually reduced till an agreement was reached, and on April 30, 1803, a treaty was signed by our ministers on behalf of the United States of America, and by Francis Barbe Marbois, the financial minister of France, on the part of that country, by which, in consideration of the payment of fifteen million dollars, the equivalent of eighty million francs, the territory of Louisiana passed to the republic of the United States. The consummation of the treaty was accompanied by no illusions on the part of the signatory parties. On the contrary they were fully aware of its import and tremendous importance. When it had been signed, Livingston, rising from the consultation table, said: "We have lived long, but this is the noblest work of our lives. From this day the United States takes their place amongst the powers of the first rank; England loses all her exclusive influence in the affairs of America." And Napoleon, showing his full appreciation of the importance of the event, exclaimed: "This accession of territory forever strengthens the power of the United States. I have just given England a maritime rival that will sooner or later humble her pride."

The patriotic and far-seeing Jefferson lost not a moment's time in securing the ratification of this treaty. As soon as it was received on this side of the Atlantic, he issued a call for a special session of congress. That body assembled on the 17th day of October, 1803, and within a month the treaty was ratified and authority conferred upon the President to take immediate possession of the newly acquired territory. To enable him to do so, he was empowered to employ the army and navy of the United States, and, if in his opinion necessary, he was authorized also to enroll the militia of the several states to the number of eighty thousand men, to enforce and secure our country's right to the ceded territory.

But no opposition was encountered to the surrender of the possession of the great purchase. France herself, on December 17, 1803, first procured its surrender from Spain, and on Tuesday, the 25th day of December, three days thereafter, Governor W. C. C. Claiborne, of Mississippi territory, having been commissioned by the President to assume the provisional government of Louisiana, appeared at the gate of New Orleans, escorted by General Wilkinson, with a small detachment of state militia. The party was greeted by a salute of twenty-one guns from the forts, and entering the city it drew up on the square known as the Place d'Arms. The ceremonies attending the formal presentation of Claiborne's credentials as a commissioner of the United States to accept the surrender of the city of New Orleans and the territory of Louisiana, were soon over. The keys of the city were delivered to him, and Lauscat, the French governor, addressing the people from the portico of the cabildo, in French, congratulated them upon their accession to liberty and absolved them from further allegiance to the sovereigns of France. Claiborne then spoke in English, assuring all present that their rights would be preserved as citizens of the republic of the United States. The fleur de lys, emblem of France, was then slowly lowered, as the stars and stripes, the banner of freedom, slowly arose to catch in the sunshine the freshening breeze from over the waters of the Mississippi. When the flags were both half way, the one descending the other ascending, a gun was fired, and at the signal the cannon on the vessels in the harbor and the batteries of the forts fired a salute, while amidst the cheers of the few Americans present, the territory of Louisiana passed forever into the possession of the United States.

It was a tremendous accession to the territory of the young republic. The very figures that attempt to convey to the mind some idea of its superficial area are themselves impressive. It more than doubled the previous land area of the United States. In round numbers it exceeded 883,000 square miles. Out of it, in addition to the present state of Louisiana, there have been carved Missouri, Arkansas, Oklahoma, Kansas, Nebraska, Iowa, North and South Dakota, two-thirds of Minnesota, one-third of Colorado, and three-fourths of Wyoming. At the time of its accession to the United States its known population did not exceed five thousand souls, nearly one-half of whom were slaves. In 1810 the first federal census showed a population of twenty thousand, of whom one-half were still negro slaves. If taken to-day,—a census of the same territory would closely approach twenty million, *all free men.*

Considered as a whole, little was really known of the vast territory of Louisiana at the time of its purchase by Jefferson. Although one hundred and twenty years had elapsed since that memorable 9th of April, 1682, when Robert Cavalier de La Salle from a lonely eminence on the delta of the Mississipi had proclaimed the sovereignty of the King of France over his discoveries, no vigorous, persistent effort had been made to explore the vast territory, either by France or by Spain during the two score and five years she had been mistress of Louisiana. Few settlements had been established and aside from the "Chain of Forts" extending in an irregular line from the St. Lawrence to the Mississippi and on to the bay of Biloxi, Louisiana was an unknown land, except possibly to the fur traders, hunters, trappers, wood rangers, and the indefatigable French priests, who appear to have visited nearly every portion of the territory.

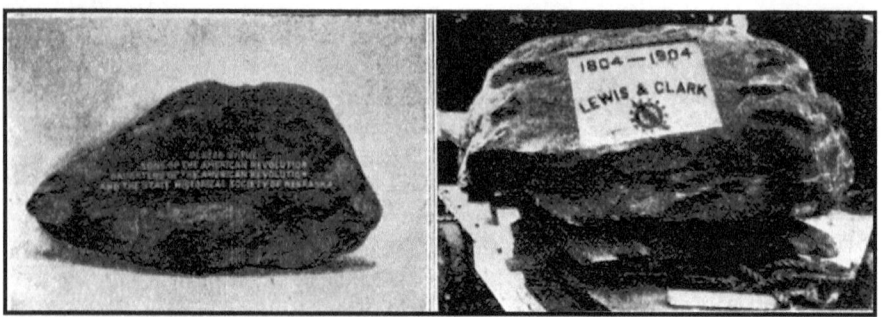

BOWLDER AT FORT CALHOUN, NEBRASKA. COMMEMORATING THE FIRST COUNCIL WITH THE INDIANS ON NEBRASKA SOIL.

But the sagacious and energetic Jefferson had matured a plan for exploring the Missouri river country, the least known portion of the territory, almost before congress had ratified the treaty under which possession was acquired. In May, 1804, he started the far-famed Lewis and Clark expedition up the Missouri, charged with the duty of exploring that great river from its mouth to its source and then on to the Pacific ocean. The report which these explorers, after an absence of two years, were able to make of the resources of the country through which they had journeyed, of its lofty mountain chains and plateaus, of its wide, rolling prairies, its forests of valuable timber, its wildernesses, rivers, native inhabitants, and its wild life of forest and plain, served to confirm the vague ideas of the times concerning the new territory as a possession of the United States.

Time, through a thousand channels, has vindicated the wisdom of Jefferson and his ministers in securing at a critical period in our country's history, by the arts of peaceful diplomacy, this great accession of territory to our beloved country.

CHAPTER III

NEBRASKA UP TO 1866

EARLY EXPLORERS IN NEBRASKA — CORONADO — MALLET BROTHERS — LEWIS AND CLARK — KANSAS-NEBRASKA BILL — TERRITORY OPENED FOR SETTLEMENT — AREA BOUNDARIES — ORGANIZATION — CENSUS — DEATH OF GOVERNOR BURT — GOVERNOR CUMING — THE FIRST LEGISLATURE STATEHOOD

> The Virgin of the wilderness,
> She sits upon her hills alone;
> Loose sprigs of cedar in her hair,
> A vine-wreath round her zone,—
> As grey-eyed Pallas pure and free,
> Expectant of the things to be.
>
> —O. C. Dake.

That portion of the "Great Purchase" which comprises the state of Nebraska was scarcely known to white men prior to the expedition of Lewis and Clark in 1804-1806. Doubtless it had been traversed, in part at least, by French-Canadian trappers, traders, and *couriers du bois*, as well as by French missionaries who followed the Indian trails to the remotest regions of all New France. But these left no records of their travels and adventures of which history can take notice. Just when the earliest visits of white men to Nebraska occurred may never be known.

In recent years efforts have been made by writers on the history of our state to connect the expedition of Francisco Vasquez de Coronado, in 1540, with Nebraska. It is claimed that this expedition not only crossed the southern boundary of the state somewhere between the eastern boundary of Gage county and points much further west, but also that it actually penetrated the state as far north as the Platte river. The most convincing evidence assigned in support of this contention is that the chroniclers of the expedition, as well as its leader, used descriptive terms, in relation to the soil, vegetation, landscape, and other phenomena observed by them, which might be applicable to southeastern Nebraska, and that Coronado himself declares that Quivera "where I have reached it is *in* the 40th degree." To say the most for such evidence it only indicates in a general way the route of the expedition. It is offset by considerations which are entitled to great weight, even in the face of Coronado's declaration. Coronado came to the New World in the train of Mendoza, viceroy of Mexico, in 1535, and had been assigned by his patron to the governorship of Neuva Galicia, a northern province of the conquered country. Like all ambitious Spaniards of that particular day, his imagination had been fired by the wonderful success of Cortez, the conqueror of Mexico, and Pizarro, the conqueror of Peru. The fabulous wealth of these vanquished nations had gone to enrich their masters to an extent of which no Spaniard had ever before so much as dreamed. Coronado, listening to the tales concerning the far away "Seven City of Cibola," whose wealth was said to rival the riches of Montezuma and the Incas of Peru, resolved to imitate the exploits of Cortez and Pizzaro by undertaking the conquest of these fabled cities of the plain. Obtaining leave from the viceroy, and assembling an army of three hundred Spanish soldiers and a band of warlike Mexican Indians and equipping them for conquest, he started from the capital of his province on the 23d day of February, 1540, animated solely by the hope of plunder. For two years this marauding, predatory expedition wandered about over the barren wastes of New Mexico and possibly eastern Arizona, reddening their trail with the blood of the simple natives and committing heinous crimes against their chastity and virtue. The "Seven Cities of Cibola" dwindled to a few isolated Zuni villages, while the search for gold, always gold, proved an evanescent dream. Finally it was found that the riches lay far away to the east in the land of the Quivera. Here, the Spaniards were told, were large cities with unmeasured treasures of gold and vast herds of buffalo and other game. The rapacious leader gave willing ear to these tales, which no doubt were meant to involve his expedition in ruin, and, turning eastward, he traversed the plains of central Kansas as far as the neighborhood of Junction City, where, recently, enthusiastic Coronadists have erected a costly monument intended to commemorate the discovery of Quivera, a name apparently used to designate a tribe of Indians in that section of country.

From photograph owned by E. E. Blackman,
president Quivera Historical Society.

QUIVERA MONUMENT
Near Junction City, Kansas

Whether Coronado came as far north as Nebraska will never be known. His declaration that he found Quivera within the 40th degree means but little. He was not engaged in exploring the country and could not have been greatly concerned about such things as degrees of latitude. Besides it is a well settled fact that in the sixteenth century a common error of about two degrees runs through all Spanish computations as respects the fixing of degrees of latitude. If correct in the assumption that he did actually cross the fortieth parallel of latitude, then Coronado was the first white man to set foot on Nebraska soil, and Nebraska was known to the Caucasian race than eighty years before the landing of the Mayflower at Plymouth Rock.

It may be recorded that the first authentic account of the visit of white men to Nebraska is found in the journals of the brothers Pierre and Paul Mallet which fell into the hands of Jean Baptiste Lemoyne, sieur de Bienville, the founder of New Orleans and for many years the French-Canadian governor of the province of Louisiana. In attempting to reach Santa Fe by way of the Mississippi these explorers, with a party of French-Canadians, in 1739 passed up the Missouri, its chief tributary, and appear to have spent the winter at the mouth of the Niobrara. In the spring of 1740 they descended the Missouri to the Platte and, following the latter stream about seventy miles, struck across the plains to Santa Fe, thus traversing a considerable portion of what is now the state of Nebraska.

Whatever may be said concerning those who may have preceded them, it is true beyond cavil that the existence of what is now Nebraska was first brought strongly to public attention by the expedition of Lewis and Clark. These explorers, paddling up the swift and dangerous current of the Missouri river, were compelled to tie their crude vessels to objects along the river banks at night and to proceed only by daylight. They camped indifferently on either side of the stream. July 15, 1804, their journal shows they first camped on Nebraska soil, at the mouth of the Little Nemaha river, near the present town of Nemaha, and on the way out their last encampment in Nebraska was made September 7, 1804, at a point a few miles below the northeast corner of the state. On their return trip the explorers floated past the northeast corner of the state, on Sunday, the 31st day of August, 1806, and passed the southeast corner on the 11th of the following September—a total of five hundred and fifty-six miles, channel measurement. Several points in Nebraska where the explorers pitched camp have been identified from the minute and accurate description supplied by the record of their movements along the course of the Missouri. Scattered along the banks of this mighty stream Lewis and Clark found many Indian tribes, amongst them the Otoe and Missouri, which long afterward became domiciled in Gage county. While encamped at Council Bluffs, a point since identified as Fort Calhoun, the explorers made the following entries in their journal:

"The meridian altitude of this day [July 31, 1804] made the latitude of our Camp 41° 18' 1.4". We waited with much anxiety the return of our messenger to the Otoes. Our apprehensions were finally relieved by the arrival of a party of about fourteen Otoe and Missouri Indians, who came at sunset, on the 2d of August, accompanied by a Frenchman who resided among them and interpreted for us. Captain Lewis and Clark went out to meet them and told them we would hold a council in the morning."

The first political event of great significance in the history of Nebraska was the enactment by congress into law of a bill entitled "An act to organize the Territory of Nebraska." As early as 1848 the organization into a territory of that part of the public domain lying west of Missouri and extending to the Rocky mountains had received serious consideration in the halls of our national legislature and in 1852 a bill for that purpose had been actually introduced in congress. The following year a bill was brought forward for the organization of Nebraska territory, which covered substantially the territory now included in the states of Kansas and Nebraska, extending from the Missouri frontier to the crests of the Rocky mountains. Neither of these measures attracted great public attention or received legislative sanction, but early in January, 1854, Stephen A. Douglas, who was then dominant in national politics, reported from the senate committee on territories, of which he was chairman, a bill to organize the territories of Kansas and Nebraska. This was the historic Kansas-Nebraska bill, the passage of which through congress stirred the nation, north and south, east and west, to its greatest depths, and aroused passions destined to be cooled only in the agonies of fratricidal strife. No such public upheaval as followed the introduction of this bill had ever before been known in the United States. The act was drawn with the politician's most consummate art and with a boldness that startled the entire country. There was no effort on the part of the projectors of this measure or any one else to disguise the fact that it repealed the "Missouri Compromise," the most obnoxious measure to the slave-holding class ever passed by the national legislature, and permitted the extension of slavery north of the famed "Mason and Dixon Line." On the other hand, the bill, with the appearance of fairness, permitted the people of each of the proposed territories to determine, as states, whether they should be dedicated to slavery or freedom. Thus by adroitly uniting the Democratic representatives in congress, both north and south, in support of his measure, and having first by substitution divided the original bill into two organic acts, one applying to Kansas and the other to Nebraska alone, Senator Douglas secured the passage of the substitute bills through both houses of congress in May, 1854, and on the 30th day of that month the act creating the territory of Nebraska received the official approval of Franklin Pierce, then President of the United States.

STEPHEN A. DOUGLAS

In the interval between the introduction of the bill and its passage, great preparations were on foot in anticipation of the act ultimately becoming a law. On the 17th day of April, in that year, the federal government, by treaty stipulations, acquired the title of the various Indian tribes to all the lands within the boundaries of the proposed territories which bordered upon the western bank of the Missouri river. On the eastern shore of that great stream, during the spring of 1854, people gathered from many states and anxiously awaited final action on the bill and the President's proclamation opening the new territory of Nebraska for settlement. No white man had previously been or was at that time allowed to enter or remain on Nebraska soil without permission from the war department and then only while engaged in hunting, trapping, or commerce with the Indians. While the act was effecting its passage through congress, the commissioner of the general land office at Washington, after a personal exploration of the eastern boundaries of Nebraska, asserted that there were not three bona fide white settlers in the entire territory. The President's proclamation declaring it open for settlement was issued June 24, 1854, and with the wave of immigration that immediately broke over our eastern boundary, the long, exciting struggle which attended the erection of Nebraska into a territory came to an end.

The area of the new territory as defined by the organic act far exceeded its present boundaries. Beginning at a point where the fortieth parallel of latitude crosses the Missouri river, that is to say at what is now the southeastern corner of Richardson county, the southern boundary line of the territory stretched away westward to the eastern boundary of Utah and the summit of the Rocky mountains, thence northward on the principal chain of those mountains to the British possessions, thence eastward on the national boundary line to Minnesota, and southward to the Missouri river, following the main channel of that stream to the point of beginning.

In addition to the present boundaries of our state, this fledgling territory embraced within its borders Montana, North and South Dakota, the northern part of Colorado, a portion of Idaho, and nearly the whole of Wyoming. It comprised a variety of soils, scenery, climate, and products. It was inhabited only by the red man and was the range of the greatest herds of wild buffalo known to mankind, as well as elk, deer, mountain lion, and many other wild and ravenous beasts. It contained vast deposits of coal, mines of precious ores, oil fields of great and unknown value, immense forests, lakes, plains, and rivers with their rich, productive valleys. Doubtless the organic act which conferred upon the new territory such magnificent proportions was passed by congress under the belief that the major portion of the great plains region of the Missouri valley was unfit for human habitation.

But the act provided that congress might, from time to time, as appeared proper or expedient, reduce the area of this territory by creating other territories or parts of territories from it, and it is by virtue of this original provision that Nebraska has suffered successive diminutions until our present boundaries were finally reached.

From photograph owned by the Nebraska State Historical Society.

FRANCIS BURT
First governor of Nebraska territory

The organic act provided for the immediate, complete civic organization of the new territory, and to this end Francis Burt, of North Carolina, was appointed governor, and Thomas B. Cuming, of Iowa, secretary of state for the territory of Nebraska. These two officials arrived at Bellevue, in Sarpy county, October 10, 1854. This small western outpost of civilization had been a station of the American Fur Company since 1804. About 1835, the Presbyterian church had established at this point a mission for the Pawnee, Otoe, and Missouri Indians, and it was the most widely known spot in the territory at that time. It was beautifully located on a rising plateau, near the Missouri river, and for some months it was the prospective capital of the new territory. On his way out to assume the duties of his office, the governor had contracted an illness, and on the 18th day of October, eight days after his arrival, in the old Mission House at Bellevue, at the foot of the hill, "Big Elk," in that remote village, he died, and Cuming succeeded to the office thus made vacant, as acting governor of Nebraska territory.

THOMAS B. CUMING
First secretary and twice acting governor of Nebraska territory

In matters pertaining to the organization of the territorial government the organic act had clothed the governor with autocratic power and authority. Amongst other things it was made his duty, immediately upon his arrival, to take a census of the people and of the qualified voters of the territory; to apportion amongst the counties the members of the two houses of the legislature, designated by the act as the council and house of representatives; to call an election for members of that body, and select a place for holding its first session. Before his arrival at Bellevue, Governor Burt had marked off the inhabited portions of the territory into counties, and the proclamation of Acting Governor Cuming, issued on the 21st day of November, 1854, calling the first territorial election, included eight counties, namely: Burt, Cass, Dodge, Forney (now Nemaha). Pierce (now Otoe), Richardson, and Washington,—all bordering upon the Missouri river.

The first official act of the acting governor was the issuing of a proclamation containing the announcement of the death of Governor Burt, and dated the day of his demise. Three days thereafter, to wit, October 21, 1854, the acting governor, in order that all absent residents might return to the territory for registration, issued his proclamation announcing that an enumeration of the census would commence on the following Tuesday, namely October 24, 1854. When completed, this census showed the entire population of the new territory to be 2,722. Upon the return of the census enumerators, Governor Cuming apportioned the thirty-nine members of the legislature provided for in the organic act amongst the eight counties already mentioned, and issued a proclamation for their election. On the 20th day of December, 1854, the election having been held, a call was issued convening the "General Assembly of the Territory of Nebraska on the 16th day of January, 1855."

This first legislature, or general assembly, as it was called, was an able and a wonderfully active body. Following the Iowa statutes, from which it borrowed with the utmost freedom, it enacted general laws for the government of the people, adopted codes of civil and criminal procedure, established numerous territorial roads, created and defined the boundaries of nineteen new counties and provided for the establishment of seats of justice therein. It passed laws for the incorporation of insurance, railroad, land, manufacturing, milling, bridge, ferry, banking, colonization, and immigration companies. It incorporated cities, of which many were mere figments of some speculator's brain, their very names having been lost in the efflux of time.

It incorporated colleges and seats of learning destined never to have faculty or curriculum, and finally, on the 16th day of March, 1853, it expired amidst a whirlwind of joint resolutions and memorials to congress.

It is foreign to the purpose of this work to pursue at length the history of the territory of Nebraska. The organic act was passed and approved May 30, 1854, and, as we have seen, it was quickly followed by executive proclamation opening the new territory to settlement. In October, 1854, on the arrival of Governor Burt at Bellevue, there were probably less than two thousand white persons in the entire territory. But the territorial period quickly passed. The national census of 1860 showed a total population of 28,841. In 1870 the census gave the state of Nebraska 123,993. As early as 1864 a movement was inaugurated which had for its object the admission of Nebraska into the Union of States. That year, on the 19th day of April, congress passed "An act to enable the people of Nebraska to form a constitution and state government, and for the admission of such state into the Union on an equal footing with the original states." After prescribing the boundaries of the proposed state, directing the election of delegates to a constitutional convention to be held for the purpose of framing a state constitution, and fixing the date for holding such convention, the act provided that the constitution of the proposed state, when framed, should be republican and not repugnant to the constitution of the United States and the Declaration of Independence. The act further provided that such constitution should, by proper articles which should be forever irrevocable without the consent of congress, provided *inter alia* that slavery or involuntary servitude should be forever prohibited in Nebraska, and that perfect tolerance of religious sentiment should be secured, and no inhabitant of the state should ever be molested in person or property on account of his or her mode of religious worship.

In compliance with this enabling act and pursuant to the directions thereof, an election was held in the territory on the 6th day of June, 1866, for the selection of delegates to the proposed constitutional convention. At the same time, by a sort of referendum, the question of statehood was also submitted to a vote of the people. The election returns showed a clear majority against statehood, and the constitutional convention which assembled in June, in conformity with the enabling act, promptly adjourned without action.

In 1866 the subject of the admission of Nebraska as a state into the Union again challenged public attention. The territorial legislature for that year, on its own motion, submitted a state constitution, prepared under its direction, to the voters of the territory, and at an election held June 2, 1866, this action of the legislature was ratified and the constitution was adopted. Congress, thereupon, under date of February 9, 1867, passed a supplemental enabling act, wherein it was specified, as a condition precedent to statehood, that the legislature of Nebraska must declare that there should never be a denial of the right of suffrage on account of race or color, by the prospective state. This condition was finally accepted, and on March 1, 1867 the territory of Nebraska ceased to be, and the great state of Nebraska came into existence.

CHAPTER IV

GAGE COUNTY

ACT DEFINING BOUNDARIES — NAME — AREA — SEAT OF JUSTICE — WHITESVILLE — PREPARATION FOR ELECTION — ORGANIZATION — FIRST MEETINGS OF COUNTY COMMISSIONERS — COUNTY SEAT

Among the nineteen counties which were created by the first session of the legislative assembly of Nebraska territory was the county of Gage. This act was entitled "An act to define the boundaries and locate the seat of justice in Gage county." In conferring a name upon the new county it was the aim of the assembly to honor the Rev. William D. Gage, a Methodist clergyman, who was then serving as chaplain for both houses of the legislative assembly.

This act became a law on the 16th day of March, 1855. As defined by the act, the county consisted of a tract of land twenty-four miles square, lying directly west of Pawnee county, which had been likewise created by this session of the legislative assembly and its boundaries prescribed by an act approved March 6, 1855. The second section of the act creating Gage county reads as follows: "William D. Gage, John B. Robinson and I. L. Gibbs be and are hereby appointed commissioners to locate the seat of justice in said county." And by the third section these commissioners or a majority of them were required to meet "at some convenient point (as may be agreed upon) on or before the 10th day of June next, or within three months thereafter, and proceed to locate the seat of justice for said Gage county." By the fourth section of the act the commissioners were required to commit their findings to writing, giving a particular description of the place so selected, and to file the same in the office of the county clerk of Richardson county, who was required to file and keep on file such findings. The place thus designated was declared to be the "seat of justice" for the new county. The act further required the setting aside of "fifty lots of land" in the town so selected to be reserved for the use of such county, the moneys arising from the sale thereof to be by the county judge applied to the erection of a court house and other necessary public buildings.

REV. WILLIAM D. GAGE
Chaplain of the first legislature

Prior to the passage of the foregoing act. Acting Governor Cuming had evidently marked out a county, lying west of Richardson, to be known as Jones county. This prospective county began at the northwest corner of Richardson county, as then constituted and which included both the present counties of Pawnee and Richardson, and apparently it was meant to extend thence northward to the Platte river, and along the south side of that stream to the western boundary of the territory, on the crest of the Rocky mountains; following this chain in a southeasterly direction to the south line of the territory and thence back again to the southwest corner of Richardson county and north to the place of beginning.

In preparing for the election of members for the first legislature, the governor detailed Jesse Lowe, the deputy United States marshal, to visit the proposed county and ascertain the number of settlers therein. He was instructed to apportion to it one or more representatives, as the number of inhabitants should require, and to arrange for the holding of an election in such county. Whether the deputy marshal actually visited the prospective county is doubtful, but on the 10th day of December, 1854, he reported to the acting governor that there were no voters in said county, "unless a few living in the neighborhood of Bellews precinct in Richardson county, and who would naturally vote in said precinct." But as we have already seen, within three months from the date of this report, a bill passed both branches of the legislative assembly and became a law, creating the county of Gage, defining its boundaries and providing for the location of a seat of justice in and for said county.

But it takes more than broad acres and legislative enactments to create a body politic. At the time the first territorial legislature sought to immortalize its chaplain, the Rev. William D. Gage, by bestowing his name on that portion of the public domain which it had erected into Gage county, there is not known to have been a single actual settler within its boundaries, and it is doubtful if at that time there was a single white person in the county. It was, in fact, more than two years after the passage of this act before a sufficient number of settlers had gathered in the county to attempt its organization.

No evidence is known to exist which shows that the commission charged with the duty of locating a county seat or "seat of justice" for Gage county ever met or acted under the authority thus conferred upon it. But at the third session of the territorial assembly, begun and held at Omaha, January 5, 1857, an act was passed (and approved February 13, 1857), locating the "seat of justice" of said county at Whitesville. The site thus selected by the assembly as the future county seat of Gage county comprised the southeast quarter of the southeast quarter of section twenty-nine in Rockford township, located a little south of the present village of Holmesville, two miles east and one half mile north of the geographical center of the county as originally created. For several years thereafter the stout oak stakes driven into the prairie to mark the corners of lots in Whitesville were plainly visible. Prairie fires finally consumed them and with their destruction all trace of the projected "seat of justice" for Gage county disappeared.

The first territorial assembly, by an act passed and approved March 14, 1855, provided that whenever the citizens of any unorganized county desired to organize the same a majority of the legal voters of the county might make application to the probate judge of the county to which it was attached for election purposes for an order calling an election for county officers in such unorganized county. The act further provided that all unorganized counties should be attached to the nearest organized county to the eastward for election, judicial, and revenue purposes. Under this act, Gage county at the moment of its creation became automatically attached to Pawnee county for the purposes specified in the act, until such date as it had perfected its own organization.

On the 5th day of August, 1857, shortly after the arrival of the company of colonists who founded the city of Beatrice, steps were initiated by them to organize Gage county, with Beatrice as the county seat, and this without complying with the provisions of the act above mentioned. The townsite enthusiasts appear to have gone through a form of an election of county officers at that time. It is said that thirty-three votes were cast and it seems that a full list of county officials were chosen. At that date there could not have been over fifty white persons within the county of Gage and it is doubtful if there were a dozen voters outside of the Beatrice Town site Company. The minutes of the county commissioners, or county court, as it was then called, in and for Gage county, begin March 13, 1858, wherein it appears that Albert Towle and H. M. Reynolds acted as county commissioners and Nathan Blakely as county clerk of said county. These minutes are the first county records of any kind in existence, and in a sense they form an unbroken, continuous record of the transactions of the county board of the county from the beginning. The minutes of the first meeting read as follows:

"Commissioners court, held March 13, 1858, at which ordered that a county election should be held on Saturday, March 28th, to relocate the county seat of Cage county; also to elect a sheriff in place of Daniel P. Taylor, who failed to qualify; also to elect a county treasurer in the place of Calvin Miller, who failed to qualify; also to elect a recorder in the place of John Hart, who failed to qualify; also a superintendent of common schools in place of N. B Beldin, who failed to qualify.

"It was ordered: That the county be divided into two precincts for election purposes; that townships one and two shall be called precinct No. 1, and that townships three and four shall be called precinct No. 2.

"Isma Mumford, John McDowell and Bennett Pike were appointed judges of election in precinct No. 2; Rankin Johnson, James Johnson and Henry Elliott judges of election for precinct No. 1. The court then adjourned."

The next meeting of the commissioners' court was held at the house of Albert Towle, October 7, 1858, and the third meeting was held at the same place November 29, 1858, both designated as regular meetings, with the same officers present as at the first meeting. The next regular meeting of the commissioners' court was held January 3, 1859; present Commissioners Towle and Reynolds and County Clerk Nathan Blakely. And on April 13, 1859, at a special meeting of the commissioners' court, there occurs the following entry:

"At a meeting at a special term of the Co. Court held at the house of A. Towle, on the 13th day of April, 1859, present: Commissioners Albert Towle and H. M. Reynolds. It was ordered and the following preamble and resolutions be adopted:

"WHEREAS. We have been officially informed by the county clerk of Pawnee county that certain individuals residing in precinct No. One of Gage county have petitioned the county commissioners of Pawnee county to issue an order for an election for the purpose of organizing said Gage county. Therefore,

"RESOLVED. That we protest against any such order being issued by the aforesaid commissioners of Pawnee county or any action being taken thereon by the citizens of precinct No. One of Gage county.

"RESOLVED. That we claim that Gage county was regularly organized by an election held on the 3d day of August, 1857; that as evidence of this fact we have the certificate from the county clerk of

Pawnee county certifying that the officers elected at the said election were duly elected. And also the fact that the county clerk of said Gage county elected at the said election was duly qualified by the county clerk of Pawnee county.

"In addition to the above the returns of an election held since the above named have been recognized by the board of territorial canvassers as being issued by a regularly organized county.

"It is ordered that the county clerk of Gage county forward a copy of the above preamble and resolutions to the county clerk of Pawnee county. Also send a copy of the same into precinct No. One of Gage county.

"The court then adjourned.

"NATHAN BLAKELY, Co. Clerk."

It is clear from this preamble and these resolutions that active steps had been taken by the county-seat promoters at Beatrice to validate the election of August 3, 1857. A second election had been held March 27, 1859, for the evident purpose of filling the county offices in all cases where the officials chosen at the first election had failed to qualify. Probably at the second election no action was taken on the county-seat matter, as specified in the commissioners' proceedings under date of March 13, 1858. Blue Springs had become an aspirant for that honor, and as both voting precincts of the county participated in the election of March 27, 1859, a contest at the polls over that question appears to have been avoided.

The location of the county seat and the insistence of Beatrice on the legality of the organization of the county in August, 1857, by the Beatrice Townsite Company had become so acute a subject of difference between the rival towns, that precinct No. 1, Blue Springs, failed to participate in the annual election held August 2, 1858. At the meeting of the commissioners' court under date of July 4, 1859, among other things, it was ordered that Albert Towle, Samuel Jones, and Nathan Blakely be allowed and paid $1.50 each as judges of election at Beatrice, August 2, 1858, and that W. D. Spencer and Myron Newton be allowed and paid a like sum each for acting as clerks of that election, but nothing seems to have been allowed any citizen of Blue Springs or vicinity for acting as a judge or a clerk in precinct No. 1 in this election.

In the spring of 1859, both Blue Springs and Beatrice attempted to assess Gage county, each claiming to have lawful right to perform that service, Blue Springs because of the assumed illegality of the county organization claimed to have been effected by Beatrice in August, 1857, and because of her pending application to the commissioners of Pawnee county for the calling of an election to effect the legal organization of the county; and Beatrice, by virtue of the election in 1857, and her assumption of its regularity. The resolutions of Commissioners Towle and Reynolds above set forth, under date of April 4, 1859, put an end to that movement on the part of Blue Springs, and both precincts of the county participated in the election of 1859. To terminate the dissension that grew out of this rivalry, the legislative assembly, at its session begun and held at Omaha, December 5, 1859, passed an act entitled: "An act to legalize the *first* organization of Gage county, the location of the county seat at Beatrice and the official acts of the officers of said county."

There can be no doubt but that the alleged organization of the county by the Beatrice Townsite Company in August, 1857, was irregular and probably illegal from its inception. There appears to be no evidence that the enthusiastic townsite boomers made the slightest effort to comply with the law then in effect, regulating the organization of counties, and this fact seems to have been recognized by the legislature in passing the above described act.

The passage of this act destroyed forever the hopes of Blue Springs respecting the county seat of the new county. This unpretentious outpost of civilization possessed many advantages which were justly counted in its favor as an aspirant to first place in civic honors. It is a romantic spot, beautifully located on the Big Blue river, and during all the times here mentioned it was a prospective station on a projected cutoff from the old military highway from Fort Leavenworth to the west, which, leaving the main road at Richmond, Nemaha county, Kansas, a few miles below Seneca, on the Nemaha river, led north-west from Blue Springs and beyond, intersecting the main road at some point east and south of the famous Rock Creek Station, in Jefferson county. Blue Springs also was on a main traveled road from Marysville, Kansas, through the Otoe Indian village to Beatrice. It possessed natural advantages for a city which were wanting to some extent in its rival. It was several miles nearer the geographical center of the county than Beatrice, and its few inhabitants were people of worth and character, equal in these respects to the Beatrice colonists. Its most serious drawback was its proximity to the Otoe and Missouri Indian reservation, the north line of which was only two miles distant.

Beatrice may have been more in line with the direct travel both east and west, and it certainly possessed the controlling advantage of a central location as respected the white inhabitants of the county at that time. In addition to these things, its destiny was in the hands of men who were fully alive to the advantages that would accrue to them by controlling the organization of the county from the very first, and by this and other methods securing at Beatrice the county seat. The changing years have probably vindicated their judgment. With its present boundaries, Beatrice is unquestionably the most desirable location as a seat for the government of our splendid county. The animosities which may have been engendered by the county-seat rivalry of more than a generation ago have long since passed away, and the two historic territorial cities, of Gage county, their early dissensions forgotten, for many years have dwelt together in the bonds of unity and friendship.

CHAPTER V

OLD CLAY COUNTY

ACT CREATING — ORGANIZATION — AUSTIN — SETTLEMENTS — PARTITIONING — JOHN P. CADMAN — JOINT MEETING COMMISSIONERS OF GAGE AND LANCASTER COUNTIES

Prior to the passage of the act creating Gage county and defining its boundaries, the first territorial assembly, on the 6th day of March, 1855, passed an act "To define the boundaries and establish the seat of justice for Lancaster county," and on the following day an act was passed creating Clay county and defining its boundaries. Gideon Bennett and James H. Decker, members of the assembly from former Pierce (now Otoe) county, and D. M. Johnson, representative from Richardson county, were appointed by the last named act as legislative commissioners "to locate the seat of justice for Clay county"; and a third section of the act provided "that the seat of justice in and for Clay county shall be called Clatonia." Both of these counties, like Gage, were twenty-four miles square, Clay lying north of Gage and south of Lancaster, but joining each, and consisting of a fine body of land, with an unusual proportion of rich upland prairie.

Clay was duly organized into a county pursuant to the act creating it and defining its boundaries, and entered upon its separate existence as such. No evidence is known to exist to show that any place was ever selected by the legislative commission as a county seat or seat of justice for Clay county. While several towns or villages appear to have been laid out on paper, there was never in fact any semblance of a town in Clay county. The nearest approach to it seems to have been a group of squatters on the public domain about what was known as Austin's mill, on Stevens (now Indian) creek. Here, in 1857, came Hiram W. Parker,

Fordyce Roper, Edward C., Charles, and Homer B. Austin, also Orrin Stevens, who gave his name to Indian creek at that point—a name which the Beatrice colonists always refused to recognize. Possibly a few other early settlers gathered near there on the public domain, and an effort was made to establish a town which could become in the course of time a county seat for the new county. Edward C. Austin had located a claim in the latter part of April or early in May, 1857, in the immediate vicinity of the present village of Pickrell. He had built a log cabin, staked out a forty-acre tract of his claim into town lots, and called the proposed town Austin. Shortly thereafter he purchased and brought to his claim a saw mill and buhrs for a grist mill, and erected the former on the east side of Indian or Stevens creek, on the north side of the present road leading east from Pickrell. A little below the mill, on the east side of Indian creek, was the surveyed town of Austin. No dwellings or other structures were ever erected on the townsite and the mill itself proved a financial failure, due in part to the fact that it was not on the line of western bound emigrant travel, and in part to the fact that there was scarcely any demand for lumber in that locality, but more to the fact that a saw mill was established about the same time in Beatrice, by the Beatrice Townsite Company. About the year 1862 the buhrs of Austin's mill were purchased by Mr. Fordyce Roper for use in a mill which he was then erecting in Beatrice. This move broke up the prospective town of Austin and nothing more was heard of it. The Austins left the country: Parker, Roper, and Stevens moved to Beatrice, and no one was left to take their places in furthering the interests of this forlorn hope.

In addition to the projected town of Austin, there was at least one serious effort to found a town in the north half of Clay county. In that section of the county, John D. Prey and family had established a residence near Roca, July 26, 1856. The following year other settlers joined them, among whom were J. L. Davidson, W. W. Dunham, and I. C. Bristol. A townsite company was formed, composed of John L. Davidson, Joseph B. Weeks, James S. Goodwin, John G. Haskins, and George L. Bristol; a forty-acre tract of land was surveyed into town lots and the prospective town named Olathe. This ambitious project was located on Salt creek, about three-quarters of a mile west of the ford where the road from Nebraska City to Denver crossed that stream, a few yards north of the spot where the present bridge at Roca is located. The Olathe quarries were only a short distance away, there was some wood along the creek, and these appear to have been the determining factors in the location of the town. Nothing came of this venture, and at the time Clay county was divided there was not a single town, village, or hamlet within its bounds.

Clay county as thus constituted was largely a treeless scope of country, rather poorly watered, especially on the upland, and it was generally thought that there was no desirable central location for a county seat in the county. Its big, rolling, unbroken prairies did not look inviting to men who were wholly dependent for so important a matter as fuel upon timber along the streams. The settlements had been confined to those localities where timber could be had. In addition to the settlement in the neighborhood of Austin's mill, others were made in 1857, in Adams township, along the Big Nemaha river at several points in the north half of Clay county, along Salt creek and its tributaries, and a few squatters on the public domain might have been found in the southwest corner of the county, along the Big Blue river.

The maintenance of county government in a county whose population was so sparse and so widely separated, would, it was thought, be an expensive and difficult problem under any circumstances, and the early settlers of the county, realizing the situation, were for the most part readily persuaded to embrace a scheme for the division of their county. This movement was started in 1863. John P. Cadman, residing near the village of Lancaster, in the neighborhood known as Yankee Hill, where the present Asylum for the Insane, at Lincoln, is located, was that year elected the representative of Gage, Clay, and Lancaster counties in the territorial legislature. He is said to have carried with him a petition signed by a majority of the legal voters of Clay county praying the legislature to divide that county and attach the north half to Lancaster and the south half to Gage county. Whether this is true or not, a bill was brought forward early in the session of the assembly, which convened at Omaha, January 7, 1864, to effect such division and distribution of old Clay county. Some opposition developed at first to this measure in the legislative body, headed by Mr. John S. Gregory, a colleague of Cadman's. But the obvious advantages of this important measure to all three counties were such that Gregory was finally induced to lend his influence to the act.

The bill, which passed the assembly on the 15th day of February, 1864, was carefully and skillfully drawn by the late P. M. Marquette. It was entitled "An act to attach the north half of Clay county to the county of Lancaster and the south half of Clay county to the county of Gage." It covered every possible contingency that might arise from the proposed division. It declared the organization of the county of Clay to be forever at an end, and constituted the board of county commissioners of Lancaster and Gage counties "A board to meet at such time and place as they might agree upon for the purpose of effecting the division of Clay county pursuant to the provisions of this act." In compliance with the terms of the act, the commissioners of Gage county on July 26, 1864, held a joint session with the commissioners of Lancaster county, represented by John W. Prey, at the home of Hiram W. Parker, the county clerk of Clay county, in Beatrice, for the purpose of effecting a settlement of the affairs of that county. The preliminary entry on the journal of the records of the county commissioners of Gage county as respects this meeting reads as follows:

"County Court, July 26, 1864. Commissioners of Lancaster and Gage.

"At a meeting of the county commissioners of the counties of Gage and Lancaster, held at the house of H. W. Parker, for the purpose of receiving the accounts, books, monies, and all and any other property belonging to Clay county, and for the purpose of a settlement of the accounts to and with the officers of the aforesaid county of Clay.

"There were present county commissioners from Gage county, Fordyce Roper, F. H. Dobbs and William Tyler. From the county of Lancaster, John W. Prey."

As illustrative of the meager volume of business transacted by a county in that early day, as well perhaps as the poverty and simplicity of the times, the remainder of the record of the meeting mentioned in the preceding paragraph may not be without interest to the reader or regarded as inappropriate to this history. It reads as follows:

ORDER OF BUSINESS

Ordered 1st.—That the account of H. W. Parker be allowed for services as county clerk (Clay County) from April 4, 1864 to July 28, 1864, 3½ months at $4.25 per month, $15.00. And that the Clerk of Clay County draw a warrant on the county treasurer for the same.

Ordered 2nd.—That John W. Prey be allowed $11.00, his per cent. for collecting Co. revenue and that the Co. clerk of Clay County draw warrant on the Co. treasurer for the same.

3rd.—That the clerk of Clay County draw warrants on the Co. treasurer for John W. Prey for $25.80, said amount having been paid out by him for non-assessed sinking fund for the year 1861.

4th.—By an examination of the Clay County record, the total amount of indebtedness was found to be $211.95.

5th.—The assessed valuation of property in the south half of Clay County for the year 1864 is $13,482.00.

6th.—The assessed valuation of property in the north half of Clay County for the year 1864 is $22,647.82.

7th.—The total amount of indebtedness to be paid by the north half of Clay County according to apportionment is $185.70.

8th.—The total amount of indebtedness to be paid by the south half of Clay County is $110.75.

Ordered 9th.—That the county treasurer of Clay County pay over all monies in his hands to their respective funds.

Ordered 10th.—That all offices in Clay County be declared vacant from this date, except precinct officers.

(Signed)
Oliver Townsend,
Co. Clerk for Gage Co.

F. Roper,
F. H. Dobbs,
William Tyler.
John W. Prey.

The reader has now looked upon the closing scene of old Clay county. Seldom have the obsequies of so important an organization as a splendid county been attended with greater simplicity or with less bitterness and dissension. It is easy to read between the lines of the act of dissolution the paramount influence of the rising city on the south and the ambitions village of Lancaster on the north, so soon to lose its identity in the noblest monument that has yet been reared to the martyr-president, the heroic Abraham Lincoln. Lapse of time has proved that the few heroic spirits of Stevens creek, Pierce, Bear, the Nemaha and Salt, would have been more than justified in persisting to the last in maintaining the separate existence of their county. The traveler who now motors over northern Gage and southern Lancaster counties is charmed with the beauty of the landscape and the fertility of the soil. Where once only a few souls gathered in isolation and loneliness along the widely separated streams within these boundaries, he finds a contented, prosperous, and happy population numbering many thousands. Where once stretched the silent and, to many, desolate prairies, he beholds wide-spreading fields, meadows and pasture lands, groves and orchards; he finds also commodious and not infrequently elegant country homes. No finer upland site for an ambitious county-seat town can be anywhere found in the west than that occupied by the present village of Cortland, near the geographical center of ancient Clay county. Within the former boundaries of this old county are several other pretty, attractive, and thriving villages, and what was Clay county in the primitive days has evolved into a district supplied with railroads, telegraph and telephone lines, schools, churches, banks, magnificent highways, and other institutions and conveniences by which modern living is both embellished and exalted.

CHAPTER VI

Topography of Gage County

Location — Townships — Area — Hydrographic Features — Stone — Clay — Coal — Water Supply — Climate — Temperature — Soil — The Prairies

The county of Gage is located in the southern part of the state of Nebraska, its eastern boundary being approximately fifty miles west of the Missouri river. On the north it is bounded by Lancaster county, on the east by Johnson and Pawnee counties, on the south by the state of Kansas, and on the west by Jefferson and Saline counties. It is a rectangular body of land, thirty-six miles in length north and south and twenty-four miles in breadth from east to west. As originally created by the territorial assembly, in 1855, it was twenty-four miles square, but as the reader will remember, in 1864, Clay county, which was also twenty-four miles square, was divided by the territorial assembly, the south half being attached to Gage and the north half to Lancaster county, thus giving to both Gage and Lancaster their present dimensions. The county is composed of twenty-four government townships, which, under article 9 of the constitution of the state of Nebraska, are each independent corporations—like counties as relates to their own internal affairs. In 1885 the county government was changed from the commissioner system to township organization, and when such change is made, boards of supervisors are required by law to select names for the various townships under their jurisdiction, by which they shall thereafter be designated. Pursuant to this provision of the law, the various townships of Gage county, beginning with the northeast, are named as follows: Adams, Nemaha, Highland, Clatonia, Grant, Holt, Hanover, Hooker, Filley, Logan, Midland, Blakely, Lincoln, Riverside,

Rockford, Sherman, Blue Springs, Island Grove, Wymore, Sicily, Elm, Glenwood, Paddock, Barneston, Liberty. With the exception of Blue Springs and Wymore all these townships are approximately six miles square. Originally Blue Springs comprised a full government township, but in 1889, for the purposes of local government, it was divided, on an east and west line through the center, into two townships. The south half was named Wymore, and in the same is situated the city of that name; the north half retained the name of Blue Springs and within its limits is the little city of the same name. It is through this division of the original township of Blue Springs that Gage county now has twenty-five townships.

The county has a superficial area of nearly 864 square miles,—approximately 552,960 acres. It has an average elevation above sea level of 1,200 feet. Its surface configuration may be described as a plain, tipped toward the southeast,—a construction which is only slightly modified locally by erosion and the direction of water courses. When it is considered that the two principal drainage systems of the county flow from the northwest in an almost due southeasterly direction, it becomes evident even to casual observation that the general surface trend also follows that course.

The hydrographic features of the county are very marked and readily traced. The Big Nemaha river enters it from the northwest, near the half-section line running north and south through Section 2, in Nemaha township, and, flowing in an almost due southeast direction across Adams township to the southeast corner of Section 36 in that township, it crosses the county line into Johnson county. With its tributary streams, it drains a large portion of Nemaha, Adams, and Hooker townships. At Sterling it receives the waters of Hooker creek, and at Tecumseh those of Yankee creek, both of considerable volume and with headwaters partly in Gage county. At Tecumseh the Nemaha has a volume of water sufficient for milling purposes if properly conserved, and for many years it was the site of a good grist and flouring mill, deriving its power wholly from the river. It crosses the Pawnee county line into Richardson county a few miles east of Tablerock, receives at Salem the waters of its South Fork from Kansas, and falls into the

Missouri river at the southeast corner of Richardson county, discharging into the Missouri a considerable volume of water.

But by far the most important element in the natural drainage of Gage county is the Big Blue river. This beautiful stream also enters the county from the northwest, in Section 19, Grant township, and, taking a south easterly course, it flows across Grant, Blakely, Midland, Riverside, Rockford, Blue Springs, and Barneston townships, crossing the state line into Kansas at a point in Section 35 in Barneston township, approximately twenty-eight miles south and seventeen miles east of the initial point. From the west it receives the waters of Swan creek at a point two and one-half miles south of DeWitt, Cub creek near Hoag, Bills creek at Blue Springs, and Big Indian creek at Wymore, with their numerous tributaries. From the north and east its waters are augmented by those of Clatonia, Soap, Smake, Indian, Bear, Cedar, Mud, Wolf, Plum, and Mission creeks with their tributaries, most of which are living streams, a number carrying considerable quantities of water. Power for all purposes is supplied by the river itself, and its value and usefulness in this respect become increasingly important with every decade. From Barneston the river flows almost due south, through Kansas, receiving the waters of the Little Blue river and other streams on its course, and, greatly augmented in volume and force, it falls into the Republican at Manhattan, Kansas. It is one of the most beautiful and interesting of all Nebraska rivers, and from source to mouth it is approximately three hundred miles in length,—channel measurement.

The drainage of the county is fully matured. From every portion of it the water is led at once by natural depressions, streams and water courses away from the land. So nearly perfect is the drainage that in case of excessive rainfall the surface water is immediately conducted into runs, creeks, and streams, and these may become swollen, overflow their banks and flood the valley and low lands, sometimes washing away the soil, destroying fences, bridges, and other structures, and often doing great damage to crops on the bottoms and sloping uplands. Damages from this source could be greatly mitigated if the farmers and other interested parties would avail themselves of the recent drainage legislation of our state, form drainage districts, if necessary issue bonds, and, by ditching, straighten the channels of the streams so as to facilitate the rapid discharge of their waters and prevent overflow. This has been done in Pawnee, Johnson, Lancaster, Nemaha, Richardson, and probably other counties of the state, to the very great profit of the sections concerned.

Both the Nemaha and the Big Blue rivers, and particularly the latter, are noted for their wide and fertile valleys. Many of their tributaries also present in a marked degree valley formation. Usually the valleys on either hand are bounded by ranges of low hills, beyond which are the uplands,—formerly prairies.

From the time white men first became familiar with southeastern Nebraska, the streams of our county were bordered by lines of timber, which under favorable circumstances often spread out over the lower bottom lands into groves of valuable oak, walnut, hickory, ash, elm, hackberry, cottonwood, willow, and other deciduous varieties of trees common to this latitude. On some of the streams the red cedar is occasionally found. From these natural sources the early settlers of our county obtained wood for fuel and lumber, logs and clapboards for building purposes, fencing and other requirements of rural husbandry. Cultivation of the land, by keeping down disastrous prairie fires and by affording strong protection to the native timber growths, has largely contributed to the spread of timbered areas. In later times the use of coal and other fuels, and of foreign lumber, by relieving the demand upon the native woods has likewise greatly augmented the natural resources of the country, so that at the present moment our timbered areas exceed by many thousand acres the natural forest resources of the county as known to the pioneers. In addition to these factors tree planting in recent years has given Gage county largely the appearance of a timbered country.

There are no mountains and no hills of unusual size or altitude in Gage county. Its most noted elevation is a round-topped hill on the eastern boundary of Riverside township, a few miles southeast of Beatrice, locally known as "Iron Mountain." Speaking generally, the configuration of the surface of the county is such that a traveler is everywhere met with a panorama of low hills, gentle slopes, short plains, and shallow ravines, all pleasingly diversified by stream and wood.

In may portions of the county a fair quality of building stone is found, and in the neighborhood of Blue Springs and Wymore are extensive quarries of conglomerate rock, which for several years have afforded an ample supply of materials for the important rock-crushing industries at those points, the products being shipped in quantities over the state and elsewhere. Sand and gravel of exceptional quality are also valuable natural products of this county, as well as clay, both common and vitreous.

Coal has not yet been discovered in paying quantities anywhere in the state of Nebraska. As far back as 1868, Prof. F. V. Hayden, then at the head of the National Geological Survey, in an address delivered to the citizens of Beatrice in the old frame school house, cautioned his audience against entertaining any hope of finding coal in Gage county in workable quantities; and in his report to the secretary of the interior at Washington in 1872, after a thorough study and survey of the resources of the state of Nebraska, says: "In regard to finding workable beds of coal within accessable depths in eastern Nebraska by deep boring, I would remark in conclusion that though not prepared to discourage all hope of success, it is proper to state that all the known facts are unfavorable."

The intervening years have only served to prove the wisdom and correctness of this eminent scientist's conclusion. Twice in Gage county deep borings have been made for coal, oil, and natural gas. The first effort was about 1875, when a boring eleven hundred feet deep was put down across the alley on the Robertson property just north of the old jail, in Beatrice, with no other result than to develop a strong flow of salt water which rose to the top of the ground with nearly artesian force. Quite recently another boring was put down, on the Farlow tract of land which now is incorporated in the golf links and Country Club grounds. A depth of six hundred feet was reached, where salt water was again found. Within a few months from this date several tracts of land in the eastern part of our county have been covered with oil, coal, and natural-gas leases. No borings have yet been made, and nothing has transpired since 1868 to discredit the cautionary remarks of Prof. F. V. Hayden.

The county is well supplied with water other than that afforded by streams. Numerous excellent springs are found in many localities. At Barneston, within a stone's throw of the old Agency building, is a splendid spring which during the Indian occupation gushed out of the ancient prairie. For many years it supplied the entire Otoe and Missouri tribes of Indians, as well as the white population at the agency, with pure, wholesome water for drinking and all domestic purposes. It has been allowed to fall into disuse and is now so filled with washings from the land and with other debris that it is a mere bog,—so much an object of danger to stock that the owner of the land where it is located keeps a fence around it. With proper development this spring is capable of supplying a city of many thousands with an abundance of the purest water, at small expense. At Blue Springs there is a succession of beautiful springs gushing from under steep embankments and forming a little stream which is called Spring creek and which debouches a few rods away into the Big Blue river. Here is an unknown quantity but certainly an abundant supply of excellent water, capable of meeting the demand of a large city. These natural water resources, besides giving a name to the beautiful city of Blue Springs, have been sufficiently developed to meet the demands of both Blue Springs and Wymore. Beatrice, as is well known, draws her entire municipal water supply for her 12,000 population, amounting to over 1,000,000 gallons a day, from what is known as Zimmerman Springs, a few miles northwest of the city,—a supply which under scientific analysis has been found to be almost chemically pure. There are other localities throughout the county where spring water of excellent quality and great purity can be obtained at comparatively small cost. Well water of great volume and purity is obtainable in every part of the county, at depths varying from a few feet in the Blue river bottom lands to much greater depths in the upland regions. There are no natural lakes in the county and no large bodies of water formed by the streams.

The climate of Gage county is moderately humid, mild and invigorating. The normal monthly temperature ranges from an average of thirty-two degrees Fahrenheit in January to seventy-six degrees in July. Nowhere in the upper Mississippi valley are the climatic conditions more equable or more conducive to healthy living for man and beast. Here one experiences in the greatest perfection the grand procession of the seasons, spring, summer, autumn, winter. The rainfall averages about thirty inches per annum and is well distributed throughout the period of plant growth, as a rule assuring abundant harvests, bountiful crops. All Nebraska, however, is in the region of occasional extremes of temperature caused by excessive drought. Once in each decade, sometimes oftener, crops may partly fail from this cause or from hot, dry southwesterly winds. The winters are sometimes severe, and other eccentricities of climate common to Nebraska and neighboring states may, and do in fact, manifest themselves in some degree in Gage county. But, all things considered, it would be difficult to find in this latitude of the entire country a more healthful or a more attractive climate.

In the early days fluctuations of temperature were more frequent and more marked than now, and the pioneers often suffered severely both from the rigors of winter and the heat and drought of summer. Fearful storms not infrequently swept over the tree less prairies, endangering the lives of man and beast, both in winter and summer. With the settlement of the country, the cessation of prairie tires, the planting of groves, orchards, and hedgerows, together with many other agencies incident to a large and progressive community, tending to ameliorate the hard conditions of pioneer life, the sudden and frequent changes of temperature to which all the northwest is subject summer and winter, have come to be regarded here with great indifference.

The soils of the county, as of nearly all eastern Nebraska, are mature and fertile. They contain the essential elements necessary to the growth and production of the fruits, grasses, and grains common to north temperate regions, and as a rule, up to the present moment, they respond bountifully to the labors of the husbandman without artificial fertilization or other expensive upkeep.

Soil may be defined as a mixture of fine earthy materials with organic matter produced by the decomposition of vegetation on the earth's surface,—as the stems, roots, and leaves of trees, grasses, and other forms of vegetation. The earthy materials which enter into soil formation are the outer portions of the earth's crust, which, by a process described as weathering, or by glacial action or other drastic force, become decomposed into fine stone, gravel, minerals, clay, sand, and silt. Types of soils are determined by the relative proportions of these materials, organic and inorganic, which by inspection or chemical analysis are found to enter into their composition.

On the basis of their origin, the soils of Gage county may be roughly classed as residual, alluvial, glacial drift, and loessial deposits. Residual soils are formed from the decomposition of limestone and possibly some other kinds of rock by a process scientifically known as leaching, in which the soluble portions of the decomposed mass disappear, and the insoluble or less soluble remain in the place where decomposition or leaching has occurred, as a sort of subsoil, and by the addition of vegetable or organic mold may mature into rich, fertile soil.

Alluvial soils are formed from sedimentary deposits arising from the overflow of streams, carrying in suspension soils and soil materials from a higher to a lower elevation. The vegetable matter such soils contain often renders them the richest and most fruitful known to man. The valleys of the Nile, the Mississippi, the upper Ganges, the Hoang-Ho. the Po, and the Danube, afford fine examples of the strength and wonderful fertility of this kind of soil.

Glacial soils are derived from those deposits which are mainly the product of glacial action, exerted through long ages in the formative period of the earth, though their immediate deposition may have been caused in part by the action of wind and water. Such soils are found as far south as the southern boundary of the great ice cap, which in the glacial or ice age covered to enormous depths the north temperate regions of the world. Soils derived from this source are scientifically described as *drift*.

Loessial soil is a loessial deposit, very homogeneous in character and rarely stratified. It usually contains large quantities of land and fresh water shells as well as the bones of extinct animals. In regions where the loess occurs it is the most recent of the soil formations. It is regarded as the sedimentary bottoms of ancient fresh-water seas and lakes. Its presence is often attributed to fierce winds which in primordial times carried the fine loamy silt to distant areas and spread it out, often in great thickness. This imperial soil, according to Professor Samuel Aughey, who was the first to occupy the position of geologist at the State University of Nebraska, veneers almost the entire glacial drift of the state. It forms the Missouri river bluffs and is thickest there, gradually thinning towards the west. A recent soil survey of Gage county showed the loess to be extensively present in various areas, principally however on the uplands. It is said to be the thickest and in the highest state of preservation about Cortland. In common parlance it is spoken of as loam, modified by descriptive terms, as black loam, sandy loam, clay loam, and the like.

To the wondering view of the early inhabitants of this section of Nebraska the object of the most striking and universal interest was the rolling prairies. Extending from the Canadian boundary on the north to the tropical gulf of Mexico on the south, and from the timbered shore of the Missouri river on the east to the foothills of the Rocky mountains on the west, its apparently illimitable expanse presented great variety of surface configuration. In its virgin state it was a source of never-ending curiosity and interest. Thickly clothed with verdure, diversified by stream and wood, and shimmering in the brilliant sunshine, the prairies of eastern Nebraska were probably the most beautiful landscape on the face of the earth. At frequent intervals were found rivers and living streams of pure water, and the dark foliage of the forest trees skirting them presented a pleasing contrast to the lighter green of the prairies. Such was the fascination which they exerted over the human mind that the first settlers were prone to wander from one high place to another to feast their eyes upon the beautiful panorama which the prairies offered.

The origin of the prairies is involved in some doubt. Even scientific men of character and great learning are not fully agreed upon this important subject. The most plausible theory which seeks to account for the presence of the great level prairies is that they were the sites of ancient shallow lakes, which gradually filled with silt washed down from the Rocky mountains, six hundred miles away, and from other sources,— first becoming marshes, which with the accumulations of vegetable matter ultimately became the high level prairies. The rolling prairies are said to bear evidence to the rush and the recoil of the fresh-water seas that followed the melting of the great ice cap, while the ravines, the hills, and the valleys were formed by the washing away of large portions of the surface in the process of continental draining.

CHAPTER VII

FLORA AND FAUNA

GRASSES — FLOWERS—FOREST AND STREAM — ANIMAL LIFE — THE BUFFALO — ELK — ANTELOPE — NATIVE BIRDS — FISH — INSECT LIFE — GRASSHOPPERS — EFFECT OF SETTLEMENT

The native flora of our county, like all the southeastern portion of Nebraska, was characterized by many forms of plant life. The most casual observer could readily divide it into the flora of the prairies and the flora of forest and stream. The prairies were clothed with many varieties of grass as well as of plants, some of which were perennial and in their florescenze beautiful. The early settlers found bottom land along the streams and other depressions stocked with the blue-stem grass, the uplands with bunch grass and other species of succulent grasses, all of which however ultimately yielded to the blue-stem as the country became settled, the uplands pastured, and the ravages of fire diminished,—eastern Nebraska thus became clothed with this the most desirable of all our native forage plants. This process was rapid in Gage county, so much so that within ten years after the first settlements were made the blue-stem could be cut for hay anywhere on the prairies. Mingled with the grasses, which spread a beautiful carpet of verdure over the earth's surface, were hundreds of flowering plants whose diversity of size, color, and perfume contributed to the beauty and interest of the primitive landscape. The graceful wild rose, representatives of the lily family, buttercups, violets, mallows, primroses, goldenrods, asters, verbenas, morning-glories, and many other well known flowering species bloomed forth over the prairies in their season,—a profusion of delicate colors. In almost no other way have settlement and cultivation wrought such radical changes as in the plant life of the prairies.

The flora of the forest and stream needs but a word. Unlike that of the prairies, which was native in its origin, the larger forms of vegetation in this portion of Nebraska are wholly due to migration. In the southern part of the state the source of forest growth is readily assignable to the nearby forests along the Missouri river. The distribution of tree, vine, and shrub seeds, of all common forests growths in this latitude, has been greatly facilitated by wind, by flood, by beak and wing, a process which has gone on from primordial times to the present moment. Shut off from germination, by the fine, compact soils of the prairies, such seeds, when transported from near by or from distant forests, have found lodgment and favorable conditions of growth in the rich alluvial soils of the streams, thus giving rise to our forests of oak, hickory, elm, hackberry, sycamore, maple, box elder, red bud, locust, willow, cottonwood, and all the other varieties of timber growth that go to make up our groves and forests. Amongst the shrubs are the plum, chokecherry, hazel nut, prickly ash, wahoo bush, red willow, gooseberry, wintergreen, and some other varieties. Of plants and vines the most beautiful and important are the strawberry, the blackberry, raspberry, several varieties of wild grape, bitter-sweet, Virginia creeper, sarsaparilla, and other climbing vines.

The hand of man has greatly modified the pleasing aspect which nature wore here in her primitive state, and has added greatly to the stock of forest trees and forest growths by the art and skill of arboriculture, while by excluding fire and other destructive agencies it has greatly increased both the quality of our growing timber and the acreage of our forests.

The animal life of southeastern Nebraska when the white man came was varied and interesting. Nearly every form of wild life common to this latitude, whether of earth, air, or water, was represented here, and, in addition, forms which are associated mainly with wide reaches of open prairies. In vast herds, aggregating many millions, here roamed the shaggy buffalo, while the shy and lordly elk in great bands fed upon the natural meadows. Both species of the American deer were native here, and droves of beautiful antelope roamed the plains. Not long before the advent of the white man, our plains were probably also the range of the caribou, the moose, and the mountain sheep. The wild fox, the sly coyote, and his large relation, the mountain or gray wolf, the lynx, the panther, the bear, the mountain lion, and other representatives of the carnivorous tribe were all at some time no doubt native to our eastern Nebraska. The rodents were widely distributed in forest and plain: they were the mole, the wood mouse, the ground gopher or ground squirrel, the pocket gopher, the common tree squirrel, the badger, the ground hog, while acres upon acres were included in the villages of the prairie dog. The strictly fur-bearing animals were well represented by the beaver, the otter, the mink, the muskrat, the raccoon, and the skunk. Frogs, toads, and other batracians inhabited the streams and marsh lands, while numerous varieties of snakes, the prairie rattlesnake, the common bull snake, the water moccasin, the puffing adder, and other forms of reptilian life abounded on the prairies and about the woods and streams.

Bird life was in evidence on every hand. The largest species were the wild turkey, goose, brant, crane, duck, and turkey buzzard; The medium-sized species were the long-billed curlew in vast flocks, the golden plover, the sand piper, several species of hawks, owls, and crows; the smaller birds and the singers, amongst others, included swallows, wrens, yellow hammers, chickadees, peewees, bluejays, meadow larks, thrush, bluebird, black bird, and many other prairie, bush, meadow, and grass species of song and plumage birds. The game and food birds aside from water fowl were wild turkeys in occasional flocks, the quail, and millions upon millions of grouse, or prairie chickens as they were commonly called.

The clear waters of the creeks and rivers were well stocked with all varieties of fish common to this portion of North America. In the smaller streams and in the deep holes in large ravines which were fed in part by springs, were found bullheads, perch, chubs, cat, red-horse, and sunfish. In the rivers and larger streams were the buffalo, pike, pickerel, gar-pike, suckers, croppies, and cat fish. In Gage county in the early days as at the present time, the Big Blue river was the one reliable source of the fish supply. In this respect it was a very notable stream, as fish abounded in it and were easily taken, and before the wash from cultivated lands had changed their character its waters were clear, sparkling, beautiful as a mountain stream—in deep places as blue as the overhanging sky. A river moss, wherever a stony formation supplied points of attachment, spread out over the bottom of the stream, sometimes from shore to shore and several inches thick, covering large areas of the channel, its individual streamers often being many feet in length and all thickly leaved. The swift water imparted a wavy motion to its mass, and its gentle rising and falling was often accelerated by large buffalo fish and other species preying upon the periwinkle, crawfish, and other small acquatic life found attached to the green moving masses of moss.

Insect life, the most numerous and varied of all forms of life, has always abounded in every portion of Nebraska. Flies, gnats, mosquitos, wasps, hornets, vari-colored butterflies, moths, grasshoppers, cycads, beetles, miriapods, crickets, spiders, bees, locusts, caterpillars, ants, and every other creeping and crawling thing native to the north temperate zone finds a natural habitat in eastern Nebraska. Of these native insects the most destructive species are the chinch bug, the army worm, the Hessian fly, the Colorado potato-beetle, and the codling moth. At varying periods of time, under favorable circumstances, great injury has been done to growing field crops by many of these insects, as well as to orchards and gardens.

But the insect that has caused the greatest and most widespread disaster to crops and vegetation in our county, as well as to the state at large and neighboring states, is the Rocky Mountain locust or grasshopper—a migratory insect, native to the high, dry plateaus of New Mexico and Arizona, the eastern foothills of the Rocky mountains, and the plains of Wyoming, Idaho, and Montana. Nothing in the natural history of the west has excited such widespread interest as the great locust plagues to which the early settlers of our state were frequently subjected and which may again become a menace to our prosperity. Unlike Pharaoh's locusts that came on an east wind, these usually came on a northwest wind, but like them "they covered the face of the whole earth so that the land was darkened; and they did eat every herb of the land, and all the fruit of the trees—and there remained not any green thing in the trees or the herbs of the field in all the land of Egypt." [Ex. 8, v. 15.]

It is not known when these pests first appeared in Nebraska. Probably before the coming of the white man they may have been here as a mere incident to wild nature. The first actual visitation known to history occurred in 1857, when they are described by the Brownville *Advertiser* as "mowing the prairies." No less than seven invasions are known to have occurred in southeastern Nebraska before the last, in 1874. They were much alike. In a few instances the corn crop was far enough advanced to escape total destruction, but in the great invasion of 1874 not a green thing escaped. The leaves on the trees, prairie grass, and herbage of every description were practically laid waste. The first intimation of disaster would be a few rapidly dropping hoppers out of the sky, mere avant couriers of the myriads of destroying locusts. The observer, glancing toward the sun, beheld the air to a depth of half a mile or more thick with the flying insects, moving with the wind and glittering in the sunshine like flakes of snow. A slight change of the high-wafting breeze or a slackening of its force, caused an immediate descent of the whole dense mass to the ground, and the whole earth, as in biblical times, was covered by hopping, flying, creeping, climbing, crawling locusts, and every edible thing perished.

GRASSHOPPER SCENE, PLATTSMOUTH, NEBRASKA, 1874

Here in Gage county up to July 16, 1874, crops of every description had never held greater promise. Fall wheat and oats were already harvested, or well matured, but on that day a devastating hot wind swept up from the southwest and the corn crop was blasted in a few hours. The grasshopper invasion which followed in the early part of August left the fields practically bare. All Nebraska, Minnesota, Iowa, Illinois, Missouri, Kansas, Arkansas, Nevada, Colorado, Texas, and the territories of Wyoming, Dakota, and Idaho were involved in the disaster. In most of this territory the crops, gardens, and orchards were in flourishing condition; everything was swept away. This invasion marks an era in the history of the states affected and in the lives of all their inhabitants, a never to be forgotten circumstance. It was the same story everywhere—destruction on a tremendous scale. It was the most startling plague of locusts of which we have any account outside of the Bible. Combined with the drought, this scourge was the cause of great destitution in Nebraska. On the 8th day of September, 1874, Governor Robert W. Furnas, by proclamation, appointed twenty prominent Nebraskans as a relief commission to receive and distribute all contributions of money and clothing in aid of those who had been, through no fault of their own, practically reduced to beggary. These gentlemen formed a corporation known in our history as the Nebraska Relief and Aid Society. This society proceeded to organize the work throughout the state. It was estimated in January, 1874, that more than ten thousand people of our commonwealth were in need of aid. In the frontier counties the suffering was acute and often pitiful, but a great many benevolent persons interested themselves in the cause of relief and much was done by private charity to mitigate the poverty and want of the times.

By January 8, 1875, the society was able to report the receipt from various sources of $37,279.73 in money and nearly an equal amount in clothing. Early in 1875 congress appropriated thirty thousand dollars in money to be used in the purchase of food supplies and five times that amount for the purchase of clothing, its beneficences to be distributed to the people of the several states who were sufferers from the grasshopper scourge of 1874. A part of these funds came of course to our state. By far the most practical and noteworthy act within our borders was the passage of a law by the legislature, under date of February 17, 1875, providing for the issuing of state bonds, to the amount of fifty thousand dollars. "For the purpose of providing seed for the citizens of counties devastated by grasshoppers during the year 1874." Most of the counties in the state, including Gage. were beneficiaries of these relief measures, and by these various means thousands of homesteaders were held upon their claims and the state was spared wholesale depopulation in many counties.

Great alarm existed during the winter of 1874-1875, as well as the following spring and early summer, on account of the billions and billions of grasshopper eggs that had been deposited in the ground the previous autumn. The exact facts of the case with respect to the deposition of grasshopper eggs staggers belief. Scarcely an inch of land or a clod of dirt but contained several nests of grasshopper eggs, closely packed in a sealed mass, about an inch in length, numbering probably one hundred eggs to a package, shaped like and about the size of a small ant egg. When hatching time came in the spring, the sight was simply wonderful. Myriads upon multiplied myriads of small, young hoppers appeared everywhere, so thick in places upon the rails of the railway tracks as to impede travel. Words fail to describe adequately the situation. The young hoppers were ravenous. In a large portion of the state every green, edible thing disappeared as if by magic. They matured rapidly and by the 20th of May or a little later the young pests got their wings and shape, after a succession of moultings, and became, by an almost instantaneous transition from a mere rusty hopper, a winged insect capable of prolonged flight. The migration began the moment their wings appeared. The young, wingless insects would begin hopping with a wind from the north, when suddenly with a mighty hop their wings would appear and, spreading them, they would sail away southward on the favoring breeze. In a few days all were gone and the replanting of the corn, oats, and gardens began. But on June 15, 1875, a south wind brought them back. Pale, anxious, frightened groups of men gathered in the cities and villages to discuss the situation, business came to a standstill, and appalling disaster seemed imminent. But Providence had intervened to avert the threatened ruin. It was soon observed that although they had settled in multiplied billions in the fields and gardens, no depredations were committed. An examination showed that every insect was the victim of more than a single species of parasite, amongst them being a small, yellowish boring beetle, at the base of the wings. None ever again rose in flight. They remained stationary a few hours and perished. Here in Gage county, where comparatively little damage had been done to the growing crops by the young hoppers, a cold rain set in the night of their return, and when it was over there was not a single live grasshopper to be found. Their bodies were washed, by wagon loads, into the draws, frequently damming them and impeding the flow of surface water from the rain. This was the last of the much and justly dreaded grasshopper scourges. More than two score years have elapsed since the final appearance of this strange and destructive migratory insect, and the state of Nebraska has become rich and powerful, but the man who was living in Nebraska in 1874 witnessed a scourge of locusts greater than that of Pharaoh.

The Grasshoppers

Edwin Ford Piper

>Down by the orchard plot a man and boy,
>The boy's hat just above the whitened floor
>Of oats half hiding the young trees and swaying
>Under a strong breeze in the blazing noon,
>The man looks upward, blinks with dazzled eyes,
>Then shading face with hand peers painfully;
>Little winged creatures drive athwart the sun,
>High up, in ceaseless, countless flight to the north,
>His, mood runs hot envisioning the past,
>"It was three years ago this very day.
>
>"Three years ago that clinging, hopping horde
>Made the earth crawl. With slobbery mouths,

All leafage, woody twig, and grain, and grass,
They utterly consumed, leaving the land
Abominable. The wind-borne plague rained down
On the full-leaved tree where laughter rippled light.
To answer odorous whispers of the flowers.
Soon, naked to the blistering sun, it stared
At the bones of its piteous comrades. Afterwards,
A jest to strangers—charity—cattle hungering—
Women and children starving! But the power of the
   creatures!
The daughters of the locust, numberless, numberless!
Jaws bite, throats suck, the beauty of lovely fields
Is in their guts, the world is but a mummy!"

Man and boy turn from the oats and the vigorous
   orchard;
But as they go the lad is looking, looking
To see, high up, like gnats, the winged millions
Moving across the sun. May God rebuke them!

   As long as the human race was represented in Nebraska by wandering savages who dwelt sparsely in widely separated communities it was possible for every form of wild life to thrive and increase, but when the white man spreads abroad over nature's wide domain, maintaining fixed habitations, he dominates all forms of life. And the settlement of Nebraska by the palefaced race has brought tremendous changes in its primitive forms. Gone are the useful buffalo, the stately elk, the deer, the antelope, from which the Indian fed and clothed himself and manufactured many of the crude utensils for his own use; gone the larger felines that preyed upon them; fish, bird, and even insect life have also been notably modified by the presence of the white man. The game birds have almost totally disappeared, with the curlews and the plovers, while the wild goose, brant, crane, and duck are rarely seen except in their long, high, semi-annual pilgrimages to and from their breeding grounds on the Saskatchewan and the far north. The denizens of the streams have been depleted both in quantity and quality, many species having wholly disappeared, as the pike, pickerel, bullhead, sucker, chub, red horse, and perch. The waters of our county no longer abound with the buffalo fish or the cat, and even the vicious gar-pike has become scarce. While these are taken in limited numbers, the carp, an alien fish, has largely supplanted them. Even the great Missouri has suffered similar depletions and invasions and the faithful and continuous efforts of the state through its fish commission to restock our streams with desirable edible fish have so far proved of doubtful value.

The beaver and the otter, which once were found in numbers about the water courses of southeastern Nebraska, have almost wholly disappeared. The mink, muskrat, and skunk are still occasionally trapped or shot, but their pursuit is no longer a profitable occupation. The wolves, badgers, mountain lions, and other noxious carnivora have either been driven away or hunted and killed, until only an occasional coyote, bob cat, or badger is found where once they abounded. Few representatives of the reptilian family remain and these are mostly of an innocuous kind.

Animal life of the state has been affected too by the additions to it which man has consciously made or which have followed his course. Besides the domestic animals which replaced the buffalo, elk, and deer and made civilization possible on the "Great American Desert," wherever man builds, plants, sows, gathers, or reaps, there is found in its greatest perfection the house fly, the Colorado potato-beetle, the chinch bug, the cut-worm, and other insects that prey upon the roots, stems, and leaves of his fields, gardens, and orchards.

CHAPTER VIII

THE PUBLIC DOMAIN

NEMAHA LAND DISTRICT — BROWNVILLE LAND OFFICE — REGISTERS AND RECEIVERS — OFFERED AND UNOFFERED LANDS — PREËMPTIONS — FREE HOMESTEAD LAW — AGRICULTURAL COLLEGE LAND GRANT ACT — OPERATION OF THE ACT — COLLEGE SCRIP ENTRIES IN TOWNSHIPS — HOMESTEAD ENTRIES

The public domain of the United States has dwindled to a mere fraction of what it was in 1854, when the territory of Nebraska was created by act of congress. The system by which the United States government undertook to dispose of its lands has worked as efficiently as any department of the public service. In every state and territory where public lands were located, and particularly here in the west, the federal land office has always proved an effective and a most important factor in the settlement and development of the country. The prospective settler has met, at the very outset of his inquiries, the organized agencies of his government, prepared to lend him all possible assistance in selecting and locating upon a tract of land.

The local land office for the district in which Gage county was situated in the early pioneer days, was established at Brownville. Nemaha county, Nebraska, under an act of congress, dated March 3, 1857, and opened for business about that time. The land district was officially described as the Nemaha District, while amongst the people it was almost universally designated as the Brownville land district. The office continued in operation at Brownville from the date of its establishment to July 7, 1868, when it was removed to Beatrice. The district was thereafter known as the Beatrice land district, and it embraced Nemaha, Richardson, Pawnee, Johnson, Gage, Jefferson, Saline, Fillmore,

Thayer, Nuckolls, and Clay counties. The office was maintained at Beatrice from July 7, 1868, to the 15th day of September, 1887, when the district was consolidated with the Lincoln land district and the records of the Beatrice office were removed to Lincoln.

For more than thirty years this office was a necessary and an important factor in the affairs of the inhabitants of the district which it served. Through its ministrations many homes were established and the foundation for many a fortune laid. The volume of business transacted at this office through the greater portion of its existence was enormous. Its officials were called upon to advise the settlers both with respect to the laws under which public lands were granted to individuals and the methods of complying with these laws once the entryman had availed himself of their benefits. The officers of the local land offices of the United States are designated as register and receiver. The fixed salary attached to each office was $500 and an additional amount, on the fee basis, was allowed, not to exceed $2,500, or $3,000 in all. The officers of the old Brownville-Beatrice land office were uniformly gentlemen of high character and excellent ability. Their names may be regarded as worthy of preservation in a work of this kind. At Brownville the officials were:

George H. Nixon, Register, April 9, 1857, temporary; April 16, 1858, permanent.

Charles B. Smith, Receiver, April 11, 1857, temporary; April 16, 1858, permanent.

Richard F. Barrett, Register, May 27, 1861, temporary; July 26, 1861, permanent.

I. Edward Burbank, Receiver, May 27, 1861, temporary.

George F. Watton, Receiver, June 21, 1861, temporary; July 26, 1861, permanent.

Sewell R. Jamison, Receiver, March 10, 1862, permanent.

Charles G. Dorsey, Register, July 25, 1865, temporary; May 16, 1866, permanent.

Theodore W. Bedford, Register, November 5, 1866, temporary.

Henry M. Atkinson, Register, March 7, 1867, permanent.

John S. Carson, Receiver, April 15, 1867, permanent.

At Beatrice the officials were:

Hiram W. Parker, Register, June 2, 1871, temporary; December 27, 1871, permanent; January 22, 1876, permanent; January 29, 1880, permanent.

Nathan Blakely, Receiver, August 10, 1869, temporary; December 28, 1869, permanent.

Robert B. Harrington, Receiver, September 10, 1875, temporary; December 17, 1875, permanent; December 22, 1879, permanent.

Hugh J. Dobbs, Register, March 7, 1884.

William H. Somers, Receiver, March 24, 1881.

Joseph Hill, Receiver, June 9, 1885, temporary.

Edward R. Fogg, Receiver, May 24, 1886, permanent.

In the beginning of the land office in the old Nemaha district, the public lands were classified as *offered* and *unoffered* lands. The former comprised all those tracts which had been formally offered by the local land office for sale at public auction, for cash, to the highest bidder, the minimum bid allowed being one dollar and twenty-five cents per acre. The unoffered lands comprised all public lands which had not been placed on sale at public auction, for cash, to the highest bidder. This distinction in the public land laws was made by act of congress in the early '40s, and continued from that time until May 18, 1898, when the law creating the distinction was repealed.

In districts where offered lands were located, those not sold at public vendue when offered, could be afterward bought without settlement for cash, at one dollar and twenty-five cents per acre. Unoffered lands were not open for cash entry. In both classes title could be acquired by entry and actual settlement under the preëmption laws of congress. Likewise military-bounty land warrants issued, under the acts of 1847 and 1855, to the soldiers and sailors of the Revolutionary war, the war of 1812, the Mexican war, and the various Indian wars, could be used in purchasing public lands of the United States, regardless of the foregoing distinction. And under the homestead act, effective January 1, 1863, this distinction was also ignored and entry could be made anywhere on the public domain on lands not reserved or otherwise appropriated by congress.

The offered lands in the old Brownville-Beatrice land district were confined to the Missouri river counties. From first to last Gage county presented a clear field for entry of land under the preëmption, homestead, and other acts for acquiring title on the public domain. Prior to the passage of the homestead law the settlers acquired title under the preemption act, where purchase was not made by military-bounty land warrants. The procedure under the preemption laws as applied by claimants was simplicity itself. It consisted in performing some act which amounted to notice to the world of an intention on the part of the settler to claim the tract selected by him—as the erection of some sort of a dwelling or the placing of a foundation for a cabin on the land selected; any act, in fact, which manifested an intent to claim a given tract of land and which at the same time amounted to notice of such intent to an adverse claimant. Such act must of course be followed by filing in the local land office a written declaration of intent on the part of the claimant to enter and purchase said land; it must also be followed by actual settlement on his part, and in twelve months by proof of settlement, of improvement, and the payment to the government of one dollar and twenty-five cents per acre in cash or in military-bounty land warrants, or, at a later date, by college scrip at the same rate per acre.

A number of preëmption filings were made on Gage county land prior to the taking effect of the homestead law, January 1, 1863, but these were followed by comparatively few final entries. In actual practice, the squatter on the public domain performed his acts of settlement, filed his declaration of intentions in the local land office to appropriate said land and pay for the same, made improvements, established his residence upon the land, and in many instances, without perfecting his entry under the preemption acts, remained in open, exclusive, adverse possession until the homestead law became effective, when he availed himself of its benefits by changing his preemption into a homestead. Once in actual possession the "Squatter Sovereign" ran little risk of being disturbed by a rival claimant. By a sort of freemasonry existing between them, the settlers allowed it to be understood that there must be no claim jumping, and claim jumpers in Gage county were pretty scarce.

The passage of the free-homestead bill by congress nearly two and one-half years before the close of the great Civil war, was followed, after the close of the war, by a tremendous influx of settlers on the public domain, wherever free homes could be found, and Gage county rapidly filled with actual settlers seeking permanent homes in this beautiful section of country, many of them veterans of the Civil war. But in 1867 this movement was suddenly and permanently halted by the operation of what is known as the Agricultural College Land Grant Act.

Whatever one may think of the beneficent purpose of this act, whereby the national legislature was induced, without the slightest financial consideration, to appropriate nearly ten million acres of the public lands of the United States for educational purposes, there can be no difference of opinion as to the improvidence and wastefulness of this legislation. As set forth in the title to the act, the purpose of this vast donation was to provide for the establishment of one or more institutions in each state, "the leading object of which shall be, without excluding other scientific and classical studies, and including military practice, to teach such branches of learning as are related to agriculture and mechanic arts, in such manner as the legislatures of the states shall respectively prescribe, in order to promote the liberal and practical education of the industrial classes in the several pursuits and professions of life."

Had the operation of this act been confined to those states and territories whose wealth consisted chiefly in the public lands within their boundaries, and which, on account of poverty, were unable to make suitable provision for the education and training of their young men and women, it would be beyond just criticism and worthy of all praise. Probably that was the original intent and purpose of the act, but the selfishness of the old and wealthy states, where there were no public lands, resulted in a distortion of the original intent, and in the end imparted to the act the appearance of a land-grabbing device of colossal proportions, by which states with large delegations in congress profited enormously at public expense.

For the bill in its passage through congress to secure the support of the representatives of those states where there were no public lands subject to entry or purchase under federal laws, an ingeneous scheme was devised whereby scrip was to be issued to all such states for the full amount of their donative shares, at one dollar and twenty-five cents per acre, for the entire acreage due them on the basis of thirty thousand acres for each senator and representative in congress. The states holding this scrip could under the law either enter land with it themselves or sell it at private sale and use the proceeds of such sale as they deemed proper to carry out the purposes of the law. The result is perfectly obvious—the weak, helpless, needy states, rich only in the public lands within their borders, were restricted to the land itself at the rate of thirty thousand acres for each senator and representative in congress, while the great, strong, healthy, powerful states took their share in scrip, and either located it themselves at the rate of one dollar and twenty-five cents per acre on vast tracts of public lands or sold it upon the market for cash. Thus Nebraska received under the act ninety thousand acres of public land, which formed the nucleus for its State University, while the great state of New York received college scrip covering 989,930 acres, part of which was sold on the market at a fraction of its face value, the remainder being used to purchase vast areas of the finest pine land in the world, in Wisconsin and Minnesota. From her donative share New York realized $6,651,473.88, which vast sum constitutes the endowment of Cornell University. Not a single state or territory failed to avail itself of the provisions of this enactment, by which a grand total of 9,597,340 acres of the public lands of the United States were nominally dedicated to the cause of higher education. Only a comparatively few, however, actually received their donative shares in land. As might have been foreseen by any patriotic and prudent statesman, the vast profit of this legislation inured to individuals. The process by which this curious and unexpected result was achieved was very simple. The scrip was thrown indiscriminately on the market and sold for cash to speculators, usually for a fraction of its nominal value, the purchaser or assignee succeeding to the rights of the states to select and pay for the public lands of the country with agricultural-college scrip so purchased, at the rate of one dollar and twenty-five cents per acre. Thus, Alabama scrip sold for one dollar and six cents per acre, leaving a margin of nineteen cents per acre profit to the purchaser; Arkansas scrip sold for ninety cents.

Connecticut scrip for seventy-five cents, Delaware ninety-two cents, Illinois one dollar, Indiana eighty-seven cents, Kentucky sixty cents, Maine and Massachusetts fifty-six cents, Maryland and New Jersey fifty-five cents, Missouri and Pennsylvania fifty-two cents, Ohio fifty-four cents, New Hampshire thirty-two cents, North Carolina forty-six cents, and Rhode Island forty-one cents per acre. Even at these low prices, some of the states were enabled, on account of the vast amount of their donative shares of the public lands, to endow most liberally the institutions founded under the act. Thus, Pennsylvania, with 780,000 scrip acres, received, at the low rate of fifty-two cents per acre, from scrip sales alone the sum of $406,000; Massachusetts, with a donative share of 390,000 acres of the public domain, from scrip sales alone received $219,000; and the other wealthy eastern states profited from scrip sales proportionally. When we take into account the fact that the populous eastern states received the lion's share of this vast donation, and that the new prairie states and territories and the northern timbered states and territories were despoiled of their rich and valuable lands under this act, to build up existing educational institutions in New England, New York Pennsylvania, New Jersey, Ohio, Indiana, Illinois, and other landless states, the improvidence and the selfishness of this legislation must be apparent to the dullest mind.

Gage county suffered severely from this wasteful policy. Speculators thronged her prairies, their pockets and carpetbags stuffed with college scrip bought at nominal figures from Illinois, Ohio, Indiana, Pennsylvania, Massachusetts, Maine, New Hampshire, Missouri, Kentucky, Alabama, Mississippi, Rhode Island, New York, and other scrip states, and in the summer of 1867 her broad, fertile acres disappeared as by magic, at the very moment when Nebraska had ceased to be a territory, when the railroads had come or were on their way, and when the pioneer days were over and immigration was setting toward her in an ever increasing stream. Keen-eyed appraisers went leisurely over our county's finest upland regions and marked for entry every desirable tract of land. The following table shows approximately the acreage thus entered in the several townships of our county during the years 1867 and 1868, by the use of college scrip:

Adams	19 sections
Nemaha	19 1-2 sections
Highland	8 sections
Clatonia	3 1-4 sections
Grant	14 1-2 sections
Holt	23 1-2 sections
Hanover	29 1-2 sections
Hooker	29 1-2 sections
Filley	19 1-2 sections
Logan	20 3-4 sections
Midland	14 3-4 sections
Blakely	11 1-2 sections
Lincoln	20 3-4 sections
Riverside	24 3-4 sections
Rockford	18 sections
Sherman	31 1-2 sections
Island Grove	15 1-2 sections
Blue Springs	7 3-4 sections
Sicily	12 1-2 sections
Elm	8 sections

 In the northern portion of the county at that time, most of Nemaha township, practically all of Highland, and a large part of both Clatonia and Grant townships had been with drawn from public entry as state selections under the grant by the general government to the state of Nebraska of 500,000 acres of the public domain for internal improvement, under the act of September 4, 1841. In 1871 these lands were opened for homestead entry, the state's application for the reservation of such lands having been rejected by the general land office at Washington, and were thus saved from the predatory effects of the Agricultural College Land Grant Act. In the south part of the county the Otoe and Missouri Indian reservation, of course, escaped speculative spoliation of the college scriptor. The dense population of those townships, where practically each quarter-section of land went to an actual settler, shows what would have taken place had not more than one-half of Gage county's fair domain gone to increase the educational facilities of the wealthy eastern states and line the pockets of speculators in college scrip.

It may interest the reader to know that, notwithstanding the donation of this large acreage of Gage county land in the way here described, a great many homestead entries were, in fact, made in the county by actual bonafide settlers prior to 1871, when the opening of the lands in the northern part of the county noticeably increased the number of such entries.

In the several townships of the county where homestead entries could be made prior to the above date, the number of such entries exclusive of cancellations, was:

Adams	46
Highland (Michael Weaver	1
Grant	46
Hanover	—
Filley	26
Midland	29
Lincoln	8
Rockford	54
Island Grove	26
Sicily	21
Liberty	20
Nemaha	—
Clatonia	9
Holt	12
Hooker	21
Logan	24
Blakely	52
Riverside	16
Sherman	9
Blue Springs	14
Elm	10

A total of four hundred and forty-four entries. Assuming that each entry covered the maximum of one hundred and sixty acres, the total acreage embraced in these homestead entries is 71,040. Subsequent to

January 1, 1871, the public lands in our county subject to homestead entry were almost wholly confined to Nemaha, Highland, Clatonia, and Grant townships, with an occasional entry in some of the other townships, usually growing out of the relinquishment and cancellation of a previous one.

In these calculations the lands of the Otoe and Missouri Indian reservation, which were ceded to the United States in 1881 and which were afterward sold for the exclusive benefit of these Indians, for cash, to actual settlers only, under virtually the same conditions and restrictions as prevailed under the homestead law, are not considered. But if we add the acreage of these lands to the acreage covered by homestead entries in our county, it will be seen that even then less than one-half the territory of Gage county passed from the government of the United States to actual settlers.

Nor are the lands the titles to which were acquired under the preëmption laws or cash entries with military-bounty land warrants, considered in the above calculations, but the lands so purchased from the United States were not of sufficient acreage to affect to any extent the foregoing results.

A moment's reflection will show the striking contrast between the beneficent influence of the free-homestead law and the effects of the agricultural-college act, not only in the early settlement and development of our county but in existing and future conditions. The one operated as a gift from heaven, descending upon an independent, self-respecting and industrious population; the other forms the basis of nearly every large landed fortune in the county. Without it there would have been no such individual domain as the Scully estate, and the problem of landlordism in Gage county would be scarcely worth considering.

CHAPTER IX

THE PIONEERS

FIRST GLIMPSE OF GAGE COUNTY — HOME BUILDING ON THE PRAIRIES — FOOD SUPPLIES — FRUITS — FISH — GAME — THE BUFFALO — CLOTHES — FOOD SUBSTITUTES — FIRST WHEAT CROP — SPRING WHEAT — COMMON SALT — SOCIAL LIFE

It should certainly be the delight of every age to pay grateful tribute to a noble or valiant ancestry. The annals of mankind have but meager interest when stripped of the personal element and confined to a bare narrative of events. But when vivified by the record of the lives of those whose heroic daring lifted them far above the ordinary, common plane of living, history may become the most pleasing and instructive of all subjects of study.

No history of our county would be complete which failed to render justice to its pioneers. Three score and four years have passed since the first wave of immigration broke over the eastern boundary of our state, which marked the close of the long struggle that attended the creation of the territory of Nebraska. Accustomed as we now are to comfortable and often luxurious homes, to cultivated fields, well kept, well traveled public highways, to groves, orchards, meadows, churches and schools, to thriving villages and cities, to newspapers, manufactories, banks, business establishments, railroads, telegraph and telephone lines, to everything, in fact, that typifies modern living, we are too prone to forget the hard, difficult pioneer days, when there were no homes save the settlers' lonely dug-out, sod-house. or log-cabin; when there were no fields or meadows save the rolling prairies, stretching away to the horizon on every hand, as far as the eye could see; when there were no highways save the meandering paths of the buffalo and Indian; when there were no orchards, towns or cities, no railroads, telegraph or telephone lines; when all the landscape was fresh from the hand of God, untouched and unchanged by the brain and genius of man.

Not only are we in our present state of happiness and prosperity prone to forget the aspect that nature wore in these primitive solitudes to the wondering view of the first inhabitants of our county, but we may even be strongly inclined to hold as of trifling consequence the sacrifices required of pioneer life and to disparage the actual hardships, dangers, privations, and suffering which they endured whose heroism and courage made it possible for the lines of civilization to be advanced upon the great plains region of the west.

The thin line of immigrants that gathered in the spring and early summer of 1854, on the eastern shore of the Missouri river, awaiting the signal to enter the new territory of Nebraska, rapidly spread over the eastern section of the territory contiguous to that mighty stream. And the early immigrants of Richardson, Nemaha, Otoe, Cass, Sarpy, Douglas, and some other of the eastern counties, on account of the navigation then existing on the river, were spared many of the privations of pioneer life. But those who later pushed on into Gage and other counties remote from this, the only source of water transportation available, experienced in every degree the hardships of isolated pioneer existence.

If we turn back the pages that cover the sixty-four years of our state's history, we will find that in 1854 when people of the New England, the Middle, and the South Atlantic states spoke of the west they meant Ohio, Indiana or, at the farthest, Michigan, Illinois.—or Iowa or Missouri when they mentioned our western border or frontier. The immigrants bound for Nebraska territory in 1854, and for several years thereafter, usually crossed the Missouri river at Omaha, Plattsmouth, Nebraska City, Brownville, or some less known village nestled amongst the bluffs on the western shore of that stream. The means of travel were in their crudest state. The intending immigrant might reach the river on foot, on horseback or by mule, ox or horse drawn vehicle, or by the deep-throated, side-wheel Missouri river steamboats, which in those days traversed the "Big Muddy" from St. Louis to the trading posts of the trappers, traders, and frontiersmen scattered along its banks to its source in the northwest. Once having crossed that turbulent stream, the immigrant did not need to be told that he was on the very confines of civilization, since the crudity and newness of his surroundings were vocal with evidence of that fact. He found himself hundreds of miles from the nearest railway, while the future of the electric telegraph was still wrapped up in a congressional appropriation of thirty thousand dollars, to enable Professor Morse to perfect his wonderful invention. Eastward across the river lay the hamlets and sparse settlements of the new state of Iowa; toward the west, from every point as far as the eye could see, stretched the territory of Nebraska, until then wholly unoccupied by civilized man. Of one thing the immigrant could feel assured,—when he turned his back upon the Missouri river and faced the western horizon he was like an army cut off from its base of supplies and lines of communication. Before him lay the undulating almost treeless prairie, rolling away to the west, north, and south like the billows of the ocean, hundreds upon hundreds of miles. It was the "Great American Desert" of the old geographers; the "Plains" of the military department at Washington; the El Dorado of the poor homeseeker; the unorganized, tenantless territory of Nebraska, inhabited only by wild animals and by the red man, almost equally wild. As he advanced westward a little in the brilliant sunlit plain, the last trace of the presence of civilized man soon vanished. The dim wagon trail grew dimmer and more uncertain and finally disappeared. Around on every hand the blue sky, descending to the horizon, encompassed him like a gigantic dome. A silence, a solitude that had brooded together over these vast areas since the world began, closed about him as his distance from the river settlements slowly increased. In these primeval solitudes he might remain for weeks, aye months, without seeing a single human face or hearing save his own, a single human voice.

Such was the face that nature wore and the conditions that life presented to those who drew the first furrows in the virgin soil of Nebraska. But the true pioneer looks beyond his present hard, uninviting surroundings, and with prophetic vision beholds states and nations arise from tenantless wildernesses and naked plains. Others may grow weary or discouraged, and abandon the enterprise,—not so the pioneer. Destiny points his course and with unswerving fidelity he calmly awaits the fruition of his hopes!

But the prospect that confronted the Gage county pioneer in that long by-gone day—three score and four years ago—was not wholly uninviting, nor his surroundings as desolate, nor his condition as desperate as to the unreflecting mind they might have seemed. Resourceful by nature, self-reliant from the hard school of experience, courageous, determined, he was his own best guarantor of the successful issue of his venture as a pioneer in the new territory. If the winds of winter whistled and roared about his lonely cabin and drifting snows almost hid it from sight, within the blazing logs glowed on the rude hearth and all was warmth and cheer. If the winter seemed long, cold, and hard, it burgeoned at last into spring, whose vernal clouds and dappled sky, whose long twilight and dawn, song of birds and distant boom of prairie chicken welcoming the rising sun, renewed his hopes and spurred him on to yet higher endeavor. Summer followed, always beautiful, with the wide billowy prairie garbed in green, white, pink, red, yellow, and gold; then autumn, with its brilliant and soothing colors outlining prairies and stream.

From drawing by Geo. Simons, in the frontier sketch book of N. P. Dodge

FIRST CLAIM CABIN IN NEBRASKA
Built by Daniel Norton, between Omaha and Bellevue, in 1853

The occupations of the pioneer were many and varied. His first care was to provide some sort of shelter for himself and family. Here in Gage county this usually consisted of a log cabin, or occasionally a sod house, generally comprising a single room, probably fourteen by sixteen feet in dimensions, of a single low story in height, built in some bend of a stream or other sheltered spot. It was often scant quarters for a family, but children of pioneer parents soon learned to accommodate themselves to their surroundings and the exigencies of circumstances. After his family the pioneer's next care was to construct shelter for such stock as he possessed and to provide for their maintenance. This shelter was apt to be a very crude affair, though warm and safe, while hay made from bluestem and other grasses, and corn grown on the newly turned sod, furnished an abundant supply of animal food.

The water supply for man and beast, and fuel being provided, the pioneer turned his attention to breaking the tough prairie sod, which was accomplished as a rule with plows constructed for that purpose, drawn by several yoke of oxen or sometimes by three or more horses or mules. The sod was usually broken to a depth of about three inches, the plows being equipped with either a standing or a rolling cutter, and the depth of the furrow regulated by a device which held the plow steadily on a level. With the pioneers, perfection in prairie breaking consisted in so turning the sod that the edges lapped in such a way as to give to a strip of breaking, the appearance of the weather-boarded side of a frame house. The breaking could be planted as a corn field either by dropping the corn in every second or third furrow and covering with the next, or by cutting a gash in the upturned sod with a sharp ax or spade and inserting the seed, firming the earth above with the foot. Pumpkin seeds, watermelon seeds, beans, and other field or garden truck were planted in the same way, and this method carefully followed was most apt to give satisfactory results. If the season were favorable, crops of sod corn were often raised yielding as high as twenty-five or more bushels per acre, and the rich, new soil produced potatoes, melons, pumpkins, squashes, turnips, and other vegetables in great profusion and of excellent quality. Ordinarily a very few months in the growing season of the year, under favorable conditions, were sufficient to place the family of the pioneer beyond the possibility of actual want, as far as good wholesome vegetables and Indian corn could insure this result.

For sugar a ready and a very wholesome substitute was found in common sorghum, and in the production of a high grade of sorghum molasses the pioneer often attained great skill, the product being wholesome and pleasant to the taste. Beginning with the first settlement of the county, and extending until long after the close of the great Civil war, this nutritious product entered largely into the dietary of the people.

The pioneers of our county found growing in great abundance along the streams thickets of wild plums and chokecherries. The plums were often of large size and delicious flavor; the cherries, large and meaty, hung in long, thick, grape-like bunches in profusion on the low bushes. These thickets were apt to be found in great perfection in the bends of the streams, forming a sort of fire break to the groves of timber, of which they were the fringe. The mold produced by their thick leaves from year to year afforded almost ideal conditions for the spread of forest growth. In the early spring, when the elms, willows, cottonwoods, box elders, oaks, and other trees along the streams were putting forth their tender young leaves and the fresh green of the prairies was beginning to show on every hand, the milk-white, fragrant blossoms of the plum and cherry thickets afforded a pleasing diversity to the landscape, often outlining the course of the streams for great distances.

In the woods were found numerous varieties of excellent wild grapes and wild gooseberries, while at the edges of the prairies the wild strawberries grew in abundance—and these formed the staple fruit supply of the pioneers. These fruits were made into jellies, preserves, jams, butters, and other forms of food for winter use, and with the thrifty housewife's tomato preserves, pumpkin butter, dried corn, and other preparations of a like character, they formed an important feature of the homely family food supply in the early days, as they virtually took the place of the orchards and vineyards of the older settled portions of the country. These native wild fruits have long since lost their value and importance as sources of food supply. The plum and cherry thickets have largely disappeared and even the wild grape and gooseberry no longer enter extensively into the dietary of the present population. The custom of pasturing non-tillable and timbered land with stock has proved almost fatal to the existence and spread of every sort of wild shrub, vine, and forest growth. The time is rapidly approaching when the scarcity and the high cost of coal and lumber will force a return, in the matter of forestation, to the primitive conditions of the country as respects the protection of growing timber from destruction by pasturage.

The food supply afforded by these sources was not infrequently supplemented by the streams, the groves, and the prairie. The waters of our county in an early day abounded with several varieties of edible fish which were easily taken by the expenditure of a little time and trouble. Many of the most desirable sort, the pike, the pickerel, the perch, the sunfish, the chub, the red horse, have long since disappeared. Throughout the pioneer days our prairies abounded with grouse or prairie chickens, the woods with squirrels, rabbits, raccoons, and quails, with an occasional flock of wild turkeys.

Prior to the advent of the white man, Gage county had been a favorite range of the wild buffalo, the elk, the deer, the antelope. As late probably as 1855, when the Otoe and Missouri tribes of Indians were transferred from the Missouri river country to our county, these great game animals were here in large herds and bands. The early settlers found their remains in every direction. They had slowly retired, however, before the red man, so that by 1857 the buffalo had wholly disappeared from the confines of our county, but still could be found in great abundance in the region west of the Little Blue river. Small bands of elk were occasionally seen in the northern portions of the county, while deer and antelope, when the first settlers arrived, were still fairly abundant, especially in the winter about the heads of draws or wherever thick underbrush afforded shelter and food.

Of all the plains animals the buffalo was at once the most picturesque and the most useful. These huge beasts ranged the prairies by millions from the Height of Land in the far north to the tide waters of the gulf of Mexico. They spread over what is now Texas, western Louisiana, Oklahoma, New Mexico, Kansas, Colorado, Nebraska, Iowa, the Dakotas, and Montana. To the Indian tribes inhabiting these regions they furnished clothing, food, materials for sewing garments, knives, arrow points, war clubs, and many other useful articles of Indian manufacture for both peace and war. The building of the transcontinental railway lines in 1867 and in subsequent years, by multiplying the means for their destruction, finally led to the wanton extinction of this wonderful and picturesque indigenous source of wealth. Such representatives of this once numerous and powerful denizen of the prairies as now remain are found only in parks or shows, in semi or complete confinement, regarded as curiosities and forming a sad commentary upon the careless wastefulness of a government to which conservation of natural resources of wealth has until recently been a subject of minor consideration—a high sounding phrase.

From such sources of food supply as here given, the pioneer was able fully to supplement the products of his raw land and stock of domestic animals and to live in security against the demands of hunger through the most strenuous times, until his harvest ripened again upon the rich soil of his homestead and the returns of his toil and foresight finally rendered him indifferent to the wild plum and grape, the bison, the deer, the antelope, and those conditions of living which his dependence on them implied.

Probably the most perplexing subject with which the pioneer had to deal concerned clothes. Even before the beginning of the war of the rebellion, in 1861, clothing materials of all kinds here in Gage county were scarce and expensive. The cost of all commodities was increased by the Civil war of 1861-1865, which also augmented the scarcity of many articles. But in the case of wearing apparel the cost was not only very much enhanced but there was often little of much value to be had. The scarcity of clothing and the materials for it, as well as the cost of all clothing materials, was manifested in many ways, but chiefly by plainness and inexpensiveness of attire. Frequently the men and boys wore coats made by wives and mothers from blankets obtained from the Indians by barter, while pantaloons constructed from meal sacks or any common, cheap material were much in evidence. Shortly before the close of the war, and for some time thereafter, army contract clothing which had been condemned and rejected by the government was to be had at fairly reasonable figures, and a civilian partly clad in army blue was a common sight on the streets of Beatrice and elsewhere long after the war had closed. Boots, shoes, socks, hats, caps, mittens, gloves, and other articles of wearing apparel for men and boys were often crude in manufacture as well as material. The common footwear for winter was brogans and cowhide boots and shoes, while in summer the country population during the war went mostly barefoot. Occasionally Indian moccasins would be worn and not infrequently rough homemade footgear, while the skins of animals—the badger, coon, coyote, squirrel, sheep, antelope, deer—were often used for caps, mittens, leggings, and vests. Leather straps, strips of buckskin, and even bedticking, often supplied the office of suspenders, and all articles of wearing apparel were more or less of home manufacture.

Wives and daughters dressed plainly in homemade garments. The sunbonnet was the most fashionable form of female headgear and crinoline was worn by all. Outside the villages, Beatrice and Blue Springs, what might be deemed a well dressed lady or gentleman was, in fact, rarely seen amongst the pioneers, and none but beggars and tramps would now think of dressing as rural folks in that far off day were forced to dress.

In addition to his other privations, the pioneer during the opening years of our county's history was frequently unable to procure tea, coffee, wheat flour, coal oil, salt, and many other commodities of common household consumption, nearer than the Missouri river, if at all. Even when procurable, such articles were expensive and the cost often prohibitive. For tea and coffee substitutes were found which were relished by many. Often a burnt crust of corn or any bread, parched corn, or even corn meal stirred with sorghum and browned over the fire to the size and consistency of grape nuts, made a substitute for coffee. For tea the leaves of summer savory and various other herbs were used in place of Bohea, Souchong, Young Hyson, and Gunpowder. The substitute for wheat flour was of course corn meal, and many a family was reared to strength and happiness largely on corn bread milk, butter, garden vegetables, and such wild meat as was available. The common substitute for coal oil for lighting purposes was the tallow candle or the old fashioned homemade lamp, consisting of some sort of receptacle, as a saucer, teacup, or tin plate, with a twist of cotton cloth for a wick, immersed in lard.

Wheat was not grown in Cage county prior to 1861 or 1862, when spring wheat was introduced, and for many years it constituted the only variety planted. At first the settlers strove to raise only enough for their own use, as there was no home market for their surplus. And in addition the manufactory of wheat flour was in its crudest state. The first mill for grinding grain of any kind in Cage county was at the Otoe reservation, and for several years corn meal and graham flour were its only products. The pioneer hauled his wheat to Brownville, Peru, Nebraska City, and even to points in western Iowa, to obtain his supply of wheat flour. But about the year 1864 Fordyce Roper came into possession of the milling franchise in Beatrice and erected a small mill, run by water power, on the present site of Black Brothers' fine merchant mill. At the same time the United States government began to make white flour at the mill on the Otoe reservation, and thereafter both points became important milling centers for an increasingly large patronage. These were toll mills, where the farmer delivered his grain at the mill in large or small quantities, divided it with the miller on the proportional basis fixed by law and waited around until his grist was ground. Sometimes this might require several days, as each customer took his turn, like buying tickets at a railway station on an excursion day. Those living close at hand could, and often did, leave their grists and return later for their share of the flour.

SALT BASIN AND SALT WORKS, LINCOLN, NEBRASKA, 1872

Spring wheat continued to be a staple crop here until about 1876, when the chinch bug became so destructive to the plant that its cultivation ceased, and fall wheat was substituted for it with more happy results, while the chinch bug as a pest disappeared. The surplus wheat crop was either hauled to market at some Missouri river point or made into flour and hauled by wagon loads to the stage stations, ranches, and military posts along the old military highway from Independence, Missouri, Leavenworth, Atchison, and St. Joseph to Fort Kearney and beyond, where it found a ready sale at good prices, along with the homesteaders' surplus butter, eggs, beef, pork, and corn.

Common salt also was a necessary article that was difficult to obtain through the ordinary channels of trade. At a very early period in the settlement of our state, the salt basin at Lincoln became a factor of much importance not only to the pioneers of Gage county but also to large areas of the settled portions of the territories of Nebraska and Kansas and the state of Iowa; for here, under favorable conditions, the settler by a few hours' labor could often obtain enough of this important substance to last an ordinary family for an entire year. Throughout the summer months, in dry weather, a thin crust of salt would be produced every twenty-four hours over the low, flat, semi-dry surface of the basin, and this could be scraped up by wagon loads. At first the settlers hauled their scrapings home and proceeded to cleanse the salt from its impurities. This was done by boiling the mass in sorghum pans or large cast-iron kettles, skimming off the impurities that rose to the surface and evaporating the strong brine in shallow vessels. From a wagon load of scrapings could be produced by this method a barrel or more of clean, pure salt in a few days, the length of time required depending upon the sun and the atmospheric conditions. Under favorable circumstances ten inches of brine could be completely reduced to high-grade salt in sixty hours.

Very shortly after the beginning of the Civil war, in 1861, there had been established at the basin a regular industry for producing salt in quantities, by evaporation. People coming from great distances for salt were enabled to exchange flour, corn, eggs, butter, potatoes, and other farm produce for salt ready for immediate use. Or upon the payment of fifty cents per hundred weight they could buy the crude salt which in fair weather had been scraped together in heaps under some sort of shelter, and by subsequent evaporation at home secure their supply of salt. This was a great convenience, since many a settler after driving for miles to obtain his annual salt supply found the basin black and bare, on account of rain, mist, fog, or exceptionally high winds, and might even be compelled to return home saltless after camping for several days on the salt flats. For a number of years several enterprising gentlemen managed to make a very comfortable living in this industry, besides enjoying in its season the fine shooting of wild goose, duck, crane, and other water fowl that in myriads frequented the salt lake at the basin.

Social intercourse and social diversions amongst the pioneers were on a plane commensurate with their lives. To those who are wholly unaccustomed to the conditions which a new country, devoid of every convenience of modern living, imposes on its adventurous first inhabitants, the life of a Gage county pioneer may seem cruelly hard and unattractive—a drab existence from which one might reasonably exclaim in the language of the Book of Common Prayer, "Good Lord deliver us." Such persons take small account of the wonderful adaptability of human nature which enables the normal man often to turn to his advantage his most adverse surroundings. And, besides, the pioneers of a new country are largely in a class by themselves. They possess the prevision of the seer of visions and the dreamer of dreams, and are endowed with the never-failing light of imagination. To such, pioneer life in the early days in Nebraska was anything but dull and uninteresting. Its great simplicity and its freedom from those exactions which wealth imposes left time for social intercourse. None were rich and few so poor as to suffer by contrast with their neighbors. Amongst the pioneers there existed a far truer sense of equality than can anywhere be found in communities where society is complex and where prevail social distinctions resting on wealth, ancestry, or position. Neighbors were few and often remote, but distance was no barrier to social intercourse in those far-off simple days. The settlers were not usually pressed for time and made nothing of traveling, even with slow ox teams, several miles to spend the day with friends. Social gatherings, picnics, Sunday schools and other religious meetings, and even dances, were apt to bring together whole townships. Innocent youthful parties were frequent, where the masculine element appeared in its smartest garments, and well greased cow-hide boots; the feminine in its prettiest pink and white, most fetching poke bonnet and newest crinoline. Tag, blindman's buff, drop the handkerchief, and other youthful games served to pass the hours. Refreshments consisted at all social gatherings of native walnuts, popcorn, and sorghum taffy, while gaiety ruled the happy throng. Dancing was always a staple amusement for the youth of the community and even for those of staider deportment and greater age. It was not the fox trot or bunny hug, not often the waltz, polka, or schottisch, but the Virginia reel or the common square dance, with the fiddles wailing out the "Money Musk," the "Arkansas Traveler," "The Girl I Left Behind Me," and other simple, lively melodies, while some one called to the waiting couples on the floor, "Salute your partners and the opposite lady"; when this act of ballroom courtesy had been performed there would come the stentorian call, "Forward four," then "Balance all" and "Swing your partners," and so on through the whole set of dancing figures till the call "To your seats" came at last, after several minutes of glorious rythmic motion in time to the rude orchestra. After a few moments of social intercourse, laughter, perchance a song, the floor manager's call was again heard good and loud, "Choose your partners for the next dance," and if the young swain was fortunate enough to lead forward the girl of his choice, his happiness was unalloyed, and in the minds of the happy sons and daughters of our pioneers was apt to be eclipsed Byron's description of the great ball in Brussels the night before Waterloo, when

> "There was a sound of revelry by night,
> And Belgium's capital had gathered there
> Her beauty and her chivalry; and bright
> The lamps shone o'er fair women and brave men.
> A thousand hearts beat happily, and when
> Music arose with its voluptuous swell,
> Soft eye looked love to eye that spoke again,
> And all went merry as a marriage bell."

CHAPTER X

"Have You an Eye," Poem by Edwin Ford Piper — Early Gage County Markets — Missouri River-Oregon Trail — Insufficiency of Local Markets — High Prices — Missouri River Points Best Purchasing Markets — Oregon Trail Best Selling Market — Its Early History — Great South Pass — John C. Fremont — Origin of Term, "Military Road" — Starting Point — Route — Marcus Whitman — Changes — Statistics on Northern Route — An Emigrant Route — Freighting — Nebraska City — Overland Stage — Pony Express — Beatrice Route — General Description.

Have You an Eye?

Have you an eye for the trails, the trails,
    The old mark and the new?
What scurried here, what loitered there,
    In the dust and in the dew?

Have you an eye for the beaten track,
    The old hoof and the young?
Come name me the drivers of yesterday,
    Sing me the songs they sung.

O, was it a schooner last went by,
    And where will it cross the stream?
Where will it halt in the early dusk,
    And where will the camp-fire gleam?

They used to take the shortest cut
    The cattle trails had made;

Get down the hill by the easy slope
    To the water and the shade.

But it's barbed wire fence, and section line,
    And kill-horse travel now;
Scoot you down the canyon bank,—
    The old road's under plough.

Have you an eye for the laden wheel,
    The worn tire or the new?
Or the sign of the prairie pony's hoof
    That was never trimmed for shoe?

O little by-path and big highway,
    Alas, your lives are done.
The freighter's track a weed-grown ditch.
    Points to the setting sun.

The marks are faint and rain will fall,
    The lore is hard to learn.
O heart, what ghosts would follow the road
    If the old years might return.[1]

    The lack of convenient markets was perhaps as serious a drawback to the early settler of our county as any of his numerous hardships. At the very beginning, of course, there was no need of markets. On account of drought, hot, dry winds, grasshoppers, or other calamity, it frequently happened that the settler had no surplus, but had to supplement the meager returns from his claim by such food as the streams, woods, and prairies supplied. But in process of time the problem of markets became immediate and insistent.

    It was often as necessary to be able to buy in a convenient market as to sell, and for many years here in Gage county merchants were able to supply to only a limited degree the necessary demands of the population.

---

[1] From *Barbed Wire and Other Poems,* by Edwin Ford Piper (1917).

Their stock in trade consisted principally of the bare necessities of life, flour, bacon, cheese, crackers, sorghum, and the like, and as they would not usually pay cash for farm products, transactions with their customers were largely a matter of barter,—calicoes for eggs, denims for gooseberries or butter. There being virtually no home market where the pioneer could both sell for cash the surplus of his labor and skill and purchase the necessary articles of consumption for himself and family, he was often compelled to seek distant markets in which to sell as well as buy. Thus many of the commonest things in use, as a hat, a bonnet, a slate, a pencil, a spool of thread, farm machinery, tools, clothing, and the like, could often be had only at some Missouri river town or village. This condition of affairs is tolerably well stated by the following extract from a letter written from the interior of the territory of Nebraska as late as January 26, 1866, in which the writer says:

"I will give you, or attempt it,—for nothing could show except the actual living here,—some idea of the life in these western wilds. In the first place we are about as near in the center of nowhere as I care to be. We are fifty miles directly west from Nebraska City, which is the nearest point where one can buy a shoe-string or a spool of thread. Farms here are 'ranches,' cattle yards 'corrals'; there are no fences of any account, people herd their cattle by day, put them in corrals by night, that is they 'corral' them."

From the beginning of our county's history in 1857 until long after the close of the Civil war, until the railroads came, in fact, prices ranged high on all sorts of commodities. This was due to two main causes, namely, a depreciated medium of exchange and the absence of anything like a system of rapid transportation.

In 1854, the year which witnessed the first immigration to our county, the whole country was laboring in the slough of a financial depression induced in part, if not mainly, by a system of state banks, commonly designated "Wildcat," which sprang into being after the dissolution of the historic United States Bank and its branches, by Andrew Jackson, President of the United States, in 1835. These banks were invariably what is known as banks of issue, and their beautifully engraved notes, containing the figure of an Indian, dog, buffalo, tree, cat, or other meaningless device, and intended to circulate as money, were so often utterly worthless as to destroy public confidence in the entire system. Gold and silver were at a tremendous premium and difficult to get. All classes of chattels as well as land had an inflated value when measured by this medium of exchange. In every case the value of a bill depended wholly on the rating of the bank issuing it, and this could be shown only by the "National Business Man's Detector," a publication intended to give the financial standing and condition of every bank of issue in the United States. The public was wholly dependent upon such information as to the solvency of the banks of the entire country.

The working of this system of exchange can be illustrated by a concrete example. An immigrant party to the territory of Nebraska, in 1859, tendered the owner of the ferry boat in payment of its passage charge at the point where they desired to cross the Missouri river, a bill issued by a newly organized bank of Indiana. The bank was not listed in the copy of the "Detector" in the possession of the ferryman, and he refused the transportation until he could telegraph to St. Joseph and receive a reply assuring him of the solvency of the Indiana bank. This took from three o'clock until seven o'clock in the afternoon. All business transactions were necessarily conducted in the same cautious and cumbersome manner. The National Banking Act of 1864 introduced a stable as well as a uniform monetary system, under the general supervision of the government of the United States, and "Wildcat" banking became a thing of the past. But to such a deplorable state had the country fallen that the issuance of the treasury notes and the national greenback currency early in the great Civil war, as war measures, acted upon the business world like the elixir of life, and this even though the greenback currency itself possessed a purchasing power far below its par value. For example, in 1863 one hundred dollars in gold would purchase two hundred and eighty dollars in greenbacks.

As the products of the soil increased, the pioneers, following a natural law of commerce, turned to the nearest cash market in which to dispose of their surplus. This was the great continental highway which was known to the traders, ranchmen, and overland stage drivers as the "Military Road," but which is now more generally and perhaps more properly designated as the "Oregon Trail." The certainty of good cash prices for almost every description of farm produce and live stock along this great thoroughfare not only relieved the settlers of the dread and fear of want, but also had the effect of steadying and stimulating prices at home, thereby creating a better home market. Through the agency of this great public roadway eastern Nebraska rapidly filled with immigrants and the slow accumulation of wealth and fixed capital set in. This great national highway was so much a part of our county's early development and entered so largely into the life of the pioneers that it deserves a place in this history.

Engraved from pencil sketch in the Frontier Sketch Book of N. P. Dodge

A MORMON ENCAMPMENT ABOUT 1846

The Oregon Trail has been described as the route of "a national movement"—the migration of a people seeking to avail itself of opportunities which have come but rarely in the history of the world and will never come again. It was a route every mile of which had been the scene of hardship and suffering, yet of high purpose and stern determination.

The known history of the great trail begins with the establishment of the fortified trading post known as Astoria, on the Columbia river, fifteen miles above its mouth, in 1811, by the agents of John Jacob Astor, head of the American Fur Company. This venture failed and in

1813 it was abandoned, but in their expeditions to and from the post the Astorians established a traveled road over most of the distance between Independence and Astoria. Later this dim trail was followed by the hunters, trappers, and traders whose occupations took them to the northwest, and finally by explorers, surveyors, Mormons, and emigrants making their way to Utah, Oregon, and California.

In 1824 the Great South Pass, at the head of the Sweetwater, a branch of the North Platte river, was discovered, which greatly facilitated western travel. In 1832 Captain Bonneville passed over this route from Independence to California, and it is claimed that his was the first wagon train over the great trail. In 1842 John C. Frémont, but recently commissioned lieutenant of a corps of topographical engineers, by the direction of the federal government, led a surveying expedition from Independence, by way of the Grand Island, in the Platte, to the Great South Pass and the Rocky mountains. This expedition was accompanied by the famous Kit Carson, as guide. It consisted of twenty-seven armed and mounted men, together with the young lieutenant and the twelve-year-old son of Colonel Thomas H. Benton, United States senator from Missouri, whose daughter, Jessie, was Frémont's wife.

In 1846 Frémont's route was followed by Joel Palmer and party, from Indiana, and by Edwin Bryant and party. In 1843 the Oregon immigration set in, and in 1847 began the great Mormon immigration to Utah, which lasted for several years. The main body of "Saints," some fifteen thousand, led by Brigham Young, set out from Florence, Nebraska, taking the already broken trail up the north side of the Platte river. But from Independence, Westport, and other Missouri frontier points the Mormons followed the southern trail to its confluence with the northern in the neighborhood of the Great South Pass. In 1849 came the gold excitement in California and a mighty emigration set in across the plains, along the old trail. The following year General Albert Sidney Johnston, who was afterward commander in chief of the Confederate armies, led an armed force of five thousand men along the trail, from Fort Leavenworth to Utah, to suppress a threatened Mormon insurrection supposed to be brewing at the time, and from this circumstance the eastern portion of this great highway was thereafter frequently designated as the "Military Road." In 1859 placer gold was discovered in the sands of Cherry creek, where the city of Denver now stands, and the following year, placer gold was discovered also in the neighborhood of Pike's Peak. The immigration that followed these several events in our country's history imparted to the old trail tremendous importance in the settlement and development of the west and northwest.

JOHN C. FRÉMONT

The actual starting point of the Oregon Trail was St. Louis, the entrepôt of western traffic. From there to the mouth of the Kansas the journey could be made by steamboat. But from the Kansas river, the upward course of the Missouri for six hundred miles was almost directly north, which rendered its further navigation for those bound for Oregon, California, and the Rocky mountain regions undesirable. Land expeditions became the recognized mode of travel from this and all upper Missouri river points to the far west and northwest. The Santa Fe Trail also had its origin at the mouth of the Kansas river, some years prior to the beginning of overland travel along the Oregon Trail.

To accommodate the travel on both these historic thoroughfares the town of Independence, Missouri, first sprang into existence, and, later, Westport, now the site of Kansas City. Here were located horseshoeing and repair shops, general outfitting and supply houses, horse and cattle markets,—everything in fact required by the caravan trade to Santa Fe and the Oregon country.

From Independence the two trails were at first identical as far out as the neighborhood of the town of Gardner, Kansas, a distance of forty-one miles. Here a signboard was erected, with an arrow pointing toward the northwest and bearing the legend "ROAD TO OREGON." Never before or since those memorable days has a wayside sign announced so long or so unusual a journey. Leading on from this point across the country in an almost straight northwest direction, the original trail crossed the Kansas river at Papin's Ferry, where the state capital of Kansas now stands, eighty-one miles out from Independence. The general itinerary of the early trail from this point to its destination was as follows: Turkey creek, ninety-five miles; Big Vermillion, 160 miles; Big Blue river, 174 miles; here the ford was first near the mouth of the Little Blue, and eight miles beyond the ford Albert Sidney Johnston's "Military Road" came in, bringing the travel from Leavenworth, Atchison and St. Joseph; later the ford was diverted to Marysville, where the junction of the two roads occurred. The trail entered Nebraska a trifle east of the southwest corner of Gage county, at a point now occupied by a monument; then on to Big Sandy, 226 miles, near its junction with Little Blue river; Platte river, 316 miles. The trail now led up the immediate valley of the Platte to the junction of the North and South Forks; Lower Ford, on the South Platte, 493 miles, where the road to the headwaters of the South Platte led away from the trail, up the south bank of the river; Ash Hollow, 513 miles; Court House Rock, 555 miles; Chimney Rock, 571 miles; Scott's Bluffs, 616 miles; Laramie, 667 miles; Big Springs, 680 miles; Ford of the Platte, 794 miles; Poison Spider creek, 807 miles; Independence Rock, 838 miles; Devil's Gate, 843 miles; Great South Pass, 947 miles. This is the most celebrated pass in the entire length of the continental divide. Here the trail passed from Atlantic to Pacific waters. Pacific Springs, 952 miles; Green river, 1014 miles; Fort Bridger, 1070 miles; junction with Sublette's Cutoff, 1146 miles. This cutoff eliminated the wide detour by way of Fort Bridger; it left the main road at Little Sandy, 969 miles, and, taking a nearly due west course, reached Big Sandy, 975 miles; then Green river, 1021 miles; Bear river, 1093 miles; Smith's Fork, 1149 miles; Thompson's Fork, 1156 miles; Soda Springs, 1206 miles; Fort Hall, 1288 miles (on the left bank of the Snake river, the third important station on the trail and the first on Columbia waters); American Falls, 1308 miles; Salmon Falls, 1439 miles; Fort Boise, 1585 miles; Powder river, 1692 miles; the Grande Ronde, 1736 miles; Umatilla river, 1791 miles; Columbia river, 1835 miles; The Dalles, 1893 miles; the Cascades, 1977 miles; Fort Vancouver, opposite the mouth of the Willamette, head of navigation on the Columbia and properly regarded as the end of the Oregon Trail, 2020 miles.[2]

BRIGHAM YOUNG

---

[2] Nota bene: All distances here given are from Independence.

Photographs by John Wright, staff artist.

SCENES AT ASH HOLLOW

The original route of the Oregon trail from the south fork to the north fork of the Platte river by way of Ash Hollow, descends northward from the plain, 3,763 feet above sea level, four miles to the river bottom, at an elevation of 3,314 feet. From the head of the Hollow, the trail, still invisible, wound to the left about a mile along the sharp-backed ridges, then dropped by a very steep descent eastward into the Hollow, which here widens into a level valley from a quarter to half a mile wide. The spring, a luxury to the emigrant, still bubbles up strongly a quarter of a mile from the mouth of the Hollow, and at the base of a cliff about 100 feet high, as shown in the middle picture. The cedar and ash trees at one time abundant here all have been cut away. Marks of Fort Grattan, occupied as a post in 1855, are visible near the river north of the east side of the mouth of the Hollow. On the west side of the mouth of the Hollow are the modest gravestones of Rachel Patterson, a girl of nineteen, who died in 1849, and of two infant children. The figure on the hill is that of Mr. Alberts, editor of the Morton History.

From the time of the Astorians (1811-1813) to the beginning of the Oregon immigration (1843) travel along the great trail was largely confined to exploring, surveying, and military expeditions and to parties engaged in hunting, trapping, and trade with the Indians. These stopped short of covering the entire distance to the Pacific coast by a direct continuous route, and it remained for Dr. Marcus Whitman to demonstrate to the world the practicability of such a highway of travel.

In 1836 this remarkable man had gone into the Oregon country as a missionary-physician, under the auspices of the American Board. In 1842 he returned to the east deeply impressed with the great value of Oregon and strongly opposed to the treaty of 1818, which established joint occupation of that territory by England and the United States. He visited Washington for the purpose of acquainting the federal authorities with the advantages that would accrue to this country by the abrogation of the treaty and the acquirement of the undisputed possession of Oregon. To prove the accessibility of Oregon to settlers he assisted in leading a large party of emigrants, in 1843, from Independence to the Columbia river. In 1844, at the suggestion of the secretary of war, he prepared a bill for passage by congress, which provided for the establishment of military posts along the trail from Papin's Ferry to the Pacific coast for the protection of emigration. Writing of this measure, to the secretary, in 1844, he says:

"I have since our last interview, been instrumental in piloting across the route described in the accompanying bill and which is the only eligible wagon road, no less than two hundred families, consisting of one thousand persons, of both sexes, with their wagons, amounting in all to more than one hundred and twenty, with six hundred and ninety-four oxen and seven hundred and seventy-three loose cattle. As pioneers these people have established a durable road from Missouri to Oregon, which will serve to mark permanently the route for larger numbers for each succeeding year."

On the arrival of these emigrants, in 1843, a provisional government was formed for Oregon, and on the withdrawal by England of her claims, Oregon, in 1848, was erected into a territory of the United States. These results are justly attributable to the indefatigable energy, courage and patriotic ardor of Dr. Marcus Whitman.

"As a highway of travel the Oregon Trail is the most remarkable known to history. Considering the fact that it originated with the spontaneous use of travelers; that no transit ever located a foot of it; that no level established its grades; that no engineer sought out the fords or built any bridges or surveyed the mountain passes; that there was no grading to speak of nor any attempt at metalling the road-bed;—and the general good quality of this two thousand miles of highway will seem most extraordinary. Father De Smet, who was born in Belgium, the home of good roads, pronounced the Oregon Trail one of the finest highways in the world. At the proper season of the year this was undoubtedly true. Before the prairies became too dry, the natural turf formed the best roadway for horses to travel on that has probably ever been known. It was amply hard to sustain traffic, yet soft enough to be easier to the feet than even the most perfect asphalt pavement. Over such roads, winding ribbon-like through the verdant prairies, amid the profusion of spring flowers, with grass so plentiful that the animals reveled in its abundance, and game everywhere greeted the hunter's rifle, and finally, with pure water in the streams, the traveler sped his way with a feeling of joy and exhilaration. But not so when the prairies became dry and parched, the road filled with stifling dust, the stream-beds mere dry ravines, or carrying only alkaline water which could not be used, the game all gone to more hospitable sections and the summer sun pouring down its heat with torrid intensity. It was then that the Trail became a highway of desolation, strewn with abandoned property, the skeletons of horses, mules and oxen, and, alas, too often, with freshly made mounds and head boards that told the pitiful tale of suffering too great to be endured. If the trail was the scene of romance, adventure, pleasure, and excitement, so it was marked in every mile of its course by human misery, tragedy and death."

PETER J. DE SMET, S. J.

"The immense travel which in later years passed over the trail carved it into a deep furrow, often with several parallel tracks making a total of a hundred feet or more. It was an astonishing spectacle, even to white men, when seen for the first time. It may easily be imagined how great an impression the sight of this road must have made upon the minds of the Indians. Father De Smet has recorded some interesting observations upon this point."

"In 1851 he traveled, in company with a large number of Indians from the Missouri and Yellowstone rivers to Fort Laramie, where a great council was held that year to form treaties with the several tribes. Most of these Indians had not been in that section before and were quite unprepared for what they saw. 'Our Indian companions,' says Father De Smet, 'who had never seen but the narrow hunting paths by which they transport themselves and their lodges, were filled with admiration on seeing this noble highway which is as smooth as a barn floor swept by winds, and not a blade of grass can shoot up on it on account of the continual passing. They conceived a high idea of the countless White Nation, as they express it. They fancied that all had gone over that road and that an immense void must exist in the land of the rising sun. Their countenances testified evident incredulity when I told them that their exit was in no wise perceived in the land of the whites. They styled the route the 'Great Medicine Road of the Whites.' "[3]

The settlement and development of the west produced many changes in the old Trail as known to Frémont, the "Pathfinder," and other early western travelers and explorers. In February, 1859, the Hannibal & St. Joseph Railroad was completed to St. Joseph, Missouri, and in 1861 it was extended to Atchison, Kansas. During the late '50s and early '60s navigation on the Missouri attained its greatest volume and towns sprung up as by magic along its banks. Each progressive step in the march of western development was reflected in the history of the old highway. Branch lines shot out from Fort Leavenworth, Atchison, St. Joseph, Brownville, Nebraska City, and other Missouri river towns, all converging upon the old trail and intersecting it before it reached Fort Kearney. The most noted of these has already been mentioned as starting from the vicinity of Council Bluffs and threading the valley of the Platte, north of the river,—the avant courier of the Union Pacific Railroad. The non-Mormon travel along this route, though bound to California, Oregon, and the northwest, followed it to Shinn's Ferry or a ford in the immediate neighborhood of Fort Kearney, and, crossing the Platte, continued on up the south side of the river, traversing the Independence trail. As time developed the necessity for diverting travel to the gold fields of Colorado and other sections of the great west, branch lines led away from the Oregon Trail, to Salt Lake City, San Francisco, Denver, and the southwest, as far even as Santa Fe, but until the construction of the Union Pacific Railroad, in 1867-1868, the Oregon Trail, its cutoffs and numerous branches leading into and away from it, was the sole connected line of travel across the continent from the Atlantic to the Pacific ocean, and the usual means of communication throughout the great plains and Rocky mountain regions of the west, as well as the entire Pacific slope.

---

[3] *Hist. Am. Fur Trade*, vol. i. Chitenden.

No statistics are available which in brief compass illustrate the tremendous importance of the great trail, considered as a unit. The following news item taken from the Dakota City *Herald*, under date of August 13, 1859, affords some evidence of the volume of travel and emigration on the route from Council Bluffs and Omaha up the Platte valley, at that early date:

"The secretary of the Columbus Ferry Company at Loup Fork informs the Omaha *Nebraskian* that the emigration across the plains up to June 25th was as follows: 1807 wagons, 20 hand carts, 5401 men, 434 women, 480 children, 1610 horses, 406 mules, 610 oxen, 6000 sheep, had crossed this ferry at that point. This statement includes no portion of the Mormon emigration, but embraces merely California, Oregon and Pike's Peak emigrants and their stock, all going westward. The returning emigration crosses at Shinn's Ferry, some fifteen miles below the confluence of the Loup Fork with the Platte. Many of the outward-bound emigrants also crossed at the same point, so it is probable that not less than 4000 wagons have passed over the Military Road westward from this city since the 20th of March."

The reader will observe from the foregoing extract that the uses made of the old trail were many and varied. In 1859 the high tide of western travel and emigration had not been reached, but from that year forward to the completion of the Union Pacific Railway, it increased by leaps and bounds. From a dim, narrow roadway, traveled at wide intervals by exploring, surveying, and military expeditions and thin lines of emigration, it expanded under its increasing usefulness into a broad, smooth, hard-beaten highway of great national interest and importance. Unlike the Appian Way and other great roads centering in Rome, the products of military necessity and ambition, the Oregon Trail in all its branches and ramifications was wholly devoted to the arts of peace and the activities of a young and mighty nation.

As a route of emigration its value and usefulness can never be exaggerated. Long before a transcontinental railway was projected, when in fact railway construction was yet in its infancy in this country, it was the means of peopling Utah, Oregon, California, Colorado, and other sections of the great west. Over it travel was maintained across the continent of North America. Travelers bent on business or pleasure and persons engaged in the diplomatic service of foreign countries freely made use of this great thoroughfare, to escape the long, tedious, and often dangerous sea voyage around Cape Horn, to and from the Orient.

The military occupation of the west by our government, and the tremendous emigration that followed it, gave rise to a freighting industry by mule and ox trains unlike anything previously known in our history, and this formed a most conspicuous element in the usefulness of the trail. No statistics are available to give an adequate idea of the tremendous volume of goods annually carried across the plains when this industry was at its maximum. As early as 1861, Nebraska City, by becoming the headquarters of the firm of Russell, Majors & Waddell, contractors for the transportation of government freight to the far west, grew quickly into one of the principal outfitting towns on the Missouri river. A census of the freighting business from that point taken for the year 1865 showed the following figures: Men employed in the movement of grain and merchandise westward, 8,385; wagons, 7,365; mules, 7,231; oxen, 50,712; freight transported, 31,445,428 pounds. When it is considered that Nebraska City was only one of several great outfitting stations on the Oregon Trail and its branches, that most of the freight was carried long distances over plain and mountain, across unbridged streams, in huge, creaking, linch-pin, thick-tired, canvas-covered wagons, capable of transporting from seven to ten tons of freight and drawn by from five to ten yoke of oxen or more, traveling at the rate of two miles an hour and requiring months to make the round trip, the gigantic proportions of this industry must be apparent to the dullest mind.

The following description of Nebraska City in its pristine days as a terminus of freight traffic is taken from a letter written from near there in 1866, and is fairly representative of the scenes constantly occurring at all, Missouri river outfitting towns for freight traffic across the plains:

The streets are not filled with carriages and gay equipages, though I saw some elegant turnouts, but there are huge freight wagons on every street, at every corner; there are hundreds of oxen and mules attached to them. Often ten yoke of oxen to a wagon,—six span, oftener four, of mules driven with one line. There is heard the lumbering of these "prairie schooners," the bellowing of oxen, braying of mules, cracking of long whips, which for me is a show of itself, to see the dexterity with which the drivers use them. There is the hallowing, yelling of teamsters, mingled with more oaths than I have ever heard before in all my life together. Everything is high in this prairie land. My mother sells some of her butter for sixty cents per pound, none less than fifty cents, and that at home; cheese thirty cents and thirty-five cents; and so on with everything. The great amount of travel on the road half a mile from us makes all the market one needs at present. Trains passing with thirty wagons (twenty-four or eighteen, those being the usual numbers) are or have been until recently of almost daily occurrence,—some going to the mountains, others going to the states. It is also the stage route (or one) of Ben Holliday's express through to California, so that we have a daily mail one day from the west, the next from the east. It seems odd in such a new country, so devoid of almost everything civilized, to see the coach daily, going and coming.

As a highway for the Overland stage from the Missouri river to the Pacific coast the great trail performed a most interesting and a most important service to the American people. Light Concord coaches were usually required for this service, and with the rapid growth of the west, the business ultimately attained huge proportions.

ONE TYPE OF THE FAMOUS CONCORD STAGE-COACH

FREIGHTING SCENES ALONG THE OREGON TRAIL

The lower view represents the freighting train known as "Bull of the Woods," owned by Alexander and James Carlisle. From a photograph taken on Main street, Nebraska City, looking east from Sixth street, and loaned by Mr. O. C. Morton. This train consisted of twenty-five wagons with six mules to each wagon, and was considered one of the finest outfits known to freighters.

From 1850 down to the date when the old trail ultimately fell into disuse the overland stage was largely devoted to the carrying of the mails. The carrying of passengers and express packages also formed important items of its receipts. At first monthly trips were made, then semi-monthly, and finally—when the overland-stage business fell into the hands of Ben Holliday, who in many respects was one of the most remarkable men of his day—a stage service was evolved in which stages ran daily on fast and schedule time from Atchison, Kansas, to Placerville, California, in the remarkably short period of seventeen days, carrying mail and passengers each way.

An important incident to the old highway was the pony express, a movement which originated, in 1860, with William H. Russell, of Leavenworth, Kansas. It was a system of mounted couriers, wholly devoted to the private transmission of letter-mail, newspapers, telegraph messages, important government dispatches, bank drafts, and the like. It followed the St. Joseph branch of the Overland trail to Kennekuk, forty-four miles out from the Missouri river, where it intersected the main Independence line, and thereafter followed the old trail to Fort Kearney, thence on up the Platte valley to old Julesburg, where it forded the South Fork, followed the old Mormon trail up Lodge Pole creek, thence through the Great South Pass to Fort Bridger, Salt Lake City, and on to Sacramento, where it connected with navigation on the Sacramento river to San Francisco. The trip from its eastern terminus, at St. Joseph, Missouri, to its western terminus usually required eight days, and the return trip the same number of days. It was inaugurated at five o'clock in the afternoon of the 3d day of April, 1860, with many demonstrations of satisfaction throughout its entire course across mountain and plain. At San Francisco cannon were fired, flags displayed, speeches made, flowers distributed, and at both terminals crowds gathered to witness the departure of the first daring rider of the pony express. The horses selected for this service were hardy and fleet plains stock. The equipment consisted of a strong, well made saddle and a mail sack of the old-fashioned saddle-bags pattern, and an emergency lariat. The rider was booted and spurred. A leathern holster on either side of the pommel of his saddle carried a navy revolver. No time was wasted at the stations where changes of horses, and often of riders, were made. Usually the rider found his mount already groomed, saddled, and held by an assistant awaiting his arrival. He had only to change his holsters and mail bags from one saddle to the other, mount the fresh steed and away with the speed of the winds. At stations where riders were relieved, the fresh rider would be awaiting the incoming man, mounted and ready to fly on his journey.

This service lasted approximately eighteen months and was discontinued only when the telegraph line, of which it was the *avant courier*, reached Fort Kearney, in 1861. It was by far the most picturesque feature of overland travel along the wonderful old trail, and no other business venture of the great plains region had a more daring or romantic history or left a more lasting impression than the pony express.

This storied old highway was reached from Beatrice and other sections of Gage county mainly by the Brownville road. This branch of the overland trail crossed the Big Blue river at the old Market street ford; it then swung northward to the river, and, taking the course of the present highway to a point about two miles west of the Cub creek crossing, it left the creek and started on its course across the high prairie on what was known as Twenty-two Mile Ridge; it struck Little Sandy creek at Thomas Helvey's ranch, and a mile further on to the west, at Shumway's ranch, it intersected the main trail. Three miles west of Shumway's, at Patterson's ranch, Big Sandy was crossed, and the traveler entered the stirring scenes and pulsing life of the great national highway.

At Big Sandy, besides Patterson's ranch, there were Slaughter's ranch, D. C. Jenkins' ranch, George Weisel's ranch, and some others. In addition to these there was a stage station, kept by Edward Farrell. From Farrell's station on the Big Sandy, the trail, a broad, smooth highway, led almost due west across Eighteen Mile Ridge, past Thompson's stage station, twelve miles out from Farrell's, to the great Hackney ranch, on the Little Blue river, near where the town of Alexandria is now located. Four miles above Hackney's was the Kiowa stage station; six miles beyond the Kiowa was the Oak Grove ranch, located near the dreaded Narrows, a point on the Little Blue river where the prairies terminated abruptly in low, steep bluffs, forcing the travel on a narrow strip of land along the river bank. A little east of the Narrows was the ranch of the ill-fated Ubanks family. Comstock's ranch was a short distance above this pass, and beyond Comstock's was the Little Blue stage station. Here the trail left the river and struck out across the Nine Mile Ridge. At Buffalo ranch it returned to the Little Blue and continued up that stream eight miles to Pawnee ranch. Four miles beyond was Spring ranch, an overland stage station, where the trail climbed a long, steep hill to the high prairie, and led on to Thirty-two Mile Creek, a station located on a little stream of that name, eight miles southwest of the present city of Hastings. From Thirty-two Mile Creek it ran in a north-westerly direction through a collection of low, rounded sand hills to the Platte river bottom, where it intersected the Nebraska City branch of the trail at Hook's ranch, nine miles this way from Fort Kearney.

From almost any point in Gage county a market could be found for farm produce in two or three days' travel, at the ranches and stations along the old trail. Money was abundant, prices good, and the excitement, romance, and thrilling adventure afforded by the trail was an added inducement to draw the pioneers and their sons to this traffic.

A person who now travels by rail or motors over country roads from any portion of south-eastern Nebraska to the site of old Fort Kearney, in the general direction held by the Oregon Trail or its branches, encounters evidence of wealth and refinement on every hand. He sees a succession of thriving cities and villages, connected by rail, telegraph, and telephone lines. Beautiful homes, smiling countrysides, and a happy, intelligent, and thriving population greet him on every hand. To such a traveler the condition of life which this same section of country presented along the old continental cross-country highway from about 1850 to 1867 would be impossible of visualization. To the traveler in those heroic days the only signs of civilized life were the old highway and its ever shifting kaleidoscopic population. The road itself constituted not the least wonderful of the objects which he encountered. It led across the naked prairie from the Missouri river,—wide, hard, and bare. It followed no definite course, unless a generally northwesterly direction could be so designated. It crossed bridgeless streams, traversed localities of great natural beauty and vast prairie meadows where millions of buffalo, elk, deer, and antelope found abundant pasturage during the greater portion of the year. On either side, stretching away in all directions, was the uninhabited and apparently limitless prairie. The few stage stations and ranches that marked its course served to emphasize the emptiness and desolation of the country through which it passed.

This great thoroughfare was traveled by as heterogeneous a mass of people as could be found anywhere in the world,—merchants, capitalists, freighters, prospectors, miners, hunters, trappers, traders, soldiers, Indians, emigrants, Mormons, gamblers, adventurers, pleasure-seekers, tourists, and the representatives of foreign nations,—passing from east to west or from west to east, all in teeming, restless activity. From the top of a Concord stage-coach, drawn by three span of horses selected for this service on account of their speed and endurance, and rushing ahead on schedule time at the rate of ten or more miles per hour, pausing at the stations only long enough to change jaded for fresh teams, the traveler might go for days without being out of sight of long trains of huge wagons drawn slowly by from six to ten yoke of oxen or half as many mules.

The pioneers either hauled their produce to the ranches or stations on the trail or sold at home, at remunerative prices, to those who were regularly engaged in freighting along the trail. Among these were Samuel Jones and his son William R. Jones, Peter Hanna, John Dunbar, Jefferson B. Weston, Joseph Saunders, David Kilpatrick, Nathan Blakely, William Blakely, Thomas and Joseph Kline, Volney Whitmore, George Whitmore, M. C. Butler, J. W. Kelly, Gilbert T. Loomis, Alvah Ayers, and many others whose names are not readily recalled. The ranches along the old trail were kept by a fearless class of frontiersmen, whose business it was to supply the freighters, soldiers, stage-drivers, emigrants, and travelers with provender for their stock, and for themselves food and drink,—quite often *drink*. Amongst the Gage county people who were engaged from time to time in the ranching and stage-driving business were Albert Holliday, who for many years kept the Hackney ranch; Charles N. Emery, first a stage-driver and then a keeper of Pawnee and other ranches; Jim Bainter; "Big" Fred and "Little" Fred Roper; Joseph B. Roper; Joseph Milligan; William E. Mudge; William Hess; Asa and John Latham; Robert Emery; Carl Emery; John Gilbert; Ray Grayson; William Blakely, and George Hurlburt.

This storied highway is now a thing of the past. The part it played in the settlement and development of the great west may never be fully understood or rightly appreciated. Over the greater part of the distance traversed by it there is left scarcely a trace. In a few years there will be none who could mark its course. But as long as men note and love the history of their country, this one fact must always remain,—for nearly three score years, beginning with the Astorians in 1811, this great national thoroughfare, with its branches and ramifications, was to the plains and Rocky mountain regions of our country, the far west and north-west, what the Union Pacific Railroad, of which it was the precursor, became on its completion over half a century ago.

> There are highways born, the old roads die—
> Can you read what once they said,
> From the way-worn ditch and the sunflower clump,
> And the needs of folk long dead?[4]

---

[4] From *Barbed Wire and Other Poems*, by Edwin Ford Piper (1917).

CHAPTER XI

FIRST ACTUAL SETTLERS

OTOE AND MISSOURI TRIBES OF INDIANS — HISTORY — RESERVATION — RELATION OF PIONEERS TO INDIANS — PLANS TO SELL RESERVATION — SALE — REPORT OF LEWIS AND CLARK — INDIAN VILLAGE — REMOVAL OF INDIAN TRIBES

The first actual settlers of Gage county were of course the Otoe and Missouri consolidated tribes of Indians. The treaty under which all their lands in the territory of Nebraska were ceded to the United States, except their reservation on the Big Blue river, was made March 15, 1854, and became immediately effective. Section 2 of the treaty required the Indians to vacate the ceded lands and remove to their new reservation "as soon after the United States shall make the necessary provision for fulfilling the stipulations of this instrument as they can conveniently arrange their affairs, and not exceeding one year after such provision is made."

The report of George Heppner, the government agent for these Indians, to the Indian Bureau at Washington, under date of November 1, 1855, conveys the information that they were then occupying their new reservation, in what afterward became Gage county, and had raised a crop of corn for their support during that season. According to this report there were at that time approximately six hundred Indians on the reservation, which was doubtless their full tribal strength.

When first known to white men, the Otoe tribe of Indians were one of a group of three related tribes, the others being the Iowa and Missouri tribes of Indians, all speaking practically the same language. They appear never to have been numerous, like the Pawnees, Comanches, and some others of the plains Indians. Their history as far as known contains little more than a struggle to defend themselves against their enemies, until they came virtually under the domination of the white man. They are first mentioned by some of the French-Canadian traders, trappers, and missionaries. Father Marquette, in 1673, apparently locates them on his autograph map about the upper Des Moines river, and Membre, the companion of LaSalle, in 1680, places the tribe one hundred and thirty leagues west of the Illinois, on the Wisconsin. In 1700, Iberville, a French-Canadian explorer and the first governor of the province of Louisiana, said that the Otoe and Iowa Indians were with the Omahas. Charlevoix, in 1721, found them on the east side of the Missouri, above the Kansa tribe, on the west side of the Missouri. In 1761 they were located on the Platte, between its mouth and the Pawnee country to the west. Here they were found by Lewis and Clark in 1804, on the south side of the river, twenty miles from its mouth; but the explorers record the fact that they had formerly lived twenty miles above the mouth of the Platte on the south bank of the Missouri river. Having been greatly diminished by war and smallpox, in 1817 they migrated to the neighborhood of the Pawnees, near the city of Fremont, under whose protection they seem to have lived for a time, and were here incorporated with the Missouris. For some time prior to 1841 the two tribes were located near the mouth of the Platte river, in the neighborhood of Bellevue. Later they removed to a reservation near Nebraska City, which in the treaty bearing date of March 15, 1854, was ceded to the United States, together with all lands in Nebraska territory save and except a reservation lying partly in the southern portion of Gage county. As before stated, Article 2 of the treaty promised that they would vacate the ceded territory and remove to the lands reserved for them by it "as soon after the United States shall make the necessary provision for fulfilling the stipulations of this instrument as they can conveniently arrange their affairs, and not to exceed one year after such provision is made."

This reservation comprised a fine body of land, ten miles north and south and twenty-five miles east and west. It extended two miles south of the state line its full length, into Washington and Marshall counties, Kansas. North of the state line it extended two and three-fourths miles into Jefferson county. That portion of it which lay in Gage county was a strip eight miles in width and twenty-two and one-half miles in length, east and west. Glenwood, Paddock, and Barneston townships lay wholly within the reservation, also the greater part of Liberty township; it included the two southern tiers of sections in Elm, Sicily, Wymore, and Island Grove townships to within two and one-fourth miles of the county line on the east. Altogether it comprised 250 sections, 160,000 acres, of which 126,720 acres lay in Gage county. It was well watered and timbered. The Big Blue river flowed through it in a southeasterly direction, across Wymore and Barneston townships, while Big Indian creek drained the northern and western portions and entered the river at Wymore. East of the river Wolf, Plum, and Mission creeks with their tributaries drained the land and supplied in great abundance water for grazing purposes. Fine groves of timber lined all the streams. Hunting and fishing offered both sport and sustenance to the noble red man and his progeny, while to the hoes, which a wise and beneficent government placed in the hands of the squaws, the rich alluvial soils of the creek and river valleys responded with bountiful crops of Indian corn, melons, pumpkins, beans, and other field and garden produce.

AR-KA-KE-TA (tribal guardian)
Head chief of the Otoes

The pioneers profited considerably from the existence of this large reservation within the county. The United States government from the first had maintained on the reservation, at the junction of Plum creek and the river, a steam saw and grist mill where lumber of all dimensions was manufactured from native timber and where corn meal and graham flour could be ground. Here also was a blacksmith shop which, in addition to the Indian blacksmithing, did custom work. From the surrounding country for miles settlers hauled their saw logs and grain to this primitive mill and battled back lumber, slabs, meal, and cracked wheat or graham flour. The mill was afterward supplied with proper machinery for making bolted flour, and then became one of the early milling points of our county.

Considerable trade, mainly barter, was carried on between the pioneers and the Indians, in which beaded moccasins, buffalo robes, dried or jerked buffalo meat, other products of the chase, and handiwork of the squaws, as well as blankets, calicoes, and other articles issued annually by the Great Father at Washington to his dusky children, were exchanged for the hogs, cattle, sheep, and cured meats of the settlers.

The personal relations between the Indians and the white settlers were ideally friendly. There were many members of these tribes that in point of worth of character measured up to the best traditions of the North American Indian. They were as a rule scrupulously honest, returning what they borrowed from their white neighbors and friends, and discharging punctually their financial obligations. They were not pilferers or thieves. They were inclined to overstay a welcome and were great beggars for something to eat. In their domestic relations they apparently led well ordered and decent lives.

In those days of primitive life the white man rarely turned his eyes toward the landed possessions of his Indian neighbors. Government land was cheap and abundant, to be had almost for the asking. No man needed to want for land; he could take it by paying a trifling fee to the officers of the government land office at Brownville. But on the admission of Nebraska into the Union as a state; on the entry by college scrip, in 1867, of the finest portions of the public domain in Gage county, and the coming of the railroads, the situation completely changed. Land began to have a value. Soon it was impossible for a man to be land poor. A homesteader who had been accustomed to regard his quarter section more as a liability than an asset, suddenly found that it possessed a cash value in the open market; that when pressed for money, by resorting to an invention known as a mortgage, he could actually borrow a few hundred dollars on his homestead. Undreamed of opulence descended upon him, and the poor homesteader, whose years had been spent in poverty and want, who was often compelled to stay because too poor to leave, suddenly found his broad acres a source of wealth, as wonderful to him as the lamp of Aladdin or the purse and hat of Fortunatus.

Under these circumstances the lands of the Indian reservation became appreciably valuable in the eyes of the white inhabitants of the two states where it lay, and in the eyes of the Indians themselves and their guardian, the United States government. Great pressure was brought, beginning with the early '70s, on the representatives of both Kansas and Nebraska in congress, to effect the sale of the reservation and convert it into a source of wealth for the white man.

In January, 1875, Hon. Algernon S. Paddock, then a citizen of Gage county, was elected to the United States senate from Nebraska. Soon after taking his seat he introduced a bill providing for the sale of that portion of the Otoe and Missouri Indian reservation lying west of range VII, and prescribing a method for conducting the sale of such lands. This act, by and with the consent of the Indians, became a law August 15, 1876, and the lands affected by it, constituting a little more than one-half of the reservation, were appraised and sold for cash to active settlers at the appraised value, in tracts not exceeding one hundred and sixty acres to any one purchaser. They attracted a fine class of settlers, and were soon disposed of at an average price of about three dollars and fifty cents per acre. With interest on deferred payments this netted the Indians over two hundred thousand dollars.

The sale of this land, which had hitherto produced nothing to its owners and which they regarded as of but little value, for practically five hundred dollars per capita, served only to whet the appetite of the Indians for that sort of tangible wealth which always bears the dollar mark. The successful outcome of this sale prompted further agitation in congress on the part of the representatives of both Kansas and Nebraska to put the remainder of the reservation on the market, and on March 3, 1881, a bill was passed by congress for that purpose, which also prescribed a method of conducting a sale of the lands affected by it. The government having purchased in the Indian territory, now Oklahoma, 129,113 acres of land as a reservation for the Otoe and Missouri Indians, immediately after the passage of this act, the remainder of their lands, after appraisement, were placed on sale, in 1883. Under the orders of the secretary of the interior, the appraisement was ignored and the lands sold at public auction for cash to the highest bidder, but to actual settlers only, and in tracts not to exceed one hundred and sixty acres to any one purchaser. The exact figures are not at hand to show the amount of this sale, but the lands brought approximately twelve and one-half dollars per acre, amounting approximately to the sum of one million dollars. In addition to removing an unassimilable element from the population of our county, these two sales brought within its jurisdiction and added to its taxable wealth a splendid body of land which in process of time has become very valuable, and thickly populated by a splendid class of American citizens.

Tradition aside, the Otoe Indians were never warlike or aggressive. They were tillers of the soil, traders and trappers, and were usually found in the neighborhood of some more powerful tribe whose protection they sought.

The Missouri tribe of Indians, who derived their name from the great river on whose shores they dwelt for many years, after having been attacked and almost annihilated, in 1720, by the Sac and Fox tribes with their allies, were dispersed. Five or six lodges joined the Osage, two or three took refuge with the Kansa, and the remainder amalgamated with the Otoe Indians. Lewis and Clark spoke of the Otoes and Missouris whom they saw in the neighborhood of Council Bluffs, as almost naked, having in fact no covering except a sort of breech-cloth and a loose blanket or painted buffalo robe thrown about their shoulders. Their villages consisted of large earthen lodges, but when traveling they found shelter in skin tepees.

The permanent Indian village was located in Barneston township, mainly on the site of the present village of Barneston. At this point there was and still is a splendid spring of purest water, similar in quality to the well known Zimmerman spring from which the city of Beatrice draws its entire supply of water. Near this spring were the agency building, the school house, Indian tepees and burial place. To the south of the village, across Plum creek, at the point where that stream enters the Big Blue river, on the small tract of level land adjacent to both these streams, were the blacksmith shop, the steam saw and grist mill belonging to the Indians, and the residences of several of the employes of the government upon the reservation. The Indians maintained an unbroken residence in this location from April, 1855, to October 5, 1882,—more than twenty-seven years,—during which period of time, under the care and tutelage of the government of the United States, its agents and employes, including several teachers, they made considerable progress in general education and in a knowledge of the useful industries of civilized life. After ceding their lands here to the United States, they removed from our county to Oklahoma, in 1882. The last glance afforded us of the aboriginal inhabitants of Gage county is presented in the following extract from the report of their agent, Jacob V. Carter, to the bureau of Indian affairs, under date of August 20, 1882. It reads in part as follows:

Soon after forwarding my last annual report dated at Otoe Agency, Nebraska, I received orders to remove the Indians in my charge from that agency to their new location in Indian Territory. Agreeable to said order, I began the work of removal at once. On September 22, 1882, I started the cattle herd, numbering two hundred and twenty-four head, in charge of competent herders, for the territory. On the 5th of October following, having completed my arrangements, I pulled out of the Agency with a train which consisted of seventy wagons and about two hundred ponies. We arrived at Red Rock on the 23d day of the same month, nineteen days out, traveling nearly three hundred miles without sustaining any loss or mishap by the way. The herd arrived on the 16th, in good condition and without loss.

It is generally understood that these Indian tribes had been greatly decimated by death, induced partly by sloth and excess wealth, until their numbers were reduced to somewhat over five hundred, in 1881. Their number was estimated as twelve hundred in 1833. Burroughs gave in 1859 their number as nine-hundred; the report of the Indian bureau at Washington for 1843 designates nine hundred and thirty-one. In 1862 the two tribes numbered seven hundred and eight; in 1867, five hundred and eleven; in 1877, four hundred and fifty-seven; in 1886, three hundred and thirty-four; and in 1906 three hundred and ninety.

CHAPTER XII

NARRATIVE OF MAJOR ALBERT LAMBORN GREEN

[When Ulysses Grant became president of the United States in 1869 he adopted the policy of placing the Indian wards of the nation as far as possible in the hands of the Quakers, a policy to which he rigorously adhered during the eight years of his incumbency in office. In June, 1869, Albert Lamborn Green, of Philadelphia, a young man affiliated with that sect, was placed in charge of the Otoe and Missouri tribes of Indians in Gage county, as the agent of the government and with the rank and title of a major in the federal army. Major Green served in that capacity several years, and became familiar with the history of these Indian tribes as well as with their manners and customs. At the request of the author of this book he has prepared the following reminiscent narrative illustrated by pen drawings prepared by himself. Those who may feel an interest in these aboriginal inhabitants of our county cannot fail to read with keen pleasure the following context:]

Man's earliest weapon was a stone, and later a rudely chipped flint, the acquisition and use of which ushered in the paleolithic age,—the initial period of all human culture and progress. It was during this earliest stage of human advancement that the region now embraced within the limits of Gage county, received its first inhabitants,—a race whose weapons and utensils, rudely chipped from the flints of the locality, still testify to its having existed. In the course of many generations, as greater skill became acquired, the paleolithic age of roughly chipped flints gradually merged into a neolithic age of finely wrought arrowheads and carefully finished weapons and utensils of stone. Such an age has likewise left its scattered memorials throughout the region. Whether both periods pertain to an identical race may never be known, but archeologists regard it as almost a certainty that the period of roughly chipped flints long antedates the Pawnee occupancy of the region. To the period of Pawnee occupancy may confidently be attributed all fragments of pottery and possibly all relics of a neolithic character. Prof. E. E. Blackman has definitely located the sites of at least five prehistoric villages within the county, the most ancient of which undoubtedly belonged to the paleolithic age. One that is known to have been occupied by the Pawnees long after the invasion of Quivira by the French traders and explorers, is located about a mile north of Blue Springs. Another, that is evidently of much greater antiquity, has been found a short distance south of Holmesville. Other village sites, both east and west of the river, bear ample evidence of the fact, that, for untold centuries, the valley of the Blue has been the abode of man.

It may have been with a people whose ancestors were of the older, or paleolithic, period, that Coronado met in 1541, and of whom Castaneda, the chronicler of the expedition, has left us so graphic a description. It is from Castaneda's account, which historians have generally regarded as authentic, that we are led to believe that Coronado's horsemen crossed the Kansas river near the mouth of the Blue and followed the course of the latter stream northward. No other river or stream flowing into the Kansas so accurately meets the description given, and the fact that the principal villages and trails or routes of travel were undoubtedly along its course lends confirmatory evidence to this conclusion. Coronado was in search of cities and towns, and the great flint deposits near the present side of Wymore had attracted to their vicinity a population whose village sites are still traceable. Thus we may safely assume that Castaneda's graphic description of the people met with, applied to the aboriginal inhabitants of this vicinity, hence a few quotations from his narrative may be in place. He says "they are very intelligent," and "able to make themselves so well understood by signs that there was no need of an interpreter"; he speaks of them as "a kind people and faithful friends"; he tells us that "the women are well made and modest," that "they cover the whole body and wear shoes and buskins made of tanned skins"; he tells us that when away from their villages, they travel with troops of dogs loaded with poles and having Moorish pack-saddles with girths, and that when the loads become disarranged the dogs howl, calling some one to fix them aright." Two hundred years after this account was written this region was still a part of that mystical Quivira described by Spanish writers as bounded on the east by the "Mountains of the Sun"—now known as the Missouri river bluffs. At that time the existence of the Blue river had become so well known to the French traders and explorers that when, in 1795, information was being obtained for the preparation of an up-to-date map of North America, showing all the latest discoveries, the Blue river was correctly located and named, at least so far as its course through Quivira was concerned, but the geographer evidently lacked information as to its further course and disposed of the problem by causing it to empty into the gulf of California. The Otoe name of the river was Nee-haun-chee, but the Indians sometimes referred to it as Nee-haunchee-toe, Big Blue river.

This ancient map locates the "Otter Nation," probably intending it for the "Ottoe Nation"—that being an old-time way of spelling the name of the Otoe tribe. At the time the map was made the Pawnees occupied the valley of the Blue as well as that of the Republican, while the Otoes dwelt near the mouth of the Nebraithka (Platte) and included in their trapping grounds the Nemahas and bluff region of the Missouri as far south as the Great Nemaha. Tradition informs us that prior to about 1720 the natives of this region possessed no horses, their only domestic animal being a tamed descendant of the large gray wolf. But about that time an expedition set out from Santa Fe to conquer the Otoes and take possession of the region for the king of Spain, and thus head off the French, whose activities as traders and explorers had extended far up the Espiritu Santo, and Nebraithka rivers. It appears that the Spanish had learned of a chronic state of warfare existing between the Osages, who lived south of the Kansas river, and the tribe they were advancing against, and decided, if possible, to engage their assistance. As the Spanish cavalcade journeyed toward the Osage domain, it met a war party of Missouris, and, mistaking them for Osages, informed them of the purpose they had in view, which was nothing less than to surprise and destroy their own kindred. The Missouris, quick to perceive the blunder the Spaniards had made, conferred together and soon informed the Spaniards that they really were

Osages returning from a war against the Otoes and that they would willingly accompany them on a war-path against their enemy. Then, secretly dispatching a courier to the Otoe village to acquaint their friends as to the situation, they conducted the Spanish party thither by slow stages, giving them to understand that they were conducting them to the town of the Osages, where they would be entertained before proceeding against their common enemy. It was customary with the Spaniards on all warlike expeditions to have a friar along to look after their spiritual interests and to act as a chronicler of their doings, and we are indebted to a friar's letter now in the archives of Spain for most of the particulars here given. The Otoes, posing as Osages at the village, received the visitors with a great show of hospitality. The interval that had elapsed between the arrival of the courier and that of the Spaniards had been employed in assembling warriors from every available source; even a band of their hereditary enemies, the Pawnees had arrived, probably from the valley of the Blue. After a night spent in feasting and dancing, the assembled warriors fell upon the drowsy unsuspecting Spaniards and killed them all, except a monk. The horses and equipage of the invaders were secured by the Indians, and it afterward devolved upon the monk to teach them how to ride—an art in which they soon became adepts. Tradition informs us that the monk afterwards escaped on the fleetest of the animals. Thus it was that in the course of time ponies superseded dogs as beasts of burden in this region. As the pony herds multiplied they came to be regarded as synonyms of wealth. The war-path became no longer a mad adventure to secure scalps that had no economic value, for an enemy's ponies were worth more than his scalp, and it usually required as much risk and bravery to secure the one as the other. The Pawnees probably occupied the valley of the Blue until about the year 1825, when they went north to join their kindred whom the Delawares had driven from the valley of the Republican. During their occupancy of this region their principal village was situated about a mile north of the present town of Blue Springs, while their winter tepees were scattered up and down the river. The enmity between the Otoes and the Pawnees was hereditary; surprise attacks and bloody reprisals had kept alive a hatred that had been nursed from generation to generation. The smoke-cured scalps of Pawnee warriors, hardened and faded with age, still adorned the Otoe medicine bags long after they had settled on their reservation.

The last attack made upon the village above mentioned by Otoe warriors occurred only a few years prior to the Pawnees' removal. A large band of Otoes were then encamped near the mouth of the Nemaha, and had cunningly timed their attack to take place at day-break of the day succeeding that on which the young braves of the Pawnee village had started on a buffalo hunt. The Otoes, bent on securing scalps as well as plunder, had killed a number of people and caused a frightful uproar and panic in the village, when a brave from the hunting party—which had encamped the evening before near the head of Indian creek—came riding into the village; he was at once killed by the Otoes, who also wounded the pony and frightened it so that it galloped back towards the camp; its return, riderless and wounded, caused great alarm and called for instant action. All the braves of the hunting party, mounted on their swiftest ponies, started at once for the home village, on reaching which, they saw at a glance what had occurred. The enemy had left, but the avengers were not long in striking their trail, which was swiftly followed; they were overtaken in a large draw near the east side of what is now Island Grove township,—a spot that was pointed out to the writer by old men of the Otoe tribe who related incidents connected with the affair as handed down to them. A fierce battle ensued—during which no quarter was given or asked. The Otoes, about thirty in number, were completely surrounded and fought desperately, but were outnumbered two to one; only one was permitted to escape and report the fate of his companions; the wounded were scalped, and both dead and wounded were burned, the Pawnees having fired the tall sloughgrass that grew in the draw.

After the Pawnees left the Blue, which is supposed to have been about 1825, the Otoes included the Blue valley in their hunting and trapping circuit, and it was seldom that the tepee of an Otoe family, or perhaps a group of tepees, might not be found somewhere along the river's course. In 1854 a reservation, comprising two hundred and fifty square miles, the greater part of which is now included within the limits of Gage county, was set apart for the Otoes, they having ceded, for a consideration to be paid in the form of an annuity, all their lands south of the Platte, except said tract. Of the one hundred and sixty thousand acres comprised in the area reserved, considerably more than one hundred thousand acres were included within the limits of the county. The site selected for their village and the agent's residence was a sightly elevation about half a mile east of the river, where a spring, that issued from a limestone ledge, afforded an ample supply of pure water. The town of Barneston now occupies a part of the site. A residence for the government agent was built about one hundred feet north of the spring. It consisted of a one and a half story frame with an ell on the rear, and contained in all six rooms with large basement. There was a latticed porch in front, with a balcony over the same, that commanded a view of the whole village; near the agent's house was a large barn and other outbuildings. A steam grist mill, saw mill, blacksmith shop, and residences for the various white employes, were located on Plum creek, about a mile from the agency. The main village consisted of about forty large earth-covered lodges of the type commonly used by tribes of Sioux origin. Each lodge was circular in form, with an entrance through a projecting passageway opening towards the east, and was usually not less than about forty feet in diameter, inside measurement. Usually several closely related families occupied a single lodge—each having a sleeping booth on a raised platform that extended around the inside space. All cooking was done at a fire of small logs that blazed in the center, the smoke escaping through a circular opening in the roof. There were also a few bark lodges of a type that were common among the Iowas and Sacs and Foxes, but they were of a less durable character than the Siouan type of habitation and were usually regarded as temporary. An agency farm of one hundred acres was broken out adjacent to the village. The white employes included a farmer, carpenter, blacksmith, miller, physician, teachers, etc. All plowing was done with oxen. All supplies were hauled from Missouri river points, usually from Brownville. A mission school, under Presbyterian auspices, was established near the reservation soon after the Indians removed there. It was established by the New York Home Mission Society of that denomination, on the north half of Section 1, township 1 south, range eight east, state of Kansas, which tract of three hundred and twenty acres the society had purchased, and on which it had caused to be erected a concrete building ninety by forty feet in size and three stories in height with an ell or wing two stories in height. The kitchen and dining room were in the latter and the school rooms and dormitories were in the main building. The buildings were about six miles from the agency and village, and about a mile and a quarter beyond the limits of the reservation. On May 10, 1857, the Rev. Daniel A. Murdock, with his wife, Prudence, and their seven children, arrived and assumed charge of the mission; three teachers were engaged, as were also a farmer, a carpenter, and a teamster, as well as two interpreters. It was the benevolent design of the society that the education of both sexes should combine industrial features. Soon after Mr. Murdock's arrival a conference was held with the chiefs, which resulted in an agreement on their part that they would promote the attendance of all children of a proper age, and in due time the school opened with an attendance of seventy-two, of whom only two were females. This was very disappointing, as accommodations had been provided for as many girls as boys. All pupils arrived almost in a state of nudity, and they were generously supplied with clothing at the expense of the society. Each day was divided into periods of hours for school-room study, for out-door play, and for farm work, and thus all was progressing favorably when the time arrived for the tribe to start on its annual fall buffalo hunt. The chiefs and heads of families then visited the mission and urgently requested that the boys be permitted to accompany their parents on the hunt, a request that could not be granted, inasmuch as it would practically break up the school for an indefinite time. It was supposed that the Indians had acquiesced in this refusal, when suddenly, on a Sabbath afternoon, all the boys disappeared and were soon en route with their parents to the buffalo region. The mission people were not only discouraged—but also dismayed, for there was no certainty as to when the children would return, and it was possible that they might be absent the greater part of the winter. A few weeks after the departure of the children an incident occurred that doomed the school to failure, through fear and distrust on the part of the Indians, causing their refusal to permit their children to attend. This incident was nothing less than a raid of hostile Sioux Indians upon the Otoe village and the mission property, during the tribe's absence on the hunt. The circumstances of their raid convinced the Otoes that their children would have been massacred if they had not accompanied them on the hunt. It seems that the Sioux, finding that the village was deserted, as any who had not gone on the hunt had fled or secreted themselves, ransacked such caches as they were able to find and then proceeded to the mission, evidently in search of the children. Finding none in sight about the premises, the leader of the band ascended the hall staircase, leading to a dormitory, when be encountered J E. Tanner, overseer of the farm, who seized him and threw him to the bottom of the stairs, where he landed very heavily. Being unsuccessful in finding any of the children, the two girls having been secreted by the teachers, the Sioux angrily departed. This was the last time that a Sioux war-party ever ventured within the limits of the county. The following spring, finding that the Indians still refused to allow their children to attend the school, Mr. Murdock resigned his charge and left the mission in charge of a Mr. Guthery, but after vainly trying to win the favourable regard and confidence of the Indians he too resigned, and the society, thoroughly discouraged, concluded to abandon as a hopeless job all attempts to educate and civilize the Otoes. The society sold the mission property, and the building was afterward partially destroyed by a tornado.

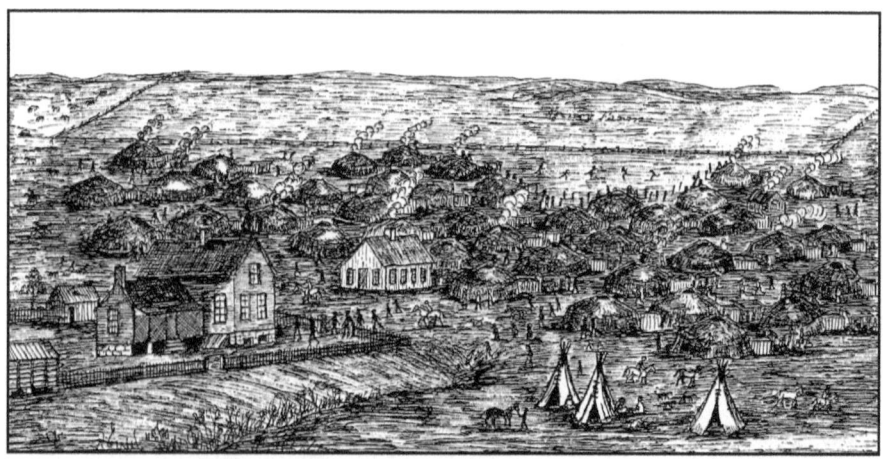

OTOE INDIAN VILLAGE, 1869-1870

No further attempt was made toward educating the Otoe children until the summer of 1869, when the administration of agency affairs was placed in the hands of a representative of the Society of Friends, by President Grant. At that time the Otoes and Missouris were, with very few exceptions, "blanket" Indians. Most of the men, both young and old, were accustomed during warm weather, to discard even the blanket and wear only a clout or breech cloth. Hats were never worn, except by the interpreter and occasionally by an Indian policeman. It was customary to shave the scalp, leaving only a lock from the center of the crown backward, to which an eagle's feather was frequently attached. They used much vermillion, indigo, yellow ocher, and white clay in facial decoration, and necklaces of woven horsehair curiously wrought with many colored bead-work by the Indian women, were worn by both sexes almost universally. The Indian women were very skilful in embroidering and decorating moccasins and leggins of deer-skin with bead and porcupine quill work. Most of the older men and women had their ears lacerated with holes, often not less than a quarter of an inch in diameter, not only through the lobe, but also through the rim of the ear from the top downward. Such holes facilitated loading the ears with large clusters of bobs,—an article of adornment made of block tin and sold by all Indian traders. It was usual for the women and girls to put a line of vermillion paint where their hair parted as well as to paint with vermillion the inside of their ears, thus adding to the fine effect of the silvery bobs. Eagle feathers, red-stone pipes, wampum, and beadwork were among their most highly prized possessions—single specimens of either being frequently valued at more than a fine horse.

While the earth-covered lodges of the village were cool and pleasant as summer habitations, they were cold and draughty in winter, the heat from the central fire escaping too readily through the great circular opening in the roof. For that reason it was customary for all to live in tepees during the winter, each family selecting a sheltered spot where water and dead wood were obtainable, and where, though often surrounded by banks of drifted snow, they existed with some degree of comfort until spring. The Indian ponies sought shelter in the timber, where they often depended on the bark of the cottonwood for sustenance. At the time the writer assumed management of the Indian agency, old Ar-ka-ke-ta was the head chief and the other chiefs were Big Soldier, Wan-na-ga-he, Medicine Horse (Shunga-mon-co), Buffalo, Pipe Stem, and Little Pipe. Ar-ka-ke-ta was a polygamist, and regarded his wives as valuable assets on account of their usefulness in cultivating the ground, providing fire-wood, and otherwise contributing to his support. He was opposed to *man*-ual labor, and was what might be termed an obstructionist, as he opposed all measures likely to promote the advancement of the tribe. In appearance he was decidedly unprepossessing and untidy; his usual facial adornment was a coating of soot mixed with mud,—which accorded well with a pessimistic state of mind that was natural to him. In 1867-1868 a party of the chiefs had visited Washington and negotiated a treaty, under the terms of which they agreed to sell the whole reservation of one hundred and sixty thousand acres at one dollar and fifty cents per acre, and Ar-ka-ke-ta posed on that occasion as a great man; the mud and soot disappeared from his face; the pessimist became an optimist, for, in his mental visions of the future, he saw his people rescued from the shackles that civilization was weaving around them, and mingling once more with kindered tribes in the far off Indian territory. When the writer arrived at the agency in June, 1869, the treaty was awaiting ratification by the senate and the tribe was consequently in a very restless condition. It soon became obvious to him that the conditions of the treaty were very prejudicial to the best interest of the Indians and that the consideration was entirely inadequate, being less than half of what might be considered a fair valuation of the land at that time. He accordingly commenced taking measures to defeat ratification, by calling a council and persuading the head men and a few of the chiefs to sign a remonstrance against ratification, and a repudiation of the action of the party that had visited Washington. This, together with a carefully prepared statement, was taken to Washington by a committee of Friends, and the result was the defeat of the treaty. The lands afterward sold for nearly ten times what they would have brought under the terms of the treaty.

OLD AGENCY MILL

In 1870, as Indian agent, I removed Ar-ka-ke-ta from the position of head chief and promoted Shunga-mon-co (Medicine Horse) to that position. This was done because of the old head chief's refusal to remove from the village and go to farming when a neat frame house and tract of choice land had been offered him. It was important that the head chief should set an example to the young men of the tribe. Medicine Horse was a man of considerable influence and of very striking appearance,— a natural orator whose flowery figures of speech always elicited cries of how! how! how! from the assembled council. He agreed that if appointed head chief he would occupy a frame house, open a small farm, and set a good example to others. When the matter was first broached to him he declared, with pretended seriousness, that he had never done a stroke of work in his life, but he was immediately contradicted by old Chief Buffalo, who affirmed that he remembered seeing him, when a boy, carrying a kettle of water for his mother. At this accusation Medicine Horse pretended to be very angry declaring that the charge was utterly false. In the course of a few days Medicine Horse, assisted by others, was busily engaged in cutting saw-logs and in due time he and his family were ensconced in a neat frame dwelling built of newly sawed cottonwood lumber. Encouraged by his example others were also persuaded to cut logs, and the agency ox-teams were kept busy hauling them to the saw mill. During the years 1870, 1871 and 1872 probably twenty-five families had tried the experiment of living in houses and cooking on stoves—at least during the summer months—the lure of tepee life proving too strong on the approach of winter for some of them. Next in importance to Medicine Horse was Big Soldier, who, in face and figure, was a replica of an ancient Roman senator. By means of facial, labial, and finger movements, he was always able to converse without an interpreter, although he seldom used an English word. In many ways he was a very remarkable man, and a typical thoroughbred Otoe.

Next in importance to the chiefs were the police, usually consisting of not more than fifteen individuals, chosen and appointed by the agent, whose duty it was to make arrests and otherwise assist in preserving order. They were commanded by a captain and lieutenant, and all provided with United States cavalry uniforms, which, however, were seldom worn except on important occasions, such as council meetings, and the execution of orders that required them to leave the reservation. All of the chiefs were Otoes except Eagle, who was a Missouri Indian and the recognized "war chief" of the combined tribes; for many years it had been his province to act as commander on all buffalo hunts or other adventurous enterprises. He was a man of commanding and dignified appearance, and despite his great age was straight as an arrow and active as a young man. An incident that came under the writer's observation while accompanying the Indians on a buffalo hunt in 1870, illustrates how punctilious old Eagle was in strictly enforcing an ancient tribal rule that forbids the killing of a straggling buffalo before the camp has been pitched and the hunters are all ready to participate in a combined attack upon the great herd. In this case it was a young chief, Little Pipe, who was the offender. Eagle's face was stern and unrelenting as he ordered the heavy pony lash applied to the culprit's naked back, but before a blow descended the young chief's brother-in-law pushed him aside and presented his own back to receive vicariously the punishment that it was feared might degrade a chief. A bloody back soon showed that while the substitution had been accepted no mercy had been shown by the old war chief. This chief's name is worthy of a place in history as the last chieftain of that Indian nation whose name is more frequently mentioned than is that of any other aboriginal people on the continent; a people who have given name to one of earth's longest rivers and to one of our nation's greatest and richest commonwealths. In 1869 there were only about eighty Missouris living, and since that time the race has practically disappeared.

It was customary for the Otoes to go on a buffalo hunt twice a year, starting on the summer hunt about the last of June and getting back usually some time in August. Late in November they started on the winter hunt, the return from which was wholly dependent on weather conditions and their success in procuring hides and meat. The depredations by hostile Indians on the Little Blue had made the settlers very distrustful of all Indians, and in order to allay fear on the part of the settlers, as well as to protect the Otoes from hostile Indians, the agent obtained from the war department an order directing General Augur to furnish an escort of cavalry for the winter hunt of 1869 as well as for the summer hunt of 1870. On the latter occasion the agent and a party of Philadelphians accompanied the expedition; they encountered a large herd of buffalo on the Sappa creek, in what is now Decatur county, Kansas.

It was an ancient Indian practice among the Nebraska Indians to make sugar from the sap of the box alder,—a practice that the Otoes continued after their settlement on the reservation. Formerly they used no tobacco, but smoked a mixture of dried sumac leaves and red-willow bark that had been in common use among all the western tribes probably for centuries. This old Quivira mixture, with sometimes a little tobacco added but oftener without any, was always adhered to by the Otoes and Missouris. The smoke produced had an acrid though not altogether disagreeable odor and was usually exhaled through the nostrils. The Indians obtained many fine fish from the Blue. They used no fishhooks, but shot the fish as they glided through the clear water, using only bow and arrows for the purpose. When heavy rains raised the water to flood tide they built seine-like barriers of willow poles and rods across the mouths of bayous and draws so that the receding waters left many fish, usually of large size, stranded behind such barriers. As long as the waters of the Blue remained clear the river abounded with gars, which often attained a large size; specimens four feet in length being frequently caught. Although the white settlers did not consider them edible, the Otoes regarded them very favourably as food. As the country gradually settled up and sediment from plowed fields found its way into the river, the gars disappeared. As late as 1869 a beaver was occasionally caught, and the commoner fur-bearing animals, such as mink, skunk, raccoon, etc., were plentiful, their furs being quite a source of profit to the Indians. The abundance and variety of plums gathered by the Indian women were surprising. They varied greatly in quality and size, a tree being occasionally found the fruit from which equalled the choicest sold in our markets to-day. There were still a few wild deer in the county as late as 1870, for at least two fawns were caught by the Indians during that year, and a large antlered buck was seen by the writer a few miles south of Beatrice.

The breaking of the prairie sod caused the total disappearance of a plant, once quite plentiful, whose bulbous root was eagerly sought for and highly prized as an article of food by the Otoes. In taste it slightly resembled a chestnut, and when divested of its thick, bark-like skin, it was as large as a hulled walnut. This plant grew to a height of from eighteen inches to two feet and had a branching top. The settlers made no use of it, but to the Indians travelling on the war-path or the hunt, when short of other food, it afforded security from starvation. It was an emergency food supply that the Indians had no doubt availed themselves of from time immemorial. The Otoes at all times relished it highly, even when they had other food in abundance. The destruction of the original sod has caused the disappearance from the county of other plants equally as interesting, but probably of none that occupied as high a place in the Indian's estimation as did this one.

For more than a decade prior to 1869 no missionary efforts had been made or religious services held among the Otoes and Missouris. They had a religion, if such it might be called, that was not based on creed, bible, or confession of faith, and that had come down to them as an inheritance from a far off past. It was the religion of ancient Quivira. The Great Spirit, Wa-con-da,—the maker of all things was to them no far off deity dwelling in a far off heaven, but an ever present actuating and controlling force in nature and in all natural phenomena; they heard his voice in the thunder and saw the ashes of his wrath in the lightning; the tornado showed his might and power; the sunshine and the gentle rain, the ripened corn, and every beneficent gift of nature, bore evidence to his favor. How many white professors of religion, seated at a loaded table, commence eating without giving a thankful thought to the Great Giver of all good:—and yet we have seen an Otoe chief, seated with his family on the ground around a pot of succotash, a mixture of boiled corn and pumpkin, before dispensing it to the members of his family pour some of it on the ground and stir it into the dirt and ashes so that the dogs could not get it, calling on Wa-con-da to accept it as a thank offering. It was the universal custom in council to pass the pipe from chief to chief, each taking a whiff or two, and exclaiming, as he exhaled the smoke, words that signified an acknowledgment of Wa-con-da's presence,—the act being in reality a smoke offering. They knew nothing of the Mosaic law, but old Chief Wan-a-ga-he once declared, striking himself upon the breast, "We know that within us is peace if we do right, but if we do wrong Wa-con-da is displeased and we are unhappy." Kindness toward each other and harmony in families were notable traits of the Otoe character that remind one of Castaneda's statement already quoted—"they are a kind people." As the ancient Jews relied upon their tribal God to aid them in battle with their enemies, so the Otoes relied upon Wa-con-da to aid and protect them on the war-path.

In the fall of 1870 Agent Green discovered that a party of Otoes were preparing for a pony raid on a distant tribe a procedure that was analogous to going on the war-path, so far as risk and excitement were concerned. The leader of the party, a notorious half-breed, known as Jim White-water (who afterward spent seventeen years in the state penitentiary for an atrocious double murder), had already nearly completed all preliminary arrangements when the discovery was made. For several days the braves whom he had selected for the party had been segregated in a tepee at some distance from the village, undergoing certain preparatory exercises, consisting mostly of chanting and drumming, while Jim sought secluded places in the timber along Plum creek where he loudly wailed and called on Wa-con-da to favour the enterprise. This segregation or separation of men from their wives for some days, before starting on the war-path, the time being taken up with efforts to win the favour of Wa-con-da by chanting and drumming, is of great antiquity. On this occasion Wa-con-da failed to render protection, for the agent wrathfully descended on the band with his police and ordered their dispersal threatening imprisonment of their leader if he attempted to leave the reservation. The chiefs at once asked for a council and informed the agent that when a war-party had gone so far with the preliminaries they could not back out without disgrace, and that in order to look their friends in the face without shame it would be necessary to give them at least six ponies, and suggested that if the agent would give one they would make up the required number. This the agent refused to do, and the chiefs silently departed, but sent a messenger to inform the agent that they had bought the war-party off with ponies.

The medicine-bag, a bundle about two feet in length, containing a mysterious assortment of relics and charms, held an important place in what might be termed the religious psychology of the Otoes. In some mysterious way it was supposed to invite the presence or favour of Wa-con-da. There was usually one of these mysterious bundles suspended in every large lodge and all were supposed to be of great antiquity, having been handed down from generation to generation. Some of them were decorated with the scalps of enemies slain in battles fought so long ago that even tradition failed to recall their story. There was no tincture of idolatry connected with these objects; they were venerated very much as shrines have been venerated by Christians and were carried by war parties in a belief that Wa-con-da, the Great Medicine (Mystery), would favour them with his protecting presence.

The Otoes and Missouris believed in a universal immortality that included not only human souls but also spirits of all animals. They believed that a pony, strangled by the side of its owner's grave at the time of his burial, accompanied him as a spirit steed to the land of the immortals, and that a dog strangled beside the grave of a little child afforded it company and protection. It was not until 1870-1871 that Agent Green succeeded in abolishing the practice of strangling ponies, but the strangling of dogs was permitted to continue during the Indians' sojourn in the county. It was not an uncommon sight to see the body of a dog, dried to a mummy, standing in an upright position with its back to a stake, to which it was tightly bound by a raw-hide thong passed around its throat.

The Otoes used no coffins, but placed their dead in a sitting posture in graves that were only about four feet in depth with an opening at the top only large enough to admit the body,—the cavity being from three to four feet in width at the bottom. The relatives, having taken a final farewell of the dead, all joined in loud wailing, while the old women, whose province it was to dig graves and conduct burials, placed a layer of heavy sticks and a buffalo robe or blanket over the mouth of the grave and piled the excavated earth upon it. If a pony was to be strangled, a saddle and bridle was usually put beside its owner in the grave, and the chosen animal, having been decorated with hand-marks of vermillion, was led to the grave-side with a lariat looped around its neck in a manner easily to produce strangulation when a squaw at each end pulled with all her strength. The pony having fallen beside the grave was allowed to remain there until dogs and wild animals had consumed its flesh; the skull was then placed as a decoration on the top of the mound, and its tail or a portion of the mane attached to a pole planted at the side of the grave. A well authenticated instance of the burial alive of an old man, with the body of his grandchild, occurred a few years prior to 1869. The story, as related by Battiste Deroin, was a very sad and pathetic one. It appears that the old man was greatly attached to the child and when it died was inconsolable; his feeble condition indicated that his own departure was not far distant, and it was in accordance with his own desire that he was placed in the grave with the little one in his embrace, that he might be its caretaker and companion through the wilderness that all must cross in order to reach the land of eternal rest. Food was placed beside him and the wailing sounded afar, as his kinsmen bade him farewell and the heavy earth was mounded above his head.

The Otoes did not always bury their dead, especially when the ground was deeply frozen. One of the strangest sights to be seen upon the reservation consisted of two ancient oaks, standing within a few feet of each other, the limbs and forks of which were laden with the mummified remains of men women and children, each wrapped in skins, old blankets, bark, etc., and bound with raw hide thongs so securely that the most violent storms had never been able to dislodge them. The trees stood at the foot of a low bluff near the principal Indian burial ground, and at a point nearly midway between the present town of Barneston and Plum creek. During the fall of 1872 a great prairie fire swept the river bottom and there being much tall grass and dry trash beneath the partly decayed oaks, they were ignited and with their gruesome burden completely destroyed. What was probably the last instance of such disposal of the dead occurred during the winter of 1870, when the writer discovered the recently placed body of a child securely wrapped and tied far out on the limb of a very tall tree that stood on the bank of the Blue at a point about a mile south of the present town of Wymore.

OLD BURIAL PLACE AND FUNERAL TREES OF THE OTOES

The first mercantile establishment in the county was on Plum creek, at a point about a mile west of the present town of Liberty, where in a log cabin, one Gideon Bennett, an Indian trader, sold beads, calico and other Indian goods, taking in exchange furs and buffalo robes, as well as crediting the heads of families against the forthcoming annuity payments. The business afterward passed into the hands of Macdonald, of St Joseph, who, in 1869, engaged Mrs. David Palmer to conduct the store. She understood and talked the Indian language and dealt fairly with the Indians. Mrs. Palmer and her husband were among the first settlers of the county and were typical pioneers. David was a stalwart mountainer, inured to hardships; the advantages of an education had been denied him, but the book of nature was ever open to his understanding. Mrs. Palmer was in many respects a remarkable woman, energetic and trustworthy in conducting Macdonald's business and quick to acquire a knowledge of the Otoe language that enabled her to transact business without an interpreter. As illustrating the versatility of her talents, the writer has in his possession a pair of heavy, gauntleted driving gloves made from a beaver skin that he obtained from an Otoe,— the palms and fingers being of deer skin, the cutting, fitting, and stitching all being the work of her hands and equal to any that are offered for sale. The vicinity of the store was settled by families from Tennessee, some of whom tried raising cotton, but soon discovered that the climate was not very well adapted to it; some of them did their own spinning and weaving of a sort of cloth, having brought the necessary apparatus with them from Tennessee. The writer remembers to have seen men's clothing made from this homespun cloth.

It was during the time that Bennett conducted the store on Plum creek that a band of Pawnees made a raid upon it. They had spent a part of the night watching for an opportunity to seize Otoe ponies, but finding them too securely corralled and guarded, had broken into the store instead. Naturally Bennett supposed that a party of Otoes must have been guilty of the affair, but investigation at the agency proved that such was not the case. The Otoes were greatly excited and their police were not long in discovering the trail of the robber band which they followed swiftly, overtaking them on the Little Blue, some miles above the present site of Fairbury. In the fall of 1869 the writer, while accompanying the Otoes on a hunt, encamped for a night near the spot where this encounter took place, at which time fragments of skulls and bones were found among the briars and underbrush that covered the spot where the Pawnees were overtaken. The Otoes claimed to have killed the entire party.

We have already referred to the hereditary hostility that existed between these Indians and the Osages,—a hostility that is known to have existed as far back as 1720, if the writings of Spanish friars can be depended upon, and which appears to have been kept alive through all the intervening years, resulting in frequent ventures upon the war-path, reprisals for ponies stolen and sometimes in bloodshed. The last raid made by Osage warriors upon the Indians of Gage county occurred in the fall of 1868; it resulted in the killing of a number of Otoe women who were at work at some distance from the village, all of whom were scalped and otherwise mutilated. The Osages were a powerful tribe as compared with the Otoes, but a party of Otoe braves at once prepared to take the war-path against them, determined either to inflict retribution or exact reparation. Having invoked the favour of Wa-conda by chanting, drumming, and wailing, in a tepee apart from the village, the party set out on their perilous undertaking. They had been gone many days and great suspense and anxiety was felt in regard to them when a messenger, announcing their approach with a great herd of ponies, arrived at the village. The greatest excitement and rejoicing ensued; heralds cried the news from one end of the village to the other, and the women and children stationed themselves on the tops of the lodges in order to get a view of the returning war party as it approached in the distance. Soon, with beating drum and loud war whoops, they filed into the village with a string of eighty ponies following in their train. Of these eighty ponies, it appears that forty had been given by the Osages on presentation of the peace-pipe at a parley held at the Osage village, the other forty had been stolen from the Osages the following night. A great war dance followed; the story of bravery and daring was loudly shouted by the heralds; feasting and rejoicing continued far into the night, but through it all a sense of hovering danger disquieted the old men of the tribe who were too well acquainted with the ways of the Osages to doubt for a moment that their painted warriors would lose little time in exacting reparation. Measures were at once taken to guard against a surprise raid. All ponies were securely corralled within the village every night and kept under watch both night and day.

It was during this period of fear and suspense, which extended into the summer of 1869, that the Pottawattamies turned a rather neat trick on the Otoes. A war-party of Pottawattamies had made a raid upon the Omahas and with thirty head of stolen ponies were on their homeward way, when, in order to mislead the Omahas and throw suspicion upon the Otoes, should the Omahas follow their trail, they made a detour through the Otoe reservation, passing in the night as near the village as possible without discovery by the Otoes. The war-party of thirty Omaha braves who a few days later, following their trail, naturally concluded that their ponies had been stolen by the Otoes and that the right thing to do would be to recoup themselves from the Otoe herds. Cautiously reconnoitering during the small hours of the night, they were greatly astonished at the unusual precautions that the Otoes had taken to protect their ponies from theft, not being aware of their recent trouble with the Osages. The ponies belonging to each family were enclosed in pens of heavy wickerwork close to the lodge entrance and from sunset until day break a watchman was on guard.

The Omaha braves, secreted in the tall sunflowers and wild hemp that formed a rank growth in the vicinity of the lodges and corralls, received no attention from the Indian dogs, though if a white man had so hidden they would have announced his presence in the noisiest manner. Slowly the hours passed until, with the first streaks of dawn, the watchmen retired and then with swift movements the silent forms of thirty nearly naked men cut the withes of bark that held the wickerwork and poles of the corralls in place, each seized a choice animal, mounted it, and all rode swiftly away. The noise of clattering hoof-beats awakened the drowsy Otoes who came swarming from their lodges, sure that the feared and hated Osages had visited them at last. It was soon found that thirty head of the very best ponies were missing. In a very short time the women and children of the village were standing on the lodges gazing afar off on the prairie where a long line of Otoe horsemen were swiftly following the trail of the stolen ponies. By noon the thieves had been overtaken and found to be Omahas instead of Osages. The entire party were taken prisoners and brought to the agency; all were in war paint and heavily armed, each man having, besides a bow and quiver of arrows, a heavy revolver of the type used by cavalrymen during the Civil war. The leader carried a war-drum which the writer still retains as a memento of the occasion. Having disarmed them as they entered the council room in charge of the Indian police, all were seated on the floor while their leader and other principal men of the party were called upon to state the circumstances of their visit. The Otoes had been furiously angry at first, but on learning all the facts connected with the affair were rather inclined to view it as a "comedy of errors" and, on advice of the agent, smoked the pipe of peace with the captured men and invited them to partake of food, as they were nearly starved. They had traveled from their village one hundred and fifty miles away, afoot, expecting to return on horseback, but the fortunes of war compelled them to return as they came. The only blood shed upon their war-path was that of a hog belonging to Elijah Filley, whose farm lay in their course. Elijah brought the bloody arrow to the agency as evidence of what he supposed to have been an Otoe depredation.

The success of the Omaha raiders in taking ponies from the corralls did not lessen the feeling of uneasiness and dread that was felt in the direction of the Osages. In fact the expectation of an Osage attack kept the Otoes on the anxious seat until the Spring of 1870, when Agent Green called a council and announced to the chiefs his intention of making an everlasting peace between the tribes. He informed them that he should at once invite the Osages to send representatives to a settlement of all differences; that forty head of ponies should be delivered to them, that being the number stolen; and that the war-path between the Otoes and the Osages should be forever ended. In due course of time a band of Osage chiefs and braves, gorgeously painted and befeathered, arrived at the agency; a council was held and many speeches in both the Otoe and Osage language were made; the great red-stone peace pipe was smoked by all as it passed from hand to hand. The agent, whom the Indian chiefs always addressed as "Un-koe" (my father) when they were assembled in council, then emphasized the importance of at once forever ending a custom that civilization would no longer tolerate.

All agreed that the words of the father were good,—a great feast followed the adjournment of the council, and the Osage warriors departed, leaving behind them a sense of peaceful security that the Otoes had not known for many long years.

After the destruction of the old mission building some years elapsed before any attempt was again made to educate the Indian children. During the fall and winter of 1869 cottonwood and walnut logs were cut and the saw mill was kept busy preparing lumber for a school house and other needed buildings. A large one-story school building was completed in 1870 and all Indian children of school age were required to attend, attendance being made compulsory. Commencing with the fall of 1869 clothing of all kinds for children was abundantly furnished by the Indian Aid Association of the Philadelphia Yearly Meeting of Friends, consequently the school children were all well clothed for the first time in their lives. The school was supplied with competent teachers from the start,—women whose faithful services entitle their names to laudatory mention in any historical account of our county's Indian population. Miss Maria VanDorn and Mrs. Nannie Armstrong were Virginians, while Mrs. Sallie Ely and Miss Elizabeth Walton were from Philadelphia. All were faithful and efficient workers in educational lines as well as in attending to the needs of the sick and aged, in distributing clothing, and in advising the Indian women in regard to sanitary living. Miss Phebe Oliver, a graduate of the Women's Medical College of Philadelphia, came to the agency as resident physician in 1870. She was very successful in the treatment of diseases of children, the prevalence of which diseases had caused many deaths previous to her arrival. Up to this time the Otoes had relied wholly on their own methods of treatment, the basic principle of which was the prevention of interference by evil spirits. Every case of sickness was supposed to result in accordance with the will of an evil spirit or influence that, unless frightened away, will interfere with the action of medicine and render a cure impossible. The course usually adopted in the case of desperate wounds or severe injuries was to shake rattles and to dance around the patient for six days and nights, fresh dancers taking the place of others from time to time. In the case of a sick or wounded horse a different method was pursued. At each administration of medicine or treatment of a wound a different colored blanket was placed upon the animal, the supposition being that this would confuse or deceive the bad spirit that interfered with the curative process, so that it would be likely to pass without recognizing the animal.

As illustrative of Otoe methods in the successful treatment of a case that the agent and his employes all considered hopeless, that of Roc-co a young brave whose skull had been split by an axe so that a portion of the brain exuded, deserves recording in these pages. It seems that Roc-co was sitting on the ground close to where his wife was cutting down a tree, when her axe slipped or glanced and cut deeply into the top of his head. The horrified woman, believing that she had killed him and knowing that his blood relatives would lose no time in taking her life for his, at once fled and secreted herself in some far-off fastness. The unconscious Roc-co was found in due time and borne to the agency. It was the opinion of all the white employes that he could survive but a short time and that he would never regain consciousness. Dr. Oliver not yet having arrived upon the reservation, the Otoe doctors begged for permission to try their skill upon him, which the agent granted. He was then taken to his own lodge and laid upon the ground with his head near a fire, beside which an Otoe drum was continuously beaten and around which a circle of Indians danced, each shaking a gourd rattle, the noise of which, together with the monotonous chanting of the relays of dancers, was kept up for six days and nights. At intervals one of the dancers stepped from the circle and taking a mouthful of a dark liquid sprayed it upon the wound. Whether it was the alternate moistening of the wound with the liquid and drying by the warmth of the fire, or the incessant noise, acting curatively in awakening dormant faith, no one can tell, but the fact remains that after six days the tribe assembled to see him led forth, pale as a ghost, tottering and leaning on a staff. His complete recovery was a matter of only a few weeks.

In the meantime diligent search had been made for Roc-co's wife, and she was very liable to perish from cold and hunger, the nights being cold and she very thinly clad. It was many days before a trace of her could be found and when at last, emaciated and worn out with anguish and physical suffering, she was found in some far off ravine, the news of her husband's survival and possible recovery came to her as a message of great joy. She had carefully evaded and eluded all searching parties, supposing their intention was to put her to death.

Among the Otoes the doctors were usually women, whose duty it was to dig the grave and bury a patient whom they failed to cure, such termination of a case entitling them to act as administrators of the personal estate of the deceased, most of which became their perquisites. Bleeding and blistering were resorted to for many pains and aches. The bleeding was done by scarifying the spot in which the pain centered and then using a sort of a suction cup made from the horn of a young buffalo, the small end of which had been perforated. The blistering was a cruel infliction usually applied on the breasts of children by inserting a piece of dry pitch in a small cut and igniting it. As several such torches were scattered over a child's breast and burned down until large blisters were produced, one can imagine the agony the little patients had to endure.

An ancient Indian custom, that survived until 1871-1872, was pony-giving and pipe-dancing. The Iowas, Omahas, and Otoes had always been on visiting terms, and always owed each other visits, in order to get back as many ponies as had been given or more. It was nothing unusual for the Otoes to give from twenty-five to fifty head of ponies to a visiting band. A man's reputation for courage and his standing in the tribe was largely dependant on the number of ponies he had given away during his lifetime. In almost every lodge there was conspicuously displayed a bundle of small painted sticks, each of which represented a pony that the owner of the lodge had given away on the occasion of a pipe-dance. The larger the bundle the greater the honor due its possessor. The daughter of a man whose display of painted sticks indicated his having given away many ponies was entitled to bear the "Kra-kah" mark,—a blue spot tattooed midway between the eye brows. The possession of such a beauty-spot was evidence that she was the daughter of a very brave and honorable personage. Agent Green found that pipe-dancing and tribal visits with pony giving were very detrimental to the tribe's advancement toward a more civilized condition. They were customs that had been in vogue for untold centuries and were among the strongest ties binding the tribes to a past age of barbarism. At a conference of United States Indian agents, held in Omaha in 1870-1871, he advocated a concerted action on the part of all the agents in the superintendancy, in putting a stop to tribal visiting, pipe-dancing and pony-giving. Each agent present agreed no longer to permit his Indians either to go on a pipe-dance visit, or to receive a visiting band from another tribe. It required some time for the tribes to reconcile themselves to this abandonment of what for centuries had been one of their chief sources of pleasure and excitement, and it was not until after a few visiting bands had been sent to their homes pony-less that the custom was reluctantly abandoned. The conclusion of a permanent peace with the Osages and the discontinuance of frequent tribal visits with their attendant excitement rendered it less difficult to induce the Indians to live in the small frame houses that the agent was building for them, and to cultivate the land.

Gradually the men were induced to wear the clothing furnished by the Indian Aid Association, though many of the older men could never be persuaded to wear trousers and often mutilated or destroyed a new pair of trousers in order to use the legs as leggings; they objected to the rest of the garment for the reason that it made the lower part of the body too warm. Efforts were made by the ladies of the agency to introduce the use of soap and towels into the domestic economy of the Otoe lodges, and considerable quantities of these were supplied by the Indian Aid Association, all of which the Indians gladly received and at once established a lively commerce with their white neighbors, supplying them with soap and towels in exchange for fresh pork, chickens, butter, and other edibles. On one occasion the Indian Aid Association sent a very large box containing enough gay creations of the milliner's art to supply every woman in the tribe with a flower or feather bedecked headpiece, either a hat or a bonnet. The next day the young braves of the tribe had bedecked themselves with the whole of this supply of gay millinery; the women had no use for it.

The Otoes and Missouris were of very pure Indian blood, except in the case of three or four individuals whose names indicated a French ancestry. Two of these men were of striking appearance and physique. Both were fairly well educated and they were of nearly the same age. One was Battiste Deroin the other Battiste Barneby. Battiste Deroin was an Otoe while his lifelong rival and competitor for the position of United States interpreter was an Omaha, married to an Otoe woman. The French blood in the veins of each had been diluted through so many generations of Indian ancestors that its existence was hardly apparent. For some reasons that had militated in his favour Deroin received the appointment as government interpreter from Agent Green, in 1869,—a position that he afterward held until the removal of the Indians from the county. Both men had great influence among the Indians and were highly regarded by many of the early settlers of the county. They were both most interesting conversationalists and well versed in all Indian lore. Battiste Deroin was a polygamist, his two wives being sisters, as he had availed himself of an Indian custom that permitted a man to take his wife's younger sister as a supplementary wife without ceremony or gift. The fact that this young woman was the beauty of the tribe and had a host of admirers and lovers caused him many a pang of jealousy that was far from being groundless. Battiste Barneby was among the first Indians on the reservation to build a frame house and occupy it as a dwelling place both winter and summer. It was provided with a wide, open fireplace, within which a cheerful tire always blazed and beside which might be often seen a nearly full-grown wild cat, either asleep or engaged in washing its face with its paw, just as an ordinary pussy does. Its sharp claws enabled it to exact due respect from the snarling dogs that tried to form its acquaintance. Mrs. Barneby wore the Kra-kah mark between her eyebrows, indicating that her father had been brave and honorable; a man of great liberality and generosity. A bundle of small painted sticks, each representing a pony given away, doubtless accompanied him to the grave. Battiste Barneby was accidentally killed, in Atchison, Kansas, in 1875 or 1876.

Perhaps no Indian was more widely known among the early settlers than old Medicine Jake, the snake doctor. Emaciated and entirely nude, except as to a breech cloth, his striking appearance was enhanced by a snakeskin bandaged around one of his skinny legs, just below the knee, as a sign or advertisement of his profession. Rattlesnakes and moccasins were quite plentiful and the Indian children were frequently bitten. It was claimed that old Jake had an infallible cure that nobody else knew how to prepare. Strange as it may seem, the Otoes were afraid to kill snakes owing to a belief that if one was killed its kindred would seek until they found the killer and inflicted revenge. Their name for snake was "wah-cun," signifying something akin to a spirit. Another remarkable character was O-thro-kes-koo-nie, known among the white people as "Hog-Jaw" because of a deformity that caused his lower teeth and jaw to project in a frightful manner,—a malformation that made the poor fellow's life miserable by creating fear and aversion whenever he appeared in the presence of strangers. Perhaps one of the strongest characters among the Otoes was Jo-John, captain of the Indian police. When Ar-ka-ke-ta was deposed and Medicine Horse made chief, Jo-John was promoted by the agent to a chieftainship, but alas, Beatrice whiskey was his undoing,—when under its influence, in a sudden fit of anger, he killed a companion by striking him on the head with a neckyoke. This act cost him his position as chief and, according to ancient custom, forfeited him his life, putting it absolutely at the disposal of the kindred of the slain. In order to save him from summary execution he was lodged in jail at Beatrice. Eventually the relatives of the murdered man were appeased by a liberal gift of ponies, and Jo-John was restored to the bosom of his family. Physically Jo-John was a splendid specimen of his race. Having a mental capacity above the average, he possessed those ancient traits of Indian character that won the confidence and esteem of the early French traders,—honesty, integrity, and truthfulness. An incident illustrating this occurred shortly before the unfortunate homicide we have mentioned. It seems that he had borrowed a small sum of money from a person living near Blue Springs, promising to repay it within a certain time and when the time was near at hand he went to the house of the lender to repay it, only to find the premises occupied by strangers, who informed him that the party he sought had removed to a distant part of Kansas. Jo-John knew nothing about bank drafts or money orders, so, mounting his pony, he set out on a long and wearisome journey to find his creditor. The trip required several days and involved much inquiry, for it was not known exactly where the party had located and an inability to clearly express ideas in English made the task he had undertaken all the harder. His perseverance, however, was rewarded by finding the party sought, who was greatly surprised by the payment of a small debt that he had forgotten all about.

The Otoes as a people were innately honest and generally careful to meet all their financial obligations. This characteristic was so well known to all Indian traders and agency employes that they never hesitated to extend them credit, knowing that on annuity payment, if not before, the debt would be paid. Perhaps next to Jo-John the finest looking and most typical specimen of an Indian warrior was Har-ra-gar-rah, son of Chief Big Soldier. He was known among the white people by the name of "Hod-de-god-die." It was the chief hope and ambition of Big Soldier's life that Hod-de-god-die should succeed him as chief, and many were the interviews he sought with the agent on that account, but the old man's hopes were doomed to disappointment for Hod-de-god-die's mental equipment and calibre would have disqualified him even had a vacancy occurred. When arrayed in full Indian costume that included a very ancient necklace of bear's claws, ears loaded with silver bobs, and face bedecked with indigo and vermillion, Hod-de-god-die presented a rather gorgeous spectacle, but the real Beau Brummel of the tribe, the acknowledged prince of all fops, was Jack Wild-Bird. To visitors he was a curiosity. He appeared to have only one serious occupation, aside from athletic games, and that was the beautification and decoration of his personality. Hours were spent in painting and decorating his face with vermillion, indigo, yellow ocher, and white clay, and experience had taught him how to produce the most startling and inharmonious effect. His head was always kept shaved to a scalp-look, from which floated a fine eagle's feather. And many hours of his time were occupied in the use of his beard-puller and in watching his face in a large hand-glass that was carried attached to his waist-cord. The beard-pullers used by the Otoes consisted of a spring-like steel coil about three inches in length which, when pressed against the face, and tightly squeezed, caught and held the small hairs and eyebrows, thus enabling the operator to extract a large number at once. These instruments were sold by all Indian traders. During warm weather Jack's only raiment, aside from his scarlet breech cloth and heavy necklaces of wampum and beads, was similar to that possessed by Adam before the apple episode, but in cold weather he fairly bloomed in gay ribbands, deer-skin leggings decorated with the stained quills of the porcupine, and the handsomest scarlet blanket obtainable. He was undoubtedly the most accomplished flute musician in the tribe, and during summer evenings the melodious strains of his flute, mingled with the far off wail of a mourner beside a lonely grave, were often aids in courting sleep. The neverfailing hospitality to be met with at every lodge rendered the matter of subsistence a minor consideration with this gay idler. In the ancient athletic games of the tribe he was a leader and expert. The village play ground was a very important feature of village life. It consisted of well-smoothed and perfectly level space about five hundred feet in length by perhaps two hundred in width. It was there that many of the young men, nude except as to breech cloth, played from morning till night through the hottest days, exhibiting a wonderful dexterity in throwing, while running at great speed, a small flexible ring, causing it to spin along the ground while each runner essayed to catch it upon a sort of a javelin that he threw as he ran. This game was rendered very exciting by the betting that accompanied it, and it was from this source that Jack Wild-Bird acquired the means that enabled him to bedeck himself so gayly.

It was a custom among the Indians to deprive a woman of the sight of one eye if she was known to have departed from the path of virtue. The writer was cognizant of a case of this kind in 1869, but occasions for the infliction of this severe punishment were very rare. Marital infelicity, caused by infidelity on the part of a wife, called for the blood of her paramour; or in lieu of that a gift of ponies proportionate to his wealth.

The adjudication and settlement of all troubles devolved upon the agent. In the course of administering justice and punishing delinquents he found it necessary on one occasion to convert the agency smoke-house into a jail, and having placed a number of youthful culprits therein, under a ten days' sentence, he securely padlocked the door. The building being an old frame structure, the prisoners had little difficulty in devising a secret exit which enabled them to spend most of their time at home, being very careful to be in jail when the meals were handed in. This free and easy manner of suffering imprisonment had been continued for several days so successfully that the prisoners grew careless in regard to being in limbo at meal-time, and their jailor having decided to pay them a visit a little earlier than usual, found the prison empty. The police were at once notified and soon reported that they had found them in the jail, where they positively declared they had been all the time.

The Otoe word for medicine had a broader meaning than we attach to its equivalent, for it is "mon-co,"—the mysterious, the occult, the incomeprehensible; even clairvoyance is not beyond its pale. A remarkable instance of an exhibition of the last named phenomena by the medicine men of the tribe occurred in 1872, while efforts were being made to recapture White-Water, the murderer, who, having escaped from the sheriff after his arrest, was in hiding somewhere on the reservation. A large party of Iowas were visiting the Otoes at the time, on account of a pipe-dance, and had joined in the hunt that was being made for the hiding-place of the fugitive. On account of a trifling peculiarity in the shape of the sole of his moccasin the searchers had discovered his trail in widely separated localities, but his cunning in eluding them was greater than their sleuth-craft. The Indians were exceedingly anxious to capture White-Water in order to show their condemnation of his crime as well as to placate the animosity it had created, toward the Indians, among the friends and relatives of the murdered men. Disappointed in their efforts after several days of search, they at length invoked the occult and mysterious power that was believed to pertain to the "Mon-co" men, with results in the direction of clairvoyance that were as astonishing as they were mystifying. An assemblage of probably two hundred horsemen, including the Iowas, was gathered at a place on the west side of the river where the prairie gradually sloped to a broad river-bottom. The medicine men in their midst chanted and danced frantically until at length two of them, mounted on swift ponies, emerged from the throng and after circling around it a few times at great speed, darted off across the prairie and out of sight,—where they went or what happened to them during their absence of perhaps twenty minutes we do not know, but when they reappeared their horses were in a lather of sweat and as they approached it became evident that both swayed and could hardly retain their seats;

a rush was made to meet them and each fell from his horse into the outstretched arms of his friends in an apparently unconscious condition. They were laid upon the ground and an excited crowd gathered closely around them. As they slowly recovered from a stupor they muttered words that were eagerly awaited for and listened to by those who were bending over them. In gasping and broken sentences they told of where they had (clairvoyantly?) seen the fugitive seated. It was on the summit of a high bluff on the south side of Cedar creek at a point that could be reached by climbing a very steep rocky gulch that extended from the bed of the creek. There, they declared, he was sitting in the tall grass and gazing watchfully over the country. The writer who accompanied the party of horsemen that at once started for the spot indicated, which was several miles distant, noticed that as they drew near, the Indians halted and were evidently afraid to approach within gun shot, and it was not until he had appealed to the police to show their bravery that they finally charged up the hill and, on the very spot designated by the medicine men, found the nest in the tall grass where he had been seated a very short time before the party charged up the hill on the prairie side, his moccasin tracks proving that he had escaped down the rocky gulch to the bed of the creek and along the edge of the creek, where his trail was followed for about a mile when it struck across the prairie towards the timber on Wolf creek.

The circumstances connected with the arrest of White-Water by Sheriff Alexander, of Jefferson county, his escape from the sheriff, and his final capture by the Indians, may be of sufficient historical interest to relate here. News of an atrocious double murder had reached us, but it was not until the arrival of Sheriff Alexander at the Agency that we learned that White-Water was suspected of the crime. On inquiry it was learned that when the Otoes returned from the hunt a few days before he had loitered behind and came in alone and very seriously wounded some hours after the crime must have been committed. The police informed us that he was living at Medicine Horse's village of bark lodges near the mouth of Mission creek, and the agent and sheriff at once proceeded to that place.

MEDICINE-HORSE'S VILLAGE

On their arrival an Indian, by a sly gesture, indicated the lodge where he slept and the agent at once entered and found him lying beside his wife on the platform of poles that, with a covering of skins, constituted his bed. On seeing the agent enter and catching a glimpse of the sheriff outside the doorway he at once realized that for him the situation was now desperate, and reaching beneath his pillow he drew forth a heavy, old-fashioned navy revolver, the very one with which the murder had been committed, and cocking it with his unwounded hand, excitedly told his wife that "now my time has come to die and these two principal white men shall die with me." He arose from the bed and, keeping the pistol pointed at the agent, backed to the rear doorway of the lodge, the agent followed closely despite his repeated threats that he would shoot, a threat that he would undoubtedly have carried into effect had not Medicine Horse arrived in the nick of time and compelled him to put up his pistol, telling him that if he killed either the agent or the sheriff the white people would wipe the tribe off the reservation. The murderer, pale with fear and suffering from his wound, was placed on a rear seat of the agency carriage with Medicine-Horse beside him as a guard as well as a friend and adviser, and driven rapidly to the agency. On arriving at the Otoe village White-Water begged to be permitted to bid farewell to a relative, and it was while doing this that he sprang away from the sheriff and with the swiftness of a deer made his escape. It was nearly two weeks after the clairvoyance episode before his capture was finally effected. It had become known that he was lurking in the timber bordering Wolf creek, heavily armed, and determined never to be taken alive; this knowledge had been obtained by secretly following and watching his wife, who had sought him out and was in communication with him. On the day of his capture the agent had gone to Beatrice, expecting to return the next day, but having finished his business by sundown, and the night being moonlight, he concluded to start back. In those days all the creeks between Beatrice and the agency were crossed by very dangerous and uncertain fords, and in order to reach the Wolf creek ford the road skirted along the creek through the timber for nearly a quarter of a mile. It was shortly before midnight when the agent reached this stage of his homeward journey, the very timber tract in which the outlaw was secreted. The moon was shining brightly and as all the curtains of the carriage were rolled up he at once realized that he was about to become a possible target to an unerring marksman. He stopped the horses, unrolled and fastened down every curtain, and then using the whip made quick time through the timber and across the steep-banked, dangerous ford. Approaching the agency with the expectation of finding all wrapped in darkness and slumber, he was greatly astonished to find the place all lighted and astir. The Indian police were standing on guard about the doors, and evidently something momentuous had occurred. Yes, White-Water had been captured, brought to the agency, and delivered to the agent's wife, who had been left in charge of affairs during his absence. She had wisely planned all arrangements to render the murderer's escape impossible, but the unexpected return of her husband was a great relief to her. The capture was effected by his kinsmen in order that no one could be held liable, or compelled to atone for his blood in case of his execution,—it being the Indian custom for kindred to exact reparation either by taking a life or exacting a heavy penalty in ponies. They had approached him with brotherly greetings that disarmed suspicion and it was his own brother who, at an opportune moment, sprang upon him and held his arms while the others bound him securely with a lariat. A farm wagon was then brought from the agency and his unhappy kindred completed their stern act of duty by delivering him into the hands of the law. The next day the Indian police, clad in their blue cavalry uniforms, and carrying a large United States flag at their head, escorted the large agency carriage containing the agent, his interpreter, Battiste Deroin, and the prisoner for Fairbury. Lack of space forbids giving details of the case; suffice to say that at a trial before Judge O. P. Mason, held some months later, White-Water was convicted of murder in the first degree and sentenced to imprisonment in the penitentiary for life. Seventeen years later he was pardoned by the governor, but his stay in prison had been an age to him. Confinement had ruined his health, his wife had married another, his kindred were mostly dead, and the beautiful valley of the Blue was no longer the home of his race.

The names of some of the leading braves and heads of families whose faces were familiar to many of the early settlers of the county may become of historic interest to future generations and well worth preserving, together with the significance of each in English. Hence we present the following:

Shun-ga-mon-co (Medicine-Horse)
Cha-pah (Buffalo's Head)
Cha-thea-ka (Buffalo's Tracks)
Hoo-gra-toe-way (Four Pillars)
E-stah-mon-tha (Iron Eyes)
Kay-tah (Turtle)
Paw-nee-inga (Little Pawnee)
Paw-nee-coo-cha (Pawnee-Killer)
Sho-cha-mon-ie (Moving Smoke)
Wah-nah-quash-coon-ie (Fearless)
Wah-cun-hun-cha (Big Snake)
Shun-ga-scaw (White Horse)
Mon-co-yo (Valley or Low Land)
Bah-thea-inga (Little Cedar)
My-um-pe (Good Land)
Nah-way-hun-cha (Big Hand)
Koth-a-inga (Little Crow)

Lont-noo-inga (Little Pipe)
Nee-ach-shinga (Little Creek)
Maw-hee (Knife)
Mah-loo-ha-la (Distant Land)
Mon-toe-pah (Bear's Head)
Mon-toe-tha-way (Black Bear)
No-ho-cha-ning-shinga (Little Brains)
Ton-nah-coo-nah (Courting Favour)
Wah-con-dah-keep-ah (Religious Head)
Wah-cun-thra-cha (Long Snake)
Whan-a-ga-he (Adviser)
Ho-mo-schu-cha (Red Elk)
Mah-sho-cha (Dust)
Chee-na-inga (Small Village)

Other heads of families, the English significance of whose names we are unable to give, but all of whom were well known to most of the early settlers of southern Gage county, were the following:

A-Gie-hi-ya
Cha-ah-gra
Har-ra-gar-rah (Police)
Ka-gra-tha
Mus-ka-gah-hay (Police)
Pah-wan-a-sha
Shoc-a-pi-ya
Poonch-e-in-do-wa
Who-ha
Ah-ga-ha-mon-nee
Cre-cah-gah
Hoth-a-coe
Gah-he-gah (Police)
Nah-pe-wah-la
Pay-ton-gah-hay
Tah-poth-ka (Police)
Noh-thra-thra-cha
Chu-sho-cha

Ah-ho-thea-ah
Ha-thon-ta
Ha-naw
Loo-he-a-mon
Noh-he-toppe (Police)
Roc-co (Police)
Um-buth-ka-day
We-ru-gri-inga
Sho-cha-inga

Among the names of prominent Otoe women who were occasional callers on the white settlers and whose faces were familiar to many of them were:

Ho-tock-a-me (Tom Boy)
Hun-gesh-cha-me
Ah-wa-soon-tha-me
Mon-ka-toe-wack-a-me
O-ma-toe-me
Mon-com-pay-me
Hoo-gla-me
Moh-sho-cha-me
Hun-do-ya-me
Tah-cha-me
Bah-ho-cha-me
Kay-lah-me
Mon-thu-bla-me

In 1875-1876 better school accommodations were secured by the erection of a large modern two-story school building, with accommodations for boarding a large number of the children. The supervision and care of the Indian Aid Association of the Society of Friends was continued from year to year, and this, combined with other civilizing influences, was instrumental in gradually changing the modes of living and habits of thought among the younger members of the tribe, but the old people adhered tenaciously to the ancient habits and customs of their race. The discontinuance of buffalo hunting, tribal visiting, pony-giving, pipe-dancing, and other episodes of Indian life that had always been of vast import to them, caused a feeling of unrest and dissatisfaction that finally culminated in a determination to remove to the Indian Territory.

In concluding this account of the aboriginal inhabitants of Gage county the writer wishes to bear testimony to their many virtues as a people,—their honesty, their never-failing generosity, their unselfish liberality, and their love and deep regard for each other in every family circle. Many interesting facts and incidents might be added, but space forbids.

CHAPTER XIII

First White Settlers

Indian Agents and Employes — Gideon Bennett — David Palmer — John O. Adams, and the Shaws — The Pethouds — The Killpatricks and Others — Settlements in Rockford Township — In Grant Township — At Blue Springs

The first white man to enter our county as far as we have any reliable information, were George Heppner, Indian agent for the Otoe and Missouri tribes of Indians, in 1855; his successor in office, William Wallace Dennison, in 1859; and a few employes of the government who had in charge the mill which belonged to the Indians and which had been hauled from Nebraska City by ox teams, in April, 1855; the blacksmith, farmer, and such other employes as the government allowed at that time. At least one white man followed the Indians from Nebraska City and engaged in trade with them on his own account. This was Gideon Bennett, who, in 1854, kept the famous ferry on which so many immigrants to the new territory of Nebraska there crossed the Big Muddy then and later on, and who obtained a charter from the first territorial legislative assembly conferring upon him and his family the exclusive privilege and franchise for operating a ferry at Nebraska City for ten years, beginning April 1, 1855. This privilege the second session of this assembly revoked. Bennett established a trading post on Plum creek, just outside the eastern reservation line and in the immediate vicinity of the village of Liberty, on Plum creek. He, however, acquired no residence in our county and remained at the trading post but a short time, when he sold it to a party named McDonald, at St. Joseph, Missouri, and returned to Nebraska City, where his family resided. Afterward he became prominent in local and territorial affairs, amongst other activities representing Otoe county in the territorial assembly of 1864. Some of his children still reside in Nebraska City. Neither Agent Heppner nor Agent Dennison removed their families from Nebraska City to the new reservation nor made any effort to acquire a residence in the county, nor did any of the other employes of the government about the Indian agency acquire or attempt to acquire a permanent residence in the county until after settlement was made at a number of other points. Some of the employes at the agency did, however, at an early date acquire a permanent residence in the county. Among these were Robert A. Wilson, who with his brother, William Wilson, came to the agency in 1855, and erected and took charge of the steam saw mill. They remained in charge of this property as millers and engineers till 1859, when both returned to Iowa. Robert A. Wilson married there and in 1861 he returned to Gage county, where he has ever since resided in Blue Springs. A more extended notice of him will be found later on in this work, in the article entitled "Blue Springs." Another of the Indian employes in an early day was Jacob Shaw. Mr. Shaw and his wife came to the Otoe agency with their only son, John Shaw, now connected with Klein's Mercantile Company, of Beatrice, in 1859, and was the government blacksmith for the Indians until about the year 1865, when he removed to Beatrice, where he and his wife and son became highly respected and prominent citizens. Mr. Shaw passed away in 1916, but his aged widow and their son survive at the time of this writing.

About the time the Indians were removed from Nebraska City to their new reservation, a young man by the name of David Palmer came to the county as an employe of Gideon Bennett at the latter's trading post on Cub creek. Just when he acquired an actual and permanent residence in the county does not seem to be settled beyond a doubt. It is certain, however, that he remained in the county from about 1855 until his death, residing during the latter part of his life on a farm owned by him in the neighborhood of Liberty. While living there he was drowned June 26, 1876, in the Big Blue river, near the Otoe and Missouri Indian village. His descendants still live in Barneston and Liberty townships. They are William Palmer, a son, of Liberty; Mrs. Flora McFarland and Mrs. Fannie Evans, daughters, of Barneston. It is to be regretted that a more authentic record of David Palmer cannot be obtained for the purposes of this history.

If we can look to neither Agents Heppner nor Dennison nor to the employes of the government about the Indian agency, nor to Gideon Bennett, nor to David Palmer, as the first white settler in Gage county, that question must be determined by considering other portions of the county.

The evidence is conclusive that white men in considerable numbers came into the county in the spring of 1857. In March of that year, in old Clay county, a lone white man is said to have stretched a piece of bark between two saplings on which was written this scrap of information: "John O. Adams claims this tract of land this 30th of March, 1857." Under the doctrine of squatter sovereignty as then applied to the preemption laws of the country, this simple act was sufficient probably to constitute a settlement upon the public domain, if followed within four months with substantial improvements and actual occupancy. After selecting this tract of land, Mr. Adams returned to Holt county, Missouri, where he spent the winter of 1856-1857, and in the following April he moved with his family upon his claim, a part of which now constitutes the townsite of the village of Adams. Having erected a small hewed-log house on his land, he, on May 17, 1857, occupied it as a residence and on the same day began breaking up the virgin soil and planting a crop of sod corn. It can hardly be questioned that his is the first claim located, his the first cabin erected (the cabin at Bennett's trading post excepted), and his the first furrows drawn within the present boundaries of Gage county—all this, even though we may concede to David Palmer the honor of being the first bona fide white settler of our county. In addition to himself and wife Mr. Adams's family consisted of seven children. They were Nelson, Nancy, Isaac, John Quincy, Leander, Naomi, and Myanna. Mr. Adams was born in New Jersey, in 1807, he married Miss Letitia Harris, a native of Kentucky, born in 1812, and removed from Kentucky to Missouri in the fall of 1856, with an ox team. He acquired a large tract of land in Adams township, and several of his children were old enough to avail themselves of the benefit of the homestead law. His wife passed away at the age of fifty-five years and his own death occurred December 24, 1867.

None of his children survive except Nelson and Naomi, who reside in the town of Adams. To this sterling pioneer a special memoir is dedicated in the biographical department of this volume.

Shortly after his arrival Mr. Adams was joined by John Stafford, H. Reynolds and brother, Charles Hickock, and Henry Golden; and in July, 1857, Stephen P. Shaw and his wife, Anna Hicks Shaw, with their sons, William, Egbert, John B., James I., and Stephen V. Shaw, with their families, and James and William P. Silvernail, sons-in-law, with their families, settled along the Big Nemaha river, in Adams township, all neighbors of John O. Adams. The Shaws were natives of the state of New York, migrated from that state to Wisconsin in 1850, and from there to Nebraska, leaving Wisconsin March 6th, with six lumber wagons drawn by eight yoke of oxen, and arriving in Nebraska July 6, 1857. In November of that year this small colony was augmented by George Gale, John Lyons, and George Noxon, who also were sons-in-law of Stephen P. Shaw. And in the same year Jacob and John Hildebrand, George Drown, William Curtis, and H. C. Barmore arrived to swell the number of this little colony of progressive citizens. All these early pioneers settled in Adams township. Some are still living, among them John B., James I., and Stephen V. Shaw. Alfred Gale, who was also a pioneer of 1857 in Adams township, and who maintained a continuous residence in that township until recently, is spending the closing years of his life in University Place, this state.

At almost the same time that John O. Adams entered the boundaries of old Clay county, John Pethoud, head of the well known pioneer family of that name, came with his friend Edward C. Austin to that county. Austin settled on Stevens (now Indian) creek, in the immediate neighborhood of the village of Pickrell, and began the erection of a log cabin on his claim. He and Pethoud were found at this work on the 15th day of May, 1857, by Jefferson B. Weston, Bennett Pike, M. W. Ross, and Harrison F. Cook, members of the locating committee of the Nebraska Association, on their way to Omaha to report to the remainder of the association the selection of the original townsite of Beatrice by this committee as the most eligible location in south eastern Nebraska for a city.

John Pethoud also drew after him a considerable following of relatives and friends, who settled in Midland, Logan, and Hanover townships, along Indian, Pierce, and Bear creeks, on the south side of the Clay county line. Amongst these were his married sons, John, Thomas, and Franklin M., with their families, and his sons, Andrew J. and James K. P. Pethoud. Soon afterward he was joined by his sons-in-law, Samuel Jones, the father of William R. Jones and Mrs. Sarah Drew of Beatrice, and John Wilson and Marvin Thompson. About the same time, as previously noted, Edward C. Austin and two brothers, with Fordyce Roper, H. W. Parker, Orrin Stevens, and a few others settled in Clay county, around Austin's mill, near the present site of Pickrell. These pioneer families were soon joined by Ira Dixon and family, Joseph Proud, Thomas Sherrill and family, M. C. Kelly, J. H. Butler, and H. J. Pierce, for whom Pierce creek was named.

SECTION OF WALNUT LOG FROM JOHN PETHOUD'S LOG CABIN ERECTED IN THE SUMMER OF 1857 ON HIS CLAIM FOUR MILES NORTH OF BEATRICE

In 1858 and 1859 settlements were made in the western part of the county, along Cub creek, by Samuel Kilpatrick and his wife, Rachael, parents of John David and Henry Kilpatrick, both deceased, and the well known railroad contractors, capitalists, farmers, and stock-raisers,

William H. Kilpatrick, Robert J. Kilpatrick. Samuel Davenport Kilpatrick, and Joseph M. Kilpatrick. About the same time, down the creek toward Beatrice from Samuel Kilpatrick's homestead. Leander Coffin, Thomas and Joseph Clyne and their mother, Elizabeth Clyne, Andrew Dean, a large family by the name of Wells, Asa F. Bailey, George Whittemore, Joseph Graff, William Blakely, Frederick Elwood, Jonathan Potts, and another man of the same surname, located claims along Cub creek or its vicinity.

Early settlements were made also along the Big Blue river, and the Mud and Cedar creeks, in Rockford township. The first settler in this township, as far as known, was James B. Mattingley, with his wife and two children. Mattingley located on lower Mud creek, in Section 33, in May, 1857. In 1858 the C. C. (Coffin) Berry family located a mile west of Mattingley's, on the Big Blue river, in Section 33 of Rockford township. In the spring of 1858 Edward Woolridge and wife, Leonard Wilson, wife and child, George W. Stark, and Solon M. Hazen located on preëmption claims in the central part of the township. They each broke out a few acres of prairie and planted a crop of sod corn. Woolridge, Wilson, and Stark built cabins on their claims and remained until their corn had ripened. This was gathered and stored in their cabins. Leonard Wilson's child died in the autumn of 1858, its little grave being the first grave in Rockford township and the beginning of what is known as the Stark cemetery. In August, 1858, Fidillo H. Dobbs located a preëmption claim in the same neighborhood. All these settlers returned to Missouri river points to spend the winter. In the spring of 1859 the Woolridges, Pottertons, Hazen, and Stark returned to their claims; the Wilsons never came back. Fidillo H. Dobbs moved his family, consisting of his wife and six children, to his claim March 13, 1859. The same year Jacob Schullenberger and family, Henry Schullenberger, wife and children, Philip B. Coffee and family, Robert Breese, John Tidler, John H. Dunn, and James W. Dunn established their permanent residence in Rockford and Filley townships along Mud creek. In 1861 these settlers were joined by William E. Mudge and family and Joseph Milligan and his wife Sally; and within the same year the Hollingsworth, Shelley, and Wild families, consisting of about twenty-five persons, settled in the neighborhood of Holmesville, along Cedar creek and the Big Blue river. They were English, were all related, and proved a welcome and valuable addition to the population of Gage county.

On the Big Blue river north of Beatrice, in Grant and Blakely townships, the first settlers were John Barrett, George Grant, and Charles Buss, about 1859. They were soon joined by a strong English colony of which the prominent members were Richard Rossiter and family, William and James Plucknett, Robert Nicholas, Richard Dibble and families. These were afterward joined by the Kinsies, two brothers, Joseph Roper and Frederick B. Roper, and members of the Quackenbush family and others.

In the southeast corner of the county settlement was made in 1859 along Plum and Wolf creeks and their tributaries, by James L. Ayers, Jonathan Sharp, Nathaniel D. Cain, Stephen B. Evans, John Palmer, Frederick Fisher, Peter Buckles, Tipton Marion, Frederick Wymore, and others.

In July, 1857, about the time the city of Beatrice was founded on an open prairie, settlement was made also in the neighborhood of Blue Springs. The first settlers of whom we have any account in that locality were James H. Johnson and his family, consisting of his wife, Martha M. Johnson, his young daughters, Mary and Martha, and his sons, Thomas, Allen, James, and Richard. Allen, a boy ten years of age, was drowned in the Big Blue river shortly after the arrival of this family on their claim, a mile and a half northeast of Blue Springs. His death was the first to occur in Blue Springs township of which we have any record. The Johnson family was accompanied in its migration by the Elliott family, which, besides Martin Elliott, the head of this pioneer family, his wife and some minor children, included his adult married sons with their families—Williams, Stephen, and Henry Elliott. With the Elliotts was also a related family named Hevener. In 1858-1859, these pioneers were joined by Rankin Johnson and family, Patrick R. Gary, a son-in-law of Johnson's, and by Jacob Poff, Reuyl Noyes, Joseph Chambers, Samuel Shaw, Rebecca Woodward, F. M. Gratiam, William B. Tyler, Wright Sargent and his wife, True Sargent, and Herbert Viney and wife; and in 1860-1861, Thomas Armstrong and family, George Desert, Dr.

J. M. Summers, and his son-in-law, James B. Maxfield, who afterwards became distinguished as a presiding elder in the Methodist Episcopal church in Nebraska. Robert A. Wilson, Dr. Levi Anthony, Lynus Knight, and King Fisher also settled in Blue Springs or in that neighborhood. The individual histories of some of these settlers will be found later on in this volume, in an article devoted to Blue Springs.

ORIGINAL CABIN ON FIRST HOMESTEAD

An interesting incident in the early settlement of Gage county is the fact that the first homestead entry under the homestead act of 1863 was made by a citizen of this county, Daniel Freeman, long a resident of Blakely township, where his homestead is located.

DANIEL FREEMAN

He had entered the service of the United States as a private in the Sixteenth Illinois Volunteer Infantry at the breaking out of the Civil war, in 1861. Shortly afterward he was transferred to the secret service of the United States, in which he continued until the close of the war, rendering almost invaluable services to the military department at Washington. In 1862 he was detailed for duty in the territory of Nebraska, and while here he visited the village of Beatrice and located a claim, in Section 26, township 4, range 5 of this county. He erected thereon a log cabin, and he moved his family to his claim prior to the first of January, 1863.

On the last day of December, 1862, Mr. Freeman appeared at Brownville for the purpose of availing himself of the benefit of the new homestead act, which went into effect at midnight, December 31, 1862. Mr. Freeman knew of the provisions of the homestead act but had no conscious intent of being the first man to profit by it. He had been ordered to report for service in one of the military departments of the country and was anxious to be away. That night he attended a dance at Brownville, and, becoming acquainted with one of the employes of the government land office, he apprised him of the fact that he desired to make homestead entry of his claim in Gage county. This accommodating official immediately after twelve o'clock, on January 1, 1863, accompanied Mr. Freeman to the land office and prepared his application for homestead entry covering the south half of the northwest quarter, the northeast quarter of the northwest quarter, and the southwest quarter of the northeast quarter of section 26, township 4, range 5, Gage county, Nebraska, and when the land office opened in the morning for business, Mr. Freeman's entry was allowed as the first under the homestead act—this notwithstanding the presence of a large number of other applicants, including Samuel Kilpatrick, who were awaiting opportunity to enter land under the new homestead act. Hon. Galusha A. Grow, the author of the free-homestead law, speaking years afterward in congress upon the beneficence of this act, among other things, said:

There are two interesting incidents connected with the final passage of the original free-homestead bill. First, it took effect on the day of Lincoln's emancipation proclamation. Second, the first settler under the homestead bill, which provided free homes for free men, was named Freeman. Daniel Freeman, of Beatrice, Gage county, Nebraska, was a Union soldier, home on a furlough which would expire on the 2d or 3d day of January, 1863. At a little past midnight on the 1st day of January, 1863, he made his entry in the land office of his district, and left his home the same day to take his place again in the ranks on the tented fields. His entry was number one, his proof of residence was number one, his patent was number one, recorded on page one of book one of the land office of the United States. The first settler under this law was a Freeman, and I trust that the last of its beneficiaries in the long coming years of the future will be a free man.

Daniel Freeman was of the sturdiest kind of New England stock. His ancestors almost from the beginning of this country have been prominent and influential citizens of their communities. Many of them, including his great-grandfather, had fought in the Revolutionary war as well as in the war of 1812 and the Indian wars of the country. He himself possessed many admirable and heroic qualities. The last visit paid to him by the author of this volume some time before his death was at his home on the old homestead. He was ill, suffering from ailments from which he never recovered. Lying on his couch, he discoursed eloquently about his family history and pointed out upon the walls of his room and in its corners, many relics of Revolutionary days, among them his great-grandfather's flintlock musket, carried in some of the first battles for liberty in Massachusetts.

Mr. Freeman was born in Ohio in 1826, and was taken by his parents to Knox county, Illinois, in 1835. In 1847 he began the study of medicine, at Peoria, Illinois. Two years later he graduated from the Electric Medical Institute at Cincinnati, and he began the practice of his profession at Ottawa, Illinois, the same year. But the great Civil war drew him into its maelstrom in 1861, and after its close, in 1865, he found occupation in the simple, uneventful life of a farmer. He served his country as sheriff in 1869-1870; he was for many years justice of the peace of his township, and he held other minor civil offices. Of this honored pioneer further mention is made in the biographical department of this work.

CHAPTER XIV

FOUNDING OF BEATRICE

THE HANNIBAL-NEBRASKA ASSOCIATION — ORGANIZATION — MEMBERS — LOCATING COMMITTEE — ITS REPORT — SELECTION OF NAME — FIRST FOURTH OF JULY CELEBRATION — ASSOCIATION MEETS ON TOWNSITE — SELECTION AND ENTRY OF TOWNSITE

The most authentic and interesting account of the early settlement of our county clusters about the beautiful city of Beatrice. Whatever credit may be due to others for the settlement, development, and progress of Gage county, there can be no doubt of the part that this city has played in all this work. The story of the founding of Beatrice reads like a romance and can never fail to have absorbing interest as a unique experiment in the settlement of the west.

Almost from the beginning of the nineteenth century the Missouri river steamboat had been an important means of communication between settled portions of our country and the western frontier. By 1854, when the territory of Nebraska was created and opened to immigration, lines of steamboats were regularly plying between St. Louis and the upper Missouri. One of these vessels was the old side-wheel steamer "Hannibal." On the 3d day of April, 1857, this staunch river boat slowly turned her prow up the current of the Mississippi, pushed off from her wharf at St. Louis, and began a long, tedious, and uneventful voyage to the settlements along the Missouri river. She was crowded with emigrants from every portion of the country, all bound for the west. Of her three hundred passengers two hundred were Mormons on their way to join a Mormon colony at Florence, Nebraska territory, and thence to move across the great plains to Salt Lake City. Of the remaining passengers many were young men, and a few were heads of families; nearly all were bound for the western frontier. Before they had been many days out from St. Louis, there sprung up between the non-Mormon portion of the passengers an acquaintance which was destined to be attended by consequences of the utmost importance to the citizens of Gage county and the state of Nebraska. On the 23d day of the voyage from St. Louis, while this great river boat was temporarily stranded on a sand bar, opposite the village of Doniphan, in Kansas territory, in a meeting called for the purpose of considering the situation steps were taken whereby thirty-five of these daring and congenial spirits bound themselves by a written constitution to remain together and settle as a colony somewhere in the new territory of Nebraska.

The minutes of this meeting when viewed by the light of subsequent events possess great interest. They read as follows:

Wednesday, April 22, 1857.

Meeting of the passengers on board the steamboat Hannibal, convened while fastened on a sand bar near Doniphan, K. T.

On motion of John McConihe, Hon. J. F. Kinney was called to the chair. On motion, John McConihe was appointed secretary.

The chairman then stated the object of the meeting to be the organization of all who were willing into one town association and the formation of a settlement in Nebraska. Appropriate remarks were made by the president, tending to show the advantages of such an association, if all the members were actual settlers, and further stated that southern Nebraska, the Nemaha country, would probably offer the greatest inducements at present.

Mr. Albert Towle was then called upon and he addressed the meeting, stating that he had traveled in the Nemaha country and that it was a beautiful and desirable section, and that a town located in its midst would thrive and prosper.

Thereupon it was resolved that a committee of five be appointed to draft articles of association and report at a subsequent meeting.

The chair appointed as a committee to draft articles of association, John McConihe, Ezra M. Drake, Timothy Elliott, Bayard T. Wise, James A. Raridon.

Mr. McConihe moved that the chairman be added to the committee as its chairman. Carried.

The meeting was large and enthusiastic, and the subject of starting new towns was generally discussed.

On motion the meeting adjourned to meet to-morrow, April 23d, at 10 o'clock A.M.

JOHN MCCONIHE, Secretary.

The second meeting also was well attended. It included probably most of the non-Mormon male passengers who were looking forward to establishing themselves in the new territory of Nebraska. The minutes of this meeting are interesting and have great historical value. They are as follows:

Missouri River Steamboat Hannibal.
April 23, 1857, 10 A. M.

Meeting called to order, Hon. J. F. Kinney in the chair. The committee appointed at the first meeting to draft articles of association reported as the result of their labors, the following:

Articles of Association.

The undersigned agree to and adopt the following Articles of Association.

First: The name of this association shall be known as "The Nebraska Association."

Second: The object of the same to select a townsite in Nebraska, either by purchase or claim; claim the same and so much land adjacent thereto as this association may agree upon, all of which shall be held by the members for the mutual benefit of all.

Third: Persons signing these articles and becoming settlers either in person or by substitute upon the townsite or adjacent land claimed as aforesaid within two months shall be entitled to an equal share in all the benefits belonging to or arising out of this association.

Fourth: The officers of this association shall consist of a president, secretary, treasurer and board of directors.

Fifth: A locating committee shall be appointed immediately, who shall proceed at the expense of this association to explore Nebraska and select a townsite and report at an adjourned meeting to be held at Omaha City on the 20th of May next, which report shall be adopted as the townsite for the town of..............

Sixth: Such townsite shall be surveyed, lithographed and divided into such number of shares as may be agreed upon, which with the claims adjacent thereto shall be the property of this association, and such number of shares as may be thought best can be sold and the proceeds of such shares applied to the carrying out of the purposes of this association.

Seventh: Assessments may be made if necessary from time to time for such expenses and improvements as a majority of the members of the association may declare necessary.

Eighth: Members who do not in person or by substitute locate upon said townsite or some claim of the association adjacent thereto within two months from the time of the report of the locating committee shall forfeit all right of membership; unless he shall be justified in his absence by the association.

Ninth: These articles may be amended or others substituted therefor by a two-thirds vote of the members, provided always that requisite notice of such proposed alteration of these articles has been given to the association at least two weeks previous to the adoption of the same and the members thereof sufficiently notified of such meeting.

Tenth: Each member shall have the benefit of such improvements as exceed in value those made by others of the association, to be ascertained and allowed in such equitable manner as may be agreed upon.

The above articles were fully discussed separately and were finally adopted unanimously. When, on motion, the secretary was ordered to copy the same preparatory to receiving signatures, and the meeting adjourned to three o'clock PM. for that purpose.

JOHN MCCONIHE, Secretary.

At the adjourned meeting, at three o'clock in the afternoon, the articles of the association were presented for signatures and were signed by the following named persons: E. A. Wilmans, Calvin Miller, E. M. Drake, William F. Buffington, John McConihe, Timothy Elliott, M. C. Barr, Gilbert T. Loomis, George W. Robb, John B. Kellogg, John Henn,

Jacob Talman, Albert Towle, Bayard T. Wise, Herman M. Reynolds, Bennett Pike, John Brown, George H. Tobey, A. Nelson, J. F. King, Norman Colson, John P. Cadman, Phineas W. Hitchcock, George A. Jackson, M. W. Ross, Edward Stewart, Jefferson B. Weston, Jesse Spielman, Jacob Zolinger, John F. Kinney, Richard Northrup, James J. Raridan, Alexander McCready, Justus Townsend.

Later, and before the boat reached its destination in Omaha, Isaac M. Steele, Alexander Lewis, Charles Dripps, James M. Green, Daniel P. Taylor, Obediah H. Hewett, John N. Newton, Joseph R. Nelson, and Logan D. Cameron were admitted to membership in the association, and at a meeting of the board of directors held in Omaha, on May 22, 1857, George D. Bonham and Joseph Milligan also were admitted into full membership in the association on the same terms as the others, namely, payment into the treasury of the sum of one hundred dollars. And at a meeting of the board of directors held at Beatrice it was "resolved that H. F. Cook become a member of the association upon payment of assessment (in place of Mr. Dripps, whose share has been forfeited) and upon payment of fifty dollars additional." As far as the records go there were no other formal additions to the membership of the association, but it is an historical fact that Nathan and William Blakely, together with Isma P. Mumford and wife, arrived on the townsite of Beatrice on July 17, 1857, and became thereafter closely identified with the history and destiny of Beatrice.

At the third meeting of the association held on board the Hannibal April 28, 1857, a census of the membership was taken with respect to their occupations and it was found that there were six lawyers, four physicians, three merchants, a mason, a bricklayer, an engineer, and a surveyor, together with a number of members without expressed occupations.

Before the "Hannibal" reached Nebraska City a committee consisting of Bennett Pike, M. W. Ross, F. A. Wilmans, Bayard T. Wise, Jefferson B. Weston, and Judge John F. Kinney, was chosen, known as the locating committee, in conformity with the 5th subdivision of the articles of association, "to explore Nebraska and select a townsite and report at an adjourned meeting (of the association) to be held at Omaha on the 20th day of May next, which report shall be adopted as a townsite," etc. At Nebraska City this committee left the boat and proceeded to discharge its duty. It divided itself into two sub-committees, Wise, Kinney, and Wilmans formed one of these, and, proceeding directly west from Nebraska City they passed over the spot where Lincoln, the state capital, now stands. The other three members of the committee, Weston, Pike, and Ross, hired a team at Nebraska City, and, with Harrison F. Cook as driver, began their search at once for a suitable location for the prospective city. Striking in a southwesterly direction, without other guide than the sectional corner stones planted by the government surveyors, they proceeded through the bright May weather to examine the country through which they took their course with the single purpose of choosing the most desirable site for a city. After several days of intelligent wandering over the springing prairies, in the brilliant sunshine lands, on a late afternoon in early May, they pitched camp on the banks of Indian creek, near where the Kees Manufacturing Company's buildings now stand, and within the present limits of the city of Beatrice. A little investigation convinced them that their quest was at an end. These clear-visioned young men noted the wide sweep of rolling plain extending in all directions from the confluence of the two streams where their camp was made; they marked the near neighborhood of several well wooded streams flowing through fertile lands into the Big Blue river; they observed that this stream, with its rock bottom and steep shores possessed at this point ample facilities and power for milling and manufacturing purposes, and that nature had given the adjacent land grades and levels that rendered the work of building a city an easy task.

Having carefully noted all these things they began their journey to Omaha, stopping a few hours on the way with John Pethoud and his friend Edward C. Austin, who were engaged in building a hewed-log house on Mr. Pethoud's claim, four and one-half miles north of the prospective city, on this side of the Clay county line.

The entire committee having assembled in Omaha and agreed upon its report, the members of the association were called together to receive it, on the 20th day of May, 1857, at the hour of one o'clock in the forenoon, in the office of the territorial secretary of state. The report was brief and was probably written by that able young lawyer, Bennett Pike. It reads as follows:

We the undersigned, locating committee of the Nebraska Association, after thoroughly exploring Johnson, Gage Clay, Lancaster and Cass counties, find the most eligible site for a town near the center of Gage county. The advantages of this place consist in its location between two tributaries of the Blue and at the junction of the western branch with the main river; in the great beauty and fertility of the adjacent prairies, in the abundance of wood and timber, in the proximity of stone fit for building purposes, and the favorable indications of coal. The prairie is four miles in width from creek to creek and is skirted on either side by the timber line along the banks of the above mentioned streams. The timber is generally oak, walnut, hickory, ash, cottonwood and elm, and is of a better quality and finer size than any other we saw in our explorations. The beauty of the situation, the central position in the county, and quality and quantity of the timber, the superior nature and location of the intervening prairie and the large extent of country tributary to it, determined us in the selection of this place as possessing all the requisites and advantages necessary to the founding and building of a prosperous and thriving inland town. All of which is very respectfully submitted, with an accompanying map of the place.

Bennett Pike.	M. W. Ross.
F. A. Wilmans.	B. T. Wise.
J. B. Weston.	J. F. Kinney.

This report was unanimously adopted and a committee appointed whose duty it was to ascertain and properly designate the exact location of the proposed townsite and have the same surveyed. Another committee was appointed, charged with the duty of reporting at an early date to the association a name for this embryo town. The last named committee, as a result of its deliberations, at a meeting of the association on May 21st, reported the names of "Wheatland" and "Beatrice". The latter was the name of Judge Kinney's eldest daughter, Julia Beatrice Kinney, and it was adopted by a vote of sixteen to nine.

The association, after appointing a committee, headed by Bennett Pike, to purchase for its use a steam saw mill, adjourned to meet at Beatrice on the 27th day of July, 1857.

JULIA BEATRICE KINNEY
1860

Most of the members of the association made their way to the proposed townsite during the month of June, and by the 4th day of July nearly all were assembled on the original virgin townsite of Beatrice. They proceeded to celebrate the national holiday, and this was the first Fourth of July celebration ever held in Gage county. Judge Kinney, who had located at Nebraska City in the practice of the law, drove across the country with his family to participate in this celebration. Though the participants were few in number, patriotic enthusiasm was much in evidence. Miss Julia Beatrice Kinney, the seventeen-year-old daughter of the president of the association, in a pleasing speech presented to her namesake the national flag which had been made by the ladies of the association at Nebraska City, and Bennett Pike replied.

Most of the members remained on the ground until the 27th day of July, the date to which the association had adjourned at Omaha in May to meet at the townsite of Beatrice, and when on that day the president of the association, Judge Kinney, directed his scholarly secretary, John McConihe, to call the roll of the members the following gentlemen responded to their names: Messrs. Pike, Towle, Wise, Weston, Jackson, Hewett, Elliott, Joseph Nelson, Northrop, Townsend, Tobey, Tailor, Wilmans, Ross, Reynolds, Johnson, Miller, Brown, Loomis, Green, and Bonham. Thirteen members, namely, Kellogg, A. Nelson, Barr, Cadman, Hitchcock, Henn, Dripps, Stewart, Zolinger, King, Raridon, Robb, and Buffington, were represented by proxy.

Judge Kinney then announced that the site selected for the location of the town was "one mile from east to west and one-half mile from north to south." Some discussion ensued, during which Mr. Bonham moved "that the townsite be so moved as to conform with the government survey and to consist of four hundred acres." After further discussion of the site of the proposed town "the whole matter was referred back to the locating committee". On the 28th day of July, that committee reported, recommending that "the eastern boundary be placed on the section line and that an addition be taken in on the west sufficient to cross the river." This report was accepted and O. B. Hewett was thereupon appointed lot agent "to donate town lots and that he be allowed to donate no more than three lots in any one block, and that no lots be donated except to actual settlers who will build thereon." A resolution was adopted that "the size of the town lots be fifty feet front by one hundred and forty feet deep, with streets eighty feet wide and alleys twenty feet wide, running one way." The Rev. D. H. May, the grandfather of Earl and Paul Marvin, was given five lots "for his kindness in coming to Beatrice and preaching the first sermon in town." A resolution was adopted donating "one thousand dollars to any competent man who will take the mill, erect the same immediately and run it under certain specified restrictions," and "Mr. Towle was allowed the privilege of occupying the association log house by unanimous consent until further action upon the subject." William H. Brodhead, who had previously been selected to survey the townsite, at this meeting of the association, July 28, 1857, was "allowed one hundred dollars and expenses for laying out the townsite and making three plats of the same" and Mr. Bonham was appointed "to confer with him about selecting lands." A half block was donated and set apart for school purposes and a committee appointed to select land for a cemetery. Mr. Pike was empowered to sell the mill if opportunity offered, and Hewett was directed as lot agent to donate two lots to the "first blacksmith who would erect a blacksmith shop in town." At an adjourned meeting of the association held July 29th at three o'clock in the afternoon, the location of the townsite was taken up and finally it was resolved "that the townsite be removed to the north so as to correspond with the government survey."

The townsite finally selected comprised the southeast quarter of section thirty-three and the southwest quarter of section thirty-four, in township four north, and range six east of the sixth principal meridian, comprising three hundred and twenty acres. It was surveyed and platted by William H. Brodhead, at that time a resident of Nebraska City, and on the 13th day of August, 1859, it was formally entered under the national townsite act, by Dr. Herman M. Reynolds, as mayor of the city of Beatrice, at the land office at Brownville, where at the same time a plat of the new town was filed, as in case of such entries the law required.

The reader has now looked upon the origin of the city of Beatrice. Glancing backward across the intervening three score years from his felicitous surroundings, it may be difficult for him to visualize the unpromising conditions that beset this beautiful city at the hour of its birth. Planted in the midst of what was virtually a primitive waste, far removed from even the confines of civilized life, no one who was not endowed with the prevision of the pioneer could have foreseen the bright future that awaited it.

The Nebraska Association continued in business until about 1870, when Solon M. Hazen of Blue Springs, who was one of the county commissioners at that time, was selected as a referee to make a division amongst the persistent members of the unsold and unclaimed lots included in the original townsite. Unfortunately his assignment of lots is not available for the purposes of this history. Few, however, of the original company were left to claim their proportionate share of the residue of the company assets. Having accomplished its original purpose and witnessed the full fruition of its hopes, the association, following Hazen's report, formally and voluntarily disbanded.

When we consider that the title to the ninety-four blocks comprising the original townsite of Beatrice, and now by far the most populous and valuable portions of the city, rests upon the entry made by Dr. Herman M. Reynolds at the United States land office at Brownville, on the 12th day of September, 1859, under the act of congress dated May 25, 1844, commonly known as the townsite act, and the steady, unwavering zeal of the body of men who for years held the destiny of our city in their hands, we are bound to yield to the founders of Beatrice ungrudging credit for all they did here. It is to their energy, enthusiasm, and prevision that we owe not only the origin of Beatrice, but also in a large measure its prosperity and happiness. Their names should be ever spoken with reverence and respect by all who take the slightest interest in her welfare, or who feel a just pride in the fact that she is as a city set upon a hill, whose light can not be hid.

CHAPTER XV

NARRATIVE OF MRS. JULIA BEATRICE (KINNEY) METCALF

[The following narrative, by Mrs. Julia Beatrice (Kinney) Metcalf, for whom the city of Beatrice was named, was prepared at the request of the author of this book. As far as known, it is the only contemporary narrative of the voyage of the "Hannibal" and the founding of Beatrice which could be procured now from any living person. Mrs. Metcalf when a girl became a resident, with her parents, of Nebraska City, in May, 1857. Later she became the wife of Julian Metcalf, a pioneer banker of Nebraska City. Until 1893 her home was in Nebraska City, when Mr. and Mrs. Metcalf removed to the Pacific coast. She is spending her declining years in the city of Portland, Oregon.]

This brief sketch of the founding of Beatrice and the events that led to it must unavoidably be somewhat biographical. To recall the incidents and experiences of sixty years ago is not an easy task, as some scenes stand out very vividly, while others have faded and grown dim.

My native state is Ohio, and Mount Vernon my native town, where I first saw the light October 29, 1839. When I was four years old my father, J. F. Kinney, dazzled by the star of empire which had led him from the Atlantic and was destined to lead him to the far-off Pacific, gathered his little family together and moved to Iowa. Here, in the small town of West Point, we lived until I was in my fourteenth year. I was always kept in school, there being an excellent one in in the place, and I do not remember ever missing a day either by illness or by the spring desire to play hooky when the flowers came and the birds sang. Not but that I had that desire, but we were taught obedience in those days.

At this time my father received the appointment of chief justice of Utah territory, which he accepted, and a change of base became necessary. After a family council it was decided that my school-life must be continued. My sister, two years my junior, now Mrs. J. A. Ware of Nebraska City, was to go on the wonderful journey across the plains with my parents and the three boys, still younger. But I was taken by my father to Georgetown, D. C., a suburb of Washington, and placed in Miss English's seminary, where I found myself in a typical southern atmosphere, my companions being daughters of old southern families. I was the only western girl there, and at first was looked at askance as coming from a daredevil region of wild Indians, tomahawks, and stampeding buffaloes. This school during the Civil war was converted into a hospital, and Miss Alcott wrote her "Hospital Sketches" from her experiences as a nurse in this and other Washington hospitals. Georgetown Heights was the fashionable place of residence for government foreign officials in 1854. Here General Badiscoe, the Russian ambassador, lived, having married a former student of Miss English's school, a beautiful young girl called when in Russia "the American rose."

My school life in Georgetown was both instructive and interesting; I was in Washington during part of two presidential administrations, Pierce and Buchanan, and recall Mrs. Pierce's sad face, in her deep mourning for the loss of her son; and also Miss Lane, President Buchanan's handsome niece, who presided at the White House during his administration. On the President's reception days we of the senior class were permitted to attend the state functions at rare intervals, chaperoned by a teacher. It all looked brilliant and gorgeous to our young eyes.

In 1856 I was graduated, being honored as valedictorian and receiving the highest prize in music. My father, having returned from Utah, came on immediately for me, and once more we were in our old home,—but how changed everything looked to me, the town so much smaller than I remembered it. Even our pleasant country home had dwindled,—the ceilings were lower, the rooms smaller; we judge all things by comparison.

The star of empire still drawing my father westward, the farm was sold, and in 1857 we all embarked at Fort Madison on the Mississippi for Nebraska the "land of broad rivers." The trip down the river was uneventful. On reaching St. Louis, the "Hannibal," long to be remembered, a large freight and passenger boat, awaited us. I suppose it was named for the great Carthaginian general who amid superhuman difficulties crossed the Alps in a week's less time than it took us to reach our goal on the Missouri river.

JULIA BEATRICE (KINNEY) METCALF, 1909   JULIA BEATRICE (KINNEY) METCALF, 1878

What a memorable journey that was! Three hundred human beings of all nationalities crowded the boat to its capacity. The morning was a typical April one, the sky bright with the mists from the two rivers floating away and the trees and grasses sparkling from the past night's shower. All were in high spirits as we started from the wharf, saluted by boats as we passed; one having once heard the "Hannibal's tremendous blast as she answered the signals can never forget it,—hoarse, deep as the lowest trombone tone, it thundered with impressive self-importance. Thus with waving hands and handkerchiefs we passed up the river on our journey to the unknown.

When night came the "Hannibal" rested from her labors, not daring to brave in the darkness her vicious enemies, the great snags and sandbars that surrounded her, thick as the "Thousand Islands" but without their beauty. Remember, there were no brilliant search lights in those faraway days. The first and last impressions of the "Big Muddy" were snags, ugly, cruel-looking things, grotesque in shape, and countless sandbars, while ever floating swiftly by were ashen gray logs, hurrying to the end, wherever that might be. It gave one a dizzy, sickening feeling to watch them. But turn your eyes from this treacherous, mighty river to the banks on either side, where were vine-covered trees, the tender spring verdure, the early flowers, the waving grasses;—all of which delighted us; at night the whippoorwills sang, and at dawn we heard innumerable birds hidden in the tree-tops.

Sometimes when the boat landed we went exploring along the shore, gathering the early wild flowers but always keeping our ears open for the tremendous blast which hurried us back to our floating home. Once on landing at a small town, two boys, eight and ten years old, went ashore to buy some shoes which they sadly needed. After the purchase a most exciting dog-fight took place; the boat whistled, but the boys, oblivious to all but the absorbing event at hand, heard it not, and the boat went on its way. Soon however the mother, missing her children, raised a cry of despair, and the mighty "Hannibal," after a mile or so, reversed her course and picked up the penitent boys, who explained that they "wanted to stay and see the end of the fight."

The chief amusements among us were chess, checkers, and dancing the old-fashioned quadrilles, for round dances were not considered proper in those days, and cards were forbidden; in fact, I believe that not one of us young people knew one card from another. So the days dragged on. It was always interesting to watch the great spars as they worked to free us from the sandbars, to hear the signals ring and the shouting of the men as orders were given; there was great rejoicing when we were on our way once more, until the creaking and quivering of the boat told us we were again aground.

It was when our steamer was on one of these sandbars, the worst we had yet encountered, that the organization was formed for the purpose of locating a town in Nebraska; a written constitution and by-laws were signed by some thirty-five men, and an exploring committee was appointed. Little did they realize then that they were making history and that a beautiful city was to spring magically on the virgin soil of the then unknown land.

These gentlemen were men of sterling worth, possessing all the energy, mental attainments and courage necessary for a frontier life, as time has proved. Their names are all emblazoned in the annals of the State History of Nebraska, so it is not necessary for me to name them here. I distinctly remember the Towle family as adding so much to our social life on the steamer, and afterward being most active in all good works and hospitality in Beatrice.

After three long weeks we reached Nebraska City, where we landed with joy; we drove at once to the "City Hotel," a small, frame, two-story building which afterward fell down and was replaced by a substantial brick hotel. The next thing to do was to find a house to live in, not an easy matter, as houses were few and far between. We found a small frame house with one room and a shed at the back, which served for kitchen and dining room. This rented for twenty-five dollars a month. Here we took up our new life. We partitioned the one room with a curtain, and this recess was my sanctum. I enjoyed playing stage effects going in and out of that curtain, and on the whole found it more interesting that a well appointed bedroom.

On July 4, 1857, the interesting ceremony of christening the new city which the company organized on the boat and had located on the Blue river, was to be celebrated, and our family, with many others, started well equipped for the land of promise. We had all the comforts and conveniences necessary for camp life, and were in joyful mood and high anticipation as we left Nebraska City behind us. The weather was perfect, for where will you find more sunshine or purer air than in our noble state? The vast, gently rolling prairies seemed like petrified waves of a gentle sea. The waving grasses, often as high as our heads, gave a wonderful effect of light and shade in their graceful undulations as the light winds passed over them.

As we journeyed we halted to gather the wild flowers, so beautiful and abundant. Here we found the blue and yellow violets, the fragrant wild roses ranging in color from the deepest tone of pink to the white, their color kissed from them by the sun. We decorated our horses and wagons with the Indian paintbrush, flaming like fire in the grass, and the golden rod, now our national flower. Sunflowers were everywhere, giving a vivid touch of color to the landscape; we went through avenues of them. Yellow and purple seemed to predominate.

Who of us can forget the first sunset on that vast uninhabited plain? As the sun sank the air was filled with a radiant glow, the hills were touched with red and violet and purple tints. A silence fell upon our little party as we gazed; the sweet song of a thrush thrilled us as though it were an evening hymn of praise. How small and material seemed our petty lives in so much grandeur! But alas, we were awakened from this poet's dream by the rattling of dishes, the steam of the coffee, the buzz of talk and the care of the horses, and as the sunset faded we ate our supper, for mortals must eat, so "it readeth in the law." Soon our camp in that vast wilderness, with no human beings but ourselves to desecrate nature's primitive domain, rested in sweet and refreshing sleep.

We were early awakened by the birds. They seemed to fill the air with melody; meadowlarks led the chorus, but over and above them all, poised high in mid-air, a bird hovered, pouring forth the most delicious trills, cadences and sparkling scales. The song floated down to us like liquid music. I think it must have been the Missouri skylark. Neocorys Spraguei, described by Audubon and by Elliott Cones.[5] "No other bird music heard in our land compares with the wonderful strains of this songster; there is something not of earth in the melody, coming from above, yet from no visible source. The notes are something indescribable, but once heard they can never be forgotten; their volume and penetration are truly wonderful; they are neither loud nor strong, yet the whole air seems thrilled with the tender strains, and the delightful melody continues long unbroken. It is only uttered when the birds are soaring." They make their nests in the prairie grasses, but are very difficult to find. We could do nothing while this heavenly song lasted, and when it ended we turned reluctantly to our morning tasks. We had an early start, hoping to reach our destination that evening. The wild

---

[5] See Cones, Birds of the Northwest, pp. 42-45.

flowers seemed more and more abundant. The purple vetch, columbine, phlox, coloring great fields with blue. There was blue-eyed grass, and, as if to enhance the delicious blueness, we heard the quiet little song of the blue-bird. Overhead flew great flocks of blackbirds, all varieties, the red-shouldered ones, the yellow-headed, and the bronze variety. Then further on we found great patches of the Prairie Snow, Euphorbia, making the ground white with a very faint tinge of pale green. We did not reach the Blue river as soon as we had hoped, so we had another glowing sunset, another song of birds, and through the night we heard the whippoorwill.

The morning brought us to our goal. The view was entrancing, the valley with its glistening river, the wooded banks, the sloping hills. No narrow outlook met our gaze, but far as the eye could reach was the limitless range of beauty, calm, peaceful with the smile of God resting upon it. All involuntarily exclaimed "Could a more beautiful spot for a city be found anywhere?"

On the 4th of July we assembled for the formal presentation of the nation's flag given by the ladies of the company. I had the honor of making the presentation. I well remember going down by the river, sitting among the willows and invoking the muse, which resulted in some four short verses of salutation to the town to be. Of course if I had dreamed that the occasion was to be historic I would have preserved them, unworthy as they were, but after the ceremony was over they were thrown on the bright, flowing river, which, unlike the traditional "Sweet Afton," bore the song of praise away from its inspirer. Mr. Pike, a cultured young lawyer, replied, somewhat embarrassed I thought; probably the combination of the Stars and Stripes and a young lady overcame him. Beatrice was christened, and my name forever honored. A shaking of hands and congratulations followed, and plans of future work were talked over by the company. All these particulars have been told so well in historical sketches of Nebraska that I will not attempt them. Our return was uneventful, but with the little pioneer party we had formed lifelong friendships which I recall to this distant day with pleasure.

Of course the habits and customs of many of the early settlers in Gage county, breaking the sod and building their cabins, impressed me as somewhat peculiar; as all nationalities were represented, this was to be expected. I remember driving with my father far out on the prairie and stopping at a cabin for dinner. Boiled potatoes in their jackets and fried pork (a good deal cheaper then than now), with saleratus biscuit very yellow with the superfluous amount of soda, made our bill-of-fare. When the good woman of the house asked me if I would take "long shortening or short shortening" in my coffee I deliberated as to what this might mean, but thought the safest way was to say "short" as that would mean less of whatever it might be, and some very coarse looking brown sugar was put into my cup. My father not liking the looks of this, said in his polite, old-school manner, "I will take long shortening, Madam, if you please"; whereupon a couple of tablespoons of very black looking molasses were poured into his coffee. The look of consternation on his face and of mirth on mine fortunately were unobserved by the hostess. Useless to say the coffee was left untasted. Here too I first heard the expression "powerful weak," speaking of a man suffering with ague, then very prevalent in some parts of the country. The phrase struck me as being comically contradictory, but physiologically it means I suppose that the weakness holds the man powerfully; at least it might be so explained. These same people in course of years developed a fine farm by their thrift and industry, and educated their children, who are now doubtless driving their autos and enjoying all the luxuries of modern life.

In 1861 I did what young ladies have done since the world began,— I married. My husband Julian Metcalf was a banker and greatly interested in our growing state.

My first visit to Beatrice was in 1864, I think; it was with my father, who, with a light top-buggy and a pair of mettlesome horses, invited me to accompany him. It was a perfect October day and I was more than delighted to go and see my beautiful namesake again. We made the drive in one day; the fast livery team seemed as fresh when we reached Beatrice as when we started. I found great changes in these few years, the town developing substantially and rapidly. We spent only a day there, as my father's business required no longer time, and we started early so as to reach Nebraska City before dark. This proved a memorable drive. When we had driven several miles we saw a vast sea of fire sweeping toward us with a terrific roar. We were on a hill which gave us a full view. The grass, dry as tinder, eight and even ten feet high, made rich fuel for the flames. It was a race for life. My father turned the horses and urged them to their utmost speed. The flying, blackened cinders of the burnt grass flew by us and over us, we could hear the rushing of the fire-storm and even feel its heat as it gained upon us. The horses seemed to understand the danger and, maddened by the crackling and roar of the flames, they raced as they had never raced before. In places burning wisps of grass carried by the fierce wind started fires on either side of us, but fortunately not near the road. With great relief we reached Beatrice in safety, for it was out of the immediate path of the fire; only the little school house was endangered, and as the fire swept over it we watched with fear and trembling for its fate. For a moment it was enveloped by the flames, with the roar and speed of a railroad train, and as they passed we saw the little frame school house unharmed; the very fury and swiftness of the fire saved it. We resumed our journey, and for twenty miles we traveled through a black, smoking country. In places we saw deer that had been chased by the fire lying by the roadside too exhausted to move as we drove by.

As night fell, one of the traces became unfastened and hitting the horse frightened him, and they both started on a wild run. They left the road and, dashing over hillocks and rough places, nearly upset the light buggy. My father was thrown out. This left the reins under the horses' feet and they plunged madly on through the darkness. My only thought was to cling to the buggy. In a short time, long to me, they broke away from it and I was left sitting in it, unharmed. At once I started in search of my father, whom I found unconscious; he had struck on his head and it was bleeding. Rubbing him and calling him, I succeeded at last in rousing him, and, urging him to walk, we started toward a distant light, which proved to be a farm house. There we were able to find a wagon and driver to take us to Nebraska City, only three miles distant.

Thus ended my first and last visit to Beatrice. But I have always kept in touch with its progress and development, and have pictures of its handsome homes and fine business buildings. If I ever go eastward again I shall certainly visit the beautiful city by the Blue, of which I am naturally proud, as I appreciate the honor conferred on me by its name.

In 1893 we moved to the Pacific coast, where my three children, two daughters and a son, were living, also my parents. We made San Diego our home, and at times Los Angeles and Portland, Oregon. At the latter place my beloved husband passed away in his eighty-third year. Blessed with perfect health and strength, surrounded with loving children, I am indeed most thankful to the Giver of every good and perfect gift who guides us all in love and wisdom.

CHAPTER XVI

FOUNDERS OF BEATRICE

John Fitch Kinney — John McConihe — Albert Towle — Joseph Rutherford Nelson — Obediah Brown Hewett — Gilbert T. Loomis — Oliver Townsend — Harrison F. Cook — Dr. Bayard T. Wise — Joseph Milligan — Bennett Pike — Jefferson B. Weston — William H. Brodhead — Dr. Herman M. Reynolds

It was no ordinary body of men who in April, 1857, while passengers on the old river boat "Hannibal," resolved to cut loose from civilization and seek fortune and happiness in that region of our country which was even then designated in the school geographies as the "Great American Desert." Although there were many other river boats beside the "Hannibal" plying between St. Louis and the Upper Missouri, we nowhere else have any account of the formation from their passenger lists of any organization similar to the Nebraska Association.

It took courage of no mean order and optimism of large proportions to hold men of learning and ability, such as for the most part composed the membership of the Beatrice Townsite Company, to what must have appeared to a reflecting mind a forlorn hope. As far as we are acquainted with their history, we must accord to them the qualities of the true pioneer, who, scorning the hard, uninviting surroundings of the moment, sees, in the changing years, mighty commonwealths develop from primeval conditions. On the date of the actual founding of Beatrice, July 27, 1857, there were not to exceed, besides themselves, twenty-five white men in Gage county as originally created. There had never been a bushel of wheat, a bushel of corn, a potato, or any sort of product raised from the soil of the county by the hand of man outside of the Otoe and Missouri Indian reservation. The first furrows had been drawn through the virgin soil in the spring of that year, by John Pethoud. There was not a government mail route or carrier, not a single stage line, not a broken road traveled by white men in the county; excepting Gideon Bennett's Indian trading post, a mile and a quarter southwest of the present town of Liberty, there was not a single place within the boundaries of Gage county where a man could buy a knife or any other article of common use, or a meal, or a garment.

A number of those who subscribed to the articles of association, or who were afterward added to the membership by the board of directors, never came to Beatrice or attempted to profit by their connection with the company, and under the eighth section of the articles of association they forfeited their membership. They were Edward Stewart, Jesse Spielman, E. M. Drake, Jacob Zolinger, William E. Buffington, Richard Northup, Norman Colson, J. P. Cadman, Alex, McCleary, Phineas W. Hitchcock, George W. Robb, John Henn, Jacob Talman, John B. Kellogg, A. Nelson, W. C. Barr, and George W. Dripps. The subsequent history of most of these persons is unknown to this historian. John B. Kellogg finally settled at Tabor, Fremont county, Iowa. Phineas W. Hitchcock, who seems never to have acted with the old town site company after the "Hannibal" tied up to the Missouri river bank at Omaha, was represented at the meeting of the association July 27, 1857, on the townsite of Beatrice, by John McConihe, who held his proxy. He was a young lawyer who found in the growing city of Omaha a most attractive field for the exercise of his talents and calling. He early obtained prominence as a politician, and in 1860 he was a delegate to the national Republican convention, at Chicago, which nominated Abraham Lincoln for President of the United States. Afterward he was United States marshal of Nebraska territory and territorial delegate to congress. In 1871, he was chosen as a Republican senator from the state of Nebraska, and served six years in that exalted position. He died of appendicitis, at Omaha, in 1881, in the forty-ninth year of his age. For several years he was proprietor of the Omaha Republican the mouthpiece of the Republican party in Nebraska, and one of the leading newspapers in this state. His son, Gilbert M. Hitchcock, is now serving his second term in the United States senate from Nebraska. Whether J.

P. Cadman, who was one of the original townsite company and dropped out at Omaha or Nebraska City, was the John Cadman who, in 1859, settled in the neighborhood of Yankee Hill, in old Clay county, who was a prominent member of the territorial legislature in 1864, and who, after the partition of Clay county, became a prominent citizen of Lancaster county, is unknown to this writer. The first president of the Nebraska Association. John Fitch Kinney, at the time of its formation was a man of mature years, and not only the most experienced in human affairs, but probably, also the most variously endowed of all members of that organization.

JOHN FITCH KINNEY

JOHN FITCH KINNEY   HANNAH D. (HALL) KINNEY

Born in New Haven, Oswego county, New York, April 7, 1816, Judge Kinney was a trifle past forty-one years of age on the 22d day of 1857, when he was chosen as the president of the Nebraska Association. He obtained his elementary education in the public schools of western New York, and at the age of fifteen entered a private school in New Haven, where he remained six months, after which he entered a private school at Hannibal, New York. After a year spent there, he enrolled himself as a student in the Rensselaer Academy at Oswego, a famous institution of learning in its day, where he remained two years. Forty years afterward he attended a reunion of its old teachers and pupils on the classic grounds of his alma mater. This proved to be a notable gathering of several hundred persons, including lawyers, judges, doctors, authors, ministers, lawmakers, and teachers, the occasion being the fiftieth anniversary of the founding of the academy. At this meeting Judge Kinney was chosen president of the alumni association.

In 1835 Judge Kinney began the study of the law, as a student in the office of Judge Orville Robinson, in the city of Mexico, state of New York. After eighteen months' application to his studies, in September, 1837, he removed to Marysville, Ohio, where he formed the acquaintance of Augustus Hall, a rising young lawyer of that city, with whom he studied law for a year; he was then admitted to the bar in Ohio. On January 29, 1839, he married his preceptor's sister, Miss Hannah D. Hall.

In 1842, another brother-in-law, Orville Hall, left Ohio and settled in the territory of Iowa, and in 1854 he was appointed by Franklin Pierce, President of the United States, to the office of chief justice of the supreme court of the territory of Nebraska. He died at Bellevue, in January, 1861, leaving two daughters and a son. The latter was the late Richard S. Hall, who for many years was a prominent lawyer of the Omaha bar and was at one time a partner in the practice of law of the late John M. Thurston, a former United States senator from Nebraska.

In 1840 Judge Kinney began the practice of his profession at Mount Vernon, Ohio, where his success was immediate. But the lure of the great west descended upon him and in 1844 he too migrated to the territory of Iowa, where he entered at once upon an active professional and political career. The mere enumeration of the professional, civic, and political honors that fell to him would be lengthy and impressive. He was an honored member of the national Democratic party, was one of its most trusted advisers, and was frequently its candidate for important offices. Before he had attained to the age of thirty-three years he had been twice secretary of the legislative council of Iowa, prosecuting attorney of his judicial district and justice of the supreme court. His opinions as a judge are found in Volumes I, II, III and IV of Green's Iowa Supreme Court Reports. In 1853 the President of the United States appointed him chief justice of the supreme court of Utah, a position which, though attended with much danger, was ably and conscientiously filled by him for two years. In the spring of 1856 he returned to Iowa, and in April, 1857, as we have already seen, he and his family were passengers on the old river boat "Hannibal," bound for the great new territory of Nebraska.

Judge Kinney's destination was Nebraska City, and on the arrival of the "Hannibal" at that little hamlet, nestled amongst the Missouri river bluffs, in the latter part of April, 1857, they went ashore and took up their residence amongst the few pioneers that had gathered at that spot since May, 1854. Here for thirty-three years, and until the spring of 1890, he made his home. He engaged in the practice of the law, with other occupations, during the greater portion of his life, and during the formative period of Nebraska's history he was not only active in his profession, but he was also one of the most useful and valued citizens of the entire state. He was a warm personal friend of the late J. Sterling Morton, and in the early days these two men bore the heat and burden of the Democratic politics in Nebraska. In 1890, he removed with his wife and a portion of his family to San Diego, California, where in 1895, Mrs. Kinney passed away, at the age of seventy-nine years. August 17, 1902, she was followed to the grave by her distinguished husband, ripe with years and clothed with honors worthily achieved and modestly worn.

Judge Kinney to the last moment of his life remained a steady friend of the little city of Beatrice. He retained his interest in the townsite till it had passed the experimental stage and was a frequent visitor here until he removed to California. The existence of our lovely city is much indebted to his prevision, ripe judgment, and persistent energy.

JOHN McCONIHE

The first secretary of the townsite association, John McConihe, was a member of an old New York family. He was born in the city of Troy, Rensselaer county, New York, September 4, 1834. When sixteen years of age he entered Union College at Schenectady, New York, from which famous institution he graduated in 1853. He studied law with his father at Troy for a few months, and then entered the Albany Law School, from which he graduated in 1855, and immediately opened an office in his native city. He had already established a practice and had been elected a member of the school board of Troy when he became imbued with a desire to try his fortunes in the "Far West." Bidding farewell to his ancestral home and making his way to St. Louis, we find him on board the old Missouri river boat "Hannibal", in April, 1857, bound for the new territory of Nebraska. He attended the preliminary meeting of the Nebraska Association, and was chosen its secretary. He participated actively in the meeting and was a member of the committee appointed to prepare the articles of association. After the organization was perfected he was chosen as a member of its board of directors and the minutes both of the organization itself and of the official board are in the scholarly handwriting of John McConihe from April 27, to July 28, 1857, these being signed by him as secretary.

JOHN MCCONIHE

Before coming to Beatrice from Omaha with the other members of the association, he had arranged to enter upon the practice of the law there. Although Omaha was at that time little more than a western village, perched on the bank of the Missouri river, it was the capital of the new territory and a most promising location for a young lawyer. After July 28, 1857, his name no longer appears in the records of the proceedings of the Nebraska Association or of its board of directors, but he complied with all the requirements of the organization, received his distributive share of the town lots of Beatrice, and it was only in recent years that his interests in the city were finally disposed of by his relatives.

Having assisted in placing the infant town upon its feet, he returned to Omaha and entered upon the practice of his profession. He was a man of many activities. In 1858 he formed a copartnership with some one of the numerous freighters or freighting concerns then to be found at every Missouri river town in eastern Nebraska, and he seems to have participated in the business until the breaking out of the Civil war, in 1861. Politically he was a Democrat, and in 1858 he was appointed private secretary to Governor Richardson; he afterward held the same position under Governor Black until the end of the latter's term. In 1860 he was an unsuccessful candidate for mayor of Omaha, and within the same year he was appointed adjutant general of the territory, subsequently leading an expedition against the Pawnee Indians.

On the breaking out of the Civil war he raised a company for the First Nebraska Regiment, and as its captain he participated with the regiment in its Missouri campaign. He was detailed to attend to certain military matters connected with the Department of Missouri at Washington. While there in the discharge of his duty, he became ill, in February, 1862, and immediately left for his home in Troy, where he was critically ill with typhoid fever for several weeks. On recovering his health, he rejoined his regiment, the day before the great battle of Shiloh, and participated with it in that terrible conflict. He was severely wounded in the left arm and while at home slowly recovering from his injury, he was appointed lieutenant colonel of the One Hundred and Sixty-ninth Regiment of New York Volunteers. In October, 1862, he went with his regiment to Washington. He later saw service in Florida, North Carolina, Bermuda Hundred, and other places. On the resignation of Colonel Buell he was made colonel of his regiment and later became a brigadier general. While leading his brigade in a desperate charge against the "Bloody Angle" at the battle of Cold Harbor, this gallant young officer was shot through the heart. With an involuntary exclamation, he died instantly. His last orders, given in the heat of battle a moment before his death, were "Cease firing. Fix bayonets. Charge. Dress up on the colors. Do not leave the colors."

Thus perished the gallant, handsome, scholarly John McConihe, a man greatly admired by all who knew him, greatly loved by his friends and kindred and deeply mourned by his native city. His remains lie under the monument in the McConihe family burial plot which overlooks the lordly Hudson from a height near the busy city of Troy. During the brief period in which he participated in the founding of Beatrice, he exhibited a genial, friendly nature that won the kindly regard of every member of the association. The great Civil war deprived Nebraska of one its ablest and most promising citizens when John McConihe gave his valuable life to his country.

ALBERT TOWLE

ALBERT TOWLE

One of the most influential members of the Nebraska Association was Albert Towle, "Pap" Towle as he was familiarly called by nearly every one of his acquaintance. Like Judge Kinney, Mr. Towle was a man of mature years and large experience in the affairs of life at the time the Nebraska Association was organized on board the "Hannibal," in April, 1857. As far as the records show, he was the only member of the organization who claimed to possess any personal knowledge of Nebraska territory or any portion of it.

Mr. Towle was born in 1817, and most of his early life was spent in the state of Illinois. He had acquired a good usable education and throughout the early history of Beatrice and Gage county he was the most all-around servicable member of the entire community. No man devoted his life more exclusively to the interests of the public and the upbuilding of the embryo city of Beatrice than Albert Towle. By nature he was highly optimistic, and there were times when but for him the venture would have entirely failed. He possessed a singular power of infusing into others his own enthusiasm and hopeful courage. His age and experience in the affairs of life gave him great influence over the young men with whom he was associated in founding and building up our city. He was present and answered to his name when the roll of members was called in the office of the territorial secretary of state May 20th and responded to his name when the roll was again called, on the Beatrice townsite, July 27, 1857. From that time till the day of his death he was rarely outside Gage county.

Mr. Towle assisted in erecting the company house and on the arrival of his family, in the late summer or fall of 1857, this log cabin was donated to him. For many years he occupied it as a home. It became widely and familiarly known as "Pap's Cabin," and for a decade besides serving as a wayside inn it was the postoffice, while its main room became a place for holding public meetings of almost every character. It was here that Mr. Towle's youngest child, Katie, was born. She was the first child born of white parents in the county and, growing to lovely womanhood in her native city, she became the wife of George M. Ayres, of Deadwood, South Dakota, who had spent most of his life in Beatrice. She died at Deadwood on the 28th day of March, 1890, at the age of 32 years. Her remains rest by the side of those of her parents in the Beatrice cemetery, near the city of her birth.

KATIE TOWLE
First white child born in Gage county

Mr. Towle was the second postmaster of Beatrice, having been appointed to that position May 22, 1860, succeeding Herman M. Reynolds who was commissioned first postmaster, in 1857. By successive appointments he held the office till his death. In addition to the office of postmaster Mr. Towle was frequently honored by election to various county offices. On the organization of the county, in August, 1857, he, with George Bonham, was elected county-commissioner of the county, and he retained the office three years,—until all questions respecting the organization of the county and the location of the county seat had been settled. He was county judge from 1861 to 1867; county treasurer in 1858-59-60 and again in 1864-65-66-67-68-69. He was for many years a notary public and a justice of the peace. The second instrument recorded in the office of the register of deeds of the county is his bond in the sum of two hundred dollars as a notary public, with John McConihe as his surety. It is dated October 9, 1857, and was filed for record June 3, 1858.

Mr. Towle early in life married Catherine Holt, a woman of ability and great force of character. She strongly supported her husband's ambitions and efforts as respected the upbuilding of Beatrice, and her practical good sense rendered her an exceedingly useful member of the community. She survived her husband ten years and rests at his side in the family burial lot in Beatrice cemetery. To this union there was born Helen, who became the wife of Jefferson B. Weston and who recently passed away at her home in Beatrice; Emer, who, about 1868, became the wife of Joseph Saunders, the first mail carrier from the Missouri river to Beatrice and one of the early and successful merchants of our city (Mr. Saunders died recently, at his home in Reynolds, Jefferson county and lies with his wife in his burial lot in Beatrice cemetery); Adelia, who became the wife of Richard C. Davis and who died in Chicago, in 1916; Mary, who became the wife of Dr. John G. Davis and who now lives in Chicago; and Katie, of whom mention has just been made.

The family of Albert Towle was one of the best known and most highly esteemed of the pioneer families of our county. The head of the family more than any other man is entitled to be known to posterity as the "Father of Beatrice. This beautiful city is in a large sense his enduring monument. He died on the 8th day of March, 1879, at his home, the story and a half brick cottage erected by him in 1869, at the corner of Fourth and Ella streets this city.

JOSEPH RUTHERFORD NELSON

Nelson was but little past twenty-one years of age in 1857, when he became a member of the Nebraska Association, and was probably the youngest man in the organization. He responded to his name when the roll of membership was called in Omaha May 20th, and again on the townsite of Beatrice, July 27, 1857, but he does not appear to have ever been active in the affairs of the association or to have accepted his distributive share of the townsite of Beatrice. It is not known to this writer how long he remained here nor where he went after leaving Beatrice in August, 1857, but in 1860 he is known to have made a trip across the plains to the Colorado gold fields. From there he went to Minnesota, thence to Wisconsin, and finally to Chicago, Illinois, where we find him in 1862. He attended a commercial college for a while in Chicago, and then found employment with the Lake Shore & Michigan

Southern Railway Company until 1867, when he returned to Beatrice. In 1868, in co-operation with Nathaniel Howard, he established at Beatrice the first newspaper in Gage county, known as the *Blue Valley Record*. The history of the venture will be found further in this volume, in the chapter devoted to the newspapers and newspaper men of Gage county. On the 8th day of September, 1869, he married, at Wayne, Wisconsin, Miss Mary Eastman. Five children were born to this union, of whom only one is living, a son, Amos A. Nelson. In 1881 Mr. Nelson engaged in the general mercantile business in DeWitt, Saline county, Nebraska, where he resided until 1884, when he removed to Texas. During the great Galveston flood he lost nearly all his property and in 1901 he again returned to Beatrice. About 1910 he removed to the state of Washington, where he has ever since resided, and he is reported to be a helpless invalid, at the age of eighty-two years. As far as known, he is the last survivor of the old Nebraska Association.

JOSEPH RUTHERFORD NELSON

OBEDIAH BROWN HEWETT

Judge Hewett was admitted to membership in the Nebraska Association April 29, 1857, at the first meeting of the board of directors on board the "Hannibal," and was thereafter for several years an active and an efficient member of the organization. He was the only one of the seven lawyers who were members of the company who engaged in the practice of his profession in Beatrice, in those far off, early years. He was the first county judge of Gage county and his name frequently occurs in the minutes of the county commissioners' court as having performed some service for the county.

He was born at Hope, Maine, September 18, 1828, and was educated through his own efforts. He entered Bowdoin College and graduated with the class of 1855. He then went to Chicago, Illinois, where he was employed for two years as a teacher. While so employed he read law and he was admitted to the bar in the spring of 1857, by the supreme court of Illinois. Almost immediately thereafter he set out for St. Louis, where we find him a passenger on board the "Hannibal" in April of that year. After the founding of Beatrice he went, in 1858, to Brownville, Nebraska, where he engaged in the practice of his profession for a short time. He spent a few months of 1859 prospecting for gold in Colorado. In October, 1867 he joined the Second Nebraska Cavalry, as a private in Company F; he was later elected captain of Company M, which he commanded until it was mustered out, in December, 1863. He was secretary of the last territorial council, in 1867, and secretary of the senate in the second state legislature. During the years 1868 and 1869, he was the county superintendent of schools for Nemaha county and he was the third mayor of Brownville. Beginning with 1868, he served the people as district attorney for four years, at a time when the district embraced nearly the whole of Nebraska south of the Platte river.

Judge Hewett was always interested in the work of education and during the greater part of his life he was active in the support and encouragement of every educational agency. He was president of the first meeting of the Nebraska State Teachers' Association and a member of the first board of education of the State Normal School at Peru, Nebraska, continuing several years in its service. Judge Hewett was an ardent Presbyterian and in his later years he was especially active in the establishment of Hastings College, of which institution his son was the first graduate. He continued in the practice of the law at Brownville until

1876, when he removed to a farm near Auburn, Nebraska, from which, in 1880, he went to Hastings. There he was engaged in the practice of the law until 1893, when he removed to Riverside, California, where he again engaged in the practice of law, afterward locating on a fruit ranch in Chino, where he died, November 10, 1898.

At Brownville, Nebraska, Judge Hewett was married in October, 1857, to Miss Mary W. Turner, who was the first milliner of that western village. She died at Hastings, Nebraska, March 22, 1891. Three children of this marriage are living, James H. H. Hewett, chief clerk of the United States land office at Alliance, Nebraska; Mrs. Katherine L. Davis, of Long Beach, California; and C. William Hewett, of Little Rock, Arkansas. Mr. Hewett was again married, at Riverside, California, in 1893, to Mrs. Mary Nance, who survived him but a short time.

Personally Obediah Brown Hewett was a man of unusually large stature; he was deliberate of speech, a good, clear thinker, and a man whose whole life was dominated by absolute integrity of purpose.

GILBERT T. LOOMIS

Gilbert T. Loomis was one of the younger members of the Nebraska Association. He was a large, good-looking, pleasant gentleman, with brown eyes and brown curling hair and beard. He settled upon the northeast quarter of section twenty-six, Midland township, now owned by Markus and Jens Jepson. It was at this point, almost due east of the quarter section line running east and west through this tract, that the old Brownville, Beatrice, Fort Kearney road forded Bear creek for many, many years. He lead the uneventful life of a farmer and was never very active in the affairs of the Nebraska Association, though he maintained his membership to the end in that historic organization, and on March 3, 1859, he went so far as to trade a yoke of oxen for the distributive share of Richard Northrop in the Beatrice townsite. The assignment describes Northrop as a resident of Tabor, Fremont county, Iowa. It bears the above date, is recorded in Book A, page 1, of the deed records of Gage county and is the first instrument of any description to be made a matter of record in the office of the register of deeds. Mr. Loomis, in 1861 or

1862, in connection with Volney S. Whitemore, bought a new threshing outfit, and for a year or two these gentlemen did all the threshing by machinery in the county. It was an old-fashioned, horse-power affair and was the first threshing machine brought to Gage county. Loomis kept with his teams and machine a large, vicious dog and there was always more or less trouble between him and the hands about the machine over this faithful but dangerous canine. He sold his farm many years ago and with his family removed to Washington, in which state both he and his wife recently passed away. Mrs. Loomis was a kindly, gentle woman, the sister of Thomas W. Brown, who in 1866-1867 was sheriff of Gage county and who now lives in Tumwater, Washington. Both Mr. and Mrs. Loomis left none but pleasant memories behind them in Gage county.

OLIVER TOWNSEND

The reader may have noticed the name of Justus Townsend amongst those who originally subscribed to the articles of association of the Nebraska Townsite Company. Justus Townsend was a young physician, who with his sister, Miss Jennie Townsend, was also a passenger on board the "Hannibal" from St. Louis bound to the new territory of Nebraska. He took an active interest in the affairs of the association from the time of its organization until the founding of Beatrice, in July, 1857, and his name is frequently mentioned in the minutes of the association's meetings. Later, returning to New York, he transferred, by assignment, his interest in the townsite to his brother Oliver, who joined the organization in October, 1857, and who never, as long as he lived, claimed a home anywhere but at Beatrice, where he became one of the most active and useful citizens of our county. The lure of the west must have been very great to have held a refined, scholarly gentleman like Oliver Townsend in the forlorn hamlet of Beatrice during its earliest years. When Townsend first saw it, it consisted of a single two-room log house. "Pap's Cabin," and a wheezy old steam saw mill, perched on the bank of the Big Blue river. All the brilliant company who, in July, had assisted in founding the future city, except Albert Towle, J. B. Weston, Bennett Pike, Gilbert T. Loomis, and M. W. Ross, had returned to Missouri river points or elsewhere to spend the winter and to earn a little money. The privations of that winter were very, very great, and these few pioneers who had been left to guard this new outpost of western civilization frequently arose in the morning with gnawing appetites and at night retired hungry to bed. But with more accurate knowledge of the food-resources afforded by the prairies, the woods, and the streams, all fear of hunger was ultimately dispelled, and returning spring brought increase of numbers and reviving hope.

OLIVER TOWNSEND

Several of the colony availed themselves of the benefits of existing land laws and located claims about the embryo city, the cultivation of which soon yielded abundance. Mr. Townsend himself established a claim upon the tract of land which now comprises Glenover Addition to Beatrice. This he fenced and farmed in part for four years before disposing of it. With the development of the city and the settlement of the county, honors, such as they were, came to Mr. Townsend. He was four times elected county clerk of Gage county, and served in that office from 1862 to 1870. He was a member of the first state legislature, having been elected to that office in 1867. He served acceptably for two years and as a legislator he participated in the stirring events which accompanied the effort to remove the capital of the state from Omaha to Lincoln. As county clerk he was ex officio one of the earliest superintendents of the common schools of Gage county, serving in that office from 1862 to 1868. When the first one-room frame school house was erected in Beatrice, in 1862, Mr. Townsend was hired to teach the first fall and winter school in that building. He was, in fact, for many years active in the civic, social, political, and scholastic life of this city, county, and state.

Mr. Townsend was widely known as a pioneer merchant, and for several years was a member of the firm of Blakely, Reynolds & Townsend, which erected the old part of the stone building now owned by Kilpatrick Brothers at the corner of Fifth and Court streets, north of the Burwood Hotel, and which conducted a general merchandise business therein for a number of years. After the dissolution of this firm by the death of Dr. Reynolds, in 1875, Mr. Townsend engaged in business on his own account, maintaining for a number of years a men's clothing and furnishings store on the north side of Court street, just east of Fifth street.

In 1880 he was married, at Nebraska City, to Miss Kate Monce, and with her he spent the latter part of his life on a small farm east of the city, on the road to the State Institution. To this union six children were born, three sons and a like number of daughters. The sons died in infancy, and the daughters are Jean, Ruth and Catherine. He died in April, 1914, in the eightieth year of his age. His devoted wife survives him, and, with her younger daughters, Ruth and Catherine, occupies the homestead, the object of the affection and tender regard of all who know her.

Oliver Townsend by disposition was open, friendly, and genial. He was a man of great personal worth, thoroughly honest and reliable in all the relations of life. He was from the very first the recipient of universal confidence and esteem from the early settlers of this portion of our state, and he retained the affectionate regard of the entire community to the last moment of his life.

HARRISON F. COOK

Mr. Cook became associated with the Beatrice Townsite Company immediately on the arrival of the steamboat "Hannibal" at Nebraska City, April 29, 1857, where he was awaiting events. Learning of the locating committee and its intended search for a townsite, he offered to hire himself as a driver for the livery team with which a part of the committee, Weston, Pike, and Ross, intended to explore southeastern Nebraska. Mr. Cook accompanied these members of the committee on their long drive across green stretches of unbroken prairie, until they finally reached the townsite of Beatrice. Early in June he came to Beatrice and was admitted into membership in the association. He returned to Nebraska City in the latter part of July and remained there until the spring of 1858. He was again in Beatrice during that year and possibly as late as the spring of 1859. He then left for Connecticut and did not return to Gage county again until about the year 1867, having been absent eight years. He engaged in farming for a while on his land, a mile and a half north of the city, on Indian creek, which is still owned by a member of his family, but later he established himself in the furniture business in Beatrice.

HARRISON F. COOK

Mr. Cook carried on this business until his death, which occurred at Beatrice, on the 17th day of January, 1908. He had witnessed the transformation of the bare, naked townsite of Beatrice into the beautiful city which it has grown to be. Not only had he witnessed but he had also been part and parcel of the growth and development for more than half a century of what was a prairie waste in 1857. No one can remember the time when he was not an enthusiast over the prospects of the city of his affections. He died universally respected by the community.

Harrison F. Cook was born at Norridgewock, Somerset county, Maine, November 4, 1830. He was married, at Stafford Hollow, Tolland county, Connecticut, March 15, 1860, to Lucinda H. Harvey, a native of that place. This pioneer husband and wife lie side by side in the old Beatrice cemetery.

Although abrupt in manner and very terse in statement, quick to take offense and slow to forget an injury, real or fancied, Harrison F. Cook was a wholesome, genuine, true man, and will live in the memory of his fellow citizens who knew and deeply loved him.

DR. BAYARD T. WISE

Dr. Wise was a young physician who found himself on board the "Hannibal" in April, 1857, bound for the territory of Nebraska. He was active in the organization of the Nebraska Association, served as its first treasurer, was a member of the locating committee, was present at the call of the roll of the members in Omaha, May 20th, in the office of the territorial secretary of state, repaired with the others to the Beatrice townsite in June, 1857, took an active part in the Fourth of July celebration, and answered to his name when the roll was called on the Beatrice townsite July 27, 1857. He remained here, however, only a few days after that time, but appears to have visited Beatrice again in 1858, while located in Plattsmouth, Nebraska, in the practice of his profession. From there he removed to Fort Madison, Iowa, where he remained until the breaking out of the great Civil war, in which he served as surgeon of the Fifth Iowa Cavalry. After the close of the war, he returned to Fort Madison, and resumed his practice for a short period of time. But Dr.

Wise found more congenial and perhaps more profitable employment as the state agent for the Phoenix Fire Insurance Company of Brooklyn, New York. For twenty-seven years he served this company as its field man in the great state of Illinois, with headquarters at Springfield. He died in the Deaconess Hospital at Indianapolis, May 16, 1908, of hardening of the liver, at the age of seventy-three years. His remains lie by those of his wife, in the beautiful Elmwood cemetery in the city of Fort Madison, Iowa.

Dr. Wise was survived by three sons, namely, Edward P. Wise, state agent of the Agricultural Insurance Company for the states of Kansas and Nebraska; Frederick T. Wise, state agent for Illinois for the Home Insurance Company of New York; and Gus M. Wise, state agent and field man for the Agricultural Insurance for the state of Indiana.

Dr. Wise was known to be a kindly, good man and a very useful man.

JOSEPH MILLIGAN

Joseph Milligan joined the Nebraska Association after its organization, his name appearing among those who answered the roll call on the Beatrice townsite July 27, 1857. He did not maintain close relations with the association and appears to have gone, in the late summer of 1857, to some Missouri river point, where he remained until about the year 1860. He then returned to Gage county, settled on a claim on East Mud creek, and resided in that vicinity, with his wife Sallie, until 1863, when he, with William E. Mudge, established Buffalo Ranch, on the old Oregon Trail, at the western terminus of the stretch of roadway know as Nine Mile Ridge, on the Little Blue river, where the village of Deweese is now located. At this time the travel on the old trail had attained its maximum and the partners flourished amazingly. But on the afternoon of the 7th day of August, 1864, a stage driver halted his panting horses in front of the ranch and shouted a warning that the Indians were murdering the ranchmen further down the road, burning the ranches and destroying property, and advising them to fly at once for their lives. Hastily attaching a team to a wagon and placing therein a few provisions and clothing, they loaded their families in the wagon and drove rapidly to Pawnee Ranch, eight miles up the road, passing the body of Patrick Burke, the first blacksmith of Beatrice, who had been killed by the Indians two hours before. They remained at Pawnee Ranch, which was then leased and managed by Charles N. Emery, throughout a determined attack made upon it by the Indians the same day, a few hours after their escape. Later they returned to Gage county, by way of the Nebraska City branch of the Oregon Trail, bringing with them Patrick Burke's team, which they turned over to his widow, Mary E. Burke. In 1865 the Indian war having been quelled, they returned to Buffalo Ranch, but the building of the Union Pacific Railway in 1866, across Nebraska from east to west, put an end to the freighting and ranching business along the old trail and the partnership was dissolved. William E. Mudge returned to Gage county, and in 1866 he took a homestead in Elm township, where he lived for many years, his death having occurred in Beatrice, in 1917. Joseph Milligan and wife went to Texas to live, where they both died many years ago. They were fine-looking people and would have been valuable accessions to any community. They were Irish and were endowed with the ready wit and good humor which characterize that race. They were both much loved and highly respected by the old settlers of Gage county.

BENNETT PIKE

Perhaps no man was more active in the affairs of the Nebraska Association while identified with it than Bennett Pike. The minutes of the organization show that much of its early success was due to his clear, logical and vigorous intellect. He was a member of the important "Locating Committee," and with Jefferson B. Weston and M. W. Ross selected the townsite for Beatrice. He prepared the report of the committee and presented it at the meeting of the organization in Omaha, May 20, 1857, in which the advantages of the site selected by the committee were set forth in detail and with great clearness. While in Omaha the company selected him as the mill agent to transport to the proposed townsite the steam saw mill which had previously been purchased and which formed practically the only asset of the association.

Mr. Pike answered to his name when the roll was called on the Beatrice townsite July 27, 1857. He took a very active part in the preliminary work of founding Beatrice. With Weston, Reynolds Towle, Townsend, and Loomis, he remained on the townsite until late in the fall of 1858, over fifteen months. In the meantime he preëmpted and purchased of the government the northeast quarter of Section 33, township 4, range 6 east, joining the townsite, north of Grant and west of Sixth street. On leaving the territory he seems to have gone to Rockport, Missouri, and during the year 1859 he engaged in the practice of law at that point, but later he removed to Saint Joseph.

BENNETT PIKE

Mr. Pike was the son of John and Elvira (Check) Pike. He was born in the town of Cornish, state of Maine, January 6, 1829, and died at Arcadia, Missouri, July 15, 1892. He was educated at Bowdoin College, Brunswick, Maine. He was colonel of the Fifty-eighth Regiment of Missouri State Militia during 1863 and 1864, at the same time representing his district in the house of representatives of the state legislature; he was also appointed brigadier general of militia. About the time the Civil war closed he was appointed federal district attorney for the Northern District of Missouri, and he served several years in that office. He was elected to congress from the Saint Joseph, Missouri, district in 1870 but was counted out; he was elected district judge for the Buchanan county district and afterward became the general attorney for the Iron Mountain Railroad Company, with headquarters at Saint Louis, Missouri. Five days after his death the Saint Louis bar held a memorial meeting in which a preamble and resolutions in regard to Judge Pike were unanimously adopted. Amongst other things are the following recitals respecting him:

Judge Bennett Pike died July 25, A. D. 1892. He ran his mortal course, and at the end bowed unmurmuringly to the arbiter of all human destines.

His was a race of varied experiences. Nature had endowed him with talents and a disposition that marked him as an important influence in his community. Personally and socially he was genial and full of sympathy, with a great heart full of love; he stooped to kiss the wounds of the sorrowing, and, with manly generosity, rejoiced with those who deservingly won life's laurels. He was a helper of his fellow kind. Distinctions came to him and he bore them with modesty, dignity and honor.

He was a member of the house of representatives of this state, and his efforts were (as in all his other walks) to the upbuilding of the public welfare and happiness, upon a broad, strong and intelligent basis.

He served as federal district attorney in this state at a time when passion ran high and prosecution was prone to take the form of persecution, but with a heart incapable of embitterment, an impartial and scrupulous mind, he stood, at once, the protector of rights and the just defender of violated law.

As a judge upon the state circuit bench he challenged the deference and confidence of the lawyers and people, neither fawning to the leadership of the one nor cringing to the impulse of the other. He was just, discriminating, learned and courageous.

For many years he was with us as a practitioner at the bar. His integrity was impregnable, his demeanor calm, gentle and dignified. His humor in conversation sprang freely as from a fountain of good nature, and if weakness he had it was his admiration and veneration for his chosen and constantly pursued profession.

JEFFERSON BURNS WESTON

No other man connected with the Nebraska Association became as thoroughly identified with the history of the state of Nebraska as Jefferson Burns Weston. From the moment of arriving in the new territory of Nebraska to the end of his long career he was a loyal and useful citizen of our state. He was widely known and was universally honored and respected throughout our commonwealth.

Mr. Weston was born March 23, 1821, in the little town of Bremen, Lincoln county, Maine. He was the son of Eliphaz and Elizabeth Longfellow Weston, natives of the Pine Tree state and both highly respected members of old New England families who traced their ancestry back to Puritan days in this country. Mr. Weston obtained his elementary education in the common schools of Maine and, having prepared himself for a collegiate course of study, he, about 1852, entered Union College, now Union University, at Schenectady, New York, which under the presidency of Dr. Eliphalet Knott (1804-1866) had become one of the foremost educational institutions in the western world and drew bright, capable young men from every portion of the country. Mr. Weston graduated in the classical course from the college in 1856, and lending ear to the call of the great west, he came first to Chicago, and, still following the Star of Empire to the cry "Westward Ho," he went, in the spring of 1857, to St. Louis, where on a soft April morning, in 1857, he joined Judge John Fitch Kinney, John McConihe (a fellow alumnus of his alma mater), Albert Towle, Herman M. Reynolds, Bennett Pike, and the rest on board the "Hannibal" in her memorable voyage to the upper Missouri. He became a leader in that band of intrepid spirits who, on the 23d day of April, entered into a written compact to remain together and found a city somewhere in the new territory of Nebraska. From the moment of its organization Mr. Weston was most active in furthering this venture into what was, in fact little more than a prairie waste. He was member of the locating committee, and with Bennett Pike, M. W. Ross, and Harrison F. Cook, reported to the organization at Omaha, May 20, 1857, their selection of the original townsite of Beatrice as the most eligible site for the prospective city. He never for a single moment wavered in his loyalty to this enterprise and throughout his life he was an efficient force in the upbuilding of Beatrice—child of his courage and brain. From May 29, 1857, when the first stake was driven on the townsite of Beatrice, with the exception of about nine years spent in Lincoln during and immediately following his six years' service as a state official, this city was his home. He retained his distributive share in the original townsite of Beatrice until it became valuable and he, more than any other of the Nebraska Association, profited from this venture.

Mr. Weston remained with Townsend, Towle, Pike, and Loomis, throughout the summer and fall of 1857 and the following winter, as a component part of the guard left behind to protect the interests of the Townsite Company. Some time in 1858, or possibly as late as 1859, he returned to Chicago and took a course in the study of the law. He was admitted to the bar and on his return to Beatrice he engaged for a brief time in the practice of his profession. But he soon turned to a more adventurous, a more profitable and (to him at that period of life) a more congenial field of activity. About 1860 he engaged in the business of freighting across the plains along the old Military Highway from Beatrice to Denver and other western points. Later he engaged in mining and other enterprises about the gold fields of Colorado, but, returning to Beatrice in 1868, he resumed the practice of the law. His professional card appears in Volume I, No. 8 of the *Blue Valley Record*, the first newspaper published in Gage county. It reads as follows:

J. B. WESTON.
Notary Public and Conveyancing.
Real Estate Agency and Law Office.
Beatrice, Gage County, Nebraska.

He continued in the practice of law at Beatrice till 1873, when, having been elected auditor of public accounts for the state of Nebraska, he removed his family to Lincoln. He served the people as their auditor from January 1, 1873 to January 1, 1879,—six years.

On the 18th day of November, 1883, Mr. Weston, having with Daniel W. Cook and others purchased the stock of the Gage County Bank, organized the Beatrice National Bank, of Beatrice, Nebraska. He was chosen the president of this institution by the first board of directors, a position which he held for over twenty years, and until his death. Of those who were associated with him at the time, namely, Daniel W. Cook, Hiram W. Parker, Cyrus Alden, Silas P. Wheeler, Nathan Blakely, and William Lamb, of Beatrice, and Nathan S. Harwood, of Lincoln, all have passed away, Mr. Cook, the last survivor, dying in March, 1916.

On the 30th of April, 1860, Mr. Weston married Miss Helen Towle, the eldest daughter of Albert Towle. To this union four children were born, namely Ralph A., Elizabeth L., Katherine, and Herbert T. Weston. Mr. Weston died September 15, 1905, in the seventieth year of his age, and in 1917 his wife followed him to the grave. Their remains rest in the beautiful Evergreen Home Cemetery, as do also those of their younger daughter, Katherine. To every loyal citizen of our county, and to every man who values worth of character, the turf that wraps their clay should be hallowed mold.

No sketch of the life of Mr. Weston would be complete which failed to take account of the remarkable influence which, without conscious effort on his part, he exercised over others. From first to last he was an important factor in the affairs of the territory and state. He was a just man, kind and sympathetic. He was remarkably deliberate and conservative in judgment, and was accustomed to take an accurate and comprehensive view of human affairs. His clear, inclusive way of looking at things made him one of the most useful citizens the state of Nebraska has ever possessed.

In his habits and association, Jefferson Burns Weston was the most democratic of men. His charity was large, his integrity above question. With a generous, open-hearted faith in humanity and a deep-rooted faith in Almighty God, he reached the end of his long journey in an atmosphere of hope, courage, and cheer that was infectious to all who came under his influence.

WILLIAM H. BRODHEAD

WILLIAM H. BRODHEAD
Surveyor original townsite of Beatrice, 1857

Though not a member of the Beatrice Townsite Association, William H. Brodhead was so intimately connected with the enterprise as to deserve a place amongst the founders of our city. In 1857 he was the best known and perhaps the most competent surveyor and topographical engineer in the territory of Nebraska, and for this reason he was employed by the directors of the Beatrice Association to survey and make plats of the original town of Beatrice. During his entire life Mr. Brodhead took a keen interest in Beatrice, and to friends here he frequently expressed an appreciation of the fact that he had been instrumental in the founding of the city.

Mr. Brodhead was born near Milford, Pike county, Pennsylvania, August 25, 1832. He died at Hailey, Idaho, October 21, 1898. At Honesdale, Wayne county, Pennsylvania, June 11, 1867, he married Eliza Avery. Surviving him are his widow and their son, W. A. Brodhead, who is a prominent lawyer of Mackay, Idaho, and the chairman of the Idaho state highway commission.

William H. Brodhead, in addition to a very accurate and useful education in civil engineering, was a lawyer of ability, having been admitted to the bar of Pennsylvania November 21, 1856. The same year he came to the territory of Nebraska, where he practised both of his professions, having been admitted to practice before the courts of the territory June 4, 1857. In 1859 he was elected a member of the house of representatives of the territory, from Otoe county, and he served during that session. His friend, the distinguished Nebraskan, J. Sterling Morton, also was a member of that legislature. In 1861 Mr. Brodhead went to Utah territory to live; there he served for a while as the federal district attorney. Although a non-Mormon in belief and practice, he was a warm personal friend of Brigham Young and was frequently the recipient of the Prophet's favor. In 1863 he located at Carson City, Nevada, where he practiced law for a few years, but, being drawn into the maelstrom of the mining excitement then rife in Carson City, he dropped the law and sought wealth as a miner. He followed this business until the fall of 1879, when he moved to Hailey, Idaho. In 1894 he was appointed register of the United States land office at Hailey, and he died just after he had completed his four years' term of office.

Mr. Brodhead was six feet four inches in height and was proportionately a large man.

As a surveyor, Mr. Brodhead was required to make three plats of the original town of Beatrice, one of which was filed in the local land office at Brownville on the 12th day of August, 1859, and one was forwarded to the General Land Office at Washington to be kept as a part of its files. The third was, of course, delivered to Herman M. Reynolds, as mayor of the city. Some dissatisfaction existed for a while over Brodhead's survey, and about the year 1875 Anselmo B. Smith was employed to resurvey the original town of Beatrice. These surveys differ slightly; the Smith survey showing a deviation from the true lines of less than three feet in some parts of the city. When we take into account the crudeness of the time and the probable haste with which the original survey was made by Mr. Brodhead, it is evident, assuming that the error did exist, that his work was well done. A careless chain carrier might easily account for this error.

DR. HERMAN MYER REYNOLDS

It would be difficult for any one to speak the whole truth about Dr. Herman Myer Reynolds without appearing to be his panegyrist. But seven days past the age of twenty-five years when he joined with Kinney, McConihe, Towle, Weston, Wise, Pike, and the others to form the Nebraska Association, on board the old steamboat "Hannibal," he was already a man of affairs and for some time had been a successful practicing physician. He was a native of Sullivan county, New York, and was a son of Andrew and Catherine Reynolds, both natives of the state of New York. The father was of English lineage, and the mother was the daughter of Garrett Van Benscoten, a Hollander and a soldier of the Revolution. Dr. Reynolds obtained his elementary education in the common schools of his native state, and in his youth entered an academy at Liberty, New York. He afterward pursued a course of study in the State Normal School at Albany, with the view of fitting himself for a teacher, and he did for a while engage in that occupation. When still a very young man he began the study of medicine, at Pittsfield, Massachusetts. His final course was taken in the great medical college at Albany, from which institution he graduated May 31, 1853, and he at once entered upon the practice of his profession at Barryville, in his native state. Afterward he removed to Scranton, Pennsylvania, where he remained two years, engaged in the practice of his profession. Dr.

Reynolds was not the man to yield to the wanderlust, as his subsequent history clearly shows, but the call of the great west was in the air. The romance, the spirit of adventure and its excitement, proved to him as to many other young men, irresistible, and him too we find, on a soft April morning, in 1857, aboard the old steamer "Hannibal," headed for the new territory of Nebraska.

With characteristic modesty, his name first appeared in the records of the townsite company amongst those who signed the articles of association, following the names of Dr. Wilmans, Dr. Wise, and Albert Towle. It is next found when the membership roll was called by the scholarly secretary, John McConihe, in the office of the territorial secretary of state, in Omaha, May 20, 1857, and when the roll was again called on the townsite of Beatrice, July 27, 1857, Dr. Reynolds was one of the members who answered "Here." Prior to coming to Beatrice, it had been arranged that the members of the association should observe some sort of order in locating claims on the public domain with respect to the townsite, so as to avoid rivalry and contests over the matter, and the first public service Dr. Reynolds was called upon to perform was to act as a member of a committee of three persons "to draft resolutions for a claim association," evidently to be given jurisdiction over this delicate subject. The importance attached by the members of the association to the subject of claims is evidenced by the fact that this committee was the first one appointed at Beatrice, July 27, 1857. At the adjourned session in the afternoon of that day, on the coming in of the report of this committee, Dr. Reynolds was chosen as secretary and treasurer for this claims association, and the next day Bennett Pike was selected as president, the other members being David P. Taylor and H. F. Cook. Their duties were plainly outlined by the proceeding of May 28, 1858, when it was resolved that "Each individual hold his own claim as at present staked out, regardless of the valuation of the same, but subject to the location of the town," and it was further "resolved that the claim club settle boundary lines of claims and that the same be referred to them," and it was at this meeting also "resolved that no one individual be allowed to hold more than one hundred and sixty acres within one mile of town."

HERMAN M. REYNOLDS

After these meetings, the name of Dr. Reynolds frequently occurs in the association's record. At a meeting of the association, held May 22, 1858, when sixty votes were cast for president of the Nebraska Association, he received fifty-seven, and was at the same time selected as a member of the board of directors. Under the federal, townsite act, the government did not recognize individuals but required at least a semblance of a village or town organization, the mayor of such body alone having authority to enter land for townsite purposes. Dr. Reynolds was chosen as the first mayor of Beatrice,—at a time when there was neither councilmen, clerk, treasurer, city attorney nor any semblance of civic organization,—in order that the law might be complied with and the land comprising the original townsite of Beatrice be purchased, pursuant to the above mentioned act of congress. An assessment was levied upon the members of the association and a thousand dollars was in some way gotten together to pay for the survey and the government price of one dollar and twenty-five cents per acre for the land and other necessary expenditures connected with the survey and entry of the townsite. On the 12th day of August, 1959, Dr.

Reynolds, as the mayor of Beatrice, entered at the government land office at Brownville the half-section of land comprising the original townsite. Most of the mayor's deeds for lots in the original townsite were executed by him.

Dr. Reynolds was also very active in the early affairs of Gage county. With Mr. Towle he served from January, 1858, to January 1, 1860, as a member of the first board of county commissioners, and after the county was divided into three commissioner districts he served on the board till May, 1860, when he resigned, so that J. M. Summers of Blue Springs could be appointed to represent that part of the county on the board. He was county treasurer in 1858 and 1859 and again in 1863; he was county judge in 1868-1869; clerk of the district court in 1866-1867; county superintendent of school in 1868-1869. He was a member of the state constitutional convention in 1866, from Gage county, and represented our county in the legislature of 1874.

Dr. Reynolds was the first resident physician of Gage county and one of the first in the state of Nebraska. In 1857, there was of course but little call for men of his profession. But, undeterred by the discouraging outlook, he took up his work as a physician amongst the settlers, and for several years he devoted his time, when called upon, simply to doing good, such compensation as he was willing to accept being usually in some sort of farm produce—butter, eggs, poultry and the like. In the first issue of the *Blue Valley Record*, of August 1, 1868, is found this card:

H. M. Reynolds, M.D.
Office Blakely, Reynolds & Co's. Store
Beatrice, Neb.

Until the last moment of his life Dr. Reynolds treasured above his earthly possessions his ability to relieve the sick, minister to the afflicted, console the dying. Until prostrated by disease, he was never known to fail, even in his busiest years, the demands upon his professional skill and knowledge. Through cold and heat, across desolate prairies, this pioneer physician went about among the people ministering with all kindness to those who sought his aid.

The Doctor frequently engaged in business ventures outside of his profession. In 1864, he put up a considerable quantity of prairie hay, and in the fall and winter he bought a large number of cattle. Roughing the cattle through the winter, he herded them on the prairie until they became fit for market, then drove them to St. Joseph, Missouri, where they were sold. So many died during the winter that his profits, if any at all, were small. A number of times he engaged in mercantile business of some kind. As early as 1859 he had a small grocery and provision store, about where the old First National Bank began business in 1872. His goods were kept in a small, round-log cabin, with the side next to Court street. Finally he and Oliver Townsend opened a general store here, later the firm became Blakely, Reynolds & Company, and still later Dr. Reynolds and Oliver Townsend erected the old part of the stone building now owned by the Kilpatrick Brothers at the corner of Fifth and Court streets, where the firm continued in business until he died, in 1875. Mr. Blakely, however, was appointed receiver of the government land office at Beatrice, August 10, 1869, and retired from the firm, being succeeded later by I. N. McConnell. This business made money for the various partners and was really the foundation of their fortunes.

Dr. Reynolds was of medium height and probably never weighed in excess of one hundred and forty pounds. When he was a young man his hair was thick, black, and curled; his complexion was dark; his eyes gray, large, and very expressive; his nose Grecian, features regular, forehead broad and high, countenance frank and open. He was a most kindly, sympathetic man and wonderfully considerate of the feelings and wishes of others.

On October 20, 1861, Dr. Reynolds married Naomi Barcus, who at this writing survives him, and with her daughters, Josephine and Ruth, the wife of Corey C. Farlow, occupies the two-story, brick dwelling house, at the corner of Market and Eighth streets, which was erected by the Doctor as a home a few years prior to his death. His widowed daughter is Mrs. Elsie Loeber, of Beatrice, and his other children are Mrs. Mollie Randall, the wife of George Randall, of Morrill county, Nebraska, and, Mrs. Hermina Sackett, the wife of Hon. Harry E. Sackett, of Beatrice.

To the last moment of conscious existence Dr. Reynolds was a most loyal citizen of the city which he was so instrumental in founding. He rarely left Gage county and his interest in its welfare was such as always to hasten his return. He died at Beatrice on the 26th day of April, 1875, after a lingering illness, and when but a few days past the forty-third year of his age. His remains lie in the Beatrice cemetery, near the city whose history is inseparably linked with his name. He was deeply loved and universally mourned. On the day of his burial, the business houses of the city closed out of respect for him. Some one has said "To live in hearts we leave behind is not to die." If this is a true saying, then Dr. Reynolds is immortal, for he can never be forgotten while the city of Beatrice lasts. As in the case of Albert Towle, Oliver Townsend, and Jefferson Burns Weston, the beautiful city of Beatrice stands as an enduring monument to the memory of Dr. Herman Myer Reynolds.

CHAPTER XVII

A ROLL OF HONOR

Gage County Territorial Pioneers — Biographical Sketches: Nathan Blakely, Charles N. Emery, Joseph Hollingworth, Hiram W. Parker, Charles G. Dorsey, Fordyce Roper, Albert L. Tinkham, Horace M. Wickham, Isma P. and Elizabeth Mumford, James B. Mattingley, Samuel Jones, Algernon Sidney Paddock.

Most of the men and women of our county whose heroism made it possible for the lines of civilization to be advanced upon these western prairies, have long since passed away. Many are now unrepresented here by posterity or near relatives. As far as possible, it is the design of the author of this history to rescue from oblivion in this chapter of his work the names of the territorial pioneers of Gage county. In a few instances names will be found here of those who were in the territory many years before they became residents of Gage county. Appended to the list of names will be found brief biographical sketches of some of these heroic dead, who, by public service, position in the county, or from worth of character, are entitled to a place in any history of the county. It is a regrettable fact that no accurate catalogue of the names of these pioneers is now in existence. The most reliable evidence is afforded perhaps by the records of the United States land office. As far as possible the writer has supplemented these records from the minutes of the meetings of the Old Settlers' Association of Gage county, the early district-court records, the minutes of the county commissioners, and the recollection of a few pioneers still amongst us.

Nebraska was admitted to the great sisterhood of states March 1, 1867. Though pioneer conditions still prevailed in many portions of the state, it may reasonably be said that with railroads built and rapidly building throughout Nebraska, fairly accessible markets for the bulk of the population, steadily rising land values, rapidly accumulating wealth, a growing independence on the part of the entire population and the political freedom which under our system of government statehood always confers, the pioneer days were at an end when Nebraska ceased to be a territory. In compiling the following list of names, where the date on which the residence of the pioneer began in our county is known it is given; where unknown, the date on which the pioneer is shown to have entered public land in the old Brownville-Beatrice land office is given as the year to which residence of the party is credited. Names appear in this roll regardless of the fact that they are found elsewhere in this history. It is hoped that as time advances, the years may render more and more apparent the value of this

Roll of Honor

Beatrice

Alexander, T. J., 1859
Alexander, William, 1859
Ashby, William H., 1865
Ayers, James L., 1860
Ayers, Patience M.
Blakely, Nathan, July 17, 1857
Blakely, Margaret Constance (Tinkham)
Blakely, William, 1857
Burke, Patrick, 1858
Burke, Mary E., 1858
Brown, Thomas W., 1860
Brown, J. L, 1860
Brown, Sidney, 1860
Bonham, G. W., 1857
Coulter, Theodore M., 1859
Cartwright, Edward, 1860
Cook, Harrison F., 1857

Chandler, Luther B., 1865
Chase, J. E., 1860
Cox, M. D., 1867
Davis, Richard C., 1860
Dorsey, C. G., 1856 (Brownville)
Dunbar, John J., 1866
Emery, Charles, 1860
Emery, Mary E., 1860
Emery, Carl, 1860
Favor, Filetus M., 1859
Gilbert, John, 1858
Griggs, L. T., 1865
Griggs, N. K. 1867
Hewett, Obediah B., 1857
Hulburt, George W., 1864
Hamma, Peter, 1865
Harrington, Silas B., 1857
La Selle, Henry A., 1866
Loomis, Gilbert T., 1857

LePoidevin, Nicholas, 1865
LePoidevin, Thomas, 1866
Latham, John W., 1864
Latham, Diana, 1864
Latham, Asa, 1864
Mumford, Isma P., 1857
Mumford, Elizabeth, 1857
Mack, Eugene, 1866
Maxfield, James B., 1860
Nelson, Joseph. R., 1857
Parker, Hiram W., 1857
Pike, Bennett, 1857
Paddock, Algernon Sidney, 1857
Pethoud, Andrew J., 1857
Reed, Israel
Roper, Fordyce, 1857
Roper, Frederick E., 1857
Sage, A. D., 1863
Stevens, Orrin, 1857
Stevens, Amasa, 1864
Sibier, Frederick, 1866
Shaw, Jacob, 1866
Shaw, Julia, 1866
Shaw, John, 1866
Stoner, William Henry, 1860
Saunders, Joseph, 1855
Saunders, Emer, 1857
Steer, William H., 1866
Snow, A. L., 1866
Snow, Emilie, 1866
Towle, Albert, 1857
Towle, Catherine, 1857
Tinkham, Albert L., 1862
Tinkham, Sarah, 1862

Tobbey, G. H., 1857
Townsend, Oliver, 1857
Weston, Jefferson Burns, 1857
Weston, Helen (Towle), 1857

ELM TOWNSHIP

Mudge, William E., 1866
Stebbins, Austin E., 1866
Worden, William A., 1866

BLAKELY TOWNSHIP

Alexander, John W., 1863
Badley, John W., 1863
Ball, Lucy A., 1865
Bailey, Asa F., 1863
Benjamin, James H., 1861
Blakely, William, 1857
Blakely, Cornelia, 1863
Claybaugh, John H., 1866
Claybaugh, Reuben, 1866
Claybaugh, Rebecca, 1866
Claybaugh, Joseph, 1866
Clyne, Thomas, 1859
Clyne, Joseph, 1859
Clyne, Margaret, 1859
Dibble, Richard, 1865
Dolen, Benjamin, 1864
Freeman, Daniel, 1866
Graff, Joseph, 1863
Jakes, John, 1862
Kilpatrick, Samuel, 1859
Kilpatrick, Rachael, 1859
Kinzie, John, 1866
Myers, Mary, 1863

McCleve, William H., 1864
Odell, Hiram S., 1859
Rogers, Washington N., 1865
Rogers, Wilber S., 1865
Rossiter, Richard, 1862
Scheve, Henry, 1865
Scheve, John, 1866
Scribner, Irving S., 1866
Sopher, Elijah, 1866
Suiter, Agnes E., 1865
Wells, Joel, 1863
Wells, Christian, 1865
Wells, Leon, 1863
Wells, James, 1863
Wells, Darius, 1863
Wells, Cyrus, 1863
Wells, B. E., 1863
Wright, Amos L., 1866
Wickham, Horace, 1859

GRANT TOWNSHIP

Barrett, John, 1858
Buss, Charles, 1859
Carnahan, Thomas, 1866
Carnahan, George, 1866
Claibourne, 1865
Claibourne, 1865
Creed, George, 1865
Gaston, George W., 1866
Grant, George, 1858
Grant, John, 1858
Grant, James, 1865
Haddlock, Alva R., 1865
Harvey, David, 1865

Kinsey, James, 1861
Kinsey, William, 1861
Lull, H. M., 1865
Nicholas, Robert, 1860
Plucknett, William, 1861
Van Clief, William, 1863

CLATONIA TOWNSHIP

Albert, Henry, 1866
Kloepper, Henry, 1866
Pitzer, Frederick, 1866
Steinmeyer, William, 1866
Steinmeyer, Henry, 1866
Steinmeyer, Frederick, 1866

SICILY TOWNSHIP

Harvey, Oliver J., 1866
Harpster, Daniel J., 1862
Lott, James L., 1864
Stebbins, Austin E., 1861

RIVERSIDE TOWNSHIP

Crites, George B., 1866
Holt, C. B., 1866
Parker, John C., 1864
Shelley, Francis, 1862

MIDLAND TOWNSHIP

Brick, Henry, 1866
Buchanan, Joe, 1865
Bull, Stephen, 1866
Barney, Joseph, 1866
Conley, Michael, 1866

Dixon, Ira, 1858
Jones, Samuel, 1857
Jones, William, 1859
Jones, Isaac, 1857
LePoidevin, Thomas, 1866
Loomis, Gilbert T., 1857
Martin, Joseph, 1860
Pierce, H. J., 1857
Pethoud, John, 1857
Pethoud, John, Jr., 1858
Pethoud, F. M., 1857
Pethoud, Thomas, 1858
Pethoud, James K. P., 1858
Sherrill, Thomas, 1860

HOLT TOWNSHIP

Austin, Edward C., 1857
Austin, Homer B., 1857
Barnhouse, John, 1866
Chesney, Warren, 1865

HIGHLAND TOWNSHIP

Michael, Weaver, 1866

BLUE SPRINGS

Armstrong, Thomas, 1860
Anthony, Levi, 1862
Chambers, Joseph
Desert, George
Elliott, Martin, 1857
Elliott, William, 1857
Elliott, Henry, 1857
Elliott, Stephen, 1857
Hager, Adam, 1859

Hager, Margaret, 1859
Hager, John, 1859
Fisher, King, 1862
Fisher, Fred, 1862
Gary, Patrick R., 1859
Graham, F. M., 1859
Johnson, James H., 1857
Johnson, Martha M., 1857
Johnson, Rankin, 1859
Knight, Lynus, 1860
Knight, Jane A., 1860
Lott, James, 1860
Max Nichols, James H., 1864
Noyes, Reuyl, 1857
Poff, Jacob, 1857
Shaw, Samuel, 1859
Sargent, True, 1859
Sargent, Wright, 1859
Summers, J. M., 1859
Tyler, William B., 1859
Tyler, Rebecca (Woodward), 1859
Wilson, Robert A., 1861

ROCKFORD TOWNSHIP

Adams, John, 1865
Andrews, Miles, 1863
Barnum, H. S., 1859
Breese, Robert, 1860
Coffee, Philip B, 1865
Coffinberry, C. C., 1858
Davis, Carroll, 1859
Davis, William, 1859
Dixon, James, 1858
Dobbs, F. H., 1858

Dunn. John H., 1860
Elerbeck, James, 1866
Freeman, Humphrey P., 1863
Graves, H. J., 1860
Hendy, Eli B., 1859
Hollingworth, James, 1862
Hollingworth, Henry, 1862
Hollingworth, Joseph, 1862
Hollingworth, James, Jr., 1862
Hayden, Stephen, 1863
Hayden, Amos, 1863
Lily, Henry D., 1863
Mattingley, James B., 1857
Milligan, Joseph, 1857
Montgomery, John, 1860
Miller, David, 1863
Miller, Catherine, 1863
Mudge, Louis C., 1866
Mudge, Franklin, 1865
Nyghart, Stodgell, 1866
Potterton, John, 1859
Schullenberger, Jacob, 1859
Schullenberger, Henry, 1859
Schullenberger, William McK., 1859
Shaw, Harley, J., 1865
Slocumb, Charles H., 1866
Stark, George W., 1858
Tidler, John, 1859
Webber, Cyrene, 1865
Weigle, Gabriel, 1863
Welsh, Alex, 1864
Wild, William, 1862
Van Boskirk, Asher, 1863
Van Bockirk, William, 1866

LOGAN TOWNSHIP

Armstrong, William, 1865
Chrisman, David, 1863
Chrisman, Marion, 1863
Chrisman, Joseph, 1863
Graves, Abraham, 1860
Graves, Louis, 1860
Graves, Enoch, 1860
Graves, Henry, 1860
Hadley, Isaac N., 1862
Mumford, J. W., 1865
Mumford, J. B., 1865
Pheaster, Johnathan, 1865
Rogers, John, 1863
Smith, Duncan, 1866
Smith, Archibald, 1866
Tanner, John, 1865
Williams, Thomas, 1865
Williams, Evan, 1865
Zimmerman, Thomas, 1862
Zimmerman, Class, 1862

NEMAHA TOWNSHIP

Sykes, George, 1865

LIBERTY TOWNSHIP

Cain, Nathaniel D., 1865
Dunn, William B., 1865
Dunn, John C., 1865
Evans, Stephen, 1866
Fisher, Sylvester, 1859
Goin, James K., 1856
Jimmerson, Allen, 1866

Jimmerson, John J., 1866
Muchmore, L. M., 1856
Muchmore, James, 1866
MacMains, A. P., 1858
Palmer, David, 1855
Palmer, John, 1866
Sharp, Johnathan, 1865
Sharp, Louis, 1865
Sharp, George, 1865
Wymore, Cornelius S., 1866

ISLAND GROVE

Bolinger, Peter, 1866
Buckles, Peter, 1864
Brown, Joel, 1866
Dewey, Timothy, 1859
Dewey, William F., 1859
Fishbaugh, John, 1864
Garaer, James I., 1866
Irby, James, 1864
Mangus, David, 1866
Marion, Tipton, 1864
Stuteman, Thomas, 1866
Tibbitts, Samuel A., 1864
Tibbitts, Thomas D., 1864
Tibbitts, Edward, 1864
Willis, Scott, 1864
Willis, Cornelius, 1864
Wymore, Cornelius, 1864
Wymore, James, 1864
Wymore, Frederick, 1863

SHERMAN TOWNSHIP

Anderson, Asa, 1865
Martin, Thomas, 1865
Smith, Abraham B., 1866
Wilkinson, George, 1866

FILLEY TOWNSHIP

Bendernagle, Andrew, 1866
Bendernagle, Philip, 1866
Blakely, Benjamin F., 1862
Dunn, James W., 1859
Franklin, George W., 1863
Kees, John F., 1866
Norton, Noah, 1866
Reese, Levi M., 1864
Scott, Wilson D., 1865

HOOKER TOWNSHIP

Fuller, George W., 1863
Fuller, John, 1863
Fuller, Mary A., 1863
Hillman, John, Sr., 1860
Hillman, John, Jr., 1860
Hillman, Thaddeus, 1860
Krause, William, 1865
Williams, Thaddeus, 1863

ADAMS TOWNSHIP

Adams, John O., 1857
Adams, Nelson, 1857
Barmore, Henry, 1865
Curtis, William, 1860
Drown, George W., 1863

Golden, Henry, 1857
Gale, Alfred, 1857
Gale, George, 1858
Hildebrand, Jacob P., 1858
Hildebrand, Leroy, 1857
Hickock, Charles, 1860
Mathews, William, 1856
Moore, B. F., 1859
Noxon, George, 1857
Lyons, John, 1857
Reynolds, H., 1857

Shaw, Stephen P., 1857
Shaw, William, 1857
Shaw, John, 1857
Shaw, James I., 1857
Shaw, Stephen V., 1857
Silvernail, James, 1857
Silvernail, William, 1857
Stafford, John, 1857
Shaw, Egbert, 1857
Whyman, Charles, 1866

NATHAN BLAKELY

Nathan Blakely was born at Roxbury, Connecticut, July 26, 1824. He obtained a good, usable education in the public schools of his neighborhood and in Roxbury Academy. In 1844 he began to teach school in Westchester county, New York, and he followed this uneventful but useful calling for a number of years, teaching thirteen terms in succession at Long Branch, the celebrated watering place in Monmouth county, New Jersey. He then returned to Connecticut and for a while engaged in newspaper work at Roxbury. In 1852 he went to Chicago, and finally he located in Iowa, where he again taught school. In 1857, in company with his brother, William Blakely, he came to the new territory of Nebraska, and, with Isma Mumford, almost by accident, stumbled upon the Beatrice Townsite Company and found the members of this company engaged in building the log house which afterward became famous in the pioneer history of the county as "Pap's Cabin." He never identified himself directly with the townsite company, but a few days after his arrival he entered the tract of land where Zimmerman Spring is now located. He lived there from July, 1857, to the spring of 1865, and the walnut grove north of the spring was planted by him. He then sold his land to Nicholas LePoidevin and moved to

Beatrice, where he engaged in mercantile pursuits and for a few years was the most active and prominent business man in the village.

NATHAN BLAKELY

In 1858 he was elected county clerk of Gage county and the first minutes of the board of county commissioners, or the county court as that board was then called, are written by Mr. Blakely's hand. In 1859 he was reëlected to the office of county clerk, and during his entire incumbency of that office he was ex officio county superintendent of public instruction, while for a brief period, in 1858-1859, he filled the office of county judge. In 1861 Mr. Blakely was elected the representative in the territorial assembly for the district composed of Gage, Johnson, Clay, and Jones (now Jefferson) counties, and in 1866 he was again elected, to what proved to be the last territorial legislature. Before the adjournment of the session, in June, 1867, Nebraska had become a state and it became necessary to elect two United States senators to represent her in congress. Mr. Blakely steadily supported for these offices Thomas W. Tipton of Brownville, and Algernon S. Paddock of Omaha. Tipton was elected, but instead of Paddock, General John M. Thayer was chosen. Mr. Blakely was elected to the first state legislature in the fall of 1868, from our county, and while still a member of that body he was appointed receiver of public moneys for the United States land office at Beatrice; he took charge of that office October 1, 1869. He served the government in this responsible position for six years, handling thousands of dollars of public money, and at the close of his service it was found that the government was slightly in his debt.

MARGARET CONSTANCE BLAKELY

In November, 1868, Mr. Blakely married Margaret Constance Tinkham, the daughter of Albert L. and Sarah Tinkham, who were also among the earliest settlers of Gage county. Prior to her marriage Mrs. Blakely had been one of the active and successful school teachers of Gage county. Her first school was at Blue Springs, and her pupils were: Carter C. Coffinberry and Hugh J. Dobbs, from what is now Rockford township; John Shaw, from the Otoe Indian Agency; and from Blue Springs, Thomas, James, Richard, and Martha Johnson, Maria Knight (afterward Mrs. Louis When), Retta Anthony (now Mrs. F. M. Graham), her brother Isaac, and two younger sisters, children of Dr. Levi Anthony. These, with Sarah Fisher and her sister, daughters of King Fisher, constituted one of the earliest schools taught in the county.

Mr. Blakely's death occurred at his home in Beatrice on his birthday anniversary, July 26, 1906, and his wife passed away, at her home,

December 6, 1908. At the time of his decease he had attained the age of eighty-two years, and Mrs. Blakely had reached the age of sixty-five. Mr. Blakely was a shrewd business man and at the time of his death was one of the wealthy men of our county. His fortune was all in Beatrice real estate and farm lands in Gage, Thayer, Nuckolls, and other Nebraska counties. After his widow's death this fortune descended to their only son, Charles, who is now a resident of Omaha. This pioneer husband and wife lie side by side in their own burial plot in Beatrice cemetery, in, as yet, unmarked graves.

From the moment of its origin until the last moment of his life, Beatrice never possessed a more loyal, enthusiastic, hopeful friend than Nathan Blakely.

CHARLES N. EMERY

Charles N. Emery was born in Industry, Franklin county, Maine, August 15, 1836. Early in 1856, with the great influx of free-soil immigration, he came to Kansas, and made his home at Lawrence, which, from 1854 to 1863, was the rallying point of the free-soilers and the headquarters of John Brown, Jim Lane, Redpath, Parsons, Eldridge, Pomeroy, and other anti-slavery leaders. His first occupation was to drive stage on the old Santa Fe Trail from Leavenworth to Topeka, Kansas, and in this capacity he made the acquaintance of nearly every prominent leader of the anti-slavery movement in the territory of Kansas.

In 1864 he came to Nebraska territory, where he was for a while in the employ of the Overland Stage Company and had charge of the station at Thirty-two Mile Creek. Later he came eastward on the Oregon Trail to Liberty Farm, and he had charge of that important station at the time of the great Sioux Indian raid on the Little Blue river in August, 1864. On the afternoon of that day a stage driver halted his team at Liberty Farm long enough to warn the inmates to fly for their lives. Mr. Emery and his family made their way quickly to Pawnee Ranch, a large station of the Overland Stage Company, so located as to be easily defended. They went through the siege from three or four hundred savages, and when the danger had subsided they made their way to

Atchison, Kansas. From that point, for a year or two, Mr. Emery engaged in freighting across the plains to Colorado. In July, 1867, he came to Beatrice, and for a while he was engaged in farming and stock raising, but on the completion of the old stone hotel building at the corner of Fifth and Court streets, he, on January 1, 1871, became its landlord. This famous old hostelry was known for years as the "Emery House," and is to this day in favor with the traveling public, under the name of the "Burwood." Beginning with 1878, Mr. Emery owned and ran a livery barn, which was located directly east of the hotel.

While driving stage over the old Santa Fe Trail, Charles N. Emery met Mary Benson, and on May 4, 1858, they were married, at Lawrence, Kansas. Here their two children were born, George E. and John C. Emery. This pioneer family from the first was prominent in the social and business affairs of Beatrice. Charles and Mary Emery were genial, optimistic, friendly people and were much loved and highly respected by the entire community.

He reached the boundaries of life when venerable in years, and on the 6th day of January, 1907, the passing Death Angel with his wing touched his companion of over forty years, and she passed peacefully from the earth forever. After their long pilgrimage together, they lie side by side, in everlasting repose, near the beautiful city which they both loved and which loved them.

JOSEPH HOLLINGSWORTH

Joseph Hollingworth was born in the manufacturing town of Melbourne, Derbyshire, England, November 2, 1836. He was the youngest of twelve children born to his parents, James and Elizabeth Hollingworth. In 1848 these fine English parents, accompanied by their four youngest children, came from England to the United States of America and settled in the then new state of Wisconsin, where the father engaged in farming and in the manufacture of lumber from the pine forests of that state. After the parents had been in this country some years they were followed by most of their other children. They were James, the eldest son; Henry and Robert; also their married daughters

Elizabeth, wife of William Wild, and Frances, wife of Francis Shelley. In 1861 all these families except Robert numbering probably twenty-five souls, migrated from Wisconsin to Gage county, Nebraska. All found homes in Rockford township except Robert, who came on later and settled in Thayer county, where he became very prominent both in public and private life. They became at once useful and valued citizens of our county and state and though all but Elizabeth Wild have answered the summons of death their posterity is to be found in numbers in the city of Beatrice, in Gage county and elsewhere in Nebraska, engaged in many vocations in the world of work. Joseph Hollingworth and his brothers, as well as Wild and Shelley, were successful farmers and belonged to the cultivated English rural class. These families all possessed the manly and womanly virtues that distinguish high-class English people wherever found.

Shortly after coming to Nebraska Joseph Hollingworth met and, on July 13, 1862, married Wealthy, the good and accomplished daughter of Rev. Albert L. Tinkham and his wife Sarah, pioneers, too, of Gage county. She was a successful school teacher. She taught the village school in Beatrice in 1861 and was teaching the second school taught in Blue Springs, in 1862, when she first met her future husband. Their marriage was from first to last a complete exemplification of perfect conjugal happiness and domestic felicity, broken only by the husband's death.

Joseph Hollingworth maintained a continuous residence here till 1882, when he went to Nuckolls county to live, on a section of land which he had purchased. In 1887 he returned to his farm in Rockford township, and in 1895 he came to Beatrice to live. After a few years spent in this city he removed to University Place and after a short time he went to California, whence eventually he went to Portland, Oregon, where he died October 23, 1914. His wife, though nearing life's boundary, still survives,—the object of the tender affection and solicitude of her children and friends.

To Joseph and Wealthy Hollingworth there were born five sons and three daughters. The sons are Arthur, Thomas, George, Albert, and Archie; the daughters are Alma, Arvilla, and Aimee. All reside in Portland, Oregon, except Albert, who for many years has made his home in Beatrice. He served during the Spanish-American war as captain of Company C of the First Nebraska Regiment of Volunteer Infantry, a company composed largely of Gage county men. He was severely wounded in battle in the Philippines but returned with his regiment in 1899, and on February 27, 1906, he was appointed postmaster of Beatrice, an office which he most ably and acceptably filled for more than eight years, maintaining, however, in some capacity a connection with the military organization of the state. When the United States entered the present world war, in 1917, he was among the first to offer his services to his country, and he is now lieutenant colonel of one of the Nebraska regiments in training for service in France.

HIRAM W. PARKER

In the history of Gage county, few men have played so important a part as Hiram W. Parker. He was born in Worcester, Massachusetts, December 17, 1827; he died at Beatrice in 1899. Mr. Parker came to Nebraska from Ironton, Ohio, in April, 1857, and in 1858 he located a claim in old Clay county, near the present village of Pickrell, and engaged in farming and stock-raising. In 1865 he removed to Camden, in Seward county, Nebraska, where he built a saw mill, and followed this, in 1871, by adding a grist mill. On the 2d day of June, 1871, he was appointed register of the government land office at Beatrice, and by successive appointments he held this office until April 1, 1884. He was county judge of old Clay county, and was the clerk of that county in 1864, when Clay was partitioned between Lancaster and Gage counties. In 1860 Mr. Parker was elected to represent Gage, Clay, and Johnson counties in the territorial assembly, and he was also a member of the state constitutional convention in 1871.

Mr. Parker was married, at Austinburg, Ohio, in October, 1852, to Almira T. Dole, a native of that state. His living children are Franklin H. Parker of Santa Rosa, California, and Louis C. Parker of Chicago, Illinois. Mr. Parker for a long time was vice-president of the First National Bank, and was also president of a brick manufacturing company and a large canning company, in both of which he lost money, and of an early-day telephone company of Beatrice. For a number of years he was a member and president of the school board of the city of Beatrice; he was also a long-time official of the Gage County Agricultural Society.

HIRAM W. PARKER

The remains of both Mr. and Mrs. Parker lie in the old Beatrice cemetery, where two children preceded them many years, and the spot is marked by a fine monument.

Though rather abrupt in manner, Mr. Parker at bottom was a good, reliable citizen, and to those who broke through his reserve he was a good friend.

CHARLES G. DORSEY

Charles G. Dorsey came to Brownville from Indianapolis, Indiana, in 1856, and engaged in the practice of the law, principally, however, in such litigation as grew out of land contests before the register and receiver in the Brownville land office. He combined with his practice a general real-estate business. On the 25th day of July, 1865, he was appointed register of the land office, and he held this position till March 7, 1867, when he was succeeded by Henry M. Atkinson, who was afterwards surveyor general of New Mexico. The land office was moved from Brownville to Beatrice July 7, 1868, and Mr. Dorsey removed from Brownville in 1869, and continued his practice before that office. His brother, George Dorsey, also came from Brownville to Beatrice, and the brothers, with I. N. McConnell, for a number of years practically monopolized the litigation before the register and receiver of the Beatrice land office, at the same time doing a very large real-estate and insurance business, from which all the partners reaped large profits. In the late '70s Mr. Dorsey engaged in the hardware business in Beatrice, and about the year 1882, he erected the double, three-story, brick building in block sixty-four of the original town of Beatrice, west of the Burwood Hotel. Mr. Dorsey continued in the hardware business in one of these storerooms for a number of years, but during the hard times in 1893 to 1898, he lost his property largely, and, with a mere remnant of his property, he moved to Kansas City, Missouri, where he made an heroic struggle to recoup his fortune. He again engaged in the hardware business and was gradually achieving success, when his death occurred.

Mr. Dorsey was for many years active and prominent in the affairs of Beatrice and Gage county. He was an able man and very considerate, as well as conservative in judgment. He was an esteemed and valuable citizen.

Before coming to Beatrice, Mr. Dorsey had been a member of the territorial legislature. While here, he was frequently a member of the city council. He was married at Peru, Nebraska, in the fall of 1871, to Mary E. Majors, a daughter of S. P. Majors, a prominent citizen and pioneer of Nemaha county, whose son, Colonel Thomas J. Majors, is a widely known citizen of the state of Nebraska. Three children were born to this husband and wife, namely: William C., Edith, and Harry Dorsey. Harry, the second son, died in Beatrice a number of years ago. The elder son, William C. Dorsey, resides at Bloomington, Nebraska, and is at the present time serving as district judge of his judicial district of the state.

FORDYCE ROPER

Fordyce Roper was one of the early settlers of old Clay county, having established his residence on Indian creek, twelve miles north of Beatrice, in 1857. He accompanied Judge Kinney, Dr. Wise, Dr. Wilmans, Dr. Reynolds, J. B. Weston, and others to the Beatrice townsite, the last of May, 1857. He became a resident of Beatrice in 1859, but in 1860 he went to Pike's Peak on a prospecting expedition for gold. He returned that fall and purchasing the buhrs of Austin's mill he removed them to Beatrice. Having acquired some interest in the saw mill at that time being operated on the bank of the Big Blue river (where Black Brothers merchant mill is now located) by one Waldripp, he proceeded to put in a dam across the river and erect a grist mill, both to be driven by water power. For some reason this venture did not prove a success, but Mr. Roper persisted in the enterprise and ultimately produced a very fair grist mill. In connection with this he developed a very efficient saw mill, planing mill, and lath and shingle industry. He was not only the first miller of Beatrice, but was also for many years one of its most important and most considered citizens. He was active in community affairs, serving the county as a commissioner from 1862 to and including 1864, and was chairman of the Gage county board when Clay county was divided, in 1864, between Lancaster and Gage counties. In 1869, on the resignation of Nathan Blakely as representative for Gage and Jefferson counties in the state legislature, Mr. Roper was elected to fill the vacancy. About the year 1875 he sold his mill to Henry Weatherald and his son Newton, and retired from the milling business. About the same time he sold his residence and removed from Nebraska to California, settling finally in Bakersfield, that state, where he died a few years ago.

Mr. Roper was the first miller of Beatrice. He had the business acumen to forsee the necessity for such an enterprise and the energy and enthusiasm which urged forward to its accomplishment. His old home stood and still stands facing South Second street where it terminates on

Scott street. It is practically unchanged from what it was when he left it. It is now occupied by Henry Von Reisen as a residence.

REV ALBERT L. TINKHAM

If worth of character and a long life devoted to the betterment of mankind are in themselves sufficient to perpetuate the memory of man, then no history of Gage county could be complete without some account of the Rev. Albert L. Tinkham.

This writer knew this good man long and well; many of the happiest recollections of his life are inseparably connected with him and his, and this sketch is written for the purpose of commemorating the life and character, and the noble and unselfish services to the pioneers of Gage county, of this heroic man.

Mr. Tinkham was born almost at the opening of the nineteenth century. He died in Beatrice at the age of seventy-eight years. He was derived from good New England stock and was endowed with all those qualities of heart and brain which win and retain the esteem of mankind. He was of a deeply religious nature and as a minister of the Gospel, he spent the greater part of his life in simply doing good. He exemplified perfectly in his long life as a Christian minister the sentiment contained in Tennyson's verse:

"Howe'er it be, it seems to me
'Tis only noble to be good;
Kind hearts are more than coronets
And simple faith than Norman blood."

Mr. Tinkham came to Beatrice in 1860. He had been preceded here by his eldest son, Gilbert, who died among strangers, in the lonely, almost desolate hamlet of Beatrice, in the winter of 1859. On arriving here with his family, Mr. Tinkham became at once a useful and an influential member of the community. He found Beatrice a mere village of log and board shanties, where people hibernated in winter and vegetated in summer. It required courage of no ordinary character to bring a young and growing family, in what seems now that far-off day, to this outpost of civilization. He was presented by the townsite company with the two lots on Ella street, in block forty-nine, where the three-story building known as the Penner Block is located, and he proceeded to build thereon a two-room, hewed-log, clapboard-roofed house, which in its day was perhaps equal to any other residence in Beatrice. It was the furthest out of any of the houses and was located on the broad, open prairie. Here he dwelt with his family during four busy years and here his son Edward was born. He was a carpenter by trade and in addition to his pastoral duties he was accustomed to labor assiduously with saw and plane. He and his son Elias built the old frame school house on the block where the old high-school building, now Central grade-school building, stands. Mr. Tinkham was a Methodist clergyman and possessed the fire and enthusiasm of the early ministers of that church,—the Wesleys, Whitfield, Cartwright. For many years he was the best known minister of the Gospel in Gage county, extending his gentle ministrations far and wide, amongst the hardy pioneers, officiating at marriages, funerals, and other services performed by clergymen; he was known by all and loved by all. In the lonely dugouts and log cabins he was a familiar figure and a welcome guest. People traveled far to hear him preach. At his maximum his voice was as mellow and resonant as a bell. No preaching could have been more simple and direct, more free from rant and cant. He possessed traits of character which disarmed emnity and left him without foe or detractor in all the world. He was gentle and considerate and endowed to a remarkable degree with the charity that envieth not, is not puffed up, that vaunteth not itself, that suffereth long and yet is kind. Strictly honorable and exact in his dealings with his fellow men he expected Almighty God to be exact with him. Not ambitions of worldly wealth or honors, he was content with a life severely simple and plain.

In early life Mr. Tinkham married Sarah Wilson, at Wilsonville, Ohio. To this couple there were born Gilbert, Wealthy, Elias, Margaret Constance, James Leroy, Thomas Alice, Edward, and Albert Tinkham. Both Wealthy and Margaret were amongst the first school teachers in Gage county. The former married Joseph Hollingworth, the latter Nathan Blakely.

In 1864, Mr. Tinkham was prevailed upon by his friends to avail himself of the benefits of the homestead law, and he entered the quarter-section of land on Bear creek on the south side of the Scott-street road, extending from Cottonwood Grove school house a little way beyond the bridge. This tract of land continued to be the family home until his death. His remains, with those of his wife and other members of his family, lie in the family burial lot in the Beatrice cemetery.

HORACE M. WICKHAM

Horace M. Wickham was born in Licking county, Ohio, September 2, 1832. His early life was spent in Andrew county, Missouri. He spent the years of 1855-1856 in Iowa, and on March 20, 1859, he became a resident of Gage county, Nebraska. During most of the intervening years up to the time of his death, September 4, 1906, he made this county his home and was by occupation a farmer. In 1867 he was elected a county commissioner of Gage county, and he served continuously in that responsible office till the year 1877,—the longest continuous service in that office of any of its numerous incumbents. On the 8th of May, 1859, Mr. Wickham was married, at the home of a Mr. Woodrow, on Bear creek, three miles northeast of Beatrice, to Lavinia Young, by Nathan Blakely, then acting probate judge of this county. Some years ago, on the occasion of a farewell party to Mr. Wickham at his home in Blakely township, Mr. Blakely, who performed this first marriage ceremony in Gage county, sent to Mr. Wickham a letter, which is not only self-explanatory but also sheds much light on the crude conditions of those early days. The letter reads as follows:

Horace M. Wickham,
    Hoag, Gage County, Nebraska.

My Dear Friend:
    I regret that my health is such that I can not avail myself of a kind invitation to meet you and your old friends in this county before you make your departure for your new home in the Platte valley, in this state.

We have always known you long and well, and we think you should have remained with us the few remaining days of our earthly pilgrimage, to cheer and comfort one another.

We have all had many joys and sorrows since we located in this wild, unsettled country so many years ago. We found many good and true friends among the old settlers of this county. We cherish the memory of many departed ones and the hearty handshake of others, who, with us, will soon bid adieu to all earthly scenes, we hope for a brighter and better life.

I have always felt a special interest in you and yours, for, in the spring of 1859, you asked me to marry you to Miss Lavinia Young. As there was no minister in this part of the country, and I being the only county official that seemed to have authority, I was compelled to perform the operation. There had never been a marriage in this county, so I could not get any information just what to say or how to proceed. I lay awake a good share of two or three nights trying to learn my piece; then I wrote it down and used to declaim it out on the prairie—a mile from any human being. As the audience neither applauded or hissed, I decided it was good.

The ordeal came, and one pleasant Sunday in May (8th), 1859, I started for Bear creek, where Mr. Woodrow and family lived, near Fulton's Spring, Miss Young living with them. On the green grass, under a new tent, I tried my very best to make Mr. Wickham and Miss Young husband and wife, and, as far as I have ever learned, I succeeded.

I don't know what I said and I never dared ask you or your wife, but as you appeared to be so smiling, I could not tell whether it was from what I had said or from your inexpressible happiness of being made a husband.

May the blessings of Heaven rest upon you and your family henceforth and for evermore, and evermore,

Your friend,
NATHAN BLAKELY.

The reader has now looked upon the first marriage solemnized in Gage county, and its commemoration by a man of keen intellect and unquestioned veracity.

Shortly after this marriage, Mr. and Mrs. Wickham went to the state of Colorado with a view of making their home there. Here the young bride was taken ill and died, at South Park, Colorado, August 7, 1860. Mr. Wickham later married, at St. Joseph, Missouri, Mrs. Isabelle Beebe, who passed away in 1873, leaving two children, Clarissa and Franklin P. Wickham.

ISMA P. MUMFORD

Isma P. and Elizabeth Mumford were amongst the first pioneers in Gage county. Isma P. Mumford was born in the state of Maryland, while Elizabeth Mallock, was born in Adams county, Ohio, in 1830. She was the granddaughter of a Revolutionary soldier and the daughter of a man who bore arms for his country in the war of 1812. When twenty-one years of age she became the wife of Isma P. Mumford. Shortly after their marriage, in 1853, they migrated from Ohio to the new state of Wisconsin, and in 1857 they came seeking a home in the new territory of Nebraska. On the way out they were joined at Plattsmouth by William and Nathan Blakely, and together these heroic pioneers of Gage county made their slow way across the unmarked, trackless prairies of southeastern Nebraska. Hearing that the Big Blue river valley offered great advantages to settlers, on account of the abundant timber and rich bottom land which lined its course, they traveled thither, and on the 17th day of July, almost by accident, stumbled upon the members of the Beatrice Townsite Company, who were engaged in erecting a company house on their townsite, which building later became the property of Albert Towle and widely famous as "Pap's Cabin." They also found a cluster of covered wagons and tents, in the neighborhood of the Kees Manufacturing plant, a little above the junction of Indian creek and the Big Blue river. Learning that the representatives of the townsite company had founded a town and purposed to remain and carry their enterprise to fulfillment, and pleased both with the prospect and company, the little party resolved to cast in its fortunes with that old guard which then and for many succeeding years held this remote outpost of civilization against all hardships, privations and discouragements.

ELIZABETH MUMFORD
The first white woman settler in Gage county

For several months Mrs. Mumford and a Miss Bailey, who accompanied the party, were the only white women in the settlement, and probably the only white women in the county. Of Miss Bailey this writer is unable to give any further account, but Mrs. Mumford enjoyed the distinction of being the sole representative of her sex in Gage county until the arrival of Mrs. Catherine Towle, in the autumn of 1857. The names of both these good ladies must be forever spoken with reverence by those for whom the early history of Beatrice and Gage county has the slightest interest. Both possessed unusual mental vigor; both were endowed with those traits of personal character that always command and retain the respect of mankind; both have long since passed to their rest. One sleeps beside her honored husband in the old cemetery, near this city, and the other is wrapped in kindred earth of a sister state. To Mrs. Towle belongs the honor of being the mother of the first child born in Gage county, a daughter, Katie Towle, and to Mrs. Mumford, the honor of being the mother of the first white male child born within the boundaries of our county. Both these children, having reached the age of maturity, were long ago gathered to the bosom of Mother Earth. Katie Towle became the wife of George V.

Ayers, of Deadwood, South Dakota. She died on the 28th day of March 1890, aged thirty-two years. Her remains lie with those of her parents in the family burial ground in the Beatrice cemetery, while the turf that enfolds a fathers and a brother's clay wraps also the dust of Dawson Mumford, he having perished in an accident, at the age of twenty-two years—the age when most men begin life.

The remaining history of Isma P. and Elizabeth Mumford may be briefly told. On August 7, 1857, at an election attended principally by the members of the Beatrice Townsite Company for the purpose of organizing Gage county by electing a complete set of county officials, Mr. Mumford was chosen county treasurer, and he held that office one year. He bears the distinction of being the first county treasurer of Gage county. During the great Indian panic of 1864, which swept over this portion of Nebraska with irresistible force, the Mumfords, with many other families, left the territory, some never to return. But in the spring of 1865 Isma P. and Elizabeth Mumford, with their children, established a home near what was know as the "Steam Wagon Road," six miles west of Nebraska City. Here, in 1873, Isma died, and his wife, in 1875, removed permanently from the state, taking up her residence with a son, in Nodaway county, Missouri, where she died in March, 1897. They were the parents of nine children, seven sons and two daughters. One son, James, became a prominent Congregational minister, and as far as known to this writer, all their children who reached maturity became useful and worthy members of society.

JAMES B. MATTINGLY

James B. Mattingly was born in the state of Kentucky, on the 8th day of April, 1818, near Elizabethtown, Harden county. In 1841 he migrated to the territory of Illinois and settled in Moultrie county. He was of a roving disposition, and leaving Illinois, about 1847, he moved to Iowa; from there, in 1849, to Platte county, Missouri. In 1857 he left Missouri and started west along the Oregon Trail in an aimless search for a new location. At Ash Point, a station on the old highway, he struck a dim trail and followed it to the Otoe and Missouri Indian village. Guided by reports of desirable locations further north, he passed the site of Blue Springs, and finally selected a quarter-section of land in the south west corner of Rockford township, on Mud creek, in June 1857. About the year 1866 he sold his homestead to James Millard, and moved to Jefferson county, Nebraska, where he entered a tract of land, eighty acres of which now form the most populous and wealthy portion of the city of Fairbury. Shortly after arriving in Jefferson county he engaged somewhat extensively in the freighting business, along the Oregon Trail, for a few months, an occupation which he had followed also while residing in Gage county. When, in 1867, the construction of the Union Pacific Railroad put an end to the freighting business along the old trail, Mattingly established himself on the Little Blue river, within pistol shot of the court house in Fairbury, in the saw-mill business, and while engaged in sawing lumber for homesteaders who were rapidly flowing into that section of country, he was visited one day by Woodford G. McDowell, a resident of Fairbury, Illinois. The St. Joseph & Grand Island Railway was pointing up the Little Blue river, and McDowell, with keen prevision, had selected the present site of Fairbury as the location for the county seat of Jefferson county. Mattingly possessed in a remarkable degree the imagination which always goes with adventure, and McDowell had no difficulty in getting him to enter into his scheme to found a town, to be called Fairbury, which should be the chief city of that entire section of country. McDowell had obtained title to eighty acres adjoining Mattingly's. They jointly laid out and platted the town of Fairbury, the history of which has more than fulfilled the dreams of both its founders.

James Bartholomew Mattingly belonged to that class of men which is ever adrift in the forefront of advancing civilization. After investing some money in the town of Endicott, in the vain endeavor to boom it into a city of importance, and losing heavily in the venture, he, with his son, Joel Thomas, his wife, and daughter Polly, migrated to the Pacific slope. All are dead now but the son, Joel Thomas, who lives at Condon, Oregon, in fairly comfortable circumstances. Mr. Mattingly himself died October 19, 1907, aged eighty-nine years. At the time of his death he was a resident of a little town in northern Washington.

James B. Mattingly was a wonderfully active man; his occupations were diverse; he was at once a soldier, a freighter on the Oregon Trail, a speculator, a farmer, a miller, a carpenter, and dabbled in many other occupations. With many faults of character and of mental equipment and attitude, he was at bottom a reliable citizen and active in the public welfare. He was county commissioner of Gage county in 1861-62-63; he was deputy sheriff, bailiff of the courts, justice of the peace and occupied other civil positions of trust, if not of profit, in Gage county. He taught the first Sunday school in Rockford township and one of the first in our county. This Sunday school was organized in April, 1859. The writer of this volume, with his brother, and Joel Thomas Mattingly were his only pupils, although the school lasted two or three years.

James B. Mattingly was as eccentric a character as he was a picturesque one, and when he died, the world could have better spared a better man.

SAMUEL JONES

Samuel Jones was born in Grayson county, Virginia, in 1826. When he was eight years of age his parents moved to Ohio, and settled near Gallipolis, Gallia county, where he grew to manhood. In 1845 he married Rebecca Pethoud, daughter of John Pethoud, one of the first settlers of Gage county, Nebraska. In 1855 he moved from Ohio to Platte county, Missouri, and after six months' residence there he moved to Jefferson county, Kansas, locating thirty-three miles west of Leavenworth. In September, 1857, he came to Gage county, Nebraska territory, and in the spring of 1858 he made preëmption filing and settlement on the northeast quarter of section 15, Midland township. He built a log house on his preëmption claim that year, the carpentry work being done by H. F. Cook, one of the founders of the city of Beatrice. With some additions to this rude structure, to accommodate his increasing family, the building constituted his home for several years, but in 1866, he began the erection of a large stone house, near the old pioneer log cabin. This was finished by 1868 and was probably the most commodious farm residence in the county. The wood work was done by Tom Redpath, who was afterward drowned while bathing in the Big Blue river above the dam, when that stream was in flood.

Samuel Jones was a farmer all his life, but during the pioneer days in Nebraska Territory he engaged in freighting and ranching to some extent, along the old Oregon Trail, and was one of the best known freighters and all around business men in the county. He was a very active man, good natured, kindly, and was heartily liked by the early settlers. He died February 8, 1872, and with his father, William Jones, and sister, Mrs. Elizabeth McDaniel, and daughter Helen, aged five years, is buried on the hill a quarter of a mile south of the old stone dwelling. His wife, Rebecca Jones, died at Gooding, Idaho, about 1901, while making her home with a daughter, and was buried there.

To these pioneer parents there were born fourteen children—eight sons and six daughters. Seven of these children are numbered with the dead. The living are William R. Jones, the eldest son, who resides in the city of Beatrice and has made his home in Gage county since September, 1857, when he was eleven years of age; the third daughter, Sarah A. Drew, wife of Lorenzo L. Drew, also lives in Beatrice; John T. Jones and Elizabeth Dwyer, son and daughter, live at Gooding, Idaho; Leroy C. Jones, another son, is United States marshal of Idaho and lives in the city of Boise; Albert Jones, a son, lives at Baker City, Oregon; Rebecca (Jones) Pethoud, daughter, lives at Cotopaxi, Colorado.

PIONEER RESIDENCE OF SAMUEL JONES

The old stone mansion erected as a family home by Samuel Jones in 1866 is in process of demolition and will soon be a thing of the past. Time was when this pioneer residence was a place of great interest and importance. It was the abode of hospitality, generous, ungrudging, and was a center of the social forces of the surrounding community. It stood, staunch and inviting, near one of the old trails that led from Beatrice up Indian creek bottom and on past its portals to the head of Salt creek, and down that stream to the salt basin, where it connected with the old trails from Nebraska City, Plattsmouth and Omaha. One after another the pioneer homes have disappeared, until at the present moment there are probably not twenty of these ancient buildings left in the county. With them are rapidly disappearing the traditions and the romance of the past.

ALGERNON SIDNEY PADDOCK

Algernon Sidney Paddock was born at Glens Falls, New York, November 9, 1830. He died at Beatrice, Nebraska, October 17, 1897. He was the son of Ira A. Paddock, a well known and prominent lawyer of Glens Falls. He received his elementary education in the common schools of his native city, and, preparing himself for college in the academy of Glens Falls, at the age of eighteen years he entered Union College (now university), at Schenectady, New York, where so many of the able men of the nation have received their education. On account of financial affairs he was compelled to leave the college when just entering upon his senior year. For a while he taught school, reading law at the same time, and, having been admitted to the bar in his native state, he, in May, 1857, came by steam boat from St. Louis, Missouri, to Omaha. He was a man of great amiability and pleasing address, and these and other qualities won him influential friends in Nebraska from the moment of his arrival. He was always an ardent, unflinching and loyal Republican, and in 1860 he was a delegate from Nebraska, to the national convention of his party which nominated Abraham Lincoln for president. In the convention Mr. Paddock, however, supported his friend William H. Seward for that office, a service which that able and good man never forgot, and in 1861, through his influence, Mr. Lincoln appointed Mr. Paddock territorial secretary of state for Nebraska, an office which he both adorned and exalted for the period of six years, retiring only upon the admission of Nebraska to the Union, March 1, 1867. At the first state legislature Mr. Paddock was a candidate for United States senator, but was defeated by General John M. Thayer, a Civil war hero of Nebraska. In 1869 he became interested in the construction of the Burlington Railroad system in Nebraska, and for a while maintained business relations with the officers of that railroad company. In 1872 he moved from Omaha to Beatrice, which was his home for the remainder of his life.

Mr. Paddock was elected United States senator for Nebraska in 1875, in place of Thomas W. Tipton, for the term of six years. In 1881 he was defeated for that office by Charles H. Van Wyck, and in 1882 he was appointed a member of the very important "Utah Commission" by his friend President Arthur, upon which body he served with great distinction until October 1, 1886, when he resigned. In 1887 Mr. Paddock was again chosen United States senator for the state of Nebraska, serving until 1893, when his place was taken by William V. Allen.

On entering the United States senate few western senators were as well equipped as Mr. Paddock for serving their section of the country. He was familiar with western conditions versed in the land laws under which title could be obtained to land in the public domain, he was acquainted in detail with questions growing out of Indian depredations, school-land selections, surveys and re-surveys of public lands, Indian and military reservations, and the necessary military equipment for all the great west. He was indefatigable in his efforts to secure proper legislation for the entire country and particularly for the western states and territories. Perhaps it is no more than just to say that Nebraska has never had in either house of congress an abler, more conscientious and more faithful and intelligent servant than Senator Paddock.

For many years Senator Paddock was not only a citizen of Beatrice but he was also a force in this community. In 1887-1888 he built the Hotel Paddock, which in many respects is the most important private property in the city of Beatrice. He platted and laid out Fairview and

Paddock additions to Beatrice, and in other ways exhibited his interest in the destiny of the fair city of Beatrice.

In his personality Senator Paddock was one of the most attractive of men. He was extremely optimistic in temperament and his faith in Nebraska was unbounded,—and this through good, as through evil report. Mr. Paddock stood four-square to all the world, and, though often subject to adverse criticism by his political opponents, no man ever had the temerity to attack him in his private life.

On the 22d day of December, 1859, Mr. Paddock married Anna L. Mack, of St. Lawrence county, New York, a daughter of Daniel Mack, an honored citizen of that state. It was a most felicitous marriage, covering a period of thirty-eight years. His devoted wife still (1918) survives him, and makes her home in Lincoln. The children of this marriage were Daniel Mack and Susan, both of whom died at an early age; Harriet, wife of O. J. Colman, of Lincoln, Nebraska; Francis Amelia, now deceased; and Franklin Algernon Paddock, of Kansas City, Missouri.

Both time and space forbid the further extension of these sketches of territorial pioneers of our county. The reader will find in the biographical department of this work and elsewhere, the life history in more or less detail of a large number of these pioneers. The chief aim of the writer in these sketches has been to show the kind of men and women who were the first to people our county, and who set in motion those forces and influences which eventuated in the creation of a great, free commonwealth, one of the most attractive and interesting in the sisterhood of states.

CHAPTER XVIII

NARRATIVE OF GEORGE GALE, WITH BIOGRAPHICAL SKETCH

George Gale was born in Columbia county, New York, May 17, 1828, and died at his home in Adams township, Gage county, January 9, 1899. He was descended from a well known family of the Empire state, members of which had participated in both the Revolutionary war and the war of 1812. His parents were Alonzo and Phoebe (Peck) Gale, both natives of Dutchess county, New York. His father was of Irish descent, his mother a Hollander. When he was six years of age his parents moved from New York to Connecticut, where he was reared and educated. March 26, 1850, Mr. Gale married Margaret M. Shaw, the daughter of Stephen P. Shaw, himself a well known pioneer immigrant to Gage county.

Shortly after his marriage George Gale moved to the new state of Michigan, and in 1854 he went still further west, settling in Neosha county, Wisconsin. From Wisconsin, in 1858, with his family and household effects, carried in two ox-drawn wagons, he migrated to Otoe county, in the territory of Nebraska. He remained in that county until 1860, when he came to what is now Adams township, Gage county, but then part of old Clay county. Here he purchased land, and in 1863, under the homestead law, he added to his purchase one hundred twenty acres more. Mr. Gale was a most reliable, conscientious man. He had a keen sense of right and was accustomed to follow the inner light of conscience wherever it led. By occupation he was a farmer, and was content with that simple, uneventful life. He was well and favorably known in Gage county and esteemed as a man of strong common sense and sturdy integrity of character. Four children were born to Mr. and Mrs. Gale, namely, Edward A., Charles F. and Margaret.

Mr. Gale was the second assessor of Gage county, having been elected to that office in 1869. For over twenty years he was a member of the school board of his school district and filled other neighborhood positions. Not only was George Gale himself thus accredited but members of his family also have been useful and esteemed citizens of our county. His sister Carrie was one of the early and successful school teachers of the county. In 1865 she taught the Beatrice Summer school and in 1866 she taught both the fall and winter terms in the old cottonwood, frame school-house in Beatrice, this writer having been much honored in being one of her pupils at the winter term. She became the wife of Louis T. Griggs, and though long since gathered to the bosom of Mother Earth both she and her husband are represented in the world of work by their children, George, Clifford, Albert, Kirk, and Mollie, all honored and useful members of society. Mr. Gale's son, Charles F., but recently deceased, was for many years prominent in the social and business life of the city of Beatrice.

The following narrative was written by Mr. Gale in 1876. Primarily it was intended as a history of old Clay county, but it is so largely devoted to the various phases of pioneer life as he saw and lived it as to impart to it historic value of a high order. It is first-hand matter and probably stands alone as a contemporary narrative of pioneer conditions in our county. It supplements to some extent other chapters of this volume, and as evidence it has the weight of an eye witness on most of the subjects considered by its author. For all these reasons, as well as from respect which the author of this work bears to the memory of Mr. Gale, his narrative is given place here. The interesting article is reproduced without formal marks of quotation.

HISTORY OF OLD CLAY COUNTY FROM ITS SETTLEMENT UP TO 1876
BY GEORGE GALE

In writing a history of this section of Nebraska, that is to say that part of it once comprised within the limits of Clay county and now attached to the counties of Lancaster and Gage, it will be necessary, or at least proper, to go back to the organization of the territorial government, and also to touch somewhat on the history of other and adjoining counties.

As is well known, the act of congress organizing the territories of Kansas and Nebraska was passed in the spring of 1854, thus opening up at once these two territories to settlement under the policy usually known as popular sovereignty, by which the question of freedom or slavery was left to a vote of the people at the time of forming state constitutions.

MR. AND MRS. GEORGE GALE

All this is necessary to be understood in order to understand why Nebraska, with a superior soil, climate and geographical position, was comparatively neglected by settlers, who agreed by common consent to make Kansas the battle-ground between freedom and slavery, and who rushed to that territory in order to assist in establishing such institutions as they personally approved.

Very little permanent settlement was made in Nebraska this year. Some towns along the Missouri river were located by parties who had been watching the land for years and waiting for it to come under the provisions of the preëmption laws. Omaha, Plattsmouth, Nebraska City, Brownville, and perhaps other towns were laid out this year.

The first session of the legislature of Nebraska was held this year, some surveying was done, and some few farm claims were taken near the river, but many of the settlers went back to Iowa or Missouri to winter.

In 1855 some farm claims were taken fifteen or twenty miles from the river, but nothing in the way of provisions was raised in this or the following year.

In 1856 people in search of first-class locations explored the country on the Nemaha, and as far west as upper Salt creek, but few, however, of the claims then taken were ever occupied by them, but were afterward taken up by others.

The first permanent settlement in Clay county was made on Salt creek by the Preys—father and sons—Mr. Davison, the Wallingfords, and others whose names are not now remembered, all of whom are now gone except the Preys.

These settlers were all driven out by the Indians in the fall of 1857. They wintered at Nebraska City and returned to their claims in the spring of 1858, but the Indians troubled them more or less for several years, as we shall have occasion to relate further on. They laid out the town of Olatha this year.

In 1857 a great many settlements were made in Clay county. On the Nemaha, Mr. John O. Adams settled early in the spring and put in and raised a crop of sod corn. Mr. John Stafford came this spring and also raised a crop. Mr. Golden and sons, Mr. H. Reynolds and brother, Charlie Hickock and, farther down the east branch, Mr. John Watson, Mr. William Freeborn, R. Swallow, B. J. Baker and others.

In July of this year came Stephen P. Shaw and sons—William, John, James, and Stephen—and James and William Silvernail. They located on the branch above Mr. Adams at Lacona, Jacob and Leroy Hildebrand also came this year, and settled on the branch known as Jake's creek, near Adams.

About the same time a settlement was made on Indian creek by E. C. Horner, Charley Austin, a gentleman named Phelps, H. W. Parker, besides others who proceeded to lay out the town of Austin, which now exists only on paper, if anywhere. Also, further down in Gage county, the Pethouds—father and son. Beatrice was also located and surveyed this season by what was and still is known as the Beatrice Town Company.

In November the Nemaha settlement was further augmented by the arrival of Egbert Shaw and John Lyons and their families. There was another settlement made this year on the head of the little Nemaha, by Mr. Noble, Mr. Rodencamp, Mr. Meecham and others, and I think they laid out a town near where Bennett now stands.

At the time these settlements were made in Clay county there had been raised in the state nothing of any consequence toward supporting the people. Everything had to be imported from the east. Those who had money could buy at the Missouri river anything they wanted but many had very little money, while some had to sell their best team or cow in order to live until a crop could be grown.

Some few who had their houses built went to the river and worked for those who had work to do and money to pay for it. However, the most of these supposed when they came that they had money enough to keep their families until they could get a crop and then make enough by farming or in some other way to pay for their land, for it must be borne in mind that there was no homestead law then. Their land was taken under the preëmption law and they did not expect the land would be brought into market for many years, and that perhaps before that time came congress would pass a homestead law and save them all further trouble. In this they deceived themselves, as they found to their great disgust a year or two afterward.

Although land could be taken from the first under the preëmption law it could not be entered at private sale until it had first been offered at public sale to the highest bidder. This being the case, the settlers felt perfectly safe with regard to their claims as long as the land was withheld from market. But in the summer of 1858, to their great astonishment and consternation, the land from the Missouri river to range 8 was advertised to be offered for sale in September. Only a few of the settlers were prepared to pay for their land, while most of them had no recourse but to hire a land warrant at forty per cent interest, for such were the very moderate terms of the gentlemen who petitioned the President to bring the land into market.

Of course they had the choice of selling their teams and fighting the battle bare-handed, or letting the matter take its own course and run the risk of their claims being bid on by speculators, and losing their land, and in some cases costly improvements besides. But as nearly every man thought his claim was the center of the universe, the very pivot around which all the rest of the world revolved, and that consequently it offered an irresistible temptation to some speculator to buy it, nearly all were frightened into buying land warrants on time, at forty per cent interest, and proving up their claims.

After this little game had been successfully played, the land was withdrawn from sale for one year. The next year, however, in 1859, it was all offered for sale as far west as to include Clay county. This produced very little excitement, people having recovered from their fright, and very little land was sold—perhaps none that was held under the preemption law. Some proved up and paid before the sale, and some let it run and took their land under the homestead law, in 1863.

We may as well say here that most of those who located borrowed land warrants on their claims lost them with all their improvements, and in some cases after paying interest at forty per cent for several years.

There were no roads at this time except Indian trails, nor bridges on the streams, and when they were obliged to go to the river or anywhere else, three or four would go together, traveling on the divides as much as possible, and when a stream had to be crossed they would take all the teams across except one, then run one of the wagons down the bank into the creek, then hitch on all the teams with chain enough to reach to the top of the bank, then pull the wagon out and then repeat the process on all the rest of the wagons.

But this was too much trouble for an everyday business and nearly every settler soon had a good bridge or a ford for his own use, which were always and for many years used by the public.

At the time of which we are treating, the settlers all used ox teams, and there were very few horses in the country.

The possession of a riding nag was an indication of the wealth of its owner, and the man who owned a horse team was set down at once as a blooded aristocrat.

In making long trips on the road they always carried their own provisions and bedding, and in winter feed for their teams. If the weather was fine they always camped out nights, but if it was cold or stormy they would always be welcome to spread their beds on the floor of some kind-hearted settler—Joe Sanders', the widow McKee's, Solonberger's, Brownell's, or almost any house from here to Nebraska City. But in the winter time Brownell's was the most popular place to stop of any on the road and your historian and nearly all of the Nemaha settlers have many times had experience of the hospitality of this genial, kind-hearted old gentleman. The old settlers of the Nemaha will never forget the nights they have lain on his floor, before the broad, open fireplace piled with blazing logs, and listened to the old gentleman's stories, and told others to match them until sometimes they would all fall asleep in the midst of a story, only to resume it at the same place in the morning.

Those were pleasant times to look back upon, but they seemed not so pleasant then, and probably if the same times were offered us now we should decline with many thanks.

These trips to the river, though not strictly pleasure parties, were occasions of considerable fun and enjoyment, provided the weather was good, but if the weather proved bad and stormy, the situation offered but few attractions, even to an old settler.

They always started on these trips in good weather, with the intention of making certain well known points each night to camp, and if no accident happened and the roads were good and if the weather was not too hot for the cattle, the points were sure to be made. Some of the most popular camping places with the Nemaha people were Syracuse ford, Brownell's, Rock ford, Delaware City, and afterward at Solenberger, Nursery Hill, Wilson Bridge, etc.

They generally managed to camp near enough to Nebraska City to go in, and get out again at night to the same place or, at least out of town. While a part of the men, and perhaps some of the women (for they liked to go to town just as well then as now), were gone, those left in the settlement looked after the families and stock of those who were gone. And when it was time for the absent ones to return, those at home would watch for the teams coming over the hill and would sometimes gather at the first house on the road to meet them and get the first news, receive their letters from friends east, and the children to receive their presents, for, in spite of poverty, something for them was sure to be found in some of the packages that came from the city.

As we have before remarked, there was a little sod corn raised in Clay county in 1857. Nearer to the river there was considerable, and it was sold for a good price to those who had not yet raised any. This served to demonstrate the fact that corn would grow in Nebraska, and to encourage the settlers to plant all they could the next year, when most bountiful crops of corn, potatoes, beans, pumpkins, squashes and all manner of garden vegetables were grown, and this was the last one and only good crop of sod corn grown in this section of country.

This success in farming solved the provision question so far as the raw material was concerned, but mills were needed to grind the corn. Several small mills were established at different places along the river this year or the year before, but the people here who were out of flour and out of money could not wait for the new crop to mature and dry sufficiently to grind. Thus they commenced living on the new corn as soon as it was in roasting ears, and as soon as they could get it dry enough to grind they hauled it to the river and had it ground, if they could find a mill that was in running order, for they were generally out of repair and sometimes our people would have to wait a week for their grinding; sometimes they would return without it and make an other trip for it; and in the meantime they would borrow meal or flour of each other until the entire stock of the whole settlement was exhausted—and then all would go to making hominy, grinding in coffee mills and Pounding in mortars or grating on tin pans, sometimes for weeks together until grinding could be had.

When the Austin mill started there was great rejoicing on the Nemaha, for now grinding could be had within from fifteen to twenty-five miles, and the trip could be made in two days. This mill only ran one day in a week and sometimes only one day in two weeks, but it proved a very convenient thing for us until we began to raise wheat, when we were again obliged to go to the city, or some other point on the river, or into

Iowa. Your historian and many others have been to Iowa to mill and been gone on the trip ten days.

The Beatrice mill was built in 1861 and burned in 1862, but it was rebuilt in 1863, and since that time there has been very little trouble about mills.

There are people who think we are not now very well provided with mill facilities, but it was worse during the days of the first settlements. One word more about the Austin mill. If from any cause the mill could not be started on the regular day, or the day had not been appointed, Mr. Austin would either ride over to the Nemaha or send a man to let us know when it would start, so that no one would come to the mill and be disappointed. Such men were millers in those days, but they are all dead, and they died poor.

The settlers commenced farming on a very small scale at first, raising garden vegetables, potatoes, etc., for their own use but nothing for sale for several years except corn, for which there was a market at Nebraska City, though after the first good crop prices were low.

In the meantime they had tried wheat to a small extent and it had not proved successful, and people had got the idea that the country was not adapted to wheat.

In the year 1858 news came of the discovery of gold near Pike's Peak, and this greatly raised the hopes of the people with regard to markets for their produce, which would not at this time pay the expense of hauling to an eastern market, but it was two or three years before their hopes were realized and the gold fields afforded a market for anything of consequence. In the meantime many of the settlers had become discouraged and had gone back to the east, to the mountains or to the war, and those who remained looked dubiously at the prospect of making homes here, with the result that there were actually less people in the territory in 1862 than there were in 1859, by about ten thousand, fully one-third of the people having left the territory.

The opening of the war had a very depressing influence on the affairs of Nebraska, especially the financial and business affairs. Coming as it did after a general failure of crops in 1860, on account of drouth, it found our people with little or nothing to sell and no market for that. It seemed as if the world had come to a stand-still. There were times when produce could not be exchanged for goods at Nebraska City, and even toward the close of the war, when confidence had become somewhat restored, it would take two bushels of wheat to buy a pound of coffee or a yard of brown sheeting, and many other things in proportion. Of course we did not put on much style in dress or live very luxuriously in any way. This state of things drove us from the Missouri river as a market and obliged us to look to the westward for the sale of our products.

There was at the opening of the war quite a large increasing population in Colorado that must be fed with produce from the east, and the people of Nebraska were quick to take advantage of this new market.

To illustrate to what expedients our people were driven during the war, take such instances as these. In the fall of 1862, I think it was, wheat was worth at Nebraska City, thirty-five cents and salt was eight dollars a barrel. How were the people to get salt? This is the way; they hitched up their teams and went to the salt basin on Salt creek, near where Lincoln now stands, scraped up the salt that rises to the surface and is crystalized by the action of the sun, hauled it home, dissolved it, purified it, boiled it down and made a very fine article of salt.

Not only were the people of this section, but of all South Platte, a part of Iowa, and the country westward to the mountains, to a great extent supplied with salt from this source. In fact manufactories of salt of considerable extent and capacity were established there, and quite a town was built up, all of which has long since disappeared.

They could not pay two dollars per pound for tobacco so they raised their own tobacco. They did not use coffee or tea every day. Sorghum syrup took the place of sugar, which was at one time two and a half pounds for a dollar. Some farmers who had heavy teams hauled their produce to Denver or went into a regular freighting business; others moved on to the lines of travel, and established ranches for the accommodation of the travel, while others staid on their farms and raised produce and hauled to the ranches and sold it, the produce being mostly corn, potatoes, pork, eggs and butter. At this time hundreds of farms were abandoned and left uncultivated in all parts of the territory.

The west was our principal market until the building of the Union Pacific Railroad, which destroyed the market for corn and drove the people of this county to raising wheat, for which we had now a pretty good market eastward.

The early settlers had the idea that wheat would not do well here until, in 1862 or 1863, some astonishingly large and good crops were raised, but for the want of a paying market very little was raised for sale until about 1866. Since that time wheat has been the principal crop grown for sale, and it was for many years considered the surest and best paying crop that could be grown.

The war found our people almost unanimous for sustaining the government. Some few secessionists were found along the river, but they speedily left Nebraska for more congenial climes. In this county a few opposed the coercion of the states, but they were generally very mild in the expression of their views.

During the winter of 1860-1861 the legislature passed a law for organizing the militia of the territory into companies, regiments, brigades and divisions, for purposes of defence in case of danger. Accordingly an election was called by proclamation, and those persons liable to military duty were required to meet at their respective county seats and organize one or more companies, according to population, by electing officers. In Clay county the able-bodied men met at Austin some day in June, 1861, and organized a company by electing for captain, Delos Mills, of Salt Creek; first lieutenant, James Silvernail, of the Nemaha; second lieutenant, H. W. Parker, of Austin; and a full set of non-commissioned officers.

Clay county had, at this time, a population of about one hundred and fifty or perhaps a trifle more, of whom about forty were voters. At the first election after the organization of the county, Nemaha precinct, composed of about one-fourth of the territory of the county, cast seven votes, being the full vote of the precinct, and as late as the division of the county the highest number of votes polled was thirteen; most of the other precincts had more.

We do not know the number or the names of all those who enlisted in the army at the different times under the different calls of the president for volunteers, but Clay county, although a frontier county, furnished a large number of soldiers, and the territory kept her quota full under all calls, without resorting to the draft. Among those who enlisted under the first call for three hundred thousand, were John Hilman, Jr., William Shaw, Egbert Shaw, James I. Shaw, William Ilaud, Charlie Austin (who went east and enlisted in an Ohio regiment), William Rudruff, and two young men on the Blue whose names are forgotten. These all, with the exception of Charlie Austin, enlisted in the Nebraska regiment and went to the front. None of them was killed in the service except William Shaw, who was killed by an accident, at St. Louis, in 1863.

Many others served for the defense of the frontier for different terms and at different times, among whom were Thaddeus Hillman, John Stafford, Nelson Adams, two young men named Etherton, on Salt creek, James Iler and several others whose names are not now known, as they were new comers and did not return to the country after their term of service expired. One son of John Hilman enlisted in an Iowa regiment and was killed in the first battle he was engaged in.

A history of this section would not be complete without an account of the division of Clay county and the distribution of its territory between the counties of Lancaster and Gage. All history has for its object the instruction of the present and future by the lessons and experiences of the past, and for this reason the history of the division of Clay county must be written.

As early as the fall of 1863, rumors of a plan for dividing Clay county began to reach the people of the several settlements of the county, but this did not arouse much interest, from the fact that no one seemed to know anything definite about it, or where the rumors came from, and further it was well known that scarcely any one in Clay county favored such division. But soon men in Beatrice would drop a hint now and then to feel the pulse of our people in this matter, but they found them all against any such scheme and for some time we heard nothing more about it, and we supposed the thing was dead. But in the fall of 1864 the matter took such shape that there could be no mistaking the fact that there were only two or three in the extreme southern and about the same number in the extreme northern part who favored the plan or assisted in carrying it out; and they were all interested in town-site speculations which the scheme was supposed to favor.

At this time Clay, Gage, and Johnson counties formed one representative district, and John Cadman managed to get the nomination for representative from this district. All this was apparent, still but few knew that this was a part of the plan to defraud the people of their rights. The plan was soon discovered, but too late to do anything of any consequence toward defeating Cadman's election. In fact, nothing could have been done under any circumstances.

This man Cadman lived on Salt creek at Saltillo, on the extreme north side of the county. He owned a town-site further down the creek, where the insane asylum has since been built, and this, if Clay county was divided, would be very near the center of Lancaster and of course would be likely with shrewd management to become the county seat of Lancaster, which was not yet located.

On the south the proprietors and people of Beatrice never felt quite sure that they could hold the county seat of Gage county at that place, because it was within six miles of the north line of the county and considerably to the west of the center of the county, while the geographical center lay on the Big Blue river and was in every way as good a place to build a town as at Beatrice. Consequently the people of that town took an active interest in the conspiracy and worked for Cadman's nomination and election.

A nomination by the Republican party was at that time nearly equivalent to an election, but Cadman did not feel safe to keep still, so he made a canvass of the three counties, telling the people of Clay and Johnson counties that if elected he would do nothing in the legislature looking to a division of the county unless he had a petition (which he felt doubtful of getting) to present, from at least two-thirds of the legal voters of the county, asking such division. The people of these counties knowing that there were not, altogether, a dozen people who would sign such a petition, he was elected.

At that time the capital was at Omaha, there were no facilities for travel as there are now, and in the winter we scarcely ever heard what was going on in the legislature until the session was over. So it was this time. Some time in March, 1865, we learned that the legislature had adjourned and one of the acts passed was an act to divide Clay county, giving the territory to Gage and Lancaster counties. The people of Clay county were thunderstruck. They had not expected such a thing. There had been no petition circulated or signed and the people were unable to conceive of such infamy and political rascality as this act revealed. It seems that the legislature had obliterated this county from the map of Nebraska at the demand of a small ring of speculators, without the consent or even knowledge of the people of the county, thus adding insult to the other wrongs consummated by this outrage.

In justice to the senators and representatives from other parts of the state, it should be stated that, in answer to our reproaches, they said that there was a petition presented properly signed and which appeared to be perfectly regular, asking them to pass such an act and they supposed that they were doing a favor to the whole people of Clay county—which proves that a forgery was committed.

The people of the county did not propose to submit to such treatment as this, but supposed that on a true representation of all the facts to the next legislature, supported by a petition of nearly the whole of the legal voters of the county, that the act would be repealed and the old county restored. Acting upon this supposition and in this belief, in the winter of 1866-1867 some of our people started out and secured the signature of very nearly every legal voter in the old county, but the work was hindered by the inclemency of the weather, by high water in the streams and by lack of facilities for traveling over the country, so that by the time the work was done and the petition was ready to send off, the legislature was adjourned and we were disappointed.

This so discouraged some that, though they most earnestly wished the old county restored, they could not be induced to take any trouble upon themselves for this purpose on the chances presented. Others never gave up their hope of remedy or ceased their efforts to attain it.

Another effort to obtain justice was made in the winter of 1868-1869, when our petition was denied, at the demand of Lancaster and Gage county delegations. Still another effort was made in 1871, when a petition signed by over four hundred legal voters was presented by Colonel H. Rhodes, representative from Johnson county, while the measure was supported by members from other counties; but, although the justice of our cause was unquestioned, we could not offer the inducement to members for votes for our measure, that Beatrice and Lincoln could for votes against it, and they refused to grant our petition. From that time all hope seemed to have died out until the session of 1875, when another effort was made for the lost cause, but with no better success than before.

In giving a history of the county division and efforts for restoration, through a period of ten years or more, we have neglected many topics of interest, which we will now proceed to take up under separate and appropriate heads.

EDUCATION

As before stated, the cause of education in Clay county looked very discouraging in the early days. The people were poor; there was no public-school fund to draw from then and very little taxable property, the land being nearly all in the hands of Uncle Sam.

The subject was taken up by the several settlements and treated according to the means and ability of the people. The first step was to form and organize school districts. The first school districts were composed of precincts of from three to five government townships, each with a township board of education whose duty it was to form sub-districts, the law not permitting the formation of a sub-district with less than ten children of school age.

There was no fund for building school houses, but the people subscribed according to their means and built log school houses, made caves or sod houses in which to teach the young idea how to shoot. Teachers' wages were low and were paid by subscription or rate bill. There were three districts laid off in Clay county in 1862—one on the Nemaha, one on Salt creek, and one on Indian creek and the Blue river—which were organized. The one on the Nemaha was divided into three sub-districts in the course of the years, but for various reasons they did not get schools running in any of them until 1864.

The first school taught on the Nemaha was taught, in the old log school house, until lately standing near James Silvernail's, by Miss Carrie Gale, now Mrs. L. T. Griggs, of Beatrice. School cost something in those days when the expense was wholly borne by three or four in each sub-district. Since that time schools have been taught regularly in nearly all the districts, both before and since the county division.

Since 1865 and 1866 the country has settled up more rapidly than before, and schools and school houses have been multiplied accordingly, and people coming to this state now need have no fears that their children need go without instruction, as our public schools will compare favorably with those of any state.

SETTLEMENTS

The settlement of this state was very slow during the war; from 1861 to 1864 a few came, mostly from Missouri, being run out by bushwackers or leaving to escape the draft. A few of these stopped in this county but most of them stayed near the Missouri river. They are nearly all gone now, some to one place and some to another. Mr. Isaac Mayo is the only one left on the Nemaha. There are a few yet on Salt creek and near Firth, of whom we may mention the Grims, Jacksons, Montgomerys and a few others. Also about this time or a little before, came from Indiana Mr. William McLane and brothers and other relatives. Further down Salt creek, Mr. Delos Mills, Mrs. Boydston, Mrs. Warner, Mr. Keyes, D. S. Brown, Fred and Carl Krul, Mr. Huskin and others. On the Nemaha, George Drown, William Curtis, H. C. Barmole, and a little later the Moore Brothers, J. H. Lynch, George Lykes and Henry Stoops, and soon after James Sykes.

On Indian creek and the Blue, the settlers were George Grant and sons, who for some time resided at Austin, and who moved to Turkey creek about this time; and near him Robert Nicholas, James and William Plucknett, and, on Clatonia and the Blue, William Van Cleit, James Krusie, Alfred Snell, and others.

After the war the settlement was rapid, and your historian was unable to keep an account of all who came, much less to name them. For several years after the war a great many soldiers found themselves, to use a vulgar but significant expression, loose-footed, and the attractions of Nebraska as an agricultural state becoming known at the east, Nebraska received a large accession of this honored class of citizens from other states.

Through all this immediate section all the claims on the streams containing bottom land or timber, were taken up in 1866 or before, and the next year prairie claims were taken, in fact early all the homestead land in the county was taken.

One thing that delayed the settlement of the section of country about Firth was the withdrawal of large tracts of land from market by the government, for railroad purposes, but this is now seen to be an advantage to the country in keeping it out of the hands of other speculators who are still holding in Gage county large tracts, above the means of settlers.

Since 1867 the improvement of the country has been very rapid, embracing the building of towns and railroads, which properly comes under another head, to which we will now refer.

TOWNS AND RAILROADS

As has been already stated, a number of towns were laid out in Clay county at an early day, but none of them ever amounted to anything. They were generally located without reference to any natural advantages of position except, perhaps, a beautiful site for building purposes, but as such sites could be had anywhere, it was not of sufficient importance to build up a town.

There was not at that time, or for many years afterward, anything in the county to build up towns. There was no water power in the county to encourage manufacturing operations, there was but one route of travel overland through the country, viz; through the Salt creek settlement from Nebraska City to Denver, Colorado, but the travel was too light and too transient to build up the town Olatha. But the principal trouble was that here were not people or capital enough to give anything a good start.

When Clay county was divided, and for years afterward, there was absolutely no town of any kind in the county. Nebraska City was the only town that could be called a market for the people of this section until about 1868.

John Adams, on the Nemaha, used to do some blacksmithing for the neighbors. He got so that he could do a good job of almost any kind, and was always willing to oblige his neighbors. John W. Prey, of Salt creek, used also to do some blacksmith work, and mend plows and wagons for his neighbors. John Stafford, on the Nemaha, made and mended shoes and boots. George Gale used to make ropes and twine, Alfred Gale used to make baskets and John B. Shaw used to make brooms. Aside from these mechanical arts practiced at home, all business had to be done a long distance from home.

After the location of the capital at Lincoln there was a market there for some of the lighter kinds of produce, and most kinds of merchandise could be bought there nearly as cheaply as at Nebraska City, but did not afford us a market for grain or other heavy produce, from the fact that there were no railroads to get it away, and up to the time of the completion of the Midland Pacific Railroad to Lincoln, in 1871, the farmers hauled all their grain to Nebraska City, and bought all or most of their heavy goods, lumber, and building material, salt, hardware, machinery, implements, etc., there. The people of this section never did much business at Beatrice until within a few years past.

The first town within the limits of Clay county that was of any use to the people was Bennett, on the Missouri Pacific Railroad. This town afforded a market for grain and made a fair trading point for the farmers of the northeastern section of the old county.

When the Burlington & Missouri River Railroad was built, a little station and trading point was established on Cheese creek, in the northwestern part of the old county, and called Highland. Other little towns were started on the Beatrice branch of the Burlington & Missouri River Railroad just outside of the limits of Clay county, and Crete, Wilber, and DeWitt are a great accommodation to many of the people of the county.

Some years previous to this, a mill was built and a town laid out in Johnson county by W. H. Mann, of Sterling, Illinois and called Sterling, but the town never made much growth until the building of the railroad. It was and still is of great advantage to some of the people of the southeastern part of the county. None of these roads run through old Clay county except to cut across a corner of it.

In 1869 the legislature offered, as a bounty for the building of railroads in Nebraska, to give twenty thousand acres of land to any company who should, by the first of January, 1871, build and operate ten miles of first-class railroad in Nebraska. About this time a company was formed and incorporated, called the Nemaha Valley Railroad Company, for the purpose of building a railroad from Rulo to Lincoln. This company and several others commenced building railroads and built ten miles of road and claimed the bounty of twenty thousand acres of land.

The legislature being in session at that time, a board of commissioners was appointed to examine and report on the several roads claiming the bounty, and on their report the legislature, while it accepted some of them, rejected the claim of the Nemaha Valley Company on the ground that it could not be rated as a first-class railroad. About this time the company became bankrupt, the work was abandoned, and the hopes of the people were frustrated.

But it was not long that this rich valley was to languish for want of railroad facilities, for a company having the means to do the work took hold of the matter and the result was the building of the Atchison & Northern Railroad from Atchison, Kansas, to Lincoln, Nebraska, in 1871-1872, thus opening up the entire valley of the Big Nemaha to the commerce of the world. Before this time this section had become pretty well settled, large farms had been opened and the want of an outlet by rail for the immense quantities of produce grown was severely felt; and when the road was completed, its benefits were immediately felt and appreciated by the people of the valley. The effects of the building of this road were to cause new farms to be opened, and old ones to be enlarged and improved, as well as the building of towns and the rise of real estate along the whole line to the distance of many miles.

Among the towns built on this road are Adams, Firth, and Hickman, all in old Clay county and consequently within the limits of this history. These towns were located and surveyed by the company.

Adams

Adams was laid out on the north half of the northeast quarter of section 27 town 6, range 8, in Gage county, in the spring of 1873, John O. Adams giving the company a half-interest in the land. William Curtis built the first house the same spring and this has been used by B. W. Anderson for a store and dwelling to the present time. After harvest of the same year Messrs. Adams and Curtis built the warehouse which is now used by R. A. Kenyon for shipping grain.

In the fall of 1874 R. A. Kenyon built and opened a store and in the fall of 1875 he enlarged his house and moved his family there, where he still keeps a store and does a good business buying grain.

The postoffice was established in 1872, with William Curtis postmaster. Mr. Burget opened a blacksmith shop there in the spring of 1875. Adams is a good point for business and would do a great deal if the railroad company would improve the facilities for doing it.

Firth

Firth was laid out on the northwest quarter of section 35, town 7, range 7, in July 1872, on land belonging to the Burlington & Missouri Railroad Company in Nebraska, which gave the Atchison & Northern a half-interest in the town.

The company commenced making improvements and others commenced building almost immediately. The first building aside from the company's improvements was a small house which was used as a saloon. Then followed the section house and depot, and A, Ellsworth's store, which was the first store in Firth. Then Lyman Wood's dwelling, then Lon Morgan's house and blacksmith shop, Champion's dwelling, Clement & Everest's store, Sweeney's dwelling, and Champion's warehouse. Albert Brown was the first station agent and operator for the railroad company. D. E. Champion commenced buying grain the 30th of September, 1872. Sweeney commenced a few days later and they soon bought together and continued together for about two years, when Champion concluded to retire from business and is not doing anything now except running a livery stable, a land agency, building houses to rent, selling implements and machinery, and running a hardware store.

Improvements from this time were rapid. Dwellings and business houses sprang up as if by magic. First one and then another branch of business was introduced, but these could scarcely keep pace with the wants of the country in their several lines. The Chicago Lumber Company established a lumber yard early in the year 1873. J. B. Hawley was agent, and was succeeded in 1875 by T. B. Barnes.

Dr. Feilds, the station agent, was the first physician to locate in Firth, followed by Dr. Murphy, and later by Dr. Robinson. Dr. Murphy brought on the first stock of drugs and started a drug store in the building now occupied as the postoffice. He sold out the stock to William Phillips, who took the stock to Hickman and sold out there. Murphy and Jewell had previously opened with a larger stock of drugs, oils, paints, etc., in Champion's new building, and sold out to W. H. Moore, who later ran the business in another building.

Clement & Everest opened the second store in Firth, occupying the stand on the corner of First and May streets east of Ellsworth's store, which was burned in November 1873, with a part of the stock.

Clement & Everest sold out to Bailey & Barnhouse. Bailey sold out to Barnhouse, who for a while ran the business alone, then sold out to Bailey Flickinger.

The first hardware store in Firth was opened by the Reed Brothers, who sold out to Champion & Hoisington. In the spring of 1874 John and George Brownell opened a new store and after a number and variety of changes they were still found in the business. In 1873 L. R. Horrum started a harness shop. He ran it for a while, and was succeeded by Charlie Flickinger, and he again by Mr. Horrum.

Spellman commenced business in Firth early in 1874. Henry Golden built and kept the first hotel. Smith & Mellinghouse started the second lumber yard in 1874 but sold out and went into the grain business.

Witzig Brothers started the second blacksmith shop and later Mr. William Cook the third. In 1875 Mr. Phinney put up the first and only mill in Firth, then sold out to John Brooks, who still runs it. In the spring of 1875 Clement & Davis started the first furniture store.

Firth since its location has grown very rapidly, partly from the fact that the country was well settled by an energetic and thrifty class of farmers who were greatly in need of business facilities, and partly from the fact that the business men of Firth were an enterprising set of men, who when they set out to build a town meant business. Such men of course will always win.

The buildings of Firth, both public and private, are of a better and more substantial character than are usually found in a new town, and the known character of its people and everything about the town, its position and surroundings point to a career of prosperity in the future.

The public school house is an honor to the town, and might be pointed to with pride by the citizens of far more pretentious towns than Firth. It cost two thousand dollars. The building of such school houses is an indication of the intelligence, liberality and far sightedness of the citizens. Mr. Beams had the honor of being the first to teach in this house.

T. S. Elsworth may be said to have been the first resident in Firth, as he was the first postmaster and merchant. Henry Golden built and kept the first hotel, D. E. Champion was the first to buy grain, Dr. Fields was the first doctor. L. N. Morgan was the first blacksmith. The first birth and the first death also occurred in his family. The oldest man in Firth is Mr. Clement, aged seventy-five years. The largest man is Mr. Champion, weight four hundred pounds. The best looking is Mr. Wood, the postmaster.

Firth has so far been remarkably free from disasters or calamities. The burning of Mr. Elsworth's house is the only fire to record since the foundation of the town. The unprecedented rise of the Great Nemaha in July, 1875, did some damage to the residents of the town, as well as to the farmers along the creek. Such a flood had never been known before since the country has been settled. The water was four or five feet deep on the bottoms.

INDIANS

When Nebraska was first settled there were several tribes of Indians in the territory. These Indians were settled (if Indians can settle) on reservations, supported and under the care of the government agents and missionaries, and were generally supposed to be friendly to the settlers. They were not allowed to leave their reservations without a permit from their agents, but being generally peaceable they were generally permitted to hunt over the country the greater part of the time.

These tribes were the Pawnees, Otoes, and Omahas, and they were friendly to each other (although they would steal each other's ponies) and were much afraid of the Sioux, Arapahoes, Kiowas, Comanches and Cheyennes, who roamed over the country to the north, southwest and west, and who occasionally made a raid on the reservation Indians, scalped a few and ran off their ponies. These were called wild Indians to distinguish them from the reservation Indians, who were supposed to have made some progress in civilization.

The most trouble the settlers had with these Indians was through their frightening the women and children, for they supposed that an Indian was an Indian anyway, and indeed they needed watching whenever they were around, for they would steal anything they could lay hands on, sometimes in the presence of the owners, and whenever they had been unsuccessful in hunting, they would steal cattle and hogs, or anything eatable. They would dig up seed potatoes and eat them, even after they were up and had made considerable growth. They would scarcely offer any violence to the whites unless they were nearly starved, and they were resisted in their thefts. A man could generally drive off any number of them, and women have been known to do it, but generally they were so much frightened at the sight of the Indians that they would give them anything that they demanded. The settlers on Salt creek had more trouble with them than any others in Clay county, because the Pawnees claimed that they had not had their pay for the land on that. In April, 1857, the Pawnees came on to that settlement and drove the settlers all away and they did not return to their claims until toward the spring of 1858. Again, in May, 1859, they became troublesome and stole some cattle, and the whites killed and scalped one of them and drove the rest away, but the settlers always lived in fear of them.

Soon after this the Arapahoes drove the Pawnees across the Missouri river into Iowa, where they remained some time, not daring to return. They also burned the Pawnee village on the Platte. When the Arapahoes returned, a part of them came through the Salt creek settlement and committed some depredations, stealing stock, burning houses, etc., and tried to carry off Miss Rebecca Prey, now Mrs. Henry Stoops, but were forced to give her up after carrying her about eighty rods.

On the Nemaha, Alfred Gale's house was attacked by Otoes in June or July of the same year, when he was alone in it, forcing the door and overpowering him and a part of them holding him while the others robbed the house of every thing that was eatable, and did not leave him enough for breakfast. The attack was made in the dusk of the evening. He had just lent his revolver and had not the least thing in the house to defend himself with.

The next day they went to John Lyon's place and tried to run off his stock, but he and J. I. Shaw were breaking prairie about a mile from them and saw them driving the cattle. They started after them and saved the stock, but one cow had two arrows shot into her about eighteen inches, but she lived and was a good cow for many years.

In 1860 seven Otoes came to the house of your historian, who would not let them in but loaded his gun with buckshot and drove them away from his stock, when they went to John B. Shaw's and finding his cattle out of sight, ran them off and killed one of them.

On Indian creek and the Blue, they were very troublesome, stealing stock and robbing houses that happened to be left alone. In July, 1861, there was a great Indian scare on the Big Blue and the Nemaha. Some way or another a story came that the Cheyennes and Sioux were coming this way, killing and burning everything they met. What the story sprung from this writer does not remember, but it created some excitement on the Nemaha. A meeting was called at John O. Adams' to consult as to what should be done, and it was decided to load up our wagons and go to the river and camp near some town until it was over, and a day was set to start.

Mr. Adams buried his blacksmith tools, and some other things that he could not take were otherwise hidden. George Gale hid his cook-stove in the brush, and some other equally foolish things were done, but before the day came to start they all, without consultation, concluded not to go and they soon found there was no occasion for alarm.

There was no more trouble with Indians in this section until the great Indian scare of August, 1864, when the Sioux broke out and killed every man and either killed or carried away every woman and child that they could get at on the Platte and little Blue, for about three hundred miles in one day, and ran off the stock and burned the ranches. Some of the ranches were well armed and defended and they escaped with only a scare.

The news of this massacre reached Beatrice and the Nemaha a day or two after it occurred, with the addition that the Indians were coming on to Beatrice, and meant to burn the towns along the Missouri river.

This news nearly made some people crazy, they loaded a few things into their wagons, gathered up their stock and started for the river. Some, nearly all, I believe, left the north branch of the Nemaha before we on the south branch heard the news. Some of these never came back on the Nemaha again, the others returned in the course of the fall.

None left the south branch at this time. In Beatrice the scare was greater than on the Nemaha. While some prepared for defense and sent out runners and scouts to find out the truth and bury those killed at the ranches, others never waited for anything, but hitched up their teams and started for the east as fast as they could go. One man drove so fast that he spoiled his team. On Salt creek all got ready to leave and some did leave and sold their land and did not return for several years, and others never came back.

OLD SETTLERS

Here is a list of the oldest settlers of the territory belonging to old Clay county, by precincts, commencing at the northeastern corner of the county.

Lancaster County

Bennett—Messrs. Rodencamp, Meecham, and Nobles, 1857.
Saltillo—J. L. Davison, Joseph Weeks, C. L. Bristo, all long since gone, so that Mr. Keyes is the oldest permanent settler, 1856.
Centerville—John D. Prey and sons, John W., Thomas R., William L., and James, David E., and George Prey, and J. F. Goodwin, 1856.
Highland—George Lougton, 1865.
Olive Branch—John and Robert Falkner, 1864.
Buda—H. Boone and Mr. Rieurd, 1865.
South Pass—William McLain, Frank and William Lorsh, and William Greer, 1864.
Panama—Curren Moore and James Platt, 1866.

Gage County

Adams—John O. Adams, 1857.
Nemaha—George Sykes, 1865.
Highland—McCollum or M. Weaver, 1867.
Clatonia—William VanCleif, 1859.
Grant—George Grant and sons, 1860.
Holt—E. C. Austin, Charley Austin, Mr. Phelps, H. W. Parker 1857, now all gone, and the oldest permanent settler is not known.
Bear Creek—John Wilson, 1858.
Hooker—John Hillman, 1860.

Alfred Gale is the longest resident in Nebraska of any person on the Nemaha, and, with the exception of the Preys on Salt creek, of any in the county. He left Kenosha, Wisconsin, in September 1856, on foot, carrying a knapsack and gun, which he carried on foot all the way to Omaha and to Nebraska City, averaging thirty-three miles per day.

CHAPTER XIX

GROWTH OF BEATRICE FROM BEGINNING TO 1870

A HARD WINTER — COMPANY ASSETS — PAP'S CABIN — MUMFORD'S CABIN — ENTRY OF THE TOWNSITE — POPULATION IN 1870 — COMING OF THE RAILROADS — FIRST SCHOOL HOUSE — FIRST BRIDGE ACROSS THE BIG BLUE — THE GOVERNMENT LAND OFFICE — IMPROVED CONDITIONS — FIRST UNITED STATES MAIL — THE STAGE ROUTES — BEATRICE OF THE SIXTIES

Few of the Townsite Company remained in Beatrice during the winter of 1857-1858. The enterprise, however, could not be wholly abandoned for even a short period of time without jeopardizing the rights of the association to the land selected as a townsite; moreover, as the association had gone through the form of organizing the county, with Beatrice as the county seat, it was considered important that some, at least, of the members of the association, including the county officials, should remain on guard. Finally it was agreed that Albert Towle, one of the county commissioners, should bring his family from Nebraska City to Beatrice, and with Bennett Pike, Jefferson B. Weston, Gilbert T. Loomis, M. W. Ross, and Oliver Townsend (who had, by assignment, succeeded to the rights of his brother, Dr. Justus Townsend, in the townsite, and who had joined the company in October), occupy the company building. During the long, cold winter Ross died, his being the first death in the county. His body was buried in the old burial ground, between Indian creek and Glenover school house, which for several years constituted the cemetery for Beatrice and surrounding country.

Those who remained in Beatrice for the winter possessed only a meager supply of provisions, but it was thought to be sufficient, with what nature provided, to last through the winter. Besides it was considered that, as a trip could be made to Brownville in a week's time, there could be no danger of starvation. The autumn days were short and a winter of great severity soon set in. As the holidays approached it became evident that it would be necessary to procure a fresh supply of food for both man and beast. Loomis possessed the only team in the company and he volunteered to make a trip to Brownville, and return as soon as possible with such supplies as were thought to be necessary to last through the winter. A common purse of such funds as the small company possessed was placed in his hands, and he was directed to go beyond Brownville into Missouri, where it was thought supplies might be procured cheaper. He was detained by the severity of the weather and was unable to return to his companions for more than a month. The occupants of "Pap's Cabin" saw their stock of provisions running lower and lower, each day bringing a visible diminution in their means of subsistence. They wondered anxiously if Loomis would ever return and went so far as to even question his honesty. The seriousness of the situation is illustrated by an incident which has been handed down from that distant day.

The family of Mr. Towle occupied the east room in the cabin and what passed for an upstairs, while the young men kept bachelors' hall in the west end. The bachelors had organized a sort of coöperative association for housekeeping purposes only, by which each took a weekly turn as cook and housekeeper. The day before Loomis returned was Sunday; the larder in the bachelors' end of the building was completely cleaned out; Mother Hubbard's cupboard was not barer. It was Pike's turn at the household duties. At the proper hour for assuming his duties, he failed to arise. When urged to proceed with the breakfast, he very logically argued that in the absence of anything to cook, breakfast was out of the question. An animated conversation ensued in which the condition of affairs was thoroughly exposed, to the enlightenment, as well as the amusement perhaps, of the occupants of the east end of the cabin. Upstairs, or more properly in the attic, the provident Mrs. Towle had suspended on nails two fair sized pieces of dried beef. A conference between her and her husband ensued, in which the relief of the famine prevailing in the west end of the cabin was agreed upon. Mr. Towle noiselessly climbed the ladder to the attic and taking one piece of the dried beef, crossed the loose floor to a point directly over the bed where Mr. Pike lay, and stealthily removing a board, dropped the beef on the breast of that gentle man, who, with ready wit, exclaimed, "Thank God, the ravens have brought us food." The arrival of Loomis removed the fear as well as the danger of starvation. It is related, however, that on account of the scarcity of meat during the latter portion of the winter, these young, college-bred bachelors did not find it beneath their dignity to search the woods for the festive raccoon, whose flesh, though eaten with relish, they never mistook for a delicacy. Spring brought complete relief, and the colonists for the first time were able to appreciate the fact that the woods, the prairies and streams about them abounded in food for both man and beast.

A number of the company returned during the spring and summer of 1858, and accessions were made from homeseekers, such as Patrick Burke, the first blacksmith, Ed. Cartwright, the noted fisherman, P. M. Favor and others. A little of the prairie on the nearby claims of members of the company was broken and planted to corn, melons and vegetables, and when the second winter came, plenty smiled on every hand.

The transition from a few covered wagons and a tent, from "Pap's Cabin" and a saw mill, in 1857, to a modern city of approximately twelve thousand inhabitants in 1918, was of course painfully slow. At first there was little at hand which by any stretch of the imagination could be regarded as valuable material for the upbuilding of a city. Supplies beyond the bare necessities of life were scarce. Brownville was the nearest trading point and between here and there lay sixty miles of prairie, practically uninhabited; the road thither was little better than a wandering trail across a prairie waste. After crossing Bear creek at a point nearly a mile north of the State Institution for Feeble Minded Youth, there was, as late as 1869 and 1870, not a single dwelling house or a place where drinking water could be obtained until Yankee creek was reached, near Crab Orchard. Settlers began to come into the county in 1858, locating usually along the streams, where wood and water could be obtained. They were mostly single men, or a husband and wife, and after spending a portion of the summer on their claims they usually returned to Missouri river towns and settlements to await the coming of spring.

At Beatrice the only tangible asset of any value possessed by the Townsite Company was the steam saw mill purchased in Omaha in May, 1857, and even this mill at first figured as a liability. At the fourth meeting of the association, on July 28, 1857, the following financial report was read:

MILL REPORT
Dr.

Original cost of mill	$2,750.00
Freight on the same	566.50
Cost of hauling mill	548.15
Cost of truck	75.00

Cr.

Paid on mill	500.00
Paid on freight	542.30
Paid on hauling	273.15

For some time this old steam mill was a source of worry to the members of the association, and possibly of some contention. The chief difficulty apparently was to find some one competent to set up and run it, but by the beginning of 1858 it was in effective operation. On the 28th day of May in that year, at a meeting of the members of the association, J. B. Weston, the agent of the company having the enterprise in charge, reported that the lumber sold from the mill amounted to $383.38. "Of this sum" he says, "five dollars in specie is in the hands of the agent." Once in successful operation, the old company steam mill, which was the first manufacturing enterprise of the county, excluding the government mill on the Otoe and Missouri Indian reservation, for many years supplied not only Beatrice but also a large area of the surrounding country with lumber of every kind and dimension, white oak, walnut, hackberry, cottonwood, the last, however, being the main reliance for building purposes. This mill did custom work on the toll system; that is, the party who hauled saw logs to it rarely if ever paid cash for the services of the sawyer, but gave in payment part of the lumber manufactured from his logs. This system has long since been abolished in Nebraska, either by law or custom, probably on account of its inherent temptation to dishonesty. The owner of the logs frequently delivered them at the mill in the winter, and at times when there was great congestion in the mill yard he might be compelled to wait many weeks before his turn came to have his logs made into lumber. He was without adequate means for checking the milling of his logs and was almost compelled to accept what the owner or lessee of the mill turned out to him. The settlers were rarely satisfied with what they received.

But with all its imperfections and the defects of the tolling system, the old company mill was not only a great convenience to the settlers but was also a positive asset in the settlement and development of the county. When Fordyce Roper, in 1861, erected the first flouring mill at Beatrice and placed a dam across the river by which to obtain power for his enterprise, he either purchased or leased the old steam saw mill from the townsite company and changed it to a water-driven mill. He operated it in connection with his flouring mill until 1869, when William E. Hill, of Nebraska City, opened a lumber yard at the corner of Fourth and Court streets and placed it in charge of William Survoss. This soon put an end to the old saw mill of pioneer days.

As already noted, the first building erected in Beatrice was the company house, which afterward became widely and favorably known as "Pap's Cabin." When the association adjourned in Omaha on May 21st, to meet in Beatrice, July 27, 1857, a number of the members of the association made their way to the townsite in June, and immediately began the erection of this building. It was located on what was afterward designated on the original town plat as block forty-six, a block which is now entirely owned and occupied by the Chicago, Burlington & Quincy Railroad Company as a site for its passenger depot. In its original state the block comprised a tract of land which terminated abruptly on the north in a steep bank that ran down six or eight feet to Ella street, which was then a flat swale leading to the river. The south third of the block also lay in a wide depression, which extended on the south nearly across Court street. This depression also led to the river, narrowing to a deep channel just before it entered that stream, where the east abutment of the present Court street bridge is located. On the south bank of this channel stood the old saw mill, a trifle north of where Black Brothers' magnificent merchant mill now stands. On the west side of the block the ground fell away rapidly toward the river, but on the east it formed part of a beautiful plateau, reaching to Third street.

After Mr. Towle moved his family to Beatrice, in the autumn of 1857, this building, which had been partly completed, was donated to him as a residence and was occupied by this genial and influential citizen as a family residence, postoffice, court room, village inn, election booth, and as the general meeting place for the entire community, until 1867, when it was sold to Job Buchanan, by whom it was eventually transferred to the Burlington Railroad Company.

The second building erected in the hamlet of Beatrice was Isma Mumford's residence and hotel building. This was located on block forty-seven, and was a story and a half, hewed-log structure, containing five or six rooms. Though suffering many modifications, this building still remains; it is just north of the Butler House and is owned and occupied by W. W. Scott as a storage building.

Beginning with 1858, a number of buildings were erected, some log, some slab and some of sawed timber. Orr Stevens had moved from the neighborhood of Austin's Mill, on Indian creek, at that time known as Stevens creek, and had settled on lot one, block forty-six. Dr. Reynolds and Oliver Townsend had a little log hut on the south side of Court street, between Third and Fourth and near them were Patrick Burke's blacksmith shop and slab shanty where his family lived. There were also a few other rude structures of which no one now remembers the use or ownership, and no reliable record exists by which their location can be ascertained. In September, 1859, when this writer first saw Beatrice, it was a mere huddle of log and slab shanties, with scarcely an effort toward a building of any pretensions. Aside from "Pap's Cabin" and the Mumford building, the most pretentious structure was the shed that housed the steam engine at the mill. Beatrice did not contain to exceed fifty actual residents all told. The prairie came down to Fifth street and the traveled portion of Court street from there to the river was a narrow wagon track, like a country road. Court was the only street that showed signs of being regularly traveled, and this was only from Fourth street on to the ford across the river just above where the bridge is now located.

In August, 1859, the members of the townsite company, after a mighty effort, raised a thousand dollars to enable Dr. Reynolds. as mayor of the town, an office required by the federal townsite act, to enter the half-section of land comprising the original town of Beatrice, and to pay the expenses attending the surveying and platting of the townsite. On September 12, 1859, a certified copy of the plat was filed in the government land office at Brownville and the entry and purchase of the land allowed. Thereafter patent was issued to Dr. Reynolds as mayor and trustee of the townsite company, and deeds and other conveyances of the lots could then be made. As far as a mere paper townsite goes, Beatrice from that moment had existence. The growth of the town, however, was slow, though constant. The county itself, in 1860, contained but four hundred and twenty-one white inhabitants, according to the federal census of that year. Of this number probably twenty per cent could properly be credited to Beatrice.

COURT STREET, BEATRICE, IN 1870.

During the decade which closed in 1870, though still a pioneer village, Beatrice increased its population to six hundred and twenty-four inhabitants. The state of Nebraska itself had come into the Union on March 1 1867, with a population of 123,993, and the old territorial organization had passed away. The Union Pacific Railroad was completed from Council Bluffs, Iowa, via Omaha, to the Pacific coast. This first great continental railway line traverses the entire length of

Nebraska from east to west. Its construction, together with the conferring of statehood upon Nebraska, was a tremendous uplift to every interest of the state. Population flowed in, capital sought investment, towns and villages sprang into existence, institutions of learning were founded, roads established, and all those elements of progress as well as of convenience and necessity, which a high degree of civilization and refinement implies, had received a mighty impetus throughout the entire state. The construction of the Burlington system, which was ultimately to gridiron a large portion of Nebraska, was under way across the state from Omaha to Denver, via Lincoln, to be followed early in the '70s by the building of the line of railway known to the early settlers as the Atchison & Nebraska. Not only Beatrice and Gage county, but also all Nebraska east of the one hundredth meridian, was pulsing with the energy and enthusiasm which a rapidly increasing population and a tremendous accession of wealth are apt to excite in a body politic at any time and under all circumstances. Before the close of 1870, steps were inaugurated for the extension of the Burlington Railroad system to Beatrice. Here it is sufficient to say that this extension, together with the other activities of the 70's here mentioned, went far toward realizing the dreams, the hopes, the visions of Kinney, McConihe, Towle, Reynolds, Weston, Pike, Townsend, Cook, and the other founders of this beautiful city of Beatrice. During this period, as if by magic, there was evolved—from the old steam saw mill, "Pap's Cabin" and the cluster of huts and slab and board shanties that earlier comprised this unknown western hamlet on the very rim of civilization under the name of Beatrice a beautiful and enterprising little city, destined to attain a position of great power and influence in the state and nation.

During this decade living conditions greatly improved in Beatrice and Gage county. As early as 1862, a small frame school house was erected on the block dedicated by the founders of the city to school purposes, where the Central grade-school building now stands. This building was a one story, single-room structure, sixteen by twenty feet in dimensions. It was built of cottonwood lumber donated by the townsite company and supplied from its sawmill, and the labor required for its erection was largely donated. As this was the first school building erected in the county, it was the subject of considerable comment by everybody. People came from far and near to look at it, and when school opened that fall, with Oliver Townsend as the teacher, many a man breathed a sigh of relief on reflecting that at last school privileges were in sight for his children.

By the close of 1870, the hardships of pioneer conditions were rapidly passing away. As a member of the first state legislature, in 1868, Hon. Nathan Blakely had procured the passage of an act appropriating one thousand acres of land in Gage county, the proceeds of which, when sold, were to be used in erecting a bridge across the Big Blue river at Beatrice. The lands thus donated were a part of a donation of five hundred thousand acres of land by the federal government to the state of Nebraska, out of the public domain in the state, to be used for internal improvement. Almost as soon as Mr. Blakely's bill became operative steps were taken to carry its purposes into effect.

On May 22, 1869, the county commissioners, Ticknor, Wickham, and Pettygrew, ordered an advertisement in the *Clarion*, a newspaper which was printed in Beatrice and which had just come into existence, calling for bids for the construction of a bridge at Beatrice across the Big Blue river, to consist of three stone piers twenty-four feet high, two spans, each one hundred and thirty feet in length and sixteen feet high, to cost not less than six thousand nor more than eight thousand dollars, and to be completed by August 1, 1870. The public lands selected by the county board to be applied to the cost of erecting this bridge, were: The northeast quarter of section 15, township 2, range 6; the southwest quarter of section 1; the southeast quarter of the southeast quarter of section 2; the northeast quarter of section 3; and the northwest quarter of section 12, all in township 4, range 6; and the north half of section 2, township 4 north, range east, Gage county, Nebraska.

There were several bids for this first county bridge. Cyrus W. Wheeler for the woodwork on the bridge bid $5,000; Michael Hinneberry for the piers alone bid $3,000; J. Killian & Son for the complete work, $8,000; Curtis & Peavy, of Pawnee City, bid $7,600 on the complete structure and were awarded the contract. This bridge was located where the old Market street ford crossed the river, immediately below Black Brothers' mill. It was a high, narrow structure, with room for only one vehicle at a time, and was perched on abutments which were said to have been filled with straw and stable manure instead of cement. The first spring freshet that took the ice out of the river, carried this bridge down with the flood. But its brief existence taught the public the value of bridges in our county, and this work has gone on until now the annual bridge budget of seventy-five thousand dollars makes the Peavey & Curtis appropriation of eight thousand look extremely insignificant.

During 1870 the old part of what is now the Burwood Hotel was erected by Woodford G. McDowell and his brother, Joseph B. McDowell, and it was opened to public patronage by a grand ball, on January 1, 1871. Prior to this, however, a frame hotel building of some pretentions had been erected by George Hulburt, at the corner of Second and Market streets, on lots 2 and 3, block 67 of the original town of Beatrice, known at the time as the Hulburt House. About 1874 title was acquired to this property by the Kansas & Nebraska Stage Company, who reconstructed the building into a large hostelry and christened it the Pacific House. For many years this old building discharged the office of a public inn. The spot where it stood is now occupied by the buildings of the Sonderegger Nurseries and Seed House.

In 1868 the government land office was moved from Brownville to Beatrice and for nearly twenty years this city was the center of activity for the entire Beatrice land district. At that time a government land office was an important institution in the settlement and development of the country. People from long distances were compelled to transact their business largely with the government officials at the land office. The counties west of Gage at that time were rapidly filling with homesteaders and other classes of entrymen, farms were being opened in all the eleven counties comprising the land district, and particularly in Jefferson, Saline, Thayer, Fillmore, Nuckolls, and Clay counties. Supplies of all kinds, including farm tools, lumber, meats, groceries, dry goods, and the like, were necessary to the settlers, and Beatrice merchants and business men profited greatly by this temporary trade.

During the time that had elapsed since that July day in 1857 when Judge Kinney directed the secretary of the Beatrice Association, young, scholarly John McConihe, to call the roll of the members of the association on the townsite of Beatrice, to the close of 1870, the people of Beatrice as well as of the county at large had accustomed themselves to the inconvenience under which they rested as respected markets, trade, mails, travel, transportation and the like. The transportation of merchandise from Nebraska City and Brownville to Beatrice had become so common as to be taken as a matter of course. When wheat became a staple crop in the county, the surplus was hauled to the Missouri river, where water transportation could be had, and the farmer loaded back with lumber, salt and other freight for Beatrice merchants, who were thus enabled not only to supply their trade with better goods and in increasing quantities, but also to carry practically everything demanded by their customers.

The carrying of the mail for Beatrice and practically all of Gage county was at first a neighborhood affair. Those whose business took them to Nebraska City, Brownville or other Missouri river towns where mail was received for the settlers, brought back with them letters, papers and other mail for their neighborhood. But in 1860 a regular mail route was established between Nebraska City and Marysville, Kansas, via Beatrice. Joseph Saunders was the first mail carrier on this route. He first rode into Beatrice with the United States mail on the evening of October 3, 1860. At that time a national election of intense interest was rapidly approaching, and as Mr. Saunders rode up to the postoffice, "Pap's Cabin," he was greeted by practically the entire population of Beatrice, all eager to hear the news. The mail was carried on horseback and the carrier was frequently forced to swim the unbridged streams. But no one ever heard Joseph Saunders complain of the hardship of his task and none ever knew him to fail in the discharge of his duties. He was, in fact, a most faithful and a most efficient public servant.

In 1868 a regular stage route was established from both Nebraska City and Brownville, via Tecumseh, to Beatrice. On August 26, 1868, the *Blue Valley Record* announced that the Kansas & Nebraska Stage Line, of which Martin V. Nichols, Cyrus P. Wheeler and Cyrus H.

Cotter were proprietors, was in perfect working order and made trips regularly to Nebraska City every other day; and later the public received the following announcement, in the way of an advertisement in the *Record*:

Kansas & Nebraska Stage Company, from Nebraska City, Nebraska, to Tecumseh and Beatrice, and intermediate points, carrying United States Mail, Passengers and Express Packages.

Leaves Nebraska City Mondays, Wednesdays and Fridays, connecting at Beatrice with a stage line to Lincoln, the Capital.

Returning, leaves Beatrice on Tuesdays, Thursdays, and Saturdays, connecting at Tecumseh with the stage line for Brownville and intermediate points, and at Nebraska City with the Council Bluffs & St. Joseph Railroad for all points east, north and south.

The Hulburt House, later and better known as the Pacific Hotel, was in those days the Beatrice stage station, and its genial proprietor, George W. Hulburt, was the stage company's agent at Beatrice.

But the aspiring entrepôt of southeast Nebraska was not long satisfied with a tri-weekly mail from Brownville and Nebraska City. Strenuous efforts were made early in 1869 to secure through the stage company a daily service. In the *Blue Valley Record* for February 20, 1869, voice is given to this longing in a brief editorial, which reads as follows:

The country needs a daily mail between this point and the river towns. This want, already a pressing one, is growing more so every day, and the increased amount of business which will be transacted here in the spring, and the rapid growth of the country will render it a demand of such a nature as not to be much longer resisted. The question of having it is only a question of time, how soon we shall have it is one which our citizens can in the main determine for themselves. Petitions should be gotten up and circulated along the route, and we, who are most interested, should be the first to move in it. Brownville and Nebraska City have already shown a willingness to assist in having it established, for they well know the importance of having close connections with this country and will not be wanting in efforts to accomplish it. The matter should be attended to at once. The roads are becoming good, the days longer and the trip can be easily made in a day. Let us for once lay aside old fogyism and inhale enough of the spirit of the age in which we live to show some energy in so important a matter.

This agitation was evidently successful, as the first number of Volume I of the Beatrice *Clarion*, issued on the 8th day of May, 1869, announced a daily mail over the Kansas & Nebraska Stage Line from Nebraska City and Brownville to Beatrice and intermediate points, connecting at Beatrice with the stage line to Lincoln and leaving Beatrice on its return trips every morning at seven o'clock, Sundays excepted, for Brownville and Nebraska City; and connecting at each point with the Council Bluffs & St. Joseph Railroad for eastern, northern and southern destinations.

These old advertisements act as little windows through which we may see into the very heart of things as they were in those far off pioneer days, half a century ago. Through them we may behold how a little western village on the bank of the Big Blue river, in a trifle more than ten years from the date of its founding on a trackless prairie waste, in 1857, had become a center for travel and the distribution of the United States mails. Nay more, they show how effectually the pioneers of our county had learned to make the most of such advantages as their surroundings afforded.

Let us take a last glance at the Beatrice of the '60s. The county officers in 1868 and 1869, most of whom were quartered in Beatrice or near it, were: Probate judge, H. M. Reynolds; county treasurer, Albert Towle; sheriff, Luther P. Chandler; county clerk, Oliver Townsend; surveyor, A. J. Pethoud; coronor, Daniel Freeman; county commissioners, William Ticknor, Horace M. Wickham and James M. Pettygrew; while Nathan Blakely represented the county in the state legislature. Albert Towle was postmaster, and the following advertisement, undoubtedly prepared by him, correctly exhibits the mailing facilities of the community on February 20, 1869.

MAILS

Arrivals and departures of mails from the Postoffice of Beatrice, Nebraska.

Falls City to Beatrice

Arrives Tuesdays, Thursdays, and Saturdays, at 6 P. M.
Departs Mondays, Wednesdays, and Fridays, at 6 A. M.

Nebraska City and Brownville, to Beatrice

Arrives at Beatrice Mondays, Wednesdays and Fridays at 4 P. M.
Departs Tuesdays, Thursdays and Saturdays, at 7 A. M.

Beatrice to Marysville, Kas.

Arrives Tuesdays, Thursdays and Saturdays, at 6 P. M.
Departs Mondays, Wednesdays and Fridays, at 6 A. M.

Plattsmouth via Lincoln, to Beatrice

Arrives Wednesday at 12 P. M.
Departs same day at 1 P. M.

Beatrice to Big Sandy

Departs Wednesdays at 6 A. M.
Arrives Thursday at 8 P. M.

Albert Towle, P.M.

The government land office was located on the second floor of Joseph Saunders' brick store, on the south side of Court street, between Third and Fourth streets, in the building now occupied in part by John Pagel's grocery store. Henry M. Atkinson was the register and John L. Carson, the well known banker of Brownville, was the receiver. The office was, however, mainly under the direction of "Jack" McFarland, chief clerk of the office at that time.

A semi-annual report of Mr. Towle, as county treasurer, of the affairs of his office from April 7 to October 7, 1869, showed total receipts amounting to $9,722.00, with a balance in the treasury of $3,323.18.

The legal profession was represented in Gage county by Jefferson B. Weston, Silas B. Harrington, Nathan K. Griggs, and Hiram P. Webb. Drs. H. H. Reynolds, Levi Anthony, and C. F. Sprague were engaged in the practice of medicine. Blakely, Reynolds & Townsend; LaSelle,

Buchanan & Son; and Joseph Saunders were the representatives of the general mercantile business. The druggists were George W. Hinkle and George W. Brock; the blacksmiths, Jacob Shaw and A. L. Snow; A. W. Proctor and D. Stewart carried on wagon-making shops, while J. W. Wehn, Jr., had a paint shop at Court and Second streets. Fordyce Roper owned the mill, which was advertised as the finest site on the Big Blue river, and in connection with it, he had a saw mill, a lath and shingle machine, and carried a large supply of all kinds of lumber. Mrs. M. F. Buchanan was the dressmaker and milliner of the town. Heard & Guffy supplied all kinds of cut stone for building purposes, from their Rockford quarry. Samuel Myers and Volney Rhodes were the harnessmakers. Warren E. Chesney was the proprietor of the Beatrice House, the old hotel erected by Isma Mumford in 1857. Charles F. Satler and Asher Van Buskirk made boots and shoes for the pioneers; while Artemus Baker, a cabinet-maker, supplied the demand for work in his line. William Hagy was just beginning to do a thriving business as a manufacturer of brick for building purposes.

CHAPTER XX

BEATRICE CONTINUED

INCORPORATION OF TOWNS BY COUNTY BOARD — PETITION TO INCORPORATE BEATRICE — ORDER INCORPORATING BEATRICE — FIRST BOARD OF TRUSTEES — INCORPORATION OF BEATRICE AS A CITY OF THE SECOND CLASS — FIRST CITY COUNCIL — POPULATION OF BEATRICE — INCORPORATION OF BEATRICE AS A CITY OF THE FIRST CLASS — ADDITIONS TO BEATRICE — CHANGED TO COMMISSION GOVERNMENT — FIRST COUNTY COURT HOUSE — LOCATION — OLD "PUBLIC SQUARE" — DESCRIPTION — COST — ABANDONED — DEMOLISHED — A NEW COURT HOUSE — COURT HOUSE BOND LITIGATION — COUNTY JAIL — THE NEW JAIL — FIRST UNITED STATES POSTOFFICES — PRESENT POSTOFFICE BUILDING — POSTMASTERS — BEATRICE CITY HALL — FIRE DEPARTMENT — LIGHTING PLANT — SEWERS — PAVING — CITY WATER WORKS

From the date of its founding, in July, 1857, to September, 1871, Beatrice had existed as an unincorporated hamlet or village. Under the law regulating the incorporation of *towns*, the county commissioners of any county in Nebraska were empowered, and in fact required, by proper order to incorporate any town within their county whenever a majority of its taxable inhabitants should present a petition praying for its incorporation. The corporate powers of every town were by law vested in a board of trustees of five members, to be elected, after the first board, by the qualified voters residing within such town; and the county commissioners at the time they declared a town incorporated were required to appoint as trustees for the town five suitable persons, who should hold their offices until their successors were duly elected and qualified. Amongst the qualifications required by law for a town trustee was that he should be a "free, white male citizen of the United States." The law vested boards of trustees of towns with the usual powers possessed by governing bodies of municipal corporations, and contained some provisions not now met with in similar statutes.

Pursuant to the requirements of this statute, on the 9th day of September, 1871, there was filed before the board of commissioners of Gage county a petition praying that body to incorporate Beatrice as a *town* and to appoint as trustees thereof, H. M. Reynolds, J. B. McDowell, Albert Towle, William Lamb, and Job Buchanan. Many of the names attached to this petition will always be prominent in every history of Gage county. For this reason, and because the petition necessarily represented a majority of the taxable inhabitants of Beatrice at that time, the names of the signers are here given. They are:

J. B. Weston	John G. Davis, M.D.
H. W. Parker	G. H. Gale
S. C. B. Dean	C. C. Freil
N. Blakely	L. M. Korner
I. N. McConnell	J. S. S. Wallace
John McGregor, M.D.	John M. Hayes
C. G. Dorsey	William Hothan
G. W. Dorsey	Byron Bradt
W. J. Pemberton	N. K. Griggs
F. T. Clifford	Israel Blythe
Oliver M. Enlow	W. D. Knowles
J. F. King	J. Buchanan
H. A. LaSelle	James Van Buskirk
A. S. Marsh	W. A. Presson
H. P. Webb	George W. Jackson
William P. Hess	L. Y. Coffin
C. N. Emery	G. F. Sprague, M.D.
George W. Hinkle	Ford Roper
J. Q. Thacker	Peter Terry
J. H. Halliday	A. P. Hazard
Daniel Freeman	A. McMeans
William H. Walker	M. L. McMeans
George W. Place	C. A. Pease
William Hewerkel	Orrin Stevens

Blauser Brown	Joseph Saunders
H. M. Reynolds	James Boyd
H. L. Wagner	Artemus Baker
James Charles	J. Fitch Kinney, Jr.
Peter Brauner	George L. Lamkin
C. H. Cotter	M. T. Wetherald
Fred Wenger	J. L. Webb, M.D.
Oliver Townsend	William Lamb
William H. Lamb	Albert Towle
Leroy Tinkham	S. W. Wadsworth
John Yohe	S. Meyers
C. R. Rogers	S. W. Allen
E. H. King	Milton Rhodes
H. Broughton	Paul Hailman
G. B. Reynolds	C. Rosenthal
D. E. Marsh	Sherman P. Lester
M. W. Beam	William A. Wagner
A. L. Snow	

Of these eighty-three petitioners, as far as known to this writer, all have passed to the great beyond, save G. B. Reynolds, H. A. LaSelle, William H. Walker, Byron Bradt, and George W. Hinkle, of Beatrice; A. L. Snow, of Milford, Nebraska; Sherman P. Lester and J. Fitch Kinney, Jr., of Portland, Oregon; and Samuel Meyers, of Bassett, Nebraska.

On the day the foregoing petition was presented to the commissioners—Solon M. Hazen, Horace M. Wickham, and James Pettigrew—that body, after declaring that it was fully satisfied that a majority of the taxable inhabitants of said town of Beatrice had signed the petition and that they had considered the same and were fully advised in the premises, ordered, "That the inhabitants residing upon the southeast quarter of section 33 and the southwest quarter of section 34, in township 4 north, of range 6 east of the 6th principal meridian, Gage county, Nebraska the same being the originally surveyed townsite of Beatrice, and all the legal additions which may now or may hereafter be attached to the said town of Beatrice, be and are hereby declared incorporated, a body politic and corporate by the name and style of the town of Beatrice.

BIRD'S-EYE VIEW OF BEATRICE, 1874

"And it is further ordered that H. M. Reynolds, J. B. McDowell, Albert Towle, William Lamb and Job Buchanan be and are hereby appointed as a board of trustees of said town of Beatrice, to hold their offices until their successors are elected and qualified."

The county clerk was instructed to notify forthwith in writing, under the seal of his office, each and all of the board of trustees of their appointment as such and to transmit to them a certified copy of the order.

On the same day the trustees thus appointed held a meeting in the rear room of Hinkle & Pease's drug store, and, having taken the oath of office, as provided by the statute, entered at once upon the discharge of their duties by electing Herman M. Reynolds chairman of the board, and appointing William A. Wagner clerk, Albert Towle treasurer, and Gilson H. Gale constable for the term of the trustees and until the successor of each was elected and qualified.

On March 18, 1873, a change was effected from town to city organization by an ordinance of that date, which reads as follows:

WHEREAS, The town of Beatrice, in the State of Nebraska, was organized as such on the 3rd day of October, A. D. 1871, under and by virtue of the provisions of chapter 53 of the Revised Statutes of the State of Nebraska, entitled "TOWNS"; and

WHEREAS, The said town now contains more than five hundred (500) inhabitants; and

WHEREAS, Said town is desirous of becoming incorporated as a city of the second class, under the provisions of the act of the legislature of the State of Nebraska, approved March 1, 1871, entitled, "An act to incorporate cities of the second class, and to define their powers," and of the amendments thereto; therefore,

Be It Ordained by the Board of Trustees of the Town of Beatrice

That the said town be, and the same is hereby, incorporated as a city of the second class, by the name of the "City of Beatrice."

This ordinance shall be published in the Beatrice *Express*, a newspaper in said town, for two (2) weeks, successively, and to take effect and be in force from and after the 5th day of April, 1873.

At the ensuing municipal election for that year, S. C. B. Dean, a lawyer of great ability and learning, was elected mayor; E. S. Chadwick, an able young lawyer, police judge; O. A. Avery, marshal; William A. Wagner, city clerk; Samuel C. Smith, city treasurer; William Bradt, C. G. Dorsey, J. E. Hill and William Lamb councilmen, of the city of Beatrice.

At this time, the population of the city had materially increased since the census of 1870, when it stood at 624. At the time the first city council was elected, in 1873, it probably exceeded 1,500. It was growing rapidly; the census of 1880 showed a population of 2,447, and it had begun to assume the proportions and attributes of a flourishing western city.

The street shown furthest north in the accompanying birdseye view of Beatrice in 1874 is Washington, the one furthest south is Scott, while Tenth instead of Thirteenth is shown as the eastern boundary of the city. The bridge in the foreground is the Curtis & Peavey bridge, on Market street; the first location of the Burlington depot is shown where Grant street apparently terminates. Roper's mill, with the dam, is properly located above the bridge. "Pap's Cabin" appears south of the string of empty cars. The old court house appears in its proper place. West of it by a little north is the original Episcopal church building. The church, with spire, in the middle foreground is the first church building of the Presbyterians. Southwest across the block is seen the old stone Methodist church, with parsonage, and southeast is the old frame school house, on the school block. Further east by south is the first high-school building. On the south the first Sixth street bridge is seen, with winding roads from east and north, across the prairie.

In April, 1891, an act of the legislature became effective which provided for the incorporation of *cities of the first class* having less than 25,000 and more than 8,000 inhabitants, and regulating their duties, powers and government. Pursuant to this statute, Lorenzo Crounse, governor of the state of Nebraska, on the 26th day of January, 1893, issued his proclamation declaring that Beatrice from and after that date was a city of the first class. In his proclamation the Governor recites the fact that the census of 1890 showed that the city possessed a population of 13,825. It can not be doubted that the actual population of Beatrice in 1890 was far short of the number of inhabitants returned by the census enumerators, and probably less even than the minimum figure for cities of the class to which this proclamation assigned Beatrice. That census has been the subject of much just criticism, which applied not only to the cities but to the entire state of Nebraska. That it was a gross exaggeration of the facts respecting the population of the state and its cities is an admitted fact.

Since the original incorporation of the town of Beatrice, in 1871, which included only the three hundred and twenty acres of land comprising the original townsite, a great many additions have been made to the superficial area of the city, until to-day it embraces approximately thirty-two hundred acres of land. The principal additions to the city are Cropsey's Addition, Weston's Additions, Smith Brothers' Addition, Fairview Addition, Paddock's Addition, Green's Addition, Grable & Beachley's Addition, Grable & Beachley's Second and Third Additions, Yule & Son's Park Addition, and Glenover Addition—on the north and west; Lamb's Subdivision, Henry H. Lamb's Subdivision, Barney's Subdivision, and Wittenberg Addition—on the east; the town of South Beatrice and the First and Second Additions to the town of South Beatrice, Cole's Addition, Riverside Park Addition, Brumback's Additions, Belvidere Heights, and Highland Park Addition—on the south; Harrington's Subdivision, McConnell's First and Second Subdivisions, West Park Addition, Scheve's Addition, Milligan's Addition and McConnell's Addition—on the west. The city also contains numerous small subdivisions, places, and irregular tracts, which by ordinance have been incorporated into the city. These additions were largely made between the years 1885 and 1890—a period which witnessed tremendous growth and expansion in all directions in Beatrice, as well as in the state at large.

From the date of its organization into a city, March 18, 1873, to May 1, 1912, the municipal government of Beatrice had been strictly representative in character. The first act of the first city council was to divide the city of Beatrice into three wards. The city government consisted of a mayor and of councilmen elected from each of the wards. Though modified to include four, five, and even six wards, the principal of representative municipal government was preserved, and the citizens at large, through their councilmen, had direct representation in the affairs of the city. The clerk, treasurer, police judge, and other administrative officers were elected by the people at the time the mayor and council were chosen. The chief of police, policemen, street commissioner, city attorney, and some other minor officers were appointed by the mayor, with the advice and consent of the council. Speaking generally, this form of municipal government up to a score of years ago was universal throughout the United States, and it is still the form under which the vast majority of cities are governed, including the great metropolitan cities of New York, Philadelphia, Boston, Pittsburgh, Chicago, and St. Louis.

About the year 1900 there arose in many of the states, a system of municipal government designated commission government or government by commission, which in a large measure did away wholly with the old representative form of municipal government. This heresy spread with some rapidity in the west and mid-west portions of the country. In 1911 the legislature of Nebraska passed an act providing for the commission form of government in all cities having more than 5,000 population, and at the election held in Beatrice in 1912 it was voted to abandon the representative form and adopt the new method of government. The centralizing of power in a few hands may possess some advantages as applied to civic affairs, but any form of government, municipal or otherwise, which abandons in whole or in part the representative principle, lays an ax at the roots of free institutions, and this because it is evident that if delegated powers may be given to two, three or five men, they can be conferred upon one, and a free community pass into the hands of a dictator. The weakness of commission government as applied to cities, and its unrepresentative character, must in time become manifest, and it is doubtful whether the people will long continue a system which in effect bars the active participation of the public to an appreciable extent in municipal affairs.

Toward the close of the period marked by the year 1870, it became apparent that the growing needs of the county demanded facilities for transacting public business. The county possessed neither court house nor jail.

The county offices were housed around town, wherever quarters could be had. If the incumbent of the office happened to live in the county seat, he carried his office around with him, or kept it at his dwelling or place of business. The board of county commissioners, or the county court, as that body was legally designated for many years, was compelled to hold its meetings at the residence of the member in Beatrice or the places of business at the county seat willing to accommodate them. The courts were held first at "Pap's Cabin," but when the Griggs & Webb building, on Court, between Third and Fourth streets, was erected, in the fall of 1868, the upper floor of that edifice was used for several years as a court room.

That a movement should be made in a rapidly growing town to secure a court house and jail was the natural outcome of these conditions, and on August 20, 1869, a petition was presented to the county court, or board of county commissioners, signed by H. M. Reynolds, Nathan Blakely, Orrin Stevens, and sixty-eight other electors of the county, praying for the submission to a vote of the people at the next general election of a proposition to bond the county in the sum of ten thousand dollars, for the erection of a county court house and jail at Beatrice, the county seat.

On the 1st day of September, 1869, the county clerk was directed to include in the call for the annual election to be held October 12, 1869, the proposition for the issuance of such bonds, and the ballots at the election fairly submitted this question to the voters of the county. The canvass of the votes showed a majority in favor of issuing the bonds, and in January, 1870, the matter of erecting the court house was taken up in earnest by the county board. On the 6th day of that month, the county clerk, Oliver Townsend, was directed to advertise in the Beatrice Clarion for bids for the erection of both a court house and a jail, costing not less than ten thousand dollars, all bids to be accompanied by plans and specifications.

About this time the question arose as to where the new court house should be erected. The founders of Beatrice had provided for county buildings by dedicating the block bounded on the north by Ella, on the east by Ninth, on the south by Court, and on the west by Eighth street;

but when it became apparent that the county commissioners were about to act in the matter of locating the county buildings, A. J. Cropsey, of Lincoln, who had been a state officer in Nebraska and who had laid out an addition on the north of the original town of Beatrice, designated and known as Cropsey's Addition, appeared upon the scene and made an offer to the county board, composed of H. M. Wickham and others, to donate block 24 of his addition to the county for court-house purposes, and the south half of block 11 for the purpose of a jail. Mr. Cropsey included also in his offer certain other inducements. The county commissioners accepted these offers and abandoned to the first comer the "public square" which the founders of Beatrice had dedicated to court-house purposes. Daniel Freeman, who was sheriff of the county in 1870-1871, quickly saw the weakness of this move and took possession of the square, fenced it and placed a couple of small dwelling houses on it. In 1873 the legislature passed an act entitled. "An Act to Quiet Title to Certain Portions of the City of Beatrice." Section 3 of the act reads as follows:

That the dedication to the county of Gage of the block known as the "public square" in the said city of Beatrice, lying between block 52 on the east, and block 51 on the west, is hereby ratified and confirmed, and the legal and equitable title thereto, in fee-simple, is hereby vested in said county of Gage, to be used as a site for public buildings, either for the said Gage county, or for the said city of Beatrice, or otherwise, as may seem proper.

In August, 1874, through the agency of a distress warrant for taxes, an effort was made by the county treasurer to dispossess Freeman. This proved abortive and in the end served to strengthen his hold on the property. (*Freeman vs. Webb et al.*, 27 Neb., 160.) No effort appears to have been made by the county at any time by direct suit to assert its title to this property, either under the act of dedication or the above described act of the legislature, and in process of time Freeman's possession, as the law then stood, ripened into a perfect title.

On the 19th day of August, 1870, the contract for the erection of a court house at Beatrice on block 24 of Cropsey's Addition to the city, was let to Binns & Fordham. The contract price of this structure was

$11,196.01, and it was to be erected in accordance with the plans and specifications furnished by the contractors and adopted by the county board. The building was a two-story, brick structure, with stone foundation and trimmings; it was about forty feet square, with both north and south frontage, connected by a straight hallway, six feet wide, through the entire building.

The lower floor of this old court house was wholly occupied by the county offices, while the upper story was used exclusively as a district court-room, with two connected jury rooms. This floor was reached by a stairway which started from the lower hallway at the middle of the east side and led directly to the second floor, terminating in a short hall which led westward to the district court room.

First Court House at Beatrice

Before the work was completed the contractors suggested modifications of the plans, which they agreed to make for one thousand dollars in addition to the contract price of the building, and which were accepted by the county board. The work progressed rapidly, and on April 19, 1871, the first court house of our county was turned over to the county and formally accepted by the commissioners—James Pettigrew, Solon M. Hazen, and Horace M. Wickham. The total cost of this old building, including a vault for the county treasurer, and all extras, was $13,914.00. The grounds about the building were planted by Mr. Cropsey with cottonwood, maple and other forest trees, and for many years served to some extent the purposes of a park.

This first court house, product of the necessities of the pioneers, remained in constant use until the spring of 1887, when several of the county offices were moved to the stone building at the corner of Fourth and Court streets, then occupied by the Nebraska National Bank. The county court and the sheriff's office were later moved to the basement in the Masonic Temple building, at the corner of Sixth and Court streets, the present site of the Beatrice National Bank. In the latter part of 1889 the court house was wholly abandoned, district court being held at first in an old frame opera house at the corner of Fifth and Ella streets, where the fine two-story Kilpatrick building now stands, and later in a hall on the third floor of the Nebraska National Bank building.

No sooner had the county abandoned the property in part than A. J. Cropsey, who after a long absence from the state had returned to Lincoln, began in the United States district court at Omaha an action in ejectment against the county, to obtain possession of the court house square, alleging that the property had been conveyed to the county for court-house purposes only, and, setting forth its abandonment by the county, charged that the title to this property had reverted to him as the grantor. After considerable evidence had been taken by deposition on both sides, the case was compromised and settled by this writer, as county attorney of Gage county, in March, 1889, by and with the approval of the county board, and a quit-claim deed taken from Cropsey and his wife for both the court house square and the half block where the county jail was located.

In 1889-1890, after arrangements had been made to erect the present court house, the old building was demolished and became a thing of the past. But to those whose memories cover its history this old building will never cease to possess a deep interest on account of the part it played in the early development of our county and state. Here many of the lawyers who are now practicing at the bar of Gage county, and many others who have died or moved away, gained their first experience in the trial of causes; here much of the important litigation, both civil and criminal, arising in our county was tried, including the two Marion murder trials (1883 and 1886), the Bradshaw murder trial (1883), the Reed murder trial (1883), the first Carson murder trial (1889), and many other cases of public interest and importance. Here also the county business was transacted from April 19, 1871, to April 1, 1887; here at desk and ledger toiled men, many of whose names are inseparably connected with the early history of our county. Among these names may be noted the following: Hiram P. Webb, John Ellis, J. F. King, E. J. Roderick, county treasurers; the lamented Daniel E. Marsh, William D. Cox, John E. Hill, A. J. Pethoud, and George E. Emery, county clerks; Oliver M. Enlow, John E. Hill (ex-officio), A. V. S. Saunders, and Frank H. Holt, clerks of the district court; Daniel Freeman, Leander Y. Coffin, Eugene Mack, Nathaniel Herron, and E. F. Davis, sheriffs of our county; C. A. Pease, J. W. Carter, Alfred Hazlett, Peter Shaffer, Joseph E. Cobbey, Ernest O. Kretsinger, and Oliver M. Enlow, county judges; Lucius B. Filley, J. R. Little, Matthew Weaverling, and M. D. Horham, county superintendents of public schools.

Few are living now of all those who in the days of the old court house were prominent in the affairs of our county. All of the old treasurers are gone; all of the old clerks but George E. Emery; all of the clerks of the district court except A. V. S. Saunders; all the sheriffs except Davis; and all the judges except Hazlett and Kretsinger, while not a single one of the old county superintendents is left.

All the days of the years of the old court house were great days for the citizens of Beatrice and Gage county. In those days were laid broad and deep, and for all time to come, the foundations of one of the most progressive, homogeneous and patriotic counties in the entire state of Nebraska.

In the year 1887 our county abandoned the commissioner system of county government and adopted the supervisor system, and at a meeting of the board of supervisors held in February, 1889, steps were taken for the erection of the present court house, on the site of the old, and a special election was called for May 7th of that year, in which a proposition for the issuance of the bonds of the county in the sum of one hundred thousand dollars for the purpose of erecting a court house at the county seat, was submitted to the voters of our county. Of the 5,059 votes cast at this, election, 2,589 favored the proposition and 2,470 opposed it, leaving a clear majority for the bonds of 139 votes. Steps were about to be taken for the issuance of these bonds and the erection of the court house, when proceedings were inaugurated by citizens of Wymore to enjoin the work on the ground that the act under which the board of supervisors had proceeded in calling the election was unconstitutional and therefore the election was void, and that the county board was without jurisdiction to bond the county for the purpose of erecting a court house. In the district court, Hon. A. D. McCandless, of Wymore, represented the plaintiffs in the action—Robert Fenton, A. Perkins, John Mordhorst, Michael Keckley, Patrick Murphy, and J. W. Bridenthal—while the writer of this history, as county attorney, represented the defendants—Thomas Yule, as chairman of the board of supervisors, and George E. Emery, as county clerk of Gage county. The cause was instituted July 8, 1889, and a temporary restraining order was granted until a hearing could be had. On July 15th a demurrer was filed to the petition, on the ground that it did not state facts sufficient to constitute a cause of action against the defendants; and on July 17th Judge Jefferson H. Broady sustained the demurrer, dissolved the injunction and dismissed the bill at the cost of plaintiffs. The cause was then appealed to the supreme court of Nebraska, where it was advanced and came up for hearing at the opening of the September term of that tribunal. At this hearing Mr. McCandless was assisted by Judge Oliver P. Mason; and the writer, as attorney for the defendants, by G. M. Lambertson. On October 30, 1889, the case was again decided in favor of the validity of the bonds, by the court of last resort in Nebraska, (Fenton, et al. vs. Yule, et al., 27 Neb. 758), and the way opened for the erection of the new court house.

At its January, 1890, session the board of supervisors adopted the plans and specifications for the present court house, prepared and submitted to them by Gunn & Curtis, of Kansas City, Missouri, and immediately advertised for bids for its erection. On the 29th day of

March, 1890, the bid of M. T. Murphy, of Omaha, for the sum of one hundred thousand dollars was accepted, upon his executing a bond, in the sum of twenty thousand dollars, to be approved by the county board, for the faithful performance of his contract. After some vicissitudes the building was finally completed, was turned over to the county board and was accepted by that board in January, 1892.

Federal Building.

Gage County Court house.

The erection of a county jail was, after the first court house, the next most urgent public need. The administration of the criminal law was reduced to almost a farce by lack of facilities for enforcing it. Whenever it became necessary to imprison persons accused of crime, the county was compelled to rely on Nebraska City, which was the nearest point within the state where jail privileges were available. This involved not only a charge for maintenance of the prisoners while in jail, but also the cost of their transportation to Nebraska City, and back again to Beatrice every time the district court set or until the criminal charge was finally disposed of. This is well illustrated in the case of the State of Nebraska vs. Lydia Armstrong, a woman who had been bound over to the district court by a justice of the peace on a common peace warrant sworn to by her husband, W. W. Armstrong. At a session of the county board held October 23, 1869, the following bills in this case were audited, allowed and paid:

L. P. Chandler, sheriff, board of prisoner at Hulbert House $4.50
A. L. Hurd, guarding prisoner 1 day..2.00
W. W. Brock, guarding prisoner 1 day...2.00
L. P. Chandler, guarding prisoner 6 days.......................................12.00
Otoe County jail, 4 days at $4 per day 16.00
Feed for team 4 days 8.00
Board for prisoner 2 days at $1.50...3.00
Expense for prisoner at Otoe County jail 30.58
A. L. Hurd, for team for conveying prisoner from
Otoe County jail to Gage County court, 4 days at $4 ....16.00
Feed for said team for 4 days..8.00
Board of prisoner 2 days 3.00
Guarding prisoner 6 days 12.00
Total $117.08

Action looking toward the erection of a jail was first taken by the county board January 30, 1872, when one W. W. Watson was appointed by the commissioners to prepare plans and specifications for a jail, and the county clerk at the same time was directed to advertise in the Beatrice *Express* for proposals for the erection of a jail at Beatrice, in accordance with such plans and specifications. But on February 24, 1872, all proposals were rejected, and, on account of cost and lack of funds, the building of a jail for Gage county was indefinitely postponed, by commissioners Solon N. Hazen, Horace M. Wickham, and Elijah Filley.

But the subject was not allowed to rest. Steps were taken by the county board to supply funds for this building, and at the regular annual election held on the 8th day of October, 1872, a proposition to bond the county in the sum of $7,000, the proceeds of which were to be used in the erection of a county jail at Beatrice, was carried by a decisive majority.

On the 9th day of January, 1873, the county clerk, William D. Cox, was again directed to advertise in the Beatrice *Express* for three consecutive weeks for bids for a county jail, all bids to be accompanied by plans and specifications, the building to consist of stone and iron, and to cost not more than $6,000—the commissioners reserving the right to reject all bids, plans and specifications. Whether any bids, or plans and specifications were filed with the county board on the $6,000 basis is unknown to this writer, but, evidently growing weary of putting the cart before the horse, that body, on the 8th day of February, 1873, adopted plans and specifications for a county jail, prepared and submitted to them by William Anyan, a well known resident and homesteader of Elm township, a farmer, a practical builder and contractor, a politician, an Englishman of talent and ability. The county clerk was a third time directed to advertise for bids for the erection of a county jail at Beatrice, in the Beatrice *Express* for three consecutive weeks, and on March 15, 1873, the county board accepted a bid submitted to it by Andrew Miller, of this city, for the erection of a jail in conformity with the Anyan plans and specifications, for the sum of $6,400, conditioned, however, upon his executing a bond to the county in the sum of $12,800 for the faithful performance of his contract. But on March 22d following, Miller appeared before the board and confessed his inability to give a bond in sufficient sum. The contract with him was thereupon cancelled, and a readvertisement ordered for bids. On April 21, 1873, the contract for the erection of a jail in accordance with the Anyan plans and specifications was awarded to T. J. Patterson for the sum of $6,364, and at a special session of the county board held May 11, 1873, the prospective jail was, by formal order of the board, located on lots 16, 17, and 18, block 11 of Cropsey's Addition to the City of Beatrice.

This old building was constructed wholly of native stone, on the corner of Lincoln and Seventh streets. It was a single story, with basement under the part devoted to the jailer's residence. The entrance was from the south, and a hall led past the living rooms to a corridor in the rear, where prisoners were allowed to exercise; beyond the corridor were the cells.

OLD COUNTY JAIL, 1874, IN PROCESS OF DEMOLITION, 1918

The building was completed and turned over to the county board in the early part of 1874, and for forty-four years it served the people as a county prison. It lacked almost every convenience for a modern jail. For years every grand jury was accustomed to condemn it as unsanitary and unsafe. In this old building all the desperate criminals of our county have been held awaiting trial, execution or removal to the penitentiary. In the old jail yard occurred the only legal execution ever had in Gage county, when Jackson Marion paid the penalty on the gallows, in March, 1886, for the brutal murder of John Cameron in 1873. Hundreds of criminals have sighed behind its iron bars, and to some it was the end of hope. If ghosts could walk and all the past be revealed, strange tales might be told of those incarcerated within its walls. In the spring of 1918, on the completion of the new jail, this old county bastile was demolished, beam by beam, bar by bar, rock by rock. The very place where it had stood so long is plowed. graded and filled, and not a trace of this sad, gloomy structure is left.

As early as 1916 the building of a modern jail was taken under consideration by the county supervisors, and a levy of one and one-fourth mills on the total valuation of the county was levied that year for the purpose of creating a fund to build a new jail. In 1917 also a levy was made for the same purpose, one and two one-hundredths mills, and on the 28th day of May, 1917, a contract for the erection of the new building was awarded to F. L. Robertson, as general contractor, the building to be erected pursuant to plans and specifications drawn by Richard W. Grant, of Beatrice, C. W. Werner, of Wymore, was awarded the plumbing contract, Baker-Hartzell Company, of Beatrice, the contract for electrical wiring and electrical appliances, while the Pauly Jail Building Company, of St. Louis, Missouri, was awarded the contract for cells and other equipment. The following table exhibits the total cost of the building, exclusive of grounds and grading:

Paid Richard W. Grant, Architect	$1,220.00
Paid F. L. Robertson, Contractor	14,841.36
Paid C. W. Werner, Plumbing Contractor	2,102.00
Paid Baker-Hartzell Co., Electrical Contractors	275.00
Paid The Pauly Jail Building Co	7,700.00
Paid for extras	87.45
Total cost	$26,225.81

NEW COUNTY JAIL, 1918

This fine, commodious jail building, which includes also a residence for the jailor or sheriff, was completed and accepted by the county board

November 27, 1917. Few, if any, counties in Nebraska can boast a more handsome, complete, modern jail building than Gage, the great third county of Nebraska.

The first United States postoffice of Beatrice was the pioneer residence of Albert Towle, commonly called "Pap's Cabin," but in 1866 the postoffice was moved to a single room in the rear of the twenty-five-foot-front, frame hardware store owned by Rainboldt & Company, on the corner of Third and Court streets, where the building of the Blue Valley Mercantile Company (wholesale grocery) now stands. The little room containing the postoffice fronted on Third street. About 1870 Mr. Towle, the postmaster, erected a narrow frame building immediately west of Saunders' two-story brick store building on Court street. The business of the office increased so rapidly that more commodious quarters became necessary, and about 1872 the postoffice was moved to the west storeroom in the Burwood hotel, where at this writing, H. P. Claussen has his shoe store. In 1886 the office was moved from the hotel building to the east room of the old Masonic Temple Block, on the corner of Sixth and Court streets, which was destroyed by fire in 1902, and on the site of which the Beatrice National Bank building now stands. In 1887 Algernon S. Paddock was elected United States senator from Nebraska, and in 1891 he secured an appropriation from congress, in the sum of $65,000, to be used for the purchase of a site and the erection of a postoffice building in the rapidly growing city of Beatrice. Of this sum, not to exceed $15,000 was to be used in the purchase of a site for the building. The northeast corner of the intersection of Seventh and Ella streets was considered the most eligible site; one hundred twenty feet of this property was selected for the site of the new postoffice building, and in July, 1891, it was purchased at a cost to the government of $15,041.74. Thereafter the United States proceeded to erect the old part of the present postoffice building on this ground, at a cost of $49,934.37, and in October, 1893, it was occupied for postoffice purposes. The material used in this structure is from the great sandstone quarries of Warrensburg, Missouri.

The business of the office increased rapidly, and in 1911 congress appropriated the sum of $62,000 for the purpose of purchasing additional land and increasing the capacity of the office. The sum of $11,000 was paid for the eighty feet of ground adjoining the original site, and an extension, with other improvements, was added to the original building, at a cost of $49,877.50. The total cost to the government of this building, including site, is the sum of $125,853.61.

The postoffice in every community is to its members the visible sign of the power and beneficence of the government. Its importance cannot be greatly exaggerated. It forms a connecting link between the citizen and the outside world. Until recent years the postal department was the sole representative in the United States of the paternal or social idea of government. It may be that the present period of the great world war will eventuate in government-owned facilities of every description, from postal to transportation and shipping.

The patrons of the Beatrice postoffice have been fortunate in the character of the men who have occupied the important position of postmaster. Since its establishment, July 16, 1857, to the present time, the following named persons have been appointed postmasters at Beatrice, on the dates here given:

Herman M. Reynolds, July 15, 1857; Albert Towle, May 27, 1860; Jacob Drum, September 1, 1879; Samuel E. Rigg, March 18, 1886; Charles M. Rigg, November 7, 1889; George P. Marvin, September 11, 1893; Alexander Graham, January 14, 1898; William H. Edgar, January 20, 1902; Albert H. Hollingworth, February 27, 1906; John R. McCann, August 19, 1914.

Some years ago the postoffice department at Washington, pursuant to acts of congress authorizing such action, established in Gage county the system of rural mail delivery, and about the same time the system of city carriers was inaugurated for Beatrice. The rural routes radiate from the Beatrice office in every direction and are served by seven carriers, while the city of Beatrice gives employment to ten carriers of United States mail within its boundaries.

In 1896 the city of Beatrice purchased lot ten in block sixty-four of the original town site and erected thereon a small, two-story, plain brick city hall. This structure, though undergoing various changes, modifications, and additions, is still too small for public requirements. It lacks nearly every appointment of a modern, up-to-date municipal building and is almost offensively wanting in architectural style and beauty.

It supplies a place, however, for a jail, the meetings of the city council, offices for the police magistrate, and chief of police and his subordinates, and several of the elective and appointive officers of the city. The day is not far distant when the growing city of Beatrice will demand a city building which besides affording ample room and facilities for the housing of the public records of the city and the transaction of municipal business will add to civic attractiveness.

Allied to the City Hall is the fire department, which includes four volunteer hose companies and a salaried force of firemen. This important branch of the public service had its origin with the organization of the volunteer companies June 8, 1886. From then until a comparatively recent date the non-salaried volunteers valiantly defended against the ravages of fire the property of the citizens of our city, in a most faithful and efficient manner. Notwithstanding the fact that since the creation of the salaried fire department the volunteer companies have been relegated to the position of reserves, they have maintained their organization intact and hold themselves in readiness to respond instantly to every call for aid. At present these companies number one hundred and thirty brave and public-spirited citizens of Beatrice.

On the first day of September, 1908, the volunteer hose companies purchased the north forty-six and two-thirds feet of lots 7 and 8, block 63. Beatrice, and, at a cost of more than thirty thousand dollars, erected thereon a fine, two-story, pressed-brick fire station, which forms headquarters for all the firemen of the city.

In this building is housed the fire-fighting apparatus of the city, at the present time consisting of a motor truck, which is a combined hose and chemical engine, a horse-drawn truck of like character, hose reels, and the hook and ladder equipment.

The volunteers also, in 1907, in commemoration of their dead, erected a splendid monument, which, fronting its main entrance, overlooks beautiful Evergreen Home Cemetery.

In many other ways this organization has written its own indelible record in the history of Beatrice. The fire chiefs have been Nathaniel

Herron (the first leader of the brave volunteers), John Schiek, John Walker, H. L. Harper, Rudolph Woelke, John Scharton, and Henry Whiteside (the present chief).

In 1912 the authorities of the city of Beatrice installed in connection with the waterworks system a municipal lighting plant, from which the streets and city buildings are now well and beautifully illuminated. Efforts have been made to secure the application of this plant to commercial purposes, but so far the voters have failed to endorse this plan. The future may see a complete revolution of sentiment with respect to the activity of the city along commercial lines.

Beatrice is also well supplied with storm and sanitary sewers, work which had its beginning about 1886, and which has been recently extended to cover large areas of the city. Perhaps no city of its size in the west exceeds our city with respect to these public utilities.

No other improvement in the city has added so much to the beauty of the city and the comfort of living in Beatrice as the street paving. This work was inaugurated in the autumn of 1886, and was largely confined to the business districts of the city. Since 1913 the paving of the streets and alleys of Beatrice has been greatly increased and been extended to include much of the residence portion of the city east of the river. This work has gone steadily forward until at the present moment Beatrice possesses approximately sixteen miles of paved streets and is probably the best paved city of its class in the state.

The outstanding indebtedness of Beatrice on account of the paving, exclusive of interest and the cost of paving the intersections of the streets, is $101,930, which is assessed against the property comprising the several paving districts.

CARNEGIE LIBRARY.

CITY WATER WORKS.

CITY HALL.

VOLUNTEER FIRE STATION.

In 1885 steps were taken by the city council to inaugurate a waterworks system in Beatrice. That year, on the twenty-first day of December, an ordinance was passed by the mayor and council which provided for holding a special election January 22, 1886, upon a proposition to issue bonds of the city in the sum of eighty thousand dollars, for the purpose "of constructing, operating and maintaining a system of waterworks for said city of Beatrice." At the election thus provided for, this proposition was carried by a decisive affirmative vote, and steps were at once taken to put into effect the wishes of the voters. The work went vigorously forward and before the closing of the year 1888 the city water-works were in operation.

The plan adopted was that known as the direct-pressure system, by which, through the agency of powerful force pumps, the water is elevated through main lines and service pipes to the consumer. In 1890 additional bonds were voted to cover the extension of the water mains. The water used by the consumers was taken directly from the Big Blue river, in an unfiltered and impure state. During the greater portion of the year it was utterly unfit for drinking or culinary purposes. In 1891 a serious effort was made to remedy this condition, and at a special election, held in Beatrice on the second day of September of that year, called for the purpose of voting on a proposition to issue additional bonds, the city council was authorized to issue the negotiable bonds of the city "to the amount of thirty-five thousand dollars ($35,000), for the purpose of constructing, maintaining and operating a system of waterworks for said city, to purchase land for the site of a water plant, and otherwise improve the waterworks system of the city of Beatrice and appurtenances, in the extension of and connection with the present system of waterworks of the said city."

At the time these bonds were voted, a series of experiments had been conducted by the water commissioner in what was then known as "Paddock's Pasture," a tract of land where the Lang canning factory and the Kilpatrick stock and storage yards are now located. From the test wells put down, the city council was led to believe that an abundance of pure water could be here obtained at a shallow depth. These bonds were issued, placed upon the market and sold for approximately their face value, and a contract for installing this plant was let to the firm of Godfrey & Means, of Fremont, Nebraska. But these contractors failed to obtain a satisfactory supply of water, though it developed that a considerable quantity of pure, wholesome water did in fact exist at that point. The money invested in this movement was wholly lost and the small brick building which was erected as a pumping station and which still occupies the small tract of ground purchased by the city, is a melancholy reminder to the tax-payers of Beatrice of this failure to secure the necessary, supply of pure municipal water.

For several years after this costly experiment, the question of an adequate supply of potable water for Beatrice was suffered to rest, though it still remained an ever-present, urgent problem to every lover of his city. About 1910 the city authorities again took up the matter and a short distance east of the Paddock pasture several test wells were put down to water bearing gravel. These, it was thought, indicated the existence of pure water in sufficient quantities, if properly developed, to meet the requirements of the city. Four large wells were put down by the city, electrical pumping apparatus was installed in them, and, in 1911, a small reservoir was built, at considerable cost, on the northern boundary of the city. Water from these wells was pumped into this reservoir and conducted by gravity through mains to the pumping station of the city waterworks. It soon became apparent that the water problem of Beatrice had not been solved, the supply from this source being painfully deficient.

At the election in 1912 a change was effected from the old plan of ward representation in the city council to the commission form of government, and the new administration applied itself at once to a solution of this ever-present, perplexing problem of wholesome water for Beatrice. Finally, on the 10th day of August, 1912, the commissioners advertised in the city press for sealed proposals "for the construction of a sufficient number of wells to supply the city of Beatrice with five hundred thousand (500,000) to seven hundred and fifty thousand (750,000) gallons of water per day of twenty-four hours, also the pumps, electric motors, pipe fittings, and all other material and equipment, including all labor necessary to install same and to deliver the above amount of water into the present water mains." Bidders were to furnish their own plans and specifications and the cost of the work to the city was to be based on the number of gallons of water that the wells and equipment should be capable of pumping into the mains for twenty-four hours.

On the 20th day of August, 1912, the Dempster Mill Manufacturing Company, of Beatrice, submitted a "proposal for wells, pump and motors for the city of Beatrice" accompanied by plans and specifications and a blueprint illustrative of the proposed wells and their equipment. This proposal was accepted, and the company entered immediately upon the work of putting down wells in the neighborhood of the

Paddock Pasture, on North Sixth street. The limitations of this volume render it inexpedient to follow the details of this movement further than to say that the company failed to develop a sufficient quantity of water from its wells to meet the requirements of its contract.

Finally it turned to the well known spring located on the farm of John H. Zimmerman, on the west side of the river, a short distance northwest of the city. The existence of this spring had been known since the first settlement of Gage county. Without development or artificial aid it sent forth a considerable stream of pure, cold water. To the Dempster Mill Manufacturing Company generally, and to its president, Charles B. Dempster, particularly, belongs the entire credit of developing this fine living spring, which is now almost the sole source of the city water supply.

The history of this venture, with its result, is well set forth in a letter by the company, signed by its president, addressed to the mayor and city commissioners of Beatrice. The general statements of this letter are pertinent to the object and purpose of this history and for that reason it is here given in full. It reads as follows:

Beatrice, Neb., Aug. 6, 1913.

Hon. Mayor & City Commissioners, Beatrice, Neb.
Gentlemen:

Without going into details with reference to our efforts to secure the city of Beatrice a sufficient supply of water, which we have been endeavoring to do since last November, we are now pleased to report that we have finally secured what we believe to be not only an ample but a lasting supply of good, pure, soft water at Zimmerman Springs, joining the city on the northwest.

We also have an option from Mr. John H. Zimmerman for the lease of these springs, together with the right of way over the land adjacent thereto, for a term of ten years, for an annual rental of $300.00 per year, with further option to purchase the springs at any time within ten years at the price of $6,000.00, together with such land as may be required, up to ten acres, at a price of $200.00 per acre. This contract or option is made direct to the Dempster Mill Manufacturing Company, but can be assigned by them to others. We believe this option is a valuable one to the city of Beatrice.

We further believe that we have secured and can deliver to the city over one and one-half million gallons of water every twenty-four hours, taking the Zimmerman Springs and the wells we put down north of the city together. The wells north of the city were put down under our contract with the city of Beatrice, dated August 20, 1912, with later amendments.

After having put down these four batteries of wells north of the city, you will remember that we were unable to secure the required amount of water to complete our contracts and that, by mutual consent, the contract was suspended until we had an opportunity to make a test of the supply of water at the Zimmerman Springs.

The test and purchase of the option of the Zimmerman Springs, as you well understand, were made at our expense and our risk, the city taking no chances in our ability to secure the water supply whatsoever. We stated that we would take the matter up with you again after we had made the tests.

Now, Gentlemen, we have not only made the tests, but have completed a permanent well, walling it up with a twelve inch brick wall, laid in cement. We have been pumping the springs almost continually for two months and the amount of water pumped increased steadily from the time we began pumping until it is now capable of furnishing 1,200,000 gallons of water per day and, at the same time, leaving three to three and a half feet of water still in the bottom of the well.

The well is dug down thirty feet deep. We also drilled five holes in the bottom of the dug well an additional twenty feet. The first two of these holes we drilled increased the flow of the water in the well about fifty per cent. It is our opinion, also the opinion of Professor E. H. Barbour, Head of the Geological Survey Department of the University of Nebraska, that by blasting and taking out the rock an additional sixteen or eighteen feet, we can increase the supply of water up to at least one and a half million gallons per day.

Professor Barbour made a special trip here at our request, while we were sinking the wells. He made a careful investigation of the formations and all conditions surrounding the springs, and stated that it was the best prospect for an ample supply of water that he had seen in the state and that it was, in his opinion, a permanent supply. He was also here yesterday, making measurements and taking photographs of the flow of the water and surroundings, and was very much pleased with the amount of water we were getting.

Now, Gentlemen, we have been to a considerable expense in our endeavor to secure the city this supply of water and, at last, we have the satisfaction of being able to say to you and to the citizens of Beatrice that we have been successful and that we have secured a supply of water sufficient to take care of the city's requirements for many years to come.

We never had figured on making a profit out of securing for the city a sufficient supply of water and we are willing at this time to turn the wells and springs over to the city of Beatrice, which shall include the option for the lease or purchase of the Zimmerman Springs together with the completed well, also the wells north of the city and the pumping machinery and equipment connected with same, also the cancellation of our contract for the water supply, and all we ask in return is that we be paid just what it has cost us to secure it, charging nothing for the risk which we have taken by virtue of the fact that had we not secured the water, we stood to lose what we had spent or invested.

The total cost amounts to $15,867.26, to which we will have to add six per cent interest from August 1, 1913.

This proposition is made to the city of Beatrice, through you as their representatives, and will hold good until September 15, 1913, which we believe will give you ample time to investigate the matter and decide whether the city wants to accept the proposition or not.

Hoping that this proposition will meet with your approval and that steps may be taken at an early date to close the matter up, in order that the main may be run into the city and the people supplied with this spring water before winter sets in, we are

                    Yours very truly,
                          Dempster Mill Mfg. Co.
                              C. B. Dempster, Pres.

At a special election held in the city May 5, 1910, the voters of the municipality had authorized the issuance of $70,000 of the bonds of the city, the proceeds thereof to be used in constructing, maintaining and operating a system of waterworks for Beatrice. On October 10th of that year these bonds had been issued and sold, and the money realized from their sale had been applied by the city authorities in enlarging the building and plant of the waterworks, installing additional machinery, including an electric pumping plant and lighting system, and in covering the expense of the various efforts put forth by the commissioners in trying to develop a sufficient water supply by the system of wells. After the development of the Zimmerman Springs proposition as set forth in the foregoing letter of the Dempster Company, it became necessary to raise money to cover the cost of acquiring the spring and the ten-acre tract where it is situated, as set out in the letter. For this purpose the special election was held in the city on the 5th day of November, 1913, at which the issuance of $30,000 of the bonds of the city was authorized, the proceeds thereof to be used to complete the waterworks system of the city by acquiring title to the spring and the ten-acre tract of land where it is located and of connecting it to the existing waterworks system of the city.

By these various steps Beatrice has finally acquired a supply of pure spring water sufficient, as far as tried, for the demands of the city, at a total cost of approximately $225,000 to the taxpayers of the municipality. After many years of operation at a steady loss, which was annually met by additional taxation, the Beatrice city water plant has reached a point where it is easily self-supporting.

CHAPTER XXI

BEATRICE CONTINUED

THE FREE PUBLIC LIBRARY — FIRST BOARD OF DIRECTORS — CARNEGIE LIBRARY BUILDING — FIRST LIBRARIAN — PUBLIC PARKS — THE OLD STONE CHURCH — THE NEW METHODIST CHURCH — THE FIRST PRESBYTERIAN CHURCH — THE EPISCOPAL CHURCH — FIRST CHRISTIAN CHURCH — UNITED BRETHREN CHURCH — TRINITY LUTHERAN CHURCH — FIRST CATHOLIC CHURCH — FIRST BAPTIST CHURCH — ST. JOHN'S LUTHERAN CHURCH — GERMAN METHODIST CHURCH — LASALLE STREET CHURCH — SEVENTH DAY ADVENTIST CHURCH — FIRST CHURCH OF CHRIST, SCIENTIST — FIRST CONGREGATIONAL CHURCH — MENNONITE CHURCH — BEATRICE SCHOOL DISTRICT — OLD FRAME SCHOOL HOUSE — FIRST HIGH SCHOOL BUILDING — SECOND HIGH SCHOOL BUILDING — THIRD HIGH SCHOOL BUILDING — GRADE SCHOOL BUILDINGS — CITY SUPERINTENDENT OF SCHOOLS

The public library of the city of Beatrice, which in the afflux of time has become a factor of inestimable importance in the intellectual life of the city, is the direct outgrowth of the activities of an organization known as the Beatrice Literary Club, founded about the year 1890, by Carroll G. Pearse (superintendent of the Beatrice city schools), Ossian H. Brainard, Alexander R. Dempster, Edward Sinclair Smith, Dr. Edward Bates, Leander M. Pemberton, Samuel S. Peters, Joseph E. Gobbey, Jr., Marion T. Cummings, Hugh J. Dobbs, and others. Prior to the founding of the library, the ladies of the Woman's Christian Temperance Union of Beatrice had for many years maintained a small circulating library in the city, this being poorly supported by voluntary contributions and paid subscriptions. It had a very limited use, on account of the small number of books of value and of the expense to patrons using it. For several years its sponsors had frequently endeavored to persuade the city to take their library and, with it as nucleus, found a municipal library supported by public tax; in this, however, they had been uniformly unsuccessful.

In the spring of 1893 the Beatrice Literary Club found itself in the possession of a considerable sum of money, the product of some very successful lecture courses given under its auspices, and resolved to undertake the service to the community of inducing the city council to accept the offer of the ladies of the Woman's Christian Temperance Union, to relieve them of the burden of carrying on a library which met the demands of the community to a very limited degree, and to found a municipal library to which every citizen of Beatrice might, under proper regulations, have full and free access. As a slight inducement to favorable action on the part of the city council, the members of the Literary Club proposed to turn over to the city the money in its treasury, to be used for library purposes. The city council gave ear to the persuasive eloquence of Carroll G. Pearse, president of the Literary Club, and, after canvassing the matter, decided to act favorably upon his suggestions. The money tendered by the club was accepted, the books and library effects of the ladies of the Woman's Christian Temperance Union were taken over by the city, and, in June, 1893, the city council, formally and in the manner provided by law, established a free public library for the citizens of Beatrice. A board of directors was thereupon appointed and for the support of the library a levy of two mills on the dollar was made upon the grand assessment roll of the city. The first board of directors was composed of the following well known citizens of the city of Beatrice: Jefferson B. Weston, three years; Cornelius Jansen, three years; Leander M. Pemberton, one year; Joseph E. Cobbey, one year; Samuel Rinaker, two years; LeRoy F. LaSelle, three years; George P. Marvin, two years; Charles G. Gilespie, one year; Hugh J. Dobbs, three years.

This board of directors organized by choosing Jefferson B. Weston, president; Leander M. Pemberton, vice-president; and Cornelius Jansen, secretary. Mary E. Abell, who had been prominent in the affairs of the former library, was elected by the board of directors as the first librarian of the municipal library. Quarters for the new library, together with a reading room, were secured on the upper floor of the new postoffice building on its completion, in October, 1893, and the Beatrice Free Public Library was formally opened to public patronage.

In December, 1902, application was made by the library board to Andrew Carnegie for an allowance out of his millions for the purpose of erecting a suitable building for the library. The application was favorably received by the great iron master, who offered to donate to the city of Beatrice the sum of $20,000 for the erection of a library building, provided a suitable site were procured and the city council would agree to make an annual levy upon the taxable valuation of the property of the city for the purpose of supporting the library. The money to purchase the present site of the library building was raised by private subscription, and lots 5 and 6 in block 36 of the original town of Beatrice, the present site of the library, were purchased for $1,600.

George A. Burlinghof, an architect then residing at Beatrice, was selected to draft plans and specifications for the library building. Contracts were let for its construction and the work entered upon in the spring of 1903, almost exactly ten years from the date of founding the library. The work progressed rapidly. The material used was Warrensburg, Missouri, sandstone and terracotta. While not fire-proof, the building is constructed on the principle known as slow combustion. This building, with its grounds, is now practically included in the Charles Park, and together they form perhaps the most interesting and beautiful spot in Beatrice.

On the completion of the building, Mr. Carnegie, being again appealed to, contributed $3,000 to be used in the purchase of suitable furniture, shelving and other fixtures for the library. The book stacks and furniture were bought of the American Library Association and were duly installed. On the first day of January, 1904, the Beatrice Free Public Library was opened to public patronage in its new and beautiful building.

Since its founding, the patrons of the library have been served by a number of efficient librarians, but by none more able or devoted than the first, Mary E. Abell. This good lady, who had been a citizen of Beatrice for many years, died while serving as librarian, on Saturday, April 4, 1903, and of the original library board, Weston, Cobbey, LaSelle, Marvin and Gillespie also have passed away. But the institution which they were instrumental in organizing remains and will long remain to radiate its beneficent influence throughout the beautiful city which it serves.

The public parks of Beatrice are Charles Park, Nichols Park, the Athletic Park, and the Chautauqua Park.

Charles Park is situated between Fifth and Sixth streets, immediately south of the old high-school building. It was purchased in part with a bequest in the will of James Charles, a pioneer resident of Beatrice and vicinity, the purchased lots being 1, 2, 3 and 4 in block 36 of the original town of Beatrice. To these were added lots 5 and 6, where the public library stands, and also Elk street between Fifth and Sixth streets, which was vacated by the city council for park purposes, and all that part of the school-house square south of the walks about the old high-school building.

Nichols Park is located a little west of the Court street bridge across the Big Blue river. It is a beautiful spot, comprising about three acres of ground between Court street and the river. Most of the land forming it was donated by Martin V. Nichols, an old and highly esteemed resident of Beatrice.

The Athletic Park is an adjunct of the city school system. The founders of this play ground were the late Daniel Wolford Cook, the Kilpatrick Brothers and S. W. Collins. After its completion, it was donated and by warranty deed conveyed to the Beatrice school district, to be forever dedicated to wholesome school sport, and other scholastic and public gatherings.

The Chautauqua Park comprises about thirty acres of land, for many years known and used as Chautauqua grounds. Beginning about 1888, the Chautauqua organization, composed of several public-spirited citizens of Beatrice, annually for several years gave a Chautauqua program on these grounds. The large assembly hall and the other structures now found there were placed on the grounds by this organization. For a dozen years or more the programs given at this place were well patronized by the people of southeastern Nebraska. Many eminent men and women have here contributed to the instruction, amusement and entertainment of large audiences. Amongst these were Thomas DeWitt Talmage, a noted clergyman of the past generation; ex-President Hayes; Sam Jones; Bishop Vincent; Frank Robinson, the travelouge entertainer; William J. Bryan; Frances Willard; Congressman Horr; Mary Ellen Lease; Edward Rosewater; Dr. Robert McIntyre; Susan B. Anthony; Dr. Henson, a noted Baptist clergyman, of Chicago; Robert LaFollette; and many others of wide reputation as speakers, lecturers, and entertainers.

After an interesting and profitable record covering many years, the organization, on account of the decrease in attendance, finally suspended operations in debt, and an action was brought against it in the district court of Gage county to foreclose a mortgage on its property, when, by an arrangement with the board of directors, the city of Beatrice intervened, paid the indebtedness, took over the property and converted it into a beautiful city park.

An important adjunct to the public-park system of the city is the use which has recently been made of the Big Blue river as a source of recreation. While always a favored means of entertainment it has grown in favor since W. E. Garrett, in August, 1907, acquired riparian rights on the river above Black Brothers' mill dam and installed a line of pleasure boats, including flat boats for picnickers. For a number of years he has given an annual evening festival on the river locally known as "Venetian Night" which attracts large and appreciative crowds, many coming from considerable distances.

The Nehaunchee canoeing club is an organization of canoe enthusiasts whose purpose is to develop a taste for this fine sport and increase the usefulness of the river as a pleasure resort.

Nothing perhaps shows the steady growth of Beatrice from a mere village of a few hundred inhabitants to a modern city of probably 12,000 people more than its church history. No movement to erect a church building in the village was inaugurated prior to the year 1868. The Methodist Episcopal denomination had possessed organizations in Beatrice, Blue Springs and other localities in the county prior to that time. Early that year steps were taken to erect in Beatrice a church for general use. The idea seemed to be that it should be open and free to all denominations; it was in effect a citizens' movement for a free church building. The location for this structure was fixed at the corner of Fourth and Elk streets, lots 7, 8, block 20 of the original town of Beatrice, and work was begun probably in the late spring of 1868. The building planned was to be a stone edifice, approximately twenty-five by fifty feet in dimensions, with a single room,—a plain building both inside and out. The stone was hauled from the quary of Hurd & Guffey, at what is now Holmesville, and the work appears to have progressed rapidly, as things went in those days. Under date of October 28, 1868, the *Blue Valley Record* says "Our free church edifice is beginning to loom up. Carr, the contractor, is a smasher to drive business. However it is no wonder, for he has the best material in the world to use in his contract." The same paper announces also that Mr. Carr, who superintended the stone work at the capitol building at Lincoln, had located permanently in Beatrice.

As the church approached completion the plan of a free church building was abandoned and the property turned over to the Methodist church organization, which completed it and occupied it for religious services in the early part of 1869. May 17, 1870, to the trustees of the church a deed was given to lot 8, block 20, by J. W. and J. B. Mumford, and on May 23, 1871, J. B. Weston conveyed to the trustees of the church lot 7 in this block, which was afterward occupied by a parsonage. This old stone structure was the first building in Gage county erected for church purposes and dedicated to the worship of Almighty God. For many years, with the parsonage, it stood at the corner of Fourth and Elk streets. Recently both lots have been purchased by the Beatrice school district and the old stone church, which had fallen into disuse, was wrecked, the parsonage moved away and the lots included in the high-school grounds. This old pioneer church building played a most interesting and useful part in the religious and social life of Beatrice for many years. In addition to the services of the church, Sunday school was held within its walls, marriages performed at its altar, the dead buried from its doors, and many a penitent found rest for a troubled heart through confession of sin and profession of faith.

The old church delighted to open its doors in hospitable welcome to religious, social and educational gatherings. The first confirmation service of the Episcopal church was held here, in April, 1871, and the first meetings of the Presbyterians were in this building, in 1869. Here the writer himself, in the unforgotten past, attended not only the religious services of the church but also debates, lectures, educational meetings, social gatherings. When its rugged walls were taken down, stone by stone, much of the past history of Beatrice may be said to have disappeared forever.

The first Methodist minister to hold service in the church as pastor was W. A. Presson, a veteran of the Civil war. After him, not strictly in order perhaps, were Revs. J. W. Wilson, David Hart, John W. Stewart, and Wesley K. Bean.

The congregation grew rapidly from the first, and the old building became inadequate to its needs. Under the ministry of Rev. Wesley K. Bean, in 1885, steps were taken to erect a new church edifice and parsonage, and as a result of that movement the fine brick house of worship located at the corner of Sixth and Elk streets, known as the Centenary Methodist Episcopal church, was erected, and it was dedicated to the worship of God in the spring of 1886.

About the year 1906 a fine pipe organ was installed in the church, the gift of Mrs. Rachael Kilpatrick and Mrs. Margaret Constance Blakely, both pioneer residents of our county. In 1915 the church was enlarged and otherwise extensively improved. The membership of this church has grown from a mere handful in 1869 to a body of nine hundred communicants. Amongst its organizations are the Ladies' Aid Society, Epworth League, the Home and Foreign Missionary Societies and the Standard Bearers.

Amongst the ministers who have occupied the pulpit of this church and given it power and influence are Wesley K. Bean, John W. Stewart, C. S. Dudley, Duke Slavens, H. T. Davis, L. J. Guild, B. F. Thomas, N. A. Martin, Ulysses G. Brown, and Benjamin F. Gaither. The present pastor is Rev. Clyde Clay Cissell.

The First Presbyterian Church of Beatrice was organized March 12, 1859, under the auspices of the Missouri River Presbytery. The charter members in the organization were Mrs. Sarah Ann Blodgett, Mrs. Mary T. Griggs, Miss Anna Griggs, Robert H. Weeden and Mrs. Lydia Weeden. Of these Mrs. Blodgett is the only survivor. The first board of trustees comprised Henry A. LaSelle, Robert H. Weeden and R. L. Blodgett. Mr. LaSelle was also clerk and treasurer of the church. In 1869 a church edifice thirty-seven by thirty-seven feet in dimensions, brick, two stories, was erected on the southwest corner of Fifth and High streets. It was completed at a cost of about $10,000 and was dedicated as a house of public worship some time in 1870. The first minister of this pioneer church was Benjamin F. McNeil, who was also county superintendent of schools. Following him there came James A. Griffith, Thomas S. Hale, L. W. B. Shryock, W. H. McMeen, H. F. White, A. B. Irving, John W. Mills, William H. Hood, John D. Countermine, William H. Kearns, L. D. Young, N. P. Patterson, and E. C. Lucas, the present pastor. Perhaps no church in the west has been served by an abler, more learned or more devoted line of ministerial leaders. Some of them, having acquired reputation and influence in Beatrice, have been called to broader fields of labor, while the present pastor, with patriotic self-denial, will soon engage in the work of his calling in distant France, during the great world war.

In 1893 the present beautiful church and parsonage were erected, at a cost of $24,000. The membership now exceeds five hundred, the attendance at Sunday school averages two hundred and fifty. The present bench of elders are: Rev. Edgar C. Lucas, Moderator; F. B. Sheldon, clerk; E. F. Kimmerly, treasurer; Dr. W. C. Purviance, G. H. Van Horn, Charles Elliott, Paul D. Marvin, J. W. Beard, J. R. Spicer, J. E. T.

Dickinson, H. A. LaSelle, and Dr. C. A. Spellman. The activities of the church are many and varied. Its societies are the Young People's Society of Christian Endeavor, Intermediate and Junior Christian Endeavor Societies, Women's Missionary Society, Ladies' Aid Society, Delta Alpha Chapter of Westminster Guild, Life Bearers and Mission Band.

In April, 1871, the first confirmation of the Episcopal church was held at the old stone Methodist church and the general services of the church began in that year. The parish was organized and admitted to the union of the diocese in 1873. The minutes of the meeting at which the parish was organized show that S. C. B. Dean was elected senior warden and John E. Smith junior warden; vestrymen, J. W. Carter, Alfred Hazlett, and A. G. Spellman. Of the incorporators only one is now identified with the parish. Mr. John E. Smith, who in 1874 was elected senior warden and who has been annually reelected since that time. The first record in the parish register is the baptism of Sarah Isabella Landy, August 13, 1871, by the Rev. Arthur E. Wilson.

The first rector of the parish was the Rev. Joseph F. Cotton, who continued in charge until 1876. The Rev. Robert W. Jones served as rector from 1877 to 1880, the Rev. William G. Hawkins served from 1880 to 1882 and was succeeded by Rev. C. L. Fulforth, who remained until 1885; the Rev. Robert Scott took charge of the parish at the beginning of 1886 and remained until 1891; Rev. J. O. Davis became rector that year and served until 1895; the Rev. W. P. N. J. Wharton served one year and was succeeded by the present rector, Rev. W. A. Mulligan, in 1896.

At the time of the organization, a wooden church was built on the site where the present church now stands. Prior to this the congregation worshiped in a small wooden school-house which stood on the block where the Central ward school now stands. During the rectorship of the Rev. Robert Scott, the present handsome stone church was built, at a cost of about $40,000. The corner stone was laid in 1889 and the church opened for service on Easter Day, 1890. In the year 1892 an excellent pipe organ was installed in the church, this being the first pipe organ in Beatrice. In 1904 the present commodious rectory was built, at a cost approximately of $5,000. In 1908 the parish was cleared of indebtedness, and the church was consecrated June 16th of that year. In 1916 a handsome stone chapel was built in the rear of the church edifice, at a cost of $6,000.

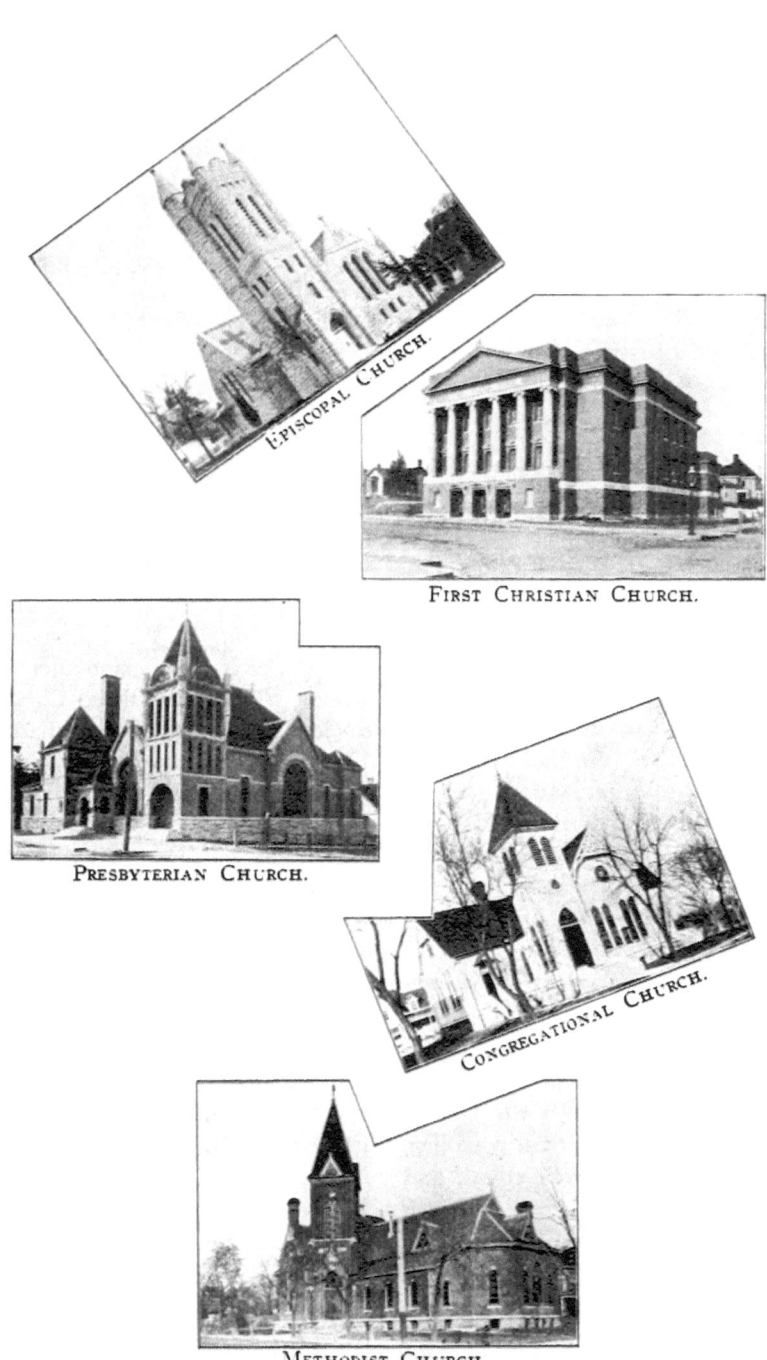

Episcopal Church.

First Christian Church.

Presbyterian Church.

Congregational Church.

Methodist Church.

The organizations of the church are the Altar Guild, Daughters of the King, Junior Auxilliary, St. Mary's Auxilliary, Red Cross Auxilliary, and Women's Auxilliary.

The following are men of Christ Church parish who have enlisted in the present world war: J. Edmund C. Fisher, Philip W. Clancy, Allen B. Ellis, Robert J. Emery, Royal Green, Edward Hackstadt, Fulton Jack, Jr., Ernest D. Kees, Clarence F. Kilpatrick, Russell A. Phelps, Samuel L. Roe, Herbert T. Schaeffer, William T. Rogers, John F. Schiek, Ralph C. Scott, Frank Hobbs, Donald N. Van Arsdale, George St. Clair Preston, Harold R. Mulligan, Clifford Rockhold, John J. Kilpatrick. Allen W. Mulligan, George W. Maurer, and Harold D. Burgess.

The Episcopalians have contributed to the beauty of the city of Beatrice in a memorable way by the erection of their stone church. No building in the city compares with it in architectural grace and churchly character. From the surrounding country on every hand, the white, beautiful spire of this sacred edifice forms the most impressive object in the landscape.

The First Christian Church of Beatrice, Nebraska, was organized the first Lord's Day in October, 1872. Rev. R. C. Barrow, laboring under the General Christian Missionary Convention, had visited the place at intervals prior to this date and baptized a few persons. Among the number thus brought together were Dr. H. M. Reynolds and wife and Mrs. Emily O. Snow, and these with a few others formed the nucleus of the congregation. Among these were John C. Past and wife, from Newcastle, Indiana; William Bradt and wife, from Rockford, Illinois; and John L. Rhodes and wife, from North English, Iowa. In the fall of 1872 John C. Past attended the state missionary convention, at Lincoln, to secure aid in holding a meeting and through this means effect an organization; the state board recommended that the brethren at Beatrice proceed to hold a meeting and if possible establish an organization, and the services of John W. Allen were secured to hold a protracted meeting, which was commenced at once. After about two weeks a church was organized with about twenty members. They were J. C. Past, Mrs. J. C. Past, William Bradt, Mrs. Bradt, Dr. H. M. Reynolds, Mrs. Reynolds, John L. Rhodes, Mrs. John L. Rhodes, Edwin Pheasant, Mrs. Edwin

Pheasant, Mr. and Mrs. Headley, G. W. Hinkle, John Ellis, Mrs. Dr. C. C. Sprague, Mrs. Chesney, Mrs. A. L. Snow, A. W. Bradt, Mrs. A. W. Bradt, and Miss Maggie Murgatroyd. J. C. Past and William Bradt were elected elders, and Dr. H. M. Reynolds and John L. Rhodes were made deacons. The elders and deacons constituted the official board. The first meetings were held in Reynolds Townsend's Hall, in the second story of the building at the northwest corner of Court and Fifth streets.

In 1874 a movement was started to build a church and $250 was paid for a lot at the northeast corner of Sixth and Ella streets. A church building was built, twenty-eight by forty-two feet, with an addition in the rear for vestry rooms, ten by twelve feet and a baptistry under the pulpit, at a cost of about $2,000. But the grasshoppers came and destroyed the crops before the building was completed, leaving the organization with a debt of seven or eight hundred dollars, because the people could not make good their pledges. In 1889 an addition was built on the north, thirty-two by forty-four feet, giving the building a T shape, with a seating capacity of five hundred. The same year they purchased the two lots at the east end of the block, where the present church building stands, and considered the construction of a new church on this site. In 1891 the United States government purchased, for a postoffice site, the lot on which the church stood, and this necessitated the removal of the church building to the lots at Seventh and Ella streets. A basement story was built level with the street under the entire building and the parsonage was moved to the north of the church. This was the home of the congregation until 1907, when the present beautiful edifice was erected, at a cost of $40,000.

At the present time the membership of the church is over twelve hundred. The number enrolled in the Sunday School is twelve hundred, with an average attendance of five hundred and twenty-five.

The first minister was the Rev. J. Madison Williams, now of Des Moines, Iowa. Those following him were Samuel Lowe, Joseph Lowe, William G. Springer, Eli Fisher, R. H. Ingram, J. D. Dabney, A. D. McKeever, F. A. Bright, Edgar Price, J. E. Davis, and C. F. Stevens, the present pastor, who has been here about six years.

The present official board is composed of J. L. Rhodes, honorary elder; D. W. Carre, H. E. Sackett, W. H. Davis, H. S. Souders, Henry Essam, J. L. Riecker, F. K. Klein, O. J. Lyndes, O. A. Burket, elders; and A. H. Voortman, Henry Fishhach, William Thomas, H. M. Smethers, P. J. Smethers, Henry Williamson, F. E. McCracken, E. L. Hevelone, W. W. Duncan, N. Thompson, Fordyce Graf, John Connor, D. G. McGaffey, H. S. Vaught, and J. W. Baumgartner, deacons. W. H. Davis is superintendent of the Sunday school. There are three Christian Endeavor Societies, senior, intermediate, and junior. There are also the Young Ladies' Circle, the Triangle Club, and the Ladies' Aid Society.

A society of the United Brethren church was organized December 14, 1874, with the Rev. W. H. Shepherd as minister in charge. Meetings were first held, on alternate Sundays, in the Baptist church, which stood where the Knox livery barn is now, on Market street between Fifth and Sixth streets. On the 20th day of October, 1876, a church was organized with the following named members: Elias Rhodes, Margaret Rhodes, Mrs. Eli Miller, Mrs. Howe, Mrs. Elizabeth Salts, Michael Beam, Mrs. Michael Beam, Elizabeth Meyers, Mary Reed, Mr. and Mrs. A. Q. Miller. The first board of trustees was composed of Elias Rhodes, Leander Swain, Michael Beam, and A. Q. Miller. Of the charter members Mrs. Eli Miller is the only one now residing in Beatrice. In 1875, by devise of Mrs. Elizabeth N. Joseph, of Aetna, Ohio, the church came into possession of one hundred and sixty acres of land near Beatrice, which they traded with William Lamb for building them a church at the southeast corner of Eighth and Ella streets. This building was enlarged in 1891 and again in 1905. The church has a membership of eighty, the Sunday school of ninety-one. The ministers who have served this congregation are W. H. Shepherd, J. H. Embree, Byron Beal, Rev. Aumiller, Robert Floyd, Rev. Landis A. Oliver, C. O. Robb, S. E. Floyd, William Burwell, Philip Surface, J. M. Haskins, E. F. Bowers, F. M. Bell, E. T. Root, J. Powers, F. M. Miller, W. F. Brink, E. A. Sharp, T. P. Cannon, W. S. Lynde, T. S. Swan, H. F. Hoffman, and S. S. Turley, the latter since February, 1918.

The Trinity Lutheran Church was organized December 9, 1883. The corner stone of the brick church belonging to this organization, at the corner of Ninth and Elk streets, was laid November 9, 1884, and the church completed and dedicated in December, 1885. It had a membership of forty-five. The ministers who have served this organization are George H. Albright, W. L. Remsburg, J. L. Motchman, W. W. Hess, J. A. Lowe, Roy M. Badger, and A. M. Reitzel. Mr. Reitzel came to the church in 1915; recently he resigned and the pastorate at this writing is vacant. The church has a membership of two hundred and fifty, and a Sunday-school enrollment of one hundred and forty, with J. H. Pletcher, superintendent.

The board of trustees of this church consists of the elders and deacons. The elders now are E. Feldkirschner, J. P. Naumann, Andrew Anderson, and T. J. Trauernicht; the deacons are F. H. Kimmerling, August Schmidt, L. K. Stevens, and C. S. Overbeck.

The first Catholic to settle in Gage county was Joseph Graff, who, in 1860, located on a claim four miles west of Beatrice. At that time the nearest priest was in Nebraska City, sixty-five miles away. Father Hoffmayer visited Gage county in 1859 and mass was offered in the log cabin of Joseph Graff, in a room sixteen by sixteen feet, and three of Mr. Graff's children were baptized. The next priest to visit Gage county was Father Ferdinand Lechleitner, who was located in Crete. He first visited Beatrice September 15, 1874, and again December 6, 1874; May 4, and June 15, 1875; May 16, 1876; May 29 and October 30, 1877. On all the above dates he held service at the residence of Joseph Graff. In July or August of 1877 Father Lechleitner presided at a meeting held at Mr. Graff's, at which it was arranged to build a church. A lot was then purchased in the block north of the Chicago, Rock Island Pacific depot, on South Sixth street, and a church forty by forty-six feet was erected thereon at a cost of $1,000. It was dedicated in 1878, and this is the first Catholic church in Gage county. The members of the organization at that time were Joseph Graff, Francis Leonard, Franz Grussel, John Russell, Thomas Grace, Anna and Marie Samletzki, Joseph Meyer, Charles Hentges and wife, Frank Hiebeler, and Charles A. Graff. The church was called St. Joseph's and was attached to the Tecumseh church until 1884. Down to this time it had been served by the following named priests: Father McNally, Father Madden, Father John Crowley, and

Father A. Havestadt, who held mass occasionally. In the spring of 1884 lots were purchased at the northeast corner of Sixth and High streets and the old church was moved to this location. Father A. Havestadt was the first resident priest, 1884-1886, and was followed by Father Thomas Quick, 1886-1889. The first parsonage was built in 1885. At the close of 1886 the number of families within the pale of the church was one hundred and eleven, or five hundred and ten souls. At the close of 1887 there were one hundred and sixty-six families; at the close of 1888, one hundred eighty-six families, or three hundred and eighty-seven persons over eighteen years of age and four hundred and eighty under that age. In 1888 a school room, thirty-eight by twenty-two feet, was added to the old church. In September, 1889, a home was opened for Ursuline Sisters, who had come from York, Nebraska, to take charge of the school. It was called St. Joseph's Convent. In December, 1889, Father A. J. Copellen assumed charge of the parish. In 1890 a tract of ten acres of land was purchased three miles north of the city, and this was consecrated as a Catholic burying ground. September 1, 1893, Father Copellen was succeeded by Rev. Michael Merkl. During the hard years of 1894-1895-1896-1897, membership in the church decreased fifty per cent; the sisters gave up the school, and at the close of 1898 there were but one hundred and thirty families. Father Merkl was succeeded by Father Petrasch, who came in 1907. He proceeded to tear down the old church, and the present brick church, school house and parsonage were erected. In 1912 Father E. Boll succeeded Father Petrasch, but the latter returned for a few months in 1916, when Father Boll left. In December, 1916, Father Bickert, the present priest, took charge of the parish. There are now one hundred and seventy-five families on the church roll, and eighty-four pupils in the school, which is in charge of three Dominican Sisters, from Racine, Wisconsin. Philip Graff, Henry Lang, John Plubeck, John Scharton, Hugh Carmichael, and Arthur Woelke constitute the present board of trustees. The following organizations affiliate with the work of the church: Knights of Columbus, Society of the Altar, Sewing Circle, Ladies' Social Club, and Blessed Virgin Mary Sodality.

The First Baptist Church of Beatrice was organized December 6, 1873, and for a while it was served by Rev. J. N. Webb, the state superintendent of Baptist churches. June 27, 1874, Rev. Thomas J. Arnold became its pastor. He was succeeded April 9, 1876, by Rev. L. P. Nason, who, in June, 1877, was succeeded by Rev. L. D. Wharton, and the latter was succeeded, November 1, 1878, by Rev. George Scott. The first church building was where the Knox livery barn now stands, on the north side of Market street, between Fifth and Sixth streets. About 1880 it was moved to the north side of Ella street, between Fourth and Fifth streets, where Kimball's laundry now stands. A few years afterward this church was moved to Grant street, between Seventh and Eighth streets. About twelve years ago the church was again moved, to Sixth Street, and placed on the alley, occupying what is now the southeast corner of Charles Park. When it was decided to locate the park upon these lots the city bought the old church property and paid the Baptists $6,000 for it, and they in turn purchased the Unitarian church building, on the northwest corner of Sixth and High streets, which they have since occupied.

The charter members of the church were John Kerlin, Elizabeth Kerlin, Mary C. Kerlin, S. A. Smith, Rhoda Smith, Josiah A. Smith, T. J. Smith, and Job Buchanan, who was also first church clerk. The trustees were John Kerlin, S. A. Smith, and Job Buchanan. The deacons of the church now are Griffith Evans, R. Davis, George Sexton, Henry Fairchild, H. M. Garrett, Fred Lloyd, F. N. Crangle, C. H. Aylesworth. The board of trustees are G. W. Thomas, Walter D. Wright, Dan Crosby, Walter Andrews, Argre Fryer; the church clerk is S. R. Jamison.

St. John's Lutheran Church of Beatrice was organized in 1880, with fifteen members. It met in various halls until the erection of its church at the corner of Fifth and Bell streets. The first minister was the Rev. Lynch. The present minister, Rev. Leonard Poeverlein, has served the church continuously since 1883. The church has a membership of fifty families. Fred Damrow, Julius Harter, and Fred Paul are trustees, John Roschefski is church clerk, and F. S. Kuhl is treasurer.

The German Methodist Church, located at the northwest comer of Eighth and Scott streets, was organized in 1886, and a church was erected in 1887, at a cost of $2,000. It had a membership of twelve when organized and now has twenty-four. As pastors E. T. Treibler, G. M.

Zwink, John Lauer, C. G. Meyer, Conrad Eberhart, John Mueller, and Edward Beck have served this church, Rev. Edward Beck being the present pastor and having been with the church since 1904. M. Buehler, Albert Eckel, and Henry Wipperman constitute the board of trustees.

LaSalle Street Methodist Church was organized in 1887, and its church was dedicated November 6th of that year, with Rev. H. C. Wells, pastor in charge. There were fifty-four charter members, and the present membership is one hundred and seventy-four. Pastors, H. C. Wells, 1886-1887; James K. Maxfield, 1887-1889; James Darby, 1889-1892; T. S. Fowler, 1892-1893; H. D. Wilcox, 1893-1895; G. W. Selby, 1895-1896; J. W. Royce, 1896-1898; D. C. Phillips, 1898-1899; A. W. Coffman, 1899-1900; E. L. Barch, 1900-1903; F. W. Bean, 1903-1905; George M. Jones, 1905-1906; J. W. Lewis, 1906-1909; B. F. Hutchins, 1909-1911; J. A. Ronsley, 1911-1912; J. B. Darby, 1912-1915; Henry Bell, 1915-1916; A. L. Pratt, 1916 to the present time. The church has been rebuilt and was rededicated in June, 1914.

The Church of the Brethren merits definite consideration in this work. This branch of the Brethren church, located at the corner of Fourteenth and Grant streets, was organized in 1881, and the church was built in 1888, at a cost of $3,000. Its ministers have been J. E. Young, J. H. Mohler, L. D. Bosserman, A. D. Sollenberger, A. P. Musselman, and W. W. Blough. At the present time the deacons are Charles H. Price, E. J. Kessler, and C. J. Lichty; the trustees are C. H. Price and E. J. Kessler; the treasurer is Miss Rebecca Essam, and the clerk is E. J. Kessler. The church has a membership of ninety-five.

The following record concerning the First Church of Christ, Scientist, in the city of Beatrice, was prepared by Leonard A. Emmert:

Interest in Christian Science was first aroused in Beatrice in the fall of 1884. A lady who had been confined to her bed several months was invited by a friend to visit her in Boston, Massachusetts. While there she was induced to take Christian Science treatments, with the result that she was healed. Upon returning to her home (Beatrice) she told of the wonderful "new religion" in Boston known as Christian Science, and of its healing power. Her recovery and the story she told interested others suffering from diseases that the doctors had pronounced hopeless.

Several decided to go to Boston, and in writing to Mary Baker Eddy, the founder of Christian Science were informed that a student of hers just finishing metaphysical college would be in Omaha in a few weeks. As soon as this student arrived in Omaha, Mrs. Elizabeth Buswell, given up by the doctors as incurable, went to her, in May, 1885, and she was healed in a week's treatment. This was the reason for many others going. All came back healed or greatly benefited.

Within a few weeks, when it was sufficiently known that the new method of healing, called Christian Science, purported to be a practical and scientific application of the truth taught and practiced by Jesus and His disciples, a number who had been interested and benefited began meeting together in the different homes. The first public meeting was held in the Masonic Hall—First National Bank Building—Easter Sunday, 1886. A charter was granted from Boston May 15, 1886. November 24, 1888, services were moved to what was then known as Gibbs Hall and on this date the First Church of Christ, Scientist, was organized and incorporated under the laws of the state. This was the first Church of Christ, Scientist, organized west of the Missouri river.

In the winter of 1890, on account of fire, the church was obliged to move again, this time taking up quarters in the LePoidevin Block. In April of the following year (1891) it became possible to secure the Brethren church edifice, located in the 1200 block of Court street. This last move proved to be an important one for the growth of the church, for shortly after locating here every department of work advanced rapidly. At a meeting of the board of directors, held June 14, 1891, it was decided to purchase a lot at the corner of Ninth and Elk streets, for the purpose of some day erecting a building. This was successfully accomplished the following month, on July 31st. It was secured from Maggie C. Blakely for a consideration of thirteen hundred dollars.

The next important step in the march of progress was the buying of the Brethren church, in the fall of 1900. It was planned that this church building was to be moved to the lot purchased, but in working out this program it developed that a more desirable location presented itself, which resulted in the directors disposing of their first purchase and buying a lot, fifty by one hundred and fifty feet, on the corner of Eighth and Ella streets. This was purchased from Cora M. Woolridge, September 22, 1900, consideration being eight hundred dollars.

In March, 1901, meetings were again held in the LePoidevin Block, while the church edifice was being moved to its new location. There it was remodeled, enlarged and refurnished throughout. This home was dedicated May 26, 1901, and remained unchanged, except for a few minor improvements, until September, 1916, when it again became possible to remodel and enlarge the structure. A beautiful foyer was added, and several large columns were placed at the entrance, which seems to be so characteristic of Christian Science churches. Meetings were resumed in the church edifice November 26, 1916. Services were held in the Commercial Club rooms while the work was being done.

Three authorized teachers have taught Christian Science in Beatrice. The first class taught west of Chicago was conducted in Beatrice, October 5, 1885.

The history of this church would be incomplete without mention being made of the nation-wide attention which was directed toward Beatrice in February and March, 1893, when a student and teacher of Christian Science was indicted, under the statutes of the state of Nebraska, for practicing medicine without legal authority. Quoting from one of the local papers, dated February 27, 1893, we find the following records made of the case: "The case of E. M. Buswell, who is charged with practicing medicine without legal authority, will be called up in the district court tomorrow. It is a peculiar case, perhaps unlike any that has gone before in the courts, and it will excite widespread interest." Quoting again from the same paper, dated March 5, 1893: "The great trial is over. The jury in the case of E. M. Buswell, charged with illegal practicing of medicine, which went out at eighty thirty yesterday afternoon, came in about nine o'clock in the evening with a verdict of acquittal. The defendant was there upon discharged. The verdict is generally regarded as what might have been expected in the face of the evidence presented." This was a victory for Christian Science which was felt throughout the United States and wrote a memorable page for the growth of the church here, and for the cause.

The history of this church is like that of most churches which started in the west—the record of a small beginning, a slow but sturdy progress, perseverance in the face of discouraging obstacles, defiance at times that seemed almost defeat. But what is here today is a testimonial of Courage—Faith—Hope—Love.

The Seventh Day Adventists of Beatrice held their first meeting July 7, 1894, and they organized a church in August, 1895, with twenty-two members. The meetings were held in homes of the members until the church was built, in 1897, on the northeast corner of Ella and Tenth streets. The first minister was Elder J. H. Rogers. The local elder is A. E. Putnam. George Stout is treasurer, and Mrs. A. E. Putnam is clerk.

The First Congregational Church of Beatrice was organized June 1, 1884. The charter members were J. M. and Matilda Wilber, Dr. Edward S. Bates and Jennie N. Bates, Gray Warner and Carrie L. Warner, W. B. Hotchkiss, Lewis R. Thomas, Ruth A. Thomas, H. S. Cox, A. R. Dempster, Jennie C. Dempster, Dr. Calvin Starr, Dr. Julia C. Starr, Mary Starr, L. E. Walker, Bessie Yule Walker, Henry D. Gates, Nellie W. Gates, Clara Bewick Colby. At a business meeting held July 20, 1884, steps were taken to provide the organization with a house of worship. On October 10, 1884, the church purchased, from Isaac N. McConnell, lots 1 and 2, block 6 of the original town of Beatrice, and began the erection of a commodious church building on the east seventy feet of these lots. It was pushed to completion and on Thursday, June 30, 1885, it was formally dedicated to the public worship of Almighty God as a Congregational church. From that date to about the 7th day of August, 1914, it was occupied by the Congregationalists of Beatrice as a house of worship. Prior to the 7th day of August, 1914, the church acquired by purchase lots 9, 10, 11, 12, block 29 of Cropsey's Addition to Beatrice, as a more suitable location, and on that date, by warranty deed, conveyed the old church property to the Evangelical Lutheran church, which has since owned and occupied it as their church. Long prior to that date the church had sold the west seventy feet of their property to Rev. E. S. Smith, one of its early pastors, who erected thereon a dwelling which he occupied as a parsonage during his pastorate. The property is now owned and occupied as a home by Miss Marie Upson. Following the sale of its property to the Lutherans, the church began the erection of a handsome brick structure on the lots purchased by it in Cropsey's Addition, on the corner of Sixth and Grant streets. This church was completed at a cost of approximately $20,000, and on the 4th day of June, 1916, it was, with appropriate ceremonies, dedicated to the worship of God.

NEW CONGREGATIONAL CHURCH

The Congregational church of Beatrice has been fortunate in the character and ability of the men who have served it as pastors during the thirty-four years of its existence. Its first regular pastor was William O. Wheedon, who served from 1884 to 1886, when he was forced to resign on account of ill health. His successor, E. H. Ashman, held the pastorate from August 18, 1886 to February 1, 1888, and was succeeded by E. St. Clair Smith, February 24, 1888, who very ably served the church as its pastor to July 31, 1892, when he resigned to accept a charge in Indiana. The church thereupon extended a call to George W. Crofts, of Council Bluffs, Iowa, and for twelve years this good and saintly man was not only a forceful factor in the Congregational church of Beatrice but also in the churches of the state and in the community at large. No minister of the Gospel ever exemplified in a greater degree the graces of its precepts than the poet-preacher George W. Crofts. In 1912 he passed to his reward, and all that is mortal of this beloved man lies in the cemetery at Council Bluffs. November 2, 1904, Mr. Crofts was succeeded by Edwin Booth, Jr., who continued in the pastorate until May 15, 1908, when he resigned, to take charge of the First Congregational church at Norfolk, Nebraska, of which he is still the pastor. He was succeeded by Fred L. Hall, whose ministry terminated July 1, 1910. Rev J. W. Ferner, of Shenandoah, Iowa, was called to the service September 23, 1910, and resigned November 8. 1914, to accept a call to the First Congregational church of Aurora, Nebraska. He was succeeded by the present pastor, Victor F. Clark.

This church, though small in numbers, enters actively into the religious and social life of the community.

Gage county has had one religious immigration, and the story of that immigration is set forth in the following narrative, prepared for this work by the Hon. Peter Jansen:

"Mennonites, called after the founder of the church, Menno Simons, a former Roman Catholic priest in Holland. Principal characteristics: Baptize only adults, upon confession of faith; opposed to all war, like the Quakers; avoid law suits; members are to be strictly honest; do not make oath, but affirm.

"They are called 'Prussian Mennonites,' which is a misconception. Their ancestors came from the Netherlands (Holland) to Prussia in search of religious liberty, especially freedom from military service, which was abrogated during the early '70s of the past century, after the Franco-Prussian war (and to avoid military service were forced out of Prussia.)

"At the instigation of Cornelius Jansen and his son Peter, the latter having settled in Jefferson county in 1874, a delegation visited Nebraska during the summer of 1876, and finally selected Gage county as the most promising and suitable place for their settlement. A dozen or more families moved to Nebraska that fall and located temporarily in Beatrice, then a frontier town of a thousand or so inhabitants. By the spring of 1877 thirty to forty families had arrived and settled within a radius of ten miles of Beatrice; most of them bought farms and grass land at from six to ten dollars per acre. The names of the most prominent families were Penner, Wiebe, Reimer, Thimm, Goosen, Claussen, Janzen, etc. Others joined them during the next few years, so that eventually a large and very prosperous settlement has sprung up.

"They built a commodious meeting house a few miles west of town, and later another one in this city. Still later they bought the old Kilpatrick church, about ten miles west of Beatrice. All three meetings are under one bishop, Gerhard Penner, now eighty-two years old, living in West Beatrice.

"At the time America entered the world war they of course were subject to the selective draft, like all other citizens; however, the government recognized their conscientious scruples against bloodshed, and designated for them, as well as for the Quakers and Dunkards, noncombatant service, under the new military law, by which they can serve their country without violating their conscience."

BEATRICE SCHOOLS

The Beatrice school district was the first district organized in Gage county. An unfortunate fire which, in 1902, destroyed the old Masonic Temple building, destroyed also all the previous records of the city schools, the superintendent at that time having his office in that building. The records of the county superintendent's office show that the Beatrice school district was organized May 10, 1868, and the school district is there numbered 15, but that date cannot represent the actual date of the organization of the district. About that time all the school districts in the county, some thirty in number, were put through a reorganization process, and numbered. The numbering began with the northeast corner of the county and without respect to the date on which the districts were organized, the aim apparently being to secure uniformity in numbering only.

Beatrice was the oldest community in the county and the most compact. Its founders were at the head of public affairs and they showed great aptitude in advancing the interests of the town. One of the first officers elected by the colony was the county superintendent of schools, and this office, through every change of the law was perpetuated in some form. It is certain that Beatrice was an organized school district under the laws of the territory of Nebraska as early as 1862, when the old frame school building was erected and the first public school was taught by Oliver Townsend.

The area of the school district in those early days is a matter of conjecture. In 1858 the territorial legislature passed an act making each government township a school district, and, under this statute, what is now Midland township then constituted a single school district, with the village of Beatrice included. This statute, however, provided for the formation of sub-districts in the township, and by various subdivisions and legislative enactments the area of the original district was reduced to its present proportions. In addition to the corporation itself, Beatrice school district now embraces several tracts of farm land, some adjacent to the city and some not.

The school history of Beatrice begins with a subscription school taught by Miss Frances Butler, in 1860, in a small frame building belonging to Fordyce Roper. In 1861 Wealthy Tinkham (later Mrs. Joseph Hollingworth) also taught a subscription school in Beatrice. After the erection of the old single-room, frame school house in 1862, on the block of ground dedicated by the founders of the city to school purposes, the public school of Beatrice became a permanent institution. This pioneer school house, the first school building in Gage county, was for many years freely used for nearly every sort of gathering, and it continued to afford the chief educational facility in Gage county until the year 1870.

It first became necessary to employ two teachers for the growing village in the year 1869. That autumn and the following winter a Mr. Hodson taught the older pupils, some thirty-five in number, in the old frame school house, and Mary L. Blodgett (later Mrs. William A. Wagner) taught the primary classes in an upstairs room in an old stone structure at the corner of Fourth and Market streets, on lot 12, block 65 of the original townsite. The Beatrice *Clarion*, the second newspaper printed in Beatrice, and the immediate predecessor of the Beatrice *Express*, occupied the ground floor of the building, below the schoolroom. Miss Blodgett's school numbered fifty-six pupils, and they, with those under Mr. Hodson's instruction, comprised the school population of the entire Beatrice school district.

In 1870 a small two-story, brick school house was erected at the corner of Eighth and Ella streets, on lots 9 and 10, block 33 of the original townsite. The building originally cost about $5,000, and, as first planned, contained four schoolrooms, two on the first and two on the second floor. Later a two-story addition was built on the north, comprising two fair sized schoolrooms, and an entry was constructed on the south, from which a stairway led to the upper floor.

FIRST HIGH SCHOOL BUILDING, 1870

This was the first school building of any pretentions in Beatrice. It was both a grade and a high school and was used as such for many years. By December 1, 1870, the two ground floor rooms of this building had been so far completed as to permit their use for the opening of the winter term of school, with H. J. Chase as principal and Mary L. Blodgett as primary and intermediate teacher. All told there were about one hundred pupils in the school, nearly equally divided between the two instructors. Mr. Chase, the principal of this early school, performed a man's work as a teacher of the older pupils. There was almost no such thing as classification, but he made a serious effort to elevate the Beatrice schools to something more than an ordinary district school. The most advanced subjects taught were higher arithmetic, algebra, book-keeping, grammar, and physical geography. The writer was a pupil of Mr. Chase, and it affords him pleasure to record his appreciation of this scholarly young teacher of that early day.

On the 5th day of January, 1878, this historian entered upon his duties as superintendent of the schools of Beatrice. At that time the old frame school house was still in use, as a primary school. In the following year another small frame school room was erected among the cottonwoods and maples at the northeast corner of the school-house square, and this also was devoted to primary instruction. By the opening of the fall term of 1879 the schools had been as carefully graded as circumstances permitted, and a printed outline course of study placed in the hands of the teachers. The board of education then consisted of Thomas II. Harrison, president; Oliver Townsend, clerk; H. W. Parker, treasurer; Peter Shaffer, Benjamin Palmerton, and O. N. Wheelock. The teachers were Hugh J. Dobbs, superintendent; Fannie B. Outcalt, assistant in the high school; Henry N. Blake, head of the grammar department; and S. W. Dodge, Amelia Marston, Mary F. Price. Mary C. F. Blake, and Mirian Blake (Mrs. R. J. Kilpatrick) as the grade teachers. At the close of the spring term of 1880 the first graduating exercises of the Beatrice schools were held, the graduates being Oliver B. Gessell, Ida Lumbeck, (both deceased) and Caroline Elwood, of Los Angeles, California. The enrollment for the school year in all departments was six hundred and eighty pupils.

This illy constructed first high-school building served its purpose until 1884, when, upon the completion of a modern, high-school building, it was demolished and every vestige of its existence effaced. The new building was erected at a cost to the Beatrice school district of $40,000, where the old frame school house had stood since 1862, and on its occupation, in the fall of 1884, it became the center of the educational system of the city of Beatrice.

West School.

High School.

Glenover School.

When the present high-school building was erected this old building became a grade school for the central portion of the city. But no change of destiny can rob it of the simple dignity of its proportions or minimize its record of scholastic usefulness. It stands in the center of the old school-house square and dominates beautiful Charles Park, the public library and its other immediate surroundings, in a way that satisfies the mind as to what a building with its history should be.

In the year 1908 the qualified electors of the Beatrice school district, at a special election called for that purpose, voted to issue the bonds of the district in the sum of $80,000 for the purpose of erecting a high-school building, and in 1909, the present high-school building was erected, pursuant to plans and specifications prepared by architect Richard W. Grant. It stands at the corner of Fifth and Elk streets, an imposing, three-story structure with a basement. The original cost of the site, building and furniture was $81,886.00.

The remaining school buildings of the city of Beatrice are as here noted: The Harrington school building was constructed in 1885-1886, at a cost of approximately $7,500; the South school building was constructed in 1886, at a cost of $8,000 (bonds); the East school building and the West school building, built on the same plan, were constructed in 1888, at a cost of $11,000 each (bonds); the Belvidere school building, at first one room, later two, was constructed in 1889; the Fairview school building and Glenover school building, built on the same plan, were constructed in 1891, at a cost of $7,500 each (bonds); addition to the West school building, four rooms, constructed in 1916, cost $13,000.

But the marshaling of physical assets, however impressive the array, can at most indicate only the wealth and power of the community. They are not the glory of our schools. For this we must look to the character of the men and women who here have received their training for the affairs of life. Measured by this standard alone the record is most excellent. Students from the public schools of Beatrice are to be found everywhere in the world of work; they honor the professions as lawyers, physicians, preachers, teachers, and they swell the ranks of those who, in the great world war, are fighting for human liberty.

The heads of the Beatrice city schools, beginning with Hodson in 1869, are H. J. Chase, Charles B. Palmer, John Ellis, John N. Fuller, H. L. Wagner, Mrs. Clara B. Colby, John N. Rhodes, Hugh J. Dobbs, L. B. Shryock, William H. Elbright, Carroll G. Pearse, J. W. Dinsmore, W. H. Beeler, Ossian H. Brainard, W. L. Stephens, C. A. Fulmer, E. J. Bodwell, and A. J. Stoddart.

Some of the men who have brought renown to the Beatrice public schools because they were at one time connected therewith are as follows: Carroll G. Pearse, superintendent back in the '80s and early '90s, has since been superintendent of schools in Omaha and Milwaukee, is now president of the Milwaukee Normal school, and is considered one of the few foremost educators of America. W. L. Stephens, superintendent of schools in the '90s, has since been superintendent of the city schools at Lincoln, and is at present in a similar position at Long Beach, California. J. W. Crabtree, one-time principal of the Beatrice high school, has since passed from normal school presidencies to the highest position in the National Educational Association, and as its secretary wields an influence undoubtedly greater than any other educator in America. In later years, C. A. Fulmer, for five years, and E. J. Bodwell, for nine years superintendent, have placed the schools at the top in the state of Nebraska. A. J. Stoddart is now superintendent, and the future will undoubtedly see the present standard maintained. In addition to these, Beatrice has enjoyed the services of many distinguished men and women who have gone far and wide through other fields. No chronicle of the Beatrice schools would be complete without mentioning Miss Juletta O. Rawles, who has been assistant principal of the high school during a period of time of such duration that the community will long know and feel the good effects of her fine personality.

Through the years old residents have seen the number of teachers grow from a small nucleus of two or three until we now have twenty-two in the high school and forty-eight in the grades; and the school enrollment grow from a few pupils in one or two rooms until last year we had 1109 boys and 1124 girls enrolled in the schools. The high school ranks third in size in the state, having now an enrollment of 490. The physical plant has grown from one little building of one room until we now have eight ward buildings and one big central high-school building. In addition to this, through the public-spiritedness of some of the citizens of Beatrice, we have the finest athletic park in the west.

CHAPTER XXII

Beatrice Concluded

BANKS — FACTORIES — WHOLESALE HOUSES — RAWLINS POST — HOSPITALS AND SANITARIUMS — NEWSPAPERS AND NEWSPAPER MEN.

For many years after the settlement and organization of our county the pioneers were wholly dependent upon foreign banking institutions in all business transactions requiring the intervention of a bank. One of the six "wild-cat" banks established in Nebraska territory in 1856, by legislative charter, was the Platte Valley Bank, at Nebraska City. It was organized with S. F. Nuckolls as president and Joshua Garside as cashier. On account of the high character of these men, this bank secured a good patronage, and it was the only territorial bank of the "wild-cat" type that survived the terrible financial panic of 1857. In 1859 it liquidated its obligations and was succeeded at Nebraska City by the private banking house of James Sweet & Company, which was organized September 19, 1859. The honorable record as bankers established by the Platte Valley Bank under Mr. Nuckolls' management, together with the confidence inspired by James Sweet and those associated with him in his private banking enterprise, drew to Nebraska City a great volume of banking business from many of the South Platte counties, including Gage. Through the cooperation of the pioneer merchants of Beatrice with these banking concerns, a regular banking business of a sort was established for Beatrice and vicinity. The process was in the main as follows: A citizen wishing to borrow a sum of money would go to Joseph Saunders or to Blakely, Reynolds & Townsend or to some other Beatrice merchant, offer his security, make his note at twelve per cent annual interest, payable in advance, and secure the money. The lender, by endorsing the note or guaranteeing its payment, could turn it in at his correspondent bank at Nebraska City and take credit for it.

But with the coming of the railroads, in 1872, all this was completely changed. To every property-owner in the county the advent of the iron horse was equivalent to unclaimed treasure-trove. That which before had possessed no market value, became marketable. Land advanced almost over night from a nominal sum to five dollars or more per acre, and found purchasers. Business quickly adjusted itself to new conditions. Grain and live stock and other products of the farm found a ready market at reasonable figures. In fact the coming of the railroads ended the pioneer days in Gage county.

In 1871 Nathan Kirk Griggs and Hiram Peter Webb began a banking business in a small way, as private bankers, in the two-story, brick building erected by them on lot 10, block 47 of the original town of Beatrice, described as No. 314 Court street. Neither member of the firm possessed sufficient capital for any but the most meager banking operations, but they did have the most desirable of all wealth,—youth, enthusiasm, self-confidence and, to a very remarkable degree, the confidence of the community,—a confidence which both well deserved. Both were well educated, both lawyers without briefs, both with character and abilities which promised much for the future. At the election in November, 1869, Webb was elected treasurer of Gage county, and by successive elections he held the office from January, 1870, to January, 1876. There were then no restrictions upon the use of the funds of the county by the treasurer, nor was he required to account for interest on such funds. Many a pioneer bank in Nebraska had its inception with the election of the county treasurer. The bank was known as the Griggs & Webb Bank and it did a large business for those crude days; it was successfully managed by Webb until 1878. In 1874 they built a two-story, stone bank building at the corner of Fifth and Court streets, and transferred the bank to this building. In 1876 Mr. Griggs, who had by that time become a prominent and successful lawyer and politician, was appointed United States consul to Chemnitz, Saxony, and on accepting this office he withdrew from the bank. Webb retired from the county treasury in January, 1876, and thereafter devoted his time exclusively to the affairs of the bank, which then became known as H. P. Webb & Company, he having associated with him in the bank Nathan Blakely and Silas P. Wheeler. Had he confined his activities to legitimate banking he no doubt would have built up a very strong institution. He was a genial, clever, accommodating man, much esteemed in the community, and drew about him a host of the warmest of friends. In an evil moment, he formed a copartnership with a man named Holt, bought both the Beatrice and DeWitt mills, and with him engaged in the milling and grain business at Dewitt and Beatrice, using the funds of his bank to finance these transactions. He was cruelly deceived and cheated by Holt, and both mills were finally destroyed by fire. The banking house of H. P. Webb & Company closed its doors in May, 1878, its assets passed into the hands of W. H. Ashby, as assignee, and Gage county's first banker, Hiram Webb, having lost what in those days was a fortune and the opportunity of great success in the banking world, broken in spirit while still a young man, left Gage county and went to Oregon, where, being deeply religious, he engaged in works of piety, and died many years ago, far from his friends. The annals of Gage county present no more pathetic ending of what might have been a brilliant and a useful life.

BEATRICE NATIONAL BANK BUILDING

Following the failure of the Webb banking concern, William Lamb, having acquired the old Webb banking house, August 1, 1879, organized a private bank bearing his name. In 1881 the Lamb banking establishment was purchased by Erastus E. Brown, of Lincoln, and reorganized June 14, 1881, as the Gage County Bank; capital $50,00, with Brown, president, Lamb, manager, and Oliver M. Enlow, cashier and attorney. In 1884 the stock of this bank was purchased by Daniel W. Cook, Jefferson B. Weston, Nathan H. Harwood and their associates, and it was then reorganized, as the Beatrice National Bank, with a capital of $50,000. President, Jefferson B. Weston; vice-president, Daniel W. Cook; cashier, C. M. Brown. The bank continued in business in the old two-story, stone building at Fifth and Court streets until December 10, 1892, when its directorate having acquired the bulk of the stock in the old Masonic Temple Building Company moved the bank to that building, on the corner of Sixth and Court streets, which had been remodeled for banking purposes. This building was destroyed by fire December 22, 1902, entailing a complete loss of the bank furniture and fixtures. The vaults and safes, however, afforded perfect protection to the books, records and funds of the bank, and at the usual hour on the morning of the 23d of December it opened for business in the old Nebraska National Bank building, secured for that purpose while its own was in flames.

Steps were immediately taken by the officers and directors of the bank to erect a modern bank building on the spot where the old Masonic Temple building had stood. This work was begun as soon as the debris of the old structure was cold, and it was pushed to completion as rapidly as possible. Almost a year was consumed in the erection of this building, and it was not till the morning of December 14, 1903, that the doors of the new building swung open to the patrons of the bank, and a new chapter was begun in its long career of usefulness and prosperity. Supplemental data concerning this institution appear in the memoir dedicated to Daniel W. Cook, in the biographical department of this history.

In August, 1872, John E. and Samuel C. Smith came to Beatrice, and on the first day of September following they opened a private bank at No. 409 Court street, in the building now occupied by Cullen & Lock as a cigar store. The brothers possessed a capital of $10,000, and the bank was known as Smith Brothers' Bank, of which John E. Smith was president and Samuel C. Smith, cashier. Both brothers were natives of Ridgefield, Connecticut; John E., the elder, was born August 6, 1842, and Samuel C. was born June 18, 1846. They were at an age when, if ever, enthusiasm and ambition have assumed full sway and they entered into the business life of our county with a vigor that was most inspiring to all who fell under their influence. They brought to their business as bankers the powerful support of a number of moneyed men both in Ridgefield and in Cambridge, New York, where the elder brother had served an apprenticeship in the banking business as an employe of the Cambridge Valley Bank, which institution he had served three years as cashier, acquiring a thorough knowledge of the business. For nearly forty-six years Smith Brothers have been prominent factors in the growth and development of the city of Beatrice, the county of Cage and state of Nebraska.

In 1877 they organized the First National Bank of Beatrice, which was chartered and commenced business in April of that year. The directors of the bank were Hon. Algernon Sidney Paddock, Hiram W. Parker, Elijah Filley, Charles G. Dorsey, John E. and Samuel C. Smith, of Beatrice, and James Ellis, of New York. John E. Smith was president; Hiram W. Parker, vice-president; Samuel C. Smith, cashier; and Frank Graham, assistant cashier. The success of this banking enterprise was immediate. The statement of its condition at the close of the first nine months of its existence comprises not only an instructive commentary on the affairs of the bank itself, but is the first bank statement ever issued by any institution in Gage county. It is dated December 31, 1877, and is as follows:

Loans and Discounts	$61,574.20	Capital Stock	$50,000.00
United States Bonds	30,000.00	Surplus and Profits	1,603.26
Other Stocks and Bonds	3,073.50	Circulation	27,000.00
Real Estate	5,978.30	Deposits	60,471.61
Furniture and Fixtures	2,006.66	Unpaid Dividends	2,500.00
Premiums	2,550.00		
Due from Banks and United States Treasurer	22,052.74		
Cash on hand	14,339.47		
Total	$141,574.87	**Total**	$141,574.87

Its wonderful growth is shown by its report to the comptroller treasury at the close of business December 31, 1881:

Loans and Discounts	$190,235.22	Capital Stock	$50,000.00
United States Bonds	50,000.00	Surplus and Profits	15,074.27
Other Stocks and Bonds	1,137.51	Circulation	45,000.00
Due from Banks and United States Treasurer	61,105.35	Deposits	204,552.11
		Re-discounts	19,000.00
Real Estate	6,861.30		
Furniture and Fixtures	2,800.00		
Cash on hand	21,487.00		
Total	**$333,626.38**	**Total**	**$333,626.38**

About the year 1885 the First National Bank building, on the corner of Fifth and Court streets was erected, and the bank was transferred to the commodious quarters arranged for it in this substantial structure.

This pioneer bank has had a remarkable career in the banking history of the state of Nebraska. In 1886, the Beatrice Savings Bank was organized and operated in connection with this institution, and from the beginning, Smith Brothers, had maintained a farm-loan department, separately incorporated however as the Smith Brothers Loan & Trust Company. All these institutions did a tremendous business, each in it's line. Through Smith Brothers Loan & Trust Company the funds of the savings bank were largely invested in mortgages on western Kansas and Nebraska land. The business thus transacted was enormous, was most conservatively conducted, and under normal conditions would have proved very profitable to all parties concerned. But the great financial panic of 1893, coupled with a series of dry seasons which beggared nearly every man in the territory where these lands were located and drove thousands out of the country, caused such shrinkage in values as to force the Smith Brothers out of business. The savings bank passed into the hands of a receiver, and the stock of the First National Bank held by them passed to L. B. Howey and those associated with him in its purchase, and John and Samuel Smith, by these transactions, turned over to the creditors of their business enterprises all their non-exempt property. The saddest part of this business tragedy consists in the fact that the assets of the two banks were what in common parlance is described as "gilt-edge." Even under the wasteful management of a receivership the assets of the savings bank paid ninety cents on the dollar of its indebtedness, and if the Smith Brothers could have been given time, the restoration of values which shortly ensued would have left their several institutions entirely solvent and them with independent fortunes. They were innocent victims of the times and the lack of confidence in all financial institutions then widely prevalent. With superb courage, they have successfully re-established themselves in a profitable farm-loaning business known as the Farmers Trust Company, but more important than all, through all reverses of fortune, they have retained the confidence and esteem of a community to whose material, social and religious development they have so largely contributed.

The reader has now witnessed the beginning of the banking business in the city of Beatrice and followed the history of its two pioneer banks to the present moment. It may be of interest, at least to those who come after us, to know that these two institutions are today stronger, more powerful and better than ever before. Since the death of Daniel W. Cook, in 1916, Wallace Robertson has been president of the Beatrice National Bank; R. J. Kilpatrick, vice-president; Daniel W. Cook, Jr., cashier; J. H. Doll, assistant cashier. Frederick H. Howey is president of the First National Bank; M. V. Nichols, first vice president; William C. Black, second vice president; R. B. Clemens, cashier; H. A. Reeves, assistant cashier. With its other activities the First National Bank, in 1909, organized and is successfully carrying on a savings bank, under the name of First State Savings Bank of Beatrice, Nebraska.

Numerous other banking ventures have been made in the city, some achieving a great success, some a dismal failure. One that in the early '80s promised to reach a position of great usefulness was The People's Bank, organized by John Ellis (a former county treasurer of Gage county), Horace L. Ewing, Warren Cole, Lafayette P. Brown, C. W. Collins and others, in 1882. Within a year after its organization Mr. Collins removed to Hebron, where he became the principal owner and president of the First National Bank of that city, an institution which he conducted to great prosperity. After the retirement of Mr. Collins, Ellis and his associates erected a splendid four-story, stone building at the corner of Fourth and Court streets, now the property of Milburn & Scott Company, and reorganized the bank into the Nebraska National Bank, with Ellis as president, Cole, vice-president, and Ewing, cashier. But the terrible financial panic of 1893-1896 found the bank unable to withstand the demands upon it, and it went down in a maelstrom of ruin. Its affairs were wound up by E. R. Fogg, the receiver, who paid about fifty per cent of the indebtedness.

In 1881 William A. Wolfe founded the German National Bank. Associated with him were George Arthur Murphy, Andrew W. Nickell, Dwight Coit and the W. H. Thrift estate; capital $100,000. Wolfe was chosen president; Nickell, vice-president; and Coit, cashier. After nearly a quarter of a century of successful business this bank liquidated in 1912, sold its building at No. 411 Court street to the Union Savings Bank, and retired from business. In 1913, Mr. Wolfe, with Dwight Coit, Hugo Ahlquist and others, organized the Nebraska State Bank, with Wolfe, president, and Coit, cashier; capital $50,000.

Another hopeful banking venture was that of the American Bank of Beatrice, organized in 1888 as the American Savings Bank, but soon changed to the American Bank, capital $100,000. The officers were: Charles E. White, president; Charles L. Schell, vice president; John Henderson, cashier. The institution occupied the banking house owned by it at No. 110 North Fifth street, and now owned and occupied by the State Savings & Loan Association. This bank also was caught in the financial storm of 1893, and closed its doors on the second day of July of that year.

About the year 1889 L. E. Walker, Thomas Yule and others organized a bank known as the Union Savings Bank of Beatrice. After a few years Mr. Walker retired and Martin V. Nichols and John H. Penner became the leading stockholders of this concern, which then became a commercial bank, under the name of Union State Bank. This bank managed to exist until quite a recent date, when the stock was purchased by Robin B. Nickell, who about the same time purchased the stock of the German National Bank and consolidated the two into a strong financial institution now known as the Union State Bank, and owned by H. C. Arnold, John Anderson and others, with Arnold, president, and Anderson, cashier; capital $50,000.

In February, 1892, the Farmers & Merchants State Bank was organized with a paid up capital of $50,000, by William P. Norcross, Milo Baker, Eugene W. Wheelock, and others, and with Norcross, president; Baker, vice-president, and Wheelock, cashier. The bank was very conservatively managed and promised a long career of usefulness in the community. It opened with a fine patronage and this was continued until the great financial panic of 1893-1896, when banking had become so hazardous a risk as to be unattractive to capital. On the 31st of December, 1896, the Farmers & Merchants Bank went into voluntary liquidation, its depositors were paid in full and the stockholders' money returned to them dollar for dollar.

In 1908 the Beatrice State Bank was organized by F. E. Allen, of Auburn, Nebraska. J. T. Harden, H. H. Waite, Frank Morrison, Alpha Graf and others; capital $50,000. This institution has had a successful career and is ably and conservatively managed. F. E. Allen is president; J. T. Harden, vice-president, and H. H. Waite, cashier.

The city of Beatrice may be said to have been a manufacturing center of consequence from the date of its origin, in July, 1857. The old steam saw mill set up by the Townsite Company, employed in the manufacture of lumber from native timber for their immediate use, was supplanted in the early '60s by Fordyce Roper's water-power saw and grist mill and shingle and lath machines, all doing custom work and finally drawing trade from considerable distances. From these early days and crude beginnings to the present time Beatrice has steadily advanced until, in a trifle more than three score years from the date of her founding, she has gained first place as a manufacturing center amongst the cities of her class in Nebraska, as respects both the variety and the value of her manufactured products.

The mere enumeration of these forms an impressive an eloquent tribute to the genius and enterprise of her citizens. The list includes valuable agricultural implements, wind mills, gasoline engines, pumps, machinery for handling hay, irrigating and ditching machinery, well-drilling devices, galvanized steel tanks, burial vaults, portable corn cribs and granaries, woven-wire fencing, wire and slat fencing, cigars, ice cream, butter, tombstones and monuments, electricity, flour, meal and other cereal products, cement building blocks, bricks and tiling, blank books, corn-husking pegs and other hardware specialties, shirts, and many other articles of daily use and consumption.

The figures are not at hand to show the value of the manufactured products of the city as a whole; but since the great Dempster Mill Manufacturing Company stands at the head of the manufacturing industries of the city, perhaps of the state, some idea may be gained of the value of its products from the fact that it has a present capital and surplus of more than one and one-fourth million dollars, that it has over five hundred employes, exclusive of its Memphis plant, and an annual pay roll of over half a million dollars.

Several of the other factories of the city make a creditable and an impressive showing. Some of the more important concerns are the Beatrice Steel Tank Manufacturing Company, Beatrice Iron Works, the John H. von Steen Company and the F. D. Kees Manufacturing Company.

In addition to its manufacturing concerns Beatrice has several allied institutions. These are the Lang Canning & Preserving Company, the Beatrice Cold Storage Company, Swift & Company's poultry house, and the Beatrice Creamery Company.

The limitations of this work make a further enumeration or description of the manufacturing interests of the city inexpedient. It is sufficient to say here that as a manufacturing and distributing center Beatrice has acquired a prestige and a momentum that assure her future growth and prosperity.

Not only has the city acquired reputation as a manufacturing center but in recent years she has also set the pace for her competitors as a wholesaling point. Here are located the great Sonderegger Nurseries & Seed House, the Pease Grain & Seed Company, the E. S. Stevens wholesale grocery, and the Blue Valley Mercantile Company, also a wholesale grocery house.

Beatrice has latterly come to occupy an enviable position as a retailing center. Her merchants are enterprising and accommodating, their stocks large and varied, and trade is attracted to the city from long distances. With her attractive business houses and her magnificent system of street lighting, Beatrice certainly in its business district approaches the "City Beautiful."

But however attractive the business portion of the city, visitors never tire of traversing the residence districts, where there are found some of the most beautiful homes in the west. The extensive paving of the streets in recent years has greatly added to the charm of Beatrice as a residence city, and latterly attention has been given to architectural form and beauty in the erection of private residences. With the constant increase of wealth, the advancing years will witness a continual accession of artistic dwellings.

Both time and space forbid extended notice of the secret societies and benevolent orders. As it has been the aim of the author to avoid anything like a directory feature in this work, it must suffice here to say that almost all the societies and different orders found in the west are represented in Beatrice. He feels constrained, however, to give place here to an organization which all delight to honor and which is not a secret society nor is it to be classed with the benevolent orders. It is a list of the living members of Rawlins Post, No. 35, Department of Nebraska, Grand Army of the Republic, which was chartered in 1880, dropped in 1881, reorganized and chartered December 27, 1882.

Avey, Samuel, Co. A, 10th Ohio Cav.
Armstrong, Thomas, Co. I, 39th Ill. Inft.
Armstrong, R., Co. F, 180th Ohio.
Arnett, Jeff (colored), Co. F, 125th U. S. Inft. (colored).
Bull, Stephen, Co. C, 186th N. Y. Inft.
Brother, Ferd, Surgeon 8th Mo. State Militia Vol.
Bress, S. W., Co. F, 18th Iowa Inft.
Black, W. H. H., Co. I, 42d Ind.
Brewster, A., Co. L, 15th N. Y. Engineer Brigade.
Brock, C. A., Co. F, 34th Ill. Inft.
Bell, William, Co. C, 1st Tenn. Inft.
Bevins, S., 1st Ohio Heavy Art.

Buck, George, Jr., Co. H, 2d Vt. Inft.
Brewster, A. W., Co. E, 128th Ind. Inft.
Calkins, D. K., Co. E, 34th Ill. Inft.
Craig, J. R., Co. B, 10th Ill. Inft.
Calland, H. S., Co. D, 92d Ohio.
Carmichael, John, Co. H, 46th Ill. Inft.
Carter, Frank, Co. A, 102d U. S. Vol. (colored).
Crangle, W. F., Co. A, 42d Ill. Inft.
Colby, L. W., Co. B, 8th Ill. Inft.
Coulter, R., Co. I, 104th Ohio.
Cousins, James, Co. G, 2d Iowa Inft. Died Feb. 23, 1917.
Confer, Daniel, Co. A, 34th Ind.
Claypool, J. W., Co. K. 143d Ill.
Davis, Samuel, Co. B, 8th Ill. Cav.
Dunn, Payson, Co. F, 37th Wis. Inft.
Decker, George, Co. E, 2d Conn.
Davis, George W., Co. A, 16th Kan. Cav.
Evans, G. D., Co. B, Wis. Inft.
Forbes, J. A., Co. F, 42d Ill. Inft.
Fletcher, J. C., Co. I, 3d Iowa Cav.
Fielder, William, Co. I. 72d Ill. Inft.
Frederick, John, Co. F, 82d Ill. Inft.
Gilmore, R. G., Co. D, 83d Penn.
Gray, L. D., Co. I. 13th Iowa Inft.
Geddes, Charles, Co. I, 16th Iowa Inft.
Gardner, R. E., Co. K, 3d Iowa Cav.
Glazier, N. Newton, Co. G, 11th Vt. Vol. (Lost left arm.)
Hemphill, R. C., Co. F, 13th Penn. Cav. Died Jan. 24, 1918.
Hutchins, T. E., Co. H, 20th Ind. Inft.
Hartwell, R. B., Co. G, 28th Iowa.
Jackson. J. W., Co. G, 124th Ill. Inft.
Kimmerly, D. J., Co. A, 13th N. Y. Died Jan. 19, 1918.
LaSelle, H. A., Co. D. 114th N. Y. Inft.
Lash, S. P., Co. H. 87th Ind. Inft.
Lilly, W. S., Co. H. 19th Mich. Inft.

Miller, S. T., Co. A, 34th Ill. Inft.
Mayborn, Thomas, Co. A, 14th N. Y.
Meeker, George, Co. G, 5th Iowa Inft.
Munson, Z., Co. H, 3d Mich. Cav.
McCrea, Ed., Co. C, 10th Mo. Cav. Died Nov. 10, 1917.
McCollery, Orvin, Co. C, 28th Mo. Died Jan. 19, 1916.
McKinney, William, Co. H, 27th Iowa.
Olsen, Iver A., Co. A, 88th Ill. Inft.
Pease, G. L., Co. F, 28th Conn. Inft.
Pfefferman, S., Co. B, 129th Ill. Inft.
Pagles, John, Co. K, 65th Ill.
Pape, Abraham, Co. F, 92d Ill. Inft.
Rice, Dr. A. T., Co. B, 91st Ind.
Randell, C. W., Co. I, 13th N. H.
Ramsey, J. H., Co. I, 3d Iowa Cav.
Reedy, A. J., Co. H, 1st Mo. Cav.
Roller, J. T., Co. D, 110th Penn. Inft. Died March 18, 1917.
Sterne, W. W., Co. K, W. Va. Cav.
Shafner, J. F., Co. B, 2d Minn. Cav.
Shottenkirk, W., Co. C, 113th Ill.
Sample, A., Co. C, 8th Iowa Cav.
Shaw, John, Co. K, 99th Ind.
Spiker, T. L., Co. G, 118th Ill. Inft.
Salts, Peter, Co. G, 76th Ohio Inft.
Smith, Charles A., Co. C, 17th Mich. Inft.
Smith, Edward, Musician 20th Ill. Inft.
Seymour, S. A., Co. E, 189th N. Y. Inft.
Thomas, Hiram, Co. D, 4th Ill. Cav.
Taylor, W. M., Co. A, 22d Pa. Cav.
Tucker, Robert, Co. H, 19th Mich. Inft.
Wilson, Charles, Co. F, 26th Ill. Inft. Died July 8, 1917.
Webb, John, Co. I, 118th Ill. Inft.
Walker, W. H., Co. E, 93d Ill. Inft.
Weston, William, Co. B, 161st Ohio Inft.

On the first day of July, 1868, there occurred in the little village of Beatrice an event of unusual significance. It was the appearance of the *Blue Valley Record*, the first newspaper published in Gage county. The proprietors of this paper were Joseph R. Nelson and Nathaniel Howard. It was a sorry little affair, judged by any standard of newspaper excellence, yet it is doubtful if any newspaper was ever more joyfully welcomed by any community. Mr. Nelson, in writing of this venture years afterward, says:

There were, I think, not a thousand people in the county, and not half of them in Beatrice.

Nat Howard and I were talking of the advantage to be gained by having a newspaper published in Beatrice, and as I had some money and Nat the brains, we concluded to go into the newspaper business. When a boy I had played often in the office of the Poughkeepsie (N. Y.) *Telegraph*, thereby gaining the only real knowledge we had with which to start our paper.

We took a sheet of wrapping paper and marked out places for ads; then we went out to find them. We found everyone interested. All subscribed and some took several copies to send to friends east. Nat went to Nebraska City and I to Brownville, and each got a few more ads. We then sent to the Adams Press Company, of New York, for a press, and on May 27, 1868, they shipped us our little press (called now Army press), which arrived in Nebraska City sometime in June.

We hurried to the city to get it, as well as the other materials, which we had bought of Tom Morton, who owned and ran the Nebraska City *News*, Sterling Morton being the editor. As we did not know the boxes, and being in a hurry, we concluded to have the cases with paper between them, and loaded them into our wagon (wagons then being the only means of transportation between Nebraska City and Beatrice) and started for home. When we arrived in Beatrice we found our type somewhat mixed, and it took us several days to sort it out. The only way we knew the boxes was by the ones that had the most of one kind in. We worked early and late, copied from Nebraska City and Brownville papers, and when we got stuck we slipped out of town to see Tom Morton, who kindly helped us, and finally we launched our first paper on the waves, and were more proud of it than a father of his first-born.

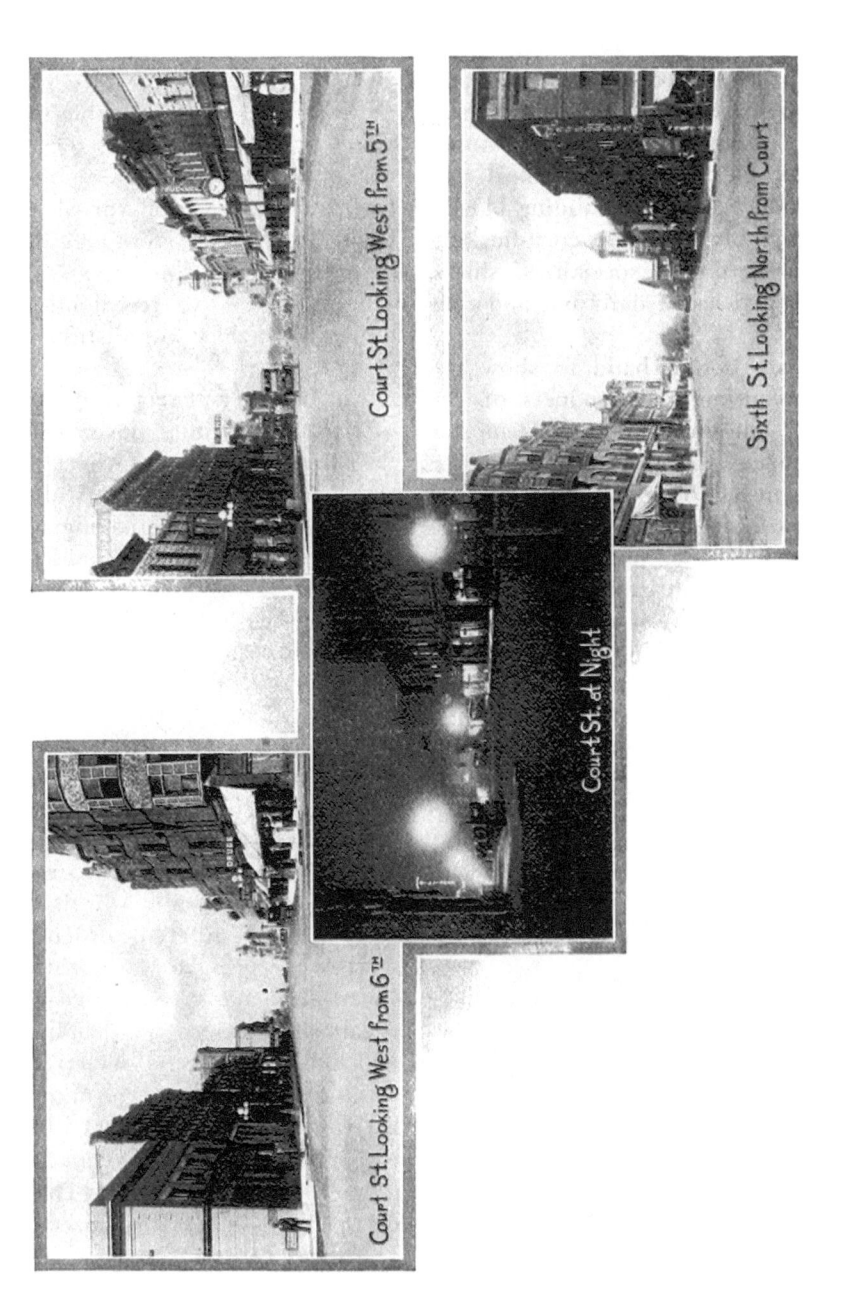

We expected encouragement from the papers, and the Nebraska City *News* and *Press* and Brownville *Advocate* gave us a good "send-off," but the galoot that ran the Marysville *Locomotive* said our paper looked as though it had been set up by a coal-heaver. That made us mad and I wanted him thrashed, for I had set it up myself, with the help of Nat Baker, a young boy, and thought I had done it extra well, but in after years concluded he was more than half right.

We printed one page at a time and had to pull type from one ad. to fix up others and sometimes made a mixed-up mess of it. We sent Warren Chesney to Nebraska City to collect, and he told us that when he presented the bill to one man he ordered him out, with a promised thrashing,—said he did not order that ad., and another thing he would not pay for one with another man's name to it. We looked over the paper and found the wooden reglet had slipped, and in putting it back we had got it in the wrong place. Warren said that when we wanted any more bills collected we could do it ourselves.

We sent Silas Harrington to Meridian to collect from a man who ran a saw mill, and told him to take it out in lumber. We did not see him for several weeks after his return, till meeting him one day and asking him where the lumber was, he pointed to his new house, and said, "There it is," and there it was, nailed fast.

We had many such trials and tribulations, with plenty of hard work, for nine months, when we sold a half interest to Mr. Hogshead. We next sold out to Theodore Coleman, and thus ended my newspaper experience.

Upon the sale of the half-interest in the *Blue Valley Record* to J. M. Hogshead, the name of the paper was changed to the Beatrice *Clarion*, the first number of which appeared Saturday, May 8, 1869, with the motto "Hew to the line, let the chips fall where they may." The publishers' names were given as J. M. Hogshead & Company, and the company consisted of J. M. Hogshead, Joseph R. Nelson, Nathaniel Howard, and Captain William H. Ashby. Of these owners all but Nelson had seen service in the Confederate army, but Howard, Hogshead, and Ashby were all fine looking, courtly gentleman, and were a welcome addition to the social and business interests of Beatrice. The biography and portrait of Joseph R. Nelson appear in Chapter XVII of this volume, entitled "A Roll of Honor."

THEODORE COLEMAN
Founder of the Beatrice *Express*

Theodore Coleman, who in 1870 purchased the Beatrice *Clarion*, gives for this history the following narrative of his newspaper experience in Beatrice:

"After having, at the age of twenty years, broken into the newspaper game in northern Wisconsin and carried on the same for several years with a measure of success that stopped short, to be sure, of illuminating the northwestern horizon with its glow, I heeded a suggestion conveyed by a letter from Joe Nelson (pardon the colloquialism touching Mr. Nelson's name), and went to Beatrice for an inspection of journalistic conditions there. My entry into Gage county was not exactly of a triumphant character, since I had to tarry three days in Iowa before the running ice in the Missouri river would allow the primitive ferry to operate across to Nebraska City; and upon finally arriving in that metropolis, it was found that transportation to Beatrice was limited to a loaded farmer's wagon, returning to his home ten miles north of my objective point. However, the walking was good and no difficulty was found in negotiating the ten miles.

"This was in 1870. The Gage County *Clarion* was the one newspaper of Beatrice at the time,—published weekly and carrying on its title page the rather startling motto (for a clarion) "Hew to the Line, Let the Chips Fall Where they May." The ownership of the *Clarion* was divided among several embryonic Greeleys and Danas and Hearsts and Northcliffes, including my friend Nelson, Mr. John Hogshead and Mr. Nathaniel Howard. Whether Captain Ashby was of the syndicate I do not know, but he had had some connection with newspaperdom in Beatrice, as I remember. I suspect there was a holding concern back of these gentlemen, for when it came to negotiations for the purchase of the *Clarion* the proposed payment of something like five hundred dollars for it on my part caused such a flurry in newspaper financial circles that frequent consultations with an unknown party to the deal seemed necessary.

"However, it went through and I acquired the property and with it the services of Mr. Hogshead, the only printer of the dissolved corporation. Changing the title of the paper to the Beatrice *Express* did not wound the feelings of the retiring proprietors, and this was done. At that time the home of the paper was the stone building on Market street near Fourth, where the newly christened *Express* was published until removal to the classic precincts of the old frame school-building then standing on Fifth street, north of Court. There we remained until the transfer to the second story of a business building on Court street.

"Certain primitive conditions obtained in Nebraska in the early '70s that somewhat hampered the production of high-class journalistic work. In the first place, mechanical facilities were so limited that in the necessary task of casting inking-rollers for our four-page forms I was on more than one occasion obliged to make a stage trip to Brownville for glue. The Clarion did not boast a job press among its assets, but its fonts of type included a few that could be used in setting up simple handbills and the like, to be worked off on the same hand-lever press from which the paper was issued in weekly installments to a waiting constituency of some three hundred or more. I soon added a rotary job-press and concomitants, and its manipulation was put into the hands of a young southerner named Bailey, who, as I recall, was an old friend of Messrs. Howard and Hogshead. The former seemed to be at the editorial helm of the *Clarion* (if the mixed metaphor may be used), with Mr. Hogshead as chief officer. John was a good printer, but it pains me to have to acknowledge that the sole effusion of his pen that sticks in my memory in connection with the last days of the *Clarion* was to the effect that a darky exclaimed as he fled from an angry bull: 'Millions for de fence.'

"It may be said without egotism that the *Express* grew apace with the growth of Beatrice, and that it was always generously supported by the people who constituted the rapidly developing community. Of these there remain with me after the elapsed half-century no memories that are not pleasant to dwell upon. Among them, I visualize now (using the familiar vernacular of that early period), Pap Towle, J. B. Weston, John and Sam Smith, Lige Filley, Judge Parker, Joe Saunders, Gil Loomis, Dan Freeman, Uncle Jimmy Boyd, Volney Whitmore, Jack Pethoud, Charley and Carl Emery, Joe McDowell, Nate Blakely, N. K. Griggs, Joe Fletcher, Colonel and Captain Presson, Oliver Townsend, Dr. Reynolds, George Hurlburt, Thacker, Dan and Alvin Marsh, Pemberton, Willard, George and Charley Dorsey, Ford Roper, Dean, Davis, et al. If Tom Shubert had been able to read and if "Old Man Chrisman" could have remained sober long enough to have achieved the same accomplishment, it is certain they would have been among the readers of the *Express*.

"Mentor A. Brown came into the office in 1873, I think, first as a most competent printer, and later as one of my successors in the proprietorship of the paper. His successful career as a newspaper man for these many years is generally known to Beatrice people. It is a matter of no little personal satisfaction that during all these forty and more years, his paper—first the *Express* and then the Kearney *Hub*—has reached my home each publication day, with his compliments. Another early employe on the Express now lives and thrives as a master printer in Los Angeles, ten miles from my own residence—John Burke. Anent

John, let this digression, if you will, creep into your veracious annals: On a day in 1884, while I was publishing the Santa Clara *Journal* in this state, a strange specimen of the now extinct *genus homo* known as tramp printer, walked into my office and asked for work. Upon close examination he was revealed as Johnny Burke. A day's work was followed by his complete disappearance, and he was not visible to me again until three years ago, when he was accidentally 'met up with' in the guise of a portly, fine appearing foreman in the office of one of the Los Angeles dailies.

"C. B. Palmer came to Beatrice as principal of the high school and soon thereafter bought an interest in the *Express*, chiefly as a means of printing and distributing a monthly educational periodical. When the election of A. S. Paddock to the United States senate took place in 1875, I conceived the idea of going to Washington and helping him run the government, which being done, the *Express* was soon thereafter sold to L. W. Colby, and my return to Beatrice was indefinitely postponed."

THEODORE COLEMAN was born in Rochester, New York, January 26, 1842, of New England (Nantucket) and Dutch lineage.

The family removed to Dubuque, Iowa, and a little later to Galena, Illinois, the lure being the lead mines of those districts. The death of his mother at Galena, in 1846, resulted in a return of the remaining members of the family to Rochester.

From Rochester another family trek was taken, in 1849, to Toronto, Canada, where Mr. Coleman's father had bought a saw mill on the shores of the bay. Theodore attended the Toronto Model School on King street, Toronto (price three pence per week), until 1852, assisting meantime in digging the first sod of Canada's first railroad, the Grand Trunk.

Back to Rochester in 1852, where the enterprising head of the family was, in 1857-1858, financially floored by building Main street bridge across the Genessee river for the city and failing to collect under his $50,000 contract because of an alleged weak abutment—that still, after a lapse of sixty years, sturdily sustains the west end of the bridge. Attendance at the public school and work in a flour mill, a grocery and on the aforesaid bridge filled the period from 1852 to 1859, when another shift of residence was made, this time to Cincinnati. Thence up the Mississippi and Chippewa rivers to Chippewa Falls, Wisconsin, went the family in 1860. There, amidst somewhat primeval surroundings, a halt was made for ten years, logging and saw-mill work occupying the men of the family. Some sort of literary work, however, had always appealed to the member under consideration, so the chance to go into the office of the *Chippewa Valley Union* as printer boy was eagerly seized. Two years thereafter Mr. Coleman bought the plant, and published the little weekly for two years, selling it out in order to piece out his disappointed school education by going for a year to Williston Seminary, East Hampton, Massachusetts, and for another year to Antioch College. Upon closing this agreeable chapter, he returned to Wisconsin and helped for a time to keep the saws running in his father's mill. Then away to Beatrice and into the newspaper work again, soon seeking a little time to go back to the northern state upon matrimonial intentions bent. The carrying out of this intention was a very fortunate achievement for him, as not a few of the present population of Beatrice who knew Mrs. Coleman would be willing to attest.

The thirty-nine years' residence in California following the close of four years of government work in Washington, has been largely taken up with newspaper publishing and editing; but for the last fifteen years Mr. Coleman has been occupied with duties of a more distinctly business character, first as secretary and business manager of an educational institution in Pasadena—Throop Polytechnic Institute and College—and later as similar officer of the Pasadena Hospital Association. His newspaper work in California was as publisher of the Santa Clara *Journal* and, in Pasadena, in an editorial capacity on the Pasadena *Star* and the Pasadena *News*. His family of two sons and two daughters, two of them natives of Beatrice, are married and all but one of the four are living in Pasadena. The oldest son is a resident of Arizona.

MENTOR A. BROWN, who succeeded Theodore Coleman in the ownership of the Beatrice *Express*, January 7, 1884, has written for this history the following interesting reminiscent narrative of his connection with the paper:

"My knowledge of the newspapers of Gage county dates from the 20th day of July, 1871. On the evening of July 19th I disembarked from a Kansas and Nebraska stage coach after a dusty ride from Crete, at the old Pacific House, of which George Hurlburt was landlord. The following morning the office of the Beatrice *Express* was discovered in a small one-room frame building that had formerly housed the public schools of the pioneer village, and it still remained in the center of a block of ground with no other building nearer than Ella and Fifth streets. This intervening space was for several summers afterward utilized by the 'fans' as a baseball park.

"Theodore Coleman was the sole proprietor and editor of the *Express*. He had purchased the plant of the *Clarion* the previous year and changed the name to the *Express*. The shop was equipped with a Washington hand-press (which served until the fall of 1883) and a limited assortment of type and other material. There was one printer in the shop, a big six-foot Mississippian named Hogshead, with the imposing front and the swing of the old-time southern colonel, sandy 'complected' and of surpassing good nature. The first 'devil' who was initiated soon afterward was 'Johnnie' Burke, who is still plying his trade and a member of the typographical union in good standing at Los Angeles. They had induced the writer to quit a job as a compositor on the Council Bluffs *Nonpareil*, to do the job printing, set the 'ads,' etc. The proprietor. Mr. Coleman, was not a skillful printer, but was a capable newspaper man, a versatile and graceful writer and also a capable business man. Charles B. Palmer, principal of the Beatrice schools, also a practical printer, became associated with Mr. Coleman in 1871, and Coleman Palmer were the publishers until January 1, 1874, when the 'cub' bought out Mr. Palmer and the firm name was changed to Coleman Brown. This partnership and business association was very harmonious, but was interrupted when Mr. Coleman accepted a position in Washington as secretary to Senator Paddock, and by the sale of his interest in the paper to Mr. Colby, in 1876. Soon thereafter the junior partner also sold his interest to Mr. Colby, but he remained in charge and conducted the business until the winter of 1876-1877, when he purchased an interest in the Fairbury *Gazette*; but in the early fall of

1877 he returned to Beatrice, having purchased Mr. Colby's entire interest in the *Express*, and became sole proprietor. The paper grew with the town, and in 1884 the *Daily Express* greeted the public. In the summer of 1888 the writer disposed of his entire interests in the newspaper and printing plant to Kilpatrick Brothers, and in October of that year he removed to Kearney, where he established the Kearney *Daily and Weekly Hub.*

"The first rival newspaper of the *Express* was the *Courier*, published by Conlee and Ritchie, about 1875. Mr. Ritchie soon retired and the paper itself lived but a short time, its career being both sensational and tempestuous. Mr. Alex W. Conlee was one of the old type of 'personal' journalists and a very interesting character. At a later date, M. B. Davis, lawyer, published the Beatrice *Republican*. The Beatrice *Democrat* was established about the middle of the '80s by George P. Marvin, a vigorous, aggressive and capable newspaper man, father of the present publisher of the Beatrice *Sun*, which later succeeded the *Democrat*.

"It might be mentioned that Beatrice was the original home of the educational journal, the '*Nebraska Teacher*,' which was first published by Mr. Palmer, printed in the office of the *Express* on a hand press, and removed to Lincoln in 1877, when the publisher removed to the capital to take charge of the preparatory department of the Nebraska State University."

MENTOR A. BROWN was born February 19, 1853, at Janesville, Wisconsin. His mother died in his infancy; his father died on Sherman's march to the sea.

Mr. Brown was reborn as printer's devil, office of *New Era,* Jefferson, Iowa, June 25, 1866. "Swarmed" July 17, 1870, and spent a year in Nebraska City, Omaha, and Council Bluffs. Found himself in Beatrice, Nebraska, July 19, 1871. Connected with Beatrice *Express* as printer, partner, publisher, and editor, until October, 1888. Nearly fifty-two years' service in "print-shop." He married and has three sons and two daughters and eleven grandchildren living; wife Sophie G., daughter of the late Captain C. J. Schmidt, of Beatrice.

The *Republican*, of which Mr. Brown speaks in his reminiscent article, was founded about 1886 by J. W. Hill, M. B. Davis later acquiring a half-interest in it. It was conducted several years by them as partners. Mr. Davis was a vigorous writer and secured for the paper a good circulation. It was a weekly newspaper and Republican in politics. About the first of May, 1892, Davis sold his half-interest in the paper to William L. Knotts and it was conducted by Hill and Knotts a short time, when Knotts acquired full ownership. About 1900 he sold it to Winfield Scott Tilton, a practical newspaper man from Kansas. The name of the paper was changed to the Beatrice *Times* and was conducted by him very ably till about 1909, when he abandoned the field and removed his press and other newspaper materials to Oklahoma.

More than twenty-one years ago Emil Schultz established in Beatrice a German-language newspaper called the *Nebraska Post*, and this has had a continuous existence till July 1, 1918, when, out of deference to public opinion, Mr. Schultz with commendable patriotism suspended the publication of his paper till the close of the great world-war now raging with the utmost fury in all western Europe—a war in which our own government has plunged with the maximum of energy and enthusiasm, in defense of democratic institutions.

COURT STREET, BEATRICE, IN 1908

CHAPTER XXIII

BLUE SPRINGS

The historic town of Blue Springs dates its origin from the year 1857, at almost the identical moment that Beatrice was founded. In July of that year James H. Johnson, Jacob Poff, Martin Elliott and his sons Stephen, William, and Henry Elliott, with their families, settled on the public domain at Blue Springs and its immediate vicinity, and, in conjunction with the government surveyors who were then engaged in surveying the public lands in that vicinity, they projected a townsite company and marked out into town lots three, hundred and twenty acres of land, comprising, with other lands, the present townsite of Blue Springs. But there was little inducement at that early day for engaging in such enterprises, and this company did not even go to the trouble of acquiring title to the lands they had selected for a townsite. The project was finally abandoned, and Reuyl Noyes and Joseph Chambers, returning from a gold-mining venture at Pike's Peak, took it up. They were enterprising young men and undertook to develop Blue Springs into an attractive frontier town. Amongst other things they attempted to divert travel from the Oregon Trail at Ash Point, near Richmond, in Nemaha county, Kansas, to Blue Springs and westward about twelve miles to the Caldwell ranch, on the old trail. It must be remembered that the Oregon Trail was to Nebraska territory in that early day what a trunk line of railway would be now to an undeveloped section of country. The principal crossing of the Big Blue river was at Marysville, in a direction south of west from Ash Point. From Marysville the trail took a northwesterly course across the southern part of the Otoe Indian reservation, to the Rock Creek stage station; part way, near the head waters of Indian creek, was Caldwell ranch. By diverting the travel by way of Richmond and Blue Springs the distance was considerably less.

These enterprising proprietors of Blue Springs and their friends, having first, in 1859, borrowed the necessary money for that purpose from Robert A. Wilson, acquired by purchase the tract of ground where Blue Springs is located, in section 17 of that township, giving him a mortgage on it. They built a double, story-and-a-half, hewed-log ranch house on the northeast corner of block 5 of the original town of Blue Springs, at the intersection of Hazen and Main streets. They also built a toll bridge across the Big Blue river, and drew a furrow from the point of departure on the old trail, past Richmond, to Blue Springs and on to the Caldwell ranch. But Seneca, the rival of Richmond, defeated this project by diverting travel from the old trail to herself. Mrs. Rebecca Woodward, who in the spring of 1859 was living at Richmond, sold her possessions there, and in anticipation of the success of the movement to divert travel to Blue Springs, moved to that place, bought the Noyes & Chambers building and immediately became a factor in the development of the village. There were at that time three other log cabins built under the bluffs along Spring creek. This was really the origin of Blue Springs. Mrs. Woodward and a number of others had bought lots in the town as originally surveyed, but on account of the Wilson mortgage, title could not be made. Chambers and Noyes finally abandoned their townsite interests and Wilson succeeded to their rights. In 1861 in order to quiet the demands of those who had purchased lots of Chambers and Noyes, Wilson caused the original townsite of Blue Springs to be surveyed and platted by Solon M. Hazen, and placed the plat thereof on record in the office of the register of deeds on the 7th day of June, 1861, whereupon he deeded to the claimants lots in the townsite as platted and recorded. Several additions have been made to Blue Springs, the principal ones being Hollister's, Blackman's, Casebeer's, and Hill's additions. The city, with its additions, now occupies a considerable portion of sections 17 and 18 of Blue Springs township.

The growth of Blue Springs was slow. In 1863, when this writer, a youth of thirteen summers, attended school there, the families living in the village and its immediate vicinity were those of William B. Tyler, Dr. Levi Anthony, Martha Johnson (widow of James H. Johnson, a first settler at Blue Springs), Robert A. Wilson, Lynus Knight, James Lott,

Thomas Armstrong, King Fisher, and Herbert Viney. About 1863 Solon M. Hazen opened a general store at the corner of Scott and Hazen streets, and in 1868 William Tichnor, at that time one of the county commissioners of Gage county, built a dam across the Big Blue river and erected a fine mill, including a saw, lath and shingle mill. This enterprise imparted to Blue Springs the character of a business center, since people were compelled to have their grists ground, their logs sawed, and their laths and shingles riven. Thereafter the village grew apace, and about 1872 there was quite an influx of immigrants from the east to Blue Springs,—the Casebeers, Gambees, Wonders, Harpsters, Shocks, and others, mostly from Pennsylvania and Ohio. The territory tributary to Blue Springs was well populated by 1870, and the village had grown rapidly during the closing years of that decade, the federal census of 1870 showing a population of 354. In 1880 the population had increased to 513; in 1890, according to the census, there were 963 inhabitants; in 1900 there were 786 and in 1910 the number was 712. While these figures show a decrease in population from 1890 to 1900, and a small decrease between 1900 and 1910, it must be borne in mind that the census of 1890, as far as population is concerned, was utterly unreliable, and there were probably no more inhabitants in the city in 1900 than in 1910; the strong probability is that there was no actual loss in population after the year 1900. Since the last census Blue Springs has grown materially and an enumeration would probably show a population of nearly a thousand souls.

Blue Springs always, even in territorial days, maintained a most enviable reputation on account of its attitude on all moral questions, and the worth of character of its citizenry. Crime is almost unknown in Blue Springs. There has never been a murder committed in that community, and prosecution for even minor offenses is almost unknown. The character of the citizens is well illustrated by the attitude of the community on the question of the licensed saloon, when that was a disturbing factor in municipal affairs throughout the state. It never looked with favor upon the saloons, although yielding occasionally to the pressure brought for them, but in 1898 this arch enemy of good morals and virtuous manhood was by the voters of Blue Springs banished forever from the community. This writer testifies with the keenest satisfaction to the high moral tone that has always characterized the beautiful city of Blue Springs.

The first bridge erected across the Big Blue river in Gage county was the Noyes-Chambers toll bridge, in the spring of 1859, which has already been mentioned. As the travel on the proposed cut-off from Ash Point to Blue Springs and beyond did not materialize, the proprietors, in the autumn of 1859, sold their bridge to Samuel Shaw, and the spring freshet of 1861 carried it away,—and nearly carried Mr. Shaw away with it. It was not rebuilt, nor was there any effort made to erect a bridge at Blue Springs until about the year 1870, when Gage county placed an iron bridge across the river at the point where the present steel bridge is found. The old bridge was moved to Beatrice and erected across the Big Blue river at the Scott street crossing. The flood of 1903 dropped it into the water and it was finally removed and rebuilt across the river a mile north of Beatrice, near the Zimmerman Springs.

THE BRIDGE AND MILL AT BLUE SPRINGS
Looking up the Big Blue river from the south

About the year 1880 John E. Smith, Samuel C. Smith and Joel C. Williams established the Bank of Blue Springs. Williams afterward acquired the stock of the Smith brothers and successfully conducted the bank for a number of years, but he was unable to withstand the difficulties of the great panic of 1893-1898, and finally, about 1895, closed the doors of the bank and liquidated its obligations as far as his shrunken assets would permit. About the year 1890 the Blue Springs State Bank was founded by O. N. Wheelock and others, which several years later passed into other hands. The present stockholders of this bank are Wm. C. Black, Jr., and Ralph Clemmons, of Beatrice; and T. J. Patton, O. E. Bishop and George F. Harris, of Blue Springs. Mr. Black is president of the board of directors and Mr. Patton is cashier.

A number of years ago the late Cochran F. Black and his brother, William C. Black, Sr., acquired by purchase the title to the Blue Springs mill and dam. This pioneer milling property was thoroughly overhauled by the new proprietors and, at great expense, one of the best mills in the county was evolved. Its present owners are William C. Black. Sr., and the estate of Cochran S. Black. This valuable property is managed by R. W. Kanagy.

In addition to the business enterprises here mentioned, Blue Springs has two grain elevators, a good lumber and coal yard, and nearly every retail business common to cities of its class in Nebraska is represented.

In 1896 M. A. Farr began the publication of the Blue Springs *Weekly Motor*, and from that day to this the city has possessed a good newspaper. The *Motor* was succeeded by the *Sentinel*, a paper established, owned, and edited by the late James H. Casebeer, and now conducted by his son Clarence Casebeer. It has always been a remarkably clean and reliable newspaper and has rendered invaluable service to its readers as a disseminator of information and a pillar of public morals.

The first school in Blue Springs was a subscription school (in 1861) taught by Miss Lucy Johnson, a daughter of Rankin Johnson, one of the early settlers of that locality. Following this, Mrs. Maria Sargent, wife of J. T. Sargent, taught a subscription school in her own house, a log cabin, and had twelve pupils. In 1862 Miss Wealthy Tinkham, afterward Mrs. Joseph Hollingsworth, taught the first public school in Blue Springs, and in 1863 her sister Margaret, afterward Mrs. Nathan Blakely, taught the second public school, with an enrollment of sixteen pupils. During the Indian troubles on the Little Blue river and farther west, 1864, 1865, 1866, little attention seems to have been given to education, but in 1869 a small school-house was erected and thereafter a school was regularly taught in Blue Springs. The district now possesses a fine, two-story, brick school-house, containing eight rooms, and employs eight teachers, with an enrollment of more than two hundred pupils.

BLUE SPRINGS HIGH SCHOOL

As early as 1859 the Methodists organized a church in Blue Springs, with John Foster as its pastor. This organization was fostered and sustained by the pioneers to a man. In 1879 the citizens assisted in erecting a stone church building for the Methodists, a movement contemporary with the building of the old stone church in Beatrice. Besides the Methodist church, the Presbyterians, the Evangelical Association, the United Brethren, and the Christian churches are represented, all owning substantial edifices for the worship of Almighty God.

Both the Masonic fraternity and the Independent Order of Odd Fellows have very strong organizations in Blue Springs, the latter having a membership of upwards of one hundred and fifty. A number of the beneficiary orders also are represented in Blue Springs.

During the Civil war, in 1863, the village of Blue Springs and its tributary territory contributed a number of volunteers to the Nebraska Second Regiment of Volunteers. The regiment was part of General Sully's command, dispatched by the government to put down the Indian uprising in Minnesota. Some of the volunteers from Blue Springs were Francis M. Graham, George Dessert, H. S. Barnum, and Edward Armstrong.

A government postoffice was established in Blue Springs about 1859, with William B. Tyler, postmaster. The mails were at first carried on horseback from Nebraska City and Brownville, and for many years the postoffice at Blue Springs served a large portion of southern Gage county with mail facilities.

Blue Springs is electrically lighted with current from the Holmesville plant. It owns its own waterworks and by an arrangement with Wymore its springs of pure water are utilized for both cities at the expense of Wymore.

The isolation of Blue Springs was broken in 1879 by the construction of the Union Pacific line of railway from Marysville to Beatrice, as well as by the extension of the Burlington line from Beatrice to the main southern line of the company. At one time, in 1880, it seemed as if Blue Springs might become the junction point, but by over-confidence and mismanagement she allowed this splendid opportunity to slip from her grasp. At first the extension of the Beatrice line was more in the nature of a disaster than a benefit. The Burlington road, for reasons of its own, refused to stop its trains or build a depot, or to recognize in any way the existence of Blue Springs, but rushed across the corporation, regardless of its public duty as a common carrier, to Wymore, which with this favoritism was growing by leaps and bounds. But in 1885 F. W. Mattoon, a citizen of Blue Springs, brought in the supreme court of Nebraska a proceeding in mandamus, to compel the road to afford Blue Springs railway facilities. The application was sustained, and thereafter the railroad grudgingly complied with the mandate of the court.

Blue Springs, though missing this great opportunity, has remained beautiful and attractive, as she was in the beginning. No "homier" place exists in all the boundaries of the state.

Amongst the sturdy pioneers who in her infancy guided the destiny of Blue Springs were William B. Tyler, Rebecca Woodward, Robert A. Wilson, Solon M. Hazen, and Dr. Levi Anthony.

Mr. Tyler was familiarly and affectionately known as "Pap" Tyler. He was of Holland extraction and in many ways possessed the shrewdness which characterized the Hollander. He was born in York county, Pennsylvania, November 16, 1801, at the very threshold of the nineteenth century. In early life he married Sarah Wilt, of his native village. In 1842 she passed away, leaving a family of four children. After the death of his wife Mr. Tyler, in 1843, enlisted in the First United States Regiment of Dragoons and he served through the Mexican war. His first term of enlistment expiring in 1848, he reenlisted and remained in the service of the United States continuously until 1854, when he was honorably discharged, at Fort Leavenworth, Kansas. He at once entered the service of the government in a clerical position in the quartermaster's department, where he remained until 1859. He then started to Salt Lake City to take a similar position under the government, but changed his mind and, in March of that year, settled at Blue Springs. He purchased a quarter-section of land a mile or so up the river from the village. In 1860 Mr. Tyler married Rebecca Woodward, who, when this writer with his parents crossed the Big Nemaha at old Richmond, Nemaha county, Nebraska, on their way to Gage county, Nebraska, kept the ranch at Richmond which was intended to be a station on the Blue Springs cut-off from the Oregon Trail, and who shortly afterward sold out at Richmond and bought the Noyes-Chambers ranch house in Blue Springs and came there to live. At the time of this marriage Mrs. Woodward was in possession of considerable means for those days, and she was probably the wealthiest person in Gage county for several years. Several of the first instruments recorded in our county represent business transactions in her name. At the time of this marriage she was about forty years of age and an amiable, accomplished, and very capable woman. She passed away in 1870, mourned by all who knew her.

Mrs. Rebecca Tyler

William B. Tyler

William B. Tyler was county commissioner of Gage county during the years of 1862, 1863, 1864, 1865, 1866, and in 1864, with Fordyce Roper and F. H. Dobbs as associate commissioners, adjusted the affairs of old Clay county after its partition between Lancaster and Gage. From 1860 until his death, in 1889, he was a judge at every annual election in the county and also the messenger who carried the returns of Blue Springs to the county clerk.

He was a kindly, genial soul, and to the last moment of his life was one of the most public-spirited citizens of Blue Springs. As a youth the writer spent nearly an entire year under the roof of William and Rebecca Tyler as a member of their household, and he desires here to testify his appreciation of their uniform kindness and goodness of heart.

Robert A. Wilson was born in Decatur, Indiana, on the 4th day of February, 1833. In 1848 his parents moved to Iowa, where his father died while yet a young man. In 1856 Mr. Wilson came to Omaha and later he went to Nebraska City, where he met Judge John Fitch Kinney, and, being a practical millwright and miller, he was about to engage with Judge Kinney to come to Beatrice and set up and take charge of the steam saw mill owned by the Beatrice Townsite Company. He was deterred from entering into this arrangement, and probably from becoming a citizen of Beatrice, by the remark of some friend to the effect that the members of the Beatrice Townsite Company were all college-bred men and knew nothing about saw mills. Mr. Wilson and his brother William did, however, about that time accept from the United States government service which took them to the Otoe and Missouri Indian Agency, where they erected the government steam saw and grist mill and ran the same until 1860. In the autumn of that year he returned to Iowa and married Miss Amelia Darner. Prior to his leaving the territory he had loaned Joseph Chambers five hundred dollars with which to purchase the tract of land where Blue Springs now stands, and had taken a mortgage upon the prospective townsite to secure this indebtedness. Learning that Chambers and his partner Noyes had disposed of their interests in Blue Springs and abandoned the projected townsite. Mr. Wilson returned to Nebraska territory and settled in Blue Springs in 1861. Shortly after his arrival he procured the services of Solon M. Hazen and surveyed and platted the original town of Blue Springs. From 1865 to 1868 he was employed in the mill of Perry Hutchison, at Marysville, Kansas. During the latter year he was interested with William Tichnor in building the dam and mill at Blue Springs.

For many years Mr. Wilson led the simple life of a farmer, on a fine tract of land adjoining the townsite of Blue Springs. Some years ago he retired from his farm and he is spending the remnant of his life in the beautiful little city of which he was the founder nearly three score years ago. He is slowly recovering from the shock of a serious surgical operation performed nearly a year ago, and he and his aged wife are the objects of the veneration and love of the entire community.

ROBERT A. WILSON
Founder and pioneer resident
of Blue Springs

MRS. AMELIA WILSON
Wife of Robert A. Wilson

Robert A. Wilson is a man of heroic stature, standing considerably over six feet, and is large of frame. Throughout his long career, until recently, he was a man of great physical strength. He is of a genial, kindly, humorous nature a good friend, an interesting companion, loyal and true-hearted.

SOLON M. HAZEN
Pioneer resident of Blue Springs

Solon M. Hazen was born in Denmark, New York, August 11, 1829. He belonged to that class of patriotic young men who came from the eastern states in the year 1857 as followers of John Brown in his efforts to save Kansas from the curse of human slavery. After spending the winter of 1857-1858 in Brown county, Kansas, he, in 1858, with George W. Stark, another anti-slavery enthusiast, came to the new territory of Nebraska and settled on land in Rockford township, this county. He built a log cabin on his land, broke out several acres of fertile Mud creek bottom, and remained here until after the presidential election of 1860, when he returned to New York and resumed his occupation as a school teacher. He also purchased a newspaper, the *Journal-Republican*, at Lowville, New York, which he conducted for three years. Later he purchased the Watertown *Herald*, at Watertown, New York, and he continued as its publisher for several years. On the 24th day of December, 1863, he married Miss Priscilla Ann Vary, and in 1868 he returned to Nebraska, which was then a state, and settled permanently in Blue Springs. Shortly after his return he opened a general store at the corner of Hazen and Scott streets, and he continued for many years in business in that location. In 1861 he surveyed for Robert A. Wilson the original townsite of Blue Springs, and later he was elected one of the county commissioners of Gage county, an office which he held for some years. In 1884 he was elected to represent the people of Gage county in the state legislature, where, as a member of several important committees, he rendered distinguished services to his constituents and to the people of the state. He served his community as justice of the peace, postmaster, member of the school board, member of the council and in other capacities.

Mr. Hazen was a tall, distinguished-looking man, slow of speech, deliberate in judgment, and very considerate of the rights and feelings of others. There were no better men than Solon M. Hazen. This historian has the kindest of recollections of this good, benevolent man. When still a mere child and at a time when there were no schools accessible to him the writer got his first lessons in numbers by the flickering light of a chip fire, in the open air, from Solon M. Hazen.

Dr. Levi Anthony was, next to Dr. Herman M. Reynolds, the earliest practising physician of reputation and standing in Gage county. He was born at Washington, Jackson county, Ohio, November 27, 1835, but from October 14, 1846, to the fall of 1849 he lived in Jackson county, Missouri. He then moved to Mills county, Iowa, and took up the study of medicine under Dr. Barrett, and he entered upon the practice of his profession in Iowa. In 1859 he moved to Peru, Nebraska, and, forming a partnership with Dr. Perry at that western outpost of civilization, he practiced his profession there until 1861. While at Peru he met Robert A. Wilson, of Blue Springs, who pursuaded him to change his location and offered to deed, and did afterward deed, to him forty acres of land in the vicinity of Blue Springs on the condition of his making such change. No time was lost by the Doctor, who was an active, decisive man, in reaching his new location. Here he soon became widely known as a physician of skill and ability. His practice extended over a large portion of Gage county and several of the surrounding counties. He made his professional calls mostly on horseback, carrying his medicine chest in large, double, leather saddle-bags, strapped to the back of his saddle. He was a most familiar figure and on account of his genial nature was a welcome visitor in the homes of the early settlers. In 1867 he moved to Beatrice and engaged successfully in the practice of his profession there, but in the latter part of 1869 the Doctor located on a homestead three-quarters of a mile south of the present city of Wilber. He acquired title to this land and made it his home for several years. When the village of Wilber was laid out as a town, in 1872, by Charles D. Wilber and Jacob Mooney, Dr. James Paddock, a young physician, came there seeking a location. Finding Dr. Anthony already on the field, he sought and was able to form a copartnership with him, and for many years these two pioneer physicians practiced their profession together at Wilber, Dr. Anthony living upon his homestead until age admonished him that the period for rest had come. He then purchased a residence in Wilber and lived there till December 4, 1891, when he passed away, at the age of sixty-six years.

In the autumn of 1864, following the Indian outbreak on the Little Blue river, in August of that year, a company of militia was raised, consisting of about one hundred men and composed exclusively of residents of Gage and Pawnee counties. Dr. Anthony was active in this movement and was elected second lieutenant of the company, which went into service in September, 1864. It was stationed at Buffalo ranch, on the Little Blue river, at the foot of Nine Mile Ridge, on the old Oregon Trail, until February, 1865, when it was mustered out of service. The company performed guard duty along the old trail, protecting the overland stage, emigrants and commercial travel each way from its stockade for a distance of forty miles.

When a very young man Dr. Anthony married Meriba Troth, October 4, 1846. To this marriage twelve children were born, Nancy Elizabeth, Hannah Retta, Mary A., Isaac T., Martha E., Eliza J., Sarah C., Orpha J., Lydia A., John F., George S., and Leon J. His wife and two of these children died before his own death occurred.

DR. LEVI ANTHONY

In his early life Dr. Anthony was an active member of the Methodist church. He later became affiliated with the Church of Latter Day Saints, at Wilber. Dr. Anthony was below average stature, was endowed with an alert mind, was genial, witty and possessed other qualities which made him a pleasant companion and a welcome visitor everywhere.

Francis M. Graham has been so long a resident of Blue Springs that few are living now who remember the time when he was not a citizen of that place. Some time prior to his arrival at Blue Springs, he had made his home with Rebecca Tyler, at Richmond, Nemaha county, Kansas, and when she sold out there and moved to Blue Springs, in the summer of 1859, he came with her, being then a youth of fifteen summers. They were much attached to each other and the relation of mother and son practically existed between them until her death. Until his marriage, in 1865, her home was his.

FRANCIS M. GRAHAM   MRS. HANNAH RETTA GRAHAM

Mr. Graham was born November 2, 1844, in Vermillion parish, Louisiana. His foster mother, Rebecca Tyler, was a southern woman. He was the son of Samuel Graham and Martha (Johnson) Graham. When quite small he was taken to Missouri to live, then to Kansas and then to Blue Springs, Nebraska. In 1865 he married Retta Anthony, the second daughter of Dr. Levi Anthony, and these worthy people have ever since made Blue Springs their home. Both are highly respected and useful members of society. They have reared a large and interesting family and are spending their declining years with their many friends, amid the surroundings of their early days. With Robert A. Wilson and perhaps one or two members of the James H. Johnson family, they are all that is left of that heroic company that created Blue Springs from a prairie waste.

Mr. and Mrs. Graham are open-hearted, friendly people whose lives are an open book to be read by all.

CHAPTER XXIV

WYMORE

The city of Wymore is located at the confluence of Big Indian creek and the Big Blue river, on the main line of the Chicago, Burlington Quincy Railroad Company across southern Nebraska, from Chicago to Denver. Here also the branch line of this company from Omaha to Concordia, Kansas, via Lincoln and Beatrice, intersects the main Denver line, imparting to the city of Wymore the characteristics of a railway center. From its beginning the city has constituted a division for the Burlington Railroad; here are found the company's roundhouse, machine and repair shops, station building and numerous other structures required at a railway division point. Here also are found the headquarters of the division officials, and the various accessories necessary to the proper operation of the railroad. Wymore is the second largest municipal corporation in Gage county and is the most important and best city of its population in southeastern Nebraska. It is thirteen miles southeast of Beatrice, joins the city of Blue Springs to the north, and is located in the midst of a wealthy, prosperous farming community.

The founding of Wymore dates from the construction of the main line of the Burlington Railroad upon which it is located. At the time of its origin the situation in Nebraska was such as to invite railroad building on a large scale throughout the eastern two thirds of the state. The main line of the Union Pacific Railway through central Nebraska had proved a surprising success as a factor in the settlement and development of all the territory tributary to it. By successive purchases and consolidations with other lines the Chicago, Burlington & Quincy Railroad Company had, by 1870, acquired a line of railway from Chicago, Illinois, to Pacific Junction, opposite Plattsmouth, Nebraska. The Burlington & Missouri River Railroad Company in Nebraska had been incorporated May 12,

1869, and in July of that year began the construction of a line of railway from Platts mouth to Kearney Junction, Nebraska, on the Union Pacific, near where the city of Kearney is located. Several years after the completion of this route, the company was consolidated with the Chicago, Burlington & Quincy Railroad Company, under date of the 26th day of July, 1880, having at that time 836 miles of trackage in southeastern Nebraska, including a railroad bridge across the Missouri river at Plattsmouth and two miles of trackage at Pacific Junction. Amongst its other activities it had constructed, in 1878, a line of railway from Hastings to Red Cloud, and thence up the Republican valley, projected to Denver. In 1871 it had also constructed a line of railway from Crete, on its main line between Plattsmouth and Kearney Junction, to Beatrice. In 1879 the Union Pacific Railway Company, then described as the Omaha & Southwestern, had built its present line of railway from Marysville, Kansas, as far as Beatrice, via Blue Springs and the Otoe Indian Agency, which was projected to a junction with its main line at Valley, via Lincoln. Almost the entire state, and particularly the South Platte country and that portion of central Nebraska which was then tributary to the Union Pacific Railway lines, was in a ferment of activity. Immigration was rushing in, following the rails, at an unheard of rate; the prairies were disappearing under the settlers' plows; in every direction towns and villages were springing up as if by magic; and everywhere in the state the railways were taxed to the uttermost to meet the demands of the ever increasing population.

Moreover the local situation by 1879 was such as to promote the increase of railway trackage in Gage county, and particularly in the southern portion. Since its completion, Beatrice had been the terminus of the Crete branch of the Burlington road. In 1877 the western portion of the Otoe and Missouri Indian lands had been placed upon the market and quickly sold to actual settlers, as by law required. This splendid tract of fertile lands was without railway facilities nearer than Beatrice or, later, than Blue Springs. Under these circumstances, it created no surprise when, in March, 1880, a party of Burlington surveyors arrived in Blue Springs from the west. They had carried a projected line of railway from Red Cloud down the Republican river to Hardy, Nuckolls county; thence across country to the head waters of Rose creek, in Jefferson county, crossed the Little Blue river at the confluence of these streams; led up historic Rock creek to the head waters of Big Indian creek; followed down the valley of that stream to its junction with the big Blue river, and, crossing the river, led away eastward to an intersection with the Atchison & Nebraska at Table Rock, and still on down the Big Nemaha to the Missouri, St. Joseph, northern Missouri, western Illinois, Chicago.

This ambitious and most successful plan of railroad building contemplated the extension of the Crete-Beatrice branch to a junction with the east and west main line. When it became evident that these lines of railway were to be pushed to immediate completion the southern half of Gage county seethed with excitement and eager anticipation. The question of greatest concern was the location of the junction, since it was evident that at that point would be developed a city of importance. Blue Springs was of course ardently hoping to become the center of all this railroad activity and to profit by securing the location of the junction of the two lines of railway. Unfortunately, and to this day to the regret of those who love it, these expectations were not to be realized. Overconfidence in her position and importance at that particular juncture in her affairs, prevented the consummation of her hopes.

The following narrative of the origin of Wymore and its early history was prepared for this work by Charles M. Murdock, who has been a citizen of that city since its founding, and who as a right-of-way agent for the Burlington Railroad Company, and at the time a citizen of Blue Springs, writes from an intimate knowledge of the facts:

"In the fore part of May, 1880, R. O. Phillips, secretary of the Lincoln Land Company, and some of the Burlington & Missouri River Railroad officials came to Blue Springs and made an arrangement with S. M. Hazen, C. W. Hill, and others in Blue Springs, for a half interest in about two hundred acres of land in sections 17 and 18, township 2 north, of range 7 east of the 6th principal meridian, surrounding where the depot at Blue Springs now stands, and to locate a depot, and not lay out or build any conflicting town interest within five miles of the depot at Blue Springs. Several business men in Blue Springs agreed to purchase from five to ten acres of the Hazen and Hill lands and pay them a stated price per acre. Then they would donate (to the Lincoln Land Company) a half-interest in the tracts they had purchased, in order to share the burden with Hazen and Hill. This arrangement was agreed to and seemed to be definitely settled. But within sixty days some of the parties who had agreed to purchase from five to ten acres of the Hazen and Hill lands went back on what they had agreed to do. They claimed the Burlington & Missouri River Railroad Company would put in the depot at Blue Springs regardless of whether they got a half-interest in the Hazen and Hill lands or not. R. O. Phillips, secretary of the Lincoln Land Company, and A. B. Smith, townsite surveyor, came to Blue Springs and tried to close the deal, but could not do it. They then had options of purchase taken on part of the southeast quarter of section 21, south west quarter of section 22, northwest quarter of section 27 and northeast quarter of section 28, township 2 north, of range 7 east, where the Burlington surveyed line crossed the Union Pacific tracks,—a move that looked very discouraging to some of the observing people in and around Blue Springs.

"Samuel Wymore then owned the northeast quarter of section 20, Blue Springs township, which joined the section in which the city was located. When he learned that R. O. Phillips, for the Lincoln Land Company, had procured options of purchase on lands east of the Big Blue river, he offered to donate a half-interest in the west half of his quarter section, which on the north joined the townsite of Blue Springs and which was crossed by the Burlington right-of-way leading eastward, if the railroad company would erect and maintain a depot on his land or at the junction of the two lines on the southeast quarter of section 20, joining his land on the south, and he signed a contract to that effect. I then went to the southeast part of Marshall county, Kansas, to see Owen R. Jones, who then owned the last-named quarter section of land, together with the north half of the northeast quarter of section 29. I took his contract for the right-of-way over the southeast of section 20 and any extra right-of-way that might be required in the construction of the railroad across or upon that tract of land. He said the railroad company ought to buy his land; I asked him his price, and he said twenty dollars per acre. He and his wife signed a memorandum contract agreeing to convey to R. O. Phillips the above described land, 240 acres, for the sum of $4,800. I sent the memorandum contracts of Samuel Wymore and Owen R. Jones to Mr. Phillips at Lincoln, Nebraska, and wrote to A. E. Touzalin what could be done with Wymore and Jones. Touzalin and Phillips were anxious to get the location at Blue Springs adjusted, and to gain time I procured, at their request. an extension of the Wymore and Jones contracts to September 15, 1880.

"But the Blue Springs location was not definitely settled and Mr. Touzalin, the general manager of the Burlington road, and other officials arranged to come to Blue Springs, and on September 17, 1880, Mr. Touzalin; George W. Holdrege, general superintendent; Tobias Castor, superintendent of right-of-way; Superintendent T. E. Calvert, and other Burlington Railroad officials came to Blue Springs from Beatrice over the Union Pacific line, in a special car. They arranged for a meeting with the Blue Springs people that evening. At the meeting the subject was fully discussed and the Blue Springs people asked for time to enable them to talk the matter over that night, and at nine o'clock the next morning they reported that they would not accept the proposition.

"Wymore and Jones were both present at the above described meeting. A deal with them was closed September 18, 1880, and it was definitely settled that a depot would be built at the junction on the southeast quarter of section 20 township 2 north, range 7 east, Gage county, Nebraska. In the latter part of December, 1880, the line was extended from Beatrice to the junction, and General Superintendent Holdrege and other officials rode down to the junction over their own new line, in a special car, January 5. 1881.

"April 7, 1881, Mr. Phillips, secretary of the Lincoln Land Company, and Anselmo B. Smith, the company's townsite surveyor, began the survey of the townsite at the junction of the two lines of railway. A. E. Touzalin, general manager of the Burlington lines, named the town Wymore after the late Samuel Wymore."

Mr. Murdock was selected by the Lincoln Land Company, an organization which every old settler will remember as having greatly influenced to its own profit the location and disposal of townsites along the lines of the Burlington Railroad system in the early history of Nebraska to handle the company's interest at Wymore. The plat of the original town of Wymore was filed for record in the office of the register of deeds at Beatrice, May 21, 1881, by which time Mr. Murdock had sold twenty lots in the townsite, upon which buildings were being erected, and within sixty days after the recording of the plat there were sixty business houses and residences erected in the new town of Wymore. Among the first to build were David Greenslate, who erected a hotel forty by forty-four feet, and two store buildings; J. Pisar, a business house twenty by thirty feet; J. Wazab, a business house twenty-four by thirty-six feet; Charles Wachtel, H. M. Leach, R. C. Welch, A. J. McClain, T. E. Cone, W. Shestak, J. Miles, M. H. Gow, L. W. Allgire, A. V. S. Saunders, David McGuire, John Vesley, F. R. Siltz. William Baxendale, P. Sullivan, H. S. Glenn, E. P. Reynolds, Sr., (hotel); James A. Myer, E. C. Pusey, H. A. Greenwood, W. H. McClelland, J. Casey, G. W. Rummel, Washburn Brothers (lumber yard); H. A. Kingsbury (lumber yard); J. S. Johnson, Joseph Grimes, O. J. King, J. D. Gallagher, J. H. Ake, George Noll, S. P. Lester (livery stable); F. J. Greer (elevator), and others.

NIAGARA AVENUE, WYMORE

The plat of the original townsite of Wymore was filed for record in the office of the register of deeds May 21, 1881. It comprised a part of the east half of section 20; it has been greatly augmented by additions, the most important of which are Ashby's Addition and Wymore's Addition, on the north and west; Summit and Railroad Additions, on the east; Hoag's, Hinkle's, and Scott's Additions, on the south and west. With these additions the city now occupies a part of sections 19, 20, 29, and 30.

The business district of the city is largely confined to the original townsite. Niagara avenue, running north to Blue Springs, is the principal business street. It is a wide, beautiful thoroughfare, and most of the business houses upon it are substantial, two-story, brick structures.

A United States government postoffice was established in the village of Wymore, October 27, 1881, with George F. Walker as postmaster. The citizens of Wymore are supplied with free mail delivery, employing two city carriers, while the rural population tributary to the city is reached by the free-delivery service of the postoffice department.

An interesting incident in the early history of Wymore was the construction and operation of a street-railway line from the Burlington station to the Union Pacific station at Blue Springs. It was a horse-car line and was built by E. P. Reynolds and his sons J. H. and Ben Reynolds, railroad contractors with headquarters at Wymore, who had completed a number of contracts for the Burlington Railroad Company on the main line from the Missouri river to Denver. This car line was carried across the Burlington right-of-way by an overhead bridge, thirty feet in width, on Ashby avenue. It was operated from 1882 till about 1892, when it was abandoned.

From the beginning Wymore grew rapidly in population and wealth. It was an ambitious and aggressive rival of Beatrice, the county seat. By 1883 it had acquired a population of approximately two thousand souls. The federal census of 1890 gave it 2420 inhabitants; that of 1900, 2626; and that of 1910, 2613. In the year 1893 those who guided its destinies conceived it possible to divide Gage county and erect a new county out of the south half, to be known as Blaine county, with Wymore as its county seat. Proper steps were taken by these enthusiasts to bring the matter to a vote at the November election. A very spirited and splendid canvass was made by the Wymoreans. Beatrice of course entered warmly into the contest, and during the latter part of the summer and early fall of 1883 a vigorous campaign was waged on the question of county division. At the election, 1332 votes were polled for division and 2801 against the project. It is to the lasting credit of Wymore that she gracefully accepted this result and, without murmur or complaint, good-naturedly has continued to play the part of the second most important city in the splendid county of Gage.

On October 25, 1881, Horace A. Greenwood, who had formerly lived at Red Oak, Iowa, established the first bank in Wymore. The following year Benjamin Burch, his son John C. Burch and M. A. Southwick came to Wymore for the purpose of engaging in the banking business and were about to start a new bank when Mr. Greenwood sold them his institution and retired for the time being from the banking business. The Bank of Wymore, under the management of its new proprietors, did a flourishing business for more than ten years, but during the great financial panic which began in 1893 and lasted for several years, the bank was forced out of business and passed into the hands of a receiver. About the time the Bank of Wymore was purchased by the Burches and Southwick, a brick bank building was erected by Joseph R. Dodds on the corner south of the Touzalin Hotel, that being the first brick bank building in Wymore, and the Citizens Bank was established in it by Elisha P. Reynolds and sons. Some years afterward this became the property of Samuel Wymore and E. C. Wilcox, with E. C. Wilcox as cashier and as the one in principal charge of the bank's fortunes. About the time of the financial stringency above referred to this bank liquidated its obligations and ceased to exist. Succeeding these two early ventures in banking, the First National Bank of Wymore was founded by Horace A. Greenwood and others, and, probably about the same time, the Farmers & Merchants Bank came into existence. These are both exceptionally strong financial institutions for a town of the population of Wymore and each possesses a fine bank building. They are owned and conducted by men of character and standing in the community and meet the ordinary demands for banking resources in a way that leaves nothing to be desired. J. A. Rueling is president of the First National; G. L. Stephenson, vice-president; John S. Jones, cashier;

and D. K. Windle, assistant cashier. Sherman Taylor is president of the Farmers & Merchants Bank; W. A. Dawson, vice-president; F. E. Lefferdink, cashier; A. L. Baker and C. F. Stillwell, assistant cashiers.

In addition to its banks Wymore is well supplied with elevators, lumber and coal yards, garages, hotels, implement houses, restaurants, general stores, grocery stores, hard ware stores, drug stores, jewelry establishments, photograph galleries, and every kind of business establishment to be found in cities of its population and class in the west.

The city obtains its water from the springs of its nearby neighbor, Blue Springs, and owns its own water system. It is well lighted by electrical current from the Holmesville Mill & Power Company.

The visitor to Wymore is always impressed by the extensive yards and shops of the Burlington Railroad Company, where hundreds of men are daily employed. The monthly distribution of wages by the company to its employes at this divisional point has been a constant and never-failing source of prosperity to the business men of the city. At present the railroad company employes 135 men in its mechanical department, 371 in its operating department, and 46 officers and clerks—a total of 552 employes of the Burlington Railroad at Wymore.

No city of its population in the state approaches Wymore in the number, acreage and beauty of its public parks. The public-park system for the city was first agitated several years ago, by Hon. A. D. McCandless, a lawyer of distinction in the Gage county bar. With intelligent persistence worthy of the cause, he has allowed no opportunity to pass for urging upon the citizens of the city and upon those in authority the desirability of adopting a system of public parks which should be more than commensurate with the immediate needs and resources of the city. Great success has crowned his unselfish and altruistic efforts. To his credit, and to the credit of those associated with him in his fine, patriotic labor, there are now eight public parks in the city of Wymore. They are as designated in the following paragraphs.

Arbor State Park consists of thirty-three acres of land in the northeast quarter of section 20, formerly known as the old Fair Ground. It was named Arbor State Park "in recognition of the loyalty of the Arbor State newspaper to the interests and upbuilding of the city of Wymore in the past quarter of a century, and of the editor of said paper for his years of faithful service as the highest office in said city, and his zealous work for the park system of said city."

McCandless Park comprises blocks 25 and 26 of Ashby's Addition to the city of Wymore, with the street lying between the two blocks, which was vacated in order to become a part of the park. It was named in honor of A. D. McCandless and in recognition of his successful work in planning and securing an attractive public parking system for the city.

Furnas Park consists of the south half of block 8 and the north half of block 9 in the original town of Wymore and the street lying between these two parcels of land, which was vacated by the city council for the purpose of being added to the park.

Rawlings Park is block 31 of the original town of Wymore and bears the name of Rawlings Park in recognition of one of its most prominent and enterprising citizens, M. L. Rawlings, who has served three terms as mayor of the city of Wymore and has been otherwise active and useful for many years in the affairs of the city.

Riverside Park lies on the east bank of the Big Blue river, between the wagon road on Bennett street and the Burlington Railroad bridge across the river.

Horseshoe Park lies south of Indian creek and west of what is known as the Marysville road, and is the property of the Lincoln Land Company.

High School Park is that portion of the high-school grounds which has been incorporated into the parking system of Wymore.

Taylor Park comprises a considerable tract of ground lying north and west of the right-of-way of the Burlington Railroad Company, in the immediate neighborhood of the depot building.

In 1916 the public-spirited citizens of Wymore began agitation for a free public library. Application was made to the great philanthropist, Andrew Carnegie, for an appropriation out of his many millions for the erection of a library building. This magnanimous builder of libraries readily donated to the city the sum of $10,000 to be used exclusively for a building, on condition that a suitable site be furnished by the citizens of Wymore and that the city authorities should annually levy a public tax sufficient to sustain the library. These conditions have been fully complied with. The library is located on the southeast corner of block 26 of Wymore's Addition, immediately west of Neuman's store, on the southeast corner of the block. The plans and specifications were furnished by Richard W. Grant, architect, of Beatrice, and at this writing the building is complete except for the placing of a furnace.

The first Episcopal church service was held in Wymore by Rev. T. O'Connell, in what is known as the Honeymoon school-house, in the fall of 1881. In March, 1884, a service was held by the Rev. C. L. Fulforth, rector of the Episcopal church at Beatrice, at which preliminary steps were taken for the organization of a parish in Wymore. A petition was prepared and was addressed to the bishop of the diocese, requesting such action. It was signed by eighteen persons, of whom eight were communicants of the church. This request was granted, and on August 17, 1884 the parish was organized under the name of St. Luke's. On the following 13th day of September, with Bishop Worthington officiating, the holy communion service of the church was celebrated for the first time in Wymore. A mission organization was adopted, with Richard Whitten as warden. On the 10th day of October, 1888, steps were taken toward the building of a church by the congregation. A lot for that purpose was donated by the Lincoln Land Company, the Bishop contributed $800 and a building was erected, this being, dedicated as a house of worship, by Bishop Worthington, April 15, 1889. The church has grown in strength and usefulness from the first day and is today one of the live, virile religious organizations of the city.

The parish of St. Mary's Catholic church was established in 1882, a pastoral residence being erected that year and later a frame church building. The priest first in charge was the Rev. A. C. Rausch, who continued his labors until 1889, when the Rev. J. C. Freeman took charge; he remained at the head of the parish until his death, in 1915. He was succeeded by Father D. J. Cronin, who is now in charge of the parish.

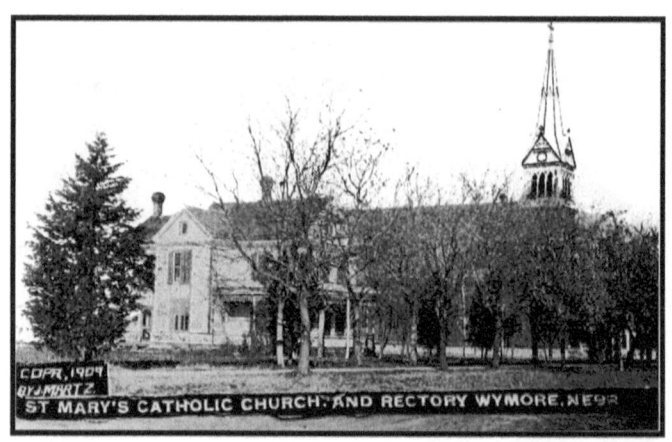

The Catholic organization owns fine church properties in Wymore, consisting of an entire block of ground adjoining the high-school block, upon which is situated the church building and a new pastoral residence, of two stories.

The Christian church was organized in 1887, by Elder Bear, of Tecumseh, the services first being held in Brownwell Hall and other places. In 1896 the present church edifice was erected. Services are regularly maintained by the church and the organization is an active factor in the social and religious life of the city.

FIRST BAPTIST CHURCH, WYMORE

The first church, organized in Wymore was the Missionary Baptist church. The organization took place September 14, 1881. Services were maintained at various places in the city until 1886, when the congregation built a frame church building, under the pastorate of Rev. A. H. Law. This building was afterward sold, and the Baptists acquired by purchase their present church, from the Congregationalists.

Since its organization a good Sunday school has been maintained and the regular services of the church have gone constantly forward. The membership of this church is quite strong and it is an influential factor in the life of the city.

About 1907 the Calvanistic Welsh church was organized in Wymore. A building was purchased and moved to its present location, where it was fitted up as a house of worship. A Sunday school and church services have since been regularly maintained.

The Free Methodist church has had an existence in Wymore since 1887, maintaining a pastor the most of the time and its organization all the time. It has a new frame church building, located in the northwest part of the city.

The Methodist Episcopal church was organized in Wymore July 20, 1883, with the Rev. C. M. Hollopeter as pastor. The church services and Sunday school were first held in Livsey's Opera House, later in the Newbranch Hall and in what is now known as the Baptist church. The first effort to secure a church building came from Mrs. William Winter, in 1885. At a family gathering at which her seven sons and two daughters were present, at her suggestion, a subscription list was started for funds to be used in purchasing a suitable site for a church building. The sum of one hundred dollars was immediately subscribed by her and her children and subscriptions continued to be taken until enough money was on hand to purchase a lot and a half in the most desirable residence portion in the city of Wymore on which to erect a church building, where the present splendid house of worship now stands. A movement was then started to secure enough money by subscription to erect a church edifice. Plans and specifications were supplied by the Methodist Church Extension Society and approved by the local board of trustees for a structure to cost approximately six thousand dollars. The building was begun in 1888 and in the following year it was completed, and dedicated, by Bishop Joyce, to the worship of God. Including the grounds, the property cost about thirteen thousand dollars. A considerable indebtedness rested upon the church, which accumulated during the hard times following 1893, until it finally amounted to $4,700. Heroic efforts were made by the pastor in charge, the Rev. A. B. Whitmer, to secure through subscriptions a sum of money sufficient to liquidate this indebtedness. He was aided by Dr. Huntington, the presiding elder of the church, and at a meeting in 1900, in the presence of a large and rejoicing congregation, it fell to the lot of the Rev. John W. Swan to commit to the flames the mortgage which had hitherto rested upon the property.

Since that date the church has erected on lots adjoining the church property, which it purchased from R. Laflin, a fine parsonage, which cost $4,250. Thus through years of toil, patience, sacrifice and self-denial, the Methodists of Wymore have succeeded in securing a beautiful and permanent church building and a roomy, homelike parsonage. The congregation is large and in a flourishing condition. Since Dr. Hollopeter's time the following named ministers have served the church: O. P. Light, C. W. Abbott, A. B. Whitmer, E. F. Gates, and O. T. Winslow.

In the neighborhood of section 16, Wymore township, are found two attractive country churches, as shown below.

In the fall of 1881, a subscription school was started in Wymore, with Miss Ormsby and Miss Mitchell as teachers. The school was held in Johnson's Hall, but as this proved too small to accommodate the attendance, another room was secured, and S. B. Bowdish was employed as principal.

TWO RURAL CHURCHES NEAR WYMORE

Early in 1882 steps were taken to detach Wymore and its additions from the Blue Springs school district, and in March of that year the city of Wymore was erected into a separate school district and numbered 114. On the organization of the district, W. H. McClelland was elected its director. He proceeded at once to take an enumeration of the district and, incidentally, a census of the population. On March 17, 1882, he reported the number of families then in Wymore to be 224; number of inhabitants, 1,280; and number of children of school age, 375.

The schools of Wymore have flourished from the beginning and the liberal-minded citizens of the city have seen to it that ample school facilities were available. The city now possesses two brick ward-school buildings of two rooms each, and a handsome, two-story, brick high-school building, containing ten rooms. The district employs seventeen teachers and the high school offers a four years' course of study, with normal training. The pupils enrolled in the schools of Wymore number 683.

HIGH SCHOOL WYMORE NEBR

The social and benevolent orders of Wymore include: Coleman Post, No. 115, Department of Nebraska Grand Army of the Republic, organized at Wymore October 7, 1882, and ever since remaining in good standing; Coleman's Women's Relief Corps, No. 65, Department of Nebraska, organized at Wymore June 12 1888, and ever since maintaining its good standing; Ancient Free and Accepted Masons, organized April 19, 1883; Independent Order of Odd Fellows, No. 105, installed February 8, 1883; Rebekah Lodge, No. 69, organized September 23, 1891; Abergeldie Castle, No. 34, Royal Highlanders; and the usual number of fraternal and benevolent orders in cities of the population of Wymore.

So rapid has been the growth of Wymore from the beginning that at a very early period of its history the necessity for some form of municipal government had become very obvious. With characteristic energy and foresight, a movement was inaugurated early in 1882, almost within a year after the founding of the city, to effect village organization under the statute which then provided that all unincorporated towns and villages in Nebraska having over two hundred and less than fifteen hundred inhabitants might be incorporated as villages. On the 22d day of June, 1882, a petition was filed before the board of commissioners of Gage county, praying for the incorporation of Wymore as a village under this statute and suggesting as suitable persons for village officials E. Hutchins to be mayor; W. H. Ashby, clerk; E. C. Wilcox, treasurer; George W. Mechling, police judge; Ben Reynolds, engineer; C. F. Washburn and E. C. Pusey, councilmen for the first ward, and S. S. Darling and A. J. Davis, councilmen for the second ward. The prayer of this petition was readily granted by the county commissioners and these recommendations approved. The organization of Wymore as a village, under the law, immediately followed.

Village government was continued in Wymore until 1884, when it was incorporated as a city of the second class having more than fifteen hundred and less than twenty-five thousand population, as provided by law. The first city officials were: Daniel McGuire, mayor; Thomas D. Cobbey, clerk; E. C. Wilcox, treasurer; A. D. McCandless, city attorney; W. H. Carmichael, marshal; James Pasco, engineer; J. M. Tout and O. P. Newbranch, councilmen for first ward, and, after the resignation of Newbranch, S. H. Craig; for the second ward, E. Snuffin and D. H. Schmitz.

Wymore appears to have always been an inviting field for newspaper men. In May, 1879, Charles M. Murdock had established at Blue Springs a newspaper called the Reporter, largely as an advertising medium for the sale of real estate, but on the 22d day of June, 1881, he removed his printing establishment to Wymore, and thereafter for many years the Wymore *Reporter* was an important factor in the settlement and development of the city. This was the first newspaper in Wymore. In May, 1881, Joseph R. Dodds, a veteran of the Civil war, came from Burlington, Iowa, to Wymore and became immediately active in its affairs. He erected the two-story, brick building on the corner of Nebraska street and Blue River avenue, directly south of the Touzalin Hotel, where later the Citizens bank was established. On the 12th day of May, 1882, from the basement of this old building, Mr. Dodds sent forth the first issue of the Wymore *Eagle*. In the fall of that year he purchased from Ashby & Scott the *Gage County Leader*, a newspaper which had been founded shortly after Murdock had brought the *Reporter* to Wymore, and this he consolidated with the *Eagle*. A little later he merged both names into the *Democrat*, bearing the following legend: "Wymore and Blue Springs." Before his death, he ceased publishing the *Democrat* and began the publication of the *Arbor State*. This bright, newsy paper is now both a daily and a weekly, and is owned and ably edited by J. W. Ellingham. In 1882, with Benjamin Burch, his son John C. Burch, and W. H Southwick, John A. Weaver, a practical newspaper man, came to Wymore from Red Oak, Iowa. In conjunction with the younger Burch he established, the *Wymorean*, a weekly newspaper which has had a continuous existence from the date of its founding and which is well established, with a circulation exceeding two thousand copies. For thirty years it has been very ably conducted by its present owner and publisher, J. M. Burnham.

Wymore is a city of many beautiful homes. The residence district lies west of Niagara avenue and is reached from the business district by ascending a gentle slope. It overlooks the beautiful valley of the Big Blue river on the north, east and south, and the valleys of Bills creek and Big Indian creek toward the west, and from almost every point presents a pleasing landscape. At an early day Elisha P. Reynolds and his sons, J. H. and Benjamin erected fine residences in this part of the city, and many others have since been erected. Here also are located the beautiful high-school grounds and a number of the churches.

CHAPTER XXV

Incorporated Villages

Adams — Barneston — Clatonia — Cortland — Filley — Liberty — Odell — Pickrell — Virginia

ADAMS

As early as 1867 a postoffice was established in Adams township, called Laona. John Lyons was the first postmaster, the postoffice being at his home, a mile and one-half west of the present town of Adams. In 1873 the Atchison & Nebraska Railroad Company built its line of railway through Adams township from Atchison to Lincoln, and in May of that year John O. Adams, in conjunction with the railroad company, laid off the south half of the northeast quarter of section 27, into a townsite and it was named Adams. Village organization was deferred until March 10, 1892. The first board of village trustees comprised the following well known residents of that place, namely: Frank E. Whyman, Henry H. Norcross, W. C. Garrison, Nathaniel C. Shaw, and William C. Gray. They were duly qualified for office by James B. Shaw, justice of the peace. F. E. Whyman was elected first chairman of the village board, W. C. Gray the first secretary, and H. L. Watson was appointed the first marshal of Adams. One of the first ordinances passed prohibited "the sale, giving away, delivering or furnishing in any manner any spirituous, malt, vinous or intoxicating liquors within the village," an ordinance which has stood intact from the beginning. The open saloon never found a place to conduct business in Adams.

The town of Adams has flourished from the beginning. It was supported by an unusually intelligent, progressive and loyal class of citizens. Amongst them the Whyman family, who came overland from western Pennsylvania, consisting of the parents and twelve children; the Adams family and the Shaw family, of whom mention has already been made in this work in the chapter on the early settlers in this county; the Silas Bryson family, who came from Ohio by boat down the Ohio river and up the Mississippi and Missouri, consisting of the parents and fourteen robust sons and daughters, who have contributed ably to the making of the state of Nebraska; William Curtis, who was the fourteenth man to make homestead entry at the Brownville land office, and his family; H. J. Merrick, who is a veteran of the Civil war and who has proved a force in the upbuilding of the village; Byron P. Zuver, Stephen Disher, John Lyons, George and Alfred Gage, L. R. Horrum and his son, Dr. J. W. McKibbin, and many other residents of the town of Adams and vicinity.

In 1874 John O. Adams, the founder of the village, and William Curtis, built the first grain elevator, and Curtis the first store building erected in Adams. In 1874 a postoffice was established at Adams, Mrs. Hannah Noxon, who had been postmistress at Laona, was appointed postmistress and for many years she occupied that position, in a manner highly satisfactory to all patrons of the office, maintaining at the same time a general store in connection with the office. In 1880 J. H. Spellman erected a store building and put in a complete stock of goods. He continued business in this building for thirty years. In 1880 L. R. Horrum, who had taken a homestead near Adams in 1868, working in the meantime at his trade as a harnessmaker in connection with his farm work, built a harness shop in Adams, and this he conducted until his death, in 1913, the business still being carried on by his son, George Horrum. The senior Horrum built the first brick business house in Adams. Dr. J. W. McKibbin, the first resident physician of Adams, located in the village in 1881, and has been in constant practice of his profession here since that time.

Early in the history of Adams, H. J. Merrick organized a patrons' cooperative company, with a capital stock of five hundred dollars, its object being the conducting of a general merchandise business. Stephen Disher became president of the company; H. J. Merrick, secretary; B. P. Zuver, manager. This was the pioneer business of Adams, it being established in June, 1874. From it has developed the Tourtelot-Barber Company, which conducts one of the best general stores anywhere to be found in a village of seven hundred inhabitants, the present population of Adams.

The grain business has been an active industry at Adams from the moment the railroad came. Many individuals and companies had helped develop it until finally the Central Granaries Company obtained control of the business. In 1908 this company sold its elevator to the Farmers Elevator Company, incorporated, with a capital stock of $10,000, held by two hundred farmers and business men of Adams and adjacent territory. J. B. Zuver was its first president, J. W. Campbell its first secretary, and J. B. Zuver its manager. The officers at present are: H. J. Merrick, president; Henry Bable, secretary; and J. B. Zuver, manager; capital and surplus, $40,000.

In 1905 W. E. Bryson and J. E. Miller erected a large, first-class flouring and feed mill, which was later sold to the Nebraska Corn Products Company, and was dismantled, the machinery being removed and the building sold to the Farmers Elevator Company.

The lumber business first operated at Adams was known as the Chicago Lumber Company, with A. Huyser, manager. This company was succeeded about 1880 by the Stewart, Chute Lumber Company and others, including M. J. Mitten, who is now engaged in that business.

The first bank at Adams was a private bank, owned by Messrs. Holber & Bauer, who began business in 1884. It was followed by the State Bank of Adams, in 1889; capital stock, $10,000. The board of directors under the original charter comprised W. P. Norcross, H. J. Merrick, J. W. McKibbin, B. P. Zuver, J. H. Spellman, W. W. Barnhouse, W. E. Bryson;—Norcross, president; McKibbin, vice-president; and Merrick, cashier. March 1, 1902, the controlling interest was purchased by C. S. Black and L. B. Howey, of the First National Bank of Beatrice, and F. B. Draper, of Lincoln, Nebraska, W. P. and H. H. Norcross retiring. Mr. Black became president and Mr. Draper the cashier, the capital stock being increased to $15,000. Directors: Black, Draper, Howey, Merrick, Barnhouse, McKibbin, and Bryson. In 1908 the bank was reorganized as the First National Bank, with a capital of

$25,000. The former officers and board of directors were retained. The institution is a depositary of the Federal Reserve Bank.

In 1908 the Farmers' State Bank was organized, with a capital stock of $25,000. President, G. W. Meeker; vice-president, W. E. Bryson; cashier, Frank O'Neal. After some changes in management, a controlling interest of the capital stock was purchased, in 1917, by Mr. Christiansen and Frank M. Stapleton. Stapleton being the cashier and A. M. Replogle the vice-president.

The bank known as the Adams State Bank was organized with a capital stock of $20,000. Officers and directors: Chris Hennies, president; Frank Schoen, vice-president; Frank Grammann, cashier; F. H. Hennies, August Hoehne, Adolph Hoehne, Thale Tholen, directors. The three banks here named are all in flourishing condition, which indicates a prosperous and wealthy community.

In the spring of 1859, Mrs. Hannah Hicks Shaw invited the settlers with their children to meet at her home to study the Bible. A dozen of all ages responded. The older ones were taught by Miss Phoebe Gale, daughter of George Gale, and the younger by Mrs. W. W. Silvernail (Rebbecca Shaw). Mrs. Shaw then visited Nebraska City and obtained second-hand Sunday-school supplies from Mr. W. L. Boydston, of the Methodist church of that place. From this lively root have sprung all the religious activities of Adams township. In 1861 D. H. Wheeler, representing the American Sunday School Union, came to the township for the purpose of establishing a Sunday school, but he found the work already advanced and in good hands. In 1861 and 1862 the school was held at a new school house in district No. 2, old Clay county, but continuing under the superintendency of Mrs. Shaw. In 1866 the school was held in a log house on what was known as Chambers' farm, and afterward at the Disher farm, now owned by S. B. Fraper; the superintendent was William Curtis. It was afterward held in a barn recently built by John Lyons, and in 1868 and 1869 again was held in the school house of district No. 2. In 1870 school district No. 30 was organized and a dug-out school-house was made on the land now a part of Adams village. In this place Matthew Weaverling (afterward, for three terms, county superintendent of schools of Gage county) taught the first school in that district. In 1871 a new frame building was erected one-half mile west of what is now the village of Adams and the Sunday school was transferred to it, where it remained until 1882, when it was transferred to the newly built Methodist Episcopal church, on the present high-school grounds in the village of Adams.

This had been a union Sunday school until this time, when the Presbyterians withdrew to their own newly built church, and organized as a denominational school, with W. C. Gray as superintendent. The remainder organized as a Methodist Episcopal school, with Silas Bryson as superintendent. In the early '70s the Baptists organized a Sunday school in school district No. 2. with J. H. Lynch and Charles Whyman as principal supporters.

The first sermon preached in Adams township was by Z. B. Truman, at the home of Stephen and Hannah Shaw, in November, 1859, followed in 1860 by Rev. Kindall, both Methodists. From this time until 1867 Rev. Luther Gibbs, a Baptist homesteader, served the people. In that year Rev. Leroy F. Britt, Methodist minister of Tecumseh, preached during the summer, and organized a class of seven persons, namely: William Curtis, Silas Bryson, Mrs. Clara Bryson, Mrs. Almira Lyons, Mrs. Letitia Adams, Mrs. Harriet Adams, Mrs. Robert Howard. Robert Howard was appointed leader. In 1868 Silas Bryson was elected leader, with Rev. George Paddock pastor in charge. In 1869-1870, Rev. A. L. Folden and Rev. J. H. Presson were pastors in charge, followed, in 1872, by T. A. Hull. In 1873-1874 J. H. Presson; 1875, H. P. Mann; 1876, N. W. Van Orsdal; 1877, T. A. Hull, who died in his chair while holding services in the Hooker school house; 1878, H. A. S. King; 1879, G. W. Walker; 1881, Isaac New—all were pastors of the Methodist congregation. Within these years the first Methodist Episcopal church was built and the congregation thereafter was served by J. W. Taylor, in 1883; B. C. Phillips, 1884-1885; J. S. Orr, 1886; M. C. Smith, 1887-1891; A. L. Folden, 1891 to 1894; J. J. Stannard, 1894-1898; Duke Slavins, 1899-1902, when the new church was built, at a cost of $10,000.

Rev. Mr. Wharton, a missionary Baptist, organized a church in 1869, with J. H. Lynch and wife, Charles Whyman and family, and others as its supporters. The First Presbyterian Church was organized February

22, 1880, by Rev. George L. Little, of Omaha. assisted by Rev. A. B. Irwin, of Beatrice. William A. Gray and F. G. Dickinson were chosen as ruling elders. This church, in connection with its Sunday school, Christian Endeavor and other organized activities, has been a directive force in the development of the moral uplift of the community. Rev. W. I. Boole is the present pastor.

The Freewill Baptists and the Christian church each has an active organization, with Sunday schools and Christian Endeavor societies in connection therewith.

The following named societies were early organized in Adams: Independent Order of Odd Fellows, Ancient Free & Accepted Masons, Grand Army of the Republic, Women's Relief Corps, Sons of Veterans, Woodmen of the World, Royal Highlanders, Independent Order of Good Templars, and others.

In November, 1905, the village board of trustees granted to E. J. Shaw and his successors, or assigns, the right to install an electric light and power plant, and this has been in constant operation since that date. In 1915 the village acquired control of this plant, enlarged its capacity and placed it on a modern basis, since which time it has been giving its patrons the best of service.

The Adams *Gazette*, Volume I, No. 1, was issued March 25, 1886, by W. H. Fitzgerald, and this was the beginning of newspaper enterprise in Adams. The paper soon passed into the hands of Mr. Snyder, who continued this publication until 1892, when M. D. Horham became editor and proprietor. In 1907 the present owner and publisher, E. W. Varner, purchased the plant and he has given to Adams and vicinity probably the best weekly newspaper now published in Gage county.

This brief summary of the origin, business interests, religious and social life of Adams was prepared in the main by Hon. Homer J. Merrick, whose life has been so long identified with the community of which he writes, and it modestly omits extended reference to the citizens of Adams and the country tributary to it. It is no exaggeration, nor is it fulsome praise, to state that no community in our county is more distinguished as possessing a large intellectual life and all those qualities and attributes of character which go to make up a loyal, enterprising and wholly reliable citizenship than the one of which he writes.

BARNESTON

The village of Barneston, one of the interesting and pretty villages of southern Gage county, stands on historic ground. It embraces within its boundaries the site of the ancient village of the Otoe Indians and their agency buildings, a location which serves as a perpetual reminder to the old settlers and their descendants of the original inhabitants of Gage county. Barneston is located on the Union Pacific Railway line from Valley, Nebraska, to Manhattan, Kansas, via Lincoln and Beatrice. It is named for Francis M. Barnes, who was a member of the original townsite company and who was affiliated by marriage with the Otoe Indian tribe, his wife being a half-blood Indian woman, a daughter of Andrew Drips. Mrs. Barnes was born November 15, 1827, in Bellevue, Nebraska, where her father was stationed as a representative of the American Fur Company. She was educated at the Convent of the Visitation, at Kaskaskia, Illinois, and in 1856, at Kansas City, Missouri, she became the wife of Francis M. Barnes. In 1859 they moved to the Territory of Nebraska, and later they settled near the Otoe and Missouri Indians in Gage county. As far as known, Mrs. Barnes is the oldest living native born Nebraskan.

The townsite of Barneston comprises the greater portion of the northwest quarter of section 18, township 1 north, range 8 east, while West Barneston, an addition to the original town, lies in the northeast quarter of section 13, township 1 north, range 7 east, where the railway line, sidetracks and station are located. The owners of the original townsite were F. M. Barnes, of Barneston; H. R. W. Hartwig, of St. Joseph, Missouri; I. N. Speer, of Hiawatha, Kansas; and H. L. Ewing, John Ellis, Charles O. Bates, and, Alfred Hazlett, of Beatrice, Nebraska. The plat of the town of Barneston was filed in the office of the register of deeds of Gage county, May 17, 1884. The plat of West Barneston was filed on August 3, 1883. The larger portion of the business establishments of the village, and nearly the entire residence district are in the original town of Barneston, which is a part of Liberty township. Some years ago, however, the county board annexed the quarter section on which the town is located to Barneston township for voting and other administrative purposes.

The surroundings of the village are romantically beautiful. Nearby on the north is Wolf creek, a living, well timbered stream, and on the south is beautiful Plum creek, a never-failing stream of water. Towards the west is the Big Blue river, and on every hand what was once a rolling prairie now shows cultivated, highly improved, thrifty farms. It is to the eastern part of the old Indian reservation what Odell is to the western part, with this difference, that about Barneston clings the romance of another race.

As early as 1873 there was a trading post at the Indian village where Barneston is now located. That year F. M. Barnes opened a store with a general stock of goods, near the agency buildings, which he maintained until the Indians removed to Indian Territory (now Oklahoma), in 1881. In 1882, prior to the founding of Barneston village, he again established a store at this point, to accommodate land seekers and the early settlers on that part of the old Otoe and Missouri Indian reservation. The first merchant in Barneston after it was surveyed and platted was Patrick Rawley, who conducted a general merchandise store there until 1910; he now lives at Falls City, Nebraska. He was soon followed by A. G. Keyes, with a hardware store. The first district schoolteacher at Barneston was a man named Harris. In 1883 he taught a school in the old Indian school building, a structure fifty by ninety feet, two stories in height. This building was located on the quarter-section of land just east of Barneston. It was erected by the United States government for the education of the Indian youths and maidens of the Otoe and Missouri Indian villages, and some years ago it was destroyed by fire.

The school district of Barneston was organized November 22, 1883, at the residence of William Tauer, and it has since been known as district No. 116. The Barneston district possesses at present a frame, two-story school house and the school district employs four teachers, with an enrollment of approximately ninety pupils. The course of study includes only two years of high-school work. Recently the district has been greatly augmented by being consolidated with districts Nos. 119, 121, 177, 136, and 137 into a county high school, with approximately one hundred and fifty pupils. It is planned to erect for the consolidated district a new school building in the village of Barneston, at a probable cost of $40,000, and when this building is completed there will be installed, with the usual grades, a high school providing four years' work.

A United States postoffice was early established in Barneston, with F. M. Barnes as the first postmaster. Those who have succeeded him are A. G. Keyes, Edwin Huddert, Jesse C. Wyatt, and Bertha Hablitzle, the present incumbent. Rural free delivery of mail is maintained at Barneston, the service now being performed by a single carrier.

The first physician in Barneston was Dr. C. S. Smith, who remained three years. Those who have followed him were Drs. Hinton, J. I. Gumaer, J. L. Kirby, U. D. Stone. G. W. Strough, F. J. Bachle, and F. J. Woods. All abandoned the field but Dr. Woods, who has pursued his calling in Barneston and vicinity so many years and so successfully that he has become not only a professional but a social and political force.

About the year 1884 James Craig opened a private bank in Barneston and he continued in business there until 1890. He was succeeded by the Bank of Barneston, incorporated, about 1890, by F. M. Barnes and C. M. Warren, of Barneston; John Ellis, Horace L. Ewing, W. F. King, and Harriet Ewing, of Beatrice; and W. Q. Bell, of Lincoln, Nebraska. This banking institution is still in existence, and is owned and officered by J. A. Spencer, president, and A. D. Spencer, cashier. Since 1903 the banking business at Barneston has been shared with the Commercial State Bank of that village. J. M. Howe is the president, and Henry Monfelt the cashier of the Commercial State Bank. Both banking institutions are in a flourishing condition.

In addition to the banks, Barneston has two general stores, a drug store, hardware store, grocery store, two restaurants, a hotel, two garages, a blacksmith shop, barber shop, lumber and coal yard, pump and plumbing establishment, two elevators, a meat market, and such other business concerns as one would expect to find in a village of like size and character.

The benevolent and other orders of the village consist of a lodge of the Ancient Free & Accepted Masons, Chapter of the Eastern Star, camp of the Modern Woodmen of America, and organizations of the Royal Neighbors and Royal Highlanders.

In 1889 the Presbyterians erected a fairly good church building in Barneston, at a cost of $1,200, and they have since maintained a church organization in the village. The Catholics also have an organization there, their church edifice having been erected in 1892, at a cost of $1,800.

By the census of 1910, Barneston was given 228 inhabitants. Its population at present (1918) is approximately 300. In general appearance Barneston is a very neat, pretty, attractive town. Its business men are active, accommodating and public-spirited. Barneston has furnished members of the legislature, Hon. A. D. Spenser having served in both branches of that body.

Among those who have been prominent in shaping the destiny of Barneston and in the management of its affairs are F. M. Barnes, W. P. Wyatt, Matthew Weaverling, C. W. Warren, George Pace, A. L. Cook, Patrick Rawley, James Ryan, William Tauer, Joseph Guittard, Jesse C. Wyatt, Julius Vogel, A. G. Keyes, G. D. Barry, William Monfelt, A. D., Hugh, and J. A. Spencer, Edward Huddert, S. S. Ratcliff, Timothy Rawley, Dennis Sullivan, James Maliscky, John Wolken, Lon Turner, Harry Zook, John Anderson, Frederick Barnes, Jacob Gutbrot, and F. J. Woods

CLATONIA

Tucked away in the northwest corner of the county is the substantial village of Clatonia, located on a creek of that name, in Clatonia township. The original townsite comprises a forty-acre tract, in sections 22 and 27. Henry Albert and J. H. Steinmeyer, both highly esteemed pioneer residents of the county, were the proprietors of Clatonia, and having caused the townsite to be surveyed and platted in the spring of 1892, they filed the plat for record in the office of the register of deeds, December 3, 1893. Some additions have been made to Clatonia and the townsite now includes about eighty acres of land. It is a station on the main line of the Rock Island Railway from Chicago to Denver, via Omaha, Lincoln, and Jansen. It is about twenty miles northwest of Beatrice and about the same distance southwest of Lincoln. Prior to the construction of this line of railroad and the founding of Clatonia the farmers of this section were without immediate market facilities for the produce of their lands, and Clatonia township and other portions of the northwest corner of the county divided their trade with Cortland, Dewitt, Wilber, and Crete; but since the founding of the village, that scope of country has been given an excellent market.

Trains began operating on the railway line in May, 1903, and Clatonia quickly grew into a thriving country village. It was incorporated as a village about 1893, with one of its founders, J. H. Steinmeyer, as chairman of the village board, and J. I. Moore as clerk. At present the village board is composed of the following well known Clatonians: E. J. Chittenden, president; J. E. McCormick, clerk; and C. A. Miller, J. H. Meyer, and H. Suders.

The first family to establish a residence in the village was that of Frank W. Jones, and Mr. Jones was also Clatonia's first postmaster. The first merchant in Clatonia was a Mr. Jacquith. The first child born in the village was Gladys Berkheimer. The first church was the German Methodist Episcopal, an organization which as early as 1871 had erected a church building on the tract of land which afterward became Clatonia. In 1903 the English-speaking Methodists organized a church and erected a house of worship.

About 1893 John H. and William Steinmeyer organized the Farmers' Bank of Clatonia, and about 1900 erected a substantial, brick, bank building, which it now occupies. Henry Albert is now president of this bank J. H. Steinmeyer, vice-president; and E. J. Chittenden, cashier. Later the Steinmeyers built a substantial village inn, and in 1894 J. H. Steinmeyer built a large grain elevator, which is now owned by the Farmers Elevator Grain Company of Clatonia.

The school district of Clatonia was organized in 1894, at the house of Henry Albert. The district has a frame, two-story school house of three rooms, employs three teachers and has an enrollment of about sixty pupils. In addition to the usual eight grades it offers a two years' high-school course of study.

In addition to the various business and other interests here mentioned, Clatonia has two general stores, two hardware stores, a lumber yard, drug store, hotel, elevator, privately owned electric-lighting plant, two garages, a blacksmith shop, and such other business enterprises as are common in Nebraska villages of its population. The village also owns its waterworks system.

The postoffice, with Mr. G. M. Ludick as postmaster, gives rural free delivery to Clatonia patrons, a service performed by a single carrier.

Clatonia has a population of 180 by the federal census of 1910. It is substantially built, many of the business houses being of brick, and is the center of a large German-American neighborhood, some of whose members were pioneers in Gage county, notably Henry Albert, J. H. Steinmeyer, Henry Steinmeyer, and William Steinmeyer.

CORTLAND

The village of Cortland is situated in Highland township, within a mile of the north line of the county. It is a station on the Union Pacific Railway line from Valley, Nebraska, to Manhattan, Kansas. The original townsite comprises the east half of the northeast quarter of section 11 in this township. The land was bought from Alfred Gale by Joseph H.

Millard, of Omaha, in 1883, about the time of the construction of what was then known as the Omaha & Republican Valley Railroad, a branch then, as now, of the Union Pacific system. Millard caused the tract to be surveyed and platted and the plat was filed for record February 4, 1884. Mr. Millard, who was afterward United States senator from Wisconsin, was at that time a director in the Union Pacific Railway Company. The station buildings and the railroad yards at Cortland are situated on this tract of land. The depot was built in the spring of 1884. A strip of land in section 17 east of the railroad right-of-way, platted in 1884 by the owner Frank H. Oberman, and Malone's Addition, on the north also platted in 1884, have been added to the original townsite.

The first merchant in Cortland was Henry Spellman, who hauled lumber from Firth, in Lancaster county, and erected a building upon the townsite in the winter of 1883-1884, where he conducted a general merchandise store. In the spring of 1884 Wallingford & Masterman established a farm-implement store in Cortland, Downs & Hickman a general store, and Fred Wittstruck erected a building used by him as a boarding house or hotel. In the winter of 1883-1884, L. A. Simmons, now sheriff of Lancaster county, erected the first residence on the townsite. Some of the early merchants in Cortland were LaSalle & Fisk, J. C. Warner and Kurtz Brothers, who conducted general stores; I. M. Scott, a hardware merchant; and Baum & Scott, druggists.

In its early history Cortland acquired banking facilities, James Scanlon and J. H. Ballard having established the Bank of Cortland about 1885. They were succeeded by Jacob Bond. During the great panic of 1893 this bank failed; but later Thomas Burling reopened it, and after conducting it for some time he was succeeded by his son, F. A. Burling. Recently the bank has been sold to R. A. Nickell. About 1912 the Farmers State Bank of Cortland was organized, with C. P. Potts, president, and E. L. Pothast, cashier. Both of these banks are well patronized and doing a lucrative business.

A postoffice was established in Highland township about 1872, with J. P. Clough, postmaster. It was located on his farm, six miles southwest of Cortland and was known as Highland Center. On the founding of the village of Cortland this postoffice was discontinued. Among those who have served as postmaster at Cortland was A. B. McNickle, now a resident of Ashland, Kansas, who was for many years justice of the peace and postmaster in the village, and who was one of the first men to locate there. Mr. McNickle was one of the first settlers in Highland township, having located on a homestead in 1872. In 1889 he was one of Gage county's representatives in the state legislature and he was always recognized as a citizen of sterling worth. At the present time Mrs. Martha Gletty is postmistress. The rural districts at Cortland are supplied with free mail delivery, this service being performed by two carriers.

The churches at Cortland are the Congregational church, the Methodist Episcopal church, the Catholic church and the Seventh Day Adventist church. The Congregational and the Catholic churches were organized in 1885 and the Methodist Episcopal church was recently organized. All these churches have substantial church buildings.

The benevolent and fraternal orders at Cortland are the Ancient Free & Accepted Masons, Modern Woodmen of America, Royal Highlanders and Knights and Ladies of Security.

Since 1884 Cortland has supported a weekly newspaper. Its founders were Conant & Bloom; it has had numerous editors and proprietors. Until quite recently it was known as the Cortland *Sun*, but it is now called the Cortland *News*.

The first school in Cortland was an ordinary district school, with the school-house located on the Union Pacific right-of-way. Later this building was moved to a better location, and it served several years as the village school-house. Cortland now possesses a fine two-story, brick school-house, with basement, which was erected in 1916 at an approximate cost of $20,000. The district employs seven teachers and there is an enrollment of one hundred and twenty-five pupils. It offers a four years' course of study in the high school, which ranks with those of Beatrice and other large cities.

Cortland has two general stores, a grocery store, drug store, three garages, blacksmith shop, meat market, two restaurants, two elevators, a lumber yard and a small private electric-lighting plant.

Although without fire protection except a volunteer brigade, the village has never suffered any disastrous fire. The federal census of 1910 gives Cortland a population of three hundred and ninety. Its present population is somewhat larger, as the village is in a prosperous, growing condition.

Cortland was organized as a village under the laws of Nebraska many years ago and has been one of the most efficiently governed municipal corporations in the county. Its present village board consists of K. Slot, Thomas Sargent, C. H. Pfeiffer, F. H. Bear and J. A. Johnson.

FILLEY

The village of Filley is a station thirteen miles out from Beatrice on the Burlington line of railroad. It is situated in the midst of a fine section of the county and since its founding has been the center of a wealthy farming community. It is located on the northwest quarter of section 28, in Filley township. It was founded by Elijah Filley, the owner of this tract of ground, in the spring of 1882 at the time of the Tecumseh-Auburn branch of the Burlington Railroad was constructed. The plat of the village was filed for record by the incorporators, Elijah and Emma Filley, April 22, 1883.

The first mercantile establishment in Filley was the general merchandise store of Lewellen & Axtell. This was followed by a hardware store belonging to Charles G. Dorsey, of Beatrice, but managed by John W. Wright, who later acquired the stock by purchase from Dorsey. Both these pioneer merchants, Lewellen and Wright, remained in business in Filley for many years and both amassed sung fortunes. Lewellen is now a prominent citizen of Thedford, Thomas county, Nebraska, and Mr. Wright died a few years ago, deeply mourned by his entire community. Dr. I. N. Pickett, now of Odell, was the first physician to locate here, though Dr. L. D. Boggs, now of Oklahoma City, who had settled on a farm in that neighborhood in 1874, had practised his profession as a physician continuously from that date and for many years thereafter, in Filley and its vicinity. His son, Dr. Charles S. Boggs, is the present resident physician.

W. A. Waddington was the first postmaster, and later, while a resident of Filley, was elected sheriff of Gage county. At present James F. Boggs is the postmaster. Filley has free rural delivery of the mails, which gives employment to two carriers.

Filley possesses two general stores, a grocery store, a restaurant, two elevators, three garages, a drug store, lumber yard, and other business enterprises usually to be found in a village of its population in this section of the country.

The fraternal and benevolent orders of Filley are the Ancient Free & Accepted Masons, Independent Order of Odd Fellows, Modern Woodmen of America, Ancient Order of United Workmen and Royal Highlanders.

In 1885 the Methodist Episcopal church building was erected, and this denomination has maintained an organization at Filley ever since. Early in the history of the village the Baptist church also was organized and a church edifice erected. This building, about 1902, was destroyed by fire and was never rebuilt, and the organization disbanded. In 1888 the Christian denomination erected a church in Filley and has since maintained its organization.

Filley school district was organized May 2, 1868, the first meeting of the voters being held at the home of Elijah Filley. The first school-teacher in the district was Matthew who taught several very successful schools here. He afterward taught in the city schools of Beatrice and was for six years county superintendent of schools in Gage county. The present school building in Filley is a substantial three-room, frame structure.

The district employs three teachers and the school has an enrollment of sixty-five pupils. The course of study at present includes two years' high-school work. June 8, 1918, on proper notices, Filley school district No. 9, effected a consolidation with districts Nos. 43, 93 and 120. The consolidated district will hereafter be known as district No. 166. This consolidated district is about to vote on a proposition to issue its bonds in the sum of $50,000, to be used in the erection and equipment of a new school building. The school population of the district is approximately one hundred and seventy-five pupils. Under the new arrangement the district will give employment to seven or eight teachers and, with the usual grades, there will be a four years' high-school course.

In addition to its other interests, Filley boasts a substantial bank, the State Bank of Filley, of which Earl Norcross is cashier and the manager in charge.

To the present world war Filley has contributed eight of its young men, namely: Ray H. Noakes, now in the aviation service in France; C. W. Hazelton, William Thomas, C. J. Saum, Milo Laflin, Elmer Hansen, now at Camp Cody; Claude Saum, at the Great Lakes Naval Training Station; Delbert Edgerton, at Camp Logan.

Filley has had several disastrous fires, but, with great tenacity, has endeavored to overcome these calamities, and the village is now substantially built up with attractive brick business houses.

At the last census the village had a population of two hundred. It probably exceeds that number now. Filley was organized into a village under the laws of Nebraska many years ago and has maintained its organization until the present time. The village board at present consists of the following well known gentlemen: T. C. Hagerman, Hans Anderson, Christ Christianson, Charles Parker, and John V. Clark.

Among those who have contributed to the growth and prosperity of the village since its founding are Elijah and Emma Filley (now of Des Moines, Iowa), Charles S. and James F. Boggs, P. T. Lewellen, John W. Wright, Hans Anderson, Daniel F. Kees, W. A. Waddington, T. C. Hagerman, P. M. Anderson, A. C. Tilton, Christ Christiansen, H. M. Miller, Charles Parker, Dr. L. B. Boggs, John V. Clark, J. F. Burbank, Earl Norcross, Dr. I. N. Pickett, and Erastus W. Starlin.

LIBERTY

The village of Liberty is located on the main line of the Chicago, Burlington & Quincy Rail road between Chicago and Denver, by way of St. Joseph. The townsite comprises a part of the southeast quarter of section 35, a part of the southwest quarter of section 36, in Island Grove township, besides a part of the northwest quarter of section 1 and part of the northeast quarter of section 2 in Liberty township; it lies within a mile of the east line of Gage county. It is the trade center of quite a scope of rich farming land in both Gage and Pawnee counties. The original townsite was owned by Nathaniel Cain, Frank Muchmore, and Allen B. Jimmerson. It was deeded by them to the Lincoln Land Company and the plat of the town was filed in the office of the register of deeds in Gage county on the 19th day of June, 1881. The railroad was built through the county in 1881 and trains began running in the fall of that year.

In the early '70s Cornelius S. Wymore had been appointed postmaster for this community and the office was called Liberty. It was on his farm, half a mile west of the present town. In 1879 he opened a drug store in connection with the postoffice. At that time the mails were carried twice a week between Pawnee City and Blue Springs. When the village was laid out, its founders adopted the name of Mr. Wymore's postoffice as a suitable cognomen for the prospective town.

The little village built up rapidly. The first merchant was E. W. Lane, who, as early as 1882, had a general merchandise store. Mr. Lane's venture was soon followed by others, and in a short time Liberty was a town of several hundred people, in which every class of business was represented,—general stores, restaurants, drug store, hardware stores, lumber yard, elevators, barber shops, meat markets and the like.

The first bank was organized in 1882 by Frank Stewart and E. E. Harden. With varying fortunes, as Harden & Stewart's Bank, Bank of Liberty, First National Bank of Liberty, it has had a continuous existence since its founding. It is now known as the State Bank of Liberty and is affiliated with the First National Bank of Beatrice. It is still the leading banking institution in the village. In the year 1917 the Farmers State Bank of Liberty was organized, and this bank also is in a flourishing condition.

The orders now in existence at Liberty are the Ancient Free & Accepted Masons, the Independent Order of Odd Fellows, the Modern Woodmen of America, with their auxiliaries, and the Royal Highlanders.

For many years the Missionary Baptists have maintained an organization in Liberty township. This church was one of the pioneer churches of the county and known among Baptists throughout the state of Nebraska. After Liberty was founded, the organization built a church building in the village, and it is still a live and active member of the Baptist denomination in Gage county. The Christian denomination also have maintained an organization in Liberty and own a substantial, well built church. At one time there were a Methodist and two Presbyterian churches in Liberty, but a few years ago these were consolidated into a Congregational church. The history of this consolidation is interestingly set forth in a statement by the Rev. N. L. Packard, which, on account of its general interest in showing what may be done in such cases, is here given in full.

"One of the most interesting attempts at church union ever known in the state was that of Liberty, Gage county. Liberty, a village of four hundred people and a well settled country adjacent, had for years tried to support five Protestant American churches. There were five church buildings and sometimes five half-starved preachers. It seemed a poor use of home-missionary funds to keep these churches running.

"Three of these churches, Presbyterian, United Presbyterian and Methodist Episcopal, felt that a union must in some way be effected. But as the three were of about equal strength, the problem which seemed impossible to solve was which one should survive and which two must be swallowed up. The matter ran on for several years, when a happy suggestion was made by a layman in the United Presbyterian church. That was for all three churches to disband and organize a Congregational church, as there was no church of this name in the place and its polity made it generally acceptable to people of all evangelical faiths.

"It was finally agreed that when eighty per cent of the membership agreed to the plan the move should be made. When the paper was circulated, almost one hundred per cent of each church signed, as well as some who were not members of any of the three. Some hoped that all five churches might combine, but the Baptists and the Disciples decided to continue their organizations.

"A committee of nine, three from each of the consolidating churches, was chosen to manage affairs until the new organization could be effected. After the local people had decided to form a Congregational church, the committee asked State Superintendent S. I. Hanford to send them a minister who could shepherd the flock and help them to organize. Rev. N. L. Packard, of Lincoln, the state general missionary, was called to the important task. He found a very delightful people to work with, and by December, 1911, property interests were arranged and a church organization effected under the name of the First Congregational Church of Liberty, Nebraska.

"The old Presbyterian church building and parsonage were turned over to the new organization, on the simple condition of their meeting some small indebtedness. The United Presbyterian church building was bought at a small figure, and both were in use for a time. At length, however, the last named building was enlarged and a basement placed under it, and the other building sold. The parsonage continued in use for the new pastor.

"The three Sunday schools were running with an average attendance of about thirty, but the new school started out with a membership of nearly two hundred, and an average attendance for the following six years of more than one hundred and thirty. The church membership was not over forty each before the union, but the new church was organized with one hundred and sixty members and has increased in numbers each succeeding year. Rev. N. L. Packard became so interested in the field that he resigned his state work and accepted a unanimous call to become pastor. He filled out six very pleasant years, and the Rev. Calvin Holbrook is at the present writing leading the church in a very successful pastorate.

"No sectarian divisions have arisen during the years and a spirit of general harmony has been maintained. Letters have come from many states in the Union, asking 'How was it done?' Just such a consolidation of church interests is demanded in many towns.

N. L. PACKARD,
Wahoo, Nebraska."

Liberty was organized as a village in 1883, under the statutes of the state of Nebraska, and it has maintained its village organization up to the present time. The present village board consists of W. D. Huntington (chairman), L. E. Baldwin, (clerk), William Harmon, Jacob Jimmerson, James Bloom, and H. H. Kirschner.

One of the first school districts organized in the county was the Plum Creek district, now Liberty district. In a reorganization in 1868 for the purpose of numbering the districts of the county, this district was given number 27, a number that it still retains. The Liberty public school, into which the old Plum Creek district has grown, is one of the highly rated schools of the county. The district owns a fine, two-story, brick school building, employs six teachers and has an enrollment of approximately one hundred and fifty pupils.

Liberty has suffered several disastrous fires, but phoenix-like, has risen from its ashes, and to-day, with a population of over four hundred, is one of the interesting and pretty villages of our county.

The Liberty *Journal* was established by a member of the well known Olmstead family, in 1882, shortly after the founding of the village. It had had a continuous unbroken existence from that day to this and is now owned and edited by J. Franklin Spence.

Some of the early settlers of Liberty township and vicinity were:

Nathaniel P. Cain, deceased, a native of Tennessee, born in 1823, homesteaded in Liberty township in 1865. Stephen Evans, deceased, a native of Ohio, born in 1823, settled in Liberty township in 1866. Sylvester Fisher, a native of Ohio, born in 1833, came to Nebraska in 1859, locating in Pawnee county, just over the line from Liberty, moved to Liberty township in 1868. James Gay, a native of England, born in 1844, immigrated to America in 1869. He located in Beatrice in 1879, and in 1880 in Liberty, where he is "The Village Blacksmith." A. P. McMains, a native of Indiana, born in 1831, came to Nebraska in 1858 and to Liberty township in March, 1860. F. M. Muchmore, deceased, a native of Ohio, born in 1832, located on Turkey creek, in Johnson county, in 1866, and in Liberty township in 1868. Cornelius S. Wymore, a native of Indiana, born in 1841, located in Pawnee county in 1861, served in Company D, Second Kansas Cavalry from 1861 to 1865, and he was first postmaster of Liberty. Peter Bollinger, native of Claibourne county, Tennessee, born in 1840, came to Liberty township in 1867. He became known as a Baptist minister, farmer, school-teacher, was a man of sterling character, able and useful, and he now resides in Graham county, Kansas. Allen B. Jimmerson, native of Claibourne county, Tennessee, settled on the southeast quarter of section 35, township 2, range 8, Gage county, in 1874, a part of his old farm being included in village of Liberty. A man of fine character, generous, friendly, honest and able, he died in 1916, leaving many descendants. Jonathan Sharp, a native of Claibourne county, Tennessee, was born June 23, 1826. He came to Liberty township in 1864 and settled across Plum creek, just south of the village of Liberty. He died about twenty years ago, a man of fine character, honest, able, active in county and local affairs, and much esteemed by all who ever knew him, for kindness of heart and generous hospitality.

Most of the men here mentioned were from the state of Tennessee. Nearly all have passed away, leaving behind them nothing but the most kindly remembrances. They would have graced any community in the world as honest, worthy, independent citizens. Such as these have given the village of Liberty high standing in Gage county.

ODELL

This neat and compact Gage county village is an important station on the main line of the Burlington Railroad system between Chicago and Denver, via St. Joseph, Missouri, and is a junction point where originates the branch line to Concordia, Kansas, via Lanham, Nebraska, and Hanover, Washington and other Kansas towns. It was the first village founded on the old Otoe and Missouri Indian reservation. Prior to the founding of Odell, William B. LaGorgue had surveyed and platted a townsite on his farm, on the south side of Big Indian creek, a mile or so from Odell, and christened it Charleston. A start had been made toward establishing a town there when, in 1880, the railroad was surveyed north of the creek and the village of Odell was founded. All who had cast in their lot with Charleston moved to Odell and were instrumental in giving that prospective village its first start on what has proved a prosperous and happy existence.

The village is located a little north of Big Indian creek, one of the prettiest and most important streams of southern Gage county. It is a living stream, and in the early days was well timbered; along its course near Odell a good quarry of limestone was found from which several of the buildings of the village were constructed. The village is planted in the midst of a thriving and wealthy farming community. Nowhere in the county are there better farm buildings, better tilled, better kept farms, better orchards, roads or school buildings than in the vicinage of Odell.

Odell is partly in Glenwood and partly in Paddock township, and is located on land originally bought by Perry Walker, in 1879, from the United States government, as agent and guardian of the Indians. He, in 1880, sold it to J. D. Myers, of Chicago, and by the latter an undivided half-interest in the tract comprising the original townsite was sold to Charles E. Perkins, representing the Lincoln Land Company, an organization composed chiefly of the officials and employes of the Burlington Railroad system. Mr. Perkins himself was at that time, or afterward, president of the Burlington Railroad Company. The original townsite covered part of the west half of the southwest quarter of section 18, township 1 north, of range 6 east, and part of the east half of the southeast quarter of section 13, township 1 north, range 5 east. It was surveyed and platted by Anselmo B. Smith, September 21, 1880. The plat was filed in the office of the register of deeds of Gage county November 11, 1884, with the Lincoln Land Company (by Charles E. Perkins, its president,) and James D. and Elizabeth A. Myers, as incorporators. It was named after LeGrand Odell, of Chicago, a friend of Myers who had induced hint to come west from Chicago and locate at Odell, and who on account of his relations with the Burlington officials or some of them, was instrumental in giving his friend a start in this venture.

The first merchant of Odell was Mike Triskey, who moved his store from Charleston to the new village on the railway line. Things moved very rapidly then. The entire county and state were new and filling with new people. Immigrants flocked to the new towns along the railroad lines, and villages were born over night. Odell soon had a supply of stores, shops and business houses of every kind, and by 1882 it was a prosperous, thriving village.

In its early history James D. Myers built what was called "The Store on the Hill," for a long time the most sightly and imposing structure in the village. Here he kept a general merchandise store and did a small banking business. But he was not a very good business man and soon others easily eclipsed him. He died some years ago, a poor man, having let slip the opportunity to make a snug fortune. His chief competitors were F. R. Joy and his sons Edward and Howard. Edward Joy, for many years the leading merchant of Odell, amassed a fortune and retired and is now living at Havelock. The father and Howard did a flourishing banking business at Odell.

Several years ago the Hinds State Bank was organized as successor to the Joy Bank. It is owned by Edward B. and Charles H. Hinds and occupies the building formerly occupied by the Joys. This bank has had a successful career and does an annual business amounting in volume to many thousands of dollars. For some time its deposits have run to nearly a quarter of a million dollars. The banking business of the village and surrounding country is shared by the Odell State Bank, with deposit accounts aggregating a quarter of a million dollars. Its owners and officers are: Thomas W, Stanosheck, president; Ernest Loeniker, vice-president; W. T. Stanosheck, cashier.

The first church organized in Odell was the Methodist Episcopal, and the organization held its meetings in a carpenter shop the first year. In 1886 J. D. Myers donated a lot upon which a small frame church building was erected, at an original cost of fifteen hundred dollars. Rev. Mr. Orr was the first pastor. The present minister in charge is Rev. H. S. Burd. The Catholics also have a flourishing organization in Odell. The first frame building erected by the church cost six hundred dollars. The present church was erected many years ago, at a cost of four thousand dollars, and the property includes a rectory or parsonage, built a dozen years ago. At first there were but eight or ten Catholic families; now there are forty-five. Several priests of great ability and learning have ministered to the parish; among them the first priest, Father Mosler, who served the parish for ten years, and the present pastor, Father W. J. McKenna. The Christian church also is one of the well established religious organizations of Odell. Its church edifice was erected in 1888 and the organization has been active in the community ever since. It frequently is without a regular pastor and is then supplied by students from Cotner University, at Lincoln.

The fraternal organizations are the Grand Army of the Republic, Ancient Free & Accepted Masons, Independent Order of Odd Fellows, Knights & Ladies of Security, and some others. The Grand Army of the Republic, once a flourishing and numerous body of Civil war veterans, has by lapse of time become reduced to five living members,—Henry Rice, E. B. Hinds, A. F. Drake, Michael Keckley, and Hubert Glasgow. While these heroes of a day long past do not meet regularly any more, they loyally maintain their organization.

The village of Odell has two lumber corporations, two elevators, two hotels, three general-merchandise stores, a drug store, harness shop, two implement houses, a furniture store and undertaking establishment, three garages, one pump shop with accessories, local telephone exchange and many other business concerns. By the last census the population of the village was four hundred and twenty-seven.

The Odell *Weekly Wave* newspaper was founded in the village in 1893, by G. W. Bede, and has had a continuous and a successful existence ever since. It is now owned and ably edited by J. P. Martin. It receives the loyal support of the community and is in a flourishing condition as a country newspaper.

The school district of the village was organized January 12, 1878, at the house of W. B. LaGorgue. The first school building was a small frame structure, to the erection of which LeGrand Odell contributed $100, the people, by subscription, $100, and the school district in bonds, $400. The present school building is a frame, two-story, seven-room structure. The district employs seven teachers and maintains a high school with a four years' course, with normal training.

Some of the men who have been prominent in the affairs of Odell are Perry Walker, William B. LaGorgue, E. B. Hinds, T. W. Stanosheck,

James D. Myers, Dr. George L. Roe, Amos Quein, F. R. Joy and his sons Edward and Howard Joy, Thomas R. Callan (the veteran merchant of Odell, whose son, now serving in the army of the United States, is postmaster of Odell), John Millhalland, Frank Styles, Eli Worthington, John Wilson, Lund Nelson, Dr. Henry Allen, Henry Rice, Hubert Glasgow, Charles N. Hinds, William M. Munns, Henry Kasparek, James F. Raney, George Williamson, Frank Truax, M. E. Shalla, H. R., Rufus, and Sidney Tincher, and Dr. I. N. Pickett.

PICKRELL

[This history of Pickrell was written by Evelyn Brinton, a high school pupil of that village.—H. J. D.]

Mr. Watson and William Pickrell owned the land where Pickrell is located. There, was some talk of having the town two miles north, but the sidetrack for the railroad was here. In the year 1884 the Pickrell brothers began to lay off the lots; some of the first lots sold for fifteen dollars and others for twenty-five dollars. Pickrell was built on the hillside, because the railroad ran on the level. The first settler was Mr. Bashaw. His home was built outside of Pickrell and afterwards moved in; the house is still standing, and Mr. William Hansel now occupies it. The first house built in Pickrell belonged to Ed. White. Mr. McKim built some of the first houses for the settlers to move into. Mrs. Edwards owned the first good building.

Pickrell was organized as a village August 14, 1913, with G. L. Mumford as chairman of the board of trustees, Dr. Amesbury Lee, treasurer, J. R. Wilson, clerk; the other members of the town board were B. E. Ridgley and J. J. Wardlaw.

The first postoffice was in the grain-elevator office. It was started in 1884. Mr. Joseph Chandler was appointed postmaster February 1, 1884. Mr. David Royer, the second postmaster, was appointed July 1, 1884. The first postoffice building burned in 1890. The first mail carrier was Roy Armstrong.

The first church was the Congregational, built in 1885, and the first minister was Mr. Bates. In 1888 the United Brethren church was built and Mr. Surface was the minister. In 1910 both the Congregational and United Brethren churches were torn down and the present United Brethren church was built.

A list of old settlers is as follows: David Royer, who now resides at McPherson, Kansas; Mr. Houdgs, deceased, place of burial southeast of Pickerell; Mr. Bergett, deceased, place of burial, Hutchinson, Kansas; Roxie Irvin, deceased; J. D. White, who resides at Gage, Oklahoma; D. Nicewonger, G. Balderson and F. J. Emal, who reside in Pickrell; S. King, John Young, Mr. Bashaw, Mr. McKin, Mr. Lockwood, Thomas Noonan, Thomas Langely, B. Bathrick, Dr. D. W. Tucker, Mr. Wilber, Mr. Chandler, Henry Latimer, and Mr. Waters.

Pickrell was started with one family; later more settlers came. There was a store, an elevator, postoffice, drug store and a few other business houses. Now we have two general stores, two elevators, three garages, a bank, an implement shop, a drug store, a hardware store, cream station, hotel, blacksmith shop, barber shop and lumber yard. The population is now between one hundred and seventy-five and two hundred. A list of the leading business houses when the town was first started is as follows: A general store, managers Mr. Royer and Mr. Bergett; a blacksmith shop, William Hunter, manager; a lumber yard, Mr. McKim and Mr. Newcomb, managers; a livery barn, Mr. D. Tucker, proprietor; a hardware store, Mr. Newcomb, proprietor. The depot agent was Roxie Irvin. The first section boss was Thomas Noonan. Mr. Davis and Mr. Chandler bought hogs.

A list of leading business houses and managers today is as follows: Bergstraesser store; managers, Bergstraesser Brothers. Rife's store; manager, Henry Dirk. Implement store; proprietor, F. C. Pape. Drug store; druggist, R. Dunkle. Lumber yard; manager, C. P. Horn. Blacksmith shop; proprietor, F. J. Emal. Cream station; manager, B. Mumford.

The first school house was built in 1885, where the present school building stands. The school district is No. 144. Some of the first teachers were Miss Proctor, Mr. Lamberti, Miss Kennedy, and Miss Hadley.

In 1912 school districts Nos. 65 and 144 were consolidated and a new brick school building built. It is now a ten-grade school. In December,

1917, the pupils of the high school surveyed the land in Pickrell that could be utilized for gardens; they found about eight acres, which is going to be used. Later the school became a hundred-per-cent school as a Red Cross society. The food-pledge cards were distributed to the parents by the school children; they were signed by the parents and returned, to be sent to the food administrator. In January, 1918, the pupils of the primary and grammar rooms went to the homes of all the people in the town and tagged their shovels. The school was very successful in the sale of thrift and war-savings stamps. There are sixty-seven on the roll. During the month of January, 1918, the school bought $1,300 worth of war-savings stamps and was awarded a banner by the county superintendent of Gage county, T. J. Trauernicht.

A list of the early preachers is: Mr. Bates, Mr. Long, Mr. Rock, and Mr. Surface. The first doctor and druggist was Mr. B. Bathrick.

The first bank was organized in 1904. F. R. Pothast is cashier and Mr. Reil, bookkeeper. The first bank building was on the north side of Main street and is still standing; in 1911 a brick bank building was erected across the street.

The postoffice is in the hardware store; William Vanderhook is postmaster. Bud is the mail carrier for route No. 2 and Earl Emal is substitute for route No. 1.

The Union Pacific Railroad was started through Pickrell in 1883 and finished in 1884.

The first grain elevator was the Omaha, in the southeast part of Pickrell, built in 1884; Mr. Cotner, manager. The next elevator was the Nebraska, with Mr. J. D. White as manager. Before the elevators were built Mr. White bought the grain and shipped it. Then the farmers bought the elevator, and Mr. White, Mr. Wardlaw, Mr. Williams and Mr. J. R. Wilson were managers. It was organized in 1905. In 1913 a new elevator was built by the farmers, and Mr. J. R. Wilson has been manager from then to the present time. There are 175 members of the Farmers Elevator Company and the capital stock is $25,000. The capacity of the elevator is 25,000 bushels.

Mr. D. Nicewonger has lived in Pickrell the longest; he came from Oregon, Illinois, when he was seven years old. Some of the leading citizens are: J. R. Wilson, C. P. Horn. F. L. Pothast, Rev. Beasley, William Vanderhook, R. W. Dunkle, D. Nicewonger, G. Balderson, Bergstraesser Brothers and F. C. Pape. We have four boys in the world war. They are David Emal, Robert Mumford, Ben Weiser, and Marion Sigler.

Pickrell has had three fires. In 1890 five buildings on the north side of Main street burned. In 1893 two livery barns burned; they were never rebuilt. The last fire was in 1910, when some of the buildings on the south side of Main street burned. There have been two floods that came to the railroad tracks but did not do any damage.

The officers of Pickrell now are: J. R. chairman; C. P. Horn, clerk; F. L. Pothast, treasurer; and the other members of the village board are Mr. Reil, B. E. Ridgley, and D. Nicewonger.

VIRGINIA

This attractive Gage county village comprises the northwest quarter of the northwest quarter of section 11, township 2 north, range 6 east. It is a station of both the Chicago, Rock Island Pacific line of railway, from Chicago to Denver and a branch of the Missouri Pacific Railway from Kansas City, Missouri, which terminates at Virginia. It has several good stores, lumber yard, implement house, garage, blacksmith shop, grain elevators and other business accessories to a thriving village. The townsite was surveyed and platted by Ford Lewis, the owner of the land, about the time of the completion of the Chicago, Rock Island Pacific Railway through that section of country. The plat was filed for record in the office of the register of deeds May 23, 1887.

The first general store was that of M. V. Drew, and this was followed almost immediately by the store of Warren Barber, who was Virginia's first postmaster. The first blacksmith was A. L. Boyer, and the first children born in Virginia were his twin daughters, Gertie and Mertie. Mr. Boyer is still the village blacksmith.

The first church organized in Virginia was the Methodist Episcopal church and its pastor, Rev. J. F. Holgate, preached the first sermon. The Christian church was erected in 1902, on a lot donated by Mr. and Mrs. Dwight Dalbey.

In the early history of Virginia, Captain Logan Enyart, of Nebraska City, opened a state bank in the village. It soon passed into the hands of George H. Gale, and later became the property of O. O. Thomas. Still later, A. W. Nickell, of Beatrice, purchased a majority of the stock and he operated this bank until his death. The present Citizens' State Bank of Virginia is an outgrowth of this early banking venture. Amos L. Wright, a pioneer of Gage county, is the principal stockholder and president of the bank and his son, Frederick A. Wright is the present cashier.

Several years ago Mr. Dalbey built a modern hotel for the village, which has added greatly to its attractiveness. There is no more "homey" public house in Gage county than this little hotel. Visitors are drawn to it from far and near and it is liberally patronized by the traveling public.

Virginia started with a single-room school house in 1887, but in 1902 the school district erected a frame, two-story school building. There are about ninety pupils in the district and three teachers are employed. On the 3d day of June, 1918, Virginia school district, No. 110, was consolidated, under the school laws of Nebraska, with districts Nos. 149, 151 and 157, into a county high-school district. The consolidated school district is preparing to erect a modern high-school building which is to cost not to exceed $50,000. The grounds for this building, not to exceed fifteen acres, will be donated by Mr. and Mrs. Dalbey. The consolidated school district will have a school population of approximately one hundred and sixty, will have a full four years' high school course, and employ from seven to ten teachers.

Virginia was incorporated as a village, under the laws of the state, about 1905, and has ever since maintained a corporate existence. As at present constituted, the village board consists of A. M. Darwin, president; W. S. McGaffey, clerk; F. A. Wright, treasurer; and N. C. Mittan and John Henzel.

Virginia is beautifully located on the high, rolling prairie of Sherman township, in the midst of a wealthy farming community, which it serves as a business and social center. By the census of 1910 it contained a population of 154. Its steady growth since then has increased this to probably two hundred inhabitants.

CHAPTER XXVI

Unincorporated Villages

Ellis — Hoag — Kinney — Lanham — Rockford — Holmesville

The unincorporated villages of Gage county are Ellis, Hoag, Kinney, Lanhan, Rockford and Holmesville.

ELLIS

Ellis is located in the midst of a prosperous farming community in Lincoln township, ten miles west by south from Beatrice. It is a station on the Chicago-Denver line of the Chicago, Rock Island & Pacific Railroad. It has a bank, the Ellis State Bank, lumber yard, two elevators, two general stores and a farm-implement store.

The Methodist Episcopal church is the only religious denomination represented in Ellis. The village forms a good rural-school district of the county, with a substantial frame building as school house. The district employs one teacher and enrolls about fifty pupils. At the last census Ellis was shown to have a population of 122. It is a good social and business center for the surrounding territory.

HOAG

Hoag is a mere hamlet on the Beatrice-Lincoln line of the Burlington Railroad, the first station out of Beatrice, with a population not to exceed 25. It has a postoffice, general store and two elevators. This is a rural school district, having a frame, one-room school house, about three quarters of a mile southeast of the village. The school employs one teacher and has an enrollment of about forty-five pupils.

KINNEY

Kinney is also a hamlet, located on the Burlington main line, first station east of Wymore, named for Samuel A. Kinney, an old resident of Island Grove township, on whose farm the village is located. It has a general store, post office and lumber yard.

LANHAM

Lanham is a village of eighty inhabitants, located twenty-five miles southwest of Beatrice, on the state line, partly in Glenwood township and partly in Kansas. It is a station on the Concordia line of the Burlington Railroad. The principal business houses are the State Bank of Lanham, general store, hardware store, drug store, restaurant, meat market, lumber and coal yard, barber shop and blacksmith shop. Its school district was organized in 1892, at the home of George Arnold. It possesses a single-room, frame school-house, employs one teacher and has an enrollment of thirty-five pupils.

ROCKFORD

Rockford is located in section 1 of Rockford township and is the first station east of Beatrice on both the Burlington and the Rock Island Railroads. It is in one of the oldest-settled portions of the county and has fifty-six inhabitants. It was founded by William Girl more than a quarter of a century ago and has slowly grown to a position of great usefulness as a social and business center of Rockford, Lincoln, Hanover, and parts of Sherman and Filley townships. Though not boastful it is a good little village and there are those yet living who love it because of early associations and the memories its name invokes.

Rockford has a general store, postoffice, two elevators, blacksmith shop and a very pretty church building, the property of the Methodist Episcopal denomination. Rockford school district No. 49 was organized at the home of Morgan Reed, upon notice to John Dunn, May 27, 1872. A few years ago it was consolidated with the F. H. Dobbs school district on the south and the T. B. Essex school district on the north, and it retains its original number, 49. A few years ago the consolidated district erected a fine three-room school house, at a cost of about $5,000. It employs three teachers and has an enrollment of about ninety pupils. In addition to the grades, it offers a two years' high-school course of study.

The early settlers in the immediate neighborhood of Rockford were F. H. Dobbs, Henry D. Lillie, George W. Stark, Solon M. Hazen, Abraham Fetro, Thomas B. Essex, John H. Dunn, John Potterton, Edward Woolridge, Jesse Willis, Humphrey P. Freeman, Peter Girl, William Girl, Calvin Miller, David Miller, Stephen Hayden, Rufus Hayden, John E. Murphy, James B. McLaughlin, Thomas M. Martin, Asa Anderson, D. J. Woods, Henry, Robert and Jacob Fry, (triplets), Morgan Reed, Daniel Fuller, James West, Charles Slocumb, Michael Weaver, John O. Adams, A. B. Smith, George Wilkinson, Andrew Kerr, Alexander Welch, Josiah Graves, Mrs. Serena Webber, Miles Andrews, Duncan Smith, Archibald Smith, Marvin Freeman, and Marion Reese.

No locality in Gage county possesses greater rural charm than that where Rockford is situated. Cedar creek and both branches of Mud creek flow through the township into the Big Blue river. They are all well timbered streams of living water. From every height of land the observer is rewarded by a most beautiful landscape of hill, dale, valley, forest, and in the growing season of the year by vistas of living green; and in the autumn by stretches of gold and brown. No other place in the county exerts as lasting an influence over the heart as the environment of the humble village of Rockford.

HOLMESVILLE

Holmesville is not only the largest but is easily the most important of the unincorporated villages of Gage county. It has a population of 175, according to the federal census of 1910. It is located in Rockford township, on the east bank of the Big Blue river. It is nine miles southeast of Beatrice and is the first station on the Union Pacific Railroad. It was marked by the early settlers as the location for a townsite and Whitesville, the first legal county seat of Gage county, was within half a mile of the townsite of Holmesville, on a tract of land afterward taken as a homestead by James Kingsford, namely: the southwest quarter of section 29, Rockford township. In a very early day, A. L. Hurd and W. S. Guffey opened a stone quarry at or near the site of Holmesville, and most of the stone used in building the first state capitol at Lincoln was hauled across country, by ox, mule and horse teams, from this quarry, in 1868.

The village was founded by Morgan L. Holmes, in 1880, the surveyed plat being filed for record in the office of the register of deeds on March 8th of that year. The founding of the village immediately followed the construction of the present line of the Union Pacific Railroad from Marysville, Kansas, to Beatrice. The first store in Holmesville was a general store opened by Thomas Patz. James Gleason, a brother-in-law of the founder of the village, James H. Davis, Abraham Petro, Eli Miller and James H. Fuller also were among its earliest business men and residents. Fuller ran a general merchandise store for many years, and up to the time of his death, a few years ago, was a well known and substantial citizen of Holmesville.

Amongst the business concerns now found in Holmesville are two general stores, hardware store and lumber yard, elevator, hotel, restaurant and meat market. But what distinguishes Holmesville from all the other villages in the county is the investment made there by J. H. Steinmeyer and his sons George W. and Robert Steinmeyer. About 1908 these public-spirited citizens of the county established the State Bank of Holmesville, with a capital of $10,000. Under the very able management of the owners this banking institution has grown to the point where it does a large volume of business in the course of a year and has deposits of over $100,000.

In addition to this bank Mr. Steinmeyer and his sons have invested heavily in a hydro-electric power and lighting plant. The building where the machinery is located is just below the dam and is of concrete and steel construction; it was begun in 1908 and completed in 1911. It generates an electric current of one million watts per hour, and from it Wymore, Blue Springs, Beatrice, and Holmesville are supplied with electricity for all purposes.

The Holmesville school district was organized August 30, 1868, at a meeting held for that purpose at the home of Amos Hayden, two miles southeast of Holmesville, on Mud creek. The first school house was a low, round-log cabin, erected by F. H. Dobbs in the fall of 1858 on his preemption claim in Rockford township. After the formation of the district, this cabin was bought, taken down and moved to the southeast quarter of section 32 and rebuilt on the northeast corner of that tract, where it was used for several years as a school house for the district. The first teacher was S. S. Switzer. After the founding of Holmesville, a frame, single-room school house was erected in the village, which by successive additions has been expanded into the present public school building. The district employs three teachers, has enrollment of about sixty pupils and offers a two years' high school course of study. Recently it was consolidated with districts numbered 19, 37, 58, 76, 133 and part of 139. The consolidated school district is about to erect a school building which, with equipment, will cost approximately $50,000. The district will probably then employ seven teachers, will have a school population of approximately 160 pupils, and will install a high school with a four years' course of study.

The Methodist Episcopal church maintains an organization at Holmesville and owns a substantial and very neat house of worship.

For many years Holmesville has been a social and religious center for the Church of the a religious denomination commonly spoken of by outsiders as Dunkards, but amongst themselves always simply called The Brethren or Church of the Brethren. This denomination had its origin in Westphalia, Germany in 1708. It was founded by Alexander Mack, as a protest against what he conceived to be the erroneous practices and beliefs of the followers of Martin Luther. Mack taught the strict observances of the forms as respects baptism, the sacrament of the Lord's Supper and other ordinances of the church. Both he and his followers were the subjects of intense persecution, and were finally driven out of Germany and compelled to take refuge in the New World. They settled first in Pennsylvania, then spread over Ohio, Indiana, Maryland, Virginia and other states, and Canada as well. The communicants of this church now number more 100,000. In doctrine the Brethren are closely affiliated with the Mennonites as opposed to war and litigation; in dress and manners they closely resemble the Quakers or Society of Friends. In Holmesville they have a small church, but a couple of miles northeast of the village the denomination owns a large church edifice, where most of its religious activities are carried on. There is really but one congregation for the two churches and they both have the same pastor, at present the Rev. Edgar Rothrock.

The Church of the Brethren in Rockford township was founded by the Rev. Henry Brubaker, under the following circumstances. John P. Crothers, of Indiana, in 1867, had entered with college scrip a large tract of land in Rockford township, much of which lay on the upland between the valleys of Mud and Cedar creeks. Knowing something of the sturdy virtues of the Church of the Brethren, he advertised largely that he would donate a quarter-section of land in Rockford township to any minister of the Brethren church who would locate upon it and organize a church of that denomination. Mr. Brubaker accepted this offer, and in 1875 Mr. Crothers conveyed to him, by warranty deed, the northwest quarter of section 21 of Rockford township. Shortly thereafter he organized the Brethren church at Rockford, with twelve members. The organization gained in membership rapidly, many of the new-comers purchasing land of Crothers, and about 1880 the large church of the Brethren was erected on the southeast corner of the southwest quarter of section 15, Rockford township. This is one of the historic churches of Gage county. It has performed a great and important service in the settlement and development of the county. Its membership is of a high order of citizens and it exemplifies in an almost perfect degree the gentle doctrines of its founder. It has grown steadily in power, wealth, influence and usefulness, until it is to-day the most lasting monument that could be erected to the venerable Henry Brubaker, who is now spending the declining years of his life in Holmesville, under its shadow.

CHAPTER XXVII

COUNTY OFFICES AND OFFICIALS

FIRST ELECTION LAW — ELECTIONS — TWO EARLY ELECTIONS — OFFICIAL ROSTER COUNTY COMMISSIONERS — ADOPTION OF TOWNSHIP ORGANIZATION — COUNTY CLERKS — COUNTY TREASURERS — CLERKS OF DISTRICT COURT — COUNTY SHERIFFS — COUNTY JUDGES — COUNTY SUPERINTENDENTS OF SCHOOLS — COUNTY SURVEYORS — COUNTY CORONERS — REGISTERS OF DEEDS — COUNTY ATTORNEYS — COUNTY ASSESSORS — TERRITORIAL ASSEMBLIES — HOUSE OF REPRESENTATIVES — MEMBERS OF THE COUNCIL — STATE LEGISLATURES — MEMBERS OF THE SENATE

At the second session of the legislative assembly of the territory of Nebraska, begun and held at Omaha December 16, 1855, a general election law was passed and approved January 26, 1856, which, amongst other things, provided that "an election for members of the house of representatives shall take place on the first Monday in August, 1856, and on the same day of each year thereafter." It was further provided that an election for a delegate to congress and for territorial and county officials should be held on the first Monday in August in 1857, and on the same day in every second year thereafter.

The official history of Gage county began on the 7th day of August, 1857, with the form of an election by the members of the Beatrice Townsite Company, for the purpose of effecting county organization by the election of a full corps of county officials. This election was wholly irregular, though held probably on the proper date fixed by statute. It required a special act of the legislative assembly of 1859 to validate this election and give effect to the official acts of the officers so chosen. In 1858 a special election was called by the county board for the purpose of filling vacancies in certain county offices where those who had been chosen the previous year had failed to qualify. For the purpose of elections, the county board divided Gage county into two election precincts. Precinct No. 1 included the south half of the county; precinct No. 2 the north half, as then organized. The dividing line between the precincts was the line between townships 2 and 3. The entire county participated in the special election, and in 1859, at the regular election, a full set of county officials was chosen by the voters of the county.

For a period of sixty years Gage county has gone through a procession of elections, uneventful as a rule, but effective in results. If that nation is happy whose annals are without interest, then the citizens of Gage county have enjoyed great felicity during these three score years, if their annual and biennial elections are to be regarded as barometers of domestic felicity.

Perhaps an incident of the election of 1859 and one of the election of 1860 may be of sufficient interest to justify their preservation in this history. Of both elections and the incidents here narrated the writer can speak with the authority of an eye-witness.

The election of 1859 occurred on a mellow day in August and was well attended by the voters of precinct No. 2. It was held in the open street, at the corner of Second and Court Streets, where the ground about the middle of Court fell away to the north in a wide depression, to include about one-third of block 46, now owned by the Burlington Railroad Company. On the southeast corner of this block, lot 12, was the plain, board shanty of Orrin Stevens, well back from Court street, near the alley, and south of the house, at the edge of the depression, stood his straw-covered shed or stable. The entire population of the county did not exceed three hundred white persons, the majority of whom were residents of precinct No. 2. The voters about the polls that day and the spectators combined probably numbered fifty persons. The voting began some time in the afternoon. Probably about three o'clock anxious inquiries began to be made as to the whereabouts of "Orr Stevens." Presently there arose from the edge of the prairie at Fifth and Court streets a fierce Comanche-like yell, and coming toward the polls the spectator saw a new, party covered wagon, drawn by a span of fine mules, plunging under whip down street toward the voting place, every crack of the whip being punctuated by yells from the driver, who stood erect in the front end of his wagon. Then the cry was raised "There comes Orr Stevens," and the crowd gathered about the voting place. The team was brought to a sudden stop in their midst, the driver, a spare, light-complexioned man, slightly above medium height, with reddish-brown hair and beard, blue eyes, high, narrow forehead, descended to the ground, and with many good-natured oaths in reply to the banter of the crowd, proceeded to take out the rear endgate of his wagon, and with the help of other willing hands, brought forth a barrel of perfectly good whiskey.

It was election whiskey furnished by the candidates and representatives of the Beatrice Townsite Company, to be used in celebrating the first general election held in Gage county. The head of the barrel was knocked in and all who would helped themselves without invitation to its contents.

The election of 1860 was of great dramatic interest throughout the entire United States. That was the election that sounded the doom of human slavery in our country. The polling place in Beatrice was at "Pap's Cabin." The population of the county had materially increased since the last election, the census of that year showing 421 white inhabitants. The voters, to the number of probably one hundred, gathered early in the forenoon about the voting place. Nebraska Territory was strongly Republican, and at this polling place but two parties were represented, "Douglas Democrats" and Republicans. The seriousness of the situation seemed to be impressed upon all those present, regardless of party. There was some delay in opening the polls, and inquiry was made as to the cause. The information was then given out that those in authority were waiting the arrival of Frederick Elwood and Johnathan Potts, who were to act as clerks of election. Presently two fresh-faced young men arrived and took their places at a table prepared and in readiness for the judges and clerks of election. They were Elwood and Potts, both residents of the Cub creek neighborhood and squatters on the public domain. Less than a year afterward they were the first to volunteer from Gage county in the service of their country in the great Civil war. They went to Nebraska City and both enlisted in Company H, First Regiment of Nebraska Volunteers, the regiment of General John M. Thayer, John McConihe, Thomas J. Majors, Silas D. Strickland, and other Nebraska heroes of that great struggle for human liberty.

The reader may find from the following official roster of Gage county officials some information which may be of interest.

COUNTY COMMISSIONERS

1857—Albert Towle, George D. Bonham.
1858—Albert Towle, H. M. Reynolds.
1859—Albert Towle, H. M. Reynolds.
1860—H. M. Reynolds (resigned, succeeded by J. M. Summers), J. T. Alexander, J B. Mattingly.
1861—J. B. Mattingly, J. C. Waldrip, J. T. Sargent.
1862—Fidillo H. Dobbs, Fordyce Roper, William Tyler.
1863—William Tyler, Fordyce Roper, Fidillo H. Dobbs.
1864—William Tyler, Fordyce Roper and Fidillo H. Dobbs.
1865—Fidillo H. Dobbs, William Tyler, H. T. Pierce.
1866—William Tyler, George Grant, H. P. Freeman.
1867—H. P. Freeman, William Tichnor, Horace M. Wickham.
1868—H. P. Freeman, William Tichnor, Horace M. Wickham.
1869—Horace M. Wickham, J. M. Pettegrew, William Tichnor.
1870—Horace M. Wickham, J. M. Pettegrew, Solon M. Hazen.
1871—Horace M. Wickham, Solon M. Hazen, Elijah Filley.
1872—W. S. Guffy, Elijah Filley, H. M. Wickham.
1873—W. S. Guffy, Elijah Filley, H. M. Wickham.
1874—Elijah Filley, H. M. Wickham, W. S. Guffy.
1875—Solon M. Hazen, Elijah Filley, H. M. Wickham.
1876—Solon M. Hazen, Elijah Filley, H. M. Wickham.
1877—Solon M. Hazen, Elijah Filley, Henry Albert.
1878—William Lamb, Henry Albert, George W. Talbot.
1879—Henry Albert, George W. Talbot, William Lamb.
1880—J. Blackman, Henry Albert, William Lamb.
1881—J. I. Gumaer, William Lamb, Henry Albert.

1882—T. B. Essex, J. I. Gumaer, Henry Albert.
1883—T. B. Essex, J. I. Gumaer, T. J. Chesney.
1884—T. B. Essex, T. J. Chesney, E. W. Lane.
1885—E. W. Lane, T. J. Chesney, J. W. Williams.
1886—Township Supervisors.

In 1885 the county adopted the township-supervisor system of county government. At first each township was represented on the county board by a supervisor, the city of Beatrice by four supervisors. This large representation, which was both cumbersome and expensive, was changed by the legislature in 1911, providing that counties under township organization should be divided into seven supervisor districts, with a supervisor for each district. Under this law township organization in Gage county has been very effective, and the county boards have uniformly been composed of men of ability and character. The limitations of this work render it impractical to set forth the names of the supervisors from the beginning of township organization in this county. At present the 1st district, composed of Adams, Filley, Hooker, Logan, Hanover and Nemaha townships, is represented on the board of supervisors by B. H. Siefkes. District No. 2, composed of Blakely, Grant, Clatonia, Highland, Holt and Midland townships, is represented by Warren E. Chittenden. District No. 3, comprising Riverside township and wards one and three of the city of Beatrice, is represented by W. P. Carrithers. District No. 4, comprising wards two and four of Beatrice, is represented by John O. Essam; District No. 5, comprising Rockford, Blue Springs, Sherman, Island Grove and Liberty townships, by J. W. Marples, resigned, John W. McFarren appointed to fill vacancy; District No. 6, composed of Wymore and Barneston townships, by Anton Scheideler; District No. 7, composed of Sicily, Paddock, Lincoln. Elm and Glenwood townships, by J. R. Sailing.

COUNTY CLERKS

1857, L. H. Johnson (failed to qualify; Nathan Blakely by appointment); 1858-1860, Nathan Blakely; 1861, C. C. Coffinberry;

1862-1869, Oliver Townsend; 1870-1871, Daniel E. Marsh; 1871-1876, William D. Cox; 1876-1882, J. E. Hill; 1882-1886, A. J. Pethoud, 1886-1890, George E. Emery; 1890-1894, Albert G. Keim; 1894-1898, Thomas E. Wilson; 1898-1902, Joseph D. White; 1902-1906, James R. Plasters; 1906-1910, Benjamin H. Conlee; 1910-1917, Jesse C. Penrod (died close of term and his deputy E. M. Burnham appointed for the unexpired term); 1917-1919, E. M. Burnham, (resigned, and Mrs. Mabel C. Penrod appointed to fill unexpired term).

COUNTY TREASURERS

1857, Isma P. Mumford; 1858-1860, Albert Towle; 1860-1862, Theodore M. Coulter; 1863, Herman M. Reynolds; 1864-1870, Albert Towle; 1870-1876, Hiram P. Webb; 1878-1882, John Ellis; 1882-1886, James F. King; 1886-1890, Evan J. Roderick; 1890-1892, Harry W. Davis; 1892-1896, Isaac J. Frantz; 1896-1898, Jacob Klein; 1898-1902, George W. Maurer; 1902-1906 William W. Wright; 1906-1910, Julian A. Barnard; 1910-1915, Elmer E. Hevelone; 1915-1919, Andrew Andersen.

CLERKS OF THE DISTRICT COURT

Prior to the passage of an act of the state legislature under date of June 22, it seems to have been the custom for judges of the district court to appoint clerks of the court in all organized counties of the territory. The act named not only authorized but also directed the judges to make such appointments. By an act of the legislature approved February 9, 1867, amending the act of June 22, 1867, the county clerks of the several counties of the state were declared to be ex officio clerks of the district court of their respective counties. This act continued in force till 1879, when an act was passed directing that in each county of the state "having a population of eight thousand inhabitants or more there shall be elected in the year 1879, and every four years thereafter, a clerk of the district court in and for such county."

The first clerk of the district court for Gage county of which we have any record was Rienzi Streeter, of Nebraska City. He was represented at the first term of the district court of which there is any known record, beginning November 26, 1863, by Oliver Townsend as deputy. At the second term of the court, held in September, 1865, he was represented by Herman M. Reynolds as deputy, and at the fall term (third), which convened October 7, 1867, he was again represented by Herman M. Reynolds. It was probably to remedy this situation that the act of June 22, 1867, was passed.

Those who held the office by appointment from the bench were H. M. Reynolds, 1867; H. P. Webb, 1868; Oliver M. Enlow, 1874; O. H. Phillips, 1876; and J. E. Hill, 1878. Those who have held the office by election under the act of 1879 are:

A. V. S. Saunders, served from 1880 to 1888, inclusive. Frank H. Holt, 1888 to November, 1891. He died on the night of the election, having been reelected for an ensuing four years' term. His wife was appointed to fill out his unexpired term, and R. W. Laflin was then appointed to hold office till the general election of 1892, when he was elected for the full term of four years. He was succeeded by John A. Weaver, who was elected at the general election of 1895, for the full term of four years. On the expiration of his term he was succeeded by Charles L. Brewster, January 1, 1900, and the latter was succeeded, in 1904, by John R. Quein, who held the office, by a reelection in 1907, till January 1, 1908, and was succeeded by Frank E. Lenhart, the present incumbent.

SHERIFFS

1857, Daniel P. Taylor, failed to qualify; 1858-1860, Philetus M. Favor; 1860-1862, Eli B. Hendy; 1862-1866, Joseph Clyne; 1866-1868, Thomas W. Brown; 1868-1870, Luther P. Chandler; 1870-1872, Daniel Freeman; 1872-1876, Leander Y. Coffin; 1876-1878, A. P. Hazard; 1878-1880, Eugene Mack; 1880-1886, Nathaniel Herron; 1886-1890, E. F. Davis; 1890-1892, William R. Jones; 1892-1896, Robert Kyd; 1896-1900, Lind Nelson; 1900-1904, William A.

Waddington; 1904-1910, Alonzo J. Trude; 1910-1915, John L. Schiek; 1915-1919, Frank W. Acton.

COUNTY JUDGES

1857, Obediah B. Hewett; 1858, Nathan Blakely; 1859-1860, William Blakely; 1861-1868, Albert Towle; 1868-1870, Herman M. Reynolds; 1870-1872, C. A. Pease; 1872-1876, J. W. Carter; Carter resigned in 1875 and Alfred Hazlett was appointed to serve remainder of term; 1876-1878, Alfred Hazlett; Hazlett resigned in 1877 and William M. Forbes was appointed to complete the term; 1878-1880, Peter Shaffer; 1880-1882, Joseph E. Cobbey; 1882-1886, Ernest O. Kretsinger; 1886-1890, Oliner N. Enlow; 1890-1896, Wilbur S. Bourne; 1896-1900, M. B. Davis; 1900-1906, Frederick E. Bourne; 1906-1910, Harry E. Spafford; 1910-1917, Herbert D. Walden, 1917-1919, J. A. O'Keefe.

COUNTY SUPERINTENDENTS OF SCHOOLS

1857, N. B. Belden; 1858-1861, Henry Elliott; 1861-1866, B. F. McNeil; 1866-1867, Nathan Blakely; 1867-1869, H. M. Reynolds; 1869-1870, B. F. McNeil; 1870-1874, Lucius B. Filley; 1874-1878, Joseph R. Little; 1878-1884, Matthew Weaverling; 1884-1888, M. D. Horhum; 1888-1892, Marie P. Upson, 1892-1894, A. A. Reed; 1894-1898, W. J. Todd; 1898-1904, A. R. Staller; 1904-1910, Anna V. Day; 1910-1915, Jessie V. Pyrtle; 1915-1919, T. J. Trauernicht.

COUNTY SURVEYORS

1857-1860, G. H. Tobey; 1861-1863, A. J. Pethoud; 1864-1868, Isaac Newton Headley; 1868-1870, A. J. Pethoud; 1870-1872, Alfred Gale; 1872-1876, A. J. Pethoud; 1876-1882, Willis Ball; 1882-1884, G. W. Minkler; 1884-1890, Willis Ball; 1890-1894, R. D. Kennedy; 1894-

1896, Joseph Pasco; 1896-1906, Willis Ball; 1906-1915, A. J. Pethoud; 1915-1919, John L. Hershey.

COUNTY CORONERS

H. M. Wickham was the first coroner, elected in 1861, served to 1862, one year; 1863-1866, J. B. Mattingly; 1866, J. L. Brown; 1867-1871. Daniel Freeman; 1871-1878, Job Buchanan; 1878-1880, Joseph C. Fletcher; 1880-1882, D. A. Walden; 1882-1884, Osceola O. Wells; 1884-1886, M. P. Walsh; 1886-1890, Frank M. Somers; 1890-1892, Osceola O. Wells; 1892-1894, Robert H. Albright; 1894-1896, Joseph C. Fletcher; 1896-1898, Louis Miller; 1898-1902, John Q. Reed; 1902-1906, Clifford W. Walden; 1906-1915, John Q. Reed; 1916-1919, the county attorney, ex officio.

REGISTER OF DEEDS

The legislature of 1887 created the office of register of deeds in counties having a stipulated number of inhabitants. Prior to that time the duties of this official had been performed by the county clerks of the several counties in the state. At the election in November, 1887, J. E. Hays was elected to this office, and he served till January 1st, 1894; 1894-1898, John T. Greenwood; 1898-1906, Charles L. Reed; 1906-1910, Charles B. Hensley; 1910-1919, John A. Weaver.

COUNTY ASSESSORS

This important, not very desirable, and poorly paid office of county assessor has been the subject of a good deal of legislation. On the 26th day of January, 1856, the territorial assembly passed a general statute respecting assessors and assessments. By that act the office of *county* assessor was created. By the act of February 22, 1873, provision was made for the election of *precinct* assessors. This was followed by an act of the legislature in 1879, becoming effective September 1st of that year, which provided for the election of *township* assessors. The general revenue law of 1903 provided for the election of *county* assessors, who should hold office for four years and be ineligible for reelection while in office. The legislature of 1913 provided that at the general election of 1916 and each four years thereafter there should be elected in each county in the state a *county* assessor, whose term of office should be four years and who should be ineligible for two successive terms. The act then provided that upon presentation of a petition to the county board not less than sixty days before a general election, signed by a prescribed percentage of the electors of the county, and praying that the question of electing the county assessor of said county be submitted to the electors therein, the county board should order that question to be submitted at the general election, and that if a majority of the votes cast should be opposed to the election of county assessors in that county, the office should cease with the expiration of the term of the then incumbent, and the duties of the office be thereafter performed by the county clerk. The last statute is the one now in force.

The condition of the Gage county records as respects this office is such as to render it extremely difficult to make up an accurate list of those who have held the office of county assessor under the act of 1856. In 1867 William Blakely was elected to that office, for a term of two years. He was succeeded by George Gale, in 1869, and at the general election of 1871 Charles H. Slocum was elected county assessor. He served until January 1, 1874, when, by the change in the law, as above noted, precinct assessors came into existence. Under the act of 1903 Walter W. Scott was the first assessor and held the one term. He was succeeded by R. C. Hemphill, in 1908. At the general election of 1911 A. K. Smith was elected county assessor, but he died before taking office, and Oliver M. Enlow was appointed to and held the office of assessor until the act of 1913 came into effect and the duties of the office devolved upon the county clerk.

DISTRICT AND COUNTY ATTORNEY

The legislature of 1885 created the office of county attorney in all counties of the state having 2,000 population. Prior to the passage of this act the duties of a prosecuting attorney had been performed by district attorneys elected for each judicial district of the state. District attorneys for the district in which Gage county is located were uniformly lawyers of ability and high character. One of the early district attorneys was the late Jefferson H. Broady, who, in the '70s, although a Democrat of the old school, was elected to the office in a strong Republican district, which at the time comprised the counties of Richardson, Nemaha, Otoe, Johnson, Pawnee, Gage, Jefferson, Saline, Fillmore, Nuckolls, Clay, Adams, Kearney, Harlan, Thayer, Franklin, and Webster. In 1883 he was elected judge of the First judicial district, then composed of Richardson, Pawnee, Nemaha, Johnson, and Gage counties, and he was reelected to the office in 1887, making eight years' service on the district judicial bench. He was a splendid citizen, an able lawyer, and a wise and conscientious judge.

Judge Broady was succeeded in the district attorney's office by John P. Maul, of Fairmont, Fillmore county, who, after a four years' term, ending about 1879, was succeeded by Judge William H. Morris, of Crete. In 1881 Robert W. Sabin, of Beatrice, was elected to this responsible office, and at the close of the two years' term he was succeeded by Daniel F. Osgood, of Tecumseh, in 1883. Before the election of 1885 occurred, the office of district attorney was abolished by the legislature and that of county attorney created.

Robert S. Bibb was the first county attorney of Gage county, being elected to that office in November, 1886. In 1888 Hugh J. Dobbs was elected, and in 1890, Charles O. Bates. Mr. Bates afterward resigned his office and left the state, whereupon his partner, Alfred Hazlett, was appointed to serve the remainder of his term. In 1892 Robert W. Sabin was elected county attorney, and after two years' service he was succeeded by George Arthur Murphy, who was reelected in 1894. He was succeeded by Samuel Rinaker, who, by reelection in 1898, held the office four years. He was succeeded, in 1900, by H. E. Sackett, who was reelected in 1902, and who was succeeded, in 1904, by Samuel D. Killen, who was himself succeeded by Menzo Terry, in 1906. Frederick O. McGirr was elected in 1908, and in the presidential election of 1912 his successor, Jean Cobbey, was elected. He served two years and was defeated for reelection in 1914, by Frederick Messmore, who was reelected in 1916 and is the present incumbent of the office.

TERRITORIAL ASSEMBLY—HOUSE OF REPRESENTATIVES

DATE	NAME	RESIDENCE	COUNTIES REPRESENTED
1859	Dr. Charles A. Goshen	Tecumseh	Gage, Clay, Johnson
1860	Hiram W. Parker	Austin	Gage, Clay, Johnson
1861	Nathan Blakely	Beatrice	Gage, Clay, Johnson
1862	Nathan Blakely	Beatrice	Gage, Clay, Johnson
1863	John Cadman	Lancaster	Gage, Clay, Johnson
1864	John Cadman	Lancaster	Gage, Clay, Johnson
1865	Herman M. Reynolds	Beatrice	Gage, Jones
1866	Hugh M. Ross	Unknown	Gage, Jones
1867	Nathan Blakely	Beatrice	Gage, Jones

TERRITORIAL ASSEMBLY—MEMBERS OF THE COUNCIL

1865	Dr. Jeremiah N. McCasland	Pawnee City	Pawnee, Gage, Clay, Johnson, Jones
1866	Dr. Jeremiah N. McCasland	Pawnee City	Pawnee, Gage, Clay, Johnson, Jones
1867	Dr. Alexander S. Stewart	Pawnee City	Pawnee, Gage, Clay, Johnson, Jones

STATE LEGISLATURE—HOUSE OF REPRESENTATIVES

1867	Oliver Townsend	Beatrice	Gage, Jones
1869	Nathan Blakely	Beatrice	Gage, Jones

Year	Name	Town	County
1871	Fordyce Roper	Beatrice	Pawnee, Gage, Saline, Jefferson and Lancaster
1873	J. B. McDowell	Beatrice	Gage
1875	J. B. McDowell	Beatrice	Gage
1877	William Anyan	Beatrice	Gage
1879	L. B. Boggs	Beatrice	Gage
	John Sparks	Beatrice	Gage
	William Curtis	Adams	Gage
1881	H. H. Silver	Silver	Gage
	Elijah Filley	Beatrice	Gage
1883	G. R. Turner	Blue Springs	Gage
	W. W. Morrison	Beatrice	Gage
	G. H. Castle	Blue Springs	Gage
1885	F. H. Holt	Beatrice	Gage
	S. M. Hazen	Blue Springs	Gage
	J. R. Buffungton	Liberty	Gage
1887	J.M. Wardlow	Pickrell	Gage
	CC. Gafford	Wymore	Gage
	J.N. Fuller	Hanover	Gage
1889	F. E. Whyman	Adams	Gage
	F. C. Severin	Cortland	Gage
	A. B. McNickle	Cortland	Gage
	W. C. Hill	Blue Springs	Gage
1891	J. W. Williams	Filley	Gage
	J. W. Faxon	Lanham	Gage
	Edward Arnold	Odell	Gage
	Henry Albert	Wilber	Gage
1893	J. M. Wardlaw	Pickrell	Gage
	H. J. Merrick	Adams	Gage
	P. H. James	Cortland	Gage
	E. B. Hinds	Odell	Gage
	F. W. Miles	DeWitt	Gage
1895	E. B. Hinds	Odell	Gage
	H. J. Merrick	Adams	Gage
	J. C. Birch	Wymore	Gage
1897	G. U. Jones	Wymore	Gage
	G. R. Fouke	Liberty	Gage
	W. E. Chittenden	Cortland	Gage
	J. H. Casebeer	Blue Springs	Gage and Saline

1899	W. E. Chittenden	Clatonia	
	T. E. Hibbert	Adams	
	G. U. Jones	Wymore	
1901	A. D. Spencer	Barneston	Gage and Saline
	T. E. Hibbert	Adams	Gage
	Henry Steinmeyer	Clatonia	Gage
	R. W. Laflin	Wymore	Gage
1903	W. E. Robbins	Cortland	Gage
	J. H. Ramsay	Filley	Gage
	S. S. Spier	Odell	Gage
	Herschel W. Smith	Tobias	Gage and Saline
1905	Robert K. Kyd	Beatrice	Gage and Saline
	James H. Casebeer	Blue Springs	Gage
	Adam McMullen	Wymore	Gage
	W. E. Robbins	Cortland	Gage
1907	Adam McMullen	Wymore	Gage
	C. W. McCullough	Blue Springs	Gage
	D. J. Killen	Adams	Gage
	C. H. Culdice	DeWitt	Gage and Saline
1909	B. H. Begole	Beatrice	Gage
	D. J. Killen	Adams	Gage
	Charles J. McColl	Beatrice	Gage
	Frank O. Ellis	Beatrice	Gage and Saline
1911	J. R. Clayton	Wymore	Gage
	H. Clyde Filley	Beatrice	Gage
	J. W. McKissick	Beatrice	Gage
	Anton Sagl	Wilber	Gage and Saline
1913	Charles F. Allen	Beatrice	Gage
	F. W. Schaupp	Virginia	Gage
1915	D. S. Dalby	Beatrice	Gage
	G. W. Burrows	Adams	Gage

STATE LEGISLATURE—SENATE

1867	Oscar Holden		Pawnee, Gage, Johnson, Clay, and Jones

Year	Name	City	Counties
1869	C. H. Gere		Pawnee, Gage, Jefferson, Saline, Lancaster
1871	A. J. Cropsey		Pawnee, Gage, Jefferson, Saline, Lancaster
1873	N. K. Griggs	Beatrice	
1875	N. K. Griggs	Beatrice	
1877	L. W. Colby	Beatrice	
1879	J. A. McMeans	Fairbury	Jefferson and Gage
1881	E. B. Harrington	Beatrice	
1883	Elijah Filley	Beatrice	
1885	W. H. Snell	Fairbury	
1887	L. W. Colby	Beatrice	
1889	J. W. Funck	Beatrice	
1891	G. F. Collins	Firth	
1893	Alex. Graham	Beatrice	
1895	Alex. Graham	Beatrice	
1897	G. A. Murphy	Beatrice	
1899	F. N. Prout	Beatrice	
1901	W. H. Edgar	Beatrice	
1903	L. M. Pemberton	Beatrice	
1905	H. W. L. Jackson	Beatrice	
1907	H. E. Sackett	Beatrice	
1909	Jacob Klein	Beatrice	
1911	Peter Jansen	Beatrice	
1913	Jacob Klein	Beatrice	Gage and Pawnee
1915	A. D. Spencer	Barneston	Gage and Pawnee
1917	Adam McMullen	Wymore	Gage and Pawnee

CHAPTER XXVIII

Hospitals

Institute for Feeble Minded Youths — Herrerlin's Hospital — New Lutheran Hospital — Fall's Sanitarium — The Mennonite Deaconess Home and Hospital.

A community is often distinguished by its beneficent institutions, both public and private. If the aphorism "Man's inhumanity to man makes countless thousands mourn," as the old school readers had it, then it must be equally true that man's humanity to man causes countless thousands to rejoice. Nothing is more indicative of the altruistic principle in human affairs than asylums and hospitals for the afflicted, the helpless, the hopeless. Though the commercial spirit may largely prevail in a community, there will always be found those to whom the cup of cold water given in kindness, the gentle word, the alleviation of pain and suffering, the care of the unfortunate, are more than gold, than much fine gold.

Beatrice is widely known on account of its being the site of the Institution for Feeble Minded Youths, as well as on account of its two private hospitals and a private sanitarium located within the city.

The state institution was created by act of the legislature of 1885, which became a law March 5th of that year. The second section of the act reads as follows:

Besides shelter and protection, the prime object of said institution shall be to provide special means of improvement for that unfortunate portion of the community who were born, or by disease have become, imbecile or feeble-minded, and by a wise and well adapted course of instruction reclaim them from their helpless condition, and, through the development of their intellectual faculties, fit them as far as possible for usefulness in society. To this end there shall be furnished them such agricultural and mechanical education as they may be capable of receiving.

The fourth section of the act provided for the location of the institution "at or near Beatrice and within two miles of the corporate limits of said city; Provided, that said city of Beatrice or the citizens thereof shall donate and convey to the state not less than forty (40) acres of land, near or through which runs a stream of living water sufficient to afford water supply for said institution, said site to be approved by the board of public lands and buildings."

Pursuant to this proviso, the money to purchase a site and thereby secure the location of the institution at Beatrice was readily subscribed by the citizens, amounting to the sum of $4,000, and the east ten acres of the northeast quarter of the northeast quarter of section 35 and the west thirty acres of the northwest quarter of the northwest quarter of section 36, in Midland township, were purchased and, by warranty deed, conveyed to the state as a site for this institution.

The ninth section of the act appropriated the sum of $50,000 for the purpose of constructing and furnishing a building for the use of the inmates, as provided by the act, and the tenth and last section reads as follows:

In order to create a fund for the support of said institution, there is hereby authorized and shall be made an annual tax levy on the taxable property of the state, not to exceed one-eighth ($\frac{1}{8}$) of one mill on the dollar; said fund shall be known as "The Fund of the Institution for the Feeble Minded."

Shortly after the passage of the act and the purchase and conveyance of the above-described tract of land to the state, work was begun on the first structure erected on these grounds. It is now used and known as the administration building.

The act establishing the institution authorized the state board of public lands and buildings to appoint a superintendent for it, to whom was to be committed its control, and also provided for the appointment of a matron, teachers, and other employes. Dr. J. T. Armstrong was the first superintendent of the institution and his wife the first matron. It was to him more than to any other man that credit is due for the founding of this great charity, one of the very few of like character in the United States. He remained superintendent until his death. The Beatrice Institute for Feeble Minded Youths stands as a lasting monument to the enthusiasm and benevolence of spirit of Dr. J. T. Armstrong, and to Frank M. Holt, who at that time represented Gage county in the legislature, and whose powerful and manly advocacy of his bill establishing the institution won him the respect and gratitude of the entire state. He died in November, 1891, on the day of his reelection to the office of clerk of the district court. Both he and Dr. Armstrong are buried in Evergreen Home cemetery. His grave is marked by a stone, the Doctor's by a monument.

The first child was admitted to the institution May 24, 1887. It is a matter of history that Orion Rossman, a boy who is still an inmate of the institution, was the third one admitted, he having entered on the 25th day of May, 1887.

A number of prominent physicians have served the state as superintendent of the institution since the death of Dr. Armstrong. They are Dr. Clifford P. Fall, of Beatrice, Drs. Sprague, Deering, Johnson, Osbourne, G. L. Roe (also of Beatrice), Thomas, and Fast. Dr. D. G. Griffiths is the present superintendent, and under his able administration, the high record of efficiency in this important trust has been fully maintained.

The state has been most liberal in providing the necessary buildings and conveniences for these youthful but hopeless wards. In addition to the buildings here shown there are an up-to-date dairy, barn, laundry, store-room, bakery, engine house, pumping station for the water supply and a large stand pipe for water service to all the buildings as well as the grounds. By successive purchases the state now owns a fine body of fertile land, comprising three hundred acres, adjoining its original forty-acre tract, and the institution is in a large measure self-supporting. There is at this time a population of six hundred children at the institution, a population which is constantly increasing. Few are ever discharged except by death, and it is a matter of record that patients of this class are as a rule short-lived.

Stone Cottage

Boys' First Cottage

Girls' First Cottage

Boys' Second Cottage

GIRLS' SECOND COTTAGE

HOSPITAL BUILDING

The state of Nebraska is entitled to the greatest possible credit for what it has done to alleviate the condition of these unfortunate children and to relieve their relatives from the great burden of their care.

In 1879 Dr. Harry M. Hepperlen established, at No. 1700 South Ninth street, a private hospital, which immediately secured a large patronage from the city and surrounding country. After several years of prosperous existence under its founder's personal care, it was purchased, in 1909, by the United Brethren church, which continued its beneficent mission until 1913, when it was sold to the Lutheran church. This organization has carefully nourished the plant, attracting a widely distributed patronage. The old building in which the hospital was first started, after some additions and changes had been made by Dr. Hepperlen, could accommodate twenty-five patients. But latterly these accommodations have been found insufficient, and the present owners are now erecting a modern hospital, to cost $150,000, and to be equipped with the latest and most modern appliances of every description for hospital work. It is the intention to spare no pains or expense to make it one of the most complete institutions of its kind in existence. It will be a fire-proof building and when opened to public patronage will contain one hundred beds. The new structure is located a little north of the old building and the latter will continue to be used, as a nurse's home.

In 1901 Dr. Clifford P. Fall established a private sanitarium in connection with his practice. It is located at No. 723 North Eleventh street. This institution has had a very successful and a very useful career. It contains twenty-five beds, has the service of eight nurses, and it is open to the use of other physicians and surgeons. Dr. Fall came to Beatrice a young man, in 1888; he is now a veteran in his profession and has achieved an enviable reputation both as a physician and a surgeon.

The Mennonite Deaconess Home and Hospital is located at Eleventh and Arthur streets. Its inception can be traced to a jubilee celebration held by the Beatrice Mennonites several years ago, for the purpose of praising the Lord for His merciful guidance during the twenty-five years of their settlement in this country of religious liberty. On this occasion the congregation was seized with a desire to make a special thanks-offering to God for all their blessings. It was at first proposed to establish a home for the aged, but it was finally determined to found a hospital, to be known as the Mennonite Deaconess Home and Hospital. By the congregation was chosen a board of directors consisting of twelve brethren, who went immediately to work, their first object being to raise the funds necessary to purchase a site and erect a suitable building. When $20,516.25 had been subscribed for the building, Hon. Peter Jansen and wife donated to the church for hospital purposes block 2 of Fairview Addition to Beatrice. The plans for the building were drawn by Richard W. Grant, architect, and the work of erecting the structure was begun during the year 1910. It was completed in 1911, and, with appropriate ceremonies, was dedicated to its work of mercy on July 16th of that year.

NEW LUTHERAN HOSPITAL

The hospital is arranged to accommodate thirty patients, and these are cared for by the sisters in a faithful and conscientious manner. It employs from eight to ten nurses, and every effort is made to alleviate suffering, mitigate despair, and awaken hope in the breasts of the despondent and afflicted. With generous unselfishness and absolute impartiality, the management invites all practising physicians and surgeons to avail themselves of its facilities.

CHAPTER XXIX

MILITARY HISTORY OF GAGE COUNTY

INDIAN RAID ON LITTLE BLUE RIVER, 1864 — FIRST MILITARY ORGANIZATION — A STAMPEDE — COMPANY C, NEBRASKA MILITIA — SIOUX INDIAN WAR, 1891 — GAGE COUNTY IN THE CIVIL WAR — THE SPANISH-AMERICAN WAR — ROSTER OF COMPANY C, FIRST REGIMENT — THE WAR.

The early annals of Gage county as respects military affairs have but little interest. The pioneers usually provided themselves with arms against the depredations of Indians and lawless persons, but within the boundaries of our county there is no well authenticated case of Indian troubles worthy of mention. The Otoe and Missouri tribes of Indians were at peace with the whites and were their allies against the encroachments of warlike tribes. Nevertheless, for a number of years the white population maintained an attitude of constant vigilance against surprises and attacks by marauding bands of savages, but until 1864 nothing like a military organization of any kind existed in the county.

That year, on Sunday, the 7th day of August, occurred what is known in Nebraska history as the Indian raid on the Little Blue river, in which several Gage county people lost their lives and property and in which the lives of many others were put in jeopardy. The Indians were Cheyennes, led by Black Kettle, One-Eyed George Bent, a half-breed, Two Face, and other chiefs. It had evidently been planned to attack the ranches and stage stations along the Oregon Trail simultaneously at a number of points, to kill the whites, destroy their property, and clear the Little Blue country as far as the Big Sandy. Patrick Burke, the first blacksmith of Beatrice, on his way up the old trail with a load of corn, about three o'clock in the afternoon, in plain sight of and within half a mile of Pawnee Ranch, was shot and killed. About the same hour an attack was made by a band of Cheyennes on Little Blue Station, or Comstock's Ranch, at Oak Grove, and J. H. Butler and M. C. Kelley, both Gage county men, were shot with arrows, and killed. A few miles further down the river the Eubank family was murdered, nine persons in all, and Mrs. Eubank, the wife of Eubank, her child and Miss Laura Roper, a Gage county girl, were carried away into captivity. In May, 1865, while quartered at Laramie, General Tom Moonlight, afterward governor of Wyoming, when about to start on an expedition against the Indians learned that two white women were with Two Face's band, near the south base of the Black Hills. Communication was opened with these Indians, and for a large number of ponies, blankets, a quantity of sugar and other things of value to the Indians, the white women were purchased from them and brought into Laramie, under an armistice, accompanied by Two Face and two of his best warriors. The women were Mrs. Eubank and Laura Roper. When the condition of Mrs. Eubank became known to General Moonlight, the armistice was violated—Two Face and his warriors were arrested and were hanged in chains, on a bluff two miles north of Fort Laramie, where their bodies remained until the crows had picked their bones. Thirty persons lost their lives at the ranches and stage stations along the Little Blue river in this raid, and the first semblance of a military organization in Gage county was a company of its citizens hastily called together by the sheriff, Joseph Clyne, for the purpose of investigating the depredations of these savages, ascertaining the true condition of affairs, burying the dead killed in the massacre, and repelling the invasion.

As far as known the members of this company from Gage county were William H. Stoner, John Gilbert, Oliver Townsend, Albert C. Howe (half-brother of Church Howe), H. M. Wickham, William R. Jones, Daniel Freeman, Thomas Pethoud, James Pethoud, Enoch Graves, Henry Graves, Louis Graves, Ira Dixon Leander Wilson, Samuel Jones, Richard C. Davis, William Alexander, Joseph Clyne, Edward Wells and his brother, from Cub creek, Mr. Bagley, also from Cub creek, and Theodore M. Coulter, a defaulting county treasurer and a prisoner in the custody of Sheriff Clyne. Stoner was elected captain of the company, and John Gilbert, who still lives, an honored citizen of Red Cloud, was chosen lieutenant. At Big Sandy this company of men was joined by a number of others, among them a man named Constable, who, in the battle which ensued, was killed, with another, whose name is not known. These men were well armed and well mounted, and, after passing Big Sandy, numbered thirty-four. On their way out they buried the dead, including Bill Kennedy, who had been killed in his cabin by the Indians, five of the Eubanks family, Kelley and Butler. They found all the principal ranches and stage stations between the Hackney Ranch and Pawnee Ranch burned, except Little Blue Station, where they found an abandoned wagon train of a hundred laden wagons, bound westward, and they found desolation and destruction everywhere. A detail of United States troops had been dispatched from Fort Kearney, under the command of Captain E. B. Murphy, to go over the Little Blue country on the same mission of the company from Beatrice, and the two companies met at Pawnee Ranch on the 14th day of August. The next day, under command of Captain Murphy, they started south in pursuit of the hostile Cheyennes, and came upon the Indians where the Fort Riley road crossed Elk creek, in northeastern Nuckolls county, ten miles south of Little Blue Station, in considerable numbers and in a warlike attitude. In the engagement which immediately ensued about three hundred warriors participated, while a still larger number appeared to be held in reserve. The entire band was moving toward the Republican river. Captain Murphy had a single field-piece, but it was disabled in firing the first round. He then deemed it best, in view of the number of Indians, to retreat and fall back to Little Blue Station, having lost two of his command. Having only limited rations, he abandoned further pursuit of the Indians and the Beatrice company returned home.

The excitement in Gage county over this Indian raid was intense. At Beatrice a sod breastwork was thrown up on the east bank of the Big Blue river, to defend the Market street ford, and, as far as possible, the men went armed and took other precautions to defend the city. The late summer and fall of 1864 was a period of great suspense and nervous strain. This is well illustrated by a stampede which occurred in the eastern portion of the county toward the end of August. One day, a little after noon, a couple of men in a lumber wagon, passed up Mud creek and reported that the Indians had attacked and were burning Blue Springs. They claimed also that they had been attacked, and, as proof, showed bullet holes in their wagon-box. About that time a confederate near Blue Springs set fire to a patch of prairie grass, and these strangers pointed to the smoke as a confirmation of their story. That was enough; the alarm spread like wildfire, and before sundown not a white person was left in Rockford, Filley, and Sherman townships. The settlers turned their hogs, cattle, and chickens loose to roam at will, loaded their women and children into wagons, and fled as best they could. That night most of them stopped on Yankee creek, about a mile west of Crab Orchard; others went on to Brownville and Nebraska City. After a day or two a company of ten men ventured back to their homes and found that the settlers had been the victims of a practical joke.

The Little Blue country, however, continued to be dangerous ground, and a call was issued by Governor Saunders for four companies of territorial militia to be used in guarding traffic, travel and the Overland Stage line along the old trail from Big Sandy to Denver. One of these was Company C of the Second Brigade, First Regiment Nebraska Militia (cavalry), raised in Pawnee and Gage counties—Alvin G. of Pawnee City, captain; William B. Raper, of Pawnee City, first lieutenant; Dr. Levi Anthony, of Blue Springs, second lieutenant. The Gage county members of the company were:

Levi Anthony (second lieutenant), John Barrett, William Alexander, James Grant, Isaac Claiborne, William Aikens, Nelson Adams, Alvah Ayers, William T. Brown, Charles Bailey, Charles Buss, Edward Cartwright, Heury Corlett, William J. Dobbs, John H. Dunn, Josiah Eastman, David K. Fisher, John J. Fisher, Francis M. Graham, Henry Graves, Henry L. McMuford, Abraham P. McManis, Joel T. Mattingley, Joseph Milligan, Francis M. Reese, D. M. Shellanberger, Horace M. Wickham, James A. Wymore.

The company was mustered into the service of the state at Pawnee City, September 1, 1864, and was stationed at Buffalo Ranch, at the western end of Nine Mile Ridge, on Little Blue river throughout the ensuing fall and winter, to guard the stage lines, ranches, stations and travel from Big Sandy to Fort Kearney. It performed this duty efficiently, was paid by the state, but rationed by the federal government, and disbanded, without being discharged, about February 7, 1865.

Our county took an honorable and efficient part in what is known as the Sioux Indian war, in 1890-1891. In that year there arose on the northwestern border of our state a religious disturbance amongst the Sioux Indians in South Dakota. A young, half-educated, Piute Indian, with a smattering knowledge of the Christian religion, appeared in Utah as the long expected Indian Messiah, who was to drive the whites from the ancient Indian hunting grounds, rejuvenate the aged and infirm, resurrect the dead, bring back to the hunting grounds the deer, buffalo and other wild game of the early days, and restore to the Indians the great northwest. This mischief-making imposter claimed to have received direct from the Great Spirit the revelation of the "Ghost Dance" as a means of spreading the knowledge of his mission abroad. This sacred rite was introduced among the powerful Sioux tribes of South Dakota at a moment when, on account of general drought, they were facing a great shortage of provisions. The subtle influence of these pretentious manifested itself at first in mutterings of discontent and finally in a general movement of large bodies of Indians from their agencies in almost open defiance of authority. The Indians of Standing Rock Agency, Big Foot's band from the Cheyenne River Agency, and the Brules at the Rosebud Agency, broke away from every semblance of control and, in open defiance of their agents' orders, refused to discontinue the dance. Disaffection was spreading to the Rosebud and Pine Ridge Agencies, which together comprised a compact body of more than ten thousand Indians, the most warlike in the northwest. In August, 1890, some of the local agents declared the situation to be beyond their control, and in November the president of the United States directed the secretary of war to take active measures to prevent an outbreak. Troops to the number of 8,000 were poured into the country and many of the Indians left their agencies and fled to the Bad Lands. With more than twenty-five thousand Indians in a state of semi-rebellion and nearly all infected by the Messiah craze and the Ghost

Dance, and impatient of restraint, the inhabitants of northern Nebraska appealed to the governor of the state for protection.

By his direction, the adjutant general supplied fourteen independent military companies, organized in places along the northwestern frontier, with Springfield breech-loading rifles, ammunition, and equipment, and in January, 1891, the two regiments of the Nebraska National Guard, under Brigadier General Leonard W. Colby, were ordered to the scene of action and stationed at or near the towns along the Elkhorn Railway, south of the Indian country. The guards did good service in quieting the fears of the people and in showing a readiness to afford protection in case of necessity.

Company C of the First Regiment was from Beatrice. It was commanded by A. A. Reed, was stationed during the Indian troubles at Valentine, Nebraska, and its services in this historic event closed the military activities of Gage county as respects Indian wars.

Our county participated to some extent in the great Civil war. The patriotic devotion of the territory of Nebraska to the Union throughout those trying days forms a most creditable chapter in its history. The news of the fall of Fort Sumter, in April, 1861, evoked a spirit of unbounded loyalty in the new territory. In Omaha steps were at once taken to aid the government by organizing two companies of infantry, one of dragoons and one of artillery. Governor Black appointed George F. Kennedy, of Florence, acting brigadier general of the First Nebraska Regiment, pending its organization and enrollment. Governor Saunders, who had succeeded to the executive chair, on May 18, 1861, issued his proclamation reciting the necessity of loyally supporting the government, and invoked the aid of every lover of his country and his home to sustain and protect it. Steps were immediately taken to organize a regiment, and on the 2d day of July, 1861, the tenth and last company of the First Nebraska Regiment of Volunteers were sworn into the service of the United States. Men were drawn from all over the territory into this regiment. From Gage county came Samuel Shaw, who enlisted in Company B, June 13, 1861; Frederick Elwood, aged twenty-three, who went from Beatrice and enlisted in Company H; Jonathan Potts, twenty-seven years old, also from Beatrice, enlisted in Company M. These heroic citizens of our county served faithfully until the end of the war, and all returned to Gage county to make their homes. Mr. Shaw some years ago went to Florida, where he died. Elwood and Potts, after many years' residence, both died in Gage county, much honored by all who knew their history. In addition to these, William, Egbert, and James Shaw (sons of Stephen P. Shaw), and John Q Adams, from Adams township, served in this regiment, being members of Company H.

The county contributed also to the membership of the Second Nebraska Cavalry Regiment, organized in 1863, to repel an invasion by the Sioux Indians in their retreat from Minnesota, following the great massacres of August, 1862. This regiment was raised in eastern Nebraska and enlisted for nine months' service, under the command of Colonel Robert W. Furnas, of Brownville. It became a part of General Sully's expedition up the Missouri river, participating in the skirmishes and the battle of White Stone Hills, South Dakota, in which the Indians were completely vanquished. Those from Gage county who took part in this campaign, as members of Company L of the Second Nebraska, were Francis M. Graham, George W. Desert, H. S. Barnum, Edward Armstrong, Thaddeus Armstrong, and John Hagar, all of Blue Springs and vicinity.

Our county can take a just pride in the record made by its citizens in the Spanish American war, in 1898. On April 20th of that year the United States presented its ultimatum to Spain, demanding that she relinquish sovereignty over Cuba before noon of April 23d and withdraw her land and naval forces from that unhappy island. Spain indignantly refused to comply with these demands, and on that day, at noon, President William McKinley issued a call for volunteers in the military and naval service of the United States. On the 25th day of April congress issued its declaration of a state of war between Spain and the United States, and the call reached Lincoln, Nebraska, on the 27th of April. At noon of the following day the companies of the First Nebraska, including Company C, of Beatrice, went into camp at Camp Alvin Saunders, Lincoln. This regiment was mustered into service beginning on the 9th day of May; on June 5th it was aboard the steamer "Senator," at San Francisco, bound for the orient; and on July 17th, the city of

Manila lay spread out before its members, from their vessel's anchorage in Manila Bay. The regiment disembarked on the 21st day of July, at Cavite, and remained in camp until August 2d, when it participated in the assault on the outposts of Manila, in which eight Nebraskans were wounded. On August 13th the regiment took an active part in the assault and capture of the city of Manila. From that time until February it was on outpost and guard duty about Manila, while Aguinaldo's rebellion was rapidly gathering head. On February 4, 1899, while stationed opposite block house No. 6, near the waterworks, on Pasig river, a squad of four armed Filipinos attempted to pass the American line. Private Grayson, of the First Nebraska, stood guard there, and when the Filipinos refused to halt, he fired on them. His fire was returned by the insurrectos, and the war of the Philippines was on. The regiment rushed to the defense of its outposts, the Filipinos attacking with vigor, and this action is known as the first battle of Santa Mesa.

COLONEL JOHN M. STOTSENBERG
Killed in action in the Philippines, April 23, 1899

The regiment participated with great renown in the second battle of Santa Mesa, February 20th; the battle of Maraquana Roads, March 5th and 6th; the advance on Mallolos; the capture of Francisco del Monte, Meycangua, Ste. Marie, Ste. Clara, March 25th; the battle of Quingua, April 23d; the battles of Calumpit, Santa Thomas, San Fernando and Calocan, May 6, 1899. Perhaps the battle of Quingua was the most sanguinary conflict in which the regiment was engaged. Amongst those who fell that day was John M. Stotsenberg, the colonel of the regiment.

The regiment sailed from Manila July 21st and reached San Francisco July 29th, went into camp at the Presidio July 30th, and was mustered out and discharged August 23, 1899, after a service of one year, three months, and fourteen days. Its losses were: Killed in battle, twenty-one; died of wounds, thirteen; died of disease, thirty—a total of sixty-four.

Company C reached Beatrice September 1, 1899, and was given a royal reception by the entire population. The roster of this company is as follows:

Captain

Hollingworth, Albert H.

First Lieutenants

Archer, Harry L.
Storch, Joseph A.

Second Lieutenants

McLaughlin, Warren L.
Wheedon, Burt D.
Dungan, William B.
Coleman, Garrett F.

First Sergeants

Wadsworth, Andrew S.
Reedy, William H.

Quartermaster's Sergeants

Pethoud, Logan L.
Johnson, Hans

Sergeants

Curtis, Orrin T.
Geddes, George L.
Hall, John A.
Murdock, Harry S.
Evans, William J.
Peters, Lehman C.
Johnson, Hans
Dudley, Howard S.

Corporals

Evans, William J.
Cook, Erastus
Bick, Frederick
Bloodgood, Edwin E.
Langdon, Oliver H.
Holbert, Andrew F.
Jones, Sherman
Truax, George Lester
Hall, Sherrill W.
Tyson, Jesse
Baird, Jesse P.
Schultz, Hugo D.
Putt, Philip C.
Peters, Lehman C.
Hall, William G.

Musicians

Stevenson, Arthur E.
Baird, Jesse P.
Roller, John S.
Tucker, Luther I.
McHugh, Joseph D.

General Roster

Ashenfelter, James L.
Ashley, Clifford L.

Beal, Eugene
Butler, Charley C.
Bick, John W.
Bowling, William W.
Bradshaw, James A.
Brewster, Charles L.
Brownell, Mike
Ball, Louis
Bowling, George I.
Barry, Joseph J.
Bloodgood, Edwin E.
Campbell, Robert
Campbell, Roy C.
Clark, Frank M.
Condon, William
Cook, Fred
Davis, Everett
Drake, Neal C. A.
Druigman, William F.
Dudley, Howard S.
Field, Charles
Folden, Charles F.
Folden, James R. C.
Gable, Louis M.
Gashaw, Nelson S.
Griffith, Norman
Hall, William G.
Hall, Sherrill W.
Hileman, Wilbert S.
Holbert, Andrew F.
Hutson, Edward J.
Harris, Frank
Johnson, Hans
Johnson, William
Jones, Charley C.

Jones, Sherman
Knouse, Frank M.
Kuhn, Fred C.
Langdon, Oliver H.
Litty, Fred L.
Macy, Bruce E.
Meeker, Orrie A.
McHugh, Joseph D.
McDaniel, Charles L.
McDonough, Michael L.
Nelson, Linus C.
Olinghouse, Henry I.
Owen, Frank
Ozman, Roscoe C.
Ossowski, Paul
Penrod, Jesse C.
Peters, Lehman C.
Peters, Martin L.
Pinson, Will H.
Powers, Mark
Putt, Phillip C.
Quein, John R.
Ragland, Simeon W
Ray, Alpheus
Reedy, William H.
Roller, John S.
Riordan, John J.
Rungan, Charles
Shultz, Hugo D.
Scott, Marion F.
Smith, Elmer W.
Spott, Thomas
Staker, Will C.
Sterne, William A.
Tatman, Harry E.

Thompson, Earl W.
Tucker, Luther I.
Tyson, Jesse
Watts, Bert W.
Willey, Frank
Wilson, John E.

Recruits

Ackerman, Paul August
Avey, Sherman H.
Burnham, Lyvenus S.
Boomer, George R.
Bishop, Fred W.
Chevrout, James W.
Epp, Henry Martin
Franklin, C. M.
Logsdon, William
Miller, Julius G.
Morris, Robert B.
Nelson, Julius M.
Pillsbury, John W.
Rowland, Ira C.
Salisbury, Clayton L.
Shaw, Herman C.
Smock, Harry O.
Stambough, William H.
Stout, Ira P.
Stout, Walter I.
Tilton, Winfield S.
Truax, George Lester
Ward, Peter
Woodbridge, William E.

Promoted

Harry L. Archer, First Lieutenant, Regimental Adjutant.
W. R. McLaughlin, Second Lieutenant, Regimental Quartermaster.

Bert D. Wheedon, Second Lieutenant, Regimental Adjutant.

Andrew S. Wadsworth, First Sergeant, Second Lieutenant, Company B.

Orrin T. Curtis, First Sergeant, Second Lieutenant, Company L.

Wounded

A. H. Hollingworth, Captain, wounded in right forearm and right thigh, near Mariquina, P. I., February 17, 1899.

J. A. Storch, First Lieutenant, wounded in right arm at San Francisco del Monte, P. I., March 25, 1899.

B. D. Wheedon, Second Lieutenant, wounded in right hip, near Mariquina, P. I., February 17, 1899.

W. G. Dungan, Second Lieutenant, wounded near Quingua, P. I., April 24, 1899.

Orrin T. Curtis, First Sergeant, wounded in right hand, at Santa Mesa, P. I., February 4, 1899.

Jesse P. Baird, Corporal, wounded in left hand, at Marilao, P. I., March 29, 1899.

Chas. Brewster, Corporal, wounded in right foot, at Calumpit, P. I., April 25, 1899.

John S. Roller, Artificer, wounded in left arm, at Quingua, P. I., April 23, 1899.

Henry Epp, wounded in left shoulder, at Santa Mesa, P. I., February 5, 1899.

Fred C. Kuhn, wounded in left thigh, at waterworks, P. I., February 6, 1899.

Roscoe C. Ozman, wounded in right forearm, at San Francisco del Monte, P. I., March 25, 1899.

Roy C. Campbell, wounded in left ankle, at Guiguinto, P. I., March 29, 1899.

George R. Boomer, wounded in left forearm, near Guiguinto, P. I., March 30, 1899.

Lyvenus S. Burnham, wounded in left shoulder, near Guiguinto, P. I., March 30, 1899.

William Logsdon, wounded in right lung, near Guiguinto, P. I., March 30, 1899.

Bert W. Watts, wounded in left thigh, near Guiguinto, P. I., March 30, 1899.

Dead

William G. Evans, Sergeant, died of blood poison, at Cavite, P. July 24, 1898.

George L. Geddes, Sergeant, died of spinal meningitis, at sea, June 21, 1898.

Bruce E. Macy, wounded in action at Marilao, P. I., March 29, 1899, died April 20, 1899.

Julius G. Miller, died of spinal meningitis, at Honolulu, October 20, 1898.

Frank Knouse, drowned in Pasig river, December 15, 1898.

The members of Company C of the First Nebraska were the only Gage county people who saw active service in the Philippine war. General Leonard W. Colby, of Beatrice, at the beginning of the war, was appointed brigadier general and assigned to a command at Anniston, Georgia. His brigade, however, was never called into service.

But all other military achievements to which Gage county may justly lay claim, pale into insignificance before its activities in the present great world war. Scarcely had the declaration of war with Germany been made by congress, in April, 1917, when historic Company C of the Nebraska National Guard, of Beatrice, commanded by Captain Charles L. Brewster, presented itself for volunteer service. At Wymore, Company F, commanded by Captain F. E. Crawford, and composed almost wholly of Gage county volunteers, left Wymore September 20, 1918, for military training at Camp Cody, Deming, New Mexico. Prior to the taking effect of the draft act of congress, many others volunteered in the army and navy of the United States for service in this the greatest and most terrible of all wars. Under the draft act, many more of Gage county's young men have been drawn into the service. The figures are not at hand to show the number of our county's citizens now serving under our country's flag in the war waged for the preservation of democratic institutions throughout the world. Including both branches of the service, it is approximately 1200. Many are already in France, a few have made the supreme sacrifice for human liberty, and many others may yet do so. Besides its man-power, the county has generously contributed of its wealth for the prosecution of this war of embattled nations. The full record of the county's patriotic contributions in this crucial epoch of the world's history must needs be left to the consideration of some later historian.

CHAPTER XXX

THE BENCH AND THE BAR

Territorial Supreme Court — Territorial District Courts — Chief Justice Ferguson — Associate Justices — First Session Supreme Court — First Term District Court — First Judicial Legislation — Gage County's First District Judge — First Term District Court in Gage County — Second Term — First Grand Jury — First Embezzlement — First Murder — Third Term District Court — First Petit Jury — First Divorce Case — State Supreme Court — State District Courts — Act Admitting Attorneys — First Lawyers in Gage County — Brief Sketches of Former Members of the Bar — Present Members

The organic act by which the territory of Nebraska was created and under which it was organized, vested the judicial power of the territory in a supreme court, district courts, probate and justice-of-the-peace courts. With respect to the supreme court, it was provided that this high tribunal should consist of a chief justice and two associate justices, to be appointed by the president of the United States, by and with the consent of the senate. Any two of the justices, the act specified should constitute a quorum. They were required to hold one term of court annually at the seat of the territorial government, and continued in office for a period of four years, or until their successors were appointed and had qualified. Their salaries were fixed at the sum of two thousand dollars per annum, to be paid out of the public treasury at Washington, and they were given authority to appoint a clerk, who held office at the pleasure of the justices and who was paid by the fees of his office.

The act further provided that the territory should be divided into three judicial districts and that a term of court should be held annually in each district, by one of the judges of the supreme court, at such times and places as should be prescribed by law. Each judge was authorized to appoint a clerk of the court for his district, "who should also be a register in chancery and should keep his office at the place where the court may be held". Clerks of the district court, like the clerk of the supreme court, held office at the pleasure of the judge appointing them, and were paid by the fees of their respective offices.

Section 17 of the organic act provided that, until otherwise provided by law, the governor of the territory might define the judicial districts "and assign the judges who may be appointed for the territory to the several districts, and also appoint the times and places for holding courts in the several counties or subdivisions in each of said judicial districts, by proclamation to be issued by him; but the legislative assembly, at their first or any subsequent session, may organize, alter or modify such judicial districts, and assign the judges, and alter the times and places of holding courts, as to them shall seem proper and convenient."

In June, 1854 President Buchanan appointed James Bradley, of Pennsylvania, associate justice of the territorial supreme court of Nebraska; in July following, Edward Randolph Harden was appointed associate justice of that court; and on October 12th President Buchanan appointed Fenner Ferguson, of the state of New York, chief justice of the court.

Immediately upon his appointment Judge Ferguson moved his family to Bellevue, where he resided until his death. He was very active in assisting the legislative assembly to frame and adopt the first code of laws enacted for the government of Nebraska Territory and in otherwise placing it in a going condition. Acting within the scope of his authority, Acting-Governor Cuming had by executive proclamation provisionally organized the territorial courts by assigning Chief Justice Ferguson to the first judicial district, as established by his proclamation. This district embraced Dodge and Douglas counties. The second district, as marked out by the proclamation, embraced the entire South Platte portion of the territory, and the third, the counties of Burt and Washington. Associate Justice Harden was assigned to the second, and Associate Justice Bradley to the third district. The proclamation provided for the holding of a term of the supreme court at the seat of government on the third Monday of February, 1855; in the first district, at Bellvue, on the second Monday in March, 1855; in the second district, at Nebraska City, the third Monday in March, and in the third district, at Florence, the first Monday in April 1855.

FENNER FERGUSON
First chief justice of the Nebraska Territorial supreme court

Pursuant to this proclamation, the first session of the territorial supreme court met in Omaha—which had been selected by Acting-Governor Cuming as the capital of the new territory—on the 19th day of February, 1855, and remained in session until the 6th day of March following. Chief Justice Ferguson presided, and during most of the session both associate justices appear to have been in attendance; a part of the time, though, we are informed, Justice Harden was ill, at his lodgings at Bellevue. J. Sterling Morton, of Bellevue, was appointed clerk of the court. On the last day of the term, just before adjournment, on motion of Attorney General Estabrook, a number of applicants were admitted to practice law in the courts of the territory, amongst them being Andrew J.

Poppleton, Andrew J. Hanscom, and Silas A. Strickland, all of whom became closely identified with the early history of Nebraska. But, on the whole, this first term of the territorial supreme court was largely a formal matter, for the purpose of effecting an organization and keeping the letter of the acting governor's proclamation.

The first term of district court in the new territory was also largely for the same purposes. It was opened at Bellevue, the oldest town in Nebraska, then situated in Douglas county, now in Sarpy county, by Chief Justice Ferguson, as judge of the first territorial judicial district, on the 12th day of March, 1855. Eli R. Doyle, marshal of the territory, was present in his official capacity, and the court appointed Silas A. Strickland, of Bellevue, clerk of the court. Several applications were made for naturalization papers by foreign-born residents of the territory and, no other important business coming before the court, an adjournment was taken until April 12.

In accordance with section 17 of the organic act, which devolved upon the legislature the duty of permanently establishing the courts of the territory, defining their jurisdiction and dividing Nebraska into judicial districts, the first legislative assembly, which convened at Omaha on the 16th day of January, 1855, having adopted in part the Iowa code of civil procedure, proceeded to enact a body of general laws, amongst which were several acts or parts of acts defining the powers and duties of the several courts of the territory and prescribing their jurisdiction. The legislative enactment constituted the district courts the great trial courts of the territory. They were given exclusive and original jurisdiction of all suits at law and chancery, except such as were within the jurisdiction of the justices of the peace and such matters as were by express enactment committed to the jurisdiction of the probate courts, and for the inferior courts it was given appellate jurisdiction. The supreme court was given appellate jurisdiction in all decrees in chancery, and was a court of last resort to which writs of error could be addressed from all final judgments at law tried by the district courts. In other words, the final judgments and decrees of the members of the court, sitting as judges of the district courts, were subject to review by the entire bench on appeals or writs of error.

Amongst other things, the legislative body divided the territory into three judicial districts, the first of which comprised Washington and Douglas counties; the second, Richardson, Nemaha, Otoe, Cass, Lancaster, Green (now Seward), Clay, Pawnee, Johnson, York and Gage, the third comprised the counties of Dakota, Buffalo, Cuming, Burt, Dodge, Loupe (now Colfax), Blackbird (now Thurston in part), Izard (now Wayne), Jackson (now the north third of Gage), and McNeal (now Stanton) counties. Chief Justice Ferguson was assigned to the first district, Associate Justice Harden to the second district, and Associate Justice Bradley to the third district. The legislative assembly designated also the time and place for holding court in the three judicial districts. In the second district, it provided that court should be held in the county of Cass on the first Mondays of April and September, in Otoe county on the second Mondays, in Nemaha county on the third Mondays, and in Richardson county on the fourth Mondays of April and September in each year, and "in all other counties in said district at such times and places as the judge may appoint."

JAMES BRADLEY
Associate Justice of the Nebraska Territorial Supreme Court

As respects Gage county, there is no known evidence that Associate Justice Harden ever called a term of court in the county. He was a southern gentleman of the old school. He was born and educated in Georgia and was appointed associate justice of the supreme court of the territory of Nebraska in July, 1854, when he was thirty-nine years of age. In May, 1860, he was appointed to a like position in Utah, by James Buchanan, who was then president of the United States. He held the first term of court in his district, as far as known, at Nebraska City, in March, 1855, and left the territory probably before Gage county had any demand for a term of district court. He returned to Georgia in time to participate in the famous secession convention of that state, in 1861, and on the breaking out of the civil war he enlisted in the Confederate army as commander of a company known as the Dalton Guards; he was afterward made adjutant of Smith's Legion. He later served as an aide on General Walker's staff, and on the close of the war he resumed the practice of the law, at Cuthbert, Georgia. He served two terms in the legislature of his state, as a representative from Walker county, and held other honorary and remunerative positions. He appears to have been a man of ability and integrity. He died at Quitman, Georgia, in 1884, at the age of sixty-nine years.

EDWARD RANDOLPH HARDEN
Associate Justice of the Nebraska Territorial Supreme Court

There exists no record of the holding of a term of the territorial district court in Gage county prior to the 26th day of November, 1863. Elmer S. Dundy, of Falls City, was appointed associate justice of the supreme court by Abraham Lincoln, president of the United States, in the early part of 1863, and was assigned to the Second judicial district. The first record in the district-court records of the county, written in Judge Dundy's own hand, reads as follows:

Be It Remembered, that at the Fall adjourned term of the Gage County District Court of Nebraska Territory, held at Beatrice in said County, on the 25th day of November, A. D., 1863, the said court having been adjourned from the first Thursday after the first Monday in September, to the 26th day of November, 1863, the following named officers were present, towit: Elmer S. Dundy, Judge

    Rienzi Streeter, Clerk, by
    Oliver Townsend, Deputy,
    C. B. R. E., Prosecuting Atty.,
    Joseph Kline, Shff.

and the following proceedings were had, towit:

C. B. R. E. was admitted to practise law in the several District Courts of this Territory, after full examination in open court, he having been first duly sworn, according to law.

On motion of Aug. Schoenheit, J. Wilson Bolinger was admitted, on certificate, to practice law in the several Judicial Districts of this Territory, having been first duly sworn, according to law.

The said sheriff returns into open court the venire heretofore issued for petit jury, and the jury being called, the following named persons were present and answered to their names:

    Wm. Blakely,
    John Badly (Bagley)
    Sam'l Kilpatrick,
    H. J. Pierce.
    J. E. Chase,
    Adam Hager,
    H. M. Wickham,

and there being no business before the Court, were thereupon discharged.

Most of the business before the court was of slight importance. There were three indictments pending for the illegal sale of intoxicating liquors, one for "malicious mischief," and a charge of riot, all of which were dismissed by the prosecuting attorney "C.B.R.E."

The civil business disposed of by Judge Dundy included nineteen cases, one of the important ones being that of Gideon Bennett vs. William W. Dennison. Bennett, the reader will remember, was an Indian trader who followed the Otoe and Missouri Indian tribes from Nebraska City to their Gage county reservation in 1855, and Dennison, the defendant in the case, was the government agent of the Indians until the breaking out of the Civil war, when he left the territory, and afterwards became identified with the Confederacy. The action was upon a claim for money due to plaintiff from defendant, and had been accompanied by an order of attachment which had been levied by the sheriff upon property belonging to Major Dennison. The record shows that the defendant had died during the pendency of the suit, and John W. Latham had been appointed administrator of his estate. The suit was revived against the administrator and judgment entered for the plaintiff in the sum of three hundred and fifty dollars and costs, the sheriff being directed to sell the attached property in satisfaction of same.

Perhaps the most important case disposed of by the court was that entitled Theodore Hill, Plaintiff, vs. The Central Overland and Pike's Peak Express Company, Defendant. This action also was upon indebtedness claimed to be due plaintiff from defendant, and the property of defendant, consisting of a number of horses, "two with docked tails"; a nine-passenger, four-horse coach, named "Red Rover"; two four-mule teams, and other chattels, had been taken by Sheriff Clyne, in satisfaction of the plaintiff's claim. A jury was waived by both parties to the suit, trial had to the court and judgment entered for plaintiff against the defendant in the sum of $1,395.67, and the sheriff was directed to sell the attached property in satisfaction thereof.

The second term of district court held in Gage county convened in Beatrice on the 7th day of September, 1865.

"Present; Elmer S. Dundy, Judge,
Rienzi Streeter, Clerk,
by H. M. Reynolds, Deputy,
Joseph Clyne, Shff.,
J. B. Mattingley, Deputy Shff."

The preliminary entries, after reciting the failure of the county to select a grand jury as by law required, directs the sheriff to call by four o'clock in the afternoon "sixteen good and lawful men, possessing the qualifications of electors in said county, to serve as grand jurors for the present term, according to law in such case made and provided."

The record further recites that the following named persons appeared as grand jurors at four o'clock in the afternoon of that day, namely:

R. C. Davis	J. Hinton
John Alexander	John T. Pethoud
William Alexander	Michael Conley
Wm. Tichnor	Wm. McCumsey
Amasa Stevens	Orrin Stevens
Jacob Shaw	Edward Cartwright
Joseph L. Brown	John Q. Adams
A. D. Sage	F. Raper

As far as the records of the district court go, this appears to have been the first grand jury called in Gage county. The term lasted a single day, but the grand jurors returned indictments against Alexander Dean, for murder in the first degree; Theodore M. Coulter, for embezzlement; and John Fishpaugh, Peter Buckles, Scott Willis and Henry Willis, for assault with intent to commit murder. One of the cases tried and decided by Judge Dundy was the County of Gage vs. Theodore M. Coulter, an action brought by the county to recover against Coulter the sum of $547.98 embezzled by him while county treasurer. The defendant made default in the case and a judgment was entered for the county against him and his bondsmen for that amount, and he was almost immediately indicted for embezzlement.

Coulter was arrested upon this indictment and he was held a prisoner by the sheriff for nearly three years. There was no jail where he could be kept and the sheriff was compelled to board and care for him at the county's expense. It was often very inconvenient for the sheriff to guard or otherwise hold his prisoner in custody. Following the great Indian raid on the Little Blue river in August, 1864, the sheriff, Joseph Clyne, was a member of a company from Beatrice who went on an expedition to the stricken section of the territory, to bury the dead and assist in repelling further invasion. He was compelled to take his prisoner along, as he could find no one willing to have him in charge. After the excitement had abated, and Coulter's bondsmen had liquidated his defalcation, the expense of providing for the prisoner and of bringing him to trial outweighed all other considerations and by common consent every opportunity was given him to escape. As a prisoner he was very much of a man of leisure, the board was good and he was clothed, fed, and sheltered at public expense. He sensed the situation perfectly, talked largely about his innocence and forcing the county to bring him to trial, and made not the slightest move toward relieving the community of his embarrassing presence. At last, in sheer desperation, he was placed in the custody of the deputy sheriff, James B. Mattingley, and by the deputy was removed to his home in Rockford township a few miles north of Blue Springs. At this home he received a meager fare and a poor quality of meals. After a few weeks Coulter took the hint and disappeared. No one ever made the slightest effort to apprehend him, and thus ended the first embezzlement case in Gage county.

The indictment of Dean for murder was also largely a farcical matter, though in a more advanced state of society he would no doubt have been immediately arrested and punished. His victim was Spencer Roberts, who owned and lived upon the tract of land where Crab Orchard is now located. He had sold to Andrew Dean, a Dane living on Cub creek, near the "First Homestead," a horse and had taken his note for sixty dollars in settlement for the animal. Roberts, who was a cattle buyer and stock dealer, called at Dean's house in his absence, to collect the note, and it was alleged he attempted to be familiar with his debtor's wife. She repelled his advances and Roberts left the premises.

He afterward returned to the house and found Dean and his neighbor, Thomas Clyne, engaged in threshing wheat with flails. He was upon the point of leaving when Dean's wife attempted to assault him, and Dean, then learning the identity of the man who had insulted her, his wife claimed, grabbed his flail and rushed to attack Roberts. Clyne stepped between the men and caught Dean's hand when in the act of striking with the flail, but the short end of the bludgeon struck Roberts, fracturing his skull, from which injury he soon expired. No effort was made to apprehend Dean and he soon disappeared. His indictment was more to save the face of the community than for any definite purpose of bringing him to punishment. This was the first murder of a white person in Gage county of which there is any known evidence, and Dean's indictment was the first one returned by a grand jury in the county, all previous criminal prosecutions having been within the jurisdiction of the justice court or, where the offense charged was beyond the jurisdiction of the justice and the offender had been bound over, no indictment or prosecution followed, a procedure illustrated in the actions of the prosecuting attorney in dismissing six criminal cases pending before Judge Dundy at the first term of the Gage county district court in 1863.

Judge Dundy continued to hold the office of associate justice of the territorial supreme court until Nebraska was admitted into the Union, March 1, 1867. At the general election of 1866, in contemplation of the change from territorial to state government, William A Little, of Omaha, was elected chief justice of the supreme court and George B. Lake and Lorenzo Crounse, both of Omaha, were elected associate justices. Before taking office Little died and his opponent at the election, Oliver P. Mason, of Nebraska City, was appointed by Governor Butler (the first of the state governors) chief justice in his stead, to serve until the next general election, when he was elected chief justice of the supreme court of the state of Nebraska.

By an act of the state legislature, approved June 12, 1867, the boundaries of the judicial districts were changed, and the counties of Richardson, Nemaha, Otoe, Johnson, Pawnee, Gage Jefferson, Saline, Fillmore, and Nuckolls, with the unorganized territory to the west, were designated as the First judicial district. The first term of the Gage county district court after Nebraska territory became the state of Nebraska, was held by Judge Mason, at Beatrice, beginning the 7th day of October, A.D., 1867. The introductory entries are in Judge Mason's own handwriting, and read as follows:

Be it Remembered, That at a regular term of the District Court of the First Judicial District, sitting within and for Gage County,

Present   O. P. Mason, Judge,
            Isham Reavis, Dist. Attorney,
            Rienzi Streeter, Clerk,
by   H. M. Reynolds, Deputy
            W. T. Brown, Sheriff,
            T. J. Chesney, Deputy Sheriff,
            Daniel Freeman, Bailiff.

The following proceedings were had and done; The court having been opened at the time prescribed by law by the Sheriff making public proclamation thereof, N. K. Griggs and S. B. Harrington were admitted to practice law in the several District Courts of the State, having been first duly sworn, according to law.

The said sheriff returns in open court a venire heretofore issued for a Grand Jury, and the jury being called, the following named persons were present and answered to their names, viz:

Richard Rossiter	A. Van Buskirk
Peter Hamma	H. D. Lilley
George Stark	H. M. Wickham
Sam'l Kilpatrick	J. M. Rodgers
J. B. Shaw	John Parker
N. Kain	H. Hollingworth
John Mumford	Alex. Welch

Absent J. J. Dunbar and A. D. Sage. A. D. Sage was excused on account of sickness, and Alexander Welch was found not qualified to act as a juror, on account of being a foreigner, and an attachment was ordered for J. J. Dunbar.

The following named persons were then summoned by the sheriff to serve as Grand Jurors and fill the panel, to wit: F. E. Roper, Christian Euster and George H. Ross.

After the Grand Jurors had all been examined by the Court touching their qualifications as such, H. M. Wickham was duly sworn as Foreman of the Grand Jury, after which the other Grand Jurors were all sworn in the oath provided by law, and after being charged by the Court retired in charge of Daniel Freeman, a sworn bailiff, to consider their indictments and their presentments.

The said sheriff also returned into open court a venire heretofore issued for a petit jury, and the jury being called, the following named persons were present and answered to their names, to-wit:

R. C. Davis	John Barrett
J. W. Mumford	Henry Shullenbarger
L. P. Chandler	F. H. Dobbs
Jacob Hildebrand	David Palmer
Amos Hayden	H. S. Barnum
Frederick Sprague	John Hillman
James Kinzie	J. W. Nickols
James Plucknett	John Lyons
Alfred Snell	William Curtiss
V. S. Whittemore	Egbert Shaw
Robert Nicholas	J. Buchanan
R. A. Wilson	William Wild

As far as disclosed by the records this was the first petit jury ever empaneled in the district court in Gage county. The term lasted two days and it must have run day and night, as a large amount of business was transacted by Judge Mason. Amongst the cases tried by him at this term was that of Hester Drown vs. George W. Drown, action for divorce. It was tried on the last day of the term, September 9th, and a divorce was denied the plaintiff and awarded the defendant, on account of plaintiff's proved moral delinquencies. This was the first divorce suit ever tried in Gage county.

OLIVER P. MASON
First Chief Justice of the Nebraska State Supreme Court

After empaneling the jury the following order was made by the court: "Ordered that the Sheriff of Gage county purchase for the use of the district court within and for Gage county, twelve chairs of good and substantial material and make, and that the same be purchased at the expense of the said county of Gage."

Within the two days' session of the court occurred the trial of The People of the State of Nebraska vs. John Fishpaugh, Peter Buckles and John Scott Willis, indicted for riot. The jury empaneled to try the case were Jacob W. Mumford, Jacob Hildebrand, Frederick Sprague, James Kinzie, James Plucknett, Alfred Snell, Robert Nicholas, V. S. Whittemore, John Hillman, F. H. Dobbs, David Palmer, and John Lyons.

"After hearing the evidence introduced as well on the part of said prisoners as on the part of the People of the State of Nebraska, and after hearing the arguments of counsel and the charge of the court, the jury retired in charge of a sworn officer to consider their verdict. And after consulting and deliberating thereon, returned into court the following verdict:

'We, the jury, find the defendants, John Fishpaugh, Peter Buckles, and John Scott Willis, guilty as they stand charged in the indictment. F. H. Dobbs, Foreman'."

This was the first trial jury empaneled and this the first verdict rendered by a jury in the district court of Gage county.

From 1867 to 1873 Judge Mason, chief justice of the supreme court, was the district judge of the First judicial district of Nebraska, and was succeeded by Daniel Gantt. The state supreme court retained its original territorial organization until the adoption of the present state constitution, in 1875, By its provision, district judges were elected and members of the supreme court ceased to be trial judges in the judicial districts. The first district judge of the First judicial district under the constitution was Archibald J. Weaver, of Falls City. He was elected to this office at the general election in 1875 and reelected in 1879. Before his second term expired, at the general election in 1883, he was elected to the Forty-eighth congress from the old First congressional district, and in the fall of 1885 he was reelected, to the Forty-ninth congress. He was a man of great force of character, of indefatigable energy and of unquestioned integrity of character. He was kindly, generous, hospitable, and one of the most companionable of men. He was of such striking appearance and commanding physique as to attract attention in any crowd. His career as a judge in the old First judicial district will never be forgotten while a single member of the bar of that district who appeared in his court remains alive. His power in the dispatch of judicial business was phenomenal and his court ran at high pressure by day and a part of every night. He had remarkable sagacity in divining the intents and purposes of men and any crooked or fraudulent deal never got by him, so far as any lawyer ever knew. He contracted a slight attack of pneumonia and, after an illness of three days, died April 18, 1887, when in the prime of life and ere he had approached the zenith of his great powers and usefulness. Perhaps no man in Nebraska had been so showered with honors and few, if any, ever had a future of greater possibilities.

Judge Weaver was succeeded on the bench of the First judicial district by Jefferson H. Broady, of Brownville, at the election of 1883.

Judge Broady served the district most faithfully for four years. Before the expiration of his term of office the legislature of 1887 authorized the election of two judges for the First judicial district, and at the fall election that year Judge Broady was reelected, and with him Thomas Appleget, of Tecumseh. At the close of his term of office Judge Broady retired from the bench, honored and respected by the entire bar of the First judicial district, having for eight busy years given power, dignity and honor to the bench of the district. He had been living in Beatrice for three or four years but in 1901 he removed to Lincoln and re-engaged in the practice of the law. He died a few years ago, mourned by almost the entire state.

In 1891 the legislature redistricted the state as respects the judicial districts. The boundaries of the old First judicial district of Weaver's and Broady's day, which comprised Richardson, Nemaha, Johnson, Pawnee and Gage, was changed to include Jefferson county. The provision for the election of two judges in the district was retained, and at the general election of 1891 Albert H. Babcock and James E. Bush, both of Beatrice, were elevated to the judicial district bench. In 1895 Charles B. Letton, of Fairbury, and John S. Stull, of Auburn, were elected judges of the district, and each was reelected in 1899. At the election of 1903 Albert H. Babcock, of Beatrice, and W. H. Kellegar, of Auburn, were elected district judges of the First judicial district. Before his term of office expired Judge Babcock died, and John B. Raper, of Pawnee City, was appointed by Governor Mickey to fill out his unexpired term. At the fall election of 1907 Leander M. Pemberton and John B. Raper were elected, and both have by successive elections held this important office till the present moment.

In 1911 the legislature, by a reapportionment of the judicial districts, created district No. 18, consisting of Gage and Jefferson counties, and Judge Pemberton was assigned for service to this district. He is the present incumbent of the office.

Speaking generally, the judges of the district court of the several judicial districts to which Gage county has belonged have been lawyers of ability and of great worth of character. Some were called to even higher service than the district judicial bench. Judge Dundy was, in

1868, elevated to the bench of the Federal district court of Nebraska, and he occupied that position until his death, October 28, 1896. Judge Weaver passed from the district court bench to a seat in congress; Judge Gantt was elected a justice of the supreme court in 1867 and at the time of his demise, in 1878, was chief justice of that great court; Judge Letton, after nearly eight years' service on the district bench of the First judicial district, was, in November, 1903, appointed one of the supreme-court commissioners, and in 1905 he was elected a justice of the supreme court of the state, a position he has since held. He is a candidate for a second reelection, with every prospect of success.

The intimate relationship which always exists between bench and bar in the public mind as well as in actual practice, gives pertinency to what will be said concerning the lawyers of Gage county.

The bar as a branch of the American system of jurisprudence was given standing by the first general assembly of the territory of Nebraska in an act approved March 9, 1855, entitled "An act regulating the admission of attorneys." It is very brief. The first section provides that "any person twenty-one years of age who can produce satisfactory evidence of a good moral character and pass an examination before either the judges of the district court or before the justices of the supreme court of this territory, shall be licensed to practice as an attorney at law and solicitor in chancery in all the courts in this territory." And, as a sort of afterthought, the second section of the act provides that "every citizen of this territory may attend to his own cases in all said courts."

At the third session of the legislative assembly, begun and held at Omaha January 15, 1857, a code of civil procedure was adopted for the territory, in which the law regarding attorneys and counselors at law was formulated very much as it now appears in the statutes of our state. Under these statutes there has been from almost the first an able, patriotic and trustworthy bar in Nebraska. No class of citizens has contributed as much toward the general welfare, the formulation and enactment of wise and wholesome laws, the enforcement of law and order and the maintenance of a high standard of moral character in the community. No other profession excels the lawyers in breadth of learning and ability. The Nebraska bar has always been an influential factor in the public affairs of our state and nation, and in every walk of life it has made a record in which all of its members may feel a just pride. Gage county and the city of Beatrice are monuments to the courage, daring and prevision of a few lawyers, who, with others, gathered into an association in 1857, on board the old Missouri River steamboat "Hannibal," and resolved to remain together and share their fortunes in the new territory of Nebraska. The senior of these in point of age and experience was John Fitch Kinney, who had already acquired reputation as a politician, law-maker, judge and advocate in the states of Ohio and Iowa, and who was the first president of the Nebraska Association, which became in effect the Beatrice Townsite Company. The secretary of this organization was a young man from the state of New York, just entering upon the practice of the law,—scholarly, courtly John McConihe, whose brilliant career as a lawyer and soldier terminated on the bloody field of Cold Harbor, in 1864. Bennett Pike, a lawyer of rare ability and a man of most affable temperament and great worth of character, was the third of this group of lawyers, who, in a sister state, achieved undying fame in a learned bar in a great city. To these were joined Jefferson B. Weston, who became one of the most distinguished citizens of our State; Obediah B. Hewett, one of the early district attorneys of the old First judicial district of Nebraska and an honored citizen for many years of Nemaha county; and Phineas W. Hitchcock, whose abilities as a lawyer won him senatorial honors in the congress of the United States.

From the first settlement of Gage county, her citizens were largely dependent upon outside counsel for such legal services as were required in those primitive days. Bolinger & Rumbaugh, at Marysville, Kansas, were frequently employed by people of Gage county in handling their affairs. Judge Isham Reavis, the father of Congressman Frank Reavis, was one of the early settlers of Richardson county, and for many years was an active practitioner in the courts of our county, as was also Thomas B. Stevenson, of Nebraska City.

The first resident lawyer of Gage county was Jefferson B. Weston, who was admitted to the bar and authorized to practice his profession about 1862, after having pursued a course of legal studies in Chicago,

Illinois. But Mr. Weston found life on the plains more attractive than life in a law office in a primitive community. For several years he engaged in freighting along the Oregon Trail, and in trade and other business ventures in the far west. It was not until about 1868, when the government land office was removed from Brownville to Beatrice and the country began to fill up rapidly with homeseekers, that Mr. Weston settled down to the practice of his profession. In 1873 he was elected, for a four-year term, to the office of state auditor of Nebraska, and was reelected for two years. On his election he moved to Lincoln, where he resided until 1880, when he returned to Beatrice and engaged in the banking business. After his election to office he abandoned the practice of law altogether.

Perhaps the most picturesque character who ever assumed to practice law in Gage county was "C. B. R. E." This man had been Charles C. Coffinberry. He had reared a family, almost all grown, to each of whom he had given alliterative names. His eldest son was Cyrian C. Coffinberry; his second son, Crosby C. Coffinberry; his third son, Corwin C. Coffinberry; his fourth son was Carter C. Coffinberry; and his handsome and very amiable daughter was Caroline C. Coffinberry, who became the wife of E. B. Hendy, one of the early sheriffs of the county. The head of the family, while a member of the Wisconsin legislature, had procured a legislative enactment authorizing him thereafter to appear as plain Mr. C. C. Berry, but his entire family repudiated this shortening of the family cognomen, and insisted upon being known as Coffinberry. This was the first family to locate on the Big Blue river in Rockford township. In the spring of 1858 they settled on the claim which was afterward the homestead of James Hollingworth, and is now owned by his son Charles, a mile and a half south of Holmesville. The eccentricities of this family were a never failing source of gossip and entertainment to the early settlers. Nothing could better illustrate this characteristic than the performance of the head of the family as a member of the bar in Gage county. As far as the records show, he was the first lawyer admitted to practice in the county, yet his name is not given, only the initials "C. B. R. E." He acted as district attorney during the first term of district court held in the county, appearing for the people in six criminal cases, where in every instance it is gravely written by Judge Dundy "The prosecuting attorney, C. B. R. E., enters a nolle prosequi, by leave of the court first had and obtained." He served repeatedly on election boards, drew money from the county treasury, executed and witnessed instruments by these initials, and even went so far as to sign the bond of County Treasurer Theodore M. Coulter for $10,000, and was sued upon this bond as C. B. R. E., the same having been approved by the county commissioners. For years, as far as the records show, this singular representative of the legal profession of our county marched across the pages of its history as "C. B. R. E."

Salmasius Bardwell Harrington was the first lawyer to open and maintain an office in Beatrice. He was born at Maysville, Chautauqua county, New York, April 16, 1829, the son of Asa and Mary (Swift) Harrington. His primary education was received in a New York Quaker school. His father died while he was a child and his mother became the wife of Parley Laflin. The family removed to Illinois in 1840, residing at first in Kane county and then in Rock Island county. He worked on a farm, attended public school, and finally entered Woodward College, at Cincinnati, Ohio. Later he read law with an uncle, Eben Harrington, and at the age of nineteen, was admitted to the bar, at Rock Island, Illinois. He engaged briefly in the practice of the law there, but his family moved to Nebraska territory in 1857, and he came with them, and located in Johnson county, near Gage, a few miles northwest of Crab Orchard, where his half-brother, Louis Laflin, still resides and where his stepfather and mother died many years ago. In 1859 he followed the gold lure to Pike's Peak, and, returning, established a ranch on the Little Blue river, at the eastern end of the Nine Mile Ridge. Here he remained a year in the midst of the exciting scenes on the Oregon Trail; he then sold his ranch to a man named Ewing and returned to Illinois, to his wife and daughter. In 1861 he enlisted in the Fifty-eighth Illinois Infantry, and he was captured at the battle of Shiloh, while serving in General Prentice's Division. He was held a prisoner in Libby Prison, from which he was finally exchanged and rejoined his regiment, with which he served until Lee surrendered, at Appomattox. In the fall of 1865 he returned to Nebraska territory, made arrangements for his family to join him, and settled at once in the practice of the law at Beatrice. He was not formally admitted to the bar of the territory, however, until the regular fall term of the district court, October 7, 1867, due no doubt to the irregularity of the sessions of the court.

He was an active, aggressive lawyer, affable in manner and made and retained friends. From 1865 until his death, much of the legal business of the county was transacted by him. He died suddenly, in his office in Beatrice, August 25, 1870, and his remains lie in a secluded spot, now almost unidentified, in the Beatrice cemetery. He was a man of many excellent qualities and great worth of character. He died at the age of forty-one years, an age when most men approach the zenith of their powers and usefulness and at a time when the new state of Nebraska contained boundless possibilities for men of his profession.

In the spring of 1869, came Nathan K. Griggs, a young man who had but recently been admitted to the bar in the state of Indiana. In June of that year he opened an office in Beatrice, but as a school teacher he found a more lucrative and a more certain means of sustenance than the law afforded. He was but a beginner in his profession, without means, and litigation was not only scarce in Gage county but was as yet a luxury. He accepted the position of village school-master for the winter of 1867-1868, and thereby did more, perhaps, to ingratiate himself in public favor than by any other course he could possibly have taken. Although a man of many activities and engaging on other occupations, beginning with 1869, Mr. Griggs found ample employment for his abilities as a rising young lawyer.

In the spring of 1868 Hiram P. Webb came to Beatrice and was admitted to practice at the bar, and that spring Jefferson B. Weston also opened a law office in the village of Beatrice. Numbers 8, Vol. I, of the *Blue Valley Record*, under date of August 26, 1868, carried under the heading "Professional" the card of Jefferson B. Weston, who announced himself as a notary public, conveyancer, real-estate agent and lawyer. Another card reads, "S. B. Harrington, Attorney and Counselor at Law and Real Estate Agent," and the third and last is "N. K. Griggs, Attorney and Counselor at law and Real Estate Agent." To these announcements, there was added, in the 22d number of the same volume of the *Courier*, under date of December 5, 1868, the following: "H. P. Webb, Attorney and Counselor at Law." At the same time there appeared in the *Record* the professional card of Stephenson & Hayward, of Nebraska City, who, among other things, announce that they "will practice in the courts of Gage county." Volume 1, No. 1 of the Beatrice *Clarion*, the successor of the *Blue Valley Record*, under date of May 8, 1869, contains the following professional card: "W. H. Ashby, Attorney and Counselor at Law and Real Estate Agent, Beatrice, Nebraska," and the public is informed also that Mr. Ashby will make collections and pay taxes for non-residents, while Stephenson & Hayward continue to announce that they "will practice in the courts of Gage county."

By 1869 this group of pioneer lawyers had found the government land office the chief source of professional business and income, and they became expert in the law and rules of practice regulating contests involving entries of public lands.

About 1870 the Gage county bar, as thus composed, was augmented by the advent of Smith C. B. Dean, and for several years he and the others named, constituted the bar of Gage county. They were all able and scholarly men, all achieved success in their profession, and all, with the exception of Ashby, have long since paid the great debt of nature.

A brief sketch of S. E. Harrington already appears in this chapter, and elsewhere in this volume will be found sketches of Weston and Webb, while in the biographical department, in the sketch of Samuel Rinaker, will be found an extended reference to the life of his partner, N. K. Griggs.

William H. Ashby was for many years a distinguished member of the Gage county bar. He was born in Livingston county, Missouri, in 1841 and grew to manhood in that state. Having obtained a good, usable education, he was on the point of entering upon a professional career when the great Civil war cut short all plans of a purely personal nature. He followed the fortunes of the southern Confederacy, at first attaching himself to the command of General Sterling Price, and took part in the battles of Pea Ridge, Iuka, and Corinth. He served in the armies of the south until the close of the war, was seriously wounded during the siege of Vicksburg, was promoted to a captaincy, and on the collapse of the

Confederacy he was paroled, May 16, 1865. Within that year he came to Nebraska City and engaged in the practice of the law. In 1869 he moved to Beatrice and with J. M. Hoggshead purchased a half-interest in the *Blue Valley Record*, changed the name of the paper to the Beatrice Clarion, and, with Hoggshead, Nelson and Howard, conducted the paper as an independent publication until it was sold to Theodore Coleman, in the spring of 1870, and the name changed to the Beatrice *Express*. For a period of six eventful and busy years Captain Ashby here successfully practised his profession as a lawyer. In June, 1875, he was appointed, by President Grant, a member of the Sioux Indian Commission and spent that summer and fall amongst the Indians of South Dakota. The commission having negotiated with the Sioux a treaty of purchase for the Black Hills region, Captain Ashby was dispatched to Washington as the bearer of its report. In June, 1877, he was sent by our government as its special representative to Panama, the West Indies, and South America, to investigate and report upon certain abuses in the importation of sugar. He was recalled from this service in 1878, and, returning to Beatrice, he resumed the practice of the law. In 1881 he became interested in the rising city of Wymore. With Samuel Wymore he purchased a tract of land adjoining the original townsite and laid it out as an addition to the city. Having sold his Wymore property at good figures he in 1886, returned to Beatrice and again resumed the practice of his profession.

Captain Ashby was thrice married, first to Miss Coila B. Lambkin, of Mississippi, in 1865; second, to Miss Lilla Shaw, July 4, 1879, from both of whom he was divorced. His third marriage proved a happy and congenial one, the issue of which was two sons and a daughter. About 1912 he removed to the state of California, and he is now living in the city of Berkeley, under the shadow of the great State University of California. His two sons are in the service of the United States in the present great world war. Captain Ashby is a man of commanding presence, a good friend, a loyal citizen, and a lawyer of more than ordinary ability.

Smith C. B. Dean was by birth, education and training, a Canadian. Before coming to Nebraska he had already acquired reputation and standing as a lawyer in the courts of Canada. His health failing there, he came to the new territory of Nebraska in the vain hope of eradicating from his system the germs of pulmonary consumption. He was a man of fine presence, possessed an excellent education and was endowed with abilities of a very high order. He was a lawyer of great learning and industry, and the pleadings and other legal documents drawn by him were models of brevity and clearness. He was about forty years of age, and on his arrival in Beatrice he formed a co-partnership in the practice of the law with Jefferson B. Weston, their office being on the ground floor, beneath the United States land office, in the Saunders store building, now No. 309 Court street. Mr. Dean took a deep interest in the general welfare of the community, was very public-spirited, and lent his assistance to the upbuilding of Beatrice and Gage county at a time when such services as he willingly rendered were of the greatest value. He was the first mayor of the city of Beatrice, in 1873, and was a potent factor in shaping its destiny. He acquired great influence in the community, and at the time of his demise his voice carried further than any other in public affairs. He died in Beatrice on the first day of May, 1877.

About 1872 the bar of Gage county received several notable accessions. In April of that year E. Sanborn Chadwick and Alfred Hazlett were both admitted to practice, and in 1873 Leonard W. Colby, Louis B. Sale, and William H. Somers were licensed in the practice of the law and identified themselves with the Gage county bar.

Mr. Chadwick was the first police judge of the city of Beatrice. He remained here but a short time, made but small impression on the community, and left here many years ago, locating in Bloomington, Nebraska, where he was for several years county judge of his county. He died there many years ago.

Mr. Sale had been a classmate of Leonard W. Colby in the University of Wisconsin and they began professional life together here as partners. He remained here but a short time, returning to Wisconsin, where he achieved professional success and where political honors came to him, amongst others, a seat in congress, to which he was repeatedly elected. While still a comparatively young man, he lost his life while bathing on a Wisconsin lake. Seeing his two sons struggling in the water for their lives, he rushed to their rescue and all were drowned.

William H. Somers came to Gage county in 1872 and was for many years a leading citizen of Beatrice, but he achieved no reputation as a lawyer, other things diverting his attention and energies. He served one term in the legislature, as a float representative from Gage and other counties. In 1881 he was appointed receiver of the United States government land office at Beatrice. At the close of his term of office, in 1886, he removed with his family to California and opened a large fruit ranch in El Cajon valley, seventeen miles up the coast from San Diego. Several years ago he disposed of this property and moved to San Diego, where he was killed, about 1908, in a street-car accident.

In 1874 Oliver M. Enlow was admitted to the bar of Gage county and he remained in the practice until his death, in 1916. He did not aspire to great eminence in the legal profession but chose rather, whenever possible, to combine it with some clerical or other occupation. He was for some time clerk of the district court, during the incumbency of Judge Gantt. He was county judge of Gage county for four years, and in the latter part of his life, for a number of years, he was deputy assessor; following the general election of 1911, on the death of A. K. Smith, who had been elected county assessor, Mr. Enlow was appointed to that office, and he was the last of the county assessors. He was a warm-hearted, generous man, much esteemed by all who knew, him.

William M. Forbes was born February 28, 1847, near Greensburg, Indiana. He came to Beatrice in July, 1876, and settled in the practice of the law. He was a graduate of the law department of the Iowa State University, class of 1874, and had been a school teacher in Burlington, Iowa. He served, by appointment, as county judge of Gage county for the unexpired term of J. M. Carter, in 1878, and in 1879 he formed a law partnership with Judge Leander M. Pemberton. After several years successful practice at the bar of Gage county Mr. Forbes removed to Topeka, where he has been a prominent member of the bar of that city. He was possessed of considerable means for a western lawyer and on his arrival in Beatrice he erected an elegant home for those early days, on the corner of Fifth and Lincoln streets, opposite the Episcopal church. He and his wife were active members of the Methodist church and were important factors in the social life of the city in that early day.

Charles O. Bates was a brilliant young man who entered the law office of Colby & Hazlett in 1875; he was admitted to the bar about 1878, and at the same time to an interest in the business of his preceptors. His success as a lawyer and politician was immediate. In 1890 he was elected county attorney of Gage county, but he resigned before the expiration of his term of office and, leaving Beatrice, finally settled, about 1891, in Tacoma, where he now resides and is a prominent member of the bar.

Albert Hardy came to Beatrice in February, 1878, from the state of New York, where he had been for many years engaged in the practice of his profession, at Sandy creek, Oswego county. He was about forty years of age and in his prime. But for some eccentricities of character, he might easily have been the head of the Gage county bar and a successful practitioner of the law. He sometimes tried cases well and often won where he should have failed, and, everything considered, he was fairly successful as a lawyer. With the exception of a year or two in Denver, Mr. Hardy followed his calling in Beatrice from the time of his arrival here until about 1906. He then went to Pierre, South Dakota, to live, and a few years ago he passed away, aged about eighty years.

Andrew J. Hale was for several years a prominent member of the Gage county bar. He was born in Chittenden county, near Burlington, Vermont, March 8, 1842. He received a general education in the common schools of his native state and in Fairfax Institute, at Burlington, where he spent three years as a student. About 1865 he graduated from the law department of Union College (now University), at Albany, New York, and in 1867 be located in Nebraska City in the practice of his profession; in 1876 he came to Beatrice and opened a law office. In the early '80s he was in partnership with Albert Hardy. In 1886, having inherited a considerable fortune, he purchased, amongst other real estate, a half-section of land a few miles southwest of Beatrice, abandoned the practice of the law and engaged in farming and stockraising. This venture proving a failure and having lost most of his property, about 1885, he left the county and returned to Nebraska City, where he died a few years ago.

Thomas Farrar Burke, a young lawyer from New England settled at Blue Springs in 1879. Mr. Burke was the possessor of a good education, was a man of great energy, and rapidly acquired a practice at the bar of Gage county. About 1882 Frank N. Prout came to the county, first to Beatrice and later to Blue Springs, where he formed a law partnership with Mr. Burke. Both were good lawyers, both ambitious and both affable gentlemen. They were prominent at our bar for a number of years and as lawyers performed a real service to the people of the state of Nebraska in the case of the State on the Relation of Mattoon versus The Republican Valley Railroad Company, reported in Volume 17 of the *Nebraska Supreme Court Reports*, at page 647. This was an action in mandamus, brought in the supreme court of Nebraska, to compel the railroad company to build within the corporate limits of Blue Springs a depot and put in the necessary sidetracks and switches for a station, and to stop its trains there for the proper transaction of business. The Crete branch of the railroad line had been extended to Wymore through Blue Springs, but the company refused to afford railroad facilities to Blue Springs, while at the same time affording its rival every possible support. The writ of mandamus was allowed against the defendant and it was compelled to furnish the city of Blue Springs with service, thereby establishing the rule that no common carrier could unjustly discriminate against a municipal corporation in Nebraska.

About twenty years ago Mr. Burke removed from Nebraska to Wyoming and located at Cheyenne, where he has attained both professional success and distinguished honors as a lawyer, having served the state of Wyoming for several years as its attorney general, and for many years has served as a member of the board of regents for the Wyoming State University.

Mr. Prout removed to Beatrice after the dissolution of the copartnership and was for a number of years city attorney; in 1898 he was elected to the state senate, from Gage county. In 1900 he was elected attorney general of the state of Nebraska and, by a reelection, he served the people in the important office four years, beginning January 1, 1901.

Since retiring from office he has practised law in Oklahoma City, Oklahoma, and in Fairbury and Humboldt, Nebraska, and has finally located permanently in Falls City, in the practice of his profession.

Nathan T. Gadd came to Gage county about 1880, and located in the practice of the law at Liberty. Mr. Gadd was an active and very useful man in his community. For several years he was an important factor not only in Liberty but in the county of Gage, and from a mere youthful beginner in the law he grew into an important and lucrative practice. When the great northwest was being rapidly settled and the Burlington Railroad was pushing a line across northern Nebraska and through to the Puget Sound country, he went to Broken Bow, in Custer county, Nebraska, where he became active in the practice of his profession. Mr. Gadd is an impulsive, warm-hearted, courtly gentleman, much esteemed by his professional brethren and given to many kindly, generous acts.

William H. Richards was admitted to the bar of Gage county about 1895. He was a man of limited education but proved to be a very good business lawyer. He is a member of a pioneer family in Pawnee county, his parents having located at the head of Turkey creek, in that county, in 1859. They were people of sterling worth of character and Mr. Richards inherited from them many of the family characteristics. From the time of his admission to the bar until he left Gage county he practised his profession at Liberty, while at the same time engaging in other pursuits. About 1908 he left the county and located at Humboldt, in the practice of the law, and later he removed to Wichita, Kansas.

W. V. A. Dodds was admitted to the Gage county bar in 1885; his practice however was very limited, as he gave his attention largely to outside matters. For several years he conducted a large farm in Gage county and later he went to Montana, where he is now located in business.

George M. Johnston came to Beatrice about 1890. He erected a paper mill near the city, placed a dam across the Big Blue river and proceeded to build up a business as a paper manufacturer. But a flood, in 1902, destroyed the water power, and the enterprise was abandoned. Mr. Johnston then engaged in the practice of the law, having been previously admitted to the bar in the state of Illinois. He was successful in his professional work and was an active member of the bar of Gage county for several years. Later he went to Missouri, where he engaged in various enterprises, and he died about 1912.

Menzo Terry, a farmer near Pickrell, who had been previously admitted to the bar, was elected county attorney, on the Democratic ticket, in 1905 and served one term in that office, during which time and for a year or two afterward he was in partnership with Fred O. McGirr. In 1910 he left this state and he is now located on a fruit farm in southern California.

Robert S. Bibb came from the Peoria, Illinois, bar to the Gage county bar in 1884. Mr. Bibb had been a member of the Illinois legislature and a practicing attorney at Peoria. Shortly after his arrival here he formed a co-partnership with A. Dodds, in the practice of the law, and about 1890 he entered the firm of Griggs & Rinaker, which was thereafter known as Griggs, Rinaker & Bibb. On the removal of Mr. Griggs to Lincoln, in 1893, the firm name was changed to Rinaker & Bibb. This firm did a large and very successful legal business until Mr. Bibb's death, which occurred May 17, 1907. Mr. Bibb was the first county attorney of Gage county, having been elected to that office in 1885. He was very prominent in the business, professional and social life of Beatrice during his entire residence here. He was an unusually good lawyer, one of the ablest trial lawyers the bar of Gage county has ever produced. Personally he was genial, kindly and considerate. He was popular with the court and with his professional associates. His final resting place is in Evergreen Home cemetery, and the spot is marked by a rugged monument which, in a sense, is indicative of his character.

George Arthur Murphy came to Beatrice from Indiana about the year 1886, and engaged at once in the practice of his profession. His success was immediate, and while he lived here he had a large and paying clientage. In 1891 he was elected county attorney of Gage county, and he was reelected in 1893. In 1898 he was elected state senator from Gage county. In 1901 Mr. Murphy removed to the state of Oklahoma and located at Muscogee, where he has since resided. He has been successful in his profession and has acquired wealth.

W. C. LeHane came to Gage county about the year 1890 and for a while was a law partner of George Arthur Murphy. In 1896 he was appointed receiver of the Beatrice Savings Bank, and his duties as receiver absorbed his time to such an extent that he practically abandoned the practice of the law. He so managed the affairs of the bank as to pay ninety cents on the dollar of its indebtedness. After the adjustment of the receivership, Mr. LeHane went to Idaho, where for a time he engaged in the practice of his profession at Boise City. Later he removed to California, and he is now living near San Francisco, in the Sacramento valley.

Charles E. Bush is a son of Judge James E. Bush. He is a graduate of the Beatrice high school, studied law in his father's office and was admitted to the bar of Gage county about the year 1891. He later removed to Oklahoma and for several years he has been located in the successful practice of the law at Tulsa, that state.

Jean Cobbey, a son of Judge J. E. Cobbey, was born in Gage county, graduated from the Beatrice high school, attended the State University of Nebraska and took a course in the law and was admitted to the bar. He began the practice of his profession in Beatrice in 1911 and in 1912 was elected county attorney of Gage county. He was defeated for reelection in 1914 and shortly thereafter removed to Nebraska City. Later he sought service in the army on the Mexican border, and when our government entered the world war, in April, 1917, he was serving as chaplain of his regiment, but he recently resigned and is now with the colors in France.

Philip E. was one of the early lawyers of Wymore. For a number of years he was successfully engaged in the practice of his profession there with E. N. Kauffman, his brother-in-law. He later removed to Omaha, where for several years he was an active member of the bar. He then located in Oklahoma City, Oklahoma, and is now a prominent member of the bar at that place.

Thomas D. Cobbey located in Beatrice in the practice of his profession in 1882. Shortly thereafter he moved to Wymore and he was actively engaged in the practice of the law there for a number of years, successfully transacting a large volume of legal business. Several years ago he moved to Denver, Colorado, and he is now one of the successful and wealthy lawyers of that city.

James A. Smith came from Iowa City to Beatrice in 1879. He was born at Geneva, Illinois, November 22, 1844. On the breaking out of the Civil war he enlisted in the First Missouri Cavalry, at St. Louis, in September, 1861. He was wounded in the battle of Sugar Creek, Arkansas, February 19, 1862, lost his right arm at the shoulder and a finger of his left hand, and was discharged September 22, 1862. He read law in the office of Governor Kirkwood of Iowa and married Calista Saunders, of Iowa City, November 23, 1868. Shortly after coming to Beatrice he was elected police judge of the city, an office which he held for several years. He died in Beatrice many years ago and his remains are buried in Evergreen Home cemetery.

John N. Richards was born in Adams county, Ohio, February 22, 1850. In 1856 he went to LaSalle county, Illinois, and in that state as a youth he engaged in farming. Having obtained a common-school education, he spent some time in the Wesleyan University at Bloomington, Illinois. He came to Nebraska in 1874 and located at Falls City, where he was principal of the city schools. He removed to Beatrice in 1877 and entered upon the practice of the law, in which he was fairly successful. He left Beatrice several years ago, and is now located at Colorado City, Colorado.

Albert H. Babcock was born at Bath, Stenben county, New York, in 1846, and when quite young was taken by his parents to Michigan, where he lived until he came to Nebraska. He learned the trade of a blacksmith and was a successful artisan. In August, 1862, he enlisted in Company H, Eighteenth Michigan Volunteer Infantry, and he was afterward promoted to the captaincy of Company E of that regiment. He continued in the service until July, 1865, having been in all the battles and marches of his command. He graduated from the law department of the Michigan University with the class of 1868, and located at Pawnee City, Nebraska, in the practice of the law, in October, 1869. There he achieved a great measure of success in his profession. In February, 1880, he moved to Beatrice and opened a law office, and for many years he was prominent in the litigation of Gage county. He was a member of the Nebraska legislature in 1873-1874, and he served both Pawnee City and Beatrice as city attorney. In 1891 he was elected district judge of the First judicial district, and served four years; he was again elected in 1903, and he served until his death, which occurred in 1907. His remains lie in Evergreen Home cemetery. As a lawyer Judge Babcock was an able counselor, careful and systematic in all he did; as a judge he upheld the best traditions of the bench, and as a man he led a blameless life in the sight of God and of all men.

James E. Bush was born in Rockville, Indiana, June 1, 1845, living there and in Kentucky until he was three years old. While he was still an infant his father died, in the Mexican war; his mother dying shortly afterward, he began life as an orphan. His elder brothers and sisters held the family together, moved from Kentucky to Peoria, Illinois, where they lived five years, and thence to Wyoming, Stark county, Illinois, in the spring of 1853. On August 12, 1862, he enlisted in the service of the United States, in the One Hundred and Twelfth Regiment of Illinois Volunteer Infantry, and he served until the close of the war. He was mustered out of the service in Chicago, in July, 1865, and returned to Wyoming, Illinois. He began the study of law in 1872, in the office of Miles A. Fuller, of Toulon, Illinois, and, having passed a satisfactory examination in the supreme court of that state, he was admitted to the bar June 5, 1875. He began the practice of his profession at Bradford, Stark county, Illinois. On May 6, 1880, he came to Beatrice and associated himself with John N. Richards. When this partnership was dissolved, in 1884, he formed a partnership with Leander M. Pemberton. In 1891, with Judge Babcock, he was elected to the district bench in the old First judicial district, and he served four years. He was defeated for reelection in 1895, and died in Beatrice on the 14th day of April, 1900. His remains lie in Beatrice cemetery and those of his beloved wife were, in September, 1917, laid by his side. Their resting place is marked by a tasteful monument.

Joseph Elliott Cobbey was born in the state of Missouri, in 1853, and when a child was taken by his parents to Benton county, Iowa, where he grew to manhood. He obtained a good education in the common schools of Iowa and at the State Agricultural College, situated in the little city of Ames. While still a very young man he entered the college of law in the University of Iowa, from which institution he graduated with honor in 1877, and he came almost immediately to Beatrice. He was employed for a while in the county treasurer's office, by his uncle, Hiram P. Webb, also in the bank of Hiram P. Webb & Company. In 1878 he began the active practice of his profession and he continued therein until his death, on the 22d day of August, 1911. He soon achieved a commanding position at the bar of his county and state, and for thirty-four years this quiet, unassuming, pioneer lawyer carried on an extended and diversified practice in the courts of this state and the federal courts.

He was prominent in city and county affairs and in the Republican party, to which he belonged. In 1879 he was elected to the office of county judge, and served two years. He was defeated for renomination by his party, and again engaged in the active practice of the law. During his professional career he served the city of Beatrice one term of two years as city attorney and was four years a member of the common council of this city. Wherever placed and whatever he did, his life and labors were characterized by the utmost fidelity of purpose and he became one of the most useful and respected citizens of our county.

In 1889 Judge Cobbey turned in a measure from the practical side of his profession and sought wealth and honor by digging about the roots and strengthening the foundations of the law itself. In 1890 he published a text book on the "Law of Replevin"; he revised it in 1893, and it is everywhere in this country regarded by the courts and the legal profession as standard authority upon that subject. Later appeared his textbook on the "Law of Chattel Mortgages," in two large volumes, equal, at least, in authority to any other American textbook on that subject. In 1901 Judge Cobbey turned his attention to the business of statute-making, and that year appeared "Cobbey's Annotated Code of Nebraska." These well known contributions to the law of the land are alone sufficient to constitute an enduring monument to his memory.

In the year 1891 Judge Cobbey was employed by the legislature of Nebraska to compile and publish the statutes of the state, and that body appropriated the sum of twelve thousand dollars to assist him in the work. This is known as the "Consolidated Statutes of Nebraska for 1891." It was followed by the "Consolidated Statutes of 1893." Both editions were annotated, and both appeared under legislative sanction as the authorized statutes of the state. These were followed by similar statutes for the years 1905, 1907, 1909, 1911. The last work came from the press only a few days prior to his death. "Cobbey's Statutes for 1911" was monumental in character. It is as nearly perfect, probably, as any work of that kind could be. In addition to his indefatigable labors as annotator and publisher of the Nebraska statutes, Judge Cobbey was employed by the legislature of New Mexico, a couple of years prior to his death, to codify the laws of that new state, and he spent nearly a year in that important, and to him agreeable, task, in the old city of Santa Fe. From this brief sketch of his life, it is evident that no other Nebraska lawyer has succeeded so completely in embedding his name in the legal history and legal literature of his state and nation.

The present bar of Gage county is composed of Wilber S. Bourne; Charles L. Brewster, now serving his country as a captain in France, in the great world war; Leonard W. Colby; Frank E. Crawford, now also a captain serving his country in France; Lloyd Crocker; Hugh J. Dobbs; John W. Delehant, now in training in an officers' camp, awaiting the call for his services under his country's flag; Alfred Hazlett; Fulton Jack; Edward N. Kauffman; Albertus H. Kidd; Samuel D. Killen; Ernest O. Kretsinger and his son, Ernest Kretsinger; Frederick W. Messmore; Adam McMullen; Leander M. Pemberton; Samuel Rinaker; Robert W. Sabin; Harry E. Sackett; Franklin D. Sheldon; Walter A. Vasey; and Herbert D. Walden. Biographical sketches appear in this volume of most of the lawyers here named.

In point of ability, integrity, learning and worth of character the bar of Gage county has always compared most favorably with that of other counties of the state. From its ranks have come judges, legislators, authors, soldiers, diplomats. Not greedy of wealth and avaricious only of honor and the opportunity of service, the lawyers of our county have steadily maintained the best traditions of this noble and learned profession.

CHAPTER XXXI

People Who Have Done Their Part in Making Gage County (Part I)

DANIEL W. COOK.—Daniel Wolford Cook lives now only in the memory of those who knew and loved him. Though passed to that bourne from which no traveler has ever yet returned, his abilities and worth of character were such as to entitle him to a place in any history of Gage county or the state of Nebraska. During a long residence in the city of Beatrice he was a potent factor in its development and in its social and business activities, and at the moment of his demise he was one of its best known and most highly respected citizens. He responded to the summons of the death angel while yet in love with life—ere he had reached the zenith of his powers and usefulness and at a period of his career when the public was turning toward him more kindly and appreciatively than ever before; when his own nature was responding more fully than ever to the social demands of the community upon him as one of its leading citizens. After an illness of more than a year, the serious nature of which he understood, and having calmly and bravely awaited the end, on Saturday, the 4th day of March, 1916, at his home on North Seventh Street, Beatrice, he passed to that house not made with hands, eternal in the heavens. All that was mortal of this good and true man now rests in his tomb in Evergreen Home cemetery, near the city he loved and where so many of his happiest years were spent.

Mr. Cook was born on the 27th day of March, 1860, in the little city of Hillsdale, state of Michigan, and at the time of his death he lacked but a few days of being fifty-six years of age, an age when most men are still in their prime. He was the son of John P. Cook and Martha Wolford, and was one of ten children born to that husband and wife, six sons and four daughters. They were John P. Cook. Lewis Cass Cook, Chauncey

F., William Wilson, Catherine, Anna, Daniel Wolford, Franklin M., Caroline and Belle Cook, of whom four are still living. They are Chauncey F. and Franklin M. Cook, of Hillsdale, William Wilson Cook, of New York city, and the youngest sister, Mrs. Belle Funkhouser, of Chicago, Illinois. In addition to this family, there were five children of the half blood, born to his father John P. Cook and Betsy Wolford. Their names were Amanda, Julia, Charles H., Martha A., and Mary Cook, and none of them is now living.

Mr. Cook obtained an elementary education in the public schools of his native city and at an early age entered the well known Baptist College at Hillsdale. Later he was a student for some time in the University of Michigan, located in the city of Ann Arbor. Without graduating at either of these institutions, he obtained a good usable education and never found himself at a disadvantage when brought into contact with people of learning and refinement.

While attending Hillsdale College Mr. Cook became acquainted with Miss Elizabeth Case, who also was a student at that institution, and in the delightful intimacy of college life a friendship was formed between them which soon ripened into romantic love, the purest of all the passions of the heart, and on the 22d day of December, 1883, they were united in marriage. The conjugal felicity of this union was never doubted by those with whom this husband and wife came in contact. It was broken only by the hand of death. Four children came to bless this union and cement the marital bond, of whom three survive. They are Daniel Cook, cashier of the Beatrice National Bank; Mary E. Ramsey, the wife of Mr. William C. Ramsey, a promising young lawyer of Omaha; and John Bradford Cook, but recently graduated from the University of Nebraska and now engaged in the banking business in the thriving western town of Scotts Bluffs, Nebraska. William W. Cook, the second and much loved son, at the age of eighteen years, was drowned while bathing in the Big Blue river, on the 27th day of August, 1905.

For many years prior to his death, Mr. and Mrs. Cook owned and occupied a beautiful home at the corner of Seventh and Summit Streets, Beatrice, erected by them in 1884. Here thirty-two years of their married life were spent together; here their children were born; and from its portals a well beloved son and husband were borne to the grave and an only and much loved daughter departed a bride. Cold indeed must be the heart that can withhold its sympathy from her to whom this spot is hallowed by so many sacred memories.

No one was less inclined to speak of himself or his family than Daniel Wolford Cook. His most intimate friends rarely heard him mention his ancestry or speak of his family beyond his immediate home circle. His reticence in this respect was the more remarkable since there is much in his family genealogy of which he was, no doubt, justly proud. His reticence on this subject was probably due to a natural reserve of character which ran through his entire life, and to a fine sensitiveness concerning his personal matters.

Mr. Cook's parents were both born and reared in the town of Cato, Cayuga county, New York. His father was born in 1812, amidst the stirring scenes of our second war with England. Early in life he married Betsy Wolford, and at the age of twenty he migrated to the new Territory of Michigan, locating first at Detroit. In 1833, about four years prior to the time Michigan was admitted into the union of sovereign states, he removed to Hillsdale county and settled in the village of Hillsdale, where he resided until his death, in 1884, at the age of seventy-two years. His first wife having died about the year 1850, leaving him with a family of five young children, he in 1854, married Martha A. Wolford, her younger sister. In his early years he was a wonderfully active and a very useful man. Shortly after his arrival in Michigan, he formed the acquaintance of General Lewis Cass, and for many years he was an intimate friend of that distinguished soldier, statesman and diplomat. He was intimately connected, almost from the first, with the social, intellectual, political, and business interests of his section of country. He was the first postmaster at Hillsdale, serving his community in that capacity for a number of years; he was one of the trustees of the state hospital at Kalamazoo, and for a long time a trustee of Hillsdale College, president of the town board of Hillsdale, and discharged the duties of other local officers. He was a delegate to two constitutional conventions of his state, twice a member of the house of representatives, and thrice a member of the state senate of Michigan. He was an exceptionally good business man and by fortunate investments in Michigan timbered lands he had amassed a fortune, which at his death amounted to nearly half a million dollars.

On his father's side, Daniel Wolford Cook was descended in a direct line from William Bradford, who came over with the "Pilgrim Fathers" in the Mayflower, in 1620, and who for thirty years was governor of Plymouth Colony. A certain Captain David Cook became the husband of Mary Bradford in the early part of the eighteenth century, who in a direct line was the great-great-granddaughter of the Puritan governor. This Captain Cook fought with distinction in the war of the Revolution, from its beginning, in 1776, to its close, in 1783. From him was descended John P. Cook, the father of Daniel Wolford Cook. On his mother's side Mr. Cook was descended from Holland and French stock, his maternal grandfather being a Hollander and his maternal grandmother, a La Rue, French. Martha A. Cook, the mother of Daniel Wolford Cook, reached the bounds of this mortal life in 1909, the object of the solicitude and affection of a host of relatives and friends. Now all that is mortal of these Michigan pioneers lies in the Hillsdale cemetery, where after having answered the call of the angel of death, they await the trump of the angel of the resurrection.

Shortly after leaving the University of Michigan, in 1879, Mr. Cook, at the age of nineteen years, engaged in the wholesale and retail lumber trade in Michigan City, Indiana, at the foot of Lake Michigan. His business was operated in connection with his father's lumber manufacturing plant at White Lake, Michigan, and in carrying it on, he was associated with his cousin, W. C. Wilson, now president of the Bankers Life Insurance Company of Lincoln, Nebraska. After several years' successful business, he sold his interest in the lumber trade at Michigan City to his partner, and in 1884 he came to Nebraska to seek fortune, happiness, and success in this new state.

Having, through the mediation of his brother-in-law, the late Nathan S. Harwood, and the late Jefferson B. Weston, purchased a controlling interest in the Gage County Bank, Mr. Cook moved his family to Beatrice in February, 1884. With Harwood, Weston, and others, he reorganized the bank into a national bank, with a capital of fifty thousand dollars, to be thenceforth known as the Beatrice National Bank, a title still worn by this well known banking institution. The first board of directors of the bank were Harwood, Cook, Cyrus Alden, Nathan Blakely, Silas P. Wheeler and William Lamb, of which Mr. Weston was president and Mr. Cook vice-president. All these gentlemen, well known in the early days, have passed away, Mr. Cook being the last survivor of this board of directors. Mr. Weston served as president of the board until his death, in September, 1905, and thereafter until his demise Mr. Cook was president of the board.

Beginning at a time when Gage county was just emerging from its pioneer days, when things were new and fresh within its boundaries, when Beatrice had but recently been advanced from a mere western village to a city under the law of less than five thousand population, the steady growth of the Beatrice National Bank under Mr. Cook's management is in a sense, typical of the growth of both the city and county. The first statement by the board of directors after he took control of the affairs of the bank, under date of September 30, 1884, showed a total volume of business amounting to the sum of $124,755.37, of which $61,235.86 were deposits. The statement of the bank issued March 7, 1916, a few days after Mr. Cook's death, showed a volume of business amounting to the sum of $1,255,020.24, of which sum $988,917.49 were deposits. Assuming the management of this bank at a time when he was not yet twenty-four years of age, the unusual abilities possessed by Mr. Cook as a business man and banker are demonstrated by the steady and rapid growth of this splendid banking enterprise. While he held its destiny in his hands not a penny of its depositors' money was lost or even jeopardized by unwise banking methods.

In the everyday affairs of the community Mr. Cook acted the part of a wise and helpful banker, readily assisting the deserving in every safe business enterprise when money was needed. He had the faculty of divining character in his customers and he was never known to err seriously in his judgment of men. He was particularly generous and helpful both in monetary affairs and in advice to young men just entering a business career and he was apt to place greater reliance upon individual honesty, when coupled with ability and energy, than upon any sort of collateral. His liberal assistance to deserving customers of his bank, his habit of taking a kind and helpful interest in their affairs and his clear, comprehensive, deliberate way of looking at things, made him one of the most all-round useful citizens of his community.

He was a man of teeming activities. In addition to the personal management of his bank he devoted considerable time to farming and the breeding and sale of live stock, and he was never happier than when going over his farm, near the village of Ellis, with some sympathetic friend. In 1891 he was induced to invest a considerable sum of money in the capital stock of the Bankers Life Insurance Company of Lincoln, Nebraska. Associated with him in this enterprise were Nathan S. Harwood, John M. Thurston, Thomas Kimball (then vice-president of the Union Pacific Railway Company), William R. Kelly, J. E. Houtz, Charles Boggs (of Lincoln), Michael Wolbach (of Beatrice), his brother, Franklin M. Cook, and his cousin, W. C. Wilson. At the time Mr. Cook became interested in this company its capital stock was $100,000, its assets $127,000. He afterward acquired the stock of his brother in this institution, and at the time of his death he was its second largest stockholder, its president, W. C. Wilson, being the largest. This company has prospered amazingly. Its capital stock still remains at $100,000, but its business has increased by leaps and bounds, until at the present moment its assets amount to $13,000,000. During his entire connection with this company Mr. Cook occupied the position of vice-president, and he was also an influential member of the finance committee. In 1911, the company erected a substantial five-story, modern building at the corner of Fourteenth and M streets, Lincoln, at a cost of $300,000, where its offices are now located.

Though never seeking any sort of lucrative office for himself, Mr. Cook always manifested a deep and an intelligent interest in public affairs. He was active in all matters relating to the welfare of his city, and in the political movements of his county and state. For many years he affiliated with the Democratic party and he was twice a delegate to the national convention of that great party. Growing dissatisfied with its attitude on the question of the coinage of silver by the federal government, as set forth in its platform of 1896, he openly withdrew from it and became an active and useful member of the Republican party. This affiliation he maintained with unswerving loyalty to the last. He was eminent in its counsels and influential in shaping its policies both at home and abroad.

From this resumé it is clear that Mr. Cook's mind was turned almost wholly to the practical side of life. He was a man of affairs, keen, active, decisive. He was broad in conception, sound in judgment, and endowed with masterful powers in organizing and conducting business affairs. For thirty years he devoted his time, energy, and splendid abilities largely to laying the foundation for his own fortune and the fortunes of his business associates. Success in his several undertakings being finally assured, he extended his interest, energies, and activities to the upbuilding of the entire community. For several years prior to his demise he served faithfully and efficiently as a member of the board of public parks for the city of Beatrice. He also took a deep and friendly interest in the Young Men's Christian Association of Beatrice, and it was largely through his efforts, enterprise, enthusiasm, and love of clean, wholesome sports that the Beatrice school district now owns what is probably the finest athletic park in the west. He passed away at the moment of his greatest usefulness, when he could have been least spared and at a time when he was rapidly winning the public appreciation which always attends unselfish efforts of a high order for the upbuilding of a community.

Mr. Cook, though not directly affiliated with any religious organization at the time of his death, was never indifferent to the claims of religion or the value of Christian character. He believed in Almighty God and in an overruling providence in the affairs of men. Himself candid and direct, he despised indirection and hypocracy in others. He was an entertaining conversationalist and was well informed as respects the leading events of our country's history, the lives and characters of the public men of our day as well as the past. He delighted in clean, pointed anecdotes, and a visit with him in his private office was always a thing to be remembered. Though sometimes abrupt in manner and outspoken, at bottom he was one of the kindest and most generous of men. Though never very demonstrative, he was capable of great depth of feeling. He rarely spoke of the death of his son William without emotion and never recovered from this wound to his affections. He loved the society of men and men were fond of him. He prized his friends as few men ever did, and once his friendship was given it was never lightly withdrawn. It is hard to reflect that the grave—the silent, remorseless grave—has closed forever over the assemblage of manly qualities embodied in Daniel Wolford Cook.

THOMAS YULE.—It was within the province of the late Thomas Yule, who served one term as mayor of Beatrice, one term as city treasurer and three terms as a member of the county board of supervisors, to have wielded a large and beneficent influence in the civic, industrial, and business affairs of Gage county, and he was exponent of that high type of manhood which ever stands indicative of usefulness and subjective honor. He impressed his strong individuality deeply upon the history of Gage county, within whose gracious borders he maintained his home for nearly thirty years prior to his death, and in a publication of the functions assigned to the one at hand it is eminently consonant that a tribute be paid to his memory and recognition be accorded to him as having been one of the essentially representative men of this favored county. His character was the positive expression of a noble and loyal nature and his genial and kindly personality gained and retained to him the high regard of all with whom he came in contact.

Mr. Yule was born in Northumberland county, England, on the 20th of October, 1832, and his death occurred at his home in Beatrice, Nebraska, on the 21st of June, 1907. He was a son of George and Elizabeth (Huggett) Yule, his father having been a civil engineer by profession and having for some time held a responsible position with the London & Northeastern Railway Company. Thomas Yule received excellent educational advantages in his native land and there continued to reside until 1853, when, accompanied by his parents and his young wife, he came to the United States, the family home being established in Columbia county, Wisconsin, where the father and son became pioneer exponents of agricultural industry. The honored father died in 1871, at the age of sixty-seven years, and his wife survived him by six years, she having been seventy-three years of age at the time of her demise. Four of their six children attained to maturity and became well established in life before the death of the parents.

On the 15th of March, 1853, was solemnized the marriage of Thomas Yule to Miss Mary Todd, who likewise was born in Northumberlandshire, a daughter of John and Mary Todd. The voyage to America on a sailing vessel of the type common to that day virtually constituted the bridal tour of the young couple, and after having been for some time associated with his father in farm enterprise in Columbia county, Wisconsin, Thomas Yule removed with his wife to the village of Lodi, that county, where he was engaged in contracting and building at the time of the inception of the Civil war. His loyalty to the land of his adoption soon found significant exposition, for on the 15th of August, 1862, he enlisted as a private in the Twenty-third Wisconsin Volunteer Infantry, with which he entered service in the Army of the West, under General A. J. Smith, and in the Fourteenth Army Corps, commanded by General Sherman. Relative to the gallant military career of Mr. Yule the following interesting record has been given: "Mr. Yule, with his comrades, in active campaign service, traveled through Kentucky, Mississippi, Tennessee, and Arkansas, and with his command participated in the first battle of Vicksburg, in the summer of 1862. He continued to take part in the various engagements in which his regiment was involved until the 11th of January, 1863, when, in the engagement at Arkansas Post, he received a wound which resulted in the loss of his right leg. The grievously wounded man was removed to the Lawson hospital, in the city of St. Louis, Missouri, where he remained until the following March, when he was honorably discharged and returned to his home, at Lodi, Wisconsin. Afterward, in recognition of his service as a soldier and the sacrifice which he had made in the cause of the Union, Mr. Yule was appointed provost marshal for his Wisconsin district. He was elected also to the offices of justice of the peace and township treasurer, both of which he retained until 1867, when he was elected register of deeds of Columbia county, an office of which he continued the incumbent eight successive years." It may further be said that in later years Mr. Yule vitalized the memories and association of his military career as a soldier of the Union by maintaining active affiliation with the Grand Army of the Republic, in which great patriotic organization he was one of the most popular and influential members of Rawlins Post, at Beatrice, Nebraska, in which he passed the various official chairs and with which he continued to be actively identified until the close of his life.

Mr. Yule never permitted himself to view his physical infirmity as a definite handicap, and it is certain that it did not interfere with his productive usefulness and service. After his retirement from the office of register of deeds for Columbia county, Wisconsin, he continued to be there associated with Miles T. Alverson in the abstract and loan business until April, 1879. He then sold his interest in the business and came with his family to Beatrice, Nebraska, where he engaged in the loaning of money on real-estate security and where he forthwith put his previous experience to effective use by turning his attention to the preparation of a set of abstracts of realty titles from the original records of the county. In this commendable and important work he had as his efficient coadjutor his son John T., and they continued to be actively associated in the conducting of the well ordered abstract business until his death, since which time the son has individually continued the enterprise, as noted in the review of his career, on other pages of this volume.

Mr. Yule entered most heartily and helpfully into the communal life of Beatrice and Gage county and his ability and sterling integrity marked him as specially eligible for service in offices of local trust. It has already been noted in this memoir that he served one term as mayor of Beatrice, a position in which he gave most progressive and efficient administration, and that he held for one term the office of city treasurer. In the late '80s he was elected representative of Beatrice township on the county board of supervisors, in which office he served three consecutive terms, during the last two of which he was chairman of the board. He was one of those interested in the establishing of the canning factory at Beatrice and became a member of the board of directors of the company operating the same, besides which he was a director of the Beatrice Street Railway Company. In politics Mr. Yule, with consummate strength of conviction, never wavered in his allegiance to the Republican party and he gave in a local way yeoman service in behalf of its cause. He became affiliated with the Masonic fraternity in 1858 and was actively identified with the various Masonic bodies in Beatrice at the time of his death.

The wife of the young manhood of Mr. Yule continued as his gracious and loved companion and helpmeet until she was summoned to eternal rest, her death having occurred April 11, 1881. They became the parents of four children, concerning whom the following brief data are available: Bessie J. became the wife of Louis E. Walker and is now deceased; John T. is individually mentioned on other pages of this publication; Albert G. was a boy at the time of his death, in 1866; and Mary Grace, who completed her education by attending Brownell Hall, in the city of Omaha, is now the wife of John Gray, living in Los Angeles, California.

In 1884 Mr. Yule contracted a second marriage, when Miss Mary H. Burke became his wife. She was born in the Dominion of Canada, but was a resident of Beatrice at the time of her marriage. No children were born of this union and Mrs. Yule survived her husband, she being now a resident of Los Angeles, California.

CLARENCE W. GRAFF.—The vice-president of the representative mercantile corporation conducting business in the city of Beatrice under the title of The John H. von Steen Company, is recognized as one of the vital and representative business men of the younger generation in his native county and is further entitled to recognition by reason of being a scion of one of the well known and honored pioneer families of the county, within whose limits his paternal grandfather, Joseph Graff, established his residence at an early period in the history of development in Nebraska. Joseph Graff became one of the pioneer exponents of agricultural and live-stock industry in Gage county and here he and his wife passed the remainder of their lives. On the old homestead farm was born Henry Graff, father of him whose name initiates this paragraph, and he was reared under the conditions and influences of the pioneer days an environment that made for the development of self-reliance, ambition, and appreciation of the true values in the scheme of human thought and action. Henry Graff received the advantages of the common schools of the locality and period and after having achieved independent success through his association with agricultural industry he was for a long term of years engaged in the agricultural implement business in the fine little town of Wymore, this county. He developed a large and prosperous enterprise in this line and continued his activities in the same until his death, in 1907. He was influential in civic affairs in his community, was a stalwart supporter of the cause of the Republican party, and though not ambitious for public office he showed his loyalty by consenting to become the candidate of his party for the office of treasurer of the city of Wymore, his service in this capacity continuing for one term. He was a communicant of the Protestant Episcopal church, as is also his widow, who still maintains her home at Wymore. Of the two children, Clarence W., immediate subject of this sketch, is the elder, and the younger, Hazel, remains with her widowed mother. Mrs. Susan (Myers) Graff, widow of Henry Graff, was born in the state of Wisconsin and accompanied her parents on their removal to Gage county, Nebraska, where her marriage to Mr. Graff was later solemnized and where she has since maintained her home, her gracious personality having won to her a specially wide circle of friends. Her father, the late Valentine Myers, likewise was one of the pioneers of this county, and became one of its substantial farmers and highly esteemed citizens.

Clarence W. Graff continued his studies in the public schools until he had completed the curriculum of the high school at Wymore, his birth having occurred in the village of Blue Springs, this county, on the 8th of October, 1889. In further preparation for the active responsibilities of life he took an effective course in the business college at Beatrice. For five months thereafter he held a clerical position in a telegraph office in this city, and he then became associated with the John H. von Steen Company, in which he is now one of the interested principals and of which he has been the vice-president since 1917. His popularity in his native county is on a parity with his recognized ability and progressiveness as a business man and he takes most loyal interest in all things touching the civic and material welfare of his home city and county. His political allegiance is given to the Republican party and he is affiliated with Beatrice Lodge, No. 619, Benevolent & Protective Order of Elks.

April 25, 1917, recorded the marriage of Mr. Graff to Miss Augusta R. Kilpatrick, daughter of Joseph M. Kilpatrick, of Beatrice, Nebraska, and they are popular factors in the representative social life of the Gage county metropolis. They hold membership in the parish of Christ Church, Protestant Episcopal, of which both are communicants.

C. C. JOHNSON, who is now living retired in the village of Filley, has proved himself a man of might, like Tubal Cain of old, and for many years he followed the sturdy trade of blacksmith, through the medium of which he achieved the prosperity that enables him to pass the gracious evening of his life in well earned peace and comfort.

Mr. Johnson was born in Denmark, on the 26th of February, 1844, and is a son of John Christ and Anna Christina (Christiansen) Anderson, the latter of whom passed her entire life in Denmark and the former of whom came to the United States in 1884, settling first in Illinois, but a few months later coming to Nebraska, where he passed the remainder of his life. Of the ten children only two are now living, the subject of this review being the elder and Nels being a resident of the city of Chicago. The father was a blacksmith by trade and after coming to the United States he lived retired until his death, the closing period of his life having been passed in the home of his son C. C., subject of this sketch. Both he and his wife were earnest communicants of the Danish Lutheran church.

C. C. Johnson acquired his early education in his native land and there learned the trade of blacksmith under the effective direction of his father. He was twenty-eight years of age when he came to the United States and established his residence in the city of Kankakee, Illinois, where he was employed three years in one blacksmith shop. He continued to follow his trade in that state for seven years and then, in 1879, he came to Gage county, Nebraska, where he opened a little blacksmith shop four miles north of the present village of Filley. When this village was platted he here established its first blacksmith shop, and he was not only the first citizen to erect a house in the village but also the first to buy a lot in the newly established cemetery, in which the remains of his stepmother were the first interred. He continued actively and successfully in the work of his trade, with a large and representative patronage, until 1902, since which time he has lived virtually retired. Mr. Johnson has gained and retained the unqualified confidence and esteem of the community in which he has long maintained his home. He has a little farm of nine acres and finds recreation in giving to the same his personal supervision. He is independent in politics and is an earnest member of the Methodist Episcopal church, as is also his wife.

In 1873 was solemnized the marriage of Mr. Johnson to Miss Anna Nelson, who likewise was born in Denmark. She is the daughter of

Christ Nelson, whose entire life was passed in Denmark, his widow having finally come to the United States and having been a resident of Iowa at the time of her death, in 1914. Mr. and Mrs. Nelson became the parents of six children, of whom three are living: Lars Jansen is now a resident of Iowa; Sena Peterson maintains his home in the state of Texas; and Mrs. Johnson is the oldest of the number. To Mr. and Mrs. Johnson have been born five children: Fritz owns and operates a farm of eighty acres, four miles northeast of Filley; Nels is a farm employe in this county, as is also Louis; Lena is the wife of Chester Hill, of Filley, and they have one son, Lloyd Everett; and Clara remains at the parental home.

JOHN O. ADAMS.—The chance traveler who might have found his way in the spring of 1857 into what is now the beautiful Nemaha valley would have seen in what is now Adams township, Gage county, something that looked like the beginning of a home, but, knowing that no settlers were in the neighborhood, he would have been at a loss to understand the meaning thereof until he chanced to notice, stretched between two saplings, a tablet of bark, upon which was written, "John O. Adams claims this tract of land, this 30th day of March, 1857."

The late John O. Adams was born in New Jersey, July 17, 1808, and when a child was taken by his parents to Kentucky. In 1838 he moved to Dubois county, Indiana, and in 1840 he married Letitia Harris, a native of Kentucky, born January 4, 1812. Mr. Adams engaged in farming in Dubois county until the fall of 1856, when he started west. On October 20th the family arrived at the home of a brother in Atchison county, Missouri. In the early spring Mr. Adams started to look over the country and find a suitable place to locate, and the result was his making a claim in Gage county, Nebraska, as above stated. This locality was known as Clay county at that time. With two covered wagons drawn by oxen which he had driven from Indiana, he and his family came to that new home. Not a wagon track was to be seen or a habitation found for many miles from the spot where he located. They had to build a bridge to cross the Nemaha river. On Section 26, Adams township, half a mile east of where the town of Adams now stands, they unloaded their goods, Mr. Adams's wife and their seven children having accompanied him.

They cut and hewed logs, and just one month from the day they arrived they moved into their new home. Here the family assiduously set about to develop a farm out of the wild and unbroken prairie. This was ten years before Nebraska became a state. No homestead laws were in existence, and Mr. Adams held squatter sovereignty over one hundred and sixty acres until he could file and prove up. Here he reared his family amid the pioneer conditions, and he prospered. Before his death he divided a section of land among his children and lived to see them all well established in life.

JOHN O. ADAMS

The township and village of Adams were named in his honor. Historians concede him to be the first permanent white settler in Gage county. He was one of the founders of the Methodist church in the township and was a devoted member. He was a Republican in politics and represented old Clay county on the board of commissioners. He was a blacksmith by trade and conducted a shop on his farm. This worthy pioneer passed from the scene of earthly activities December 24, 1887.

His wife had preceded him to eternal rest many years previously, her death having occurred November 21, 1867.

They became the parents of eight children, concerning whom the following data are available: Nelson A. resides at Adams; Nancy became the wife of B. P. Zuver and is now deceased; Isaac and Leander are deceased; John Q. was the next and his whereabouts are unknown; Naomi became the wife of Thomas Davis Mosby and lives in Adams township; Anna is deceased; and one child died in infancy.

CALVIN STARR, M. D.—Dr. Calvin Starr, who was nearly ninety-four years of age at the time when he passed from the stage of life's mortal endeavors, came to Nebraska at the beginning of the decade following its admission as one of the sovereign states of the Union, and Gage county was favored in having eventually gained him as a citizen and as an able and distinguished representative of the noble profession to which he gave himself with all of earnestness and self-abnegation for more than sixty years. To his name and memory the county shall ever pay a tribute of veneration and affection, and this publication would stultify its consistency were there failure to enter at least brief record concerning the singularly interesting and truly unassuming and exalted life record of this venerated citizen, who passed to eternal rest on the 25th of November, 1915, at his home in the city of Beatrice.

Dr. Starr was one of the favored mortals whom nature launches into the world with the heritage of sturdy ancestry, a splendid physique, a masterful mind and energy enough for many men. Added to these attributes were exceptional intellectual and professional attainments and the useful lessons of a wide and varied experience stored away. He was a type of the true gentleman and a representative of the best in the communal life, dignified and yet possessed of an affability and abiding human sympathy that won him warm friends among all classes and conditions of men.

Dr. Starr, a scion of one of the honored pioneer families of the old Buckeye state, was born on the old homestead farm of his parents, in Franklin county Ohio, and the date of his nativity was April 2, 1822. It is worthy of special note that this ancestral homestead, now in part occupied by the city of Columbus, capital of Ohio, was an integral portion of the original tract of land deeded by the government to an ancestor of Dr. Starr in recognition of his services as a patriot soldier in the war of the Revolution. An appreciable portion of the original allotment of land remained for several generations in the possession of the Starr family, and Dr. Starr himself owned at one time a part that now lies between the Ohio State University and the state capitol.

The youngest in a family of eleven children, all of whom attained to years of maturity, Dr. Starr passed the period of his childhood and early youth under the sturdy and invigorating discipline of the home farm, his father, John Starr having become one of the substantial exponents of agricultural industry in Franklin county, where he reclaimed a productive farm from the virtual forest wilderness. John Starr was born in Nova Scotia, and as a young man he established his residence in Connecticut, where was solemnized his marriage to Miss Betsey Havens, a native of Groton, that state. In 1812, John Starr and his wife removed to the wilds of Ohio and settled in Franklin county, the site of the present capital city of the state having at that time been marked by a single log house. Living up to the full tension of pioneer life, John Starr and his noble wife passed the residue of their lives in Franklin county. He was a man of strong mind and sterling character—a citizen who was influential in community affairs, he having been in his young manhood a successful teacher and the passing years having continuously widened his intellectual horizon. His death occurred in 1837, and his widow survived him by thirty years, she having passed to the life eternal in 1865. Both were devoted Christians in faith and service, and in politics Mr. Starr was to be found a staunch supporter of the cause of the old-line Whig party.

Dr. Calvin Starr acquired his preliminary education in the common schools of his native county and later he completed a four years' course in Central College, at Blendon, Ohio, where his alert mind and distinctive ambition enabled him to make the best possible use of the higher academic advantages thus offered. In consonance with well formulated plans he finally began the study of medicine under private preceptorship, in accordance with the custom of the day, and in the furtherance of his technical education he took two full courses of lectures in historic old Starling Medical College, which is now a part of the University of Ohio. In completing his admirable fortification for the work of his exacting profession Dr. Starr entered the Homeopathic Medical College at Cleveland, Ohio, one of the first and most important Homeopathic colleges in the west, and in this institution he was graduated February 21, 1851, with the well earned degree of Doctor of Medicine. In this connection it may consistently be stated that at the time of his death Dr. Starr was the oldest alumnus of this college, which, about the year 1912, was removed from Cleveland to Columbus, where it became the constituent Homeopathic medical school of the University of Ohio. The Doctor, a pioneer of the benignant system of Homeopathy in the west, ever retained a deep affection for his alma mater, and after his death his widow, Mrs. Julia C. Starr, M. D., received a letter from a member of the faculty of the college, the context of the communication containing statements that are worthy of preservation in this connection: "In the death of Dr. Starr our college loses its oldest alumnus, and one whose name was frequently mentioned in faculty meetings, especially in connection with the oil painting of Hahnemann that Dr. Starr presented to the college. It is a privilege granted to but few men to be permitted to engage actively in the practice of medicine for more than sixty years, and to his family it is an occasion of just pride to know that the husband and father was permitted to accomplish so great an amount of good in the world." It may further be noted that the Hahnemann portrait thus presented by Dr. Starr now occupies a place of honor in the Homeopathic building of the University of Ohio and that since his death there has been attached thereto a metal plate with the following inscription: "Calvin Starr, M. D., Class of 1851, Donor."

After having been graduated, with high honors, Dr. Starr began his professional novitiate by engaging in active general practice at Xenia, Ohio, but one year later he removed to Springfield, that state, where he remained five years. Becoming convinced that a greater field of usefulness lay open for him in connection with the rapidly developing west, Dr. Starr removed to Iowa City, Iowa, in the year 1857, and as one of the most able and honored pioneer physicians of the Hawkeye state he continued in active practice at Iowa City for twenty years, within which he built up a large and representative professional business, besides contributing much to civic and material progress and prosperity in his home community.

In 1877, ten years after Nebraska had gained the dignity of statehood, Dr. Starr came with his family to this now favored commonwealth, and after successfully continuing in practice at Nebraska City for five years he came, in 1882, to Beatrice, judicial center of Gage county, which place remained the central stage of his earnest and able professional activities during the remainder of his long and useful life, he having been a veritable patriarch of the community at the time of his death. In his profession and as a man he was ever one to remember and aid "those who were forgotten" and he bore optimistic cheer and encouragement as well as professional ministration to those in suffering or distress, so that it may well be understood that he was loved in every community in which he had lived and labored. At this juncture may consistently be reproduced an appreciative estimate that was a part of an obituary article published in a Beatrice paper at the time of his demise:

"Dr. Starr had marked abilities as a physician and as a man of high moral character and kindly disposition. On account of his advanced years, nearly ninety-four, he had been confined to his home for some time, but his influence has continued to go forth with all who came to see him. He inherited those virtues which go to make sterling manhood, but he did not rest content with mere ancestral bequest. While true to the faith of his fathers in every essential, yet he thought for himself and followed the truth as God gave him to see it, the finest product of his religious belief being a character that gave him the absolute confidence of his fellow men—and that is the final test of religion." The Doctor was an active member and liberal supporter of the Congregational church of Beatrice, as is also his widow.

As a young man Dr. Starr wedded Miss Sophia J. McPherson, of Xenia, Ohio, and she passed the closing years of her life at Iowa City, Iowa, where she died April 23, 1876. Of this union were born five children, concerning whom the following brief data are given: George B. now resides in the state of California; Clarence A. is a resident of Winona Lake, Indiana; Emma H. was a resident of Lincoln at the time of her death; and Mary P. and John A. maintain their residence in California, the former being the wife of W. S. Brayton.

On the 27th of June, 1878, was solemnized the marriage of Dr. Starr to Dr. Julia C. (Candee) Scudder, of Muscatine, Iowa, her first husband having been Horace Scudder, and the one child of this union was Horace, Jr., who died in 1906. Mrs. Starr was born at Muscatine, Iowa, and is a daughter of Sheldon N. and Lucy A. (Starr) Candee, the former a native of Connecticut and the latter of Ohio. The parents were numbered among the honored pioneers of both Iowa and Nebraska and they passed the closing-period of their lives in the latter commonwealth, the father having devoted the major part of his active career to the carriage-factory business, and both having been residents of Beatrice, Nebraska, at the time of their death.

Dr. Julia C. Starr, a woman of high professional attainments, became the able and valued coadjutor of her husband in the control of their large and representative joint practice in Gage county, and she still maintains her office at the attractive home at 409 North Sixth street, Beatrice. She was graduated in the medical department of the University of Iowa, at Iowa City, and an unequivocal success has attended her benignant service in the practice of her profession, in which she has gained status as one of the leading women physicians and surgeons of Nebraska. She still continues in active practice and her gracious womanhood and gentle sympathy have enhanced the effectiveness of her earnest labors in the alleviation of human suffering, the while she has gained the affectionate regard of all who have received her ministrations and counsel. She has a large practice, in connection with which she spares herself neither time nor effort, and she insistently keeps in touch with the advances made in medical and surgical science, through recourse to the best standard and periodical literature of her profession, the while she is a gracious and popular figure in the representative civic and social life of her home city, where her circle of friends is coincident with that of her acquaintances. No children were born of her second marriage, but the Doctor holds hallowed memories of the gracious relations that obtained at all times during the years of her conjugal and professional association with the honored subject of this memoir.

WILLIAM HOLM has identified himself most fully with the civic and material interests of Gage county, for he is not only a representative merchant in the village of Virginia, but is also the owner of a well improved farm estate in Sherman township. He is a native son of the west and has exemplified its progressive spirit in the varied activities that have brought to him a generous share of temporal prosperity.

Mr. Holm was born in Pottawatomie county, Kansas, on the 6th of January, 1873, and is a son of Charles J. and Louise (Anderson) Holm, who were born and reared in Sweden, where their marriage was solemnized. In 1865 the parents came to the United States and settled in Kansas, where the father became a pioneer farmer of Pottawatomie county and improved his farm of one hundred and twenty acres, and where he passed the remainder of his life. William Holm was the youngest member in a family of four children and was six years of age at the time of his mother's death. John E., the eldest of the children, is a farmer in Kansas; Charles A., who was for several years engaged in the plumbing business at Virginia, Gage county, is now a resident of Lincoln, Nebraska, and is a traveling salesman; and Frank has the active charge of the fine Gage county farm of his brother William, of this review. For his second wife Charles J. Holm wedded Miss Lottie Carlson and the one child of this union is Emma, the wife of Walter F. McGaffey, of Virginia, Gage county. Charles J. Holm was a Republican in politics and he and each of his wives held the faith of the Methodist Episcopal church.

The public schools of the Sunflower state afforded to William Holm his early educational advantages and the same were supplemented by a course in shorthand and typewriting in Pond's Business College, in the city of Topeka, as well as by further commercial instruction in the Kansas City Business University. In his youth, after leaving the farm, Mr. Holm became associated with the retail lumber business, at Olesburg, Kansas, and in the spring of 1893 he came to Gage county and established his residence in Virginia. Here for two years he conducted a lumber yard, and for seventeen years thereafter he was successfully established in the hardware business, besides serving simultaneously as postmaster of the village. He finally sold his hardware stock and business and eighteen months later he purchased the stock and business of J. S. Hubka. He expanded the business by installing a large and well selected stock of general merchandise and has since conducted a most substantial and prosperous enterprise. He is the owner of a well improved farm property of three hundred and twenty acres, and the same is under the active charge of his brother Frank, as previously noted. On this place he is giving special attention to the raising of full-blood Holstein cattle, besides which he is developing a successful dairy business in the connection.

In 1896 Mr. Holm wedded Miss Bessie Wright, who was born and reared in Gage county, and who is a daughter of Amos L. Wright, a retired farmer residing in the village of Virginia, this county. Mr. and Mrs. Holm have two children—Grace A., who is a student in the Beatrice high school; and Mildred Genevieve, who had the distinction of receiving first prize as the best baby girl at the Gage county fair in 1917. Mrs. Holm is an active member of the Christian church.

Mr. Holm has been active and liberal as a citizen of intense public spirit, has held various township offices, and commands inviolable place in popular confidence and good will.

NELSON ADAMS.—The subject of this record has the distinction of being the oldest living settler in Gage county. When a lad of sixteen years he arrived in what is now Adams township, in company with his father, John O. Adams, who was the first permanent settler of the county. Mr. Adams was born in Dubois county, Indiana, February 24, 1841. He grew to manhood on the pioneer farm in Nebraska and at an early age began to aid in the development and improvement of the old homestead. In September, 1864, he enlisted in Company C, Second Nebraska Regiment, for a term of four months, or during the war. He was sent to Fort Kearney and from there to Camp Blue, where the winter was passed. In the spring of 1865, the regiment was honorably discharged and young Nelson returned home. The next year he was united in marriage to Miss Laura Haskins and they settled on a farm he had purchased. But they were destined to enjoy their companionship for only a brief season, for four months and eight days after their marriage Mrs. Adams passed away. In April of that year Mr. Adams made a trip of over five hundred miles, into Colorado. He drove overland from Nebraska City with a load of produce—eggs, butter, corn, etc.—and the

Indians made it so uncomfortable for him that he was compelled to hasten to Denver. He had entered a homestead in Section 25, Adams township, and had built a log house sixteen by twenty-two feet in dimensions. He returned from the west and in 1868 he married Miss Lydia J. Wilson, a native of Putnam county, Indiana. Of this union were born two children, Nancy E, who is the wife of C. B. Ashcroft and resides in Wyoming, and Letitia O., who died in childhood. The mother of these children passed away, and the present Mrs. Adams was in her girlhood Emily J. Dilworth. She is a native of Grant county, Kentucky, where she was born April 7, 1843. Her parents, Lindsey and Sarah (Simpson) Dilworth, came to Nebraska in 1863, settling in Johnson county. They gave the name to the town of Crab Orchard, from the large number of wild crab-apple trees growing in the vicinity. By a former marriage, to William H. Stoner, who was a Union soldier in the Civil war, Mrs. Adams became the mother of three children, the eldest of whom is William H. Stoner, who resides in Cass county, Minnesota, and is the only one now living. At the time of her marriage to Mr. Adams, Mrs. Adams was the widow of G. T. Simpson, and their one son, Hugh M., died at the age of seventeen years.

NELSON ADAMS

Nelson Adams successfully followed farming until 1902, when he retired, and he now makes his home in Adams. He has been a witness of the vast changes which have taken place in Gage county, having been a member of the first family to establish a home here. Mr. Adams is a Methodist in religious belief, and in politics is a Republican. He held various township offices years ago, but is now retired from all activities.

ELIJAH FILLEY.—In the summer of 1867, the year that marked the admission of Nebraska to statehood, Hon. Elijah Filley, a young man of industry, self-reliance, and courage, came with his wife to Gage county and numbered himself among its sterling pioneers. He and his faithful wife ran the full gamut of pioneer experience and their reminiscences of the early days are most graphic and interesting. They made the overland journey to Nebraska with teams and wagons and girded themselves with the indomitable valor and undauntable purpose that are ever the prerequisite of success under the conditions that must obtain in opening a new country to civilization and progress. Mr. Filley has been in the most significant sense the architect of his own fortunes and few men have played a larger or more benignant part in connection with the development and upbuilding of Gage county along both civic and industrial lines. Of this no further assurance need be given than the statement that a township and a village of the county have been named in honor of this venerable pioneer citizen, while it has been his to represent Gage county in both houses of the state legislature, to gain through his own ability and well ordered energies a substantial fortune, the while he has so ordered his course as to merit and receive at all stages the unqualified respect and confidence of his fellow men. It is most gratifying to be able to present in this publication a tribute to Mr. Filley as a pioneer of pioneers and to enter brief review of a career that has been marked by earnest and honest endeavor. He and his wife now live in gracious retirement in the city of Des Moines, Iowa, and though venerable in age the years rest lightly upon them, while they find a full measure of satisfaction in reverting to the attractive social and material conditions and environment which they have aided in creating in Gage county, Nebraska. Mr. Filley was born in Jackson county, Michigan, on the 28th of November, 1839, and is a son of Ammi and Mary (Marvin)

Filley, both natives of Bloomfield, Connecticut, where they were reared and educated. Ammi Filley, a member of one of the early colonial families of New England, was born January 2, 1808, and he continued his residence in Connecticut until 1833, when he immigrated to Michigan, which state was not admitted to the union until 1837. He became one of the pioneers of Jackson county, where he reclaimed a farm from the forest and where he continued his active alliance with agricultural industry about thirty years. In the summer of 1867 he retired from the active labors that had so long been his portion and accompanied his son Elijah, of this review, to Gage county, Nebraska, where he remained until his death and where he received during the intervening period the deepest filial care and solicitude on the part of his son and the latter's family. He was seventy-two years of age at the time of his death, which occurred May 13, 1880. Ammi Filley was one of the gallant sons of the nation who went forth in defense of the Union when the Civil war was precipitated on the country. In response to President Lincoln's first call, he enlisted as a private in Company D, Second Michigan Cavalry, and with this gallant command he served through out the entire course of the war. He was a skilled sharpshooter and participated in many of the important battles marking the progress of the great conflict. He took part in the siege of Vicksburg and the famous charge at Fort Donelson, and previously had been with his command in heavy campaigns and engagements in the southern states farther to the east. In later years he found pleasure in vitalizing the associations of his military career by affiliation with the Grand Army of the Republic. Ammi and Mary (Marvin) Filley became the parents of four sons and two daughters, and of the number only Elijah is living in 1918.

Elijah Filley was but five years old at the time of his mother's death, and the home was broken up. For about three years thereafter he lived in the home of a man named Crandall, a farmer in Jackson county, Michigan, and his father then contracted a second marriage and re-established a home for his children. However, with so little consideration and kindness did the stepmother treat Elijah Filley that he was compelled to leave home when about twelve years of age, and the immature youth began to provide for himself by taking up the arduous work of plowing for a neighbor farmer for a compensation of six dollars a month. In reminiscent way he frequently reverts to this period of his life, when he drove the plodding ox-team to the plow and did other heavy farm work. He continued to be employed by the month as a farm hand during the summer seasons and attended school during the intervening winter terms, the while he worked mornings and evenings to pay his board.

In 1858, when nineteen years of age, Mr. Filley went to Joliet, Illinois, and there he was employed by the firm of Poole & Ring on one of the canal boats on the old Michigan Illinois canal until the freezing of the canal put a stop to such navigation. During the following winter he was employed in sawing wood for use on railroad locomotives, and he recalls that the buzz-saw used for the purpose was operated by a treadmill on which power was furnished by horses. In 1859 Mr. Filley went to Odell, Livingston county, Illinois, and after working for a time on a farm in that vicinity he made his way to LaSalle county, that state, where for three years he was engaged in herding, driving, and dealing in live stock, in the employ of William Strawn, an extensive farmer and stock dealer of the day. In company with Mr. Strawn he made the overland trip to Cedar Rapids, Iowa, and incidentally accumulated a herd of one hundred and forty-six fat cattle at Des Moines, Iowa. With this large herd they then started for Chicago, but Mr. Strawn was summoned to his home, when fifteen miles east of Des Moines, so that Mr. Filley alone had charge of driving the cattle through to the future metropolis of the west. During his three years of association with Mr. Strawn he gained knowledge and experience that proved of inestimable value to him in later operations of an independent order that enabled him to lay the substantial foundation for his success. After leaving Mr. Strawn he continued to be engaged in farming in Livingston county, Illinois, until 1867, in the summer of which year he provided himself with three covered wagons and three good teams, and with these set forth on the overland journey to the new state of Nebraska, his young wife accompanying him on this momentous trip. In due course of time they arrived in Gage county, and here Mr. Filley utilized the money which he had previously acquired to effect the purchase of six quarter-sections of government land, besides which he filed claim on a homestead of equal area. His horses died soon after his arrival in the county and he finally acquired ox teams and began breaking the virgin prairie soil to pay for his oxen. He continued to break soil for others for about three years and in the meanwhile established a pioneer home on his own land. Instead of following the custom of the majority of the early settlers by providing a dug-out or sod house, Mr. Filley determined to make a residence of less primitive type. In the meanwhile he and his wife lived in a tent and around the same they eventually built a stone house of one room, this structure having in later years been familiarly known as "The Old Stone House," and constituting one of the veritable landmarks of this section of the state. Mr. Filley himself quarried the stone and burned the lime for mortar, while Mrs. Filley hauled the material to the site of the new home by means of the ox team. Together these ambitious pioneers mixed the mortar and laid the walls of the little dwelling, after which a roof was constructed. They lived in the one room during the first winter and in the following summer they added to the domicile, eventually making the house one of good size and excellent provisions for comfort. In this dwelling they continued to maintain their home for sixteen years.

Soon after coming to Nebraska Mr. Filley put his previous experience to good use by buying cattle to stock his large farm, and soon he developed a prosperous business in the feeding and shipping of cattle. On the completing of the railroad line to Beatrice he had the distinction of loading the first carload of cattle ever transported from Gage county to Chicago by rail. Later the railroad was extended to the present village of Filley, which was named in his honor and which is situated on a part of his old farm. He there erected a large grain elevator, the same having thereafter been utilized by him for many years in connection with his extensive operations in the buying and shipping of grain.

When the Burlington & Missouri River Railroad was completed from Beatrice to Nebraska City, Mr. Filley, in the summer of 1883, founded on the line the town which bears his name and which, as before stated, is located on one of his farms. In 1885 the county authorities conferred upon him a merited distinction, in that they authorized the changing of the name of Mud Creek township to Filley township, a fitting tribute to the sterling pioneer who was the first settler within the limits of that township. Mr. Filley was for a long term of years recognized as the most progressive and substantial farmer, stock-feeder, and stock-shipper in this section of the state, and among his early enterprises of importance was also the owning and operating of a threshing outfit.

About the year 1890 Mr. Filley sold the major part of his large and important real estate and business interests in Gage county, and settled on a tract of one thousand acres which, in an early day, he had purchased in the adjoining county of Jefferson. This property he improved in excellent order and he operated the same successfully in connection with his extensive stock business for several years—until, in fact, he met with an accident that nearly resulted in his death. He then decided to sell his property and retire from active business, and since that time he and his devoted wife have lived in the serene enjoyment of the gracious rewards of former years of earnest endeavor.

In politics Mr. Filley has been a recognized stalwart in the ranks of the Republican party and as a progressive citizen he wielded much influence in shaping the governmental policies that brought normal development and growth to Gage county. He was elected county commissioner and in this office served two terms, of three years each. In 1881 and 1883 he represented Gage county in the state legislature, and soon after his retirement from this office he was elected state senator from his district, in which position he served until 1885. His record as a legislator has become a very part of the history of the state and is illumined by his characteristic loyalty and public spirit. Mr. Filley has been affiliated with the Masonic fraternity since 1866, was made a Master Mason and also a Royal Arch Mason in Fairbury, Illinois. He then settled in Nebraska and was a charter member and helped to organize the Blue Lodge, No. 26, also the chapter and commandery at Beatrice, Nebraska. Then he organized Temple Lodge, No. 175, at Filley, and of this he served as master for about twelve years.

Matured and invigorated through the herculean labors and hardships of the pioneer days, the physical constitution of Mr. Filley has been sturdy and thus he retains, as he hears the eightieth milestone on the journey of life, the mental and physical vigor of a man many years his junior, while his loved wife has been his devoted companion and helpmeet for more than half a century—a woman whose strength has been as the number of her days and who had a remarkable share in pioneer experience in the great west, as will be attested by statements yet to be made in this context.

On the 4th of November, 1863, was solemnized the marriage of Mr. Filley to Miss Burd, of Pleasant Ridge, Livingston county, Illinois. She was born in Will county, that state, November 6, 1844, and is a daughter of Silas and Betsey Ann Burd, the former of whom was born in New Jersey, December 8, 1818, and the latter of whom was born in the state of New York, on the 13th of September, 1817. Silas Burd numbered himself among the pioneers of Illinois and later emphasized his pioneer experience by removing with his family to Texas, this action having been taken primarily for the benefit of the health of himself and his wife. Mrs. Filley was a girl of twelve years when the family thus removed to the Lone Star state, and the greater part of the journey was made with teams and wagons. Georgetown, Texas, was made the destination and from that head quarters Mr. Burd engaged in buying and selling cattle and horses. Mrs. Filley accompanied him in his trips about the country to buy stock, and finally, with a herd of about eighty cattle and several ponies, they started overland for Chicago in the spring of 1858. In the meanwhile Mr. Burd had traded his wagons for a top buggy, cattle, etc., and in starting forth on the long journey a sturdy yoke of oxen was provided for the transportation of the camp outfit. The family started on this return trip when Mrs. Filley was a girl of about fifteen years and she assisted in driving the ox team. They had proceeded as far as Waco, Texas, when the father was so stricken with illness as to be unable to proceed farther, and in the camp which they made he died on the 22d of February, 1859, leaving his wife ill in bed and with the care of their two sons and three daughters. Mrs. Filley, the eldest of the children, bravely assumed the care of her mother and the directing of family affairs in general after the remains of the loved father had been laid to rest in Texas soil. After the grass came up in the following spring the little family resumed their weary journey to the east, with the cattle and general camp equipment. On they drove through Texas and the Indian Territory, where they were urged by each successive Indian tribe encountered to give one or more head of the little band of cattle, in order to obtain permission to pass on unmolested, but Mrs. Filley, with a courage and tact beyond her years, contrived to gain this permission without sacrificing the live stock, only one beef steer having been contributed to the Indians. Continuing in the saddle every day, she led the outfit onward until they crossed the Mississippi river at Alton, Illinois, where they were joined by a brother of her mother. Thus reinforced the party continued the journey to Livingston county, Illinois, and in the village of Avoca the family rented a house until the live stock could be sold in the Chicago market, to which Mrs. Filley assisted in driving the cattle from the Texas wilds—in fact she thus made the entire trip from Texas to Chicago on the back of a little Texas pony. After the sale of the cattle the family purchased a farm in Livingston county and there Mrs. Filley remained until her marriage, within a few years after which it was again her portion to endure the trials and vicissitudes of pioneer life, as noted in foregoing paragraphs.

Mr. and Mrs. Filley became the parents of six children, concerning whom the following brief data are given: Fitch died at the age of twelve years; Hiram is now a resident of the state of Arkansas; Emma died at the age of eighteen years; Oscar Elijah died in April, 1916, aged forty-six years; Charles Elmer was four years of age at the time of his death; Daisy C. is the wife of Murray A. Scoular, of Des Moines, Iowa.

The foregoing record, implying much to him who can read between the lines as well as appreciate the data of the context itself, will be read with pleasure by the many friends of Mr. and Mrs. Filley in Gage county and will prove a definite and worthy contribution to the generic history of this favored section of Nebraska, as their names merit enduring place of honor and distinction on the pages of Gage county history.

SAMUEL RINAKER.—No history of Gage county or the state of Nebraska would be complete without the name of Samuel Rinaker. For nearly a third of a century this able and scholarly lawyer has made his home in the city of Beatrice and has engaged in the active practice of his profession in the state and federal courts. During this entire period of time he, with the several firms of which he has been a member, has enjoyed a lucrative practice at the bar of this county and state. He has been professionally connected from the beginning of his career as a lawyer here with a large portion of the important litigation arising in this section of the country, and by sheer force of character, learning and abilities of a high order, he has embedded his name deeply and permanently in the legal history of his state and country.

Yours truly,
Samuel Rinaker

Mr. Rinaker was born at Carlinville, Macoupin county, Illinois, on the 14th day of September, 1860. He is the second son of the late John

I. Rinaker and Clarissa Keplinger, his wife. Besides Samuel, the surviving children of these worthy parents are the eldest son, Thomas Rinaker, a prominent lawyer of Carlinville and for many years his father's partner in the practice of the law; John I. Rinaker, a well known and successful architect of the city of Springfield, Illinois, and Judge Lewis Rinaker, who after several years' successful practice at the Chicago bar was elected judge of the county court of Cook county, Illinois, and held this important office four years.

Shortly after locating in Beatrice, Mr. Rinaker married Miss Carrie Palmer Mayo, who like himself was a native of Carlinville and who was the daughter of Samuel and Elizabeth (Palmer) Mayo. Her father was a prominent and influential citizen of Macoupin county and her mother was a sister of the late General John M. Palmer, of whom further mention will be made later on in this sketch.

Mr. and Mrs. Rinaker occupy a handsome and attractive home at the corner of Fifth and Washington streets, Beatrice. Their marriage has proven to be a happy one—lapse of time serving only to cement more firmly the marital bond. To Mr. and Mrs. Rinaker two children have been born, Samuel Mayo Rinaker, a son, and Miss Carrie Rinaker, a daughter. The former after graduating at the Beatrice high school in 1905, with highest honors, entered the Nebraska State University in the autumn of that year and after two years spent in that institution, successfully passed a competitive examination for a Rhoades scholarship in Oxford University, England, as a representative from the state of Nebraska. In 1910 he was graduated with honors from that historic institution and, returning to the United States, he entered the law department of Harvard University. After a three years' course at Harvard he took his degree as Bachelor of Laws in the spring of 1914 and in the fall of that year he went to Chicago, Illinois, where he is now well established in the practice of his profession. The daughter, Miss Carrie Rinaker, also graduated from the high school of Beatrice, as a member of the class of 1909, and in the autumn of that year was matriculated as a student of Vassar College, Poughkeepsie, New York. She attended this institution for some time and is domiciled under the paternal roof.

While pride of ancestry is not a marked characteristic of the American citizen, it is, nevertheless, not only natural but highly commendable that one should feel a just pride in the fact that he has descended from ancestors who were more than ordinarily distinguished in their day and generation. With this thought in mind it is hoped that a brief account of the parents of Samuel Rinaker will not be deemed inappropriate in this sketch of their son.

His father, John I. Rinaker, was one of the best known and widely influential citizens of the great state of Illinois. He was born in Baltimore, Maryland, in the year 1830. He was bereft of his parents when a child six years of age and was taken to Illinois, where for a few years he made his home with the family of John T. Alden of Sangamon county. When ten years of age he was thrown on his own resources and found a home and occupation on a farm. He acquired the rudiments of an education by attending the common schools of Illinois in the winter time. By great industry, thrift and economy, as well as by close application to his studies, he was finally enrolled as a student in the Illinois College at Jacksonville, where he remained for some time, and later entering McKendree College at Lebanon, Illinois, he was graduated from that institution with the class of 1851, receiving afterward from his alma mater the degree of Doctor of Laws. Animated by an ambition to give full scope to his abilities, he entered upon the study of the law in the office of John McAuley Palmer, at Carlinville, shortly after his graduation. His preceptor, in addition to being a lawyer of renown, became afterwards distinguished as a general in the Union army during the great Civil war and as a politician of more than ordinary ability. His services as major general of volunteers began in 1862, and he closed his military career as a commander of an army corps under General Sherman, in 1865. He was elected United States senator from Illinois in 1869 as a Republican and again in 1891, as a Democrat, and he closed his political career as a candidate for the presidency of the United States as a sound-money Democrat, in 1896.

General Rinaker was admitted to the bar at Carlinville, in 1854, and was immediately successful in his profession. In 1862 he took an active part in organizing the One Hundred and Twenty-second Regiment of

Illinois Volunteer Infantry, was elected and commissioned its colonel and served throughout the remainder of the great Civil war at the head of this gallant regiment—participating in its marches, sieges, battles, victories. He was seriously wounded in the battle of Parker's Cross Roads, December 31, 1862, but as soon as he recovered he rejoined his command, and on the 13th day of March, 1865, a month before Lee surrendered to Grant at Appomattox Court House, Virginia, he was breveted brigadier general of volunteers, on account of "great and meritorious services". At the close of the war he returned to Carlinville and resumed the practice of his profession. He rapidly achieved success as a lawyer and great prominence as an orator and politician. He began life as a Democrat but in 1858 became affiliated with the rising, young Republican party, and to the end of his long and useful life he remained a loyal member of that great national organization—eminent and influential in its counsels, honoring it and frequently honored by it, and he closed a conspicuously honorable political career as a member of the congress of the United States to which he was elected in 1894, from the Sixteenth congressional district of Illinois—a district then and now strongly Democratic. He died at Eustis, Florida, where he was spending the winter with his wife, on the 15th day of January, 1915, in his eighty-fifth year, bequeathing to his posterity the example and influence of a life crowded with duties faithfully performed and of honors modestly and worthily borne. His venerable wife, though near the bounds of life, still survives her distinguished husband, the object of the tender solicitude and veneration of a host of relatives and friends.

Samuel Rinaker spent his childhood, youth and early manhood in the little city of Carlinville and acquired his elementary education in the public schools of that city. At the age of sixteen he entered Blackburn College, also located at Carlinville, from which institution he graduated in the classical course with the class of 1880. He then pursued a course of study in the business college at Jacksonville, Illinois, and having through these agencies laid the foundation for the study of the law he entered the law department of Yale College (now University) prosecuting his studies during the years of 1882 and 1883 in that historic institution and afterward completing his legal studies in the law office of his father and brother at Carlinville. He was admitted to the bar of Illinois in the autumn of 1884, by the supreme court of that state. In February, 1885, he came to the city of Beatrice, then a bustling, growing, promising western town of probably five thousand people. Upon his arrival here he formed a partnership for the practice of the law with the late Nathan Kirk Griggs, under the firm name of Griggs & Rinaker.

Both partners were splendidly endowed with all those qualities of intellect, learning and character which are indispensable to great success in the legal profession. Mr. Griggs was from Indiana. He came to Beatrice in June, 1867, and was therefore a pioneer lawyer of Gage county. He was a man of boundless energy and teeming industry, a careful practitioner of the law and a most formidable antagonist in the trial of causes. Besides being an unusually skillful and adroit trial lawyer he was an office lawyer of exceptional ability. He was forty-four years of age and at the very zenith of his powers. He brought to the co-partnership a wide experience as a lawyer, politician and legislator. He had served the United States six years as our consul at Chemitz, Saxony, a period which had produced the same effect on his mind and character as a college education might have done, and he was cosmopolitan in learning, taste, sympathy. He was the most variously endowed of any of the lawyers of the state with whom he was contemporary, being at once poet, singer, composer of songs and music, orator, writer, and lecturer— and excelling in all. As an indication of the esteem in which he was held as well as an indication of the mental equipment and attitude of its writer, on certain matters, attention is called to the following letter:

Carlinville, Ill., August 26, 1910.

Hon. N. K. Griggs, Lincoln, Nebraska.
Dear Sir:—

Several days ago I had the pleasure to receive a copy of your address, entitled "Christ in America's Life," for which accept my thanks. I was pleased with the ideas which you advanced therein and with the striking and elegant manner in which you expressed them. You show that Christianity is the vital and conservative force in all moral progress, the solvent of the refractory problems that confront human society in its onward march to a higher and better destiny. You make plain that religions are the creations of men, but that Christianity is the gift of God to man, that it is a force irresistible, immaculate and immortal and that while permeated with that force, America will lead the world to the longed for Golden Age.

JOHN I. RINAKER.

The junior member of this law firm was by education, training, ambition and abilities well calculated to supplement the experience and abilities of its senior, and he possessed necessary qualities to success which Mr. Griggs lacked to some extent. The success of the firm was immediate and lasting and each partner grew toward the intellectual stature of the other with a uniformity and certainty rarely seen in such relationships.

In 1890 Mr. Griggs accepted an appointment from the Chicago, Burlington & Quincy Railroad Company as its attorney for the western division of this great corporation and was assigned to the state of Wyoming and other inter-mountain states. He held this position until his death, which occurred while he was journeying to the northwest from his home in Lincoln, in the service of his company, at Alliance, Nebraska, on Sunday morning, September 4, 1910, he being found dead in his berth on the sleeping car at that time and place.

After Mr. Griggs accepted this appointment the late Robert S. Bibb was admitted to the co-partnership which thereafter for some time was known as Griggs, Rinaker & Bibb. But in 1893, on the removal of Mr. Griggs to Lincoln, his name was dropped from the firm name, which thereafter was designated as Rinaker & Bibb. Following the death of Mr. Bibb, in May, 1907, Mr. Rinaker practiced his profession alone until the year 1909, when he became associated with Mr. A. H. Kidd, of Beatrice, in the practice of the law under the firm name of Rinaker & Kidd, a title by which it is still known and under which it does business.

His natural amiability of character and great adaptability to the profession of the law, have enabled Mr. Rinaker always to take a leading place in the business of his several firms, and this by common consent stripped of every semblance of jealousy or envy. The volume of business with which he has been professionally connected in the various courts of the state and country has been great and varied in character. He has numbered amongst his clients, public officials and public bodies, railway companies, banks and banking institutions, manufacturing and mercantile concerns, loan associations and agencies, general corporations, firms and individuals. His practice has not been confined to the courts of the state of Nebraska alone, but it has embraced the courts of several other states and the great national courts of the country.

Mr. Rinaker is a trained and skillful trial lawyer; he possesses an accurate and a usable knowledge of the rules and principles of the law and their practical application to the trial of causes. He is eminent in counsel, clear and concise in statement, whether of fact or law, discriminating and logical in argument courtly and dignified in address, fair, just, dispassionate. Though earnest and forceful in presenting his case to court or jury he is suave, self-possessed, deferential. He is a successful trial lawyer and as an advocate and minister of justice, no member of the legal profession in Nebraska is held in higher esteem or commands greater consideration from judges and courts than Samuel Rinaker.

Though eminently qualified for public life, whether in the judicial, legislative or administrative branches of our government, Mr. Rinaker has, in the main, steadfastly refused to enter the political arena as a seeker of office. In 1896 he was put forward by his friends as the Republican candidate for county attorney of Gage county and was triumphantly elected. He was reelected to the same office in 1888. With these exceptions he has never permitted his name to be brought forward for any political office whatsoever. He has, however, served his community most acceptably as a member of the Beatrice school board, and since it was founded, twenty-five years ago, to the present moment he has been a director of the Free Public Library of Beatrice. The fact that so far his friends have failed to induce him to look with favor upon a political career has been a source of deep regret to his many friends, both at home and abroad in the state.

The talents and abilities which mark Mr. Rinaker for a useful and a successful public career have not been lost to his fellow-citizens but have served more fittingly to qualify their possessor for the duties and activities of professional and social life. Mr. Rinaker is a citizen of the utmost loyalty and public spirit. He takes an active and a sympathetic interest in the social, intellectual and business affairs of his community, and by his comprehensive way of looking at things, the accuracy of his judgment and the probity of his character he is everywhere accorded a first place as a citizen of his county and state. He is a member of the Commercial Club of Beatrice, the Beatrice Club—a social organization,—and the Golf Club of his city. For many years he has been a member of the board of directors of the First National Bank of Beatrice and the First Savings Bank, an adjunct institution. He is a Mason, a Knight Templar and a Modern Woodman. For a man with only a moderate fortune, his charities, though discriminating, are large and varied. Without advertising the fact he always contributes to every worthy enterprise or beneficence applying to him for assistance.

In politics, Mr. Rinaker has always affiliated with the Republican party and as a trusted leader in that great party he has been very influential in formulating and directing its policies and activities in both the state and nation.

If to gain and through long years of association to be able to hold the esteem of an entire community; if to so discharge the duties of an advocate and a lawyer as to dignify and ennoble that great and learned profession, if to command through the third of a century the profound respect of the bench and bar of a great state furnish sufficient evidence of worth of character, then the case for Samuel Rinaker is complete. Time may bring additional honors; it may enlarge his field of activities and usefulness, it may broaden his acquaintance; but it cannot augment the esteem, confidence and affection with which he is regarded by those who already know him.

HARRY M. HEPPERLEN, M. D.—No member of the medical profession in Nebraska has shown a greater appreciation of the exactions and responsibilities of his humane calling or has more thoroughly equipped himself for the work of the profession than Dr. Hepperlen, whose attainments are of high order and who has gained specially high reputation as a surgeon. He is distinctively one of the leading physicians and surgeons of southeastern Nebraska, has been established in practice at Beatrice since 1898 and his is the distinction of having founded the first hospital in this city. In this connection he manifested not only his professional zeal and loyalty, but also his liberality and progressiveness as a citizen. The hospital which he established constituted the nucleus of the present admirably equipped and conducted Lutheran Hospital, and Dr. Hepperlen continues his effective and valued services as chief of the surgical staff of this admirable institution. The hospital is situated about one mile distant from the center of the city of Beatrice and one block distant from the beautiful city park, which formerly was the Chautauqua assembly grounds of this city. The hospital occupies a modern three-story building, and in its general equipment and appointments it is maintained at the most approved standard, with facilities for the care of eighty patients. In connection with the hospital is conducted a well ordered training school for nurses, and the institution as a whole is a source of pride and satisfaction to the citizens of Gage county, besides standing as a monument to the initiative ability and professional zeal of its founder. As a surgeon Dr. Hepperlen controls a practice that in scope and importance is especially noteworthy, his services being demanded through a wide territory of the middle west,—particularly in Nebraska and Kansas. Many delicate surgical operations, both major and minor, stand to the credit of the Doctor, and in the field of surgery he is frequently called upon as an authority by his professional conferees. He is an enthusiast in the work of his profession, keeps in closest touch with the advances made in medical and surgical science, has a comprehensive and select library of standard medical works and has made valuable contributions to the periodical literature of his profession. He is an active member of the American Medical Association and the Nebraska State Medical Society, as well as the American College of Surgeons. As a public-spirited citizen he is found arrayed as a staunch advocate of the principles of the Republican party.

Dr. Harry M. Hepperlen was born in Lycoming county, Pennsylvania, January 26, 1868, and is a son of John and Mary (Michael) Hepperlen, who removed from the old Keystone state to

Nebraska in 1880 and established their home in Jefferson county, where the father became a substantial and influential citizen. Dr. Hepperlen acquired his earlier education in the public schools of Jefferson county, this state, and supplemented his training by attending during three winter terms the select school conducted at Beatrice by Professor Blake, an educator of exceptional ability. After having formulated definite plans for his future career Dr. Hepperlen entered Keokuk Medical College, in the city of Keokuk, Iowa, and in this institution he was graduated as a member of the class of 1891, with the degree of Doctor of Medicine. It has already been intimated in this context that Dr. Hepperlen has spared neither pains nor effort in fortifying himself for his profession, and in assurance of this it may be noted that a few years after receiving his degree he took effective post-graduate work in historic old Jefferson Medical College, in the city of Philadelphia, from which institution he received in 1896 the supplemental degree of Doctor of Medicine. Thereafter, in 1897-8, he took a two years' post-graduate course in the University of Vienna, Austria, where he specialized in surgery, as had he also at Jefferson Medical College.

In 1891, soon after his graduation, Dr. Hepperlen engaged in the practice of his profession in the village of Harbine, Jefferson county, and there he continued his residence and professional headquarters until he went abroad for further study. Upon his return to the United States, in 1899, Dr. Hepperlen established his residence in Beatrice, where he has since maintained his home and been a valued and honored figure in the community life. Here he founded soon after his arrival a small hospital, the same having but six beds as total accommodation for patients, and within the nine years that the hospital was conducted by the Doctor he brought about its splendid development and increased its accommodations to thirty-six beds. In 1912 the institution was acquired by the Brethren church, under the auspices of which it was conducted until 1914, with Dr. Hepperlen as head of its surgical staff and a valued factor in the general administration of its affairs. In 1914 the hospital, by sale, passed to the control of the Lutheran church, under the auspices of which it has since been conducted.

August 8, 1899, recorded the marriage of Dr. Hepperlen to Miss Rosa B. Warner, and they have four children, namely: Mary Bernetta, Joseph Price, Fanstella May, and Harry Michael, Jr. Mrs. Hepperlen is a member of the Presbyterian church.

REV. FRANZ ALBRECHT.—In a double sense is this honored citizen a faithful and prolific worker in the harvest, for not only is he serving with consecrated zeal as a clergyman of the Mennonite church but he is also actively and successfully identified with the basic industries of agriculture and stock-growing, as the owner of a well improved farm of one hundred and sixty acres, the northeast quarter of Section 19, Blakely township.

Mr. Albrecht was born at Lindenau, in Silesia, Prussia, and the date of his nativity was January 10, 1876. He is a son of Henry and Helena (Penner) Albrecht, of whose five children he was the second in order of birth; Henry, the eldest son, is a prosperous farmer of Jefferson county, this state; Helena is the wife of David Jansen, of that county; Abraham is a resident of Inman, Norton county, Kansas; and Jacob died when an infant. The father was born August 20, 1845, and continued his residence in his native land until 1884, when he immigrated with his family to the United States. On the 12th of September of that year he established the family home near Beatrice, and for five years thereafter he was employed as a farm workman. The succeeding nine years found him engaged in farming on rented land and he then purchased a farm near Hoag, in Blakely township. He acquired this property in 1897 made excellent improvements on the same and at the time of his death, in 1909, he was the owner of a valuable landed estate of three hundred and twenty acres. He was a son of Jacob Albrecht, who passed his entire life in Prussia and who was a farmer by vocation. His widow later removed to Russia, and there her death occurred. The mother of Rev. Franz Albrecht was born in Prussia on the 7th of April, 1847, and since the death of her husband she has resided with her son Franz on the old homestead farm. Her parents, Cornelius and Adelgunda (Dau) Penner, passed their entire lives in Germany and her father was a cloth and linen weaver. He whose name introduces this article was a lad of eight years at the time when the family came to America and established a home in Gage county. Here he was reared to adult age under the benignant influences of the farm, the while he made good use of the advantage afforded in both the German and English schools of the locality. In 1902 he entered Bethel College, at Newton, Kansas, and in this institution he was graduated as a member of the class of 1905, after the completion of a Bible course and other work of a preparatory order for ordination to the ministry. He became a clergyman of the Mennonite church in 1905, and has since been the able and zealous pastor of the church of this denomination in his home neighborhood, besides which he gives ministerial service to other Mennonite church organizations in the county—a man of strong intellectuality, of much ability as a pulpit speaker, and of utmost zeal in all departments of his service. Mr. Albrecht has resided on the present homestead farm from the time his father purchased the property and his heritage from his father's estate included the one hundred and sixty acres to the management of which he gives his effective attention, as one of the progressive and representative farmers and stock-raisers of Blakely township.

On the 5th of November, 1909, was solemnized the marriage of Mr. Albrecht to Miss Mary Wiebe, who was born in Prussia and was a young woman at the time of the family immigration to America, her parents, Herman and Wilhelmina (Hein) Wiebe, having been born and reared in Germany and the mother having passed to the life eternal in 1884. Mr. Wiebe has been a resident of Gage county since 1894 and lives upon his well improved homestead farm, north of the city of Beatrice. Mr. and Mrs. Albrecht have two children—Margaret and Dora H.

JOHN S. GOODBAN.—Along manifold lines has this honored pioneer exerted benignant influence during nearly a half century of continuous residence in Gage county, and he is now living virtually retired, his attractive home being in the village of Cortland. He is a man of broad intellectual ken, high ideals, and gracious personality—a citizen who commands the fullest measure of popular confidence and esteem.

Mr. Goodban was born in Erie county, Pennsylvania, October 21, 1846, and is a son of William and Margaret (Langley) Goodban. William Goodban was born in Kentshire, England, February 22, 1804, and he continued his residence in his native land until 1840, when he came to America and settled in the state of New York. In 1842 he removed to Erie county, Pennsylvania, where he passed the remainder of his life, his death having occurred in October, 1861. His first wife, whose maiden name was Hannah Langley, died when comparatively a young woman, four children having been born of their union—Edward, Esther A., Hannah C., and one who died in infancy. Edward died when thirty years of age and both Esther and Hannah likewise are deceased, the former having become the wife of P. J. Mosier, and the latter having been the wife of T. C. Golden. For his second wife William Goodban married Miss Margaret Langley, a sister of his first wife, and she passed to eternal rest when eighty-three years of age. Concerning the children of this marriage the following brief data are available: Margaret became the wife of J. Kellogg and is now deceased; Sarah M. is the widow of C. L. Porr and resides in the city of Burlington, Iowa; William remains on the old homestead farm in Erie county, Pennsylvania; John G., the immediate subject of this review, was the next in order of birth; Mary S. is the wife of S. Henry, of Dunkirk, Ohio; Henry F. is a resident of Ragan, Harlan county, Nebraska; Arthur J. is deceased; and Ninetta E. is the wife of L. Darling, of Chandlers Valley, Pennsylvania.

In the old Keystone state John S. Goodban was reared and educated, his scholastic discipline having included an effective course in the Pennsylvania Normal School at Edinboro. His career as a representative of the pedagogic profession covered a period of nearly fifteen years—1868-1882—and he proved a most successful and popular teacher. In 1867 Mr. Goodban numbered himself among the pioneers of Butler county, Iowa, and in that state he continued his service as a teacher, besides following agricultural pursuits, until 1870, when he came to Otoe county, Nebraska. In 1872 he established his home in Gage county. Here he continued to teach in the district schools during the winter terms for the ensuing decade, and in the meanwhile he carried forward the improvement of his farm. In Section 14 Highland township, one mile south and one-half mile west of Cortland, he entered a pre-emption claim of one hundred and sixty acres, and here he established his home. He broke the prairie soil and made it available for cultivation, set out forty acres of timber and with the passing years so developed and improved his land as to make it one of the valuable farms of the county. He was specially successful in the raising of Red Polled Angus cattle and Poland-China swine, but did not make stock-raising subordinate to agricultural enterprise. Besides his old homestead he became the owner of other lands, and he continued his active association with farm industry until 1913, since which time he has lived virtually retired in the village of Cortland, where he owns his home property and also business buildings. He is also a stockholder and director of the Bank of Cortland. He has never abated his interest in educational affairs and served a number of years as a member of the school board of his district while still residing on the farm. Well fortified in his opinions concerning public affairs, he is a stalwart advocate of the principles of the Republican party, and he and his wife are members of the Congregational church, he being treasurer of the church of this denomination at Cortland, in 1917-1918, and having previously served a number of years as a member of the board of trustees.

February 25, 1871, recorded the marriage of Mr. Goodban to Miss Emma J. Mosher, who likewise is a native of Pennsylvania and who was a resident of Iowa at the time of her marriage, her father, the late P. J. Mosher, having been a pioneer of the Hawkeye state. In conclusion is given brief record concerning the children of Mr. and Mrs. Goodban: Eva is the widow of J. Yarnall and resides at Cortland; Carrie L. is the wife of F. Hoffman, of Ragan, Harlan county, Nebraska; Nettie E. is the wife of C. P. Jones, of Highland township; Winifred died at the age of two and one-half years; and Arthur J., whose natural mechanical talent has been so developed as to make him an expert machinist, conducts an automobile garage at Cortland, with a well equipped machine and repair shop in connection therewith, besides which he is manager of the Cortland electric-lighting plant and system, he having been one of the organizers of the company which installed this important public utility, and being one of its stockholders.

CLIFFORD P. FALL, M. D.—For a period of virtually thirty years Dr. Fall has been established in the practice of his profession at Beatrice, judicial center of Gage county, and the unequivocal success which he has achieved in his exacting vocation fully attests to his high professional attainments and his facility in the effective application of his technical knowledge. The Doctor has long controlled a substantial and representative general practice, commands inviolable place in popular confidence and esteem and is essentially one of the representative physicians and surgeons of Gage county.

CLIFFORD P. FALL, M. D.

Dr. Fall was born in Boone county, Indiana, on the 9th of February, 1863, and is a son of David and Annie (Kernodle) Fall, the former a native of North Carolina and the latter of Virginia, both families having been founded in the fair southland many generations ago. The parents of Dr. Fall were children at the time of the immigration of the respective families to Preble county, Ohio, in the pioneer days, and they were reared and educated in the old Buckeye state, their marriage having been solemnized in Union county, Ohio. David Fall became a successful farmer in Boone county, Indiana, and there his death occurred when his son, Clifford P., subject of this review, was but two years of age. Dr. Fall was reared in his native county and there received the advantages of the public schools. Though his youthful experience had to do principally with the basic art of agriculture, he had the ambition that led him to seek a broader sphere of endeavor in choosing his life vocation. He took up the study of medicine and finally went to the city of Chicago, where he was matriculated in the College of Physicians & Surgeons. In this celebrated institution he was graduated as a member of the class of 1888 and in April of that year, shortly after receiving his well earned degree of Doctor of Medicine, he came to Nebraska and established his permanent residence in the progressive little city of Beatrice, which has continued as the stage of his earnest and successful professional endeavors during the intervening period of thirty years.

Dr. Fall has significantly amplified the scope of his professional work and made a valuable contribution to his home city through his conducting of a well equipped sanitarium and hospital which is known as the Beatrice Sanitarium. This institution was founded by Dr. Fall and Dr. G. A. Harris about the year 1902, and from a modest inception is has been developed into a well ordered hospital of modern equipment and facilities, the same providing for the accommodation of twenty-five patients. Dr. Fall served four years as a member of the Nebraska state board of health, and at the time of the Spanish-American war he served as special contract surgeon at the United States military cantonment at Chickamauga, for a period of three months. He is an active and valued member of the Gage county Medical Society and the Nebraska State Medical Society, besides holding membership in the American Medical Association. Through recourse to the best standard and periodical literature of his profession and through individual study and research Dr. Fall insistently keeps in touch with the advances made in medical and surgical science, and brings to bear in his practice the results of this consistent application. Though he has subordinated all other interests to the demands of his profession he has been an exponent of loyal and progressive citizenship and gives allegiance to the Democratic party, his predilections never having been such as to lead him to seek or desire political office of any description. He not only gives his attention to his large private practice, but also has the active supervision of the Beatrice Sanitarium, of which he is now sole proprietor. He was one of the organizers of the Beatrice Building & Loan Association, which has developed a large and prosperous business that extends into the various sections of Nebraska, and of this progressive association the Doctor has been president from the time of its organization. In the Masonic fraternity Dr. Fall has completed the circle of each the York and the Scottish Rites, in the latter of which he has received the thirty-second degree. He is past exalted ruler of Beatrice Lodge of the Benevolent & Protective Order of Elks, and is a member of the Presbyterian church.

In the year 1885 was solemnized the marriage of Dr. Fall to Miss Annie Kemper, who was born in the state of Wisconsin, and they have two children,—Hazel F., who is the wife of Carl F. Shafer, of Beatrice, and Frederick who remains at the parental home.

FREDERICK H. HOWEY.—The business career of Frederick H. Howey has been significantly characterized by courage, self-reliance, and progressiveness, as well as by that dynamic initiative and executive ability that brings normally in its train a full measure of success. His resolute purpose and inviolable integrity have begotten the popular confidence and esteem that are so essential in the furtherance of success in the important line of enterprise along which he has directed his attention and energies, and through the medium of which he has gained secure status as one of the representative figures in the financial circles of Nebraska. During practically his entire business career Mr. Howey has been closely associated with banking enterprise, and there is needed no further voucher for the precedence he has gained, than the statement that he is now president of the First National Bank of Beatrice; president of the First State Savings Bank of the same city; president of the State Bank of Liberty, Gage county; treasurer of the National Accident Insurance Company of Lincoln, Nebraska; and a director of the Farmers' Bank & Trust Company of Fort Collins, Colorado. As a banker Mr. Howey has shown special constructive talent, and through his effective policies and efforts he has furthered the success of every financial enterprise with which he has become associated. As one of the representative business men and progressive and public-spirited citizens of Gage county he merits specific recognition in this publication.

Mr. Howey was born in the vicinity of Columbus, the fair capital city of Ohio, on the 9th of December, 1868, and is a son of Rev. John D. and Lina E. (Bowman) Howey.

Rev. John D. Howey was born November 21, 1831, and was summoned from the stage of life's mortal endeavors on the 29th of December, 1894. After completing a four years' course in Jefferson College, at Pittsburgh Pennsylvania, and a two years' course in the Allegheny Theological Seminary he entered the ministry of the Presbyterian church, in which he was ordained in 1858. For the long period of thirty-eight years he continued as an able and faithful clergyman of the Presbyterian fold, and his earnest labors terminated only when death set its seal upon his mortal lips. He was a man of fine intellectuality and labored with all of consecrated zeal and devotion in the vineyard of the Divine Master. He held pastoral charges in Ohio and Illinois prior to becoming one of the pioneer ministers of the Presbyterian church in Nebraska, in which state he established his residence in 1884. Here he served in various pastorates, and though his death occurred in the city of Lincoln he was at the time maintaining his home at Hastings, this state. He was born and reared in Pennsylvania and was sixty-three years of age at the time of his death, his memory being revered by all who came within the sphere of his kindly and benignant influence. Mrs. Lina E. (Bowman) Howey was born at Neilsburg, Pennsylvania, in 1835, a daughter of John and Nancy Bowman. Her marriage to Rev. John D. Howey was solemnized in the year 1861, and she survived him by nearly a quarter of a century. Mrs. Howey passed the closing period of her life in the home of her daughter Ivie, wife of William C. Black, Jr., of Beatrice, and she passed to eternal rest July 19, 1917, after a lingering illness and when in her eighty-second year. For more than twenty years this gracious gentlewoman had been a resident of Beatrice and was here a member of the First Presbyterian church, in the work of which she took an active and devoted interest. Concerning the children of Rev. and Mrs. John D. Howey the following brief data are available: W. Clement is living retired on a small farm homestead near the city of Lincoln, this state; Loyal B. is president of the City National Bank of Lincoln; Frederick H., of this review, was the next in order of birth; Clyde G. is an osteopathic physician and is engaged in the successful practice of his profession in the city of Philadelphia, Pennsylvania; Miss Marie T. has held responsible clerical positions in connection with the banking business for a long term of years, was for some time in the employ of Hon. William Jennings Bryan, and she now resides in the city of Los Angeles, California; Ivie B. is the wife of William C. Black. Jr., and they maintain their home at Beatrice.

Frederick H. Howey acquired his early education in the public schools and after the removal of the family to Nebraska, when he was about sixteen years of age, he continued his studies in the schools of the cities of Lincoln and Fairmont, where his father held pastoral charges. Mr. Howey early began to depend upon his own resources and he has been in the truest sense the artificer of his own fortunes as one of the world's productive workers. At the age of eighteen years he left the gracious environment of the parental home and found employment as a clerk in a dry-goods establishment in the city of Lincoln. His judgment and ambition prompted him to further reinforce himself by taking a course in bookkeeping and accounting, and for this purpose he pursued his studies in a business college at Lincoln. Soon afterward he found employment as bookkeeper in the State National Bank of Lincoln, and after four years of effective service with this institution he was elected cashier of the Bank of Marquette, in the village of Marquette, Hamilton county, where he remained one year—in the later '80s. For a short time thereafter he held a position in the American Exchange National Bank in Lincoln, and he then purchased an interest in and assumed the position of cashier of the First National Bank at Humphrey, Platte county, at the time the same was organized as successor of the Citizens' State Bank. He played a large part in the upbuilding of the substantial business of this institution and continued the incumbent of the office of cashier until 1897, when he resigned his position and came to Beatrice, where he was elected vice-president of the First National Bank. This office he retained until 1911, since which time he has been president of the institution, his administration in each of these offices having been potent in furthering the advancement of this representative institution, which bases its operations on a capital stock of one hundred thousand dollars, the while its surplus fund and undivided profits have now attained to the significant aggregate of more than sixty thousand dollars. Since 1909 Mr. Howey has served also as president of the First State Savings Bank of Beatrice, which has a capital stock of twelve thousand five hundred dollars, surplus and undivided profits of six thousand dollars and deposits to the amount of more than one hundred thousand dollars. Under his careful and progressive régime the First National Bank has made a wonderful advancement in the volume of its business, and its deposits are now in excess of one million dollars, the bank having been founded in 1877, and being one of the leading financial institutions of southeastern Nebraska. It has previously been noted that Mr. Howey is president also of the State Bank of Liberty, and it may further be stated that this institution has a capital stock of twenty-five thousand dollars and deposits of approximately three hundred and fifty thousand dollars.

In 1907 Mr. Howey became associated with his brother Loyal B. in the organization and incorporation of the National Accident Insurance Company, at Lincoln, and the same has operations based on a capital stock of one hundred thousand dollars, he being treasurer of the company and his brother the president. Unequivocal success has attended the underwriting business of this corporation, and in extending health and accident indemnity the company now has in force policies representing about four million dollars. Its thorough reliability and able executive control have caused this company to have a remarkable growth within a decade, and it now has an extensive and representative list of patrons throughout the state of Nebraska, as well as a good business in other states of this section of the Union.

As a broad-gauged and liberal citizen Mr. Howey has always shown vital interest in community affairs, and he has served three years as a member of the Beatrice school board. He has been active in the local councils of the Republican party, as attested by the fact that he has served since 1916 as treasurer of the Gage county Republican committee. He is, however, essentially a business man and has not deviated from his course to become an aspirant for public office of any kind. He and his wife are active members of the First Presbyterian church of Beatrice and he is affiliated with the local organizations of the Masonic fraternity, including Mount Herman Commandery of Knights Templars, as is he also with Beatrice Lodge of the Benevolent & Protective Order of Elks.

In 1894 was solemnized the marriage of Mr. Howey to Miss Eva Tamblyn, who was born at Mason City, Illinois, and who was reared at Altona, Knox county, Illinois, in which state she was graduated in the Musical Conservatory of Knox College, at Galesburg. A pianist of exceptional ability, she was a successful teacher of music prior to her marriage, and she is a leader in church work and the literary and musical circles of Beatrice, where she is a popular factor in the representative social activities of the community. Mr. and Mrs. Howey have three children Earle T., who was born in 1896, was a member of the class of 1920 in the University of Nebraska, where also he is affiliated with the Phi Kappa Psi fraternity, but in December, 1917, he enlisted in the regular army of the United States, for service in the great European war; Katharyn, who was born in the year 1897, is a member of the class of 1919 in the University of Nebraska, where she holds membership in the Delta Gama sorority; and Walden H., born in 1900, is a member of the class of 1919 in the Beatrice high school.

SOLOMON HARPSTER was one of the strong and worthy pioneers who came to Nebraska in the year that marked the admission of the territory to statehood, the first year of his residence within the borders of the new commonwealth having been passed in Richardson county, and his home having been established in Gage county in 1868. He contributed to the civic and industrial development and progress of the county, represented the best in communal life and spirit and bore with fortitude and unwavering faith and confidence the hardships and trials of frontier life. He gained inviolable place in popular confidence and good will and was long and familiarly known in Gage county as "Uncle Sol Harpster." This sterling pioneer, whose death occurred in 1894, is consistently given a tribute of honor in this publication.

MR. AND MRS. SOLOMON HARPSTER

Solomon Harpster was born in the state of Pennsylvania and was seventy years and twelve days of age at the time of his death. He became a resident of Ohio when about nine years of age, remained in the old Buckeye state until 1867, when he came with his family to the newly created state of Nebraska and, as previously noted, established himself in Richardson county, whence he came to Gage county about one year later. In this county he secured a homestead of one hundred and sixty acres of wild prairie land, in Sicily township. It is interesting to record that this land, to which he received a deed from the government, has never passed from the possession of the family, by members of which it is still held. Mr. Harpster reclaimed his land and developed the same into one of the valuable farm properties of the county. In Ohio his health had been considerably impaired, but he found the climate and vital influences of Nebraska so invigorating that he became a man of robust health. He labored with characteristic zeal and ability in furthering the development of his farm and in aiding the general advancement of the county along civic and material lines. He lived in this section of Nebraska during the early pioneer days in which hardships and privations drew men together in strong ties of friendship and helpfulness, and his genial personality gained to him the sobriquet of Uncle Sol, by which he was known to all the early settlers.

Mr. Harpster superintended the building of the bridge across the Blue river at Blue Springs and also the erection of the first county jail, at Beatrice. He was careful and upright in all of the relations of life, had a fine sense of personal stewardship and was never known to use profane language, tobacco or intoxicating liquors. Both he and his wife were lifelong and zealous members of the Evangelical church. In coming to Gage county he transported his family and effects with wagon and ox team, and the oxen he there after utilized in breaking his land and otherwise carrying forward the development of his farm.

In Ohio was solemnized, June 16, 1850, the marriage of Mr. Harpster to Miss Judith Beck, and they passed the closing years of their lives in their pleasant home in the village of Blue Springs, his death having occurred in December, 1894, and his widow having entered into eternal rest in March, 1911, when seventy-seven years of age. They became the parents of four children: Malissa is the widow of Samuel Mowry, to whom a memoir is dedicated on other pages of this volume; Alonzo is a boilermaker by trade and is employed in the shops of the Chicago, Burlington & Quincy Railroad at Wymore, this county; George resides in the city of Lincoln and is a conductor in the service of the Chicago, Burlington & Quincy Railroad; and Miss Sue remains at the old home of her parents at Blue Springs.

JOHN L. ANDERSON.—Definite efficiency has characterized the service of Mr. Anderson in the responsible office of cashier of the Union

State Bank, of Beatrice, and his administration has done much to conserve the success that has marked the history of this important and representative financial institution of Gage county, the while his personality and civic loyalty have gained to him inviolable place in popular confidence and esteem.

Mr. Anderson was born in Cook county, Illinois, on the 31st of August, 1875, and is a son of John P. and Carrie (Berendutt) Anderson, the former of whom was born in Scotland and the latter in France, their marriage having been solemnized in the state of Illinois. John P. Anderson received in his youth good educational advantages, including a course in the Bryant & Stratton Business College in the city of Chicago, and he became a business man of marked circumspection and progressiveness, so that success came to him as a natural prerogative. In Illinois he was engaged in the furniture business but about the year 1885 he came to Nebraska and established the family home in the city of Omaha. There he conducted for two and one-half years two well ordered retail groceries, and in 1888 he came to Gage county and engaged in the same line of mercantile enterprise at Beatrice. He built up a large and representative business and continued as one of the leading merchants and most highly honored citizens of Beatrice until his death, when about fifty-five years of age, his widow being still a resident of this city. Of their two children the subject of this review is the elder, and Sylvia is the wife of Charles D. Loper, secretary of the wholesale woolen house of Mullin & Company, of Chicago. John P. Anderson was liberal and public-spirited in his civic attitude, gave his allegiance to the Republican party, and was an earnest communicant of the Protestant Episcopal church, as is also his widow.

John L. Anderson, the immediate subject of this sketch, acquired his early education principally in the public schools of the cities of Omaha and Beatrice and at the age of sixteen years he assumed a clerical position in the First National Bank of Beatrice. In this institution he won promotion to the position of assistant cashier, of which he continued the incumbent several years. On the 4th of July, 1912, he purchased stock in the Union State Bank of Beatrice, of which he has since continued to serve as cashier and to the upbuilding of which he has contributed in large measure. The bank was founded in 1902, bases its operations on a capital stock of fifty thousand dollars, has surplus and undivided profits of six thousand dollars, and its deposits now aggregate more than eight hundred and fifty thousand dollars. When he took the position of cashier the institution had deposits of only one hundred and fifty thousand dollars, and the remarkable increase since that time gives a measure of testimony to his efficiency of administration and to his unqualified personal popularity.

As a broad-minded and progressive citizen Mr. Anderson manifests lively interest in all things touching the communal welfare and his political allegiance is given to the Republican party. He is prominently identified with the time-honored Masonic fraternity, in which his affiliations are here briefly noted: Beatrice Lodge, No. 19, Ancient Free & Accepted Masons, of which he is past master; Livingston Chapter, No. 10, Royal Arch Masons, of which he is past high priest; Rabona Council, Royal & Select Masters, in which he has passed various official chairs; and Mount Herman Commandery, No. 7, Knights Templars, of which he is past eminent commander. He is one of the charter members of the Beatrice lodge of the Benevolent & Protective Order of Elks and served for a long period as treasurer of the same. Both he and his wife are zealous communicants of Christ church, Protestant Episcopal, and he has been a member of the vestry of this parish since 1915.

In the year 1907 was solemnized the marriage of Mr. Anderson to Miss Charlotte P. Smith, who was born and reared in Nebraska and whose father, Samuel C. Smith, has been long and prominently identified with the banking business in Beatrice. Mr. and Mrs. Anderson have one son, Peter, who was born on the 19th of November, 1909. Mrs. Anderson, a woman of culture and most gracious personality, is a leader in church, musical, and social activities in her home city. She was afforded the advantages of St. Gabriel's School at Peekskill, New York, and later pursued a course in voice culture under the preceptorship of Mrs. Morris, a leading teacher of music in the city of New York. She is the popular chatelaine of one of the attractive and hospitable homes of the city of Beatrice.

HENRY J. WIEBE.—This representative agriculturist and stockgrower of Blakely township has been a resident of Gage county for forty years. He was about sixteen years of age when he came with his widowed mother and younger brother to Beatrice and by making good use of the advantages here offered he has made his way forward to the goal of independence and marked prosperity. He is the owner of a valuable farm property of two hundred and twenty acres, one hundred and sixty acres being in Section 20 and the remaining sixty acres in Section 17, Blakely township. With the effective cooperation of his sons Mr. Wiebe is now identified with the farming and stock-raising operations on an aggregate of four hundred and sixty acres, and since 1916 he has given special attention to the breeding and feeding of thoroughbred short-horn cattle.

Mr. Wiebe was born in Prussia, Germany, on the 28th of February, 1863, and is a son of Jacob and Emeline (Penner) Wiebe, his father having been a prosperous farmer in Prussia at the time of his death. The subject of this review acquired his early education in the excellent schools of his fatherland and on the 18th of August, 1878, in company with his widowed mother, his younger brother and his one sister, he set sail for the United States. Disembarking in the port of New York city, the family came forthwith to Nebraska and settled at Beatrice. In this locality the two sons found employment at farm work, and concerning the younger son, Jacob W., individual mention is made on other pages, the daughter, Anna, being now the wife of W. A. Penner, of Beatrice, and the devoted mother having here continued to reside until her health became impaired and she was moved to visit her old home in Germany. In June, 1883, she returned to Germany, and there her death occurred in the following year, when she was nearly fifty years of age. This revered pioneer woman was a devoted Mennonite in religious faith and assisted in the organizing of the first church of this denomination in Gage county.

After the family home had been established in Gage county, Henry J. Wiebe attended the public schools of Beatrice for six months, at the time when Hugh J. Dobbs was the superintendent, and as a student both here and in his native land he gave special attention to botany and chemistry. His recompense for his services during the first year of his residence in Gage county was only fifty dollars, and he continued his activities as a farm employe for seven years, during the last of which he received wages of one hundred and eighty dollars. Thereafter he was associated with his brother in farming on rented land for one year, and in 1886 he purchased his present homestead farm of one hundred and sixty acres. The place was improved with a good house but with the passing years he has made further improvements that mark the farm as a model according to twentieth century standards. In 1907 he erected the present large barn on his farm, the same being thirty-six by sixty feet in dimensions. With increasing prosperity he added to the area of his farm and he gives his attention vigorously to diversified agriculture and the raising of superior live stock. In the season of 1917 he had one hundred and fifty acres devoted to corn and eighty-six acres to oats. He is a Republican of independent proclivities and he and his wife are earnest members of the Mennonite church, in which he is a teacher in the Sunday school.

March 10, 1887, was the date of the marriage of Mr. Wiebe to Miss Mary Wiebe, who came with her parents from Prussia to America in 1876. Her father, John G. Wiebe, became a successful lumber dealer at Beatrice, and of him mention is made on other pages of this work. Mr. and Mrs. Wiebe have eight children, the two elder sons, Gerhard R. and Henry P., being progressive farmers of this county, and all of the other children remaining at the parental home, namely: Alfred, Rudolph, Arnold, Oscar, Gertrude, and Kate.

CARL SONDEREGGER.—One of Nebraska's sterling pioneer citizens who has here had the prescience and energy to make the most of the opportunities offered in connection with civic and material development and progress. Mr. Sonderegger has achieved large and worthy success through his association with agricultural industry and later as an aggressive exponent of the nursery business. His original dwelling in Jefferson county was a "dugout" of the most primitive pioneer type, the same being established on the embryonic farm which figured as the stage of his vigorous activities in the early days. In evidence of his ability and worthy achievement stands his now extensive and well ordered nursery and seed industry, high-grade fruit and ornamental trees, shrubbery, seeds of all kinds, etc., being now shipped from his well equipped nursery plant into the most diverse sections of the Union, the while the little farm dugout pales into retrospective obscurity when it is recognized that the home of the Sonderegger family in the city of Beatrice is conceded to be one of the finest residence properties in the county, the building being a commodious structure of modern architectural design and most attractive appointments. Mr. Sonderegger has proved himself one of the world's constructive workers and in the furtherance of his own prosperity has aided also in the civic and material development and progress of the county and state of his adoption. As one of the honored and representative citizens and business men of Gage county he is especially entitled to recognition in this history.

Carl Sonderegger was born in the fair little republic of Switzerland, on the 31st of January, 1856, and is one of the eight surviving children of Conrad and Lena (Hohl) Sonderegger, both of whom passed their entire lives in Switzerland. Of the children only two came to America,— Carl, subject of this review, and Arthur, who is now a representative civil engineer residing at Los Angeles, California. The father was identified with farm industry in earlier days, but achieved his success principally as a manufacturer, and he accounted well for himself in all of the relations of life, his father, Conrad Sonderegger, likewise having been a farmer and manufacturer in Switzerland. The family has been notable for the sturdiest of physical powers and for incidental longevity, and in this connection it may be noted that not until their final illness were either the parents or the paternal grandparents of Carl Sonderegger known to be sick for even a day. Jacob Hohl, maternal grandfather of Mr. Sonderegger, was a citizen of prominence and influence in Switzerland, where he served as governor of his canton and held for forty years the office of mayor of the city of Heiden.

In his youth Carl Sonderegger received good educational advantages, and, like many another son of Switzerland, he acquired full command of both the German and French languages. As a youth he became associated with his father in the manufacturing of the fine Swiss embroidery, and finally his youthful ambition led him to sever the home ties and come to the United States, where he felt assured of better opportunities for attaining independence and prosperity through his own effort. In 1875 he came to America and in the same year he numbered himself among the pioneers of Jefferson county, Nebraska. He purchased a tract of one hundred and sixty acres of unimproved land, twenty miles west of Beatrice, and developed the same eventually into one of the valuable farms of this section of the state. There he continued his successful activities as an agriculturist and stock grower for a full quarter of a century, and at the present time he owns his admirably equipped nursery farm of one hundred and twenty acres, the soil being specially available for the propagation of high-grade nursery stock and its fertility being perpetuated through proper scientific treatment.

In initiating his nursery industry Mr. Sonderegger began operation on a modest scale, and the first catalogue which he issued contained only four pages. He has brought to bear the best scientific methods and the most scrupulous care in the development and upbuilding of the enterprise, and the business now demands the issuing of large catalogues annually, an average of one hundred thousand of these attractive catalogues being distributed each year. In the year 1900 Mr. Sonderegger established the headquarters of his nursery business in the city of Beatrice, and the industry has in its splendid development contributed much to the industrial and commercial prestige of the city and county. Mr. Sonderegger is imbued with the most vital spirit of civic pride and loyalty and has been specially influential in the development of the attractive system of public parks in Beatrice, where he is now chairman of the municipal board of park commissioners, his political allegiance being given to the Democratic party. As a matter of commercial expediency Mr. Sonderegger has incorporated his business under the laws of Nebraska and with the title of the Sonderegger Nursery and Seed House. Operations are based on a capital stock of one hundred thousand dollars, but all of the stock is held by members of the Sonderegger family, so that it is a close corporation, the subject of this sketch, as may be inferred, being the executive head of the business. He is a member of the directorate of the Union State Bank of Beatrice and also of that of the Bonner Portland Cement Company, of Kansas City, Missouri. He is affiliated with the Beatrice lodge of the Benevolent & Protective Order of Elks and he and his wife are active members of the Christian church in their home city.

In the year 1875 was solemnized the marriage of Mr. Sonderegger to Miss Babetta Hohl, who likewise was born and reared in Switzerland and who joined him in America within a short time after his immigration to this country. Most gracious have been the relations of the family home circle and in the concluding paragraph of this article are given brief data concerning the children of Mr. and Mrs. Sonderegger.

Clara married and resides in La Crosse, Wisconsin. Charles, who is associated with his father in business, married Miss Mabel Jones and they have two children,—Carl and Morris; Lydia is the wife of Charles Hughes, a farmer of Jefferson county, this state, and they have three children,—Clara, Leo and Lucille; Leo, who is now engaged in business in New York city, married Miss Louise Getzentanner and has two children,—Leo and Louise; Frederick, who is associated with his father's nursery business, wedded Miss H. Sonderegger and they have three children,—Frederick, Arnold and Margaret; Ernest has more special connection with the seed department of the Sonderegger nursery: the maiden name of his wife was Helen Loeber and they have no children; Lena is the wife of Ralph Rosezell, who is engaged in the photographic business in Beatrice, and their two children are Richard and Catherine; Arthur, who is connected with the nursery business of his father, wedded Miss Ruth Atwater, and they have one child, Phyllis; Hilda is the wife of Clayton Harris and they reside at Los Angeles, California; and Helen remains at the parental home.

FRANK W. JONES.—The attractive little village of Clatonia claims Mr. Jones as one of its liberal citizens and representative business men. Here he has developed a prosperous enterprise in the handling of lumber and building supplies, and in connection there with he keeps pace with the modern trend by acting also as agent for the celebrated Overland automobile for this part of the county.

Mr. Jones was born on a farm near the city of Dixon, Illinois, on the 8th of April, 1870, and is a son of George H. and Jane A. (Whitcomb) Jones. He is the eldest in a family of four children and concerning the others the following brief data may consistently be entered: Elva is the wife of James E. McCormack, who is a partner in the business of the subject of this sketch; Cyrus P. is a prosperous farmer in Highland township; and

Verna remains with her widowed mother in the pleasant home in the village of Cortland, this county.

George H. Jones was born in the state of Maine, in 1847, and was nine years of age when he accompanied his parents on their removal to Illinois, where he was reared and educated and where he continued his residence until 1872, when he came to Nebraska and became one of the pioneers of Gage county. He entered claim to a homestead of eighty acres in Highland township; in 1874 he purchased from the railroad company an adjoining eighty acres, and in 1884 he added another eighty acres to his valuable landed estate. His old homestead place is situated in Section 30, and he owned also the northwest one-half of Section 31 in the same township. He made the best of improvements upon his land and was one of the prominent farmers of the county for many years. For a time he rented his farm and he was engaged in the mercantile business in Cortland, Nebraska, about two years. Finally he retired again from his farm and moved to Cortland, where he remained until his death, in 1909. Mr. Jones was a man of sterling character and marked ability, so that be consistently was called upon to serve as a member of the county board of supervisors—an office in which he made a record for liberality and progressiveness. He was a staunch supporter of the cause of the Republican party and was an active member of the Methodist Episcopal church, as is also his widow. Mrs. Jones was born near the city of Philadelphia, Pennsylvania, and was a resident of Illinois at the time of her marriage. She is one of the loved pioneer women of Gage county and is now about seventy years of age. She still resides at Cortland.

Frank W. Jones was a child of two years at the time of the family removal to Gage county, where he was reared on the home farm and early gained experience in herding cattle on the prairies, besides which he recalls as a part of his experience in the pioneer days the occasional seeing of deer in this section of the state. He was afforded the advantages of the public schools and continued to be associated with his father in farm industry until the removal of his parents to the village of Cortland, where for the ensuing two years he clerked in his father's general store. The next year there found him employed as assistant in a lumber yard, and on the 14th of February, 1893, he removed to Clatonia, where for the following year he had charge of the lumber yard of his uncle, H. H. Jones. He then opened a general merchandise store in the village and for the following eleven years he successfully conducted this business. In 1893 he was appointed postmaster of Clatonia, and of this office he continued the incumbent until he sold his mercantile business and formed a partnership with James E. McCormack, with whom he has here been associated in the retail lumber trade since that time. He is the owner of his attractive residence in Clatonia and also of other realty in the village. Taking a loyal interest in local affairs, Mr. Jones was the one who prepared the petition that led to the incorporation of the village of Clatonia, and since that time he has served several terms as a member of the municipal council. His political allegiance is given to the Republican party and he and his wife hold membership in the Methodist Episcopal church.

December 21, 1893, recorded the marriage of Mr. Jones to Miss Ella L. Albert, a daughter of Henry Albert, of whom specific mention is made on other pages of this work, so that further record concerning the family is not demanded in the present connection. Mr. and Mrs. Jones have but one child, Izetta, who was born July 27, 1896, and who remains at the parental home—a young woman of culture and one who is a popular figure in the social activities of her home community. Miss Jones was for two years a student in the high school of Lincoln, Nebraska's capital city, and thereafter she was for two years a student in the high school at University Place. She is now attending Wesleyan University, at University Place, Lancaster county. She taught two terms of school in Grant township and proved herself a successful worker in the pedagogic service.

BENJAMIN F. STEINMEYER, who is one of the progressive and successful exponents of agricultural and live-stock enterprise in his native county and a member of one of the well known and influential pioneer families of this section of Nebraska, was born in Clatonia township, on the 27th of January, 1883, a son of William and Louisa (Schlake) Steinmeyer, of whose ten children the firstborn was John, who died in infancy; Sophia, who was born April 11, 1873, remains with her widowed mother; Ella died in early childhood; Henry, a representative farmer of Clatonia township, was born April 13, 1878; Anna is the wife of Fred Carsten, of Hallan, Lancaster county, her birth having occurred February 5, 1881; Benjamin F., immediate subject of this review, was the next in order of birth; William, who was born April 5, 1885, has the management of the old homestead farm, in Clatonia township; Jennie, who was born February 16, 1887, is the wife of A. P. Kost, of St. Joseph, Missouri; Edwin, who was born February 25, 1890, is a prosperous farmer of Clatonia township, and his twin brother, Albert, died at the age of nineteen years.

WILIAM STEINMEYER

The late William Steinmeyer was born in the province of Hanover, Germany, July 9, 1839, a son of John Henry and Elizabeth (Fradiker) Steinmeyer, there having been five other children,—Frederick, Henry, Mary, Ann and Emma. John Henry Steinmeyer immigrated with his family to America in 1857, and after a voyage of eight weeks on a sailing vessel they landed in Baltimore, Maryland. The family home was established in Scioto county, Ohio, where John Henry Steinmeyer continued his residence until the autumn of 1865, when he came with other members of his family to Nebraska Territory. In the following spring he came to Gage county and filed claim to a homestead of one hundred and sixty acres in Clatonia township, the present thriving village of Clatonia being on the tract which he thus secured prior to the admission of Nebraska to the Union. He reclaimed his pioneer farm to cultivation and he and his wife here passed the remainder of their lives.

William Steinmeyer was reared and educated in his native land and was eighteen years of age at the time of the family immigration to America. Upon coming with his father to Gage county, Nebraska, in the spring of 1866, he took up a homestead of one hundred and sixty acres, in Section 28, Clatonia township, this place being an integral part of the large and finely improved landed estate which he eventually accumulated and which is still owned by his widow. Of the conditions that here prevailed at the time when Mr. Steinmeyer initiated his pioneer experience the following interesting statements have been written: "The embryonic farm bore little resemblance to its condition in the present day, the plowshare never having passed over it and not a building having been erected for the shelter of man or beast. Mr. Steinmeyer was prepared, however, for this state of things and after finding a temporary home he began to gather together implements for the cultivation of the soil, while he girded himself earnestly and staunchly for the developing of a productive farm from the prairie wilds." Mr. Steinmeyer made the best of improvements upon his original homestead, and the buildings and general attractiveness of the place to-day evidence his industry and good management. On the old homestead he continued to reside until his death, which occurred July 3, 1911, and he was one of the honored pioneer citizens of the county when he was thus called from the stage of life's mortal endeavors. He became the owner of a fine landed estate of one thousand four hundred and sixty acres in Gage county, five hundred acres in Missouri and three hundred and twenty acres in Kansas. His sons utilize the various farms for their productive activities as agriculturalists and stock growers. He was a stalwart Republican in politics was loyal and progressive as a citizen and his ability and popularity gave him marked influence in community affairs. He served two terms as treasurer of Clatonia township and was a charter member of the German Methodist church that was organized by his father in Clatonia township, his widow likewise being an earnest member of this religious body.

MRS. WILLLIAM STEINMEYER

January 19, 1870, recorded the marriage of Mr. Steinmeyer to Miss Louisa Schlake, who was born in Prussia, February 12, 1851, a daughter of Henry and Mary (Tieman) Schlake, the former of whom passed his entire life in Germany and who was survived by five children,—Mary Ann, William, Charlotte, Louisa and Caroline. The devoted mother came to America in 1870 and came with her daughter to Gage county, where she died four weeks later. Mrs. Steinmeyer was reared and educated in her native land and was about seventeen years of age when, in 1869, she came to the United States in company with her sister. She remained for a time at Aurora, Illinois, and after a few months came to Gage county, Nebraska, where her marriage was shortly afterward solemnized. After the death of her husband she removed to the village of Clatonia, where she and her eldest daughter have an attractive home, and she still retains ownership of the valuable farm property accumulated by her honored husband. All of her ten children, of whom mention has been made in an earlier paragraph, received good educational advantages, including those of the college at Warrenton, Missouri.

Benjamin F. Steinmeyer, the immediate subject of this review, was reared on the old home farm, and after completing the curriculum of the district schools he was for some time a student in the Central Wesleyan College, at Warrenton, Missouri. He has never found it expedient or a matter of desire to deflect his course from farm industry and he is now successfully carrying on progressive enterprise as an agriculturist and stock-grower in his native township, where he operates a part of the family estate, in Clatonia township. His political support is given to the Republican party and at Beatrice he is affiliated with the lodge of the Benevolent and Protective Order of Elks, besides which he is a member of Blue Valley Lodge, Ancient Free & Accepted Masons, at Wilber, Saline county.

On the 2d of June, 1915, Mr. Steinmeyer wedded Miss Alice Balderson, who was born at Crete, Saline county, October 1, 1890, a daughter of Jacob and Carrie (Schnacker) Balderson, who removed eventually to Wilber, that county, where the father is living retired, Mrs. Balderson being now deceased. Mr. and Mrs. Steinmeyer have a fine little son, George Benjamin, who was born August 6, 1916.

TAMME R. ZIMMERMAN, a venerable and highly honored citizen who is now living retired in the city of Beatrice, is a man who has proved one of the world's productive workers and one who has merited the distinctive prosperity that is his in the gracious evening of his long and useful life. He is the owner of two thousand acres of land in Texas, and in Nebraska he owns sixteen hundred and eighty acres in Gage county, four hundred and eighty in Red Willow county, three hundred and twenty in Cherry county, and one hundred and sixty in Franklin county. In his extensive operations as a farmer and ranchman he made a specialty of raising the best type of live stock, and his energy and good judgment made his success assured and cumulative.

Mr. Zimmerman was born in the province of Hanover, Germany, October 14, 1834, and is a son of Frank and Anna (Dorn) Zimmerman, of whose family of two sons and three daughters only the two sons are now living, Claus being a resident of the village of Pickrell, this county, and having celebrated in 1918 his eighty-seventh birthday anniversary. The parents passed their entire lives in Germany.

The subject of this review was but two years old at the time of his mother's death and only six years of age when his father died. Thus he was early thrown on his own resources, and how effectively he has lived up to the responsibilities devolving upon him is shown in the unqualified success which he has won through his own efforts. As a boy and youth in his native land he was able to attend school only one month each year, and there he continued to be employed at farm work until 1856, when he came to America and found employment on a farm in Menard county, Illinois. In 1859 he there took unto himself a wife, and in the following year he and his young wife came to Nebraska Territory and numbered themselves among the early pioneer settlers of Richardson county. In Franklin precinct of that county he purchased forty acres of raw prairie land, upon which he built a primitive log house, and there he continued his farming activities two years. In 1862 he came to Gage county and bought one hundred and sixty acres of land in Logan township. Here he began vigorously the agricultural and live-stock enterprise that brought to him ever-increasing success with the passing years, and as his financial resources were augmented he added gradually to his landed estate, while eventually he accumulated valuable property in other counties of Nebraska, as well as his extensive land holdings in Texas. He continued as one of the representative exponents of farm enterprise in Logan township until 1904, since which time he has lived in well earned retirement, with a comfortable and attractive home in Beatrice.

In 1859 Mr. Zimmerman married Miss Catherine Miller, who was born in Germany and who came with her father to the United States in 1855, the family home being established in Illinois. Mrs. Zimmerman passed to the life eternal on the 11th of July, 1910, a devout communicant of the German Lutheran church. Of this union were born eight children: Mrs. Anna Dorn lives in Franklin county; Mrs. Abbie Meints is a resident of Logan township, Gage county; Mrs. Fannie Baughman lives near Pickrell, this county; Eilert is living on his father's old homestead farm, in Logan township; Rachel and Renken are deceased; Mrs. Tillie Frerichs resides in Logan township; and Mrs. Mary Huttenmaier lives on a farm five miles east of Beatrice.

On the 6th of December, 1911, Mr. Zimmerman wedded Mrs. Julia (Matthews) Ayers, widow of Jonathan Ayers. By her first marriage Mrs. Zimmerman has three children William is a resident of Dodge City, Kansas, where he holds the position of inspector in the service of the Atchison, Topeka & Santa Fé Railroad; Harry is superintendent of the plant of the great packing house of Swift & Company in the city of St. Paul, Minnesota; and Mrs. Effie Grace resides at Downs, Osborne county, Kansas. Mrs. Zimmerman was born in Warren county, Pennsylvania, and was five years old when her parents, Ansel and Barbara (Dias) Matthews, became pioneer settlers in Iowa, her father having been a native of Massachusetts and her mother of Indiana. After her marriage to Jonathan Ayers, Mrs. Zimmerman came with her husband to Gage county and made settlement on the Otoe Indian reservation, in 1878, their elder son having been the first white child born on this reservation. Mr. Zimmerman is a Democrat in politics and is a member of the Lutheran church, Mrs. Zimmerman being a member of the Methodist church.

REV. LEONARD POEVERLEIN, the honored pastor of the parish of St. John's German Lutheran church in the city of Beatrice, has retained this incumbency since the 13th of December, 1883, and is one of the revered pioneer clergymen of the Lutheran faith in this section of the state—the devoted shepherd of his flock, the friend of all humanity, and the earnest vicar of the Divine Master whom he has served with all of consecrated zeal.

Mr. Poeverlein was born in the Kingdom of Bavaria, Germany, December 25, 1848, a son of George and Maria (Fakelmeier) Poeverlein, who passed their entire lives in that part of the German empire. In his native land Mr. Poeverlein was given excellent educational advantages in his youth and in preparation for the responsible work of the ministry he completed a most thorough academic and theological education in the Lutheran seminary at Neuen Dettelsau, Germany, his ordination to the ministry having occurred in 1873. Prompted by faith that in America he would find a field for effective service in his chosen calling, Mr. Poeverlein came to this country in the autumn of 1873, arriving in New York city on the 25th of September, and a few weeks later continuing his westward journey to Dubuque, Iowa. Soon afterward he became pastor of a small church organization at Iowa City, where he remained until the spring of 1874, when he came to Nebraska and, on the 18th of April, entered upon pastoral duties in Nemaha county. One year later he went to Rockport, Missouri, where he held a pastoral charge until December 13, 1883, since which time he has been pastor of St. John's church in the city of Beatrice. Under his faithful pastoral and executive direction this parish has prospered both spiritually and temporally, and the congregation now includes fifty families or more, with a roll of one hundred and fifty communicants. Mr. Poeverlein has been earnest not only in his church activities but also as a loyal and public spirited citizen interested in furthering the communal welfare along all lines, and he has the high esteem of the people among whom he has so long lived and labored.

In 1876 was solemnized the marriage of Mr. Poeverlein to Miss Louisa Hemperer, who was born and reared in Clayton county, Iowa, and of the four children of this union, the firstborn, Charles, died at the age of seventeen months; Matilda, who remains at the parental home, was graduated in the Beatrice high school, and is now a popular teacher in the public schools of her home city; Heade, likewise a graduate of the Beatrice high school, is now an efficient teacher in the public schools at Columbus, Platte county; and Freda, who remains with her parents, was graduated in the local high school and also the Beatrice Business College.

ALFRED HAZLETT.—Judge Hazlett was born and reared in Indiana county, Pennsylvania. To the country public schools of his native commonwealth he is indebted for his preliminary educational discipline, which was supplemented by a course of higher studies in Jefferson College, at Cannonsburg, Pennsylvania. In preparing himself for his chosen profession, he prosecuted his studies under the tutorship of former United States Senator Edgar Cowan, of Greensburg, Pennsylvania, and in June, 1871, he was admitted to the bar of his native state.

In the fall of 1871, having just arrived at the age of his majority, with all of his vital and youthful ambition, he came to Nebraska, and established his residence in Beatrice, where he has since continuously resided.

In the year 1876, at Omaha, Nebraska, was solemnized the marriage of Judge Hazlett to Miss Sibbie Cotton. They have no living children. Those of the early pioneers now living, and who knew him from the time of his location in Nebraska, were impressed with his tall, manly, dignified figure, and pronounced him the man that he was subsequently found to be. He was strong in mind and still at his present age is maintaining a fine, shapely physique. Of Scotch-Irish descent he was born strong for decision, judgment, and with pronounced self-independence. During all of his life he has had a dislike for the affected or pretentious, and despised hypocrisy, deceit, and dishonesty. Perhaps, on account of this one permanent feature in his character, he has always refrained from entering into what he has termed the tainted cesspool of politics, although his friends many times have urged and beseeched him to run not only for state, but for national office.

Within a period of some forty years of his professional activity, in Gage county, Judge Hazlett won, and still maintains, for himself a reputation for being one of the strongest, and most resourceful trial lawyers in southeastern Nebraska. No member of the Gage county bar has participated in so many contested cases, both of a civil and criminal nature as he, and with so great a success. His whole aim in his work was not so much for the money he could obtain from his clients but to win their cases. His judgment of men is recognized by all, and this attribute alone has never failed him in selecting the jury, and in questioning the witness. The make-up of his machinery is grand, in this: He is honest; he is keen, with a bright mind stored with legal lore; in appearance he is somewhat austere—and yet no one is more gentle in spirit—and retiring; he stands as one of our central figures; he has a liberal education, and is an able advocate. Those who have seen him in our different courts, in important cases, and have heard him address a jury, say that for forensic eloquence and convincing argument few, if any, surpass him. He is indeed a strong man, by reason of his force of character and his ability as a lawyer, and he has been and is a potent factor in the affairs of men. In all of his active professional life it is to be said that he is possessed only of a modest estate in worldly goods, and this fact is a genuine testimonial to his honesty and self-sacrifice. He has often said that there is no grander type of manhood on earth than an able, cultured, honest lawyer.

MRS. SOPHIA H. DOLE.—More than casual distinction attaches to the personality and record of this venerable and revered pioneer woman, for not only has she been a resident of Nebraska since the territorial period of its history and endured her share of the hardships and vicissitudes that marked the early stages of development and progress in this now favored commonwealth, but it has also been within her province to found and upbuild in her home city of Beatrice a most prosperous and representative business enterprise—that conducted under the corporate title of the Dole Floral Company. Though this gracious gentlewoman celebrated in 1917, the eighty-first anniversary of her birth, she still takes vital and earnest interest in the world's work and fortunes, and incidental to the activities of preparation for the nation's participation in the stupendous war in Europe she has been found busily applying herself in skillful knitting of garments and supplies for the Red Cross service and otherwise "doing her bit" to exemplify the ardent patriotism of American womanhood.

Mrs. Dole was born in the state of New York, on the 6th of October, 1836, and is a daughter of P. J. and Mary (Derbyshire) Hooker, who were pioneer settlers of Seward county, Nebraska, and whose names merit enduring place on the roster of those who aided in the civic and industrial development of the territory and state. Mrs. Dole was reared and educated in her native state and after two of her brothers had returned home after valiant service as soldiers of the Union in the Civil war, the entire family came to the Territory of Nebraska, in 1866, settlement being made in Seward county, the father, two sons, and two daughters taking homesteads. The comparative isolation and the primitive conditions that marked the life of Mrs. Dole during the pioneer period of her residence in Nebraska, could not in the least curb her intellectual activity or her ambitions, and she has grown in mental stature with the passing years, has shown abiding human sympathy and tolerance and has manifested her stewardship in kindly words and kindly deeds. Mrs. Dole has been a member of the Congregational church since she was fourteen years of age, and has exemplified her Christian faith in her daily life. Her marriage to J. G. Dole was solemnized in the year 1869, and her husband devoted the major part of his active career to brick manufacturing, he having been a resident of Beatrice at the time of his death, April 19, 1903.

Mrs. Dole has maintained her home at Beatrice, judicial center of Gage county, since 1889, and in establishing and developing the now extensive business of the Dole Floral Company she has demonstrated not only her executive ability and mature judgment, but also exemplified her desire to provide for humanity the gracious natural products that make for beauty and good cheer. Of this company specific mention is made on other pages. In her venerable years she is sustained and comforted by the filial devotion of her five children, concerning whom the following brief data are available: Edward W. is engaged in farming and is the subject of an individual record on other pages of this volume; Walter A., who was long and actively associated with the Dole Floral Company, has sold his property interests at Beatrice and is at the time of this writing, in the winter of 1917, making provisions to establish his home in the state of Georgia; Anna D. is the wife of George M. Johnston, who is manager of the Dole Floral Company, and who is individually mentioned on other pages of this publication; Ella S. is the wife of Frederick von Boskirk, who is a successful farmer of Gage county and whose life work is portrayed elsewhere in this volume; and Elbert J. is engaged in the photographic business in the city of Lincoln, this state.

JAMES B. McLAUGHLIN was a gallant young veteran of the Civil war when he made his first visit to Nebraska, in the year that marked the admission of the state to the Union, and in the autumn of the same year he returned to Illinois, where he wedded the gracious young woman who was to prove his devoted companion and helpmate during the remainder of his long and useful life and who is still living. In the spring of 1868 they settled in Sherman township. James Brady McLaughlin was a man of sterling character and high ideals, and he bore his full share of the burdens and responsibilities incidental to the march of progress in a pioneer locality, as proved by his civic loyalty and influence during the many years of his residence in Gage county and by the success which attended his activities as an exponent of agricultural and live-stock industry. He was one of the honored and venerable pioneer citizens of Rockford township at the time of his death, which occurred September 12, 1914, and it is fitting that in this history be entered a tribute to his memory.

Mr. McLaughlin was born at McKeysport, Allegheny county, Pennsylvania, on the 5th of January, 1841, and was a son of David and Hannah (Brady) McLaughlin, both natives of Westmoreland county, that state. The paternal grandfather of the subject of this memoir was John McLaughlin, who came from Scotland to America when he was a youth of sixteen years and who passed the residue of his life in Pennsylvania. The maternal grandfather was a cousin of Samuel Brady who achieved historic reputation as an Indian hunter. For fully a quarter of a century David McLaughlin served as a pilot on boats plying the Ohio river, and in 1857 he removed with his family from Pennsylvania to Rock Island county, Illinois, where he became a prosperous farmer and where he died in 1870, at the age of fifty-seven years, his widow having survived him by a number of years. They became the parents of eight sons and one daughter and all save one, the daughter, are deceased.

JAMES B. MCLAUGHLIN AND FAMILY

James B. McLaughlin gained his youthful education in the schools of the old Keystone state and was sixteen years old at the time of the family removal to Illinois, where he supplemented his education by attending school during several winter terms, when his services were not in requisition in connection with the work of the home farm. Mr. McLaughlin was twenty years of age at the outbreak of the Civil war and in 1862 he enlisted, for a three months' term, as a private in Company F, Sixty-ninth Illinois Volunteer Infantry. He was assigned to guard duty over the great number of Confederate prisoners held at Camp Douglas, Chicago, and in the autumn of 1862, he was an escort of such of these prisoners as were taken to Vicksburg, Mississippi, for exchange. He continued in service three months after the expiration of his term of enlistment and then received his honorable discharge, at Camp Douglas. In 1865 he again enlisted, for the duration of the war, and after being mustered in he was sent to New Orleans, whence he was transferred to Mobile. Finally he was assigned to guard duty at Montgomery, Alabama, where he was taken ill with fever and confined in a hospital two months. He was finally discharged, on account of physical disability, and he arrived at his home in Illinois in the autumn of 1865. There he remained until 1867, when he came to Nebraska, and after a tour of investigation he decided to establish his residence in Gage county. In Section 1, Sherman township, he entered claim to a homestead of one hundred and sixty acres, and also made entry on an additional two hundred acres in the same township. He then returned to Illinois, and in March, 1868, he there wedded Miss Phoebe King, who was born in New York city, on the 30th of August, 1843. Her father was an expert in cotton manufacturing and as such was employed in various important cotton mills in the eastern states. Mrs. McLaughlin is a daughter of James and Charlotte (Allen) King, who were natives of Manchester, England, where the father was overseer in a large cotton factory until 1840, when he came with his wife and two children to the United States, Mrs. McLaughlin having been the sixth of the ten children born. Two of her brothers are deceased and three of her sisters are living in 1918. She received good advantages and developed her marked musical talent under most favorable auspices. At the age of twenty-one years she went to Illinois and engaged in the teaching of music, which she there continued until her marriage. It may well be understood that her musical talent came in for marked appreciation in the pioneer community after she came with her husband to Gage county, and both became zealous in church work, as members of the Methodist Episcopal church, as well as popular factors in the representative social activities of the county. In pioneer reminiscence Mrs. McLaughlin states that in early days she and her husband attended church services in the old Dobbs school house, where they also served in the sessions of the Sunday school. On many an occasion Mr. and Mrs. McLaughlin were dinner guests in the home of Mr. and Mrs. F. H. Dobbs, and she states that no family in Gage county has been more benignant in influence than the Dobbs family, both in the pioneer days and in later generations, her kindly mark of appreciation being one that will be specially appreciated by the editor of this history of the county. In the early days Mrs. McLaughlin often rode home on horseback after having visited at the residence of "Father and Mother Dobbs," and frequently one of their young sons would be her escort.

Mr. and Mrs. McLaughlin remained on their farm in Sherman township until 1881, when they sold the property, with the intention of removing to California. After a visit to the old home in Illinois, however, they decided to return to Gage county, and here Mr. McLaughlin purchased the farm of one hundred and sixty acres on which he passed the remainder of his life and on which his widow still maintains her home, near the village of Rockford. He made excellent improvements on the place and it is one of the attractive rural homes of Rockford township. No children were born to Mr. and Mrs. McLaughlin but they adopted and reared a boy and girl, the latter of whom is deceased. The home of Mrs. McLaughlin is endeared to her by the hallowed memories of the past, and in the association with friends who are tried and true she is passing the gracious evening of her life in peace and comfort, loved by all who have come under her gentle influence.

In politics Mr. McLaughlin was a stalwart supporter of the cause of the Republican party, he was actively affiliated with Rawlins Post, No. 35, Grand Army of the Republic, at Beatrice, and was also a member of the Masonic fraternity. His life was guided and governed by the highest principles of integrity and honor, and naught better than this can be said of any man.

CHARLES R. HITE, president and general manager of the Blue Valley Mercantile Company, of Beatrice, has the securest of status as one of the representative business men and progressive citizens of the fine metropolis and judicial center of Gage county. He was born at Marion, Iowa, February 2, 1862, and is a son of Eli and Elizabeth (Runner) Hite, the former a native of Ohio and the latter of West Virginia, their marriage having been solemnized in Iowa, where the parents of Mrs. Hite established a home in the early '50s. Eli Hite was reared and educated in Ohio and became a pioneer settler near Marion, Linn county, Iowa, where he owned land and reclaimed a good farm. Later he was thirty years engaged in the express and transfer business at Shenandoah, Page county, Iowa, where he died when about seventy-seven years of age and where his widow still resides, the subject of this review being the eldest of the three children; Addie became the wife of Marshall Morgan, who is now deceased, and she maintains her home in the city of Beatrice, Nebraska; and Frances is the wife of Michael Gauss, who is engaged in the drug business at Sheridan, Iowa. Eli Hite was a Democrat in politics and was a member of the Methodist Episcopal church, as is also his venerable widow. His father, John Hite, passed his entire life in Ohio, where the family was founded in an early day, and he was a farmer by vocation. John Runner, maternal grandfather of the subject of this sketch, was pioneer in Iowa, where both he and his wife died.

In the public schools of Shenandoah, Iowa, C. R. Hite continued his studies until he had attained to the age of fifteen years, and thereafter be served a three years' apprenticeship to the baker's trade, at Shenandoah. In the same town he then clerked five years in the grocery department of a general store, and in 1887, as an ambitious young man of twenty-five years, he came to Nebraska and settled at Giltner, Hamilton county, where he was employed three years in a general merchandise establishment. He then became associated with James Sherard in purchasing the store and business, and Mr. Hite continued as a member of the firm for the ensuing three years. For several years thereafter he was a successful traveling salesman for the wholesale grocery house of Hargreves Brothers, of Lincoln. Upon severing this alliance he assumed a similar position with the wholesale grocery house of Groneweg,

Schotgen & Company, of Lincoln, with which concern he was connected in this capacity until 1904. In the meanwhile he had established and maintained his home in Beatrice, and in the year last mentioned he here became associated with three partners in establishing a fruit and vegetable business. Two years later the business was incorporated under the present title of the Blue Valley Mercantile Company, and the scope of operations was extended to include a wholesale grocery and confectionery business, the operations of the company being now based on a capital stock of two hundred and fifty thousand dollars and its trade being extended and well established throughout Nebraska and Kansas, so that the concern has contributed much to the commercial precedence of Beatrice, where is maintained the large and well ordered wholesale house. It has already been noted that Mr. Hite is president and general manager of the company; Gilbert L. Griffith is vice-president; and Harry S. Ahlquist is secretary and treasurer. Besides these executive officers the directorate of the company includes also William E. Rife and Joseph Bouske. When the principals in the company established the original enterprise each made an investment of only two thousand dollars, and at the time of incorporation the capital stock was placed at thirteen thousand dollars. No better evidence of the splendid growth of the enterprise can be offered than the statement that the capitalistic investment is now two hundred and fifty thousand dollars and that the annual business averages fully seven hundred and fifty thousand dollars, a corps of seven efficient traveling salesmen being retained and the number of employes at headquarters being about fifteen. It is an admirable record of achievement that has been made by Mr. Hite in the business world and his success has been won entirely through his own ability and efforts. He is liberal and public-spirited in his civic attitude, as behooves one who has been thus greatly prospered in business, and his political allegiance is given to the Republican party. He holds membership in the United Commercial Travelers' Association, is a member of the Congregational church, and his wife holds membership in the Episcopal church.

December 31, 1891, recorded the marriage of Mr. Hite to Miss Jemima Armstrong, who was born in Scotland, and who was a child at the time when her parents came to the United States and settled in Illinois, where her father engaged in farm enterprise. Mr. and Mrs. Hite have two daughters, both of whom remain at the parental home and are popular figures in the social life of Beatrice: Ethel received the advantages of the public schools of Beatrice and also completed a four years' course in the Nebraska Agricultural College; the younger daughter, Hazel, has been graduated in the Beatrice high school.

FRANK T. SCHOWENGERDT, M. D., whose character and professional attainments have given him secure vantage-ground as one of the representative physicians and surgeons of Gage county, is established in the general practice of his profession at Cortland, where he has maintained his residence since 1911. He is a valued member of the Gage County Medical Society, and is identified also with the Nebraska State Medical Society and the American Medical Association.

Dr. Schowengerdt was born in Warren county, Missouri, December 2, 1875, and is the younger of the two surviving children of John and Amelia (Schaake) Schowengerdt, the former of whom was born in Franklin county, Missouri, in 1846, a member of a sterling pioneer family of that state, his parents, Mr. and Mrs. Frederick Schowengerdt, having come from Germany to America about the opening of the nineteenth century and having established their home in Missouri, their acquaintanceship having been formed and their marriage solemnized after they had come to the United States. John Schowengerdt, a farmer by vocation, passed his entire life in Missouri, where he died on the 11th of October, 1888. His first wife, mother of the Doctor, was born in Germany, in 1854, and her death occurred in 1882. For his second wife John Schowengerdt married Emma Niemeyer, who was born in Warren county, Missouri, and of the three children of this union the two survivors still reside in Missouri. Emma, the other surviving child of the first marriage, is the wife of William Dorsett and they reside at Alton, Illinois.

Dr. Schowengerdt passed the period of his childhood and early youth on the home farm and as a lad of thirteen years began working on the farm of his uncle, Frederick Schowengerdt, of Osage county, Missouri. In the meanwhile he had made good use of the advantages of the public schools and in 1894 he entered Central Wesleyan College, at Warrenton, Missouri, in which institution he pursued a general academic course during a period of three years. In 1897 he was matriculated in the Marion Sims Medical College, in the city of St. Louis, which institution is now the medical department of St. Louis University, and in this celebrated institution he was graduated as a member of the class of 1902, with the degree of Doctor of Medicine. He gained most valuable clinical experience by serving eleven months as an interne in the Alexian Brothers' Hospital, St. Louis, and three months in the St. Louis Female Hospital. In 1903 he engaged in the practice of his profession at Morrison, Missouri, whence, three years later, he removed to Brownsville, Texas, in which place he continued in the active practice of medicine until 1911, when he came to Gage county and established his home at Cortland. Here he has built up a substantial and representative practice that attests alike his professional ability and his personal popularity. The Doctor gives unswerving allegiance to the Republican party, is affiliated with the Masonic fraternity and the Modern of America, and he and his wife hold membership in the Methodist Episcopal church. When the United States entered the European war, in 1917, Dr. Schowengerdt made application for appointment as medical officer in the Medical Reserve Corps of the army, but physical inability caused his application to be rejected.

July 8, 1903, Dr. Schowengerdt wedded Miss Mary E. Smith, who was born and reared in Osage county, Missouri, a daughter of George and Henrietta Smith. Mr. Smith was born in Germany, came to America when young, and was a loyal soldier of the Union in the Civil war, he having thereafter become one of the prosperous farmers of Osage county, Missouri. Dr. and Mrs. Schowengerdt became the parents of five children—Irene, Waldo, Grace, Gladys, and Frances. Waldo and Gladys died in early childhood and the other children remain at the parental home.

HOMER J. MERRICK.—If a man comes of a good family he ought to be proud of it and he performs an immeasurable duty when he employs the best means to preserve the family record in enduring form, that future generations may receive instruction through principles and influences, personality and careers of the ancestors.

The subject of this biography can trace his ancestry from the same source that gave the world such persons as John Greenleaf Whittier, Ralph Waldo Emerson and Frances Meriam Whitcher. The Merricks are descended from the Welsh Royal family and King Elwood I of England, and the first representative of the family in this country, came over in 1636.

The parents of our subject were Austin and Sylvia (Whitcher) Merrick, natives respectively of Connecticut and Vermont. The paternal grandfather was accidentally killed on the Erie canal while making a trip to western Pennsylvania. His wife was named Alden, and was a direct descendant of John Alden, whom Longfellow made famous in his poem entitled "The Courtship of Miles Standish." The maternal grandparents were Stephen and Esther (Emerson) Whitcher, who were probably uncle and aunt of the poet, John Greenleaf Whittier, and Grandmother Whitcher was closely related to that other distinguished author, Ralph Waldo Emerson. Frances Meriam Whitcher, author of the "Widow Bedott Papers," was a sister of the mother of Homer J. Merrick, of this review.

Austin Merrick located at Pleasantville, Venango county, Pennsylvania, and was a merchant and farmer who resided there until his death, in 1875, at the age of seventy-five years. He was married three times, the mother of our subject being his second wife. She passed away in Pennsylvania in 1849, at the age of forty years.

Homer J. Merrick was born at Pleasantville, Pennsylvania, November 18, 1846. He was reared on a farm and attended village school until the outbreak of the Civil war. When just past his seventeenth birthday he enlisted, in December, 1863, in Company B, One Hundred and Eleventh Pennsylvania Volunteer Infantry, for three years, or during the war. His regiment was detailed to Bridgeport, Alabama, where it arrived in time to join the Atlanta campaign and participate in the battles of Resaca, Dallas, Kenesaw Mountain, Peach Tree Creek, and the Siege of Atlanta, and thereafter it was with General Sherman on the historic march from Atlanta to the Sea. Subsequently the command went up through the Carolinas and was present at the Grand Review at Washington, the greatest military pageant ever seen on the western hemisphere.

Returning home, Mr. Merrick attended the State Normal School at Edinboro, Pennsylvania, two years, and later was a student in a commercial college at Cleveland, Ohio. In 1869 he came to Gage county, Nebraska, and took a homestead of one hundred and sixty acres, in Section 22, Adams township. He purchased a wagon, team of horses and some implements and began farming. His first home was a dug-out in which he lived and kept bachelor's hall the first year. He boarded then with neighbors, breaking prairie for them. He would haul grain to Nebraska City and bring back to Beatrice a load of lumber, the trip requiring five days. As time passed, he prospered. In 1875 Mr. Merrick bought land in Section 16, Adams township. This he improved with good buildings, and there he continued his operations as an agriculturist, meeting with the success which always comes as the reward of industry and intelligently directed effort.

Lucy A Merrick

On the 21st of December, 1870, Mr. Merrick was united in marriage to Miss Lucy A. Lyons, a native of Kenosha county, Wisconsin. Her parents, John and Almira (Shaw) Lyons, became residents of Gage county in 1857, settling in Adams township, where they spent the remainder of their lives. The father was a native of Litchfield county, Connecticut, and the mother was born in Dutchess county, New York. The ancestors of Mrs. Merrick were of English descent. Her grandfather, John Lyons, was born in England. On the maternal side is shown a direct descent from Richard Hicks, who came to America from England on the ship "Fortune," in 1621, this being the second vessel to arrive after the "Mayflower." Mr. and Mrs. Merrick became the parents of seven children, as follows: Frank A. and John H. are deceased; Julia, is the wife of Dr. Turner, of Sterling, Nebraska; Dell, is the wife of J. M. Burnham, of Adams township; Olive R. is the wife of R. B. Winter, of Adams township; Homer C. resides in Adams; and Sylvia is deceased.

Mr. Merrick contributed his full share to the agricultural development of Gage county, and until 1907 was engaged in general farming and the raising of Shorthorn cattle, both branches of his business yielding him a substantial income. He made judicious investments in farm lands and is today the owner of thirteen hundred acres. In 1893 his neighbors, recognizing his ability and worth, elected him to represent them in the lower house of the state legislature. He was reelected, and served two terms, to the entire satisfaction of his constituents. Among the many measures which he introduced and which have found place on the statute books of this commonwealth was a bill authorizing the building of the Soldiers' Home at Milford. His community has been benefited by his wise council and he has efficiently filled all of the offices of his township. In 1898 he received an injury which necessitated his leaving the farm, and he was appointed and served as postmaster of Adams for five years. He was one of the organizers of the First State Bank of Adams, which is now the First National Bank, and he has since helped to shape its policy by serving as a director. He is now vice-president of the institution, of which he was cashier for one year. Mr. Merrick is president of the Farmers' Elevator Company of Adams and was at one time interested in a hardware business. His religious belief coincides with the doctrines of the Methodist church, of which he and his wife are members. In politics

Mr. Merrick is a Republican, and fraternally he is a member of the Ancient Free and Accepted Masons and several of the other Masonic bodies. He maintains pleasant relations with old army comrades by membership in Sargeant Cox Post, No. 100, Grand Army of the Republic. Mr. Merrick is an honorable representative of a noble family, and while he has achieved success which places him among the men of affluence in his county and state, he has not been remiss in any duty and enjoys the respect and confidence of all with whom he has come in contact.

ROBERT H. STEINMEYER, cashier of the State Bank of Holmesville, of which his father, John H. Steinmeyer, is president, is a member of a prominent and influential Gage county family, concerning which adequate mention is made on other pages of this work. Mr. Steinmeyer was born in Saline county, Nebraska, August 25, 1889, and in his youth he attended the public schools of Clatonia, Gage county, besides having taken a higher course in an academy in the city of Lincoln. His active career as a business man has been marked by his close association with banking enterprise, and he is giving most efficient service as cashier of the State Bank of Holmesville, which bases operations upon a capital stock of ten thousand dollars, and which now has in surplus and undivided profits a fund of more than one hundred thousand dollars, the substantial institution proving an important adjunct to the industrial and commercial facilities of this section of the county. In addition to his executive service at the bank Mr. Steinmeyer has developed a prosperous business in the buying and shipping of livestock.

In politics Mr. Steinmeyer is found aligned as a loyal supporter of the cause of the Republican party and he has served as township clerk, as has he also as a member of the school board of Holmesville. He is an appreciative and popular member of Beatrice Lodge, No. 619, Benevolent & Protective Order of Elks, of which he is serving, in 1918, as esteemed lecturing knight. His wife holds membership in the Brethren church.

October 15, 1913, recorded the marriage of Mr. Steinmeyer to Miss Mabel Gish, who was born and reared in this county and who is a daughter of James W. Gish, a representative farmer of Rockford township. Mr. and Mrs. Steinmeyer have one child, Phyllis, who was born in 1917.

JOSEPH C. DELL merits consideration in this history as one of the representative farmers and valued citizens of Rockford township, and also by reason of being a member of one of the sterling pioneer families of the county, where the family home was established when he was a lad of twelve years.

Mr. Dell was born in Owen county, Indiana, October 8, 1863, and is a son of Isaac and Lydia (Summers) Dell, both natives of Ohio, where the former was born March 4, 1834, and the latter on the 5th of August 1838, their marriage having been solemnized in Indiana. Isaac Dell was an honored pioneer who passed the closing years of his life in Gage county, where he died June 1, 1904, and his widow now resides in Rockford township. They became devout members of the Church of the Brethren, in which he gave earnest service as a minister for many years. Isaac Dell was a son of Peter Dell, who was born in Pennsylvania, of German ancestry, and who removed from that state to Ohio, whence he later went to Indiana, where he resided a number of years. He then returned with his family to Ohio, where he continued to live until his death, he having been a cabinet-maker by trade. Jacob Summers, maternal grandfather of the subject of this review, removed from Ohio to Indiana, in which latter state he passed the remainder of his life, a farmer by vocation. Isaac Dell acquired in his youth the trade of carpenter and he followed the same in Owen county, Indiana, until 1869, when he removed with his family to Harrison county, Iowa, where he became a pioneer contractor and builder. In 1876 he came with his family to Gage county, where he purchased and improved a farm, besides continuing for many years in the active work of his trade, in which connection he erected many buildings of excellent order that still remain as evidences of his skill as a carpenter. He was a man of fine mind and fine character, ever commanding the unqualified respect of his fellow men, and he was one of the honored pioneer citizens of Gage county at the time of his death. He took loyal interest in community affairs and was a Republican in politics. Of his family of two sons and six daughters all are living except one daughter: Ida is the wife of John G. Van Dyke, a farmer near Grand Junction, Colorado; Julia is the wife of John A. Cullen, a farmer near McPherson, Kansas; Joseph C., of this sketch, was the next in order of birth; Jacob is a prosperous farmer in Rockford township and is also a minister of the Church of the Brethren; Mary, who became the wife of William H. Pair, is deceased; Martha is the wife of Irvin Frantz, of Sherman township; Hattie is the wife of Henry J. Frantz, of the same township; and Susan is the wife of Alvah C. Heaston, who is engaged in the automobile business at Lincoln, Nebraska.

Joseph C. Dell acquired his preliminary education in the public schools of Iowa and after the family removed to Gage county he continued his studies in the district schools and also in the select school of Professor Blake, at Beatrice. His entire mature life has been marked by active association with the basic industries of agriculture and stock-growing, and through the medium of the same he has achieved definite success and advancement, his prosperity representing the direct result of his own efforts. His original independent farm operations were conducted on land which be rented, and finally he purchased eighty acres in Rockford township, to which he added, two years later, by the purchase of an adjoining tract of eighty acres. After making good improvements on this farm he traded the property for his present fine homestead farm, which now comprises three hundred and sixty acres, with the best type of buildings, the handsome house having been erected by him, as have been also the other excellent farm buildings which mark the place as a model farm. Mr. Dell is the owner also of a landed estate of twelve hundred and eighty acres in western Kansas.

In the year 1888 was solemnized the marriage of Mr. Dell to Miss Mollie Cullen, daughter of James K. and Christena Cullen, who were born in Virginia and who came to Gage county in 1885. Concerning the children of Mr. and Mrs. Dell the following brief record is offered: Claude has the supervision of his father's large landed estate in Kansas; Ernest is associated in the management of the home farm; Lela is the wife of Earl Frantz and both are attending school at McPherson, Kansas, Mr. Frantz being a minister of the Brethren church; Carl Dell likewise is attending school at McPherson; and Milton, Joseph C., Jr., and Lois remain at the parental home.

Mr. Dell and his family are earnest members of the Church of the Brethren, and in politics he is aligned with the Republican party. As a progressive farmer he is giving special attention to the raising of pure-bred Short-horn cattle and Percheron horses, and at the time of this writing he has about fifty head of horses and an equal number of cattle on his farm. His progressiveness extends also to his status as a citizen and he takes deep interest in community affairs, though he has no ambition for public office.

SAMUEL MOWRY, to whom this memoir is dedicated, was one of the honored pioneers of Gage county and more than thirty years ago he was summoned to "that undiscovered country from whose bourne no traveler returns." To him, as a man of sterling character and worthy achievement, a tribute is due in this history of the county in which he established his home in the year following that in which the Territory of Nebraska was admitted to statehood.

SAMUEL MOWRY

Samuel Mowry was born in Darke county, Ohio, on the 19th of June, 1847, and was a son of Jacob and Susan Mowry, who were natives of Pennsylvania and who became early settlers in Ohio, where they passed the remainder of their lives. Samuel Mowry was reared on the farm of his father and gained his youthful education in the schools of his native county. In 1868, as an ambitious and resolute young man of twenty-one years, he severed the ties that bound him to the old Buckeye state and set forth to establish a home in the west. In that year he arrived in Gage county, Nebraska, and here he obtained a homestead of one hundred and sixty acres, the same constituting the southwest quarter of Section 7, Blue Springs township. Not a furrow had been turned on the prairie land and on the same no improvement of any kind had been made. Mr. Mowry's first house on his homestead was a little and primitive shanty, ten by twelve feet in dimensions and constructed of lumber cut from the native cottonwood trees, the logs having been hauled by him to Blue Springs, where they were sawed into rough boards. As he had learned in his native state the trade of stone mason, Mr. Mowry was able to provide somewhat better foundation for his modest house than those commonly in evidence in the pioneer community. He excavated a cellar and walled it up with stone, this being covered with a board roof. This embryonic house served as his place of abode several years. He set resolutely to work in subduing the virgin prairie and making it available for cultivation, and as the years passed he developed a productive farm, besides making good improvements on his farm. Here he continued his vigorous and productive activities as a farmer until the close of his earnest and useful life, his death having occurred on the 28th of February, 1887. He was a man of strong and noble character, was a loyal citizen, a true friend and a devoted husband and father—a person whose death entailed a distinct loss to the community in which he had long lived and labored to goodly ends. His political allegiance was given to the Republican party, but he never sought or desired public office of any kind. He was an earnest and consistent member of the Methodist Episcopal church, as is also his widow, who has been a resident of Gage county since her childhood.

MRS. SAMUEL MOWRY

After coming to Gage county Mr. Mowry was here united in marriage to Miss Malissa Harpster, who was born in Seneca county, Ohio, and who is a daughter of the late Solomon Harpster, to whom a memoir is entered on other pages of this volume. Mrs. Mowry shared with her husband in the trials and responsibilities of pioneer life and after the gracious marital ties were severed by the death of Mr. Mowry she remained on the farm for a number of years, during which she showed marked acumen and judgment in its management. For several years past she has maintained her home in the village of Blue Springs, and few of the pioneer women of the county have a more interesting fund of reminiscences pertaining to the pioneer period of Gage county history. April 10, 1918, represented the fiftieth anniversary of the day when with her parents she crossed the Blue river and entered the little pioneer hamlet of Blue Springs, this county, the village at that time having had but one store. Concerning this primitive mercantile establishment Mrs. Mowry has given the following statement: "About all that was sold in the store was green coffee, brown sugar, calico and patent medicine, and more of these commodities were sold to the

Indians than to white persons, simply by reason of the fact that the Indians were greatly in preponderance in the locality at that time." Mrs. Mowry was a girl when she thus came with her parents to Gage county and she states that at the pioneer home of the Harpster family it was not unusual even to look up from work and see one or more Indians peering in at the window. Mr. and Mrs. Mowry became the parents of four children, of whom two, George and Frederick, died in infancy. Edgar married Miss Anna Brinley and they reside in the city of Lincoln, this state, and Miss Leafy remains with her widowed mother in the pleasant home at Blue Springs.

THOMAS M. MARTIN was an honored pioneer who established his residence in Gage county in the year that marked the admission of Nebraska to statehood, and his was also the distinction of having been a gallant soldier of the Union in the Civil war. He reclaimed and developed one of the fine farm properties of Sherman township and there continued his residence until the time of his death, which occurred January 27, 1917. A man of sterling character and one who accounted well for himself in all the relations of life, it is fitting that in this history he incorporated a tribute to his memory.

Thomas M. Martin was born in Union county, Indiana, on the 20th of December, 1836, and was a son of Thomas and Mary (Miller) Martin, the former a native of Scotland and the latter of Pennsylvania.

The subject of this memoir was but three years of age at the time of his father's death, and the widowed mother eventually came to Nebraska and took up a homestead claim in Pawnee county, where she passed the remainder of her life. She contracted a second marriage and had two children by each marriage, all being now deceased.

After his marriage, in 1859, Thomas M. Martin continued his association with farm enterprise in Clinton county, Indiana, until the outbreak of the Civil war caused him to subordinate all else to tender his aid in defense of the Union. In August, 1862, he enlisted as a member of Company K, Seventy-second Indiana Volunteer Infantry, and with this valiant command he continued in service more than three years—until the close of the war. Mr. Martin took part in many of the historic campaigns and battles of the great conflict between the states of the north and the south, and among the various engagements in which he participated may be noted the battles of Chickamauga, Stone's River, Missionary Ridge, Selma (Alabama), and Hoover's Gap. He was with his regiment in the Atlanta campaign and was present at the battle of Atlanta, the burning of that city, and with Sherman on the subsequent march to the sea. In later years he vitalized the more gracious associations of his military career by his affiliation with the Grand Army of the Republic. After the close of the war Mr. Martin continued his association with farm activities in Indiana until 1867, in the autumn of which year he set forth, in company with his wife and their three children, for the frontier as represented in the new state of Nebraska. The long and weary journey was made with a team and covered wagon and thirty-four days elapsed before the little family party arrived in Gage county, on the 4th of October. Mr. Martin entered claim to a homestead of one hundred and sixty acres, in Section 19, Sherman township, and here initiated the reclaiming of a farm from the prairie wilderness. He and his brave and loyal wife endured to the full the tension incidental to frontier life and in the early days he was compelled at times to seek outside employment in order to provide for the needs of his family. With a courage equal to that which he had evinced as a soldier on the battlefields of the south, Mr. Martin girded himself for the winning of the victories of peace, and with the passing years success and independence crowned his earnest efforts. He developed one of the fine farm properties of Sherman township, and this estate, still retained by his widow, comprises two hundred and eighty acres, Mrs. Martin still remaining on the fine old homestead which is hallowed to her by the gracious memories and associations of the past. In the early days the home was isolated, with the nearest neighbors far removed, and Mrs. Martin frequently passed many weeks with her children in the pioneer home without seeing any other white person than the members of her own family, though Indians were still much in evidence. For a number of years Mr. Martin gave his attention to the operation of a threshing outfit, and on one occasion he handled work of this order on the site of the present court-house in the city of Beatrice. He was a Democrat in politics and was always a leader in the supporting of measures and enterprises tending to advance the civic and material welfare of his home community and county.

In Clinton county, Indiana, in the year 1859, was solemnized the marriage of Mr. Martin to Miss Mary Dailey, who was born in Washington county, that state, on the 4th of September, 1840, a daughter of James and Elizabeth (Feeler) Dailey, the former a native of North Carolina and the latter of Virginia; they were pioneer settlers in Indiana, where they passed the remainder of their lives and where the father was a prosperous farmer. In conclusion of this paragraph is given brief record concerning the children of Mr. and Mrs. Martin: Mary E. is married and resides in the state of Colorado; James W. is a prosperous farmer in Sherman township; Charles W. is engaged in farm enterprise in Rockford township; T. Malon is a substantial agriculturist and cattle-grower in Colorado; John M. rents the old homestead farm, on which he and his wife remain with the widowed mother, and of him more specific mention is made elsewhere in this volume; Lillie is the widow of William R. Rainey and resides with her mother on the old home place; and Ira Jackson is a substantial farmer near Liberty, this county.

From another source have been gained additional data of genealogical and personal order that will consistently supplement the foregoing narrative. Thomas Martin, father of the subject of this memoir, was born in Scotland, in the year 1809, and at the age of fifteen years he came to America in company with his father and two brothers, settlement being made at Louisville, Kentucky, the father later removing to Indiana and buying a tract of land, which he divided among his sons. Thomas Martin was a young man when he wedded Miss Mary Miller, who was born in Pennsylvania, in 1812, a daughter of Peter and Kate (Hafford) Miller, who removed to Indiana soon after the close of the war of 1812. Thomas Martin died in 1838 and his widow passed away in 1876. They became the parents of six sons and one daughter, all of whom are now deceased.

Thomas M. Martin made his initial visit to Nebraska in 1858, a year prior to his marriage, and it was not until after he had later made a fine record as a soldier in the Civil war that he finally came with his family to Nebraska and established a permanent home, as noted in preceding paragraphs. He never sought office, but did well his part in the advancing of the communal prosperity, his interest in his old comrades of the Civil war having been shown through his affiliation with Scott Post, No. 37 Grand Army of the Republic, at Blue Springs.

FREDERICK L. POTHAST has been cashier of the Farmers' State Bank of Pickrell from the time of its organization, in 1904, has been a resourceful and progressive executive and wielded primary influence in the upbuilding of this substantial financial institution of Gage county. He is not only one of the principal stockholders of this bank but is also the owner of a valuable landed estate of four hundred acres in Gage county—two hundred and forty acres in Holt township and the remaining one hundred and sixty acres in Highland township; his farms are leased to and operated by efficient tenants.

Mr. Pothast was born in Stephenson county, Illinois, June 4, 1878, a son of David and Mary (Wendt) Pothast. He was but two years old at the time of his father's death, and his mother later became the wife of Frederick J. Smith, to whom a memoir is dedicated on other pages of this work, so that further review of the family history is not demanded in the present connection. Mr. Pothast was a child of two years when he accompanied his mother and stepfather to Gage county, where he was reared to manhood and was given the advantages of the public schools of the village of Cortland. After his graduation in the high school he taught two terms of district school and in 1898 he entered a commercial college in the city of Omaha. In this institution he was graduated in the following year and he then entered into partnership with his stepfather, Mr. Smith, in the general merchandise business at Cortland, the enterprise having been conducted under the firm name of F. J. Smith & Company. In 1901 Mr. Pothast and his brother Edward L. engaged in the agricultural implement business at Cortland, and after he sold his interest in this business, in 1903, he was for about one year a traveling representative for the International Harvester Company, in the meanwhile maintaining his headquarters in the city of Lincoln. In May, 1904, Mr. Pothast became the organizer of the Farmers' State Bank at Pickrell, and of the same he has since been the cashier, as previously noted. In a frame building on the north side of the main street of the village the bank initiated business, after having been incorporated with a capital stock of five thousand dollars. Here operations were continued until 1912, when was erected the present modern and handsomely appointed bank building, and the business of the institution is now based on a capital stock of twenty thousand dollars, while its deposits are in excess of three hundred thousand dollars. The bank has been a valuable medium for the facilitation of industrial and commercial activities in this part of the county and is conducted with conservative policies but also with well ordered progressiveness. Edward Bauman, a representative farmer of Holt township, is president of the institution, and its vice-president, Christopher Spilker, is likewise one of the prosperous farmers of Holt township.

Though he is distinctly liberal and loyal in his civic attitude and a staunch supporter of the principles of the Republican party, Mr. Pothast has manifested no ambition for public office or political preferment of any kind. He is affiliated with the Masonic fraternity, as a member of the Beatrice lodge, Ancient Free & Accepted Masons, in the city of Beatrice, and he and his wife are zealous members of the United Brethren church at Pickrell, he being a member of its board of trustees and having contributed liberally to the erection of the present church edifice.

December 12, 1900, recorded the marriage of Mr. Pothast to Miss Delia Clark, who was born in Virginia and who was a child at the time when the family home was established on a pioneer farm in Lancaster county, Nebraska, where she was reared and educated. She is a daughter of T. A. and Iva (Kincheloe) Clark, both of whom likewise were born in the historic old Dominion state. The father died when about seventy-five years of age, and the mother is still living, at Firth, Nebraska. Mr. and Mrs. Pothast have two winsome little daughters, Audrey and Mildred.

ROBERT NICHOLAS.—A history of Gage county would be incomplete without a record of the man whose name introduces the review. Mr. Nicholas was one of the very early pioneer settlers in Gage county, having come to Nebraska in 1860 and having settled in Gage county several years prior to the admission of the state to the Union.

Robert Nicholas was born in Glanstonbury, Somersetshire, England, in December, 1832, and his death occurred on his old homestead in Gage county, Nebraska, in 1913. His gracious wife, whose maiden name was Mary Ann Plucknett, was likewise born and reared in Glastonbury, England, but their acquaintanceship was formed in the state of Illinois, where their marriage was solemnized and whence they came to Gage county in the territorial period of Nebraska history. Here Mrs. Nicholas passed the remainder of her life, and she was one of the venerable pioneer women of the county at the time of her death, in 1910, at the age of seventy-six years. Robert Nicholas was reared and educated in his native land, and was an ambitious youth of eighteen years when he came to the United States and established his residence in Ohio. From that state he later removed to Hancock county, Illinois, where his marriage occurred and where he continued to be identified with farm enterprise until 1860, when he set forth for Nebraska Territory, transporting his family and little supply of household goods by means of wagon and ox team. Upon his arrival in Gage county he entered claim to a homestead of wild prairie land in Sections 29 and 30, Grant township, where as soon as possible he completed a rude log house as the family domicile. With the ox team he then began vigorously the breaking of the virgin soil, and he and his noble wife endured the trials and hardships of the early pioneers. With the passing of the years prosperity attended the energetic and efficient efforts of Mr. Nicholas and he added materially to his landed estate. He continued farming until his death and developed one of the best farms in Gage county. He raised and fed cattle upon a large scale, and was one of the first men in Nebraska to raise hay from the tame grasses. In the early days trains would be stopped when passing his farm in order that the passengers might view his fine fields, and officials of the railroad company sent samples of his timothy and clover back to the east, in exploiting the fine resources of this section of Nebraska. Before the admission of the state to the Union and prior to the Civil war, Mr. Nicholas hauled wheat by team and wagon to St. Joseph, Missouri, and from the money received in payment for the same he purchased a corn-planter. This was the first implement of the kind put into commission in Gage county, and when he arrived in Beatrice the citizens gathered about to view the novelty, most of then not knowing to what purpose the machine was to be applied. On the old homestead were born all the children of Mr. and Mrs. Nicholas, and it may well be understood that to these children many gracious memories attach to the place.

ROBERT NICHOLAS

Mr. and Mrs. Nicholas were the parents of six children, as follows: Frank E. is successfully established in the creamery business in Dewitt, Saline county; Alfretta is the wife of Walter W. Barney, president of the State Bank of Dewitt; Norton B. died when about five years of age; Jessie N. is the wife of Frank Buss, of Hunter, Oklahoma; George is now postmaster of Dewitt, and concern-him a record will be found on other pages of this publication; Elizabeth is the wife of Frank O. Ellis, of Beatrice.

MRS. ROBERT NICHOLAS

MARTIN F. EICKMANN.—That surety of vision and judgment that makes for definite success in connection with the practical affairs of life is being signally exemplified in the business career of Mr. Eickmann, who is a young man well entitled to classification among the efficient and progressive business executives of Gage county and its metropolis. He has, won advancement through his ability and efficient service and now holds the responsible office of secretary of the German Savings & Loan Association, one of the strong and well ordered financial and fiduciary institutions of this section of his native state.

Mr. Eickmann was born in Thayer county, Nebraska, on the 9th of July, 1889, a son of Christ and Mary (Sorge) Eickmann, both natives of Germany—the former having been born in Brandenburg, in 1861, and the latter in the province of Hanover, in October, 1866. Christ Eickmann was a boy at the time of the family immigration to America and was reared and educated in the state of Wisconsin, where he received the advantages of the public schools of Fond du Lac and where also he served an apprenticeship to the tailor's trade. He was eighteen years of age when he accompanied his father to Nebraska, the journey being made from Omaha to Grand Island by way of the Union Pacific Railroad and from the latter point they walked overland to their destination in Thayer county, this state. Though he had virtually no financial resources he purchased one hundred and twenty acres of land in Thayer county eventually, and with the passing years substantial success crowned his activities as an agriculturist and stock-grower. He became one of the representative farmers of Thayer county, where he continued to reside until his death, which occurred in July, 1908, his widow being still a resident of that county. His father, Christ Eickmann, Sr., likewise became a pioneer farmer of Thayer county and after there acquiring one hundred and twenty acres of land the father returned to Wisconsin to make provision for bringing the remainder of his family to the new home. He achieved independence and prosperity in connection with the development of the natural resources of Thayer county and there he and his wife passed the remainder of their lives, he having followed the trade of wagonmaker during the period of his residence in Wisconsin. Frederick Sorge, maternal grandfather of the subject of this review, came with his family to America in 1862 and became one of the very early settlers of Thayer county, where he developed a valuable farm, and he is now a resident of the village of Deshler, where he is honored as one of the sterling and venerable pioneer citizens of Thayer county. Christ Eickmann, Jr., was a man of splendid energy and of superior mentality, so that he was well equipped for leadership in community affairs. In a basic way he gave support to the principals of the Democratic party but in connection with local matters he held himself independent of strict partisan lines. He served for a number of years as a member of the school board of his district and otherwise he gave his earnest support to those things that tend to advance the general welfare. His religious faith was that of the German Lutheran church, of which his widow likewise is a zealous communicant. Of their five children four are living and of the number,

Martin F., of this sketch, is the eldest; William remains with his widowed mother on the old homestead farm in Thayer county, as did also Richard until he entered the national army being raised to represent the United States in the great European war, he being at the present time (in the winter of 1917) with his command at Camp Funston, Kansas; Arthur, youngest of the four sons, remains on the old home farm.

Martin F. Eickmann acquired his preliminary education in the Lutheran parochial schools of Thayer county and supplemented this by an effective course in Northwestern College, at Watertown, Wisconsin, his uncle, Martin Eickmann, having been at that time a member of the faculty of that institution. Prior to the death of his father Mr. Eickmann had completed a course in the preparatory department of this college, and as the eldest son he thereafter gave his attention for a short time to the management of the home farm. His tastes and ambition, however, lay in other directions, and he came to Beatrice, where he completed a course in a business college, after which he obtained a clerical position in the Union State Bank of this city, at a salary of fifteen dollars a month. He so applied himself as to make the best possible use of the experience gained, and by faithful and efficient service he won advancement. He continued with this banking institution from 1909 to 1914, in which latter year he was elected secretary of the German Savings & Loan Association, a position of which he has since continued the efficient and popular incumbent, this institution having been founded in 1913. By his own efforts Mr. Eickmann has achieved success and an inviolable reputation, and in the city of Beatrice he is the owner not only of his own attractive residence property, but also of a number of vacant city lots. His political allegiance is given to the Democratic party and he and his wife are active communicants of the German Lutheran church.

On the 14th of October, 1914, was solemnized the marriage of Mr. Eickmann to Miss Blanche M. Purdy, who was born and reared in this county, her father, William W. Purdy, being now a resident of Beatrice, where he follows the trade of plasterer and controls a successful contracting business in this line. Mr. and Mrs. Eickmann have a fine little son—Martin F., Jr., who was born July 9, 1917.

EUGENE P. MUMFORD.—He whose name introduces this review is not only one of the progressive and representative business men of Gage county, but is also a descendant of one of the well known and influential pioneer families of this part of the state. The name of Mumford is prominently linked with the early history and industrial development of Gage county, where its original representatives settled in territorial days. Eugene is upholding the honors of the family name, and his business life has given impetus to industrial and civic advancement in Gage county. By reason of his being reared and educated on the broad prairies of Nebraska, with fresh air and sunny skies, and under the freedom of pioneer days, he learned the first principles of good citizenship from early experiences on the farm, and he has kept pace with the march of development and progress.

"Gene," the name by which he is generally known, was born in Lafayette county, Wisconsin, on the 1st day of April, 1863. He is a son of John B. and Mary A. (Roach) Mumford, the former of whom was born in Maryland, of English parentage, on September 20, 1829, and the latter of whom was born in Adams county, Ohio, of Holland and English lineage.

John B. Mumford first came to Gage county, Nebraska, in May, 1860, in company with his brother Ismay, who was the first county treasurer of the county, and whose son Dawson Mumford was the first white boy born in the county. John B. Mumford returned to Wisconsin, and in 1865 he again came to Gage county, with his brother Jacob. He settled on one hundred and sixty acres of land, ten miles north of Beatrice on Bear creek, one of the best farming localities in the county. To this in later years he added by the purchase of two hundred and forty acres, making his estate one of four hundred acres. On his farm he continued to reside during the remainder of his life.

Mr. Mumford was an enterprising citizen and had much to do with the development of the county, and it may be said of him that he continued to contribute his quota to the county's progress until his death, February 14, 1904. His widow, now (1918) eighty years of age, still resides in Gage county, having moved to Beatrice after the death of her husband, and is one of the venerable and revered pioneers of the county, she being among the very few of the original settlers left. Of the nine children born to Mr. and Mrs. Mumford, six survive: Sarah E. is the wife of William A. Foreman, who was a successful farmer and is the owner of a good farm of four hundred acres, located six miles north east of Beatrice. They have now retired and live in Beatrice. Charles B. is noted for his love of fine horses and has owned many good ones. Of late years he has been engaged in the automobile business at Beatrice. Eugene P. was the next in order of birth. Ida N. is the wife of Lawrence W. Epard, and they reside upon the old homestead of her father, adjoining the old home place, John B. Mumford having relinquished the homestead in the early days to his sister. Frank W. is still living in the old home where he was born. He is also an extensive live-stock shipper. Luther E., former principal of the Beatrice high school, is now living in Lincoln, Nebraska, and is engaged in school work.

The late John B. Mumford took a decided interest in political and public affairs, and was always a Democrat. He did much to advance the party but never consented to be a candidate for office. His religious faith was that of the Methodist Episcopal church, and his venerable widow is a member of the Christian church.

Eugene P. Mumford was about two years old at the time the family moved to Gage county. He profited by the advantages of the country school and later attended the Blake Select School of Beatrice, but never completed the regular course of study. He has devoted much time to reading, and had the good fortune of having association and friendship with such pioneer characters as J. B. Weston, George P. Marvin, Judge Alfred Hazlett, R. S. Bibb, and D. W. Cook, for all of whom he had much respect and who contributed much to his fund of useful information. He is a Democrat politically, as were his ancestors "from the time the memory of man runneth not to the contrary." He belonged to the old school known as "gold" Democrats, and was opposed to free silver during the campaign on that issue. He was a student of Adam Smith on finance and believed in a commodity basis for value. He has done much, with the assistance of his brother Frank, to build up the ranks of the party and has been twice recognized for loyalty. He was appointed revenue collector for the southeast division of Nebraska during President Cleveland's administration, and although he filed his resignation at the end of four years, he was retained two years under President McKinley, owing to his familiarity with the service, and to the exigencies of the Spanish-American war. He was selected by Governor John H. Morehead as private secretary to that able executive during his several terms as governor of Nebraska. Mr. Mumford is now engaged in business at Beatrice. His reputation for absolute reliability in all transactions and his wide acquaintanceship and knowledge of affairs have established for him a good business in the real estate and insurance enterprise, including the rental of properties, of which he has farm and city property to look after. He also has a furniture store, which he conducts with the assistance of his nephew, C. D. Mumford.

On the 22d of June, 1898, Mr. Mumford was united in marriage to Lenda Mostert, who was born near Milwaukee, Wisconsin, and came to Nebraska in 1878, when seven years of age. Mrs. Mumford is of German lineage, her people coming from Bavaria. She was studious during her school days and in 1888 was graduated with honor in the Beatrice high school. For ten years thereafter she was an instructor in the Beatrice schools. Mrs. Mumford has always been active in school affairs, and is held in high regard by her many friends and associates. She is a member of the Trinity Lutheran church and has taken an active part in the work of that organization. She is at the present time treasurer of the Young Women's Christian Association and is now serving her third term. Mr. and Mrs. Mumford are the parents of one son, Paul E., who was graduated at the Beatrice high school in the class of 1918.

CHARLES H. OJERS has been a resident of Nebraska for nearly half a century and since 1889 he has been numbered among the honored citizens and representative farmers of Lincoln township, Gage county, where he has made the best of improvements on a farm of one hundred and sixty acres that constitutes the northeast quarter of Section 3, this property having been a heritage received by his wife from the estate of her father, who was an influential pioneer of Nebraska.

Mr. Ojers was born in Steuben county, New York, on the 15th of May, 1851, and is a son of John A. and Phoebe A. (Huntley) Ojers, the former of whom was born in the city of London, England, in 1821, and the latter of whom was born in Steuben county, New York, in April, 1823, a representative of one of the well known pioneer families of that section of the Empire state. In his native city John A. Ojers gained his youthful education and also served a thorough apprenticeship to the shoemaker's trade. As a young man he came to the United States and, as a skilled workman, found employment at his trade. After his marriage he continued his residence in the state of New York until 1856, when he removed with his family to Illinois and established his residence in Ogle county, where he continued in the work of his trade for a number of years. In 1874 he and his wife came to Nebraska, where he passed the remainder of his long and useful life, his death having occurred at Dewitt, Saline county, in 1909, at which time he was eighty-eight years of age. His venerable widow, who celebrated in the spring of 1917 the ninety-fourth anniversary of her birth, is one of the revered women of Gage county and is passing the gentle evening of her life in the village of Wymore.

Charles H. Ojers was five years of age at the time of the family removal to Illinois, where he was reared to manhood and where his educational advantages were those offered by the common schools. There he gave his attention principally to farm work, being employed by the month, until he had attained to his legal majority, when, in 1872, he came to Nebraska and rented land in Johnson county. Under these conditions he there continued his operations as a farmer until 1887, when he removed to Saline county and settled on a farm of one hundred and sixty acres which his wife inherited and which they still own. In 1889 they came to Gage county and established their home on their present attractive farm, upon which he has made admirable improvements in the way of buildings and other permanent evidences of thrift and good management, and which he has made one of the fine farms of Lincoln township. He has been a vigorous and productive representative of farm industry during the many years of his residence in Nebraska and has achieved success worthy of the name. He is progressive and judicious in his business policies and in addition to his valuable farm holdings he is a substantial stockholder in the Blue Valley Mercantile Company of Beatrice. Though he has had neither time nor inclination for political activity or public office of any kind, he accords loyal support to the cause of the Republican party, and he is affiliated with the Independent Order of Odd Fellows.

MR. AND MRS. CHARLES H. OJERS

On the 20th of August, 1871, was solemnized the marriage of Mr. Ojers to Miss Fannie R. Rathburn, who was born in Ogle county, Illinois, and who is a daughter of the late Job B. Rathburn, an honored pioneer who accumulated a very extensive and valuable landed estate in southeastern Nebraska and was one of the prominent and influential citizens of Gage county at the time of his death. Of the four children of Mr. and Mrs. Ojers, Charles, who was born in 1872, died at the age of five years; George L., born in 1874, died in early childhood; Annie R., who was born in 1874, is the wife of Edward Zobel and they reside with her parents on the latter's homestead farm, of which Mr. Zobel has much of the active management; and Addie R., who was born in 1881, is the wife of Essa A. Lash, a prosperous farmer in Saline county, where he operates a farm owned by his wife's father. Mr. and Mrs. Lash have six children—Lloyd, Myrtle, George, John, Mary, and Gertrude.

JEFFERSON B. WESTON.—Not too often and not through the agency of too many vehicles can be recorded the life history of one who lived so honorable and useful a life as did the late Jefferson B. Weston, who wrote his name in large and indelible characters on the history of the state of Nebraska, within whose borders he established his home three years after the creation of the original territory and fully six years prior to the reduction of its area to the present limitations. He was one of the founders and builders of this now noble and opulent commonwealth and he gave the best of an essentially strong and loyal nature to the service of the territory and the state; his life course was guided and governed by the highest principles of integrity and honor. As offering a somewhat intimate and assuredly earnest and consistent estimate of the man and his services, there is all of propriety in perpetuating in this memoir the following extracts from an appreciative article that appeared in the *Beatrice Sun* at the time of the death of Mr. Weston, who passed from the stage of life's mortal endeavors on the 15th of September, 1905, minor elimination and paraphrase being indulged in the reproduction of these excerpts:

"Mr. Weston was born at Bremen, Lincoln county, Maine, on the 3d of March, 1831, and thus he was nearly seventy-five years of age at the time of his death. He was a scion of the staunchest of colonial New England ancestry and in his personality always manifested the sturdy and rugged characteristics of a strong and worthy ancestry. When he was about twenty years of age Mr. Weston entered Union College, at Schnectady, New York, and in this institution he was graduated as a member of the class of 1856. In less than a year thereafter he joined the exodus of emigrants who were pushing their way westward, and in April, 1857, he came to the new territory of Nebraska, which then extended from the Missouri river west to the Rocky mountains and from the fortieth parallel to the Canadian border. He was one of the leaders of that band of intrepid men and women who, on board the old river boat 'Hannibal,' on the 3d of April, 1857, while stuck on a sand bar opposite Doniphan, Kansas, entered into a compact to remain together and locate somewhere in the new territory of Nebraska, with the definite purpose of there founding a city. He was the principal member of the committee representing this company of pioneers, and this committee, upon personal inspection in May of that year, determined upon the site which comprises the original town of Beatrice as the location of the prospective city to be founded by these sterling pioneers, and Mr. Weston was one of the enthusiastic young men who made prompt answer when the roll of this company was called on the site of Beatrice, June 27, 1857. From the date of his arrival in the territory Mr. Weston identified himself fully and vigorously with the activities of pioneer life. In the early days he engaged in various freighting ventures and with ox teams crossed the plains to Denver and other points, besides having gained his quota of experience in trading with the Indians and with mining enterprise. Early in his career he was admitted to the territorial bar, and for some time prior to 1872 he gave considerable time and attention to the practice of his profession, as one of the pioneer members of the bar of Gage county and its judicial center.

"In the autumn of 1872 Mr. Weston was elected auditor of public accounts of the state of Nebraska, and by successive re-elections he continued the incumbent of this office from January, 1873, until January, 1879. From 1873 to 1886 he and his family resided in the city of Lincoln, capital of the state, but with this exception he held continuous residence at Beatrice from 1857 until the time of his death.

"From the brief data here presented it will be seen that Mr. Weston was closely identified with the history of Nebraska from the beginning. He belonged to that class of frontiersmen who have in a large degree the constructive faculty. Possessed of the true pioneer spirit which looks far into the future and sees states rise from tenantless wildernesses and naked plains, he never wavered from his trust that here God had marked the outlines of a great commonwealth. He lived to see the justification of his faith and to participate in a large measure in the fruition of his hopes.

"Not only was Mr. Weston the possessor of a liberal education but he was also a man of large intellectual life. Deliberate and conservative in his judgment, he was accustomed to take an accurate and comprehensive view of human affairs. His clear, comprehensive way of looking at things made him one of the most useful members of the community in which he lived and also a useful and valued citizen of his state. His charity was large, his kindness of heart without bounds, and in his habits and associations he was the most democratic of men. With a generous, open-hearted faith in humanity and a deep-rooted faith in God, he came to the end of his long journey in an atmosphere of hope, courage and cheer that was infectious and touched all who came within the sphere of his benign influence. Men loved him, and to hundreds in his home community and in other portions of the state the world will be lonelier and less inviting without Jefferson B. Weston."

Measured by its beneficence, its rectitude, its productiveness, its unconscious altruism, and its material success, the life of Hon. Jefferson B. Weston counted for much, and Nebraska is perpetually favored in that as a young man he allied himself with all of thoroughness and completeness with its interests, grew with its growth and dignified and honored the territory and the state by his character and his achievement. Standing in the light and unassuming glory of life and character like this, those of the younger generation of Americans may gain lesson and inspiration and feel the thrill of buoyant loyalty and patriotism, the while there can not fail to be appreciation of the splendid and ever widening influence which such a life implies.

In the stability of his mature judgment Mr. Weston was well fortified in his opinions concerning economic and governmental policies, and he gave his political allegiance to the Republican party. Mr. Weston was associated with other representative citizens in the founding of the Beatrice National Bank, which received its charter in the autumn of 1883, and by the original board of directors he was elected president of the institution, an office of which he continued the incumbent until his death—a period of nearly a quarter of a century.

In 1860, at Nebraska City, was solemnized the marriage of Mr. Weston to Miss Helen Towle, who was born at Hennepin, Illinois, a daughter of Albert and Catherine (Holt) Towle, who likewise were numbered among the honored pioneers of Nebraska. Mrs. Weston survived her honored husband and in her gentle and gracious womanhood she proved a true complement to his virile and upright manhood, so that the home relations were ideal during a devoted companionship that continued nearly half a century and that was broken only by the death of the husband and father. Mrs. Weston passed to the life eternal on the 25th of February, 1917, and her memory is revered by all who came within the compass of her gentle and gracious influence. Mr. and Mrs. Weston became the parents of four children— Ralph A., Elizabeth L., Herbert T., and Katharine. Ralph A. is now a resident of Millet, Alberta, Canada, and Katharine, who became the wife of Thomas E. Wing, was a resident of Scarsdale, New York, at the time of her death. Elizabeth L. and Herbert T. remain in Beatrice.

JOSEPH LUTHER WEBB, M. D.—Large, definite, and benignant was the impress which this honored pioneer left in connection with this history of Gage county, and no work purporting to give record concerning those who have here been the vigorous apostles of civic and material development and progress can be consistent with itself if there is failure to accord an earnest tribute of recognition to Dr. Webb. He was one of the very first physicians to establish residence and engage in practice in the little frontier community which was the nucleus of the present city of Beatrice, and it has well been said that "all through the rest of his life he was closely associated with every movement looking toward the development, growth, and social and material well-being of the community.

Dr. Webb was born on a pioneer homestead farm near the city of Springfield, Illinois, and the date of his nativity was August 1, 1837. He was a son of Luther Hiram Webb and Martha (Bellows) Webb, both representatives of sterling families that were founded in New England in the early colonial period of our national history. The Doctor was the sixth in order of birth in a family of seven children and the youngest of the number was Hiram P., who likewise became prominently identified with pioneer activities in Gage county, Nebraska. Concerning the early period in the career of Dr. Webb the following record has been prepared, and it is worthy of perpetuation in this connection: "When the Doctor was but ten years old his father and elder brother died, only a day apart, leaving the widowed mother and the surviving children on the pioneer homestead. In the face of most strenuous hardships and trials the devoted mother struggled to keep her family together and saw to it that each child was cared for and afforded the best educational advantages offered in that pioneer locality, the capital city of Illinois having been a mere village at that time. After having availed himself of the advantages of the local schools, Dr. Webb went to Springfield, the state capital, and there he prosecuted his study of medicine in the offices of several of the leading physicians of the place, this method of preliminary training having been commonly in vogue in the locality and period. At this time Abraham Lincoln, Stephen A. Douglas and many other men who attained to eminence were residing in Springfield, and the ambitious young student came to an appreciable extent under their influence, his life ever afterward having shown the strong characteristics that such association tended to develop. With characteristic ambition and zeal Dr. Webb pursued his medical studies and finally he found it possible to enter the Eclectic Medical Institute in the city of Cincinnati, Ohio, an institution of celebrity at the time and one notable for leadership in the development of medical reform and advancement,—one that continues to the present day as a strong and influential school of medicine. In this college the Doctor was graduated as a member of the class of 1871 and in the same year he established his permanent residence in Gage county, which he had previously visited. In 1867 the new country represented in Nebraska, which was admitted to statehood in that year, was being much talked about and exploited in the eastern states, and a group of young men from the vicinity of Springfield, Illinois, and including Dr. Webb and his brothers, decided to pay a visit to this new land of promise. Accordingly, they set forth, and they made the trip partly by stage, partly by rail, partly on horse back, and for a considerable distance on foot, gaining much from each experience. Before returning the Webb brothers had acquired in Gage county a tract of land, as an investment. They then returned to their home in Illinois and after having prepared himself thoroughly for the work of his chosen profession Dr. Webb reverted to the favorable impression which Nebraska had made upon him, with the result that, in 1871, he came to Gage county and established himself as one of the pioneer physicians and surgeons in the embryonic city of Beatrice.

"The country was sparsely settled and the practice of medicine must needs be carried on without the aid of any of the modern conveniences, such as laboratories, hospitals, telephones, automobiles, consultants, and stores where needed appliances could be obtained. The life of the self-abnegating and faithful physician was full of exposure, long and irregular hours and all manner of incidental hardships. Dr. Webb's ministrations in the early days often involved the making of trips that required several days to complete, and on numerous occasions he found his buggy unavailable for further progress, so that he would proceed on horseback and at times even on foot—moved by an inviolable sense of stewardship and consecrated professional zeal. Travel would follow the trails and ridges, streams were to be forded, and the Doctor must needs be both physician and nurse in cases of emergency. Still, the services thus rendered seemed to be more on a basis of friendship than mere remuneration, and the heartfelt appreciation and affectionate regard which these old-time physicians won proved a greater and worthier recompense than that of mere money. Such close and inviolable relationships are seldom possible between the physicians of the present day and their clients. Later in life Dr. Webb was pleased to recount, with animation and appreciation, many stories of experience gained during these early years, when the buffalo, the Indian, the desperado sometimes crossed his path. He had unexpected meetings with many whose names are prominently associated with frontier annals in the west, as well as border outlaws and other insubordinate characters, but his genial personality and indomitable courage were such that such encounters never resulted in specially unpleasant experiences."

Dr. Webb was humanity's friend in the highest sense of the expression, was tolerant and kindly in his judgment, and he labored earnestly and efficiently in the alleviation of suffering and distress—a guide and counsellor to many of the representative pioneer families of Gage and adjoining counties. He continued in active practice until within a few years prior to his death, and even after his retirement many of his former clients refused to receive ministration from any other source. He was loved and revered in the county which so long was the stage of his earnest endeavors, and the entire community manifested a sense of personal loss and bereavement when he passed from the scene of this mortal life. Pertinent, indeed, are the following quotations: "Dr. Webb was a man of vigorous health, regular habits and temperate living.

He was active in church and other Christian work, true to his friends and possessed of an exceptionally broad education, with a philosophy in life that made him a pleasant member of any group in which he appeared. He made a trip into the country on the morning of May 12, 1911, returned and was with his family at noon. He went to his downtown office as usual, and there he was suddenly taken ill, passing into unconsciousness about sundown, and his death occurred near midnight. His demise was so unexpected that it came as a distinct shock to the community when it was announced the next morning."

DR. JOSEPH L. WEBB, SR.

Associating themselves with other representative citizens, Dr. Webb and his brother Hiram P. were closely identified with the early development of the community. They gave freely of their time and energy in the furtherance of every movement that seemed to promise good to the interests of the commonwealth, and the early annals of Gage county history give record of much which they did to accelerate social and material progress in the county and especially the city of Beatrice.

On the 2d of October, 1873, was solemnized the marriage of Dr. Webb to Miss Kate Louise Sheppard, daughter of G. W. Sheppard, who had come with his wife and children from England to America in the preceding year and who established a home in Gage county. In conclusion of this memoir is given brief record concerning the children of Dr. and Mrs. Webb, the latter continuing to occupy the attractive old homestead in the city of Beatrice and being an earnest member of the Episcopal church: Hiram L., eldest of the children, now resides near the city of Binghampton, New York; James Edgar died in infancy; Dr. Joseph Lewis Webb is individually mentioned elsewhere in this volume; and Kate L. remains with her widowed mother, being prominent in the women's activities of the Centenary Methodist Episcopal church of Beatrice and also in the local and national affairs of the Young Women's Christian Association, the while she is a popular figure in the representative social life of her native city.

HON. LEWIS B. BOGGS, M. D., a man of distinguished intellectual and professional ability and high ideals, came with his family to Gage county in 1872, and it was given him to wield a large and benignant influence not only as a pioneer physician and surgeon of this section of the state, but also as a man of affairs and a citizen whose civic loyalty and exceptional talents made him a most influential factor in public affairs in the county and state of his adoption. Now venerable in years, he and his wife maintain their residence in Oklahoma City, Oklahoma, to which state they removed from Gage county in 1894. As sterling pioneers who represented the best in civic life in Gage county for many years, it is fitting that they be accorded recognition in this history.

Dr. Lewis Bowen Boggs was born at Newcastle, Indiana, September 3, 1828, the fourth in order of birth in a family of seven children. His paternal grandfather, Andrew Boggs, was born and reared in Ireland and upon coming to America established his residence in Virginia, in which historic old commonwealth he passed the remainder of his life. James Boggs, father of the Doctor, was born in Virginia, where he was reared and educated, and as a young man of twenty years he went to Indiana and settled in the pioneer town of Newcastle. There was solemnized his marriage to Miss Martha Stinson, who was born in eastern Tennessee, October 26, 1806, her parents having removed from Tennessee to Indiana and having become pioneer settlers in Henry county, where they passed the rest of their lives, the father, John Stinson, having there become a prosperous farmer. James Boggs continued his residence in Henry county, Indiana, until his death, November 7, 1842, and he there reclaimed and improved a valuable farm, his status having been that of a substantial and influential citizen of that section of the old Hoosier state. His widow survived him by nearly a decade and was summoned to the life eternal on the 6th of March, 1852.

Dr. Lewis B. Boggs was but fourteen years of age at the time of his father's death and was thus early thrown upon his own resources. For a time he worked for his board and clothing, in the meanwhile finding it possible to attend school during the winter terms. His alert mentality was on a parity with his ambition, and he determined to obtain a liberal education. He continued to be associated with farm enterprise until he had attained to the age of twenty years, when he entered Wabash College. In this institution he completed the full classical course, and after leaving college he was employed for one year in a grain elevator at Michigan City, Indiana. At Leesburg, that state, he then took up the study of medicine, under effective private preceptorship, and he applied himself with such characteristic diligence and receptivity that three years later he was able to engage in active general practice, at North Manchester, Indiana. There he remained until 1858, when he removed to Neponset, Illinois, which locality continued to be the stage of his effective professional labors until 1865, when he returned to Indiana and established himself in practice at Argos, Marshall county. There he retained a large and representative general practice until 1870, when, on account of his impaired health, he turned over his practice to his younger brother. In 1872 he came with his family to Gage county, Nebraska, where he purchased one hundred and eighty-five acres of land in what is now Filley township. For this property he paid only four and one half dollars an acre and with the passing years he reclaimed it into one of the fine farm properties of the county. Here he gave his attention primarily to the raising of live stock, and when it became known throughout the pioneer community that he was a skilled physician and surgeon he was prevailed upon to resume here the practice of his profession, in the meanwhile continuing his farm enterprise with the effective assistance of his sons. Within a short time he built up a large practice, the same extending over a radius of twenty miles, and he devoted himself earnestly and unselfishly to the alleviation of human suffering under conditions that involved arduous work and many hardships. This pioneer physician thus gained the affectionate regard of the entire community and his name is revered in the county where he thus lived and labored to goodly ends.

In 1887 Dr. Boggs retired from the active practice of his profession, but he still retained most vital interest in community affairs and those of governmental and general public order. He became deeply interested in the cause of prohibition and was associated with others in establishing a prohibition publication to which was given the name of the *New Republic*. He was actively associated with the management of this periodical, which was made an influential organ of the cause. Dr. Boggs was reared in the faith of the Democratic party but prior to the Civil war he had become a staunch abolitionist, doing all in his power to remove the institution of human slavery from the nation.

In 1876 Dr. Boggs was elected representative of Gage county in the Nebraska legislature, and he made a characteristically effective record in the promotion of wise legislation. He was assigned to important committees of the house of representatives, including the judiciary committee, and his loyal activities as a legislator were of that exalted order which was to be expected of a man of his temperament and ability. The Doctor has for many years been affiliated with the Masonic fraternity and he was one of the founders and a director of the first banking institution established in the village of Filley. He was loyal and liberal in the support of measures and movements tending to advance the general well-being of his home county. He was one of the most influential representatives of the Prohibition party in Gage county and in 1884 was a presidential elector on the party ticket. He acquired a large landed estate in Gage county and was the true apostle of civic and industrial progress.

In LaPorte county, Indiana, on the 26th Of October, 1854, was solemnized the marriage of Dr. Boggs to Miss Virginia R. Fraser, a daughter of James and Sarah (Campbell) Fraser, the former of whom was born at Alexandria, Virginia, July 3, 1798, and the latter in the city of Washington, D. C., in the year 1808. The parents were married in the city of Washington and in 1834 became pioneer settlers in LaPorte county, Indiana, in which state they passed the remainder of their lives. Mrs. Boggs was born in LaPorte county, March 28, 1836, and was there reared and educated, she having been the third in a family of eight children. Dr. and Mrs. Boggs became the parents of a fine family of thirteen children, and of the nine now living the names and respective dates of birth are here noted: James F., January 7, 1856; Charles S., June 19, 1857 (individually mentioned on other pages of this work); Eva L. (wife of P. E. Plumb), November 19, 1858; Mary Ellen (wife of William H. Andrew), August 5, 1860; Luther A., April 16, 1862; Thomas W., March 8, 1864; Benjamin F., March 16, 1866; Alice C. (wife of H. H. Halliday), March 4, 1868; and Minnie (wife of George Scott), February 11, 1881.

GUSTAVUS A. ERICKSON merits consideration in this work by reason of his secure status as one of the representative farmers and citizens of Sherman township. He was born in Mercer county, Illinois, on the 2d of August, 1871, and is a son of Peter and Susan Erickson, both natives of Sweden. Peter Erickson was reared and educated in his native land and was a sturdy and ambitious youth of twenty years when he came to the United States. For some time thereafter he was employed at Galesburg, Illinois, where his marriage was solemnized, and in 1876 he removed with his family to Iowa, where he remained until 1884, as a farmer, and whence he then came to Gage county, Nebraska. Here he became the owner of a half-section of land, in Sherman township, and he developed this into one of the well improved and valuable farm properties of the county. He finally sold one hundred and sixty acres, but the remainder of the place he retained in his possession until his death, in 1901, his widow being now (1918) seventy-eight years of age. Of their four children three are living and of that number the subject of this sketch is the eldest; Minnie is the wife of E. G. Crook; Frank is deceased; and Ida is the wife of William Kresbaugh, who has charge of the old homestead farm of Peter Erickson. Mr. Erickson was a Republican in politics and was an earnest member of the Luthern church, as is also his venerable widow. He came to the United States without other reinforcement than his individual energy and determined purpose, and he achieved worthy success through his association with farm enterprise.

Gustavus A. Erickson was a lad of five years at the time of the family removal from Illinois to Iowa, and in the latter state he received his early education in the public schools. He was thirteen years old when his parents came to Gage county, and here he continued to attend school at intervals, the while he assisted materially in the work of the home farm. After beginning independent operations as a farmer he utilized rented land for five years, and he then purchased eighty acres of his present farm, the place now comprising one hundred and sixty acres. In addition to this homestead he owns other Gage county land of such amount as to make the area of his estate in the county four hundred acres, besides which he is the owner of four hundred acres in the state of Kansas. He has made excellent improvements on his homestead farm and in addition to carrying on well ordered operations as an agriculturist he raises each year a large number of cattle and swine of good type.

Mr. Erickson is a stalwart Republican and he is serving in 1918 as chairman of the township board. He is affiliated with the Masonic fraternity and the Modern Woodmen of America and his wife and children hold membership in the Christian church.

In 1893 Mr. Erickson wedded Miss Mary Mangus, who was born in Illinois and who is a daughter of William Mangus, who came with his family to Gage county in 1883 and who was here the owner of a valuable farm estate of four hundred acres at the time of his death, he having been born in Virginia and his wife, who survives him, having been born in Illinois. Mr. and Mrs. Erickson became the parents of five children, all of whom are living except the third, Nellie, who died at the age of two years; Oliver is a sophomore in a leading dental college in the city of Omaha; Walter is now associated with his father in farm enterprise; and Edith and Alva are attending the local district school.

AMOS L. WRIGHT is one of the honored territorial pioneers of Gage county and has become one of the specially successful exponents of industrial and business enterprise in this section of the state—an influential citizen who now resides in the village of Virginia, Sherman township, and who is properly given a tribute in this history of the county to whose development and progress he has contributed in generous measure.

Mr. Wright was born in Menard county, Illinois, on the 27th of February, 1844, and there he gained ample experience in connection with the work of the pioneer farm, the while he made excellent use of the educational advantages that were afforded him, as shown by the fact that he became a successful and popular representative of the pedagogic profession after he became a pioneer of Gage county, Nebraska, where he taught school three winter terms. He was an ambitious young man of twenty-two years when, in 1866, he came to Nebraska Territory, which was admitted to statehood in the following year. Here he found work as a farm hand, at a compensation of ten dollars a month, and finally he began the breaking and improving of his homestead of one hundred and sixty acres, in Section 10 Blakely township. In 1868 he hauled from this pioneer farm to Nebraska City three wagon-loads of wheat, representing his entire crop for that season, and for the same he received sixty cents a bushel. That the loads were not large in volume is vouched for by the fact that the sacks of grain were hauled on a wagon without sideboards. In 1867, with ox and horse teams, he broke up a part of his land, and in that year he was a member of a company, including Jacob Rutherford and seventeen other pioneers, who made their way to the west to assist in quelling insubordinate Indians, he and Mr. Rutherford being now the only surviving members of this expedition against the Cheyenne

Indians, but in the connection they failed to encounter a single Indian except one who was dead.

MR. AND MRS. AMOS L. WRIGHT

Mr. Wright reclaimed his farm into one of the productive tracts of Blakely township and there remained until 1886, when he removed with his family to Sherman township, where he purchased a tract of six hundred and forty acres—the south half of Section 14 and the north half of Section 23. On this fine estate he made the best improvements and engaged extensively in general farm industry, including diversified agriculture and the raising of live stock. Later he was engaged in the grain and lumber business in the village of Virginia, but he still retains possession of his land in Gage county. He passes a portion of each year with his children, in Gage county, where are many associations and memories that are hallowed to him and where his circle of friends is limited only by that of his acquaintances, and the intervening periods he customarily utilizes in visiting his daughter in California.

In Gage county was solemnized the marriage of Mr. Wright to Miss Clara Wickham, who was born in Holt county, Missouri, July 27, 1848, and they became the parents of three children: Frances A. is the widow of Joseph E. Penry and resides at Bostonia, California, she being the mother of three children; Bessie is the wife of William Holm, a representative merchant at Virginia, Gage county, and they have two daughters; and Fred A. is individually mentioned in this publication.

Amos L. Wright is a son of James and Elizabeth (Offiel) Wright, natives respectively of Ohio and Kentucky. James Wright removed, in company with one of his brothers, to Illinois in the pioneer days, and there he remained until 1867, when he came with other members of his family to the new state of Nebraska, where his son Amos L. has located in the preceding year. Here he became a pioneer farmer, though in earlier years he had given much attention to work at the carpenter trade, he and his brother John having built an old-time box bridge across the Sangamon river at Springfield, Illinois, in the pioneer days. James Wright died on his farm in Saline county, Nebraska, at the age of seventy-one years, his wife having preceded him to eternal rest. His father, George Wright, was riding horseback along one of the narrow pioneer roads of Ohio when a falling tree killed both the rider and the horse.

JACOB KLEIN.—The career of this honored pioneer merchant of the city of Beatrice has been significantly characterized by courage, confidence, progressiveness and impregnable integrity of purpose. None has a more secure status as a representative citizen and business man of southeastern Nebraska, and to the people of Gage county his name and achievement are practically as familiar as the name of the county. Aside from being the executive head and the founder of one of the largest and best ordered department stores in this section of the state and having other capitalistic interests of important order, Mr. Klein has been signally loyal and helpful as a public-spirited citizen and as one who has been a force in the furtherance of the civic and material advancement and prosperity of the community in which he has maintained his home for more than forty years and to which he came as an ambitious young man with very limited financial resources but with the fullest measure of determination and resourcefulness. He eminently deserves classification among those self-made men who have distinguished themselves for their ability to master the opposing forces of life and to wrest from the hands of fate a large measure of success and an honorable name. Mr. Klein has not only been the dominating force in the upbuilding of the extensive mercantile business now conducted under the corporate title of Klein's Mercantile Company, but has identified himself also with the development and promotion of other business enterprises of importance, has been the loyal supporter of all measures tending to conserve the general wellbeing of his home city, county and state, and has been called upon to serve in various positions of public trust, including that of member of the state senate.

In the Upper Palatinate of the Kingdom of Bavaria, Germany, and not far distant from the historic old city of Bingen, on the Rhine, Jacob Klein was born March 31, 1846,—a scion of old and honored families of that section of the German empire, where his paternal grandfather, John Klein, a weaver by trade and vocation, passed his entire life, as did also the maternal grandfather, Conrad Weiser, who gave his allegiance to the great fundamental industry of agriculture. Mr. Klein is a son of Jacob and Margaret (Weiser) Klein, both likewise natives of Bavaria, where each was born in the year 1805. The parents passed the closing years of their lives in Livingston county, Illinois, where the mother's death occurred in 1874 and that of the father in 1879, their marriage having been solemnized in 1832 and both having been earnest communicants of the Lutheran church. Of their five children the subject of this review is the youngest and the other two now living are Charles, who is a resident of Montana, where he is a retired farmer, and Katherine, who is the widow of Louis Moschel and maintains her home in the city of Beatrice.

In the year 1855 Jacob Klein, Senior, immigrated with his family to the United States, and soon after landing in the port of New York city he continued his westward journey and settled in Tazewell county, Illinois. He had incurred an indebtedness of six hundred dollars incidental to transporting the family to America, and thus a double responsibility rested upon him after he had established a home in this country. For the first year he was employed by others, and he then rented a farm from an Englishman who furnished him with all requisite tools and appliances, and he continued his operations on this farm, in Tazewell county, for a period of nine years. His energy and good judgment brought him a full measure of success as an agriculturist, though in his native land he had followed the trade of weaver. Through his operation in the control of the farm mentioned Mr. Klein accumulated a sufficient reserve of money to justify him in purchasing a farm of his own. Under these conditions he bought, at the rate of twenty-five dollars an acre, a tract of eighty acres in Livingston county, Illinois, and to the improving and cultivating of this homestead he continued to give his attention until the death of his loved and devoted wife, in 1874, when he sold the property to his son, Philip C., with whom he remained until he too passed to the life eternal, about five years later. The son Philip was a resident of Illinois at the time of his death and the other deceased member of the immediate family circle was John, who died when about seventy-nine years of age.

He whose name introduces this review acquired his rudimentary education in his native land and was a lad of about ten years at the time of the family immigration to the United States. He was reared to manhood under the sturdy discipline of the farm and in the meanwhile he profited by the advantages afforded in the schools of Tazewell county, Illinois, his attendance in the same having continued at intervals during a period of three years, the while he was not denied a full quota of strenuous and practical experience in connection with the work of the home farm. Like many another reared under similar conditions, he has rounded out his education through effective self-discipline and through the lessons gained through his long and successful business career, so that he has become a man of broad mental ken and mature judgment. Mr. Klein initiated his independent career as a farmer when he was about twenty-three years of age, and he continued his active alliance with farm industry in Illinois until 1873, when, at the age of twenty-seven years, he came to Nebraska and numbered himself as one of the pioneers of Gage county. His marriage occurred about two years previously and upon coming to this county he established the family home in the small but aspiring little city of Beatrice. Here he forthwith formed a partnership with Charles Moschel and Emil Lang and they engaged in the retail grocery business, under the firm name of J. Klein & Company. Success attended the enterprise and within a few years its scope was enlarged by the addition of departments devoted to dry goods and men's clothing. The partnership alliance continued until 1887, in January of which year the three principals made an equitable division of the business and stock, Mr. Klein at this time taking control of the dry goods and clothing department of the enterprise. With characteristic energy and good judgment he made himself a leader in anticipating the demands of the public incidental to the development and growth of the county and its judicial center, and finally he developed the large and important general merchandise business which marks the present department store of Klein's Mercantile Company as one of the most metropolitan and efficiently conducted institutions of the kind in this part of the state. For the accommodation of the large and constantly increasing business Mr. Klein erected the large and substantial brick block which bears his name, the building being two stories in height, not including basement, and occupying a ground area twenty-five by one hundred and ten feet in dimensions. Here is conducted under most favorable conditions and arrangement the general department store, and every department is known for efficiency and acceptability of service, so that the substantial enterprise has the firmest of foundations, even as the executive policies attest to the sterling integrity and the progressiveness of Mr. Klein, as well as of his sons, who have become his valued coadjutors in the control and management of the important enterprise,—the reputation of the concern constituting its best commercial asset. In 1901 the business was incorporated under the present name, Klein's Mercantile Company, the charter given under the laws of Nebraska designating the capital stock at one hundred and twenty-five thousand dollars. The honored founder, as president and general manager of the company, continues as the executive head of the business, his eldest son, Jacob A., who is individually mentioned on other pages, being vice-president of the company; the second son, Frederick K., being secretary and treasurer, and the youngest son, Frank E., likewise being actively associated with the business.

In noting the financial and civic status of Jacob Klein at the present time it is interesting to record that when he came to Beatrice his available capitalistic resources were summed up in about five hundred dollars. His success has not been an accident but rather the logical result of well applied energy and ability, and his many friends in the community honor him the more for the fact that he has always been an earnest and productive worker. His communal loyalty has led him to make his liberality keep pace with his cumulative prosperity, and thus he has given capitalistic co-operation in the furtherance of other business enterprises. Among his other and noteworthy connections may be mentioned his active and prolific association with the Gage County Agricultural Society, he having been one of the twenty progressive citizens who organized this society.

Well fortified in his convictions pertaining to governmental and economic policies, Mr. Klein has always been found arrayed as a staunch supporter of the cause of the Democratic party, and he has been influential in its councils and campaign activities in this part of the state. He served one term as treasurer of Gage county, has been a valued member of the Beatrice board of education, and the high popular estimate placed upon him was significantly shown when, in 1909, he was elected representative of the Fourteenth district in the state senate. He proved a well poised, sane and vigorous figure in the deliberations and work of the senate and those of the various committees to which he was assigned, and was given the best of popular commendation through his re-election in

1913. He and his family are communicants of the Lutheran church and he takes deep satisfaction in giving to his gracious and popular wife a due mede of credit for the aid she has given him in the furtherance of his success, the while her gentle and kindly personality has gained to her the affectionate regard of all who have come within the sphere of her influence.

In the year 1871 was solemnized the marriage of Mr. Klein to Miss Catharine Moschel, who was born in Germany and who came with her widowed mother, Mrs. Margaret (Schantz) Moschel, to America in the year 1865, the father, Christian Moschel, having died in Germany about the year 1854, his vocation having been that of cabinetmaker. The widowed mother brought her five children to the United States and the home was established in Illinois, the mother having there passed the residue of her life, her death having occurred on a farm near Chenoa, McLean county, in 1886. Three of her sons, Louis, Charles, and Daniel, became pioneers of Gage county, Nebraska, where they settled in the '70s and all became representative citizens of the county. Mr. and Mrs. Klein have four children, and in a preceding paragraph it has been noted that the three sons are actively associated with the business founded by their father. The only daughter, Ida M., remains at the parental home and is a popular assistant to her mother.

HERMAN M. REYNOLDS, M. D.—For all time must Gage county pay a tribute of veneration and honor to the late Dr. Herman Meyer Reynolds, who was one of the foremost pioneer physicians and surgeons of this part of the state, who wielded large and beneficent influence in the furtherance of civic and material development and progress and who was a leader in all movements tending to advance the welfare and growth of the beautiful little city of Beatrice, the metropolis and judicial center of Gage county. He aided in upbuilding Beatrice from a frontier village to its present status as one of the vigorous and important municipalities of Nebraska, and his was the distinction of being elected the city's first mayor. His life was significantly one of service, was marked by unwavering optimism and abiding human sympathy, and even this succinct record concerning his life and labors can not fail of lesson and incentive. He was one of the best known and most beloved pioneer citizens of Gage county at the time of his death, which occurred on the 26th of April, 1875.

Dr. Reynolds was born at Shelldrake, Sullivan county, New York, on the 15th of April, 1832, and was a scion of one of the old and honored families of that section of the Empire state. A youth of alert mind and valiant ambition, Dr. Reynolds early determined, after having availed himself of the advantages of the common schools, to prepare himself for the medical profession, and finally he provided ways and means to complete a course in a medical college in the city of Albany, New York. After having received the degree of Doctor of Medicine he engaged in the practice of his profession, and his ability soon gained him recognition, with the result that success attended his earnest efforts in the work of his chosen calling. For two years prior to coming to the west the Doctor was engaged in practice in the city of Scranton, Pennsylvania, and he was one of the leaders in the fine colony that came to Gage county, Nebraska, and located the town site of Beatrice, the county seat. He was thus one of the founders of this city and had the distinction of being not only its pioneer physician and surgeon, but also the first man elected as chief executive of the municipal government of the ambitious little city. In the work of his humane mission Dr. Reynolds spared himself neither mental nor physical effort in the pioneer days, and he rode on horseback over the Nebraska prairies for miles in every direction from Beatrice, to carry relief and solace to those in affliction and distress. He ministered with all of his unselfish zeal and marked ability in the work of his profession and his kindliness and sympathy transcended mere vocation to become an actuating motive for helpfulness. Under these conditions it may well be understood that his name and memory are held in lasting reverence in the community in which he lived and labored to goodly ends. In the attractive brick residence which the Doctor erected at 800 Market street he passed the closing period of his life, and there his venerable widow has maintained her home for more than forty years, the place and the community being endeared to her by the hallowed memories and associations of the past and hers being gracious status as one of the loved pioneer women of Beatrice. In this connection it may consistently be noted that the first home provided for

Dr. and Mrs. Reynolds in Beatrice was a pioneer log cabin, the same having been situated at the corner of Fourth and Court streets. Mrs. Reynolds has thus witnessed the development of Beatrice from a frontier hamlet into a populous and prosperous city of twelve thousand inhabitants, and though she has passed the psalmist's span of three score years and ten she retains in splendid degree her mental and physical vigor and finds that in the gracious evening of her life her lines are "cast in pleasant places," her circle of friends in the community being limited only by that of her acquaintances. Dr. Reynolds was a man of vigorous intellectuality and mature judgment, was well fortified in his views concerning governmental and economic policies, and gave his political allegiance to the Republican party, his religious faith having been that of the Christian church. He and his wife were charter members of the church of this denomination in Beatrice and Mrs. Reynolds is still active in its work.

At Beatrice, Nebraska, on the 20th of October, 1861, was solemnized the marriage of Dr. Reynolds to Miss Naomi Barcus, who was born at Covington, Indiana, on the 20th of October, 1841, and who was an infant at the time of the death of her father, Jesse Barcus. Her widowed mother, whose maiden name was Mary Blodgett, later became the wife of Thomas Sherrill, and in 1859 they came to Nebraska and numbered themselves among the earliest settlers of Gage county, where they passed the residue of their lives. Mrs. Reynolds was reared and educated in the old Hoosier state and was about eighteen year age when she accompanied her mother and stepfather to Gage county, Nebraska, so that it may readily be understood that hers are vivid memories touching the conditions and influences that obtained in the early pioneer days. Dr. and Mrs. Reynolds became the parents of six daughters and one son, two of whom died in infancy; Elsie is the widow of George W. Loeber and maintains her home at Beatrice; Mollie is the wife of George F. Randall, a large rancher in Morrill county, Nebraska, Redington being their postoffice address; Ruth is the wife of Charles C. Farlow, of Beatrice, and Mr. Farlow is serving, in 1918, as deputy treasurer of Gage county; Miss Josephine is an efficient and popular teacher in the public schools of Beatrice and remains with her widowed mother at the old homestead; and Hermina is the wife of Harry E. Sackett, a representative Gage county lawyear, to whom is accorded mention on other pages of this work.

JOHN W. WRIGHT was a man whose sterling character gave him excellent equipment for being master of his own destiny, and though his financial resources were of the most limited order when he came to Gage county, forty years ago, he so directed his activities as to achieve large and worthy success. He was a pioneer merchant and farmer of this county, commanded the unqualified respect of all who knew him and it is most fitting that in this history be entered a tribute to his memory.

John Wesley Wright was born in Hawkins county, Tennessee, May 27, 1852, and there he was reared and educated. At the age of twenty-four years he drove with team and wagon from Tennessee to Illinois and settled in Macoupin county, where he found employment at farm work, including the cutting of wood, his compensation at the start being only eight dollars a month. The following year was marked by his turning his attention to independent farm enterprise in that county, and there also the ambitious young man, on March 18, 1877, wedded the gracious young woman who was to continue as his devoted companion and helpmeet during the remainder of his earnest and worthy life. In 1878 Mr. Wright made, with team and wagon, the overland trip from Illinois to Gage county, Nebraska, and his wife joined him within a few months thereafter, she having made the journey by railroad. Soon after his arrival in the county Mr. Wright purchased land in Filley township, the farm now owned by John A. Burbank, and with characteristic vigor and resourcefulness he initiated the improvement and development of this place. When the village of Filley was platted Mr. Wright erected one of the first buildings in the new town and assumed the management of one of the first mercantile establishments there opened. Later he purchased the stock and business and for twenty-one years thereafter he there conducted a substantial and prosperous business as a dealer in hardware, agricultural implements, and groceries. After selling his original farm he purchased one hundred and sixty acres in Filley township just outside the corporate limits of the village of the same name, and upon this homestead he erected good buildings and made other improvements of excellent order. Here he became a most successful and progressive exponent of agricultural and live-stock enterprise and he eventually added much to the area of his landed estate, so that he left to his family at his death a valuable farm property of two hundred acres, his widow still remaining on the attractive homestead and having at all times been the popular chatelaine of a pleasant home known for its gracious hospitality.

Mr. Wright was a man well fortified for leadership in community affairs and while he had no desire for political preferment he was a stalwart advocate of the principles of the Republican party and showed his civic loyalty by his efficient service in the office of justice of the peace. He became a member of the Masonic fraternity when he was twenty-one years of age and continued his active affiliation throughout the remainder of his life. He was an earnest member of the Methodist Episcopal church, to the support of which he contributed liberally and with a high sense of personal stewardship, and his widow likewise is a zealous member.

In the year 1877, as previously intimated, was solemnized the marriage of Mr. Wright to Miss Ella E. Fetter, who was born and reared in Macoupin county, Illinois, and who is a daughter of Adam and Amelia (McDonald) Fetter, the former of whom was born in Germany and the latter in Morgan county, Illinois, where her parents were pioneer settlers. Mr. Fetter became a prosperous farmer in Illinois and there he and his wife continued to reside until their death, when well advanced in years. Of the eleven children born to Mr. and Mrs. Wright all are living except the last, who died in infancy; Clara is the wife of J. R. Landon; Cora B. is the wife of William B. Little and they reside in the city of Omaha; Charles is a bachelor and remains with his widowed mother, he having active management of the home farm; Minnie is the wife of Elon E. Hill of Omaha; Alice remains at the maternal home, as do also James and Lillie; Otis is married and resides in the village of Filley; Ella is the wife of Guy Steece, a farmer in Logan township; and Marie is the wife of Edward Dobbs, of Logan township.

AARON PALMER.—An indomitable energy that has triumphed over seemingly great obstacles, as well as varied misfortunes, is that which had dominated Aaron Palmer during the varied stages of a remarkably earnest and productive business career in which he has rallied to his cause splendid initiative ability and has made each recurrent stroke of adverse fortune but a spur to renewed effort. Depending entirely upon his own resources he has pressed forward along the line of worthy ambition and that he has arrived at the goal of substantial success and influence in connection with business operations needs no further voucher than the fact that he is now president of the A. Palmer Company, of Beatrice, which conducts the largest and most complete house-furnishing establishment in the entire state of Nebraska, this important enterprise being controlled by himself and his wife, the latter of whom is secretary of the company, even as she has been his devoted and efficient coadjutor throughout the entire period of their ideal marital companionship. Mr. Palmer is widely known through Nebraska as the "Fire King," and this title has been gained through his having purchased and sold a greater number and quantity of stocks of merchandise salvaged from tires than has probably any other one man in Nebraska—in fact the foundation of his success having been laid through this means. The company of which he is now the executive head gives special attention to the buying and selling of bankrupt stocks, fire stocks, first and second hand goods, etc., and a prosperous business has been developed. The extensive and well ordered business establishment of the A. Palmer Company at Beatrice gives twenty-six thousand square feet of floor space in the main sales and display rooms, at 119-123 North Fifth avenue, and in the company's warehouse and manufacturing building, at 417 Ella street, are utilized twelve thousand seven hundred and fifty square feet of floor space. The operations of the company are based on a capital stock of fifty thousand dollars, and of this the stock has been issued to the amount of thirty-one thousand dollars. The modern storage building owned and occupied by the company is a four-story structure with double walls and is moisture-proof. All save a few shares of the stock of the company are owned by Mr. Palmer and his wife.

Aaron Palmer, known and honored as one of the most substantial and progressive business men of southeastern Nebraska and as a citizen of loyalty and liberality, has the distinction of being a native of Nebraska and a scion of a family that was here founded in the early territorial days. He was born in the old frontier town of Brownville, Nemaha county, this state, on the 9th of February, 1857—a decade prior to the admission of the state to the Union—and he is a son of James and Elizabeth (Bell) Palmer, the former of whom was born in Missouri and the latter in Illinois, her mother having been a childhood schoolmate of Abraham Lincoln. James Palmer came from Missouri to Nebraska in 1856 and became one of the early settlers at Brownville, in which vicinity he began the development of a small farm, besides raising various garden products that found ready demand in the frontier settlement. He died at Brownville when he was but forty years of age, leaving his wife to care for their seven children, of whom the subject of this sketch was the eldest. Mrs. Palmer bravely faced the responsibilities that devolved upon her and in providing for her fatherless children manifested the utmost self-abnegation and maternal solicitude. She continued to reside in Brownville until her death and was one of the revered pioneer women of Nebraska, her death having occurred when she was about seventy-two years of age.

Reared in his native town to adult age, Aaron Palmer was about twenty-three years old at the time of his father's death, and as the eldest of the seven children, he applied himself earnestly to aiding his mother in caring for and rearing the younger children, to the support of whom he continued to contribute until they were old enough to assume individual responsibility for their own maintenance. Under such conditions it may readily be understood that the early educational training of Aaron Palmer was limited to a somewhat irregular and desultory attendance in the pioneer schools at Brownville, but his alert and receptive mind later enabled him to profit largely through the lessons learned under the preceptorship of that wisest of all headmasters, experience. In aiding in the support of the family he applied himself to whatever work he could obtain, and finally he learned the trade of baker, in a modest bakery at Brownville. With this line of occupation he there continued his association until 1887, when he came to Beatrice and opened a bakery and restaurant. He had no available capital and thus initiated this enterprise on credit. The venture proved a failure, notwithstanding his earnest and assiduous efforts, and within a year he came to involuntary liquidation, with an indebtedness of about eighteen hundred dollars. Thus temporarily astride the back of adversity, Mr. Palmer did not falter in courage or determination, and in order to provide for his family and rid himself of the burden of debt he gained appointment to the position of city mail carrier in Beatrice, in which capacity he continued to give effective service for eleven years, within which he brought himself triumphantly out of debt and also accumulated a modest reserve of sixteen hundred dollars. In 1894 the general merchandise establishment of Begole & Van Arsdale, of Beatrice, was destroyed by fire, and Mr. Palmer purchased the damaged goods salvaged from the fire, though he had only the sixteen hundred dollars to apply on the purchase price. He borrowed the balance required and in the sale of this stock of merchandise he made a profit of about two thousand dollars. Since that time he has continued to deal extensively in bankrupt and fire stocks, in which field of enterprise he has developed from a small inception a business that is now the largest of the kind in Nebraska. It has been consistently stated that in the Palmer establishment may be purchased anything from a needle to a piano, and the display of merchandise includes clothing, dry goods, hardware, stoves, and general house furnishings of every description.

Mr. Palmer has had no communion with apathy or idleness, has been a productive worker and has been found busily at work at all stages of his career. Essentially a business man, he has had neither time nor desire to enter the turbulence of practical politics or to seek public office, though he is liberal and public-spirited in his civic attitude and gives staunch support to the principles and policies for which the Republican party stands sponsor. Widely known throughout this section of the state, he has by his earnest and honest endeavors entrenched himself firmly in popular confidence and esteem, and this has contributed much to the success of his present important business enterprise. In the Masonic fraternity he has completed the circle of the York Rite, his maximum affiliation being with Beatrice commandery of Knights Templars, besides which he holds membership in the adjunct Masonic organization, the Mystic Shrine.

On the 11th of January, 1879, was officially recorded the marriage of Mr. Palmer to Miss Della Furlow, who was born in the state of Maine, but who was a child at the time of her parents' removal to Nebraska, where she was reared and educated, her father having been one of the pioneer settlers of Nemaha county. Mr. and Mrs. Palmer have no children, but in their attractive home they delight to extend welcome and entertainment to the young folk of the community as well as to the friends of their own generation. Mrs. Palmer is an active member of the

Presbyterian church of Beatrice, and is affiliated with the representative Masonic subsidiary body known as the Order of the Eastern Star.

WILLIAM C. MOORE.—In Sections 35 and 36, Holt township, Mr. Moore and his wife are the owners of a fine rural estate of three hundred and twenty acres, and Mr. Moore, whose farm experience has touched various sections of Nebraska, looks upon Gage county as one of the best and most attractive districts for the successful prosecution of agricultural and live stock industry that can be found within the limits of this progressive state. He has made his farm property one specially notable for thrift and good management and is essentially one of the representative citizens and substantial farmers of Holt township.

MR. & MRS. WILLIAM C. MOORE

Mr. Moore was born at Waterloo, Blackhawk county, Iowa, March 27 1865, being the youngest in a family of ten children, of whom eight attained to maturity. He is a son of Jacob and Catherine (Waltz) Moore, the former of whom was born in Germany, March 27, 1821, and the latter of whom was born in Dauphin county, Pennsylvania, August 28,

1821. Jacob Moore was about eleven years old when he accompanied his parents on their immigration to America, and the family home was established in Pennsylvania, where he was reared to adult age and where his marriage was solemnized. In 1857, within a short time after their marriage, Mr. Moore and his wife left the old Keystone state and made their way to Green county, Wisconsin, both having walked a large part of the intervening distance. He became a pioneer farmer in that county, where he remained until about 1864, when he removed to Blackhawk county, Iowa, where he repeated his pioneer experience as an agriculturist. One of his sons, John W., went forth as a soldier of the Union in the Civil war; he enlisted in a Wisconsin volunteer regiment of infantry and took part in many engagements marking the progress of the conflict between the north and the south, he having been with Sherman on the historic march from Atlanta to the sea. This honored veteran of the Civil war is now venerable in years and maintains his home in Newburg, Oregon. Jacob Moore became a farmer in Iowa, where he remained until 1874, when he came to Nebraska, the closing period of his life having been passed in Hamilton county, this state, where he died March 27, 1877. He had been an invalid for eight years. A man of sterling character and indefatigable industry, he had the distinction of being a pioneer in each of three different states, and he lived a righteous and upright life, so that he commanded unqualified popular esteem. His widow long survived him and was a resident of Newburg, Oregon, at the time of her death, in June, 1906. Both were reared in the faith of the German Lutheran church but after their removal they became members of the Dunkard church, with which they continued to be affiliated during the remainder of their lives.

William C. Moore gained his preliminary education in the schools of Iowa and was nine years of age when his parents numbered themselves among the pioneers of Hamilton county, Nebraska, where he continued to attend school until he was fifteen years of age. When eleven years of age he received an injury that compelled him to abandon his school work for a year, and as a youth he turned his attention to farm work, his initial experience as a farm hand having been gained when he was a lad of fifteen years. At the age of nineteen years he rented land in Hamilton county, where he conducted independent farm operations for the ensuing four years. He then established the first dray line at Stockham. He later became the owner of a homestead farm in the southern part of Lincoln county, and after selling this property, in 1889, he became associated with his brother John W. in purchasing of Daniel and William Nicewonger a general merchandise store and business in the village of Pickrell, Gage county. In 1893 the subject of this review sold his interest in the business to his brother and resumed his active association with farm enterprise, by renting a farm located to the east of Pickrell, in Holt township. In 1895 he purchased forty acres in Section 23 of that township, for a consideration of eleven hundred dollars, and about six years later he sold the property for two thousand dollars. In 1899 Mr. Moore purchased the Jersey Smith farm of eighty acres, and this constitutes an integral part of his now large and admirably improved landed estate in Holt township. Energy, progressiveness, and correct business policies have enabled Mr. Moore to achieve unqualified success in the different departments of farm industry and he is one of the substantial and influential citizens of Holt township, where he has been called upon to serve in various public offices of minor order and where he is now a director of the school board for District No. 57, his political allegiance being given to the Republican party and he and his wife being active members of the United Brethren church.

February, 1891, recorded the marriage of Mr. Moore to Miss Mary Lewis, who was born in Holt township, this county, November 8, 1870, a daughter of John E. and Sarah M. (Williams) Lewis, the former a native of Wales and the latter of the state of New York. Mr. Lewis became a pioneer of the state of Wisconsin, where he remained until 1868, when he came to the new state of Nebraska and became one of the earliest settlers in Holt township, Gage county, where he reclaimed and improved a valuable farm property and where he and his wife passed the residue of their lives as honored pioneer citizens of the county. Mr. Lewis died May 2, 1913, at the age of seventy-two years, his wife having passed away February 17, 1905, at the age of fifty-two years. Of their eight children all are living except one, only two of the number being residents of Gage county and the others maintaining their residence in

Scotts Bluff county. Concerning the children of Mr. and Mrs. Moore the following brief record is given: John is associated with his father in the management of the home farm; Eva, who was graduated in the high school at Beatrice, is a successful and popular teacher in the district schools of the county; Walter assists in the work of the home farm; Myrtle likewise was graduated in the Beatrice high school and is an efficient teacher in the district schools of her native county; Sarah is a member of the class of 1919 in the Beatrice high school; Edward and George remain at the parental home; and one son died in infancy.

Mr. Moore has been in the most significant sense the builder of the sturdy ladder on which he has risen to the plane of independence and worthy prosperity, and he is today not only the owner of a valuable landed estate and a stockholder in the farmers' grain elevator at Pickrell but is also entirely free from indebtedness. He had made good improvements on his farm property and has availed himself of the most modern farm machinery and accessories, including an elevator for the transfer ring of the various grain products raised on his broad and fertile acres. In short, he is a successful exponent of modern and scientific farm enterprise.

THE DOLE FLORAL COMPANY.—In the year 1916 was celebrated the twenty-fifth anniversary of the founding of one of the large, important, and interesting industrial enterprises of Beatrice and Gage county, that of the Dole Floral Company, and this publication exercises a consistent function when it gives special recognition to this representative corporation, for in the upbuilding of its business has been exemplified the splendid energy and initiative ability of its honored founder, Mrs. Sophia H. Dole, who, while representing all of gracious womanhood, has proved herself one of the most successful business women of Nebraska, has made of her individual success a medium of leverage for the uplifting of civic and material prosperity in her home city and county, the while she has ever retained an inviolable place in the affectionate regard of the community in which she has lived and labored to goodly ends. Of the inception and growth of the business founded by this representative exponent of business enterprise in the city of Beatrice, a brief, pertinent, and interesting record was given in the anniversary catalogue issued by the Dole Floral Company in 1916, and it is pleasing to perpetuate in more enduring form this record:

"In the spring of 1891 Mrs. Sophia H. Dole, with an investment of one dollar for flower pots and seventy-five cents for seeds, and with a hot-bed sash for a greenhouse, began the ornamental plant business at 617 Mary street. In the autumn of the same year a small greenhouse was built. The next year Josiah G. Dole and his two sons, Edward W. and Walter A., became associated with Mrs. Dole, under the firm name of S. H. Dole & Sons, and thereafter the greenhouse was enlarged from year to year until the location was outgrown. In 1898 three acres of land were leased and a new range of greenhouses was built at 609 Mary street. The business was incorporated in 1904, under the title of the Dole Floral Company. Capital stock was offered for sale and five acres of land were purchased by the company at the corner of Fifth and Hoyt streets. On this specially eligible site was erected in 1905 the present range of greenhouses, which has since been notably enlarged, in consonance with the constantly increasing demands placed upon the company in connection with its growing trade. The result is that at the present time the company has twenty-five thousand feet of glass, besides well equipped work and storage rooms.

"Our first down-town salesroom occupied a little building that was only five by seven feet in dimensions, at 114 North Fifth street. In 1908 the company purchased a lot at 518 Ella street, and in the following year there was erected on this site the present Dole building, a substantial brick structure of two stories. The building has since been enlarged and is now equipped with a large and modern case for the preservation of cut flowers and with an artificial ice refrigerating plant."

In a progressive policy that implies the giving of thoroughly metropolitan service the Dole Floral Company has equipped its attractive salesrooms with the most modern appointments and facilities, and the establishment is a source of pride to the city of Beatrice and its people. The large display cases in which the cut flowers are preserved after being taken from the greenhouses have cold air supplied from the company's artificial ice plant, which is operated by electricity and which has a capacity for the production of four tons of ice every twenty-four hours. The company has an attractive automobile delivery car, which is utilized not only in delivering floral products to patrons in Beatrice but also in transporting fresh-cut flowers from the greenhouses each morning, for display and sale at the down-town store. The propagating facilities controlled by the company are of the most approved order and the concern offers roses, carnations, sweet peas, and all other of the popular varieties of flowers, the same being grown entirely at the conservatories of the company. Large shipments are made to other cities and many towns in this section of the state, and demands come also from points even farther removed. The company gives the best of service in the supplying of cut flowers, bedding plants, house plants, and bulbs. Special attention is given also to the producing of artistic floral designs for decorative and funeral purposes, and the company maintains a department for the handling of the finest varieties of gold fish.

The Dole Floral Company now bases its operations on a capital stock of fifty thousand dollars, and the personnel of its executive corps is as here noted: Edward W. Dole, president; Victor Ryhd, secretary; and George M. Johnson, treasurer and manager. Of each of these officers more specific mention is made on other pages of this volume, and similar recognition is given also to the popular founder of the enterprise, Mrs. Sophia H. Dole.

CHARLES F. BONHAM was one of the organizers of the State Bank of Ellis, a thriving village of Gage county, and has been cashier of this well ordered institution since 1909, his administration having proved potent in the upbuilding of the substantial business of the bank.

Mr. Bonham was born in Andrew county, Missouri, December 7, 1871, and is a son of William and Mary Ann (Nicholson) Bonham, of whose four children he was the third in order of birth, Eunice, the firstborn, having been about three years of age at the time of her death; William B. died at the age of twelve years; and Clarence L. is now engaged in the banking business at Ayr, Adams county. William Bonham was born near the city of Milwaukee, Wisconsin, in 1841, a scion of a sterling pioneer family of that state. His parents, David and Rebecca (Weaver) Bonham, were natives respectively of England and Wisconsin, and from the Badger state they finally removed to Missouri, making the long overland journey in a covered wagon that was drawn by a mule and a blind horse, besides which they had an ox team. David Bonham engaged in farming in Missouri and there he and his wife passed the remainder of their lives. They became the parents of eight children and four of their sons were soldiers of the Union in the Civil war— David, Jr., Robert, John, and James—all now deceased.

William Bonham became a substantial farmer and influential citizen of Andrew county, Missouri, and later was engaged in farming in Gentry county, that state, where for a number of years he was engaged also in the agricultural-implement business, at King City. He came to Nebraska about the year 1892 and he reclaimed and developed a good farm in Furnas county, where he passed the remainder of his life, his death having occurred in 1902. His widow, who was born in Indiana, in 1846, and whose death occurred in 1906, was a daughter of John F. Nicholson, who was a gallant soldier of the Union in the Civil war. William Bonham and his wife were most zealous members of the Methodist Episcopal church and in politics he gave his support to the Republican party.

Charles F. Bonham was reared on the farm of his father in Missouri and after having profited duly by the advantages of the district schools he continued his studies in the village schools of King City until he had completed the work of the tenth grade. Later he completed a commercial course in Wesleyan College, at Cameron, Missouri, and after his graduation he became bookkeeper for his father, who was then engaged in the implement business at King City. In 1892 he resumed his association with farm enterprise in his native state and in 1894 he accompanied his parents to Furnas county, Nebraska, where he was engaged in farming until 1909, when he came to Gage county and became cashier of the State Bank of Ellis, of which position he has since continued the efficient and popular incumbent. This bank was organized in 1907 by his brother Clarence and eight representative farmers of this section of the county, and in the general record concerning the banking interests of the county, on other pages, due mention is made of this prosperous institution, of which Temple E. Pierce is president and Albert C. Pefferman, vice-president.

Mr. Bonham takes vital interest in all things touching the wellbeing and advancement of his home village and county, is a Republican in his political allegiance, is affiliated with the local organizations of the Independent Order of Odd Fellows and the Modern Woodmen of America, and he and his wife are zealous members of the Methodist Episcopal church at Ellis, of which he is serving as a steward in 1917-1918. He is the owner of village property in Ellis, including his pleasant home, and also has a well improved farm property of three hundred and twenty acres near Wilsonville, Furnas county.

January 7, 1893, recorded the marriage of Mr. Bonham to Miss Elsie Timmons, who was born in the state of Illinois, a daughter of Ephraim Timmons, and of this union have been born three children: Lee D. is assistant cashier of the Union State Bank in the city of Beatrice; Ada died at the age of two years; and Russell died in 1915, at the age of seven years.

ARNOTT D. McCANDLESS.—Each successive stage of a life that has been worthily lived bears its full measure of compensation, and the man who has passed life's meridian, who has stored up the lessons of rich and varied experience, and who has wrought wisely, justly, and effectively, must find each successive year thereafter radiant in personal contentment and gracious in memories. Such a sane, direct, and productive life has been that of Arnott Duncan McCandless, who is one of the representative members of the bar of Gage county and whose buoyant optimism has enabled him to get the best out of life in its varied relations. He is a writer of exceptional talent and another dominating attribute of his makeup is his love for the vital sports afield and afloat, in which domain of recreation he has gained distinct prestige. He is engaged in the practice of his profession in the city of Wymore and his status as a citizen, a lawyer, and as a genial and popular man makes it specially pleasing to accord him recognition in this history.

Mr. McCandless is of staunch Scotch ancestry on both the paternal and maternal sides, as the respective names fully indicate. He was born on a farm six miles east of Macomb, McDonough county, Illinois, on the 27th of August, 1849, and is a son of William Wallace McCandless and Sarah (Duncan) McCandless, both natives of Pennsylvania. A literal and fully substantiated fact pertinent to the McCandless family is singularly in consonance with a statement all too tritely made concerning the founding of other families in America. That is, the original progenitors of the McCandless family in this country were the proverbial three brothers, but it has been clearly established that one of the number established a home in Pennsylvania, that another located in the south and that the third became a seafaring man. From the one who settled in the old Keystone state the subject of this review is descended.

Arnott D. McCandless was five years old when his parents removed from McDonough county, Illinois, and settled on a farm one half mile southwest of Aledo, Mercer county, and he was a lad of about thirteen years when his loyal and patriotic father went forth to battle for the nation's integrity as a soldier of the Union in the Civil war. On the 14th of August, 1862, William W. McCandless enlisted as a private in Company H, Eighty-fourth Illinois Volunteer Infantry, and with his command he set forth from Quincy, Illinois, marched across Kentucky and on to Nashville, Tennessee, the soldiers of his regiment sleeping at night under the open sky, as they were not provided with tents. Mr. McCandless was destined soon to sacrifice his life in the righteous cause, for he was killed at the battle of Stone River, on the 31st of December, 1862, little more than four months after he had enlisted. He had become the father of six children, and his widow and two of her married daughters eventually came to Nebraska and settled in Box Butte county. While visiting at the home of her son Arnott D., of this review, at Wymore, the widowed mother was summoned to eternal rest, her death having occurred in 1910, at which time she was eighty-eight years of age.

Arnott Duncan McCandless attended the district schools in Mercer county, Illinois, and thereafter attended for two years a Presbyterian select school in that state. He was at this time about eleven years old and thereafter he attended school only three months until after he had attained to his legal majority. The death of his father compelled him to assume heavy responsibilities when he was but a boy, and through his application to farm work he aided in the support of his mother and the other members of the family. His insistent determination to broaden his education led him to take his Latin grammar into the field with him, in order that he might apply himself to study during his all too few leisure moments. In the meanwhile his advancement had been such that he proved himself a successful teacher during four months of pedagogic service in the district schools of his native state.

ARNOTT D. MCCANDLESS

Soon after reaching his legal majority Mr. McCandless entered the law office of Isaac N. Bassett, a leading lawyer at Aledo, Illinois, and, at a stipend of sixteen dollars and seventy-five cents a month, he here took charge of a set of abstract books, the while he vigorously applied himself to the study of law. In 1874 he had so effectively absorbed and assimilated the science of jurisprudence that he was admitted to the

Illinois bar, at a session of the supreme court of the state held at Ottawa. In 1875 Mr. McCandless went to the new town of Creston, Iowa, and became one of its pioneer lawyers. There he built up a substantial practice and there he continued his professional activities until 1882, when he again evidenced his predilection for being in at the start of things in a new town, as he cast in his fortunes with the village of Wymore, Gage county, Nebraska, a place that had been founded about one year previously. A man of vigorous thought and action, he proved a staunch force in furthering civic and material development and progress at Wymore, and he has continued as one of the valued and public spirited citizens of this thriving little city, even as he has been recognized as one of the able and representative members of the bar of the county. For fifteen years after their marriage Mr. McCandless and his wife kept their text books constantly at hand in their home and devoted themselves earnestly to study and reading, vying with each other in enthusiasm for advancement along educational lines.

In 1873 Mr. McCandless wedded Miss Gertrude Cabeen, who was born at Keithsburg, Illinois, a daughter of Richard C. Cabeen, an early settler and influential citizen of Mercer county, that state. Mr. and Mrs. McCandless have no children, but their devoted companionship during the long years has been of ideal order—intensified, as it were, by their having had no child to divide even measurably their interests.

In politics, as in other matters of vital importance, Mr. McCandless thinks and acts for himself, and he has not been constrained by strict partisan dictates. In his home village he is affiliated with Wymore Lodge, No. 104, Ancient Free & Accepted Masons; Hiram Chapter, No. 28, Royal Arch Masons; and Cypress Council, No. 22, Royal and Select Masters.

For many years prior to the death of his loved mother Mr. McCandless made regular visits to her and his two sisters, in Box Butte county, and incidentally he made interesting hunting expeditions in Cherry county. As he says, he "loves to sleep out on the sand hills, with only a blanket for protection, to breathe the air no one else ever breathed, and to determine the time of the night by observing the position of the Great Dipper." Along literary lines Mr. McCandless has gained no little repute by reason of the specially original and interesting articles which he has contributed to the periodical known as "Forest and Stream," his articles having been entitled "Days in Cherry County" and "Boyhood Days in Illinois." These articles have attracted wide attention on the part of devotees of outdoor sport, and Mr. McCandless has not only received letters of marked appreciation from the editor of "Forest and Stream," but they have led also to his being called upon to act as escort to wealthy and influential sportsmen in expeditions in western Nebraska. Among such millionaire sportsmen with whom Mr. McCandless has been thus pleasantly associated may be mentioned Mr. Wilbur, of Philadelphia, Pennsylvania, and Mr. Liles, of Aurora, Missouri. Mr. McCandless is an expert shot and has made splendid record at the traps, in which connection he has come in close competition with Thomas Marshall, of Keithsburg, Illinois, the two having become acquainted when they were boys.

Even this brief article indicates the broad mental grasp of Mr. McCandless and shows that while he has concentrated and won success in his profession he has had appreciation of other things that go to make up the full and complete life, and that he has made the passing years count not only in achievement but also in giving the benefices of happiness and contentment.

JOHN STROUGH.—In the career of the late John Strough, who was a resident of Gage county for more than a score of years, success and honor were inseparable, and he made his life count for good in its every relation. His sudden death, as the result of heart disease, occurred at his home in the city of Beatrice, November 23, 1917, he having been stricken while engaged in his customary evening work about the home, at 1423 High street.

Mr. Strough was born in Henry county, Indiana, on the 28th of January, 1844, and was a son of John and Sarah (Miller) Strough, who reared to years of maturity a family of eleven children. John Strough, Sr., was born in Pennsylvania, in the year 1808, and in the earlier part of his career he followed the trade of tailor. As a young man he went to the historic old state of Virginia, and later he numbered himself among the pioneers of Henry county, Indiana, where he became a prosperous farmer and where his death occurred on the 20th of May, 1863. His wife was born in Rockingham county, Virginia, in which state she was reared and educated, and there their marriage was solemnized, her father, George Miller, having been a native of Pennsylvania; she was born about the year 1835 and passed to eternal rest about 1887, her first three children having been born in Virginia, prior to the family removal to Indiana, where she continued to reside until her death.

The subject of this memoir was reared on the old homestead farm in Indiana and acquired his early education in the pioneer schools of Henry county, that state. At the time of the Civil war he gave efficient service as a soldier in an Indiana volunteer regiment, and his service covered practically the entire period of the conflict between the North and the South. In his native state his marriage was solemnized in 1867, and in 1870 he removed with his family to Holt county, Missouri, where he purchased a farm of one hundred and sixty acres, near the village of Craig. There he continued his successful activities as a farmer until 1890, when he and his wife established their home in Gage county, Nebraska, after he had disposed of his farm in Missouri. Upon coming to Gage county Mr. Strough purchased one hundred and sixty acres of land in Section 33, Holt township, and, with his progressive policies and mature judgment he there proved notably successful in his farm enterprise, the while he made excellent improvements on the homestead. He remained on the farm until 1908, when he retired from active labors and removed with his devoted wife to the city of Beatrice, where he passed the residue of his life, secure in the high regard of all who knew him.

Mr. Strough was well fortified in his convictions concerning governmental policies and was a stalwart advocate of the principles of the Republican party. He took deep interest in community affairs and while living on his Gage county farm he served as a member of the school board of his district. His religious faith was that of the Presbyterian church and his widow holds membership in the Congregational church of Beatrice.

In the year 1867 Mr. Strough wedded Miss Sarah Ann Bowers, who was born in Henry county, Indiana, April 14, 1849, a daughter of George and Lydia (Weane) Bowers, both natives of Rockingham county, Virginia, where the former was born in the year 1819 and the latter on the 9th of August, 1831. Upon his removal to Indiana, Mr. Bowers became a pioneer of Henry county, and there he became a substantial farmer and influential citizen of his community. He was one of the venerable pioneer citizens of the county at the time of his death, in 1891, at the age of seventy-two years, and his widow, who attained to the age of eighty-one years, was a resident of Henry county, Indiana, at the time of her death, in 1908. Since the death of her honored husband Mrs. Strough has continued to reside in the attractive home which he provided upon their removal to Beatrice. In conclusion is given brief record concerning their children, eleven having been born to them and two of the number having died in infancy: Laura is the wife of Giles Laughlin and they reside near Sheridan, Arkansas; Mary B. is the wife of Thomas Harding, a prosperous farmer of Holt township, Gage county, Nebraska; Joseph Leonard resides in Beatrice, this county, where he operates a garage; Dora E. is the wife of John Coonley, who is engaged in the grocery business in West Beatrice; Lloyd L., who owns and resides upon his father's old home farm in Holt township, is individually mentioned on other pages of this volume; Rufus F. is engaged in the oil business in the city of Beatrice; Jesse F. is a resident of Ottumwa, Iowa; and Nona E. is the wife of William Sherwood, a prosperous farmer in Logan township.

ANDREW J. REEDY.—In nearly every village in the United States are to be found men who fought that our nation might remain an indissoluble union, and one of such men is Mr. Reedy, of Blue Springs, this county.

Andrew Jackson Reedy was born in Morgan county, Indiana, January 1, 1839 and is a son of William and Nancy (Cannedy) Reedy, the former born in Ireland and the latter in Scotland; they migrated to West Virginia with their respective parents and in that state their marriage occurred. With hearts full of hope and courage they traversed the wilds of Ohio and crossed over into Indiana, where they cleared a space for their rude log cabin and where William Reedy became a pioneer farmer. Sons and daughters grew up around them, and they became the parents of a fine family of sixteen children. Three of this large family are now living; George Reedy, a Civil war veteran, is living retired at Nebraska City, Nebraska; Polly, widow of John Busha, resides at Council Bluffs, Iowa; and Andrew J. Reedy is the subject of this sketch. In Morgan county, Indiana, the mother of these children passed to the life eternal. Her husband later contracted a second marriage and by this union six children were born. The latter years of the life of William Reedy were spent in Oregon, where his death occurred. He was a Douglas Democrat in politics and was a captain in the Mexican war.

The educational advantages that the times afforded in the boyhood of Andrew J. Reedy were very meager, but such as they were he profited by these. When a youth of seventeen years he went to Missouri to farm and was called from the plowing of his land to take up arms for his country. He was in the service for a few months with the contingent from Harrison county, Missouri, but soon enlisted with Missouri cavalry, from Gentry county, in which command he served two years, two months, and seven days. He participated in the vigorous action incidental to the historic Price raids, fighting every day against General Price from the Ozarks to Fort Scott. In 1863 he was in the raid for Quantrell, and one time was taken prisoner by the rebels, but he made his escape from them.

After the war Mr. Reedy went back to the peaceful occupation of tilling the soil in Missouri. It was here that he married Sarah Ann Lowe, who has been his faithful companion all of these years. She has borne him twelve children, ten of whom are living, as follows: Andrew lives at Blue Springs; Florence first married O. T. Randall and is now the wife of Samuel Price, a farmer near Kansas City, Kansas; William resides at Blue Springs, Daniel in Iowa, and Alonzo at Lincoln, Nebraska; Luther is in the military service of the United States as a member of a machine gun company; Lucy, widow of Fred Stratford, is now employed in Palmer's store at Beatrice; Salome, widow of George Densmore, is living in Lincoln; Mary is the wife of John Herman, of Wymore; and Harry is in the war service of the United States.

Mr. Reedy farmed in Missouri until 1878, when he went to Kansas, and in 1886 he came to Gage county, where he continued farming until his retirement to Blue Springs twenty years ago. In politics Mr. Reedy has voted with the Republican party. He is a member of the Rawlins Post, Grand Army of the Republic, at Beatrice, and is one of the valued members of the community in which he has long resided, he having given many useful years to agricultural industry.

FREDERICK W. MESSMORE.—In the year that marked the semi-centennial of the admission of Nebraska as one of the sovereign states of the Union, Gage county numbered as one of its most efficient and valued officials Frederick W. Messmore, who is still serving as county attorney and who has the further distinction of being one of the youngest men to be the incumbent of such office in the entire state. He is making a splendid record as a public prosecutor and through his official activities is enhancing his reputation and is solidifying his status as one of the representative members of the bar of Gage county.

Mr. Messmore was born in Boone county, Iowa, on the 11th of July, 1889, and is a son of H. A. and Clara J. (Davidson) Messmore, both of whom likewise are natives of the Hawkeye state, where the respective families were founded in the early pioneer days. H. A. Messmore was reared and educated in Iowa and there became actively identified with railway operations, as a conductor on the line of the Chicago & Northwestern Railroad. About the year 1907 he removed with his family to Nebraska and established his residence at Randolph, Cedar county, where he successfully conducted a hotel, later continuing in the same line of enterprise in turn at Laurel, that county; Geneva, Fillmore county; and Nelson, Nuckolls county. In 1915 he and his wife established their home at Beatrice, and here it is his intention again to engage in the hotel business within the near future. Mr. Messmore is unwavering in his allegiance to the Democratic party, he and his wife hold membership in the Presbyterian church, and in the time-honored Masonic fraternity he has received the thirty-second degree of the Ancient Accepted Scottish Rite, besides being affiliated also with the Mystic Shrine. Of the four children of Mr. and Mrs. Messmore, the subject of this review is the younger of the two now living, and Sylvia is the wife of T. O. Hester, a banker at Wiota, Cass county, Iowa.

FREDERICK W. MESSMORE

The preliminary educational discipline of Frederick W. Messmore was acquired principally in the public schools of the city of Council Bluffs Iowa, where he completed the curriculum of the high school and also took a course in the Northwestern Business and Normal College. After his graduation in the same he followed the trend of his ambition and well formulated plans by enrolling himself as a student in the Creighton Law School, in the city of Omaha. In this well ordered institution he was graduated as a member of the class of 1912, and his admission to the Nebraska bar was virtually coincident with his reception of the degree of Bachelor of Laws. In 1913 Mr. Messmore entered, with characteristic vigor and earnestness, upon his professional novitiate, and he was favored in being at this time able to associate himself with General L. W. Colby, of Beatrice, one of the leading members of the Gage county bar. He maintained this alliance until his election to the office of county attorney, in 1914, and the estimate placed upon his administration of the affairs of this important office was unequivocally shown in his reelection in 1916.

Mr. Messmore is a most vital and effective advocate of the principles and policies for which the Democratic party stands sponsor and is one of the influential young men in its councils in his home county. Mr. Messmore is affiliated with the Masonic fraternity, the Benevolent Protective Order of Elks, the Delta Theta Phi college fraternity, and the Modern Woodmen of America, in which last mentioned organization he is past worthy advisor. He and his wife hold membership in the Methodist Episcopal church.

In April, 1913, was solemnized the marriage of Mr. Messmore to Miss Jennie Frances Saxe, who was born at Belden, Cedar county, Nebraska, a daughter of Allison and Frances (Boughn) Saxe, and she was reared in the home of her mother's uncle, Zack Boughn, who was one of the pioneer settlers of this state. Mr. and Mrs. Messmore have no children.

FRANK OVERBECK has been a resident of Gage county for nearly two score years and through his able and vigorous activities as a farmer he has achieved substantial prosperity. He is the owner of a well improved landed estate of three hundred and twenty acres, in Section 16, Holt township, and here he is now living virtually retired, his two sons having the active management of the farm property.

Mr. Overbeck was born in Prussia, Germany, July 26, 1841, a son of Frederick and Lizzie (Teisenbrink) Overbeck, who passed their entire lives in their native land. Frank Overbeck was reared and educated in Germany and there gained his initial experience in connection with farm industry. In May, 1882, he came to the United States and landed in the port of New York city. Shortly afterward he came to Nebraska and established his residence in Gage county, where he found employment as a farm workman. He continued to be thus engaged about five years and then engaged in farming in an independent way. He was encouraged to take this course by his friend Frederick Pohlman, who came to the farm on which Mr. Overbeck was at the time employed and made inquiry as to the amount of money the latter had available. Mr. Overbeck stated in reply that he had saved three hundred and twenty-five dollars, and Mr. Pohlman then said that he would lend him an additional one hundred dollars and that with the combined sum he could find him a farm that he could rent. Preparations were made by the two friends going to Dewitt, where Mr. Overbeck purchased a team of horses and the required agricultural implements, he having given his note for the purchase price of the team. He then rented the farm of John H. Steinmeyer, who established himself in the grain and elevator business at Dewitt, and on this farm Mr. Overbeck continued operations two years. He then purchased a Scully lease of land in Hanover township, and there he continued his successful activities as an agriculturist and stock-grower until he purchased his present homestead farm of one hundred and sixty acres, upon which but little improvement had been made at the time. He has developed his farm until it is now one of the model places of Holt township, the additional tract of one hundred and sixty acres having been purchased somewhat later and the farm being all in one body. Mr. Overbeck has erected good farm buildings and each of his sons has an attractive house on the half-section of land which has been under their effective management since their father retired from the labors that were so long his portion. Mr. Overbeck is a Republican in politics and is a communicant of the Lutheran church, as are also the members of his family.

As a young man Mr. Overbeck wedded Miss Caroline Stolde, who was born and reared in Germany and who there passed her entire life, her death having occurred in 1882, and she having been survived by four children. In the same year Mr. Overbeck came to America with three of his children, Henry, the eldest of the four having come to this country a short time previously, and being now a resident of Jefferson county, Nebraska; Lizzie is the wife of Charles Gerhardt, of Beatrice; Frederick is a prosperous farmer in Hanover township; and Charles is engaged in the real-estate business in the city of Beatrice.

Prior to coming to the United States Mr. Overbeck contracted a second marriage, with Miss Lizzie Hansjurgen, who was born in the year 1853, and whose death occurred April 13, 1913. Of the eleven children of this union six are living: William is a successful farmer in Hanover township; Frank is associated in the operation of the home farm of his father; Ernest is engaged in farm enterprise in Holt township; John is the other son who farms a portion of his father's place; Herman is a farmer in Nemaha township; and Edwin is engaged in farming in Saline county.

CHARLES M. MURDOCK, of Wymore, is not only one of the honored pioneer citizens of Gage county, but also a representative of a family whose name is one of singular and significant prominence in connection with the early annals of Nebraska, the subject of this review having gained wide and varied experience in connection with life on the frontier and his noble father having been one of the early missionaries to the Indians in Nebraska. A wealth of interesting data may be gleaned concerning this family, and the record cannot fail of enduring historical interest.

Charles M. Murdock was born in Greene county, Pennsylvania, August 29, 1843, and is a son of Rev. Daniel A. and Prudence L. (Smith) Murdock, both likewise natives of the old Keystone state. Rev. Daniel A. Murdock received a liberal education and as a young man he entered the ministry of the Presbyterian church. His marriage to Miss Prudence L. Smith was solemnized April 6, 1841, and concerning their nine children the following brief record may be entered: Lysander B. was born March 24, 1842, and died January 10, 1858; Charles M., of this review, was the next in order of birth; Mary F. was born August 25, 1845, and her death occurred December 5, 1863; Alonzo D. was born November 11, 1847; Bashford E. W. was born May 11, 1850, and died July 24, 1888; Alfaretta L. was born September 22, 1852; Dualla R. was born October 2, 1854, and her death occurred June 25, 1908; Effie T. was born June 30, 1858, and her death occurred March 19, 1864; and Daniel A., Jr., was born January 18, 1861.

The following specially interesting record is taken in large part from an admirable account prepared by Charles M. Murdock, to whom this sketch is dedicated. In the spring of 1853 Rev. Daniel A. Murdock removed with his family to the pioneer wilds of Iowa and established a home near Bloomfield, Davis county, but removal was soon afterward made to the vicinity of Holleyville, Page county. In September, 1856, Mr. Murdock and his wife, in company with their neighbors, Mr. and Mrs. Hayes, drove overland in covered wagons from Page county, Iowa, into the Territory of Nebraska, and they decided to locate in Richardson county, near the present village of Stell. This sturdy pioneer clergyman purchased in that locality a tract of land, and within a short time thereafter he returned to his home in Iowa. In the same year he was requested by the Presbyterian Missionary Society, of New York city, to accept the position of missionary to the Otoe and Missouri tribes of Indians in Nebraska and Kansas, and he accepted this responsible post. On the 7th of April, 1857, in company with his wife and their seven children, Rev. Daniel A. Murdock left Page county, Iowa, with teams and covered wagons and set forth for his new field of service. When they arrived at Sidney, Fremont county, Iowa, they found that the Missouri river was so high as to make it impossible to cross the same. The family therefore remained at Sidney until the 6th of May, when they crossed the river on a ferry boat, at Weeping Water, just above Nebraska City. Three days later the pioneer missionary arrived with his family at the Indian trading post conducted by Gideon Bennett, on Plum creek, and one mile west of the site of the present village of Liberty, Gage county. The next day the family continued its journey a distance of about seven miles and arrived at the Otoe and Missouri Indian mission building, in Marshall county, Kansas. Here the Presbyterian Missionary Society had purchased half a section of land, the north half of Section One (1) in Township One (1) south, Range Eight (8) east, and erected thereon a concrete building forty by ninety feet in dimensions and three stories in height, this building having been about forty rods south of the Kansas and Nebraska territorial line and one and one-half miles distant from the east line of the Otoe and Missouri Indian reservation. Soon after the arrival of the Murdock family at this frontier mission the seven chiefs of the Otoe and Missouri tribes came to visit the new incumbent at the mission. Here Arkeketa and the other six chiefs held conference and decided to send their children to the mission school. Mr. Murdock treated them with great consideration and explained to them the purpose and object of his coming as a missionary. From New York were sent two women to become teachers of the young Indians, and about seventy-five boys and two girls came to receive instruction. With its various attaches the mission represented a busy little community, and the Murdock family passed the first summer very pleasantly. When the Indians were about to set forth on their autumn hunting trip for buffalo, they asked Mr. Murdock to permit the Indian boys in the school to accompany them on the expedition. The missionary tried to persuade them to let the children remain in school. The elder Indians seemingly gave their consent to this plan, but a little after dark the same evening "all of the Indian boys at the mission vanished like a flock of quail." While the Otoes were on this hunting expedition a band of Sioux Indians, who were not on good terms with the Otoes, appeared at the mission, evidently in search of the Indian boys, whom they doubtless wished to scalp or kidnap. When they found the boys absent they did not molest the mission, the two Indian girls having in the meanwhile been secreted. When, upon their return, the Otoes learned of the visit of the Sioux their superstitious minds led them to believe that a miracle had been wrought, in that the boys had been absent, and they did not permit the youngsters to return to the mission in sufficient number to justify the continuing of the school. Only two of the Indian boys came back to the mission. The result was that the mission was given up in the autumn of 1857, the land and buildings being later sold by the missionary society.

In 1861, however, Rev. Daniel A. Murdock and his family again occupied the mission building. In the interim he had removed to Doniphan county, Kansas, whence he went to Lawrence county, Missouri, to assume charge of a college at Mount Vernon. When the Civil war broke out he found his sympathy with the Union cause to be a source of trouble in his community, and he returned to Nebraska and settled on a tract of land which he had previously entered as a preemption claim, in Pawnee county. The next spring he went with his family to Washington county, Kansas, and within a short time thereafter he was made chaplain of the Thirteenth Kansas Infantry. In this capacity he served until his death, which occurred at Springfield, Missouri, on the 5th of April, 1863. A godly and righteous life marked by self-abnegating service was that of this pioneer clergyman and missionary, and his final days were given to his country's service in the Civil war. Mrs. Murdock subsequently contracted a second marriage and removed to Wray, Colorado, where her death occurred January 18, 1899, her remains being laid to rest in the cemetery at Gage county, Nebraska.

Charles M. Murdock was a lad of about ten years at the time of the family removal to Iowa, and was reared under the conditions and influences of frontier life, his educational training having been received largely under the direction of his father and mother, both of whom were persons of superior intellectuality. He accompanied his parents on their various removals, as noted in the preceding context, and was able to attend the college of which his father was the executive head in Missouri. On the 11th of July, 1862, about one month prior to his twentieth birthday anniversary, Mr. Murdock tendered his aid in defense of the Union. At Marysville, Marshall county, Kansas, he enlisted as a member of Company K, Ninth Kansas Cavalry. The command went to Fort Leavenworth, Kansas, in September, 1862, and there received a complete outfit. It thence marched to join the army in the field in southwestern Missouri, where it thus joined the active forces on the 2d of October following. Under the command of General Blunt the Ninth Kansas Cavalry participated in the following named battles and other engagements: Newtonia, Missouri, October 3d; Neosha, October 4th; Cane Hill, Arkansas, November 28th; Prairie Grove, December 7th; Van Buren, December 28th. The command then marched to Fort Scott, Kansas, and for the remainder of the winter it was employed in escorting trains loaded with supplies from that place to the Army of the Frontier, in Arkansas. In the performance of this duty, Mr. Murdock's company had frequent engagements with guerrilla forces, which attempted to capture the trains under its escort. In March, 1863, the regiment was stationed at points on the Kansas Missouri state line, from the Missouri river to the Osage. Company K was stationed at Aubrey, in Johnson county, Kansas, and during the following year was engaged in scouting and fighting guerrillas and bushwhackers through the border tier of counties in Missouri. Mr. Murdock continued in service until victory had crowned the Union arms and peace had been re-established. He proved a loyal and gallant soldier, always at the post of duty, and was never wounded or captured. His record was one that shall ever reflect honor upon his name, and he was mustered out July 17, 1865, duly receiving his honorable discharge.

After the close of the war Mr. Murdock settled in Washington county, Kansas, and for several years thereafter he was engaged in freighting across the plains. He was well acquainted with William Hecock, commonly known as "Wild Bill," and has been in the room in which this frontier character shot McCandless and four others of his gang, at Elkhorn Station, in Jefferson county, Nebraska. Those were strenuous times and Mr. Murdock, known for his courage and self-control, was elected and efficiently served as sheriff of Washington county, Kansas. He relates many thrilling tales concerning the problems and danger which he faced in the performance of his official duties. The courthouse of Washington county was destroyed by fire while he was serving as sheriff, and he was employed by the county to draft a new set of abstract books, as the original county records had been destroyed in the fire.

On the 18th of August, 1874, Mr. Murdock came to Gage county, Nebraska, and established his residence at Blue Springs, where he engaged in newspaper enterprise. He founded the Blue Springs *Reporter*, of which he became editor and publisher, and later he was editor and publisher of the Wymore *Reporter*. He was appointed right-of-way representative for the Burlington Railroad in this section of the state and was instrumental in locating and naming the present thriving city of Wymore, where he has maintained his residence since 1881. He also gave efficient service in obtaining the right of way through Gage county for the Chicago, Rock Island & Pacific and the Union Pacific Railroads. A man of broad views, mature judgment, and utmost civic loyalty, Mr. Murdock has done much to further material and social advancement in

Gage county, and he so thoroughly grounded himself in the science of jurisprudence as to gain admission to the Nebraska bar. In later years he has given his attention principally to the practice of law and to the handling of real estate.

Mr. Murdock has given unswerving allegiance to the Republican party from the time of attaining his legal majority, and his loyalty to the party has been intensified by the thought that it represented the cause for which he fought at the time of the Civil war. He perpetuated the more gracious memories and associations of his military career by affiliation with Coleman Post, No. 115, Grand Army of the Republic, at Wymore. He is a charter member of this post, was elected its first commander, and is serving as its commander in 1918.

On the 25th of March, 1868, was solemnized the marriage of Mr. Murdock to Miss Jane E. Pasko, who was born in Wisconsin, and they celebrated their golden wedding anniversary in the spring of 1918, their long companionship having been one of ideal order. Of their six children only two are living: Arthur A. is engaged in the newspaper business at Dewitt, Saline county; and Glenn E. is in the employ of the Chicago, Milwaukee & St. Paul Railroad, at Great Falls, Montana.

Mr. Murdock is a recognized authority on historical data in Kansas and Nebraska, and has dates and names at his tongue's end—an evidence of his remarkably vigorous and retentive memory. He figures as a pioneer of both Nebraska and Kansas, and has lived up to the full tension of life on the frontier, even as he has done his part in the progressive movements that have compassed the development of these two opulent commonwealths.

ALBERT MILLER is one of the sterling pioneer citizens whose alert mentality, fine observative powers, and distinct intellectuality make his reminiscences of the early days specially graphic and interesting, and it has been through his own industry and good management that he has gained place as one of the prosperous exponents of farm industry in the county that has represented his home for nearly half a century, and to the development and progress of which he has contributed his quota. He is the owner of a well improved landed estate of two hundred and eighty acres, in Section 2, Logan township, and in the management of the place he is assisted most effectively by his only son, Eilert, who is a bachelor, so that the two reign supreme in the pleasant home, the devoted wife and mother having passed to eternal rest December 4, 1891.

MR. AND MRS. ALBERT MILLER

Mr. Miller was born in Germany, in February, 1847 and is a son of Eilert Miller. Mr. Miller was little more than an infant at the time of his mother's death and was six years old when he came with his father to the United States, settlement being made in St. Clair county, Illinois, where the father died a few months later. The orphan boy was taken into the home of a family by which he was reared to adult age on a farm in that county, and the somewhat meager education which he gained in his youth has since been supplemented by extensive and careful reading of the best in general and current literature, as well as by the diversified experiences of a singularly active and earnest life. In St. Clair county, Illinois, Mr. Miller continued his alliance with agricultural industry until he came to Gage county, Nebraska, in 1870, his wife, whose maiden name was Rachel Jurgens, having likewise been a native of Germany and having accompanied him to Gage county, where she passed the remainder of her life, the son Eilert being the only surviving child.

Upon coming to this county Mr. Miller purchased one hundred and twenty acres of land in Section 2, Logan township, and with the passing years he has transformed this virgin prairie land into one of the fine farms of the township; where he has acquired a valuable estate of two hundred and eighty acres. His original domicile on the farm was a primitive dug-out of the pioneer type, and this was replaced by a log house which he occupied until he erected his present frame house, which he has kept in excellent repair, besides supplying other farm buildings of good type. Mr. Miller had his full share of trials and vicissitudes in the pioneer days, as did other early settlers of the county, and he went twelve miles across the prairie to Beatrice for his mail, the present attractive county seat having been a mere hamlet at that time and its postmaster having been Oliver Townsend, who, as Mr. Miller has facetiously stated, "kept postoffice in his overcoat pocket." From his youth Mr. Miller has been an earnest communicant of the Lutheran church, and the first meeting of the Lutheran society organized in Logan township was held in his home, the little dug-out, as was also the first school meeting for the district. Mr. Miller has liberally done his part in support of progressive measures and movements, has continued active in the affairs of the Lutheran church, and is one of the honored and influential pioneer citizens of Logan township, where his circle of friends is coincident with that of his acquaintances. His political allegiance is given to the Republican party and in the early days he had to go to Beatrice, the only polling place, to cast his vote. He served one year as township assessor and held for a quarter of a century the office of treasurer of Logan township.

FRANK BERAN, a representative farmer of Glenwood township, is farming four hundred and eighty acres of land in Section 8. Mr. Beran is a son of Anton and Pauline (Shalla) Beran, who had three children, but he is the only one who survives; the mother is deceased. Anton Beran was married the second time, to Josephine Beran, and the family history is recorded in another portion of this volume.

Frank Beran was born November 16, 1876, in Washington county, Iowa, where his parents had followed their farming operations previous to their coming to Gage county in 1878. At that time Mr. Beran was just a babe in arms and he has passed practically all of his life thus far upon Gage county soil, growing up with her sons and receiving the education of her institutions. From 1900 to 1902 he rented land from his father and in the latter year he purchased his present farm, where he is enjoying the fruits of the labors of years gone by. He is a breeder of Duroc-Jersey hogs and is attending efficiently to his large and well improved farm.

February 27, 1900, Mr. Beran married Millie Vavruska and they are the parents of five children who are growing up in their home and being educated in the district school—in short, receiving the preliminary discipline that shall prepare them for the good citizenship necessary to make happy homes and national wellbeing. They are as follows: Frank, Alfred, Adolph, Rose, and Benjamin. Mrs. Beran was born March 7, 1878, in Marshall county, Kansas, and is a daughter of John Vavruska, who, after years of active farming life, is now retired and living in Wilber, Nebraska.

In politics Mr. Beran is loyal to the Democratic principles and in 1913 he was elected township clerk, in which position he is still serving his community.

CARL F. WOLLENBURG.—As an exponent of most modern and scientific policies as applied to farm industry Mr. Wollenburg stands forth prominently as one of the distinctly representative and influential agriculturists and stock-growers of his native county. He is a member of one of the sterling and honored families of the county and by his own energy and well directed efforts he has made his way to the goal of success and prosperity, as evidenced in the fact that he is the owner of a valuable landed estate of two hundred and eighty-eight acres, eligibly situated in Sections 3, 4, and 10, Blakely township, his homestead place being in Section 4 and on rural mail route No. 3 from the village of Dewitt, Saline county. Mr. Wollenburg is associated with his brother Henry in operating each season a thoroughly modern threshing outfit, and in his plowing and various other work for which the modern device is available he utilizes a high-grade tractor. These statements indicate unmistakably his progressiveness, which is further shown in his use of the best of farm implements and machinery and the general air of thrift and good management that pervades his fine farm property.

Mr. Wollenburg was born on his father's old homestead farm in Grant township, this county, and the date of his nativity was March 7, 1882. He is a son of the late William Wollenburg, to whom a memoir is dedicated on other pages of this volume, so that there is not demand for a further review of the family history in the present connection. In the Lutheran parochial schools and the district schools Mr. Wollenburg gained the discipline that matured his mental powers as a boy and youth, and he has shown his good judgment by his continued association with farm enterprise, through the medium of which he has achieved splendid success. In 1913 he purchased his first land—a tract of one hundred and twenty acres, in Sections 3 and 10, Blakely township—and with increasing prosperity he continued to make judicious investments until he has accumulated one of the finely improved and well ordered farm estates of his native county. In making this excellent account for himself in his independent activities Mr. Wollenburg has not become self-centered but has at all times shown loyal interest in community affairs, his political support being given to the Republican party and both he and his wife being communicants of the Lutheran church.

On the 25th of April, 1905, was solemnized the marriage of Mr. Wollenburg to Miss Matilda Schafer, who was born near Wilber, Saline county, and is a daughter of Henry Schafer, who was born in Germany and who was twelve years old when the family came to the United States and settled in Illinois. Mr. Schafer came to Gage county about 1887, he being still a resident of this county, where his wife died a few years ago. Mr. and Mrs. Wollenburg have six children—Matilda, Elsie, Wilhelmina, Carl, Theodore, and Helen, the twin sister of Helen having died in infancy.

REV. J. B. REENTS has been a faithful and zealous worker in the vineyard of the Divine Master and is one of the able and honored members of the clergy of the German Lutheran church in Nebraska. He has served since 1902 as pastor of what is familiarly known as the Hanover German Lutheran church, the present edifice of which is in Logan township, near the Hanover township line. This splendid organization claims precedence as one of the strongest and wealthiest rural churches in the entire state and offers a splendid field for the earnest and consecrated labors of its honored pastor.

REV. J. B. REENTS

Mr. Reents was born in the province of Hanover, Germany, January 15, 1874, a son of John and Jennie (Straate) Reents, both likewise natives of that historic province, where the father was born February 11, 1834, and the mother November 21, 1833, their marriage having been solemnized in 1858. In his native land John Reents continued to be actively identified with farm enterprise until the death of his loved wife, in 1911, and in the following year he came to America, the residue of his life having been passed in the home of his son J. B., the subject of this review. Both he and his wife were most devout communicants of the German Lutheran church and exemplified their faith in their noble and gracious lives. Of their five children the eldest is Joost, who is now a prosperous farmer near Clara City, Chippewa county, Minnesota; Bernard likewise is a prosperous farmer in that county; Ailt is engaged in farming near Allison, Butler county, Iowa; Rev. J. B., of this sketch, was the next in order of birth; and Theda is the wife of William Kramer, a farmer near Bristow, Butler county, Iowa. Three of the sons served the required term in the German army.

ZION'S LUTHERAN CHURCH

Rev. J. B. Reents acquired his early education in his native land, where he completed a course in a teachers' preparatory school. He was eighteen years of age when he came to the United States, in 1892, and has been a resident of Nebraska since 1900. After coming to this country he maintained his residence for three years at Nora Springs, Iowa, where he was a student in a seminary, and for one year thereafter he continued his studies at Cedar Falls, that state. Thereafter he was for five terms a successful teacher in the public schools of Iowa, after which he entered Wartburg Seminary, in the city of Dubuque, Iowa, in which institution he completed a thorough course in philosophy and theology and was graduated as a member of the class of 1900. In the same year he was ordained a minister of the German Lutheran church, and was assigned to the pastoral charge of the Lutheran church located four and one-half miles north of the village of Pickrell, Gage county, Nebraska. There he continued his service until February, 1902, when he assumed his present important pastorate, in charge of Zion's German Lutheran church in Logan township, near the Hanover township line. The original church building was located in Hanover township, within a comparatively short distance from the site of the present edifice, and the name of "Hanover Church" is still familiarly applied. The present fine church edifice, which was dedicated in 1917, is one of the best church buildings in the entire state and has been definitely proclaimed as "probably the most beautiful rural church in the west." The edifice was completed at an approximate cost of forty-five thousand dollars and it is pleasing to record that all money necessary for the construction and equipment of the building was raised before the work of construction was initiated— and that without calling for any assistance of financial order save from members of the congregation itself. The church is beautiful in its interior design and appointments, is equipped with a pipe organ of the best modern type, and it was dedicated without one cent of indebtedness, the normal seating capacity of the edifice being eight hundred. In this connection the following brief record is worthy of perpetuation: "The Hanover German Lutheran church was organized, with ten members, March 14, 1874. In 1875 a parsonage was erected, but this was destroyed by a tornado, on June 26th of the same year. Church services were held in the school house of the district No. 38 until 1881, when was erected a church building that was thirty by forty-six feet in dimensions. This soon proved too small, and an addition was made in 1898. A belfry also was built at this time and a bell of two thousand pounds was installed, this being now in the new church edifice, on the opposite of the road from the old church building. The pastors of the church from its organization to the present have been as here noted: Rev. Mr. Martin, Rev. William Ehmen, Rev. Theodore Seylor, Rev. O. Lompe, Rev. Wolfgang Hertel, and Rev. J. B. Reents, the pastorate of the present incumbent having covered a period of nearly sixteen years. Constructed of cream-colored brick and notable for the beauty and consistency of its architectural design, the new church edifice presents a very handsome appearance, two tall spires adorning the façade. Standing on a hill, the church is visible for a considerable distance in each direction and the chimes that have been installed in the taller spire can be heard for miles."

This vigorous and noble parish organization claims a membership of one hundred and fifty families—the largest congregation in Gage county and the largest of the Lutheran faith in the entire state. The present pastor, a man of fine intellectuality, is an earnest pulpit orator, unselfish and indefatigable in all pastoral duties, and an able and progressive executive. He takes deep interest in all things touching the communal welfare and his influence is in all ways beneficent, the while he has the unqualified esteem of all who know him. His political allegiance is given to the Democratic party.

On Christmas day of the year 1900 was solemnized the marriage of Mr. Reents to Miss Louisa Hertel, daughter of Rev. Wolfgang Hertel, who was the immediate predecessor of Mr. Reents as pastor of the Hanover Lutheran church. Mr. and Mrs. Reents have six children: John is attending college at Sterling, this state; and the other children remain at the parental home—Walter, Irene, Arthur, William, and Bernhard.

ALBERTUS H. KIDD.—This representative member of the Gage county bar has shown in his professional activities and service the power of concentrating the full forces of the individual and raising them to the plane of large achievement. He has demonstrated his ability not only as a lawyer but also as a citizen well qualified for leadership in movements and enterprises contributing to the general wellbeing of the community, and thus, while never wavering in his fealty to his profession, he has directed his energies also in successful exploitation of the basic industrial resources of Gage county and in fostering the progressive policies that make for civic and material advancement and prosperity in the communal life. Mr. Kidd has been engaged in the active practice of law at Beatrice, judicial center of Gage county, since 1891, and since 1909 he has maintained a professional alliance with Samuel Rinaker, with offices in the First National Bank building. The firm of Rinaker & Kidd is uniformly conceded to be one of the strongest in the southern part of the state, and this fact in itself vouches for the character and technical ability of the principals in the firm. As a lawyer Mr. Kidd has achieved high repute and has definite professional prestige throughout southeastern Nebraska—a prestige based on results achieved.

Albertus H. Kidd is a scion of sterling American colonial stock in both the agnatic and distaff lines, and takes definite pride in reverting to the fact that both paternal and maternal ancestors were numbered among the patriot soldiers of the Continental Line in the war of the Revolution. Family tradition is to the effect that the historic character, Captain Kidd, was of the same family line, and the subject of this review has never found it consonant to criticise the somewhat misdirected energies of the redoubtable captain, who under more favorable circumstances probably would have marked his career with worthy achievement as remarkable as were his storied exploits of seeming depredation.

Mr. Kidd was born at Ada, Allen county, Ohio, on the 19th of March, 1863, and is a representative of one of the honored pioneer families of the old Buckeye state, within whose borders were born his parents, Rev. Jeremiah W. and Elvira (Lillibridge) Kidd, both of whom passed the closing period of their lives in the state of Illinois. Rev. Jeremiah W. Kidd, a man of broad intellectual ken and fervent piety, prepared himself for the ministry of the Methodist Protestant church, and as a clergyman of this denomination he was called to service in Illinois in the year 1874. In that state he held thereafter pastoral charges in many different counties, and he was a revered patriarch of Bureau county, Illinois, at the time of his death, which occurred when he was nearly ninety years of age, his devoted wife having preceded him to eternal rest by many years. He labored with all of consecrated zeal in his chosen calling for a long term of years, and his ministerial services were given first in Ohio, later in Indiana, and finally in Illinois. Both the Kidd and Lillibridge family lines trace back to staunch English origin and both families sent representatives to America in the early colonial period of our national history, as previously intimated in this context. Mr. Kidd of this review has in his possession a comprehensive genealogical record of the Lillibridge family, and data therein presented show that members of the family in various generations have been prominent and influential in American affairs and in varied walks of life.

Albertus H. Kidd was about six years of age at the time of the family removal from Ohio to Indiana, and was a lad of about eleven years when removal was made to Illinois, in which latter state he acquired the major part of his early educational discipline, which included the curriculum of the high school at Wyoming, Stark county. Thereafter he pursued higher academic studies in a college at La Harpe, that state, and he put his scholastic acquirements to practical test and utilization by entering the pedagogic profession, as a teacher in the public schools of Illinois. In the meanwhile he had formulated definite plans for his future career, and in consonance therewith he began reading law under the effective preceptorship of the firm of Matthews & Peacock, of Monmouth, Illinois. With characteristic earnestness and zeal he applied himself to the study of the involved science of jurisprudence, and he proved himself well fortified in the same when he applied for and received admission to the bar of Illinois, in 1887. In the same year Mr. Kidd came to Nebraska and engaged in the practice of his profession at Alma, Harlan county. There be continued to reside until 1891, when, for the purpose of obtaining a broader field of professional endeavor, he came to Gage county and established his residence at Beatrice, where he has continued in the practice of his profession during the intervening period of more than a quarter of a century and where he has won secure vantage-ground as one of the leading members of the bar of southeastern Nebraska.

In Gage county Mr. Kidd has entered most loyally and fully into the communal life and has exemplified specially vital and well ordered progressiveness and public spirit. He served six years as a member of the board of education of Beatrice and for fifteen years as a member of the board of directors of the Beatrice public library, of which he is still a member. While he gives unfaltering allegiance to the Republican party and has accorded yeoman service in behalf of its cause, Mr. Kidd has considered his profession worthy of his undivided fealty and thus has manifested no desire for political office. His civic loyalty was shown, however, in two terms of effective service as city attorney of Beatrice. He was for four years the president of the Gage County Crop Improvement Association and his interest in agricultural industry has been shown in his ownership and improvement of several farms in Nebraska, in which connection it may be noted that he is at the present time the owner of a fine farm in Midland township. He gives a general supervision to the operations of this farm and is active in the improving of the grades of live stock in this section of the state, as well as in the advancing of scientific methods in agricultural enterprise. Mr. Kidd is president of the State Savings & Loan Association, of Beatrice, one of the substantial and important financial institutions of the county, and he is also a stockholder in the First National Bank of Beatrice. He is an influential and appreciative member of the Beatrice Commercial Club and has served for years as a member of its board of directors. In connection with the various movements incidental to the nation's participation in the great European war, Mr. Kidd is now Federal Food Administrator for Gage county.

In the year 1888, at La Harpe, Hancock county, Illinois, was solemnized the marriage of Mr. Kidd to Miss Elizabeth Gilliland who was born in Schuyler county, that state, and they have two daughters—Dora A. and Norma J., both of whom were graduated in the Beatrice high school and also in the University of Nebraska. The elder daughter remains at the parental home and Miss Norma J. is assistant secretary of the Young Women's Christian Association in the city of Lincoln, this state.

JAMES K. P. PETHOUD was a lad of fourteen years when he came with his parents to Nebraska Territory and his father became one of the earliest settlers of Gage county, where the family home was established nearly a decade prior to the admission of Nebraska to statehood. Here the subject of this memoir was reared to manhood under the conditions and influences which marked the initiation of civic and industrial development in this section of the state, and thus he was the more strongly fortified in mature years to carry forward his quota of the important work which has made Gage county one of the opulent and attractive divisions of a great and prosperous commonwealth. He was one of the world's constructive workers and was one of the honored pioneer citizens of the county at the time of his death, which occurred on the 7th of June, 1896. Adequate record concerning the family history is given on other pages of this work, in the specific tribute dedicated to John Pethoud, father of him whose name introduces this article.

MR. AND MRS. JAMES K. P. PETHOUD

James Knox Polk Pethoud was born in Lawrence county, Ohio, November 24, 1844, and was named in honor of the Hon. James Knox

Polk, who had in that year been elected president of the United States. He received his early education in the schools of the old Buckeye state and in 1858 accompanied his parents to the frontier wilds of what is now Gage county, where he assisted in reclaiming a pioneer farm and where, upon attaining to his legal majority, he entered claim to a homestead of one hundred and sixty acres of land in what is now Section 10 Midland township. For about three years after his marriage he and his wife remained on the old homestead farm of his father, in order that they might give proper filial care to his venerable parents and after he had instituted the improvement of his own farm his parents there remained with him until they were called from the stage of life's mortal endeavors. Mr. Pethoud was a man of superabundant energy and ambition and thus he was specially successful in his progressive activities as an agriculturist and stock-grower. He continued to maintain the active supervision of his fine farm property until the time of his death, and though his early educational advantages were of necessity very limited, he profited greatly from the lessons of experience and became a man of broad views and mature judgment, even as he was one of sterling integrity of character. His political allegiance was given to the Democratic party, but he pursued the even tenor of his earnest and unassuming way with no desire for political activity or preferment. He was one of the sturdy yeomen who aided in civic and material development and progress in Gage county, true to the duties and responsibilities that devolved upon him and known for simple and unpretentious rectitude.

As a young man Mr. Pethoud wedded Miss Nancy Melissa Bunker, who was born in the state of Indiana, November 12, 1844, and who was reared in the state of Iowa, where her parents were pioneer settlers. She was a daughter of Daniel Bunker, a descendant of Nathaniel Bunker, who owned the farm on which was fought the great Revolutionary battle of Bunker Hill. Chief Justice Chase, of the United States supreme court, was a scion of the Bunker family and it was through his genealogical research that definite proof was given that the celebrated battle was thus fought on the property of his forebear, whose name is thus perpetuated in history. Mrs. Pethoud survived her husband by more than a decade and was one of the venerable and loved pioneer women of Gage county at the time of her death, June 3, 1908. They are survived by only one child, Miss Arabella Pethoud, who remains on the old homestead farm which her father obtained from the government under homestead entry in the early pioneer era, the place being endeared to her by the hallowed memories and associations of the past and the pleasant home being known for its generous hospitality.

JOHN R. McCANN, who has held since 1914 the office of postmaster of the city of Beatrice, was born at Mount Sterling, Brown county, Illinois, on the 11th of January, 1868, and is a son of Thomas and Bettie (McEntee) McCann, both natives of Ireland. Thomas McCann was born in the city of Dublin, November 12, 1839, the youngest child and now the only survivor in a family of four sons and three daughters. Thomas McCann was a lad of about ten years when he accompanied his parents to America, the voyage having been made on a sailing vessel of the type common to that period and the family having landed in the port of New York city on the 5th of June, 1849. From the national metropolis the parents, Thomas and Rose McCann, proceeded to Cincinnati, Ohio, the journey having been made by canal and the Great Lakes, prior to the time when railroad facilities had been provided. After remaining about three months in Cincinnati the family went by steamer down the Ohio river and across the Mississippi to St. Louis, Missouri, where the home was maintained until 1854. Removal was then made to Brown county, Illinois, where Thomas McCann, Sr., purchased land, near Mount Sterling. There he developed a productive farm and there he and his wife passed the remainder of their lives, both having been communicants of the Catholic church, to the faith of which the later generations of the family have adhered. The father of the postmaster of Beatrice was reared to manhood on the pioneer farm in Brown county, Illinois, where he owns and still resides upon the old homestead farm which was obtained by his father nearly sixty-five years ago. Mrs. Bettie (McEntee) McCann was born in County Cavan, Ireland, in 1838, and her parents, Mr. and Mrs. Patrick McEntee, were pioneers of Brown county, Illinois, where they continued to reside until their death. Mrs. McCann passed to the life eternal in 1879, and of the seven children John R., of this review, is the eldest; Thomas M. is a resident of the city of Chicago; Rose is the wife of Henry Moss, of Mount Sterling, Illinois; Elizabeth is the wife of James W. Brady, of Mount Sterling; Clara died at the age of eighteen years and George in infancy; and Miss Anna remains with her venerable father on the old homestead farm.

John R. McCann was reared to the sturdy discipline of the farm and acquired his youthful education in the public schools of his native county. At the age of seventeen years he went to Jewell City, Kansas, where for a period of about two years he was employed in a wholesale grocery establishment. He next went to Mankato, Kansas, and there he learned the tinner's trade. After about two years his health became impaired to such an extent that he sought a less sedentary occupation and entered the employ of the Carpenter & Gage Nursery Company, at Fairbury, Jefferson county, Nebraska, where he had previously worked at his trade for some time. In 1888 Carl Sonderegger, who was the proprietor of the German Nursery at Fairbury, had occasion to make a trip to Switzerland, and he engaged Mr. McCann to assist in the management of the nursery during his absence. Mr. McCann continued his alliance with the Sonderegger nursery and in the meanwhile lived in the home of Mr. and Mrs. Carl Sonderegger until the time of his marriage. He became a traveling representative of the concern and after his marriage he resided at Dewitt, Saline county, until 1893. Save for a brief interval he continued in the employ of Mr. Sonderegger for a period of fifteen years, during which he sold nursery stock to the value of thousands of dollars, the while his relations with his honored employer were ever of the most gracious and mutually appreciative order. Mr. McCann established his residence in Beatrice in 1893 and here he continued his active connection with the Sonderegger nurseries, as a salesman, until 1898, when he here engaged in the real-estate business. His operations in this field of enterprise extended into Texas, Florida, and Georgia, where his transactions involved the handling of much land and also the promotion of immigration to those states. He continued as a successful exponent of important real estate operations until his appointment office of postmaster of Beatrice, a position of which he has been the valued incumbent since 1914, as previously noted in this context.

Mr. McCann is unwavering in his allegiance to the Democratic party, and he has been active and influential in its councils in Nebraska, where he served three years as a member of the Democratic state central committee.

On the 17th of June, 1889, was solemnized the marriage of Mr. McCann to Miss Grace E. Gast, a daughter of William and Sarah (Moyer) Gast, who were pioneer settlers in Saline county, Nebraska. There Mr. Gast became the owner of an entire section of land and developed a large and valuable farm estate, his holdings including land also in Gage county. His widow now resides at Dewitt, Saline county. Mr. and Mrs. McCann became the parents of two children, Ethel G., who died the 28th of December, 1916, and Edith Grace, who is the wife of Walter C. Magee, of Beatrice, Nebraska.

MR. AND MRS. JOHN E. MURPHY

JOHN E. MURPHY.—The history of Gage county tells what has been done during the fifty years of struggle, striving, and working toward the creation of a great county. It must tell of the individual achievements of the men who have taken an active part in the work of development and progress. These men are the foundations of the social structure of Gage county. One of the number is John E. Murphy, who is a son of Patrick and Catherine (McCaffrey) Murphy, early pioneer settlers on the former Otoe Indian reservation in Gage county. Patrick Murphy was born in Ireland and when a youth he there wedded Miss Catherine McCaffrey. The young couple left their native land to seek their fortune in the United States, and they landed in Brooklyn, New York, where Patrick worked as a laborer. By hard work and patient saying he was finally able to buy thirty-two acres of land near Tribes Hill, New York.

In 1878, when the eyes of the east were directed upon the new western lands being opened for settlement, Mr. Murphy decided to come to Nebraska and seek better opportunities for acquiring a living and competence. This entailed a long and weary journey over rough roads that were not drained, while in many places there were virtually no roads at all. Finally, after weeks of travel, Mr. Murphy and his family arrived in Lincoln, Nebraska. Here he heard of the Otoe Indian reservation land being opened up for settlement. He came to Gage county, and on the reservation purchased a squatter's right to one hundred and sixty acres of land, a few miles from the present village of Odell. Here the family was soon settled on the pioneer farm, and the father, with his only son, John, broke the virgin land, wresting from the soil in due time its treasures of wheat and corn.

Mr. Murphy gave unstintingly of his time and talent to the community at large. As other settlers came in, there was need of civic and religious organizations. He was among the first to give aid in the organization of Paddock township and also to organize a school for the education of the children. Mr. Murphy gave liberally of his time and money to organize the Catholic church at Odell, and later he helped in the organization of the Catholic church at Wymore. All during his life thereafter these institutions received liberally of his support. In all of his labors on the farm, in the church and community Mr. Murphy's devoted wife shared. She was born March 12, 1827, in Darlyn, County Fermanagh, Ireland, and she came to this country with her young husband, settled with him in the Otoe Indian reservation, and shared with him all of the hardships and trials of pioneer life. They became the parents of six daughters and one son. Mrs. Murphy lived to the venerable age of ninety years and six months, and passed the declining period of her life in the home of her youngest daughter, Mrs. Rose Masek, where she died September 23, 1917. Of the children the following record is given: Mrs. Mary McCarthy resides at Wymore, this county; Mrs. Katherine Hatmaker is deceased; Mrs. Julia Comer resides in Paddock township; John F. is the only son and is the subject of this sketch; Mrs. Susan McCaffrey is a widow and resides at Hastings, Nebraska; Mrs. Abbie Stanosheck lives at Odell, Gage county, Nebraska; and Mrs. Rose Masek, of Odell, is deceased.

John E. Murphy was the fourth child and only son born to his parents. He was born October 1, 1863, at Tribes Hill, New York. His education was received in New York prior to his coming to Nebraska with his parents. He was 15 years old when they arrived on the Otoe Indian reservation and he helped his father to build their cabin, break the land, and perform the various other duties that were to be done on a pioneer farm. He remained on this farm until he went to Odell, to serve as a clerk in a general merchandise store. He remained thus engaged until 1900, when he went into the general merchandise business for himself. He successfully conducted the enterprise until 1914, when he disposed of the business, and he has since devoted his time to the real estate and insurance business.

In 1904 the Odell Independent Telephone Company was organized and Mr. Murphy was the leading spirit in the organizing of this company, of which he was elected secretary and treasurer. This substantial company has a modern building, erected at a cost of five thousand dollars, and in this the business is conducted. Mr. Murphy was interested also in a cider and vinegar manufacturing company that was organized in 1907, and in 1913 the factory at Odell, Gage county, was transferred to Atchison, Kansas, where it is now located. Mr. Murphy was secretary and treasurer of the company until March, 1917, when he sold his interest in the business.

The marriage of John Murphy and Katie A. Stanosheck was solemnized May 4, 1892. Mrs. Murphy was born in Iowa City, Iowa, and is a daughter of Albert and Pauline Stanosheck. (See Thomas W.

Stanosheck sketch for the family history). Mr. and Mrs. Murphy became the parents of nine children: Frank E. is an electrician for the Atchison Railroad Specialty Company, at Atchison, Kansas; Ruth is a teacher in the high school at McCook, Nebraska; Rosa and Lillian are twins, Rosa being a dressmaker and remaining at the parental home, and Lillian being a teacher at Culbertson, Nebraska; Adelaide died at the age of twelve years; Marie is attending the high school at Odell; Frances is attending the public schools; and John and Catherine, twins, are at home. The children have received the advantages of the schools of Odell, and the family is popular in the social life of the community.

Mr. Murphy votes the Democratic ticket and has held offices of trust in his community. He has served as a member of the city council of Odell and as township clerk. He affiliates himself with the Knights and Ladies of Security, the Ancient Order of United Workmen, the Royal Neighbors, the Modern Woodmen of America, and the Benevolent and Protective Order of Elks. He has real estate in Nebraska, Kansas, South Dakota, and Colorado. He is ever alert to the civic needs of Odell and is a citizen of utmost loyalty and progressiveness.

JOHN H. MENTER.—The great basic industries of agriculture and stock-growing yield substantial and worthy rewards to the man of enterprise and good judgment, and this is definitely signified in the prosperity that has attended the efforts of Mr. Menter as one of the vigorous and resourceful farmers of Grant township, where he is the owner of a valuable landed estate of two hundred acres, besides which he is the owner of three hundred and twenty acres in Deuel county, this state.

Mr. Menter claims the old Buckeye state as the place of his nativity, but the year 1918 records for him thirty years of continuous residence in Nebraska, where he has achieved substantial success and independence entirely through his own ability and well ordered efforts. Mr. Menter was born in Wood county, Ohio, October 21, 1868, and is a son of Frederick and Mary (Schuerman) Menter, the latter of whom, a native of Prussia, Germany, died in 1874, at the age of thirty-six years, after having become the mother of four children, of whom three are living: Henry is a resident of Toledo, Ohio, and Louis of Pemberville, that state. The father ultimately contracted a second marriage and of the children of this union five are living, all being residents of the state of Michigan—Edward, William, Carrie, Katherine, and Ida.

Frederick Menter was born in the province of Hanover, Germany, May 20, 1840, and was six years of age at the time of the family immigration to America, his parents having settled in Wood county, Ohio, where they passed the remainder of their lives, his father having there become a prosperous farmer. Frederick Menter was reared and educated in Ohio and there he continued his alliance with farm industry until 1907, when he removed with his family to Huron county, Michigan, where, at a venerable age, he still resides on his well improved farm, the religious faith of the family having been for generations that of the Lutheran church.

John H. Menter grew to maturity under the invigorating discipline of the old home farm in Ohio and in the meanwhile profited by the advantages afforded in the district schools of the locality. In 1888, shortly before attaining to his legal majority, he came to Nebraska, where for the ensuing nine years he worked as a farm hand, principally in Gage and Saline counties. His compensation during a considerable part of this period was only fourteen dollars a month, but he carefully saved his earnings and kept fully in view the goal of his ambition—that of becoming an independent exponent of farm enterprise. In 1896 he rented land in Webster county, and later he farmed on rented land in Adams and Saline counties. In 1911 Mr. Menter purchased his present Gage county farm, on which he has since made many excellent improvements of permanent order, including the erection of a barn and other farm buildings. His energy and progressiveness have enabled him to make his place stand forth as one of the best improved and effectively operated farms in Grant township, his attractive homestead being situated three miles southeast of the village of Dewitt, Saline county, from which he receives service on rural mail route No. 3. He gives his attention to diversified agriculture and stock-growing, and is making a specialty of raising graded swine. He gives loyal support to measures and enterprises tending to advance the civic and material welfare of the community, has served as road supervisor, and he and his family hold membership in the Lutheran church.

February 22, 1896, recorded the marriage of Mr. Menter to Miss Mary Ulrich, daughter of Charles G. and Johanna (Graff) Ulrich, concerning whom further mention is made on other pages, in the sketch of their son Edward W. A. In conclusion is given brief record concerning the children of Mr. and Mrs. Menter: Carl has the management of his father's farm property in Deuel county; Alfred is associated in the work and management of the home farm in Gage county; Gertrude is deceased; and Arthur, John, Alice, and Paul remain members of the gracious home circle.

CHARLES B. MUMFORD.—From the early pioneer period in its history to the present time Gage county has claimed members of the Mumford family as sterling and valued citizens, John B. Mumford, father of the subject of this review, having been one of three brothers who came from Wisconsin to this county in the '60s, and each of these brothers, John B., Ismay, and Jacob, having taken vigorous part in the furtherance of the initial development and upbuilding of the county, where the family name has always stood forth for civic loyalty and progressiveness and for the intelligent and productive industry which makes for individual success and communal advancement.

John B. Mumford was born in the state of Maryland, where his parents established their home upon coming from England to this country, and he became one of the pioneer settlers in Wisconsin, where he engaged in agricultural pursuits and became one of the substantial citizens of Lafayette county. His initial visit to the Territory of Nebraska was made in the year 1860, when he accompanied his older brother, Ismay, to what is now the opulent and beautiful county of Gage, and of the conditions that then obtained in this locality some idea is conveyed by the statement that Dawson Mumford, son of Ismay, was the first white child born within the limits of this county. The general historical department of this publication shows also that Ismay Mumford was the first treasurer of Gage county. After this pioneer visit to Gage county John B. Mumford returned to Wisconsin, but in 1865 he brought his family to Gage county and here established a permanent home. He purchased four hundred acres of land, reclaimed and developed one of the excellent farms of the county, and he continued to reside on his well improved homestead farm, in Logan township, until his death, when seventy three years of age, his venerable widow still surviving him and being one of the loved pioneer women of Gage county: her maiden name was Mary A. Roush and she was born in Ohio, the original American progenitors of the Roush family having come from Holland in the early period of our national history. John B. and Mary A. (Roush) Mumford became the parents of nine children, and of the six now living Charles B., of this review, is the second eldest; Sarah, the eldest, is the wife of William A. Foreman, of Beatrice; Eugene P. is individually mentioned within the pages of this publication; Ida and Frank remain on the old homestead farm of their father, the former being the wife of L. W. Eppert, who is associated in the work and management of the place; and Luther A., formerly principal of the Beatrice high school, is now engaged in the school-textbook business in the city of Lincoln, capital of Nebraska. John B. Mumford was a leader in the local councils of the Democratic party, though never consenting to accept public office, and his religious faith was that of the Methodist Episcopal church, his venerable widow being a devout adherent of the Christian church.

Charles B. Mumford was born in Lafayette county, Wisconsin, and was a small boy at the time the family home was established on the pioneer farm in Gage county, Nebraska, where he was reared to manhood and received the advantages of the common schools of the period. It can well be understood that in his boyhood and youth he acquired full fellowship with the sturdy work of the farm, and in initiating his independent career he naturally continued his allegiance to the great basic industry of agriculture. For a period of years he was numbered among the progressive and successful farmers of Logan township, and in 1894 he removed to Beatrice, the county seat, where he engaged in the livery business. A number of years later he sold this business and turned his attention to the buying of horses, which he sold for local use, besides developing a substantial enterprise in the shipping of horses to various central markets. A thorough judge of values, he made a definite success of the business and was one of the prominent shippers of horses from this state. In the spring of 1915 Mr. Mumford gave evidence of his appreciation of the modern trend of progress by identifying himself with the automobile business. He erected a large garage building on Seventh street and there installed the best of equipment, including a general repair shop and a line of automobile supplies and accessories, his broad experience and aggressive policies having been potent in the upbuilding of a very prosperous business and his active control of the same having continued until September, 1917, when he sold both the building and the business to the present owner, Austin Krous. Since that time he has renewed his allegiance to his former line of business and gives his attention to handling horses, both in placing them on the market and in fitting them for service. He is at the time of this writing the owner of two fine standard bred horses which are making good account of themselves in turf events. Mr. Mumford is well known throughout this part of Nebraska, and his genial personality, as combined with his sturdy integrity in all of the relations of life, has gained to him a wide circle of friends. He is a staunch supporter of the cause of the Republican party, though he has manifested naught of ambition for public office, and his wife is an active member of the Christian church.

As a young man Mr. Mumford wedded Miss Martha Dearborn, and she is now deceased. She is survived by three children: Charles D., who is associated with his uncle, E. P. Mumford, in the furniture business in Beatrice, where he was formerly employed fourteen years in the furniture store of Walter Scott; Leslie is now a resident of San Francisco, California; and Mabel is the wife of N. Townsend, a prosperous farmer in the vicinity of Taco, in the Canadian northwest.

In September, 1904, was solemnized the marriage of Mr. Mumford to Miss Mae Van Boskirk, who was born in Linn county, Iowa, a daughter of Lincoln and Celia (Freer) Van Boskirk, whose marriage was solemnized in Wisconsin, whence they eventually removed to Iowa, from which state they came to Gage county, Nebraska, in 1885, establishing their residence in Beatrice, where Mr. Van Boskirk erected a large and attractive residence at the corner of Seventh and Summit street—this being the present home of Mr. and Mrs. Mumford. Mr. Van Boskirk was a second cousin of Abraham Lincoln, and in the early territorial days he acquired a large tract of land in Nebraska, the patent to the same having been signed by President Johnson, and this property still continues in the possession of the family. More detailed mention of the Van Boskirk family is made on other pages, in the review of the career of Frederick Van Boskirk, a brother of Mrs. Mumford. Mr. and Mrs. Mumford have one daughter, Clara Belle, who was born February 28, 1912.

JOHN B. RENARD is a successful farmer and stock-raiser who owns a valuable and well improved farm in Section 1, Glenwood township. As a representative citizen of that township he is entitled to recognition in this history of Gage county.

MR. AND MRS. JOHN B. RENARD

Mr. Renard was born at Keokuk, Lee county, Iowa, May 5, 1862. His parents, Adam and Catherine (Wofe) Renard, were natives of Germany, and both passed the closing period of their lives at Keokuk, Iowa, where they had resided for many years and where the father was a cabinet maker by trade and vocation. John B. Renard was one of seven children, four of whom are living, he being the only one in Nebraska. When a young man he made his way to Page county, Iowa, where he remained two years, and he then came to Gage county, Nebraska. Here he farmed in Rockford township for one year, and for the ensuing five years he was engaged in farming in Logan township. For the past twenty-eight years he has conducted successful operations on four hundred and twenty acres of land in Sections 1 and 12 Glenwood township. Here he has erected a splendid set of buildings, among the finest in the county, and is here engaged in general agricultural and stock-raising enterprise. He has the cooperation of Herman Lenger, who is a bachelor brother of Mrs. Renard, and who makes his home with the Renard family.

Mr. Renard chose as his wife Miss Lottie Lenger, who was born in Warren county, Missouri, her parents having been early settlers of Gage county, Nebraska, and a record of the family being given elsewhere in this volume, in sketch dedicated to Lewis D. Lenger, of Beatrice. Mr. and Mrs. Renard are members of the Christian church at Odell. Mr. Renard takes an active interest in the affairs of his community and was one of the organizers of the Odell Telephone Company, of which he has been president for many years. He assisted also in organizing the State Bank of Odell. Fraternally he is a member of Odell Lodge, No. 97, Independent Order of Odd Fellows. He is a Republican in politics and has given years of service in the office of justice of the peace. Mr. and. Mrs. Renard indulge themselves in travel and have recently made an extended trip on the Pacific coast. They are folk of sterling worth and have a host of friends.

REV. VICTOR F. CLARK.—The honored pastor of the First Congregational church of Beatrice is a man of high intellectual attainments and has labored with all of consecrated zeal and devotion in the work of the ministry, besides having wielded much influence in the field of educational service. He was reared to manhood in Nebraska, where the family home was established prior to the admission of the state to the Union and when he was a lad of about ten years. His high sense of stewardship has been shown in every pastoral charge which he has held and also in all other relations of life, the while his benignant influence has touched most helpfully the general communal life in every place that has figured as the stage of his earnest and prolific endeavors. There are many points of surpassing interest in both his personal and ancestral history and he takes pride in being a scion of one of the sterling old colonial families of New England, that gracious cradle of much of our national history. Mr. Clark plays a large part in the community life of Beatrice, aside from his ecclesiastical functions, and for this reason, as well as on account of his being the spiritual and executive head of one of the important church organizations of the city, he is specially entitled to the tribute which is perpetuated through the medium of this publication.

Rev. Victor Fremont Clark was born at West Haven, Rutland county, Vermont, on the 20th of August, 1856, and is a son of Rev. Elipha Lyman Clark and Nancy (Munger) Clark, both natives of Whiting, Addison county, Vermont, where the former was born February 27, 1813, and the latter on the 6th of March, 1815. The father died in April, 1873, and the gracious and devoted wife and mother passed to the life eternal in the following year, both having been representatives of honored and influential pioneer families of the old Green Mountain state. Rev. Elipha L. Clark, a man of fine intellectuality and exalted character, as a youth prepared himself for the legal profession and was admitted to the bar of his native state. After having been for a time engaged in the practice of law he followed the course of his earnest conviction pertinent to his personal stewardship and entered the ministry of the Baptist church, as a clergyman of which he labored for many years, a true disciple of the Divine Master and one who gave himself with devotion to the aiding and uplifting of his fellow men. He bore to the full the "heat and burden of the day," garnered a rich harvest and also a gracious aftermath, and proved himself the friend and counselor of all who came within the sphere of his influence. In 1866 he came with his family to Nebraska Territory and entered claim to one hundred and sixty acres of government land in Seward county. There he gave his attention to the development of his farm, the while he continued his activities as one of the pioneer clergymen of the territory and state, and he was one of the revered citizens of Seward county at the time of his death, which occurred on his old homestead farm. His was definite leadership in popular sentiment and action in the pioneer community, he was stalwart in his allegiance to the Republican party, and he served as representative of Seward county in the last session of the territorial legislature, as well as in the first legislature under state regime. He became the father of eleven children, of whom only four are now living, and of the number: the subject of this review is the youngest.

Rev. Elipha L. Clark was a son of Elipha and Jemima (Moulton) Clark, and a grandson of Isaiah and Eunice (Moore) Clark, whose marriage was solemnized December 24, 1778, at Simsbury, Connecticut, and who removed in the same year to Vermont, their son Elipha having been born in that year and his death having occurred in 1813, the parents having passed the remainder of their lives in the old Green Mountain state and the family name having stood exponent of strong and noble manhood and gentle and gracious womanhood as one generation has followed another onto the stage of life.

Augustus Munger, maternal grandfather of the subject of this review, was born at Whiting Vermont on the 22d of May, 1794, and his wife, whose maiden name was Temperance Babcock, was born June 30, 1793, their marriage having been solemnized February 22, 1813, and both having passed the remainder of their lives at Whiting, Vermont, where the former died in May, 1841, and the latter in the year 1870. Augustus Munger was a son of Moses and Mercy (Baker) Munger, their marriage having occurred November 21, 1793. Moses Munger was born in the west parish of South Brimfield, Massachusetts, October 21, 1769, and his wife was born in 1778. Both were residents of Whiting, Vermont, at the time of their death, he having passed to eternal rest on the 11th of January, 1861, and she in the year 1840. Moses Munger was a son of Jehiel Munger, who was born at Brimfield, Hampden county, Massachusetts, June 3, 1737, and whose marriage to Elsie Rogers was celebrated in 1758, she having been born at Brimfield in the year 1738 and both having passed the closing years of their life at Whiting, Vermont, where Mrs. Munger died in 1798 and where he passed away August 3, 1817. Jehiel Munger was a distinguished patriot soldier in the Revolution, in which he rose from the rank of sergeant to captain. He took part in important engagements marking the progress of the great war for independence, including those of Concord and the Brandywine, and in the "piping times of peace" he manifested the same spirit of loyalty and patriotism. This sterling Revolutionary soldier erected as a home for his family the first two-story house built at Whiting, Vermont, and in the same were frequently held church services, he having been a deacon of his church. Authoritative family records still extant show that Nicholas Munger, who was born and reared in England, came to America in 1639 and established his home in Massachusetts. He married Sarah Hall, in 1659, and their son Samuel, born in 1665, married Sarah Hand. The next in line of descent to the subject of this review was Nathaniel, who was born in 1712, a son of Samuel and Sarah (Hand) Munger, and in 1736 Nathaniel wedded Elizabeth Bullen, they having become the parents of Colonel Jehiel Munger, of whom mention has been made.

As previously stated in this context, Rev. Victor F. Clark was about ten years of age at the time when the family home was established in Nebraska Territory, which in the following year gained the dignity of statehood, and he was reared thereafter under the benignant influences of the pioneer farm and those of a home of distinctive culture and refinement. After having made good use of the advantages afforded in the schools of the locality and period he entered Tabor College, at Tabor, Iowa, and in the preparatory department of this institution, which was founded in 1866, under the auspices of the Congregational church, he continued his studies until his graduation. Thereafter he was a student in the college proper until he went to Chicago, in 1880, and entered the theological seminary. In this institution he was graduated as a member of the class of 1883, his ordination to the ministry of the Congregational church having occurred in that year. His first pastoral charge was at Milburn, Illinois, where he remained four years and he then devoted a year to effective post-graduate study in Princeton University, New Jersey. For the ensuing four years he held a pastorate at David City, Nebraska; the next five years found him as pastor of the Congregational church at Holdrege, this state. He then accepted a call to the pastorate of the Congregational church at Livingston, Montana, where he remained six years. He then returned to Nebraska and became pastor of the Congregational church at Neligh, Antelope county, an incumbency from which he retired six years later, to become pastor of the church at Ashland, Saunders county. After two years of characteristically earnest and fruitful service in this pastoral charge Mr. Clark was tendered and accepted the position of state secretary of Doane College, at Crete, this state—an institution maintained under Congregational church auspices. In this position Mr. Clark did effective work in promoting the interests of the college and after three years he resigned his post to accept, in 1914, the pastorate of the First Congregational church of Beatrice. Here he has done much to further the spiritual and material prosperity of his charge and has gained to his church many new members. He is not only a forceful and eloquent pulpit orator, but his every utterance bears the impress of sincere conviction and utmost altruism, while his entire freedom from intellectual intolerance makes his work in his high calling the more effective and benignant. Aside from his pastoral functions of direct order he has marked executive ability, and has shown splendid success in gaining the earnest coöperation of the people of the various churches which he has served.

It is to be presupposed that a man of such patriotic ancestry would manifest a deep interest in the welfare of the nation and the state, and the civic loyalty of Mr. Clark is shown in his giving his influence and aid in the support of measures and enterprises tending to advance the general wellbeing of the community. He pronounces himself an independent Republican in politics and while he has never sought public office he has yielded to urgent importunities and is giving effective service at the present time in the office of probation officer of Gage county. He is affiliated with the Independent Order of Odd Fellows and the Modern Woodmen of America.

In August, 1879, Mr. Clark wedded Miss Katie M. who was born at Tabor, Iowa, a daughter of Daniel Woods. Mrs. Clark passed to the life eternal in 1886 and is survived by one son, Roy Victor, who is engaged in the insurance business at Wilmington, California. In 1888 was solenmized the marriage of Mr. Clark to Miss Alice Mathews, who was born in the state of Wisconsin, a daughter of Charles and Myra (Simmons) Mathews, the former of whom was born at Norwich, Vermont, in 1825, and the latter at Kinderhook, New York, in 1831; she died in 1857, in Wisconsin. Mr. Mathews was a carpenter by trade and became a successful contractor, his home having been established near the state line between Wisconsin and Illinois for many years and his death having occurred in the latter state, in 1895. Mr. and Mrs. Clark have but one child, Martha Leavitt Clark, who was graduated in the high school at Crete, this state, where she is now a member of the class of 1919 in Doane College.

ANTON NOVOTNY.—The Bohemian farmer is industrious and accumulative. His pinched opportunities for advancement in his native land make him appreciative of the opportunities offered in the new world. This nationality is found in great numbers in Elm township, and Anton Novotny is a son of Bohemian parents, Frank and Mary (Vostry) Novotny. With their family of nine children, the youngest, Anton Novotny, but a child in arms, the parents settled in Pawnee county, Nebraska, in 1878. There were years of hard work and many deprivations facing this sterling pioneer couple, who were called upon to feed and clothe the large family of children, but Frank Novotny lived to see his children all grown to manhood and womanhood. He passed away in 1906. He was born in Bohemia in the year 1829. His wife, Mrs. Mary (Vostry) Novotny, was born in Bohemia, and since her husband's death she has made her home with her youngest daughter, Mrs. Emma Fritz, of Washington county, Kansas. The following is brief record concerning the children: Louisa died in Bohemia; Katherine is the wife of Anton Blecha, living near Oklahoma City, Oklahoma; Anna is the wife of Amos Hubka, living in Washington county, Kansas; Mary is the widow of Joe Herring, and lives in Washington county, Kansas; Joseph is a resident of Washington county, Kansas; Frank lives near Virginia, Gage county, Nebraska; James lives near Gretna, Nebraska; Louis resides in Washington county, Kansas; Anton, of this sketch, was next in order of birth; Amos lives near Wheatland, Oklahoma; and Emma is the wife of John Fritz, of Washington county, Kansas.

MR. AND MRS. ANTON NOVOTNY

Anton Novotny was born October 15, 1876, in Bohemia, and he was only fifteen months old when his parents immigrated to the United States. He received his education in the rural schools of Pawnee county, Nebraska, and early began to assist in the work of the home farm. He left the parental roof in 1901, when he married and bought land south of Virginia, Gage county. This place he farmed until 1906, when he purchased one hundred and sixty acres of land in Section 34, Elm township, where he has since resided. February 19, 1901, Mr. Novotny married Miss Mary Chadima, who was born in 1878, in Iowa. Her death occurred October 20, 1916, and she left three sons to be cared for by their father—Alvie, Fred, and George.

Mr. Novotny is a Democrat in politics but has never sought any political honors. He is a member of Western Bohemian Lodge, and is a shareholder in the Farmers' Telephone Company at Odell, this county. His sons remain on the farm with him and help him in the many ways in which boys of such age can be of use.

WILBUR S. BOURNE.—This representative member of the Gage county bar has been established in the practice of his profession at Beatrice, the county seat, for the past thirty-five years, and he has exemplified in his activities the best ethics of his profession, which he has dignified alike by his character and achievement. He is now (1918) serving as city attorney, and his inviolable hold upon popular confidence and esteem has been shown by his having been called upon to serve in various other offices of public trust. He presided six years on the bench of the county court of Gage county, has held the offices of city clerk and member of the board of education of Beatrice, and in 1898 he was elected mayor of the city, an office in which he gave a most able and popular administration, marked by well ordered progressiveness, his tenure of the position of chief executive of the municipal government having continued for two years. Judge Bourne is unswerving in his allegiance to the Republican party and has given effective service in the furtherance of its cause. In the Masonic fraternity he has completed the circle of the York Rite, in which his maximum affiliation is with Mount Herman Commandery of Knights Templars, besides which he holds membership in the adjunct Masonic organization, the Ancient Arabic Order of the Nobles of the Mystic Shrine, his affiliation in this being with Sesostris Temple, in the city of Lincoln, Nebraska. Both he and his wife are active and valued members of the Christian church of Beatrice.

Wilbur S. Bourne was born at Macomb, McDonough county, Illinois, on the 22d of June, 1854, and is a son of Rev. Milton Bourne and Melvina (Gardiner) Bourne, the former of whom was born in the state of Massachusetts and the latter in that of New York, she having been the second wife of Rev. Milton Bourne, and the latter having been the father of five children by his first marriage and five by the second. One of the sons, Milton, Jr., went forth from Illinois as a valiant soldier of the Union in the Civil war. Rev. Milton Bourne was a child at the time of his parents' removal to the state of Vermont, where he was reared and educated. He entered the ministry of the Methodist Episcopal church and became one of its pioneer clergymen in Illinois, where he formed the personal acquaintance of his historic contemporary, Peter Cartwright, while he was presiding elder of the Monmouth district of the Methodist church in Illinois at a time when said district comprised fully one-third of the entire state. Rev. Milton Bourne labored with all of zeal and self-abnegation in his chosen calling and the closing period of his life was passed on a farm in McDonough county, Illinois, where he died when his son William S., of this review, was a lad of nine years, his loved wife surviving, him by a number of years.

Wilbur S. Bourne passed the period of his childhood and early youth in his native county and after having profited by the advantages of the public schools he provided ways and means that enabled him to supplement this training by a course in a normal school of Illinois.

In 1878, with a team and old-time "prairie schooner," Mr. Bourne and his young wife made the overland journey from Illinois to Nebraska, and for the ensuing year he was here engaged in farming, in Gage county. He then returned to Illinois, where he completed his interrupted law studies and gained admission to the bar. In 1882 he returned to Nebraska and established his home at Beatrice, where he has since continued in the practice of his profession and where he is not only a representative member of the bar of south eastern Nebraska but also one of the most honored citizens of Gage county.

In the year 1878 was solemnized the marriage of Judge Bourne to Miss Georgia Rile, who likewise was born and reared at Macomb, Illinois, and they have three daughters: Fannie L., who is the wife of Edward Buhler, of Lincoln, Nebraska, and Etsel and Velma, who remain at the parental home.

GEORGE W. PITTS.—The early '80s saw great numbers of farmers coming to Gage county and possessing themselves of their several portions of land. They built their sod huts and set themselves with a will to win the wild prairie to fertility. One of these men is George W. Pitts, who for nearly forty years has tilled Gage county soil on Section 7, Glenwood township.

Mr. Pitts came to Gage county February 22, 1880, and purchased one hundred and sixty acres of land from the government, for $3.50 an acre. As far as the eye could see there was nothing to obstruct the view of the rolling prairie with the exception of one lone tree, which Mr. Pitts cut down to provide fuel for cooking the first meal after the family arrival in the county.

Mr. Pitts was born September 16, 1844, in Ross county, Ohio, where his parents, George and Lucinda (Turk) Pitts, followed their farming operations upon coming from Pennsylvania, their natal state. It was in the year 1840 they established their Ohio home and in 1848 the father was called to his eternal rest. His widow later married a Mr. White, and her last days were spent in Kansas, where her death occurred in 1882.

The early days of Mr. Pitts' life were spent amid the rural environments of Ohio, and it was here he met and married, in 1865, the companion of these many years, Albina Runnels. She was born October 17, 1845, in Licking county, Ohio, and is a daughter of Sollis and Eliza (Nash) Runnels, who were born in Vermont and became pioneers of Ohio, where they passed the remainder of their lives.

In 1869 Mr. Pitts and his good wife removed to Washington county, Iowa, where he continued farm operations until 1880, when he made selection of his present farm of one hundred and sixty acres, in Gage county, Nebraska. Mr. and Mrs. Pitts are the parents of the following named children: Flora, the wife of D. Baker, living in Idaho; Sollis, a resident of Alda, Nebraska; Cora, the wife of H. Coleman, living at Diller, Nebraska; Walter, residing in Louisiana; Arthur, of Thedford, Nebraska; and Eva, wife of O. A. Dean, farming the home place of subject. One child died in infancy.

Mr. and Mrs. Pitts are members of the Methodist church and in politics he is independent of partisan lines.

SAMUEL D. RUTH.—Controlling a large and representative trade, the John H. von Steen Company holds prestige as one of the leading business corporations of Gage county and its progressive metropolis, and more specific mention of this important Beatrice business house is made on other pages of this publication. Of this company Mr. Ruth is the secretary, and his activities as an executive and a progressive business man have inured materially to the success of the enterprise with which he is thus identified.

Mr. Ruth was born in St. Clair county, Illinois, on the 29th of March, 1873, and he received his early education in the schools of his native state. He was there graduated in the McKendree College as a member of the class of 1898. He then came to Beatrice, Nebraska, and entered the employ of the John H. von Steen Company, with which he has since maintained his alliance and in connection with which he has advanced to the responsible office of secretary, of which he has been the incumbent since 1908. He has entered fully into the general communal life of his adopted city and is essentially liberal and progressive in his civic attitude. He gives his political allegiance to the Republican party and he and his wife hold membership in the Mennonite church.

In the year 1904 was solemnized the marriage of Mr. Ruth to Miss Marie C. Dueck, who was born in the city of St. Louis, Missouri, and their two children are Clinton and Mildred.

JOHN W. McKISSICK is known and valued as one of the loyal and influential citizens of Gage county, which he has represented in the Nebraska legislature, and he is now an executive of the pure-food department of the state, in which position he is serving his fourth consecutive year, his official duties demanding virtually his entire time and attention and involving his traveling through all parts of the state. He maintains his home in the city of Beatrice, and this history of Gage county properly accords to him specific recognition.

Mr. McKissick is a native son of the west and during the course of his earnest and constructive career he has exemplified most fully the progressive western spirit. He was born near Hamburg, Fremont county, Iowa, on the 2d of November, 1875, and is a son of William A. and Ruth (Utterback) McKissick, both likewise natives of Fremont county and both representatives of pioneer families of that section of the Hawkeye state. William McKissick was born June 11, 1842, on the same farm as was his son John W., of this review, and in Fremont county,

Iowa, he passed the closing years of his life. He was a son of Cornelius McKissick, who was born in Scotland and who was a boy at the time of the family immigration to the United States, where he was reared and educated. The family home was established in Missouri, and from that state he removed to Fremont county, Iowa, in 1830. He was the first settler of that county, where he took up a squatter's claim and where eventually he developed a valuable farm property. He became one of the influential citizens of Fremont county and remained on his old homestead until his death, in 1894 a patriarchal pioneer who had been a leader in the march of development and progress in the great empire of the west and whose name and achievement merit enduring place in the annals of Iowa history. Cornelius McKissick assisted in the construction of the pioneer stage road between St. Joseph, Missouri, and Council Bluffs, Iowa, and in compensation for his services he received an allotment of land in Iowa, which was under the territorial jurisdiction of Michigan Territory at the time when he there established his home on the frontier. His wife survived him and remained on the old homestead until her death, at the remarkable age of one hundred and two years. Mrs. William A. McKissick is a daughter of James R. Utterback, who was born in Indiana and who was the second person to make settlement in western Iowa, Cornelius McKissick having been the first settler.

William A. and Ruth (Utterback) McKissick became the parents of seven children, of whom John W., of this review, is the eldest son; Edward resides at Riverton, Iowa, and is engaged in the telephone business; Mattie is the wife of Ora Hatton, of Fremont, Nebraska; Miss Stella remains with her widowed mother in the pleasant home at Riverton, Iowa; Winnie is the wife of Herbert Jones, a farmer near Riverton, Iowa; Nellie is the wife of Frederick Beam, who is engaged in the agricultural implement business at Riverton; Gosper is associated with the Palmer Company, in the metropolis of Gage county, Nebraska.

William A. McKissick had a broad experience in connection with life on the frontier, and it is worthy of record that he made, with wagon and ox team, eight trips across the plains in the early days. On the last of these venturesome journeys he made his way to California, where he remained seven years and was engaged in the buying and selling of horses. Upon his return to Iowa he brought with him from the Pacific coast several horses, besides which he was accompanied by some faithful Indians. Mr. McKissick gained through his own ability and efforts a generous measure of success and prosperity and he wielded much influence in his native county, where he was held in unqualified popular esteem. He was sixty-three years of age at the time of his death, December 18, 1908, and, as before intimated, his widow now resides at Riverton, Iowa. Her father, James R. Utterback, settled in Fremont county, Iowa, in 1833, and there he remained on his original homestead until his death, in April, 1893, his wife having passed away in 1883. William A. McKissick was a staunch supporter of the principles of the Democratic party and his religious faith was that of the Presbyterian church, of which his widow has long been a devoted member.

John W. McKissick, the immediate subject of this sketch, acquired his youthful education in the public schools of Riverton, Iowa, and he passed his childhood days on the old home farm of which mention has been made in preceding paragraphs. As a lad of thirteen years he accompanied one of his brothers to western Nebraska, where he passed about two years on a large ranch owned by his father. During the ensuing two years he was at the parental home and in the meanwhile he continued his educational work. In 1895 he settled in Polk county, Nebraska, where he continued his successful activities in connection with agricultural and live-stock industry until 1902, when he came to Gage county and established his residence in the city of Beatrice, where he has since maintained his home. Here he engaged in the insurance business, in connection with which he was made general agent for the Nebraska Mutual Life Insurance Company, of Hastings. For a few years he held the position of actuary of this company, besides having served for a term of years as a member of its board of directors. Since 1914 he has been one of the most efficient and valued executives of the Nebraska pure-food department, and he is doing also an important work as secretary of the Municipal Code Commission, of Lincoln, this state. This commission was organized for the authoritative handling of the work of codifying the ordinances of cities and minor municipalities, and in each instance it makes a definite guaranty to the accuracy of its work and to the legal impregnability of the same. The commission has already produced valuable work in its special province and this has been in connection not only with Nebraska municipalities, but also those of other states of the Union. In this connection it is interesting to record that the commission is at the time of this writing, in the summer of 1918, completing the codification of the ordinances of Gage county's judicial center and metropolis, the city of Beatrice.

Admirably fortified in his opinions concerning economic and governmental policies, Mr. McKissick is a staunch advocate of the principles of the Democratic party and has been an influential figure in the party councils in Nebraska. He served from 1911 to 1915 as representative of Gage county in the lower house of the Nebraska legislature, and here made an excellent record in the furtherance of wise legislation and the forwarding of the interests of his constituency. He is prominently affiliated with the Independent Order of Odd Fellows and he is serving in 1918 as deputy grand master of the Nebraska grand lodge. He has passed the official chairs also in the Modern Woodmen of America.

On the 26th of February, 1895, was solemnized the marriage of Mr. McKissick to Miss Della E. Swan, who was born in Polk county, Nebraska, January 8, 1876, and who is a daughter of William H. and Ida (Blowers) Swan, the former a native of Iowa and the latter of Indiana. Concerning the brothers and sisters of Mrs. McKissick the following brief data may consistently be given: William H. and Clara reside in the city of Beatrice and the latter is the wife of Rudolph R. Woelke; Harry is a resident of Shelby, Polk county, this state; Jennie is the wife of Edward Clobes, of the same place; Minnie is the wife of Andrew Peterson and they likewise reside at Shelby, as do also the younger children—Perry, Pearl, Vernal, and Floyd. The names and respective dates of birth of the children of Mr. and Mrs. McKissick are here noted: William A., March 26, 1896; Ida Ruth, December 5, 1897; Bertha June, June 24, 1901; Frances Gertrude, December 19, 1903; and Woodrow Wilson, July 26, 1913.

REV. WILLIAM T. McKENNA.—The life work of a priest of the Holy Roman Catholic church is essentially one of self-sacrificing devotion to the needs of his people, his church, and the Divine Master whom he serves. The work demands years of preliminary study and preparation, for the highest of intellectual standards and the broadest of practical humanitarianism are demanded, the while there can be in prospect no temporal rewards commensurate with the service to be rendered, save the satisfaction of having labored faithfully and well in behalf of Christ and humanity. Father McKenna has measured up fully to the demands and exactions of his high calling and is one of the representative members of the Catholic priesthood in this section of Nebraska. He is pastor of St. Mary's church at Odell, and commands the high esteem and affectionate regard of the members of his parish, as well as the confidence and good will of the entire community.

Father McKenna was born on Prince Edward Island, Canada, on the 21st of September, 1873, and he received his preliminary educational discipline in the rural schools of his native province. He remained with his parents on the home farm until he was a lad of twelve years, and was then sent to a Canadian college in which he prosecuted his studies of preparatory order as well as along higher academic lines. In 1893 he entered St. Mary's Seminary at Baltimore, Maryland, and in this institution he completed the philosophical and ecclesiastical studies that prepared him for the priesthood. In this celebrated theological seminary he was graduated in 1896, and in the same year he was ordained to the priesthood. Shortly afterward he was assigned to a pastoral charge at Fairbury, Nebraska, but after three months of service at that place he was transferred to Nebraska City, where he remained six years and gave effective pastoral service, in the parish of St. Mary's church. In July, 1916, Father McKenna came to Gage county and assumed his present charge, as pastor of St. Mary's church at Odell. He has been since that time the zealous and devoted shepherd of this fold and has given earnestly of his time and talents to the furtherance of the spiritual and temporal wellbeing of his parish.

CHARLES D. KNOX has the best of modern facilities in the conducting of his successful livery and transfer business in the city of Beatrice, and is one of the wide-awake and progressive citizens of the Gage county metropolis. He was born in Belmont county, Ohio.

November 23, 1855, and is a son of Isaac and Jane (Foster) Knox, who were born and reared in West Virginia, where their marriage was solemnized, and who removed thence to Belmont county, Ohio, where the father engaged in agricultural pursuits. In 1865 Isaac Knox removed with his family to Illinois, and later he became a pioneer settler in eastern Kansas, where he entered claim to a quarter section of land near the present town of Erie. There both he and his wife passed the remainder of their lives. Of their ten children the subject of this sketch was the sixth in order of birth and of the number six are now living. Isaac Knox was a gallant soldier of the Union in the Civil war, his service covering a period of about three years; his political allegiance was given to the Republican party and both he and his wife were earnest members of the Christian church. James Knox, father of Isaac, was a native of Ireland and was a resident of West Virginia at the time of his death.

Charles D. Knox acquired his early education in the schools of Illinois and Kansas, and he has just claim to pioneer distinction in Nebraska, to which state he came in 1873. He settled in Seward county and later took up land and engaged in farm enterprise in the south western part of the state. Still later he engaged in the stage and livery business at Grant, Perkins county, where he continued operations in this line of enterprise for ten years. He then returned to the eastern part of the state and engaged in the livery business at Seward, judicial center of the county of that name. Several years later he established himself in the same business at College View, a suburb of the city of Lincoln, and in 1913 he came to Beatrice and purchased the livery and transfer business which he has since conducted with marked success. That his establishment is thoroughly modern in its equipment needs no further voucher than the statement that he now operates a number of taxicabs and other motor vehicles, his business being the most important one of the kind in the city. In politics Mr. Knox gives his allegiance to the Republican party, he is affiliated with the Independent Order of Odd Fellows, and his wife is a member of the Methodist Episcopal church.

In 1879 Mr. Knox wedded Miss Arpha Hickman, who was born at Newton, Iowa, and they have four children: Clarence B. is now engaged in buying and shipping horses at Beatrice; Clara is the wife of Chas. B.

Hand, of Seward, this state; Fern remains at the parental home; and Eva is the wife of Frank R. Shelley, of whom mention is made on other pages of this volume.

HARVEY O. MASON, owner of an excellent farm of one hundred and sixty acres in Section 1, Lincoln township, was born in Ontario county, New York, March 21, 1841, and has been a resident of Nebraska since 1867, the year that marked the admission of the state to the Union. His life has been one of varied experiences and consecutive productiveness, and he stands forth as one of the sterling pioneer citizens of Gage county.

In a little log house of one room, in Farmington township, Ontario county, New York, Harvey O. Mason was born March 21, 1841, a son of Robinson and Mary (Brandt) Mason, of whose six children he was the fourth in order of birth; Hannah E. and Samuel are deceased; George is a resident of Fort Dodge, Iowa; and Franklin and Byron are deceased. Robinson Mason was a representative of one of the pioneer families of Ontario county, New York, where he was born, in Farmington township, in August, 1813. He continued his alliance with farm enterprise in the old Empire state until 1848, when he removed with his family to Chicago, Illinois, the future metropolis having then been little more than a straggling village. It was his intention to buy land in Illinois, but his wife found so little appeal in the west that he consented to return to New York. At Churchville, that state, he engaged in the general merchandise business, but about a year later he removed with his family to Wisconsin and engaged in the same line of business at Port age City. Two years later he became identified with lumbering operation near Grand Rapids, that state, and in 1856 he became a pioneer in the same line of enterprise at Chippewa Falls, Wisconsin, in which locality he became the owner of three thousand acres of valuable timber land. In his lumbering camps he gave employment to sixty men, and work was continued night and day, with consistent shifting of the working forces. In 1864 Mr. Mason returned to the state of New York and purchased a large farm, besides which he became concerned in the oil development business in Pennsylvania. Finally he established the home of his family in Monroe county, New York, after which he went to South Pass,

Wyoming, and engaged in mining for gold. He shipped in from Chicago, via the Union Pacific Railroad, his ten-stamp quartz mill, and from Bryan, Wyoming, he hauled the mill across the desert to South Pass—one hundred and ten miles distant. John C. Fremont, the great "pathfinder," had visited South Pass in 1848 and the name was given to the point in honor of the expedition which he led through this newly discovered pass to the Pacific coast. Mr. Mason failed to develop gold in vein quality, and finally abandoned his undertaking. The government then employed him to saw lumber for use at Fort Stambaugh, besides finally purchasing his power plant. Mr. Mason eventually returned to his family and he was a resident of Monroe county, New York, at the time of his death, in 1885. His wife was born in Ontario county, New York, in 1815, and her death occurred in September, 1890.

Harvey O. Mason attended school in Farmington and Churchville, New York, and also at Portage, Wisconsin. One of his school mates at Churchville was that noble and revered woman, Miss Frances E. Willard, founder and president of the Woman's Christian Temperance Union, and their friendship endured until this gracious gentlewoman passed to eternal rest, in 1898. Mr. Mason was associated with his father's business activities until 1865, when he engaged in the meat business in the city of Chicago, where also he became a member of the Board of Trade. In 1866 he sold his interests in Chicago and returned to the state of New York, but in the following year he came to the new state of Nebraska and purchased land in Douglas county, three miles south of Omaha. In 1870 he sold this property, and thereafter he remained in the state of New York until 1874, on the 9th of May of which year he arrived at Beatrice, the judicial center of Gage county. The following day he went by stage to Plymouth, Jefferson county, in which locality he purchased land and engaged in farming on an extensive scale. In 1887 he sold his property in that county and settled on his present attractive homestead in Gage county. For eighteen years, while continuing his association with the management of his farm, Mr. Mason was a traveling representative of the Beatrice Creamery Company, one of the foremost concerns of the kind in the west. He has stood exponent of broad-ganged and progressive citizenship, has achieved independence and prosperity through his own efforts and is one of the well known and highly esteem citizens of Gage county. His political allegiance is given to the Republican party and he and his wife hold membership in the Presbyterian church.

In February, 1869, Mr. Mason wedded Miss Jennie Shindoll, who was born in Racine county, Wisconsin, in 1857, a daughter of John G. and Mary (Nelson) Shindoll. In conclusion is given brief record concerning the children of Mr. and Mrs. Mason: Luella is a popular teacher in the schools of Long Beach, California; Byron, who is engaged in the drug business at Riverton, Wyoming, married Miss Mary Griffeth of Chicago, and they have one child; George is a successful ranchman near Blackfoot, Idaho; Gertrude is the wife of D. M. Bendernagel, of Lincoln township, Gage county; Harvey is a successful farmer in Riverside township; Roy is a resident of Deadwood, South Dakota; Elmer resides at Riverton, Wyoming; Esther is a trained nurse at the Green Gables Institute, Lincoln, Nebraska; Marjorie remains at the parental home; and two children died in infancy.

HENRY ALBERT.—The attractive village of Clatonia claims as one of its honored citizens this venerable and revered pioneer, whose has been a large and beneficent part in connection with the development and upbuilding of Gage county along both civic and industrial lines. Mr. Albert is president of the Clatonia Bank and is the owner of a valuable landed estate of eight hundred acres in Sections 23, 25, 26, and 27, Clatonia township, besides which he has six hundred and forty acres in Hand county, South Dakota, and a fine farm of one hundred and thirty acres in Allen county, Kansas. As an extensive landholder he has done most effective service in connection with the march of progress in the nation's great empire of the west.

Mr. Albert was born in the province of Hanover, Germany, on the 24th of April, 1837, and while he has attained to the age of four score years he exemplifies in his sound mental and physical powers the effectiveness of right living and right thinking during the course of a signally active and useful career. Mr. Albert is a son of David and Katherine (Kinker) Albert, of whose four children he is the firstborn; Mrs. Elizabeth Shaffer, the next in order of birth, remains a resident of

Hanover, Germany; Eberhart has been a resident of Gage county since 1874 and is now living retired in the village of Clatonia; and Katherine, who is the widow of August Struckmeier, likewise maintains her home in this village, her husband having been another of the honored pioneer setters of Clatonia township.

David Albert continued his residence in the Hanovarian fatherland until 1874, when, in company with his wife, he came to America, to which country three of their children had preceded them, and they gained likewise a pioneer distinction by joining their two sons and one daughter in Gage county, the closing years of their earnest and upright lives having here been passed in the home of their daughter, Mrs. Stuckmeier.

Henry Albert is indebted to the excellent schools of his native land for his early educational discipline, and he was but fifteen years of age when his father provided him with sufficient funds to pay the cost of the ocean voyage. It was in the year 1852 that the United States thus gained this youthful immigrant. Mr. Albert landed in the port of the national metropolis and soon afterward made his way to Ohio, where he turned his attention to the vocation of teaming and where he continued his residence until he manifested his unbounded and insistent loyalty to the country of his adoption by going forth as a soldier of the Union in the Civil war. In response to President Lincoln's first call for volunteers, he enlisted, July 15, 1861, at Cincinnati, as a private in Company M, Second United States Artillery, with which gallant command he saw wide and varied campaign service in Virginia, North Carolina and other sections on which were staged activities incidental to the great conflict between the north and the south. He was a member of the famous brigade commanded by General Custer, who later sacrificed his life in conflict with the Indians in Montana, and he participated in many engagements, including a goodly number of the important and sanguinary battles marking the progress of the war. His military career in the field extended from July 15, 1861, until he received his honorable discharge at Light House Point, Virginia, on the 16th of July, 1864, at which time he was near the spot on which, about one year later, General Lee made his historic surrender. It may well be understood that Mr.

Albert has continued to feel vital interest in his old comrades and that he signalizes the same through his active affiliation with the Grand Army of the Republic, as a member of which he was one of the organizers of Rollins Post, No. 35, at Beatrice, Nebraska, of which he served as senior vice-commander, his present affiliation being with the post in the city of Lincoln.

HENRY ALBERT

After the close of his military career Mr. Albert continued his residence in Ohio until the spring of 1865, when he came to Nebraska

Territory and numbered himself among the early pioneer settlers of Nebraska City, Otoe county. He arrived in Gage county on the 1st of April, 1866, and soon afterward entered claim to a homestead of one hundred and sixty acres, in what is now Clatonia township. This ambitious young veteran of the Civil war was fertile in resources and expedients, as befits one who essays the burdens and responsibilities of a pioneer, and in instituting the improvement of his land he purchased four yoke of oxen at Nebraska City, from which point he drove them overland to his embryonic farm, fully seventy-five miles distant. With these faithful but plodding animals Mr. Albert broke about one hundred acres of his land, and in the meanwhile he constructed a rude "dugout" as a domicile for himself and his devoted young wife, who proved his true helpmeet in these days of struggle and hardship. It may be mentioned also that he assisted in the construction of the little dugout which was placed in commission as the first schoolhouse in Clatonia township. The passing years rewarded the earnest and indefatigable activities of Mr. Albert with cumulative success and prosperity and he finally developed his old homestead into one of the fine farms of this section of the state. He erected on the old homestead modern buildings, besides making other improvements of the best order, and there he continued to reside for the long period of thirty-eight years, in the meanwhile having gained recognition as one of the most substantial and influential citizens of the county.

In 1912 Mr Albert sundered the gracious associations of the old farm and removed to the village of Clatonia, where, in a commodious and modern home known for its generous hospitality, he is now living in semi-retirement, though his important capitalistic and landed interests make imperative demands upon much of his time and attention. He owns one-third of the stock of the Clatonia Bank, of which he has been president since 1894, and his mature judgment and conservative policies have made this institution a valuable factor in the furtherance of the civic and material interests of this section of the county.

In 1876 Mr. Albert was elected a member of the board of county commissioners, and incidental to his effective service in this important office he was a member of the committee which had the supervision of matters pertaining to the erection of the county court house, as well as that in charge of the building of the bridge across the river on Court street. He served six years as county commissioner and did much to advance public improvements of an enduring order as well as to provide for the county effective governmental policies. In politics Mr. Albert has never wavered in his allegiance to the Republican party, and he reverts with satisfaction to the fact that his first presidential vote was cast for Abraham Lincoln. In 1901-02 he represented Gage county in the state legislature, where he made his influence distinctly felt in the promotion of wise legislation, though he was of the minority forces in that signally Populistic session of the legislature. He has served as mayor of Clatonia, was one of the organizers and original members of the school board of this village, and has given his service in other village offices. Mr. Albert is an active member of the Methodist Episcopal church of Clatonia and contributes liberally to the support of the various departments of its work.

At Portsmouth, Ohio, on the 9th of April, 1865, was solemnized the marriage of Mr. Albert to Miss Emma Steinmeyer, who was born and reared in Germany and who became a resident of Ohio soon after coming to the United States. Mrs. Albert shared with her husband in the tension incidental to pioneer life in Nebraska and lived to enjoy the gracious rewards that eventually attended their endeavors. She was summoned to the life eternal on the 14th of December, 1909, at the age of sixty-three years, secure in the affectionate regard of all who knew her. She was a devout member of the Methodist Episcopal church and exemplified her faith in her daily life and her association with others. Of the ten children born of this union brief record is here consistently given: Anna died when about twenty years of age; Ella is the wife of Frank W. Jones, of Clatonia, who is individually mentioned on other pages of this work; John died at the age of about thirty-three years; Frank resides upon and has active charge of the old homestead farm of his father and concerning him specific mention is made in this volume; Mrs. Minnie Latshaw and her husband reside at Chetek, Barron county, Wisconsin; Benjamin is a resident of Clatonia township and a sketch of his career appears on other pages; Augusta is the wife of J. W. Lydick, of Clatonia;

Daniel is a resident of Clatonia township and is represented individually elsewhere in this publication; Alma became the wife of Roy Barker and is now deceased; and Clara is the wife of Edward Chittenden, who is an executive in the Clatonia Bank.

On the 12th of July, 1911, Mr. Albert contracted a second marriage, when Mrs. Augusta Kroff became his wife. She was born and reared in Lippe, Germany. By her first marriage she became the mother of six children, all of whom are living. She was a resident of Lincoln, Nebraska, at the time of her marriage to Mr. Albert, and she is the gracious and popular chatelaine of their pleasant home at Clatonia.

ELMER L. HEVELONE.—The efficient and popular secretary of the State Savings & Loan Association of Beatrice became a resident of Gage county when he was a lad of six years, and that in his character and achievement he has proved fully equipped for keeping pace with the march of development and progress in this favored commonwealth is attested by the fact that he has been called upon to serve in various positions of distinctive responsibility and trust, including that of treasurer of Gage county. He has been in the most significant sense the builder of the ladder on which he has risen to the plane of definite success and prestige, and his activities have been varied, though each stage of his career has been marked by his consecutive advancement, the while he has so ordered his course as to merit and retain the inviolable confidence and esteem of all with whom he has come in contact in the varied relations of life.

Mr. Hevelone, though imbued with the utmost loyalty to Nebraska and fully appreciative of its manifold attractions and advantages, takes a due measure of satisfaction in reverting to the old Buckeye state as the place of his nativity,—perhaps in consonance with the humorous paraphrase which Hon. Chauncey M. Depew once made of a familiar quotation, his version being as follows: "Some men are born great; some achieve greatness, and some are born in Ohio." Mr. Hevelone was born in Seneca county, Ohio, on the 12th of May, 1874, and is a son of Sylvester and Cynthia C. (Wonder) Hevelone, the former of whom was born in Pennsylvania and the latter in Ohio. Sylvester Hevelone was born on the 28th of December, 1847, and was young at the time of the family removal from Pennsylvania to Ohio, where his marriage was later solemnized. In the climacteric period of the Civil war he manifested his intrinsic patriotism by tendering his services in defense of the Union. In 1864 he enlisted as a member of Company A, Fifty-fifth Ohio Volunteer Infantry, and with this gallant command he continued in active service until the close of the war. Mr. Hevelone lived up to the full tension of the great conflict between the north and the south, participated in numerous engagements of important order and as a soldier made a record that shall ever reflect honor and distinction upon his name and memory. In later years he vitalized the more gracious associations of his military career by retaining active affiliation with the Grand Army of the Republic. His political allegiance was given to the Republican party and both he and his wife held membership in the Evangelical church.

After the close of the Civil war Sylvester Hevelone continued his association with agricultural pursuits in Ohio until 1880, when he came with his family to Nebraska and settled in Gage county, where he established the family home on a farm owned by his father-in-law, George Wonder, in Blue Springs township, near the present thriving village of Blue Springs. He marked the passing years with earnest and well directed endeavor and became one of the substantial farmers and influential citizens of his township. Both he and his wife passed the closing years of their lives at Blue Springs, where his death occurred in the year 1897 and where she was summoned to the life eternal in 1908. They are survived by eight children, concerning whom brief mention may consistently be made at this juncture George D. resides at Blue Springs and is a farmer by occupation; Samuel J. is a successful farmer in Riverside township, this county; Sidney F. is engaged in the merchandise business at Beatrice, the county seat; Ralph R., of Alma, Harlan county, is a farmer by vocation Emma P. is the wife of David I. Ault, of Alma Harlan county; Eva P. is the wife of Frank Hatch, of Greeley, Colorado; Alice T. is the wife of Abraham L. Bowers, of Edinburg, Texas; and Elmer L., the immediate subject of this review, was the first in order of birth.

Reared to the sturdy discipline of a semi-pioneer farm, Elmer L. Hevelone acquired his early education in the excellent public schools of

Gage county, and in 1890 he completed an effective course in the Beatrice Business College. As a boy and youth he had found both diversion and valuable experience by working about the depot of the Chicago, Burlington & Quincy Railroad at Blue Springs, and there he learned efficiently the art of telegraphy. As a skillful operator he was given employment by the railroad company mentioned, and for a time he was in service at Atchison, Kansas. Later he became station agent for the same company at Kesterson, Jefferson county, Nebraska, where he served in this capacity until 1899, when he was transferred to a similar post in the village of Filley, Gage county, where he remained thus engaged until 1901. For eighteen months thereafter he gave his attention to the buying and shipping of grain, with headquarters at Tecumseh, Johnson county, and from 1903 to 1906 he was Burlington station agent at Blue Springs, near the old homestead farm.

In the year 1906 Mr. Hevelone was appointed deputy treasurer of Gage county, under the administration of Julian A. Barnard, and of this position he continued the incumbent four years. His efficiency and his strong hold upon popular confidence and good will then marked him as a logical candidate for the office of county treasurer, and to this responsible position he was elected in 1910, as the candidate on the Republican ticket. He received at the polls a most gratifying support, and the high estimate placed upon his administration was shown in his re-election at the close of his first term, without opposition in either political party. By a change in the state laws during his second term the adjustment was such that instead of serving for a total of four years, the regular two terms of the previous regulation, he retained the office for five consecutive years. His ability in the management of the fiscal affairs of the county marked Mr. Hevelone as a man well fortified for the administration of financial business of a general order, and after his retirement from the office of county treasurer he was chosen president of the Farmers & Merchants Bank at Wymore, this county.

Of this position he continued in tenure two years, and in 1914 he became a stockholder and director of the State Savings & Loan Association of Beatrice, which is recognized as one of the strong, well ordered and representative financial institutions of southeastern

Nebraska. In February, 1917, Mr. Hevelone was elected secretary of this banking corporation and as such he has the active administration of its large and substantial business, with incidental status as one of the efficient and representative figures in financial circles in this part of the state. The State Savings & Loan Association of Beatrice was organized and incorporated in the year 1890 and it has proved a valuable conservator of civic and material progress and prosperity in Gage county. Of this institution Albertus H. Kidd, of Beatrice, is president; Thomas J. Chidester, of Western, Saline county, is vice-president, Mr. Hevelone being its secretary, as already noted, and Louis Graff holding the office of treasurer. The assets of the institution are $1,700,000.00 and it gives special attention to the handling of savings accounts and to assisting in the purchasing and improving of real estate.

Mr. Hevelone, as intimated in a preceding paragraph, is a veritable stalwart in the local camp of the Republican party and as a citizen he stands exponent of the loyalty and public spirit that are potent in the furtherance of the general wellbeing of the community. He is one of the active and valued members of the Beatrice Commercial Club and served two years as its president. He is affiliated with the Masonic fraternity, the Eastern Star, the Benevolent & Protective Order of Elks and the Royal Highlanders. Both he and his wife hold membership in the Christian church in their home city and are popular factors in the representative social life of the community.

On February 23, 1898, was solemnized the marriage of Mr. Hevelone to Miss Anna M. McVey, who was born in the state of Missouri a daughter of Solomon and Lean (Kibler) McVey, the former of whom passed the latter years of his life in Gage county, Nebraska, and Republic county, Kansas, his widow being now a resident of Blue Springs. Mr. and Mrs. Hevelone have one child—Maurice Sylvester, born October 23, 1905, at Blue Springs.

JOSEPH MANGUS, who has figured as a successful farmer and stockman in Gage county, was born in Macoupin county, Illinois, August 17, 1871, and is a son of William and Catherine (Garst) Mangus, a record of whom appears elsewhere in this volume.

Joseph Mangus was educated in the public schools of Illinois and attended school for a short time after coming to Nebraska. He came to Gage county with his parents in 1881. He has always followed farming, beginning by renting land and later buying one hundred and twenty acres in Sherman township. After operating this for a few years he purchased eighty acres on Section 33, Rockford township, where he established his home. There were no buildings on this farm when Mr. Mangus bought it, with the exception of a small shack. Mr. Mangus greatly improved this farm, upon which he erected a fine two story house, a good modern barn, and other buildings.

On September 2, 1915, Mr. Mangus was united in marriage to Miss Margaret Hutchinson, daughter of James and Frances (Combs) Hutchinson, who were born in Illinois and who removed to Kansas in 1882. Mr. Hutchinson now makes his home in Missouri, his wife having passed away several years ago.

Joseph Mangus and wife are members of the Congregational church. Mr. Mangus is independent in politics and has never desired or held public office, thinking it better to devote his entire time and energy to his farm and the raising and feeding of live stock, in which line of enterprise he has been successful.

WALTER H. DEBOLT.—If perseverance, self-reliance and worthy purpose constitute the genius of success, then there is no need for indirection or puzzling in determining the forces that have been brought to bear in gaining advancement for Mr. DeBolt, who has depended entirely upon his own ability and resources in making his way in the world, who has shown himself a master of expedients and who has pressed steadily forward to the goal of ambition. He is now one of the stockholders of the John H. von Steen Company, one of the leading wholesale concerns of Beatrice, Nebraska, and has an active part in directing the executive policies and general business of this representative corporation, which is engaged in the wholesale and retail lumber business.

Mr. DeBolt can well claim to be intrinsically an American of Americans, as he is a scion of a family that was founded in this country prior to the war of the Revolution. In 1772 three brothers, George and

Henry DeBolt, each bearing a personal name spelled according to the French method and the original French surname of DeBaul, immigrated from the fair French province of Alsace—the present stage of much of the frightful military operations incidental to the great European war—to America, little wotting that more than two centuries later the land of promise to which they thus made their way would become involved in warfare in their native province, to which William and Henry finally returned, the brother George remaining to perpetuate the family name and honors in the new world and to become the worthy ancestor from whom the subject of this review traces his lineal descent, the presumption being that this founder of the family in America established his residence in the historic Old Dominion—Virginia. Isaac DeBolt, grandfather of him whose name initiates this article, was born and reared in Ohio, and thus is given assurance that his parents were numbered among the pioneer settlers of the Buckeye commonwealth.

Walter H. DeBolt was born at Edinburg, Johnson county, Indiana, on the 27th of July, 1860, and is a son of George and Mary (Webb) DeBolt, both natives of Indiana, where their marriage was solemnized. In 1866 George DeBolt removed with his family to Sterling, Illinois, but in the following year he numbered himself among the pioneers of Moulton, Appanoose county, Iowa. In the spring of 1878, with team and wagon, he made the overland journey from the old home in Iowa to the state of Nebraska, and became one of the early settlers of the village of Utica, Seward county, where he opened a shop for the repairing of wagons and where he maintained his home for many years. He passed the closing period of his life at St. Petersburg. Florida, where he died at the age of eighty-three years, his wife having been seventy-seven years of age when she was summoned to eternal rest and her death having occurred at Seward, Nebraska.

Walter H. DeBolt was a lad of about seven years at the time when the family home was established in Appanoose county, Iowa, where he early became inured to active labor and responsibility, the while he made the best use of the educational advantages afforded him in the public schools. Through his own resources Mr. DeBolt defrayed the expenses of his course in the Iowa Normal School at Moulton, and it is a matter of record that he attended extra classes three evenings a week, under the instruction of Mrs. H. M. Bushnell, who now resides in the city of Lincoln, Nebraska. He applied himself diligently to study during the midnight hours, found employment through the day and bent every energy to bringing himself up to the standard of his class, in which he was three years behind in his studies, owing to the conditions under which he applied himself. Of his indomitable perseverance and his marked mental receptiveness no further voucher need be asked than the statement that he made good on all his studies, though covering three years' work in one, and was triumphantly graduated in regular order with his class, that of 1877, besides having had the distinction of delivering the valedictory address.

Reinforced with the academic honors thus sturdily won, Mr. DeBolt set forth, in 1878, to join his parents in Seward county, Nebraska. Upon his arrival in Seward county he found employment at farm work, and though he had received absolutely no experience in the job assigned to him, he contrived, with much mortification of the flesh, as we may well imagine, to turn out his share of work in the binding of grain in the trail of a Marsh harvester. In the Spring of 1880 Mr. DeBolt went to Montana, and he passed four years moving about in that frontier section of the country. He then returned to Nebraska, where for several years he was identified with the lumber business, a portion of the time in the position of auditor for the Searle & Chapin Lumber Company, of Lincoln. In 1909 he came to Beatrice, still in the employ of the company mentioned, and front this center he continued his activities as auditor until he accepted a place as traveling salesman for the John H. von Steen Company. In this capacity he made an admirable record of productive business and finally he became a stockholder of the company, besides which he has served as a member of its directorate since 1914. He now remains at the headquarters of the company and is actively identified with the general management of its extensive business. Mr. DeBolt has lost none of his characteristic nerve and energy and holds prestige not only as one of the representative business men of the Gage county metropolis and judicial center but also as a progressive and wide-awake citizen who is always ready to lend his influence and cooperation in the furtherance of measures for the general good of the community. He has not been assailed by ambition for political office but has never swerved in his allegiance to the cause of the Democratic party.

In 1888 was solemnized the marriage of Mr. DeBolt to Miss Alice Corkens, daughter of James Corkens, of Beaver Crossing, Seward county, and they are popular factors in the social life of their home city; they have no children.

SILAS BRYSON.—No one who knows the facts concerning the early settlement of Gage and Johnson counties would consider the history of these counties complete were the story of the Bryson family omitted from its pages. Silas Bryson was one of the greatest and noblest of the early pioneers of this vicinity.

Silas Bryson was born June 20, 1835, in Athens county, Ohio. There he spent his boyhood days and he completed his education at the Zanesville Academy. On April 12, 1855, he was united in marriage to Clarinda Young, of Morgan county, Ohio. To this union were born fifteen children, twelve of whom are still living at the opening of the year 1918.

SILAS BRYSON

MRS. SILAS BRYSON

In April, 1862, the Bryson family came to Nebraska Territory and settled in what is now Johnson county, near the Bents Mills. Here they remained four years and they removed to Gage county and established their home near Adams, where Silas Bryson continued to reside until the time of his death. Shortly after coming to Nebraska the family had reason to be considerably in fear of the Indians, and on one occasion word came of an Indian uprising. All of the neighbors for miles around banded together and started for Nebraska City, sixty miles distant. Terrible rain storms came on, all the bedding became soaked, the victuals were ruined and the settlers were in dire distress. The third morning Mother Bryson arose in camp and announced her intentions of going back home. She said, "This style of living is worse than the Indians, and I am going back." Her courage inspired the crowd and by night the next day all arrived at home and found that their habitations had not been disturbed or their property molested. One winter when meat was scarce Father Bryson saw a fine big turkey coming into the clearing from the woods, and running back for his gun he soon brought the turkey down. This was the day before Christmas, and there was surely holiday rejoicing in the pioneer home. The older children have often said, "It was the finest Christmas dinner we ever had and no turkey since has tasted half so good."

Mr. Bryson was one of the early pioneer school teachers of Gage and Johnson counties, where he spent thirty-five years in the noble work of moulding the characters of Nebraska boys and girls. He organized the Adams Methodist Episcopal Sunday School and for seventeen years was its superintendent. Mr. and Mrs. Bryson were charter members of the Methodist Episcopal church of Adams. Their oldest grandson, Dr. Roy D. Bryson, is one of the Nebraska surgeons in the war and is now in France. Three other grandsons, Edgar Evans, Horace Patch, and Frank L. Bryson, and a grand-son-in-law, James F. Brown, also are in the government service in connection, with the great world war. Mrs. W. W. Barnhouse, eldest daughter of Mr. and Mrs. Silas Bryson, lives at Wheeler, Kansas; William E. makes his home at University Place, Nebraska; three daughters, Mrs. George Horrum, Mrs. Viola Sheppard, and Mrs. Mollie Barmore, live at Adams, Gage county, as do also the sons David F., the well-known auctioneer, and John A.; one daughter, Mrs. Jennie Patch, lives at Canby, Oregon; Mrs. Ruth Bassett lives at Bayard, Nebraska; S. Y. resides at Grand Island, this state; George lives at Arcadia, Nebraska; and another daughter, Mrs. Gertrude Evans, lives at Lincoln, Nebraska's capital city.

Although the members of this good family are much scattered, yet their influence is still felt throughout Gage county. Mother Bryson passed to her reward on April 2, 1909, and Father Bryson remained with us until November 10, 1915, when he answered the summons of his Maker and joined the heavenly assembly around the throne of God.

JAMES W. SHELLEY, whose mental, moral, and physical powers well fitted him for enduring the trials and responsibilities of pioneer life and who marked the passing years with large and worthy achievement, came to Gage county in the territorial epoch of Nebraska history and here played a prominent and influential part in connection with civic and material development and progress. He was one of the honored pioneer citizens of the county at the time of his death, which occurred October 24, 1908, and this history properly pays a specific tribute to his memory.

Mr. Shelley was born in Derbyshire, England, February 5, 1843, a son of Francis and Frances (Hollingsworth) Shelley, who, in 1855; came with their family to the United States and established a home in Portage county, Wisconsin, in which state they remained until 1861, when they came to Nebraska Territory and numbered themselves among the very early settlers of Rockford township. Though Francis Shelley had followed in his native land the trade of shoemaker he showed versatility and adaptability when he became a pioneer farmer in Gage county, and he developed a good farm in the township mentioned. On the old homestead, in Section 19, he passed the remainder of his life, his death having occurred May 25, 1884, at which time he was seventy-two years of age; his widow survived him by nearly a quarter of a century and passed to the life eternal in 1897, at a venerable age, their children having been six in number.

James W. Shelley acquired his early education in his native land and was twelve years old at the time of the family immigration to America.

He continued to attend school in Wisconsin, but there his advantages along this line were meager. He was a sturdy youth of eighteen years when he accompanied his parents to Gage county, Nebraska, and he drove an ox team through from the former home in Wisconsin. In 1864 he took up a homestead claim of one hundred and twenty acres, and while giving vigorous attention to reclaiming and improving this land he continued to remain at the parental home for six years after acquiring the property. With increasing prosperity, he made judicious investment in adjoining land and finally he developed a well improved landed estate of more than four hundred acres, the while he stood forth as one of the energetic and progressive exponents of agricultural and livestock enterprise in this section of the state. He provided excellent buildings for his farm property and was known and valued as a leader in community affairs in Rockford township, where he continued to maintain his residence until his death, his venerable widow, one of the revered pioneer women of the county, being now a resident of the city of Beatrice. Mr. Shelley was a man whose course was ever guided and governed by the highest principles and his broad range of vision made him naturally a leader in community affairs. Conscientious in every relation of life, he voted in consonance with his convictions and was a stalwart supporter of the cause of the Prohibition party. He and his wife became early members of the Methodist Episcopal church at Holmesville, a village not far distant from their farm, and he served a number of years as a member of the board of trustees of this church. He was zealous in the support of educational work and served three years as moderator of his school district.

January 1, 1870, Mr. Shelley wedded Miss Mary E. Bailey, who was born in Kenosha county, Wisconsin, January 31, 1851, the fourth in a family of eight children, and she was twelve years old when the family came to Gage county, in 1863, her parents, Asa F. and Jeanette (Ford) Bailey, having here passed the remainder of their lives, the father having been born in New Hampshire, of Colonial ancestry, and the mother having been a native of the state of New York. Mrs. Shelley shared with her husband in the vicissitudes and labors of pioneer life and prior to their marriage she had been a successful and popular teacher in the rural schools of Gage county. A woman of gracious personality, she is loved by all who have come within the sphere of her influence and she has many interesting reminiscences concerning the pioneer period in Gage county history. Of the children of Mr. and Mrs. Shelley, Violetta died at the age of eight years; Anna remains with her widowed mother at their pleasant home in the city of Beatrice; William is a substantial farmer in Rockford township; Eloise is the wife of Robert H. Whittaker, a prosperous farmer in Rockford township; Harriet E. died in 1915, at the age of thirty-three years; Merton J. at the time of this writing, in the spring of 1918, is in government service, as a member in the aviation corps at Waco, Texas; Gilbert R. has the management of his father's old homestead farm; Frank R. is president of the Northwestern Business College at Beatrice, and is individually mentioned on other pages; and Harold E. is now a member of the United States army forces in the cantonment at Fort McArthur, Waco, Texas, where, as an aviator, he is preparing to take his place as a patriot soldier in the great European war. It will be noted that three of the sons are in the aviation corps—located at Fort McArthur, Texas.

VIRGIL E. McGIRR.—The city of Beatrice proves a most attractive residence place for those who have been successful in farm enterprise in the county and who have achieved the independence that justified their retirement from active labors. Among the many popular citizens who are thus enjoying the attractions and privileges of the judicial center of the county is Mr. McGirr, who has been active not only as a representative of farm industry but also has been a successful exponent of the real-estate business. He was born in Kankakee county, Illinois, January 31, 1875, and thus is in the very prime of life. He is a son of Francis M. and Judith (Barkey) McGirr, and adequate record concerning the family is given on other pages, in the sketch of Dr. John I. McGirr.

Virgil E. McGirr was eleven years of age at the time of the family removal from Illinois to Gage county, and in the public schools he here continued his studies until his graduation in the Beatrice high school, as a member of the class of 1894. He continued his active association with farm enterprise until he had attained to the age of twenty-seven years, and he then established his residence at Beatrice, where he served three years as deputy sheriff of the county. For several years thereafter be was successfully engaged in the real-estate business; and his operations included the selling of land not only in Nebraska but also in other states of the Union. He built up a substantial and prosperous business and since his withdrawal from this line of enterprise he has lived virtually retired. He is the owner of a well improved farm of two hundred and sixty-five acres, in Holt township.

In politics Mr. McGirr is found aligned as a stalwart in the camp of the Democratic party and he has been influential in its local campaign activities. He has twice been his party's candidate for sheriff of Gage county, and on one occasion reduced materially the large Republican majority, his defeat being compassed by only twenty-seven votes. He served six years as chief of police at Beatrice, and gave a most efficient and satisfactory administration. Mr. McGirr has passed the various official chairs in the local lodge of the Independent Order of Odd Fellows, is now president (1918) of the Beatrice aerie of the Fraternal Order of Eagles, and he is affiliated also with the Benevolent & Protective Order of Elks. In their home city both he and his wife became members of the Centenary Methodist Episcopal church, with which he is still actively identified.

December 22, 1898, recorded the marriage of Mr. McGirr to Miss Bessie Hoopes, who was born in the state of Iowa and whose death occurred February 15, 1902. In 1905 Mr. McGirr wedded Miss Bertha G. Skinner who was born in Kansas, and they have three children— Francis D., John, and Paul. There are no children resultant of Mr. McGirr's first marriage.

FRANK W. ACTON.—In the administration of the office of sheriff of Gage county Mr. Acton has so ordered affairs as to prove conclusively the wisdom of the popular estimate that placed him in this exacting position. His experience in connection with police and constabular service has covered a period of fully a quarter of a century, and thus he was specially well fortified for assuming the office of sheriff of Gage county, to which he was elected in 1914, and reelected in 1916, at the close of his first term.

Sheriff Acton claims the Hawkeye state as the place of his nativity and is a representative of one of the sterling pioneer families of that commonwealth. He was born on a pioneer farm in Henry county, Iowa, October 21, 1857, and is a son of William N. and Mima E. (Cook) Acton, the former of whom was born in the state of Maryland, in 1820, and the latter was born in Ohio, in 1827. William N. Acton was a boy at the time of his father's death, which occurred in Maryland, and he was reared and educated principally in the state of Ohio. His energy, self-reliance, and ambition led him as a young man to number himself among the pioneer settlers of Iowa, where he entered claim to one hundred and sixty acres of land, in Henry county. He improved this property and after perfecting his title thereto he finally sold the farm and removed to Montgomery county, that state, in 1865. There he continued his successful activities in agriculture and stock growing until 1892, when he removed to Kansas and purchased a tract of land. In the following year he came to visit at the home of his son Frank W., at Wymore, Gage county, and here he was attacked with severe illness, in November of that year, his death having here occurred on the 2d of February, 1894. His loved and devoted wife survived him by nearly fifteen years and was a resident of Furley, Kansas, at the time of her death, in July, 1908.

William N. Acton was essentially a self-made man, and he achieved definite and worthy success in connection with normal lines of industrial and business enterprise, the while he so ordered his course as to merit and receive the unqualified respect and esteem of his fellow men. His religious faith was that of the Protestant Episcopal church and his wife held membership in the Methodist Episcopal church, she having been a daughter of Jesse Cook, who was born in Pennsylvania, whence he removed to Ohio, and who removed from the old Buckeye state to Iowa in the pioneer period of the history of the latter commonwealth; he became the owner of a valuable landed estate in Iowa and there he and his wife passed the residue of their lives. William N. and Mima E. (Cook) Acton became the parents of six children, and of the number the present sheriff of Gage county, Nebraska, is the eldest; A. B. is a representative merchant in the village of Furley, Sedgwick county,

Kansas; Ella M. is the wife of A. M. Stanley, a merchant at Palms, California; O. D. is a successful carpenter and contractor at Colfax, Iowa; J. L. is associated with his brother A. B. in the general merchandise business at Furley, Kansas, as is also C. M., the youngest of the children.

Frank W. Acton received excellent educational advantages in his youth, and after having availed himself of the privileges of the public schools of Mount Pleasant, Iowa, he entered the University of Iowa, graduating as a member of the class of 1875, and receiving the degree of Bachelor of Arts. He defrayed the expenses of his higher education largely through the revenue received from his effective services as a teacher in the public schools, his pedagogic work having included three terms of service in the district schools of Iowa, two terms in the schools of California, and two in Kansas. At Red Oak, Iowa, Mr. Acton gained his initial experience as a member of a police force.

In 1910 Sheriff Acton removed from Wymore to Beatrice, Nebraska, the capital of the same county, and here he soon afterward assumed the position of deputy sheriff, under the administration of Sheriff J. L. Schiek. Prior to this he had served for twenty years as a member of the police force of Wymore, Gage county, in which thriving little city he held also, for fourteen years, the position of street and water commissioner. Known and honored in Gage county, Mr. Acton retired from the position of deputy sheriff only to assume the more important post of sheriff. In connection with the conscription of the young men of the United States for service in the great European war Sheriff Acton is serving as a member of the exemption board for Gage county. As a stalwart in the camp of the Republican party he has at all times taken an active and loyal interest in political affairs and has been influential in the local councils of his party. The sheriff is prominently affiliated with the Knights of Pythias, in which he is past chancellor, besides which he has on several occasions served as a delegate to the Iowa grand lodge of this order. He holds membership also in the Improved Order of Red Men and the Fraternal Order of Eagles.

In the year 1881 was recorded the marriage of Mr. Acton to Miss Mary E. Harris, who was born and reared in Jefferson county, Iowa, and she was summoned to the life eternal in 1911, her memory being revered by all who came within the sphere of her gracious influence. Mrs. Acton is survived by two children: Paul holds the position of bookkeeper in the offices of the warehouse of the Chicago, Burlington & Quincy Railroad at Wymore, this county; and Maude is the wife of Paul W. Hitchins, foreman in the establishment of the Dempster Mill Manufacturing Company, at Beatrice. Christine, a foster daughter of Mr. and Mrs. Acton, is now the wife of R. M. Burroughs, an electrician at Scotts Bluff, Nebraska. Mrs. Acton was a devoted member of the Christian church and active in its work.

I. T. MERCHANT, the efficient postmaster at Adams, Gage county, claims the old Buckeye state as the place of his nativity. He was born in Paulding county, Ohio, on the 19th of March, 1856, a son of Isaac and Nancy (Caylor) Merchant. The father was born at a place eighteen miles southwest of Washington Court House, Ohio, on the 25th of November, 1823. He was a prosperous farmer in Ohio at the time when the Civil war was precipitated, and he showed his intrinsic patriotism by enlisting in an Ohio volunteer regiment and by serving valiantly with the same during the period of the great conflict between the states of the north and the south. When his country no longer needed his services as a soldier he returned to Ohio, and in 1866 he removed to Kingston, Missouri. In that locality he was engaged in farming until the time of his election to the position of county judge. In this office he served until 1873, when he came to Lincoln, Nebraska. In the following year he went to Custer county, this state, where he took up a homestead claim and became one of the pioneer settlers of that large and now prosperous section of Nebraska. He there continued his agricultural activities until 1885, when he sold his farm and established his residence at Broken Bow, the county seat, where he practiced law for several years thereafter. In 1911, after having spent some time in a visit to his native state, Mr. Merchant came to Adams, Gage county, where he passed the closing period of his life in the home of his son, the subject of this review, his death having here occurred November 10, 1913. His wife was born February 5, 1830, her birthplace having been not far distant from that of her husband, in Washington county, Ohio. She died at Broken Bow, Nebraska, January 22, 1892, and in the cemetery at that place were laid to rest the mortal remains of both her and her husband. They became the parents of ten children, concerning whom the following brief record is available: Mrs. T. J. Todhunter lives at Washington Court House, Ohio; John was a soldier of the Union at the time of his death, which occurred in a hospital at Memphis, Tennessee, within the progress of the Civil war; George W. is a resident of Bedford, Iowa; Mrs. W. H. Huffer lives at Urbana, Ohio; the subject of this sketch was the next in order of birth; Mrs. John Armstrong resides in San Francisco, California; Emma and William are deceased; and Mrs. R. D. Ross lives at Anselmo, Custer county, Nebraska.

I. T. Merchant continued his studies in the public schools until his graduation in the high school at Kingston, Missouri, as a member of the class of 1873. In 1873, as previously noted, the family removed to Lincoln, Nebraska, and there he became bookkeeper in his father's hotel. In the following year he accompanied his parents to Custer county, this state, where he entered claim to a homestead and engaged in the feeding of sheep and cattle. He finally disposed of his farm interests and removed to Broken Bow, where he became deputy sheriff of Custer county. Thereafter he was appointed postmaster at Broken Bow, an office of which he continued the incumbent until 1890. Thereafter he was there engaged in buying and shipping grain and live stock until 1893, when he became a keeper in the shops of the Nebraska penitentiary, at Lincoln. The next year he went to Toronto, Canada, where he became actively identified with lumbering enterprise.

In 1900 Mr. Merchant established his residence at Liberty, Gage county, Nebraska, where he continued to be engaged in the buying and shipping of grain for the ensuing nine years. He then removed to the village of Adams, this county, and here he was successfully engaged in buying and shipping grain and other farm produce until 1913, when he was appointed postmaster of the village, a position in which he has since continued his effective administration.

At Broken Bow, Custer county, on the 4th of September, 1880, was recorded the marriage of Mr. Merchant to Miss Sarah E. North, who was born in the Dominion of Canada and who is a daughter of Samuel and Mary (Kilpatrick) North, natives of Ireland. Mr. and Mrs. Merchant have one son, T. O., who has become a member of the national army and who is, in the spring of 1918, stationed at Camp Cody, New Mexico. Mr. and Mrs. Merchant belong to the Methodist Episcopal church, and in politics he is a Democrat. He has rendered efficient service as a member of the township board, as justice of the peace and as police judge. In a fraternal way he is affiliated with the Independent Order of Odd Fellows. Mr. Merchant is a man of ability and civic loyalty and he takes deep interest in all things pertaining to the communal welfare.

DAVID F. BRYSON.—Some one has said, "Expect great things, attempt great things and great things will result." This may not be true in every instance, but in the case of David F. Bryson it most undoubtedly is. Nebraska might be called "The young man's state," for she has within her borders many brilliantly successful young men. In this class should be included the subject of this review.

David S. Bryson is a native of Gage county, born in Adams township, July 1. 1872, and he is a son of Silas and Clarinda (Young) Bryson, a record of whom appears elsewhere in this volume. David F. Bryson spent his boyhood days on his father's farm in Adams township. He attended the district school in acquiring his early education and assisted in the work of planting, cultivating, and harvesting the crops. On reaching man's estate he engaged in farming on his own account, and no man in Gage county has met with greater success in his chosen calling. He is the owner of six hundred acres of well improved land and leases 1700 acres. He is a breeder of pure-bred Angus cattle, and deals extensively in cattle and hogs, which he buys and ships. He is the best known and most successful auctioneer in southeastern Nebraska, making a specialty of selling fancy live-stock, as well as land.

December 24, 1891, Mr. Bryson married Miss Martha L. Kensing. Her father, August Kensing, was born in Germany and came to America when a lad of sixteen years. He worked as a stone-mason and on a farm until 1861, when he enlisted as a soldier in the Civil war, serving under General Ulysses S. Grant. He was a loyal and valiant soldier, and after being captured by the enemy he was held a prisoner at Andersonville until his exchange was effected. He was mustered out at the close of the war, in 1865, when he went to Iowa and located on the farm where he remained until the time of his death. The mother of Mrs. Bryson was born in New York state, June 5, 1847, a daughter of Solomon and Martha (Davis) Perrin. She is now the widow of David J. Olmstead, and makes her home with her daughter.

MR. AND MRS. DAVID F. BRYSON

Mr. and Mrs. Bryson became the parents of ten children: Velma is the wife of Guy Atkins, of Adams, Gage county; George Douglas died in infancy; Reuben K. married Belle Hargis, and lives at Adams; Elnora May, Frank LeRoy, Martha Pearl Joy, David Silas, Alma Clarinda, June, and Queenie Hazel are still under the parental roof; and James I. died in infancy.

Mr. and Mrs. Bryson are members of the Methodist church, and in politics Mr. Bryson is a Prohibitionist, the cause of temperance finding in him a stalwart champion.

With no unusual advantages, except a laudable ambition and abundance of self-reliance and ability, Mr. Bryson has so intelligently directed his efforts that to-day he stands in the front rank of the men of large affairs in his native county.

HARRY R. BROWN, M. D., a successful and representative physician and surgeon of the younger generation in Gage county, is established in the practice of his profession in the city of Beatrice and also holds the position of assistant surgeon of the German Lutheran hospital in his home city.

Dr. Brown was born in Jefferson county, Nebraska, on the 9th of January, 1883, and is a son of Joshua P. and Dora Bell Brown, both natives of the state of Pennsylvania. Joshua P. Brown was born in the year 1856 and is a son of Orlando Brown, who likewise was born and reared in the old Keystone state and who died in 1915, at the patriarchal age of ninety years. Joshua P. Brown was for many years a successful teacher in the schools of Pennsylvania and finally he came to Nebraska and became a pioneer teacher in the schools of this commonwealth. He purchased land in Jefferson county and there reclaimed and developed a good farm. He there continued his active association with farm enterprise until 1909, when he removed to Kansas, in which state he had become the owner of two sections of land. He and his wife now maintain their home at White City, Kansas, and both are members of the Methodist Episcopal church. Mr. Brown is a man of broad intellectual ken and high ideals, and he has proved successful in the lines of productive enterprise along which he has directed his energies. His political allegiance is given to the Republican party and he has served in various township offices and as a member of school boards since he came to the west. He is affiliated with the Independent Order of Odd Fellows, of which he became a member while he was still a resident of

Pennsylvania. Levi K. Karschner, father of Mrs. Joshua P. Brown, continued his residence in his native state of Pennsylvania until he came with his family to Nebraska and became a pioneer settler and homesteader in Jefferson county. He made the long journey to this state by means of wagon and ox team. Mr. and Mrs. Joshua P. Brown became the parents of four children and of the two surviving Dr. Brown of this review is the elder; Merle is now (1918) attending school at Manhattan, Kansas.

Dr. Harry R. Brown acquired his early education in the public schools of Nebraska and in the same he continued his studies until his graduation in 1901, in the high school at Tobias, Saline county. In 1901-1902 he was a student in the University of Nebraska, and he then entered Marion Sims Medical College, now the medical department of the St. Louis University, in the metropolis of Missouri, and in this celebrated institution he was graduated as a member of the class of 1907. After thus receiving his degree of Doctor of Medicine he initiated the active practice of his profession at Dakin, Nebraska, where he built up a substantial business and where he continued his activities until 1915, when he removed to Beatrice, where he has since been associated in practice with Dr. Harry M. Hepperlen, of whom specific mention is made on other pages of this work.

In March, 1910, was solemnized the marriage of Dr. Brown to Miss Alta Briggs, daughter of Russell Briggs, who came to Nebraska in the pioneer days and who now lives on his extensive cattle ranch near Broken Bow, judicial center of Custer county. Dr. and Mrs. Brown have two children—Harry R., Jr., and Helen Loure.

Dr. Brown is found arrayed in the ranks of the Republican party, he is affiliated with the local organizations of the Benevolent & Protective Order of Elks and the Modern Woodmen of America, and both he and his wife are communicants of Christ church, Protestant Episcopal. The Doctor has gained special prestige through his ability as a surgeon and has to his credit many delicate operations, both major and minor.

FRANCIS ELIAS, M. D., established his residence in the thriving little city of Wymore in the year 1911, and here he has since been engaged in the successful practice of his profession, in which his ability and effective service have given him secure place among the representative physicians and surgeons of Gage county.

Dr. Elias was born in the state of Kansas, on the 17th of June, 1883, and the place of his nativity was his father's home farm, in Clay county. He is a son of Henry A. and Emma (Younkin) Elias, the former of whom was born in Pennsylvania, and the latter in Illinois. In the early '70s Mr. and Mrs. Henry A. Elias removed from Illinois and numbered themselves among the pioneer settlers of Clay county, Kansas. There Mr. Elias reclaimed and developed a valuable farm property and since his retirement from active farm enterprise he and his wife have maintained their home in the city of Manhattan, Kansas. In the Sunflower state were born their three children—Anna, who is the wife of Rev. Mr. Tannehill, of Centralia, Kansas; Mary, who is the wife of Jacob Nelson, of Wakefield, that state; and Dr. Francis Elias, who is the immediate subject of this review. Henry A. Elias is aligned in the ranks of the Republican party and while residing on his farm in Kansas he was called upon to serve in various local offices of public trust. Both he and his wife are members of the Methodist Episcopal church.

Dr. Francis Elias acquired his preliminary education in the public schools of Clay county, Kansas, and the discipline included a course in the high school. In preparing for the profession of his choice Dr. Elias entered the medical department of the University of Kansas, and in the same he was graduated as a member of the class of 1910. After thus receiving his well earned degree of Doctor of Medicine he was engaged in practice at St. George, Kansas, about one year. He then, in 1911, came to Gage county, Nebraska, and established his residence at Wymore, where he has since continued in active general practice as a well fortified physician and surgeon who keeps in full touch with advances made in the profession that has enlisted his earnest and effective services. The Doctor has developed a substantial and representative practice and is one of the loyal and progressive citizens of Wymore. He holds membership in the American Medical Association, the Nebraska State Medical Society, and the Gage County Medical Society. In 1915 he took an effective post-graduate course in the medical department of the famous Johns Hopkins University, in the city of Baltimore, Maryland. He gives undivided allegiance to his exacting profession but is loyal to all civic duties and responsibilities, his political support being given to the cause of the Republican party. In his home city he is affiliated with Wymore Lodge, Ancient Free & Accepted Masons, and Hiram Chapter, Royal Arch Masons.

The year 1911 recorded the marriage of Dr. Elias to Miss Olive Todd, who was born and reared in Clay county, Kansas, where her parents, Mr. and Mrs. Jonathan Todd, still maintain their home. Dr. and Mrs. Elias have three children—Houghton, Winfield, and Allison.

DWIGHT S. DALBEY has identified himself most closely and loyally with the interests of Gage county, where he has been influential in public life and civic and industrial affairs, and where he has been called upon to serve in various positions of distinctive public trust, including that of representative of the county in the Nebraska legislature.

Mr. Dalbey was born in Christian county, Illinois, on the 22d of September, 1878, and is a son of William M. and Mary N. (Hall) Dalbey, the former a native of Ohio and the latter of Illinois. Dwight S. Dalbey found the period of his boyhood and early youth compassed by the benignant influences of the old home farm in Christian county, Illinois, and in his native state he continued his studies in the public schools until he was graduated in the high school at Taylorville, as a member of the class of 1897. For the ensuing two years he was engaged in independent farm enterprise in his home county, and he then entered the college of agriculture of the University of Illinois, in which he was graduated in 1902 and from which he received the degree of Bachelor of Science. His definite proficiency was recognized by his being appointed an instructor in agronomy in the agricultural college after his graduation, and after serving in this capacity about eighteen months he resigned the position and went to Arkansas, where he purchased a one-third interest in a large cotton plantation, near Marianna. He gave the greater part of his time to the supervision of this plantation until his marriage, in 1903, after which he continued his residence at Jerseyville, Illinois, the old home of his wife, until 1907, when they came to Gage county, Nebraska, and established here their permanent home, their removal having been prompted by their desire to assume personal direction of the large landed interests which Dalbey had received in this state as a heritage from her father. Mr. Dalbey found in the new home splendid opportunities for the utilizing of his vital energies and the exercising of his progressive civic policies. His ability and personal popularity soon brought him into service in offices of local trust, for in 1910 he was elected a member of the board of supervisors of Gage county, the efficiency of his service having led to his reelection thereafter for three additional terms. He was a member of the board at the time when was constructed the first concrete bridge in the county, and he had been so conspicuously influential in bringing about this modern improvement that, at the suggestion of the supervising engineer, the new bridge was named the Dalbey bridge.

In 1915 Mr. Dalbey was elected representative of Gage county in the lower house of the Nebraska legislature, as candidate on the Republican ticket, and it should be recorded that he ran ahead of the party ticket in this election, as did he also at the time of his reelection, in 1917. He has proved a most valuable working member of the house and the various committees to which he has been assigned, and has done much to further the interests of his constituent district, as well as wise legislation for the state at large. Mr. Dalbey is a stalwart advocate of the principles and policies for which the Republican party has ever stood sponsor in a basic way, and he and his wife are active members of the Presbyterian church. Mr. Dalbey was president of the Beatrice Young Men's Christian Association for a number of years and is now director. He has been a member of the Beatrice library board for eight years, and is president of the Cornhusker Highway, which runs through Beatrice from Marysville, Kansas, to Sioux City, Iowa. He also is a director in the Beatrice National Bank, and has been a director of the Commercial Club for ten years.

Mr. and Mrs. Dalbey own about eight thousand acres of Nebraska land—in Gage, Otoe, and Pawnee counties—the same being a heritage which Mrs. Dalbey received from her father, the late Ford Lewis, to whom a memoir is dedicated on other pages of this publication. They are unflagging in their efforts to further the prosperity of the two towns founded by the latter's father—Virginia, in Gage county, and Lewiston, in Pawnee county the first having been named for Mrs. Dalbey, whose Christian name is Virginia, and Lewiston having been given its name in honor of its founder, the late Ford Lewis. Mr. and Mrs. Dalbey are prominent in connection with the representative social activities of Gage county and the city of Beatrice, in which they have a beautiful home, and they retain also the fine old Lewis homestead at Jerseyville, Illinois, between which city and Beatrice they divide their time. They have a host of friends in Nebraska—in fact, it may consistently be said that the number is limited only by that of their acquaintances. Mrs. Dalbey has been specially active in philanthropic and charitable work since establishing her home in Gage county, and is doing a generous share in the war activities to which the women of America are devoting themselves so loyally and effectively. She has served two terms as regent of Elizabeth Montague Chapter of the Society of the Daughters of the American Revolution, in the city of Beatrice, and at the time of this writing, in the summer of 1918, she is state corresponding secretary, and has been chairman of the state committee of the Nebraska Society of the Daughters of the American Revolution, which has as its special function the prevention of desecration of the nation's flag. At Virginia, this county, the town named in her honor, Mrs. Dalbey has erected a most modern and attractive hotel, known as the Virginia Inn, and at Lewiston, Pawnee county, named in honor of her father, she and her mother erected the Lewiston Hall, a most modern building for general public assemblage and community use. At both Lewiston and Virginia Mrs. Dalbey donated public parks, and in 1918 she donated a site of fifteen acres at each of the towns for the new consolidated schools.

December 23, 1903, recorded the marriage of Dwight S. Dalbey to Miss Virginia Lewis, the only daughter of the late Ford Lewis, of Jerseyville, Illinois, where Mrs. Dalbey was born and reared, her early educational advantages having included those of the public schools of her native city and those of Monticello Seminary, at Godfrey, Illinois.

JOHN H. VON STEEN, a man of admirable and pronounced initiative and constructive ability, has been the primary factor in the developing of one of the largest and most important industrial and commercial enterprises of Gage county, and he is one of the most valued and influential citizens and business men of Beatrice, where he is president and treasurer of The John H. von Steen Company, a pioneer concern which controls an extensive wholesale and retail business in the handling of building material, coal, etc., besides having developed an important and prosperous industry in the manufacturing of the woven-wire fence designated as the "Beatrice Barbed Border," and also of the celebrated "Beatrice Portable Corn Cribs." Basing its operations upon large capital and most progressive policies, this company is one of the foremost of the kind in Nebraska, and it maintains four branch yards, under the following titles and at the designated locations, at other points in the state: Hallam Lumber & Coal Company, Hallam, Lancaster county; Huntley Lumber & Coal Company, Huntley, Harlan county; and The John H. von Steen Company, Bruning, Thayer county, and Strang, Fillmore county. In addition to being the founder and president of The John H. von Steen Company of Beatrice, Mr. von Steen is executive head also of the subsidiary companies just mentioned. The business of The John H. von Steen Company is widely disseminated throughout Nebraska, and the corporation handles all kinds of building material on a large scale, at both wholesale and retail.

In 1879, about two years after he had established his residence at Beatrice, John H. von Steen here engaged in the retail lumber business. The enterprise which he thus established on a very modest scale formed the nucleus around which has been developed the great business enterprise of which he is now the head. In 1892 he expanded his enterprise to include the wholesale dealing in building material, supplies, and accessories, and in 1908, under the provisions of the laws of Nebraska, The John H. von Steen Company was incorporated with a capital stock of one hundred and fifty thousand dollars, fully paid in. Under date of March 6, 1912, the company's charter was so amended as to permit its increase of authorized capital to two hundred thousand dollars, almost fully paid now. The history of the enterprise has been one of consecutive growth in scope and importance and has been marked by those legitimate and honorable commercial policies that must underlay all worthy success along such lines. Mr. von Steen has been president and treasurer of the company from the time of its incorporation and the other members of the executive corps are here designated: Clarence W. Graff, vice-president, and Sam D. Ruth, secretary. In addition to these officers the directorate of the company includes also John H. Pletscher, and Walter H. DeBolt.

John H. von Steen was born near the city of Dantzic, capital of the Prussian province of the same name, and the date of his nativity was May 15, 1852. He is a son of John H. and Johanna (Zimmerman) von Steen, who were born and reared in that same province, where the father followed the vocation of farming until 1875, when he came with his family to America. He and his wife were zealous members of the Mennonite church, the tenets of which deprecate all activities of military service, and his principal reason for leaving his native land was to avoid, in consonance with his religious views and firm personal convictions, conscription of himself and his sons for service in the German army. In 1877 John H. von Steen, Sr., established the family home at Beatrice, and here he and his wife remained as honored and valued citizens until they were summoned to the life eternal, secure in the high regard of all who knew them.

The subject of this review received in his native city excellent educational advantages, besides which he passed four years in the cities of London and Liverpool, with the primary object of familiarizing himself with the English language and business methods. He accompanied his parents to America when he was twenty-five years of age and he has resided continuously at Beatrice since 1877. Here he was employed eighteen months in the lumber yard of LePoidevin Brothers, and in 1879 he engaged independently in the retail lumber business, on part of the grounds where the Burlington Railroad station now stands. Energy, integrity, faithfulness, and broad vision insured cumulative success to the ambitious young man, and that he has wrought earnestly and well needs no further voucher than his status to-day as one of the most substantial men of affairs in this section of the state of his adoption. While thus promoting his individual advancement Mr. von Steen has at all stages been mindful of his civic responsibilities and has stood forth as a liberal and public-spirited naturalized American citizen, his course in all of the relations of life having been such that he has gained and retained the inviolable confidence and good will of his fellow men.

The political allegiance of Mr. von Steen has been given to the Prohibition party, but he is primarily and essentially a business man and has had no ambition for political activity or preferment. He was reared in the faith of the Mennonite church and has been an earnest and active member of the same from his early youth to the present time. He is one of the influential representatives of this denomination in Gage county, has for many years been a valued teacher in the Sunday school of the Mennonite church in Beatrice. He attended the general conference of the Mennonite church held in California in the summer of 1917, and incidental to his trip to the Pacific coast he, with his wife, visited the Yellow-stone National Park—an indulgence that afforded them special satisfaction, this also being true in connection with his annual vacations, which are usually given to travel for recreation.

In 1882 Mr. von Steen wedded Miss Mary McKibbin, who was born at Fishlake, Indiana, and whose death occurred in 1893, she having been a devout member of the Mennonite church. She is survived by two daughters Edith, who completed her education in Bethel College, at Newton, Kansas, and who is now the wife of Professor D. H. Richert, a member of the faculty of that institution; and Ada, who is the wife of Dr. Louis E. Penner, a representative physician and surgeon engaged in practice at Beatrice. In 1895 Mr. von Steen contracted a second marriage, when Mrs. Katie (Ruth) Hirschler became his wife, and she is now the worthy chatelaine of their beautiful home, on North Fourth street, in Beatrice.

HENRY J. TROEMPER, D. V. S.—Broad and accurate technical knowledge and marked facility in making practical application of the same have given to Dr. Troemper definite prestige as one of the able and representative exponents of the veterinary profession in this section of the state, and, with residence and professional headquarters in the city of Beatrice, he has developed a substantial and important practice, his efficient service being of special value in its direct pertinence to the large live-stock interests of this section of Nebraska. He is a young man who is an enthusiast in his profession and in connection with his widely extended professional practice he is the proprietor of the Beatrice Veterinary Hospital, a well ordered institution of the best modern facilities.

Dr. Troemper was born at Alma, Waubaunsee county, Kansas, on the 9th of December, 1883, and is a son of Christian and Ursula (Myer) Troemper, the former of whom was born at Pottsville, Pennsylvania, and the latter in Germany. Christian Troemper was a pioneer in the state of Kansas, where he entered claim to a homestead of one hundred and sixty acres, in Waubaunsee county, and where he eventually accumulated and improved a large and valuable landed estate. He still continues his activities as one of the representative agriculturists and stock-growers of that county and is an honored citizen of his community. His wife died June 7, 1917, at the age of sixty-eight years.

Reared to the sturdy discipline of the farm, Dr. Troemper early learned the lessons of practical industry, the while he made good use of the advantages afforded in the excellent public schools of his native commonwealth. In formulating plans for his future career he followed the course of his ambition by entering the Kansas City Veterinary College, after having previously been for two years a student in the State Agricultural College of Kansas, at Manhattan. During the vacation of his freshman year in the veterinary college Dr. Troemper fortified himself by practical experience gained along the line of his chosen profession, this service having been given in Kansas City. In his junior year he gave to the government efficient professional service in the work of eradicating an epidemic of scab in sheep in the state of New Mexico, his headquarters for this interval having been in the city of Albuquerque. He was graduated in the Kansas City Veterinary College as a member of the class of 1908, and in August of that year, after having thus received his degree of Doctor of Veterinary Surgery, he established his residence in Beatrice, where he has built up a large and representative practice that extends over a radius of many miles from the judicial center of Gage county. His veterinary hospital has the most approved appliances and facilities for the treatment and general care of horses, cattle and other animals, and he has made the same an institution of much value in this section of the state.

In politics Dr. Troemper is found aligned in the ranks of the Democratic party, he is affiliated with the Masonic fraternity and both he and his wife hold membership in the Methodist Episcopal church.

In 1910 was recorded the marriage of Dr. Troemper to Miss Nannie Hadinger, who was born and reared at Shickley, Fillmore county, Nebraska, and they are popular factors in the representative social activities of their home city.

GENERAL LEONARD WRIGHT COLBY was born in Cherry Valley, Ashtabula county, Ohio, August 5, 1846, the fifth son of the seven children born to Rowel and Abigail (Livingston) Colby. His parents were Americans and natives of Grafton county, New Hampshire. When he was about four years old his parents removed to a farm five miles from Freeport, Stephenson county, Illinois, where he resided until his enlistment as a private soldier in the great war of the Rebellion and his assignment to the Eighth Regiment of Illinois Volunteer Infantry, with which he served until the close of the war. He was wounded on April 9, 1865, in almost the last battle of the Civil war, and was recommended for promotion and commission for gallant and meritorious services in the charge at Fort Blakely and the siege of Mobile, Alabama, where he captured a Confederate flag. After his discharge from the Union army, in 1865, he with about fifty others from his regiment enlisted with the forces of Maximilian, serving with the rank of captain for several months, until his resignation, in December, 1865. On his return home he entered the high school at Freeport, Illinois, from which he graduated in July, 1867, with the highest honors of his class. In the fall of the same year he entered the University of Wisconsin, in the regular classical course, and he was graduated in June, 1871, with the degree of Bachelor of Arts, again taking the highest honors of his class. He was graduated also from the military and engineering courses at the same institution, obtaining the degrees of Civil Engineer and Mechanical Engineer and the recommendation for a lieutenant's commission in the United States army. During the last two years of his college course he was commissioned and served as captain of the university cadets at Madison, Wisconsin. Thereafter he was graduated from the law department of the university, with the degree of Bachelor of Laws, and in the fall of 1872 (August 22d), he came to Nebraska and opened a law office in Beatrice, being associated in business with Lynus B. Sale, a former college friend. In 1874 the University of Wisconsin conferred upon him the degree of Master of Arts. On June 25, 1875, he became associated with Alexander W. Conley in the organization of a company of state militia at Beatrice, and was commissioned first lieutenant of such company, which was designated as the Paddock Guards, in honor of United States Senator Algernon Sidney Paddock. In the summer of 1877 he was commissioned captain by the governor of Nebraska and placed in command of four companies of mounted rifles. He marched his battalion from Beatrice to Red Cloud, thence to northern Nebraska and Wyoming in pursuit of bands of marauding Indians. On his return he was commissioned captain of the Paddock Guards, which command he held until June 13, 1881, when he was commissioned colonel of the First Regiment Nebraska National Guard. He had command of the Nebraska state troops and six companies of United States regulars during the labor strike in Omaha in March, 1882, at which time the city was placed under martial law; he was re-commissioned colonel July 10, 1884, and before the end of his term, on April 11, 1887, was promoted, by appointment and commission, to brigadier general and placed in command of the First Brigade, comprising two infantry regiments, a troop of cavalry, and a battery of artillery. On April 11, 1890, his commission as brigadier general was renewed for another term of three years.

During the winter of 1890-1891 General Colby and his command were called into active service on the occasion of the uprising of the Sioux Indians of Pine Ridge and other agencies in South Dakota and Nebraska. The command took part with great credit in the engagement at Wounded Knee and many skirmishes along the borders of the Bad Lands, where the hostile Indians were located, and won the congratulations of Major General Nelson A. Miles, of the United States army, who complimented General Colby on his successful management of the Nebraska troops. On his return home General Colby was presented with a gold medal for "gallant and efficient services rendered the state of Nebraska." The fourth day after the battle of Wounded

Knee, when the detail went out to bury the dead, an Indian baby girl about four months old was found on the battlefield, tied, in the usual fashion, on her dead mother's back, and found under a covering of snow. Her head, hands, and feet were frozen in the severe storm that followed the battle, but under proper care she fully recovered. The child was taken by General Colby to his home, was given the Christian name of Margaret Elizabeth, and the Indian name of Zintkala Nuni meaning in the Sioux language "Lost Bird." She was reared and educated at his home, being given all the advantages of civilization.

April 10, 1893, General Colby was for the third time commissioned brigadier general of the Nebraska state troops, and in July of the following year his command was again called into active service, in the suppression of the strike at the packing houses in South Omaha, where order was restored without damage or casualty. In December, 1896, during the progress of the Cuban revolution against Spain, General Colby commenced the organization of the American-Cuban Volunteer Legion, and in the following year he completed the enrollment of twenty-five thousand American volunteers, with headquarters at Matamoras, Mexico, and raised one million two hundred thousand dollars for the establishment of the Cuban republic. Upon the destruction of the battleship Maine, in Havana harbor, he tendered the services of the Cuban Legion in the approaching war between the United States and Spain. General Colby was commissioned June 3, 1898, by President McKinley, as brigadier general of United States Volunteers; he was first assigned to the command of the Third Brigade, First Division, Third Army Corps, stationed at Chickamauga Park, Ga.; for some weeks he had command of the First Division of the Third Army Corps, and was the ranking general in command at the time of the great review at that camp. He was afterward given command of the Second Brigade, Second Division of the Fourth Army Corps, and was thereafter for some time in command of the camp and the division at Anniston, Alabama. In January, 1899, he was sent to Havana, Cuba, and upon his return to Washington, the last of February of that year, he was mustered out of the service, with the rank of brigadier general of volunteers. Upon his return to Nebraska, General Colby was appointed adjutant general of the state, which office he held from May 6, 1901, to February 20, 1903. On August 8, 1906, he was placed on the retired list, with the rank of brigadier general.

In November, 1876, General Colby was elected state senator to represent Gage and Jefferson counties, and in 1886 he was reelected to the state senate, to represent Gage county. During the latter term he introduced fifty bills of importance, of which about thirty passed the senate, and of the latter number more than half became laws. In June, 1891, General Colby was appointed by President Harrison as assistant attorney general of the United States, his duties embracing, among other important litigation, the defense of claims for damages against the government and Indian tribes. These involved over ten thousand cases in the court of claims and the United States supreme court, and over forty million dollars. Upon his retirement from the department of justice he was employed by the Creeks, Cherokees, and Seminoles, three of the civilized tribes of Indians in Indian Territory, as their attorney in Washington, D. C., and during this employment he obtained a judgment against the government and in favor of the Cherokee Nation for the sum of $6,742,000.

Since the declaration of war against the imperial government of Germany, General Colby has been active in all patriotic and war measures in the interest of winning such war. At the commencement he tendered his services to the United States and to the state of Nebraska and requested to be recalled from the retired list into active service. He has been placed on the list of officers subject to call by the war department, and, having the personal assurance of Secretary of War Baker that his services will be required in the near future, he has passed his physical examination for such service. In the meantime he has served as government agent and attorney for the draft board, as chairman of the Gage County Council of Defense, as a member of the War Works Committee, and has taken an active part in the campaigns for the several Liberty Loans, the Red Cross and Y. M. C. A. drives in the county and district.

General Colby has had a law office at Beatrice and been engaged in the practice of his profession in the several courts of the states and nation and has maintained his residence at Beatrice during all of the years since his location in the state in August, 1872. He is a member of the Society of Foreign Wars, Loyal Legion, Grand Army of the Republic, Spanish-American War Veterans, Aero League and Naval League of the United States, the Blue Lodge and Royal Arch Masons, the Red Men, Knights of Pythias, Nebraska State Historical Society, Nebraska Pioneers, the Nebraska and American Bar Associations, the Republican Club, and the Christian church at Beatrice.

Marie Möller Colby, wife of General Leonard Wright Colby, was born in Robel, Mecklenburg-Schwerin, Germany, and is a daughter of

John F. Moller and Marie Henrietta (Muller) Moller, both being of pure German stock, and of long established and well known families in the fatherland. The parents left their old German home on account of political oppression and came to the United States to enjoy the blessings of a free government, arriving in Lancaster county, Nebraska, in April, 1875, and locating on a farm three miles west of Firth. Six years later they moved to Roca, and on April 1, 1882, they removed to Beatrice, which has since been the family home. Mrs. Colby is the second of seven children, all of whom are living.

Yours Cordially,
Marie Möller Colby

Mrs. Colby was educated in the public schools of Beatrice and at the Western Normal College at Lincoln, and later took a course in the Academy of Fine Arts in Philadelphia. She has added to her general knowledge by systematic courses of reading, a Chautauqua course, travel in this country, Canada, Cuba, and Mexico and by thorough business training. She is a member of several social organizations and clubs of the city, and in addition to attending to her many business interests has time for church and social work, and to assist her husband in his many duties as well as manage her domestic affairs and care for her attractive home.

THOMAS LePOIDEVIN.—This venerable citizen of Gage county is now living retired in the city of Beatrice, the prosperity that is his representing the results of his use of the advantages that have been afforded with the development of the natural resources of this favored section of the state, he having come to Gage county shortly before the admission of the state to the Union and having become one of the pioneer representatives of agricultural industry in Midland township. As a sterling citizen who has contributed generously to the material upbuilding of Gage county, he is entitled to recognition in this history.

As his name indicates, Mr. LePoidevin is of French lineage, and he was born on the beautiful island of Guernsey, in the English channel, on the 25th of March, 1840, the eldest of the seven children of Job and Rachel LePoidevin, both of whom were born on the island of Guernsey, descendants of old and honored families of that island, many of the inhabitants of which still speak the old Norman French language. John, the second son, is a resident of Odell, Gage county; Rachel died at the old home on the island of Guernsey; Joseph is a resident of the state of New York; Amelia is living on the island of Guernsey; Alfred is a resident of New York state; and Alice died on the island of Guernsey, where the parents passed their entire lives. In the schools of his native island Thomas received his limited educational training in his youth, and it later became his to profit by the lessons gained and under the direction of that wisest of all teachers, experience. Within the reign of Queen Victoria of England he served seven years, in the English militia, and this experience is one to which he often reverts with special satisfaction now that England and France have become allied in fighting for humanity in the greatest war in the annals of history, for he feels a natural and inherent loyalty to both England and France.

In 1863, at the age of twenty-three years, Mr. LePoidevin came to the United States. Within a short time after arriving in the port of New York city he made his way to Racine county, Wisconsin, where he found employment at farm work. He continued his residence in the Badger state until 1866, when he came to Nebraska Territory and entered claim to a homestead of one hundred and sixty acres, in what is now Midland township, Gage county. He forthwith began with vigor the work of reclaiming and developing his pioneer farm, and the first dwelling which he there erected was a modest house constructed of rough lumber from the native cottonwood timber, the little home being fourteen by sixteen feet and one and one-half stories in height,—a home superior to those of the average pioneers of the county, many of whom used primitive dugouts and sod houses. As prosperity attended his efforts Mr. LePoidevin made gradual improvements on his farm, to which he added by the purchase of an adjoining tract of eighty acres, and be provided a substantial and commodious house as the home for his family. In his pioneer experiences he relates that he cut his first crop of wheat with an old-time cradle, and that in those early days there were but two threshing machines in the entire county. He took a great interest in the movement which brought statehood to Nebraska and gave his help in other enterprises for the general good of the community. With the passing years he developed one of the valuable farms of Gage county, where he still retains ownership of a fine estate of two hundred and forty acres, well improved. He remained on his old homestead until 1903, when he removed to the city of Beatrice, where, still hale and vigorous, he and his devoted wife are enjoying the rewards of former years of earnest toil and endeavor, and where they are known and honored as venerable pioneer citizens of the county. Both are earnest members of the Christian church and he is a Republican in politics. He has never sought public office but while residing on his farm he served for a number of years as school director for his district.

On the 5th of December, 1867, he married Miss Teanna Tanner, who was born in the fair little republic of Switzerland, on January 16,

1847, and who was about eight years old when her parents, John and Babette Tanner, came to America and established their home at Etna, Licking county, Ohio. From that state they came to Nebraska in the year 1867, and the father obtained a homestead of one hundred and sixty acres, east of Beatrice, both he and his wife having passed the remainder of their lives in this county and their names having a place on the roll of the pioneers of this section of the state. Mr. and Mrs. LePoidevin became the parents of ten children, and it is most gratifying to record that death has never yet invaded the family circle. In conclusion is given brief record concerning the children: Adelia is the wife of Lincoln Thornburg, a successful farmer of Midland township; Almeda is the wife of Edward Essam, living five miles east of Beatrice; John is a prosperous farmer in Rockford township; Bertha, who resides at Beatrice, is the widow of Hanford Chase; Mabel is the wife of Merl Hughes, of this county; Ezra is a successful farmer and resides eight miles north of Beatrice; Charles is a representative exponent of agricultural industry in Midland township; and Marie, Josephine and Ceba remain at the parental home,—an attractive residence at 522 South Ninth street, Beatrice.

JOHN S. JONES has been a resident of Gage county since his childhood and has here, in his mature years, found ample opportunity for the achieving of success worthy of the name. Here he has been closely identified with banking enterprise during the entire course of his active business career, and of the same he is now a prominent representative in the county. He holds the position of cashier of the First National Bank of Wymore, which is recognized as one of the leading financial institutions of Gage county, and to the advancement of the interests of which his careful and progressive administrative policies have largely contributed. Mr. Jones is essentially one of the representative citizens and business men of the thriving little city of Wymore and is properly accorded consideration in this history, a publication on whose advisory board he has served during the period of compilation.

John S. Jones was born on a farm near Williamsburg, Iowa, and the date of his nativity was August 3, 1877. He is a son of John S. and Ann S. (Lloyd) Jones, both natives of Wales and representatives of staunch old families of that portion of the great British empire. John S. Jones, Sr., was born in Wales in September, 1844, a son of Thomas Jones, and in his native land he was reared and educated. As a youth he became associated with the great coal-mining industry in Wales, and he was twenty-seven years of age when he came to the United States. His prior experience readily gained to him employment in coal mines in Pennsylvania, but after remaining about two years in the old Keystone state he removed to Iowa county, Iowa, and turned his attention to farm enterprise, in the vicinity of Williamsburg. There he continued operations along this line for a period of four years, and he then, in 1881, came with his family to Gage county, Nebraska, and established his residence on a farm four miles south of Wymore. There he gave his active supervision to the work and improvement of his farm until the time of his death, which occurred July 10, 1888. His marriage to Miss Ann S. Lloyd, daughter of John and Elizabeth Lloyd, was solemnized in Wales and his young wife accompanied him on his immigration to America; she is still living and resides with her youngest daughter, at Wymore. John S. and Ann S. (Lloyd) Jones became the parents of eight children, all of whom are now married and well established in life, all save the eldest of the number having been born after the family home was established in the United States. The names of the children are here noted in the respective order of birth: Elizabeth, Sarah Ann, Maggie, John S., Jr., Mary Ella, Robert V., Edith, and Luther Ellis.

John S. Jones, Jr., the immediate subject of this review, was about four years old at the time of the family removal to Gage county, and here he has since maintained his home. He was but ten years of age at the time of his father's death and as he was the eldest son large responsibilities thus early fell upon him in connection with the work and management of the home farm. He was associated with his devoted mother in carrying forward the activities of the farm until he had attained to the age of twenty-four years, his educational advantages in the meanwhile having been those of the district schools and of the high school at Wymore, where he was a student two years. Upon leaving the farm Mr. Jones assigned its management to his brother Robert and became bookkeeper in the First National Bank of Wymore. One year later he was tendered and accepted the position of assistant cashier of the newly organized State Bank of Wymore, of which he was made cashier two years later. In 1907 this well ordered institution received charter as a national bank and was incorporated with a capital stock of fifty thousand dollars. Mr. Jones continued as cashier of the bank until its building was destroyed by fire, in 1910, and in that year its stockholders and directors made a move of distinctive expediency and wisdom, in purchasing the stock and business of the First National Bank. Upon the consolidation of the two institutions the title of First National Bank of Wymore was retained, and Mr. Jones has continued as cashier of the vital and substantial institution to the present time. The bank bases its operations on a capital stock of fifty thousand dollars, its surplus fund is ten thousand dollars and its deposits are now in excess of six hundred and fifty thousand dollars.

Mr. Jones is loyal and progressive as a citizen and is always ready to given his co-operation in the furtherance of projects advanced for the general good of his home city and county. In politics he is found staunchly aligned in the ranks of the Republican party, and he and his wife are active members of the Methodist Episcopal church of Wymore. Mr. Jones is affiliated with Wymore Lodge, Ancient Free & Accepted Masons, of which he is past master; with Hiram Chapter, Royal Arch Masons, of which he is past high priest, and with Mount Herman Commandery, Knights Templars, in the city of Beatrice, besides which he holds membership in Sesotris Temple of the Mystic Shrine, in the city of Lincoln, and in Violet Chapter, Order of the Eastern Star at Wymore, of which latter he is serving as worthy patron in 1918, his wife being likewise affiliated with this chapter. Mr. Jones takes specially deep interest in educational affairs and is serving at the time of this writing as president of the Wymore board of education.

On the 28th of June, 1905 was solemnized the marriage of Mr. Jones to Miss Mary Elizabeth Roberts, who was born near Iowa City, Iowa, on the 9th of January, 1878, her parents soon afterward coming to Gage county, Nebraska, where they still maintain their home. The names and respective dates of birth of the three children of Mr. and Mrs. Jones are here entered: Gordon John, October 12, 1908; Eleanor May, May 19, 1911; and Dwight, July 4, 1914.

In connection with the nation's participation in the great world war Mr. Jones has been very active in Red Cross and Liberty Loan work, with a spirit of loyalty that prompts him to give to the government and its gallant military and naval forces every possible assistance.

SIMON B. HARTZELL, a progressive farmer of Rockford township, was born March 21, 1879, and was an infant at the time when his parents established their home in Gage county. He is a son of Eli E. Hartzell, who is now living retired at Holmesville, this county. Eli E. Hartzell was born in Mahoning county, Ohio, March 19, 1837, and his parents, George and Jane (Smart) Hartzell, who were born and reared in Pennsylvania, removed in an early day from the old Keystone state to Ohio. Eli E. Hartzell received in his youth the advantages of the common schools and as a young man he went to Indiana, where he engaged in the lumber business. Later he resided, for intervals of varying duration, in Michigan, Kentucky, Ohio, and Pennsylvania, and in 1881 he came with his family to Gage county, Nebraska. He settled in Riverside township, and there he continued his successful activities as a farmer for fully twenty years. Several years ago he removed to Arkansas, but after remaining there a short time he returned to Gage county, where he has since lived virtually retired and where he now maintains his home at Holmesville. His wife, whose maiden name was Miralda Quigley and who was a resident of Mahoning county, Ohio, at the time of their marriage, was born December 13, 1840, a daughter of Dr. Quigley, her father having been a physician and having been engaged in the practice of his profession in Ohio for more than half a century. Eli E. and Miralda Hartzell became the parents of seven children: Willis is deceased; Rush and Jay are engaged in farm enterprise in Nemaha township, this county; Homer is a resident of Portland, Oregon; Mary, who became the wife of Rev. Gustave Briegleb, is deceased; Simon Bert, of this review, was the next in order of birth; Harry is a physician and surgeon by profession and is engaged in practice at Eldorado, Kansas.

Eli E. Hartzell, who has passed the age of four score years, is one of the venerable and highly honored citizens of Gage county, and is a man of broad mental grasp, a citizen who has been loyal in all of the relations of life. His religious faith is that of the Methodist Episcopal church.

Simon Bert Hartzell gained his early education in the schools of Gage county, including the public schools of the city of Beatrice, and his initial activities as an independent farmer were conducted on land owned by his father. Later he was engaged for eleven years in the operation of a farm in Hanover township, under a Scully lease, and three years ago he purchased his present fine farm, in Rockford township, the same comprising two hundred acres. When he purchased the property it was not provided with buildings, as those formerly on the place had been swept away by a cyclone, a few years previously, the disaster being the more malign by reason of the fact that on the farm two persons were killed at the time. Mr. Hartzell erected a good house on the farm and also provided a modern barn and other requisite farm buildings. He gives his attention to diversified agriculture, raises and feeds cattle for the market and is proving successful in all departments of his vigorous farm enterprise.

Mr. Hartzell married Miss Jewell Hickman, who was born in Macoupin county, Illinois, and who is a daughter of the late J. T. and Sarah (Piper) Hickman. Mr. and Mrs. Hartzell have four children— Ruth, Blanche, Simon B., Jr., and Raymond.

Mr. Hartzell is a member of the school board of his district and he and his wife hold membership in the Methodist church.

DAVID GRAF has been a resident of Gage county since 1875 and for more than forty years he and his wife have maintained their home on their present farm, in Section 4, Midland township. His sons now have the active management of his extensive farm estate and he and his wife are, under most gracious environment and associations, enjoying the generous prosperity and comfort that properly crown their former years of earnest endeavor—sterling pioneer citizens to whom is accorded the fullest measure of popular esteem.

David Graf was born on his father's farm in Northville township, LaSalle county, Illinois, September 27, 1845, the second in order of birth in a family of six sons and four daughters, and of the number seven are still living. The honored father, Samuel Graf, was born and reared in the fair little republic of Switzerland and was a young man when he came to America and in the state of Pennsylvania found employment at his trade, that of tailor. In Somerset county, that state, was solemnized his marriage to Miss Louise Anna Parker, and about the year 1833 they numbered themselves among the pioneer settlers of La Salle county, Illinois. There Mr. Graf reclaimed and improved one of the excellent farms of Northville township, and upon this homestead he and his wife passed the remainder of their lives, he having passed away in 1876, at the age of seventy-five years, and his widow having been one hundred years of age at the time of her death, which occurred in October, 1916. Both were zealous members of the Presbyterian church.

DAVID GRAF

David Graf was reinforced for his later service through the experience he gained on the old homestead farm in Illinois, where his early educational advantages were those afforded in the district schools of his native county. There he continued his active association with farm enterprise until he had attained to the age of twenty-seven years, when he found employment as a farm hand, working by the month. In 1875 he came to Gage county, where his father had purchased for the sons six eighty-acre tracts of land, and on one of these tracts, east of Beatrice, the subject of this sketch initiated his independent activities as a farmer. The following year he purchased his present homestead place of one hundred and sixty acres, in Section 4, Midland township, where he and his gracious wife have continuously maintained their residence during the long intervening years, which have been marked by constantly increasing prosperity, won through earnest and honest endeavor on their part. On the place the original home of the family was a frame shanty that had been erected by the previous owner, Andrew J. Pethoud, who was one of the earliest settlers of the county and did much important surveying work in the early days. This primitive house continued as the Graf abode for fifteen years, and then removal was made to the commodious and attractive frame house which Mr. and Mrs. Graf now occupy, the buildings which he has erected on his farm property being among the finest in the township and being kept in the best of repair—a fitting token of thrift and prosperity. Mr. Graf is now the owner of a fine landed estate of two hundred acres and his wife owns farm property of equal area in the same township. Vigorous and progressive policies always marked the activities of Mr. Graf as an agriculturist and stockgrower, and the principles which he thus inculcated in his sons have caused them to follow with equal efficiency the same policies in their management of the fine estate owned by him and his wife.

In LaSalle county, Illinois, March 3, 1875, recorded the marriage of Mr. Graf to Miss Adeline Hazemann, who was there born March 25, 1856, her parents, Jonathan G. and Amelia (Smith) Hazemann, having been natives of France and having become pioneer settlers of LaSalle county, Illinois, where they passed the residue of their lives. Mr. and Mrs. Graf have four children: Alpha D. and John G. remain with their parents and have the active management of the home farm; Clarence D., who is a successful farmer in Filley township, married Miss Elizabeth Jensen and they have three children; Fordyce H., the maiden name of whose wife was Hazel Burket, is serving, in 1917-1918, as city clerk of Beatrice, judicial center of the county.

MRS. DAVID GRAF

Mr. Graf has been distinctively the supporter of civic and industrial progress and development in Gage county and while he has shown loyal interest in community affairs and given staunch support to the cause of the Democratic party he has never consented to serve in official positions other than those of road supervisor and school director. He and his wife are earnest members of the Reorganized Church of Latter Day Saints, and they are genial and kindly pioneer citizens whose circle of friends in Gage county is limited only by that of their acquaintances.

GEORGE HUNKLE, secretary and manager of the Farmers' Elevator Company, at Holmesville, in Rockford township, is one of the leading exponents of the grain business in this part of the county and is held in high esteem in the county that has represented his home for more than thirty years. He was born in the state of New York, June 1, 1876, and as he was left an orphan in early childhood he has no definite information concerning the family history. He was placed in an orphans' home in New York city, and when nine years of age he was sent with other boys from that institution to Nebraska, where he became a member of the family circle of William Woolsey, a farmer in Lincoln township, Gage county. Here he was reared to manhood and received the advantages of the local schools. He remained with his foster-parents until he had attained to his legal majority and for some time thereafter he was independently engaged in farm enterprise in Lincoln township. He then went to the village of Ellis, where he learned the trade of telegraphist, and after having been employed as an operator at Jansen and Plymouth, Nebraska, he returned to Ellis, Gage county, and engaged in the grain business. In December, 1901, he was made manager of the firm's business and of this position he continued the incumbent until the business was sold to Black Brothers, with whom he continued in a similar capacity, at Holmesville, until they sold their elevator and business to the Farmers' Elevator Company, in 1913, since which time he has given most efficient service as secretary and manager of this company. Mr. Hunkle is a Republican in politics, and is affiliated with the Ellis Lodge of the Independent Order of Odd Fellows, as is he also with Beatrice Lodge of the Benevolent & Protective Order of Elks.

In 1912 Mr. Hunkle wedded Miss Fannie Lemmel, who was born in Saline county, this state, a daughter of Philip and Eliza Lemmel, the former of whom is deceased and the latter of whom now resides in the city of Beatrice. Mr. and Mrs. Hunkle have a fine little son, Donald G.

CHARLES J. McCOLL has been a resident of Gage county since 1888 and in the city of Beatrice he has long controlled a substantial and representative business as a skilled painter and paperhanger, his pleasant home being at 225 North LaSelle street. A scion of the staunchest of Scottish ancestry, Mr. McColl was born in Argyleshire, Scotland, on the 13th of August, 1852, a son of James and Mary (McGinness) McColl, who the next year, 1853, immigrated to America and established their home in York county, Province of Ontario, Canada, where the father became the owner of a small farm and where he and his wife passed the residue of their lives. Of their eleven children the subject of this review is now the only survivor. After the death of James McColl his widow engaged in the dairy business, and by her energy and ability she made the enterprise distinctly successful. Both were members of the Presbyterian church.

Reared to adult age in York county, Ontario, Charles J. McColl received in his youth but limited educational advantages, but in connection with the practical affairs of life he has effectively made good this handicap. In the city of Toronto he learned in his youth the trade of painting and graining, and after there following his trade for a number of years he decided to identify himself with the progressive western section of the United States. On the 1st of May, 1888, he arrived in the city of Beatrice, and here he has since continued his residence, the while he has been consecutively engaged in business as a painter and paperhanger, in which field of enterprise he has built up a prosperous business that makes him one of the leading exponents of the same in the judicial center and metropolis of Gage county.

March 6, 1881, recorded the marriage of Mr. McColl to Miss Susan Bates, who was born in Huron county, Ontario, Canada, a daughter of Thomas and Susan (Sterling) Bates, the former a native of Ireland and the latter of Scotland. In Canada Mr. Bates followed the trade of plasterer and there both he and his wife continued to reside until their death. Mr. and Mrs. McColl became the parents of three children: Ethel died at the age of twenty-three years; Eva is a popular teacher in the Central school in the city of Beatrice, and Mary is an efficient teacher in the high school at Shickley, Nebraska. Mrs. McColl and her daughters are members of the Presbyterian church.

Mr. McColl is affiliated with the Knights & Ladies of Security, the Order of Ancient Foresters, and the Ancient Order of Shepherds, in each of which he has passed all of the official chairs. In politics he has been a staunch Republican during the entire period of his residence as a naturalized citizen in the United States, and he has been influential in political affairs in Gage county. While a resident of St. Thomas, Canada, he served as a member of the city council, and this experience gave him special resourcefulness when he was called upon to give similar service as a member of the city council of Beatrice. His ability and popularity marked him as an eligible candidate for higher official preferment, and in 1908 he was elected representative of Gage county in the Nebraska legislature, in which he served one term. Though the lower house of the legislature was strongly Democratic, Mr. McColl proved a strong minority leader and was assigned to various important committees, including those on public lands and buildings, towns and cities, and labor and insurance.

JACOB ESSAM has been a resident of Gage county since he was a youth of eighteen years and by his well ordered industry and enterprise has gained secure vantage-place as one of the representative farmers of Midland township, where he is the owner of a well improved farm property of four hundred acres, his attractive homestead place being situated in Section 24, on rural mail route No. 3 from the city of Beatrice, which is about four and one-half miles distant.

Mr. Essam was born in Schuyler county, Illinois, May 10, 1863, was there reared on his father's farm and there acquired his early education in the district schools. He is a son of James and Susanna (Fitz) Essam, both natives of York county, Pennsylvania, where the former was born April 8, 1834, and the latter on the 12th of May, 1840. James Essam was a young man when he removed from the old Keystone state and settled in Illinois, where his activities as a farmer were carried on first in Fulton and later in Schuyler county. In 1880 he disposed of his property in Illinois and came with his family to Gage county, where he purchased one hundred and sixty acres of land, in Logan township. He improved one of the excellent farms of the county and continued to reside on the old homestead until his death, which occurred August

22, 1902, his widow having been summoned to the life eternal on the 5th of May, 1909. Both were earnest members of the Dunkard church and exemplified their faith in their daily lives, their names meriting enduring place on the roster of the honored pioneers of Gage county. Of their eight children the firstborn is Henry, who is a prosperous farmer in Riverside township; Jacob, of this review, was the next in order of birth; Mary is the wife of James Canning and they reside in the state of Kansas; Edward is a successful farmer in Logan township; Miss Rebecca resides in the city of Beatrice, and is the homekeeper for her bachelor brother, John, the next younger of the children; Charles likewise resides in Beatrice; and Harvey resides upon and operates his father's old home farm, in Logan township.

As previously intimated, Jacob Essam was a youth of eighteen years when he accompanied his parents to Gage county, and for some time thereafter he was employed by the month at farm work, his compensation being twelve and one-half dollars a month. For several years he farmed on rented land and it was about twenty-five years ago that he purchased one hundred and sixty acres, the old homestead of his father-in-law, in Midland township. This proved to be the nucleus of the large and valuable landed estate of four hundred acres which he has since accumulated through his energetic and well directed activities as an agriculturist and stock-raiser, and he has made many permanent improvements of excellent order on his property, including the rebuilding and remodeling of the house on his homestead and the erection of other farm buildings of model type and facilities. Mr. Essam is one of the substantial and popular citizens of Midland township, where he has served fifteen years in the office of township treasurer and for many years as a member of the school board of his district. He is independent of strict partisan lines in politics and gives his support to men and measures meeting the approval of his judgment. His wife is an active member of the Christian church.

February 14, 1880, recorded the marriage of Mr. Essam to Miss Mary E. Bartram, who was born in Macoupin county, Illinois, a daughter of William and Mary Bartram, with whom she came to Gage county, Nebraska, in 1878, her parents settling on the farm which is now the homestead of Mr. and Mrs. Essam, both having here passed the remainder of their lives and Mr. Essam having purchased the farm at the time when the property was placed on sale in the final adjustment of the estate. Mr. and Mrs. Essam have four children: James, the maiden name of whose wife was Esta Doan, is a prosperous farmer in Midland township; Bessie is the wife of Ezra LePoidevin, a farmer in Holt township; Evart remains at the parental home and is associated with his father in the work and management of the farm; and Gilbert, who married Miss Pearl Bible, is one of the progressive young farmers of Midland township.

JOHN W. BURGESS, treasurer of the Dempster Mill Manufacturing Company, which is the most important industrial corporation not only in the city of Beatrice but also in Gage county, has been for more than thirty years actively and prominently identified with the civic and business affairs in Beatrice and he is properly accorded recognition in this history.

John Warren Burgess was born in Cook county, Illinois, on the 3d of November, 1865, and is a son of Eli and Marietta (Childs) Burgess, who were born in Saratoga county, New York. Their marriage was solemnized in the old Empire state and thence they removed to Cook county, Illinois, prior to the Civil war. Eli Burgess was a man of staunch character and of much intellectual ability. In the earlier period of his career he was a successful teacher in the public schools and thereafter he was engaged in the mercantile business for some time. He became a farmer near Dundee, Illinois, and finally removed from the farm to that village, where he continued to be engaged in mercantile enterprise until his death, his wife also having there passed the closing years of her life. They became the parents of four sons, of whom the eldest is Edwin A., a civil engineer by profession and a resident of the city of Chicago; Arthur C. still resides at Dundee, Illinois, where he is a representative business man; William E. is deceased; and John W., of this review, is the youngest of the number.

The lineage of the Burgess family traces back to Welsh origin and the Childs family was one of early settlement in the state of New York, where members of the family married representatives of the fine old Van

Tassell family, whose name is linked with the founding of the early Holland Dutch colonies in the Empire state.

The early educational advantages of John W. Burgess were those afforded in the public schools of his native state, and after having attended the high school at Dundee he was for one year a student in Wheaton College, at Wheaton, Illinois, after which he completed a normal course in what is now Valparaiso University, at Valparaiso, Indiana. As a representative of the pedagogic profession he taught in the public schools of Henry and Kane counties, Illinois, besides which he gave effective service in the office of superintendent of schools for the latter county.

In the autumn of 1887 Mr. Burgess came to Beatrice, Nebraska, where he has since been actively associated with the Dempster Mill Manufacturing Company, of which he is a stockholder and director and of which he has served long and effectively as treasurer. He has done much to further the upbuilding of this large and important industrial corporation and as a citizen has shown marked loyalty and progressiveness. He and his wife hold membership in the Presbyterian church.

In December, 1891, was solemnized the marriage of Mr. Burgess to Miss Sarah E. Dempster, who, like her husband, was graduated in the institution now known as Valparaiso University. Mr. and Mrs. Burgess have three sons: Warren C., who is a graduate of the University of Colorado, is now in the employ of the Westinghouse Electrical Manufacturing Company; Harold D. is a student, in 1918, in the University of Kansas; and John Paul is a student in the Beatrice high school.

JOHN I. McGIRR, M. D.—In promoting general efficiency along all lines of human endeavor there has come in these later years a distinct recognition of the supreme value of concentration of effort, and this is specially true in the medical profession, in which exponents find the maximum success and are able to give the most benignant service through devoting their attention to perfecting themselves and exploiting special departments of practice. In Gage county Dr. McGirr has gained exceptional prestige by such concentration and he gives his time and attention primarily to the diagnosis and treatment of diseases of the eye, ear, nose, and throat. He maintains his residence and professional head quarters in the city of Beatrice and is known, through his character and high professional attainments, as one of the representative physicians and surgeons of this part of the state.

Dr. McGirr was born at Reddick, Kankakee county, Illinois, on the 23d of March, 1873, and in his native commonwealth he received his rudimentary education, his age at the time of the family removal to Nebraska having been twelve years. The Doctor is a son of Francis M. and Judith (Barkey) McGirr, the former of whom was born in the fair Old Emerald Isle, a scion of a family of patrician antecedents and superior educational status, and the latter of whom was born in the state of Pennsylvania, their marriage having been solemnized in the state of Illinois. Francis M. McGirr was reared and educated in his native land, where he received excellent advantages, his father, Joseph McGirr, who continued to maintain his home in Ireland until his death, at the venerable age of eighty-five years, having been a man of fine intellectuality and having served many years as a schoolmaster, in which connection it may be noted that he spoke and taught eight different languages. Francis M. McGirr was a young man when he came to the United States and that his loyalty to the land of his adoption was of perfervid order needs no further voucher than the statement that he went forth as a valiant soldier of the Union in the Civil war, in which conflict he served three years, as a member of Battery K, First Illinois Light Artillery. During his later years of residence in Nebraska he perpetuated the more gracious memories of his military career through affiliation with the Grand Army of the Republic, and in all of the relations of life he exemplified the same instinctive loyalty and high sense of personal stewardship that prompted him thus to defend in his young manhood the righteous cause through which was perpetuated our national integrity. His wife was a girl at the time of her parents' removal from the old Keystone state to Illinois, where she was reared and educated, her father, the late Enos Barkey, having finally removed with his family to Nebraska and become one of the early settlers of Gage county, where he was a prosperous farmer and where he and his wife passed the residue of their lives.

After the close of the Civil war Francis M. McGirr engaged in farming in Kankakee county, Illinois, and in that state he remained until 1885, when he came with his family to Nebraska and purchased land in Gage county. Here he developed one of the valuable farms of the county and he continued to reside upon his old homestead until 1901, when he removed to the city of Beatrice, his death having here occurred in 1905, and his widow having passed to eternal rest in 1913. Mr. McGirr was one of the honored and influential citizens of Gage county, a man of broad mental ken and well fortified convictions, and he commanded the unequivocal respect of his fellow men. He was reared in and ever held to the faith of the Catholic church, and his wife was a member of the Mennonite church. They are survived by four children: Edward B. is successfully engaged in the real estate business at Beatrice; Frederick O. is engaged in the practice of his profession at Beatrice, as a representative member of the Gage county bar, and is serving, 1917-1918, in the office of supreme court commissioner; Dr. McGirr, of this review, was the next in order of birth; and Virgil E. is a retired farmer residing in Beatrice: he served as deputy sheriff of Gage county and for several terms as chief of police of Beatrice.

As previously stated, Dr. McGirr was a lad of twelve years at the time of the family removal to Nebraska, and he was reared to maturity in Gage county, where he continued to attend the public schools until he had profited by the advantages of the Beatrice high school. Thereafter he pursued higher academic studies in Western Normal College, in the city of Lincoln, and in preparation for the work of his chosen profession he went to the city of Omaha, where he was matriculated in the medical department of the University of Nebraska. Here he completed the prescribed curriculum and was graduated as a member of the class of 1897. After thus receiving his coveted degree of Doctor of Medicine he engaged in the general practice of his profession at Ellis, Gage county, where he remained three years. In the meanwhile he determined that he could expand his field of service and usefulness by devoting himself to special phases of professional work, and to fortify himself properly for such service he took effective post-graduate work in a leading medical school of New York city and later in one of the important institutions in

Vienna, Austria. In each of these connections he gave special attention to study and clinical work pertaining to the diseases of the eye, ear, nose, and throat, and in 1901 he established his residence in the city of Beatrice, where he now gives his close and efficient attention to his special domain of practice, in which he has gained repute as one of the leading eye, ear, nose, and throat specialists in this section of the state, so that his practice is derived in appreciable part from points outside of local environs. The Doctor controls a large and representative practice, keeps in close touch with the advances made in medical and surgical science and is unremitting in his study of the best standard and periodical literature of his profession. He holds membership in the American Medical Association and is one of the active and valued members of the Nebraska State Medical Society, of which he has served as vice-president, and of the Gage County Medical Society, of which he was formerly secretary. The Doctor owns his attractive residence property in the city of Beatrice and also a valuable farm near Pickrell, this county. As a broad-gauged and progressive citizen he gives his cooperation in the furtherance of measures and enterprises tending to conserve the communal welfare, and his political allegiance is accorded to the Democratic party. He is prominently identified with the Independent Order of Odd Fellows, in which he is affiliated with both the local and encampment bodies, as well as with the auxiliary organization, the Daughters of Rebekah, and he is past grand of Beatrice Lodge, No. 187, of the Odd Fellows, besides having represented the same as a delegate to the grand lodge of Nebraska. He gives liberal support to the Baptist church of Beatrice, of which his wife is an active member.

In June, 1915, was solemnized the marriage of Dr. McGirr to Miss Myrtle Gue, who was born and reared at York, the judicial center of the Nebraska county of the same name, and the one child of this union is a son—John I., Jr., born November 6, 1916.

JOHN PETHOUD.—Ten years prior to the time when the Territory of Nebraska was transformed into a new state of the Union the late John Pethoud became a pioneer of what is now Gage county, and his was the distinction of turning the first furrow that was ever plowed on Gage county soil. A man of superior intellectuality and dauntless spirit, Judge Pethoud represented the finest type of pioneer, and it was his to wield large and benignant influence in the formative period of the history of southeastern Nebraska. This publication exercises a most consistent function when it accords a tribute to his memory.

John Pethoud was of French ancestry and was born in Lawrence county, Ohio, in August, 1798, the place of his nativity having been a tract of land that had been a French grant to the Pethoud family. His parents were called upon to meet the trials and hardships incidental to the pioneer period in the history of the old Buckeye state, and there he was reared to manhood, his early educational advantages having been limited, as a matter of course, but his alert mind and broad intellectual grasp having eventually made him a man of exceptional mentality and mature judgment. In his native state he became familiarly known as Esquire Pethoud, doubtless owing to the fact of his having served in the office of justice of the peace.

In 1857, in company with Edward Austin and H. J. Pierce, Judge Pethoud set forth for the wilds of Nebraska Territory. The three venturesome pioneers made the journey down the Ohio river and up the Mississippi and Missouri rivers by boat and upon arriving at some point near the Nebraska line, they bought ox teams and wagons, with which they continued their way to what is now Gage county. Within the limits of the county as then existing Judge Pethoud entered a preemption claim, for which he paid two hundred dollars. Gage and old Clay counties then lay contiguous and he built his modest frontier house on the Gage county side of the line, thus becoming the first settler in Gage county as then constituted. The land which he thus obtained from the government is now owned by David Graf and lies in Midland township. On this pioneer farm Judge Pethoud continued to reside until his death, which occurred September 5, 1883, after he had attained to the venerable age of eighty-five years. He was buried on that farm.

Judge Pethoud was a great reader and student, was well informed concerning history and current events, and though he was not specifically a professor of religion he was a deep student of the Bible, with which he was familiar from cover to cover, and he had an abiding appreciation of the spiritual verities of the Christian faith. He was a man of strong convictions and prejudices, but both were usually well taken, and he guided his life according to the highest principles of integrity and honor. Though he was a resident of Gage county, he was called upon to serve as the first judge of the probate court of Clay county.

In Ohio was solemnized the marriage of Judge Pethoud to Miss Mary Thompson, who was born in Pennsylvania, and she shared with him in the experiences of life on the frontier after their home had been established in Nebraska. Concerning their children brief record is given, in conclusion of this memoir: Mrs. Cynthia Ann Blankenship was a resident of Ohio at the time of her death, which occurred more than sixty years ago; Elizabeth was the wife of John Wilson, one of the early pioneer settlers of Logan township, Gage county; Francis M. was a resident of Midland township at the time of his death, and to him a memoir is dedicated on other pages of this volume; John T. is deceased, as are also Mrs. Rebecca Jones, Andrew J., and James K. P. All of the children except the eldest became residents of Gage county and the family name is one that has been signally prominent and honored in connection with the county's history.

KIRK GRIGGS.—In Sections 30 and 31 Blakely township is situated the well improved farm estate of Kirk Griggs, the place comprising six hundred acres and being given over to diversified agriculture and stock-growing. The owner has gained special success and precedence as a breeder of Holstein cattle, Hampshire swine, and Shire horses, and has made numerous exhibitions of his fine stock at various county fairs. He is one of the most progressive stock-growers of the county that has represented his home from the time of his birth and in which his parents were pioneer settlers.

Mr. Griggs was born at Beatrice, this county, on the 8th of January, 1873, and is a son of Lewis T. and Caroline (Gale) Griggs, of whose five children he was the fourth in order of birth; Mollie is the wife of Frederick W. Daniels, of Sheridan, Oregon; George L. is a resident of the city of Alliance; Clifton C. resides at Eureka, Utah; and Burt resides at Buffalo, Wyoming. Lewis T. Griggs was born in Ohio, on the 17th of April, 1843, a son of Lucien and Mary T. (Kirk) Griggs, and in the old

Buckeye state he was reared on the home farm, with such educational advantages as were afforded in the common schools of the locality. He was a youth of eighteen years at the inception of the Civil war and he tendered his aid in defense of the Union by enlisting, early in 1862, as a member of the Eleventh Indiana Cavalry, with which gallant command he participated in many battles and important campaigns, it having been his fortune to receive a wound while taking part in the battle of Chickamauga. He was with his command in the battle of Fort Donelson and those of Lookout Mountain and Vicksburg, besides which he was with General Sherman on the historic march from Atlanta to the sea. In 1864 he was promoted to the office of first lieutenant, and as such he served until the close of the war, when he received his honorable discharge. After the war he returned to Indiana, to which state his parents had removed from Ohio, and in 1866 he and his half-brother, Thomas J. Griggs, each entered claim to a homestead of one hundred and sixty acres in Pawnee county, Nebraska Territory. On his pioneer homestead, seven miles southeast of the present thriving town of Liberty, Lewis T. Griggs erected a small house, the material for which he transported with team and wagon from Nebraska City. He instituted the development of his farm and in due time perfected his title to the property. In 1869 he wedded Miss Caroline Gale and soon afterward they established their residence at Beatrice, which was then a mere frontier village. On the site of the present Beatrice National Bank he had a little store in which he engaged in the handling of agricultural implements and machinery, and here he continued his successful operations in this line of enterprise until 1883, when he removed with his family to Atchison, Kansas, where he became a representative of one of the leading harvesting machine companies, the death of his wife having there occurred in 1885. Soon afterward he returned to Beatrice, and thereafter he was a traveling salesman for agricultural implements until 1888. In that year he removed to Newcastle, Wyoming, prior to the extension of the railroad to that locality, and there he became a successful exponent of stock-raising industry, with which he continued to be identified until his death, which occurred November 11, 1908. He was one of the influential pioneers of Weston county, Wyoming, where he served as clerk of the court and also as county attorney, he having studied law previously and having been admitted to the bar in the early '70s. At Newcastle, Wyoming, he engaged in the practice of his profession, as one of the leading members of the bar of Weston county, and in a fraternal way he was affiliated with the Masonic fraternity, the Independent Order of Odd Fellows, the Knights of Pythias, and the Grand Army of the Republic, in which last named organization he was a charter member of Rawlins Post, at Beatrice. His wife was born in the western part of Massachusetts and was reared by kinsfolk, members of the Gale family having been numbered among the early settlers of Gage county. Coming to this county prior to the admission of Nebraska to the Union, Mrs. Griggs became one of the early and popular teachers in the village schools of Beatrice, she having been, in fact, one of the first teachers thus rendering service in the little frontier village that has become one of the attractive and prosperous cities of the state. She was forty-two years of age at the time of her death, June 13, 1883, and was a devoted member of the Methodist Episcopal church. Upon coming to Gage county, in 1867, Mrs. Griggs, two years prior to her marriage, entered a homestead claim, and a considerable part of this property is now included in the Glenover addition to the city of Beatrice.

Kirk Griggs, immediate subject of this review, was born in a house that stood on the site of the present Beatrice high school building, and his youthful education was gained in the schools of this city and those of Newcastle, Wyoming, where the family home was established when he was a lad of twelve years. That he profited by these advantages is shown by the fact that he proved himself eligible for pedagogic honors and was for six months engaged in teaching in a rural school in Wyoming. In that state he remained on his father's extensive cattle ranch until he had attained to the age of twenty years, and for sixteen years thereafter he was successfully identified with railroad construction enterprise, with Kilpatrick Brothers and later with the McArthur Company, leading New York contractors in this line of enterprise. His first service was in the capacity of stenographer, but later he became allied closely with the practical executive details of construction work, in which connection he organized camps of workmen, acted as auditor and superintendent and proved in all ways a vigorous and resourceful executive.

In 1913 Mr. Griggs purchased of his former employers, Kilpatrick Brothers, his present fine landed estate in his native county, and in the same year he erected his present modern and attractive residence, at a cost of six thousand dollars. His farm is one of the best improved and most effectively equipped of all in the county, and on the same he has two artesian wells, the while his modern facilities including a gas-lighting system for his house. After his return from the west Mr. Griggs purchased the house of his birth, in the city of Beatrice, and this property he finally sold to the board of education as a site for the present modern high school building. A man of thought and action, Mr. Griggs has become one of the representative agriculturists and stock-growers, as well as a popular and representative citizen of his native county. His political support is given to the Republican party and he is serving at the time of this writing as a director of school district No. 22. Both he and his wife are active members of the Christian church.

June 12, 1901, recorded the marriage of Mr. Griggs to Miss Mabel C. Pyrtle, the younger of the two children of James and Nancy E. (Murphy) Pyrtle, the former of whom was born in Missouri, in 1847, and the latter in Indiana, on the 15th of September, 1852. Mrs. Griggs, prior to her marriage, had been for five years a successful and popular teacher in the schools of Gage county, her work including four years' service in the city schools of Beatrice. Mr. and Mrs. Griggs have four children—Theodore, Roger, Gale, and Jessie M.

HENRY FISHBACH.—Under the general communal conditions and exigencies of the present day no city can claim definite metropolitan facilities if there has been failure to provide proper accommodations for the conserving of food stuffs, and Beatrice is signally favored in this respect, as the city takes just pride in the excellent service given by the large and modern plant of the Beatrice Cold Storage Company, of which Henry Fishbach was the founder and of which he has continuously been the executive head. In establishing this important enterprise Mr. Fishbach demonstrated alike his civic loyalty and his progressiveness as a business man, and through his careful and effective administration the business has been developed from a modest inception to one of large volume and definite success.

Mr. Fishbach was born at Franklin Grove, Lee county, Illinois, on the 16th of October, 1859, and is a son of Philip and Catherine (Hausknecht) Fishbach, both of whom were born in the now devastated province of Alsace-Lorraine, which was then an integral part of French domain and which has again become the stage of terrible polemic activities incidental to the great war in which France is again arrayed against Germany. The parents of Mr. Fishbach were young at the time of the immigration of the respective families to America and both families established residence in the state of Illinois, in the pioneer history of that commonwealth. Philip Fishbach devoted the greater part of his active life to his trade, that of stone-cutter, and both he and his wife continued their residence at Franklin Grove, Illinois, until their death—folk of sterling character and honored by all who knew them. To the public schools of his native county Henry Fishbach is indebted for his early educational training and there he continued to reside until he had attained to the age of nineteen years, when he went to the state of Colorado and turned his attention to farm work and other service that would give him a living recompense. He remained in Colorado three years and then returned to Illinois, where he was engaged in agricultural enterprise, in Lee county, until 1884. In the year last mentioned he came to Gage county, Nebraska, and though he had virtually no financial resources he had an abundance of ambition and self-reliance, as shown by the fact that he purchased eighty acres of land, in Greenwood township, assuming indebtedness for practically the entire purchase price. The land had received but the slightest improvement, and for the first seven years of his residence on his embryonic farm Mr. Fishbach used as his house a primitive granary that had been constructed on the place. Energy and industry brought returns, and eventually Mr. Fishbach was able not only to clear himself of the burden of debt but also to add eighty acres to the area of his landed estate. He made good improvements upon his farm property, brought the greater part of the land under effective cultivation, and there continued his vigorous activities as an agriculturist and stock-grower for a period of nine years. That he had been successful is shown by the fact that in 1893, in company with his wife, he visited the great World's Columbian Exposition, in the city of Chicago, and in this connection his alert mind caused him to see an opportunity for the development of a prosperous business enterprise in his home county. His attention was called, while in Chicago, to a carload of live poultry that was being sent in for the use of consumers in the city, and he soon decided to establish himself in the poultry business in Gage county. To carry out his plans he purchased the small poultry business that had been established by a man named

Greening, at Beatrice, and two years later he removed his business to the site of his present well equipped cold-storage plant, his original place of business having been in a building that was only ten by twelve feet in dimensions. Bringing to bear his characteristic energy and good judgment and having secure place in popular confidence and good will, Mr. Fishbach caused his business to expand substantially and normally in scope and importance, and to keep pace with demands he enlarged his quarters from time to time. In 1906, as a matter of business expediency, he effected the incorporation of the Beatrice Cold Storage Company, of which he has since been the president and active manager. His plant for cold-storage is of modern type in all respects and as an important adjunct to the same he has established a plant for the manufacturing of ice, besides conducting a creamery in connection and doing also a substantial business in the manufacturing of ice cream for the trade. Natural ice is harvested to supplement the artificial supply, and the company now controls an extensive business in the buying and shipping of poultry and eggs, with branch headquarters in the Nebraska towns of Norfolk, Fremont, Columbus, Wakefield, and Blair. In connection with the Beatrice plant of the company an average of eighty-five employes is retained, and at times the roster of employes includes as many as one hundred and fifty persons. Mr. Fishbach deserves much credit for the success which he has achieved and also for having given a substantial and progressive industrial and commercial enterprise to Gage county and its judicial center. He takes loyal interest in all measures and enterprises tending to advance the civic and material progress and prosperity of his home city and county, is the owner of two of the well improved and valuable farms of Gage county, each comprising one hundred and sixty acres, and recently, in connection with the national movement for the conservation of food products, he has had the distinction of being called to the national capital for conference with the food administrator, Mr. Hoover, in connection with the poultry, egg, and cold storage business, as one of the leading exponents of these lines of enterprise in Nebraska. His advice in this conference has been of definite general value in connection with conservation policies. In politics Mr. Fishbach gives his allegiance to the Republican party, and he and his wife are earnest members of the Christian church.

As a young man of twenty-five years Mr. Fishbach wedded Miss Mary Ellen Wolf, who was born at Leaf River, Ogle county, Illinois, and she passed to the life eternal in 1895, being survived by four children, concerning whom the following brief data are entered: Ralph is the manager of the Beatrice Cold Storage Company's plant at Norfolk, Madison county, Nebraska; Eulalie, a young woman of much business ability, as well as social popularity, is treasurer of the company of which her father is president; Oscar is identified with ranching enterprise in the Canadian northwest; and Ethel is the wife of William Myers, who is associated with the Beatrice Cold Storage Company as an employe at the headquaters in Beatrice.

On the 6th of March, 1898, Mr. Fishbach contracted a second marriage, in his union with Miss Laura Peck, who was born in the state of Kansas, and their attractive home is brightened by the presence of their three children—Agnes, Bertha, and Priscilla.

HEINRICH REIMER.—Though Mr. Reimer claims the great empire of Germany as the place of his nativity he was not yet two years of age at the time of his parents' immigration to America and his entire experience has been gained in association with conditions and influences of the middle western states of the Union. He was yet an infant at the time when the family home was established in Gage county, in the pioneer days, and here he has made the best possible use of the advantages and opportunities afforded him, as is evident when it is stated that he is now numbered among the representative exponents of agricultural and live-stock industry in Blakely township, his well improved farm, of one hundred and fifty-five acres, being situated in Section 21, that township, and on rural mail route No. 1 from the city of Beatrice, which is about eight miles distant from his home.

Mr. Reimer was born in Prussia, Germany, December 13, 1874, and is a son of Bernhard and Helen (Goosen) Reimer, who became the parents of six sons and seven daughters, the father having had also two children by his first marriage. In 1876 Bernhard Reimer came with his family to the United States and engaged in farming in Iowa, but before the close of that year he came to Gage county and established the family home on a pioneer farm three miles west of Beatrice. He developed and improved this property into one of the productive farms of the county and there he continued to reside until his death, in 1896, at the age of sixty-four years, his devoted wife having passed away in 1885, at the age of forty-two years. Both were zealous members of the Mennonite church and assisted in the organization of the church of this denomination in their home district in Gage county.

Heinrich Reimer was reared under the influence of the pioneer farm and early began to lend his aid in its work, the while he profited duly by the advantages afforded in the local schools. In 1900 be rented a portion of the lands belonging to his father's estate, and a few years later he purchased his present farm, upon which he has made good improvements, including the erection of a modern barn that is thirty-six by sixty-four feet in dimensions. Thrift and enterprise have given him place among the most progressive and successful agriculturists and stock-raisers of Blakely township and he is one of the stock holders of the farmers' grain elevator in the village of Hoag. He is a Republican in politics, and he and his wife are earnest members of the Mennonite church.

April 27, 1900, Mr. Reimer married Miss Agatha Penner, who was born and reared in Gage county and who is a daughter of Rev. Gerhard Penner and Anna (Froese) Penner, her parents having been members of a sterling Mennonite colony that came from western Prussia and settled in Gage county in 1874. Mr. Penner is now pastor of the Mennonite church at Beatrice and is one of the revered pioneer citizens of Gage county. Mr. and Mrs. Reimer have one child, Gerhard, who was born October 27, 1902.

LOUIS GRAFF.—Successfully established in business in the city of Beatrice, Mr. Graff is a scion of one of the most honored and influential territorial pioneer families of Gage county and takes just pride in claiming the county as the place of his nativity. He was born on the old homestead farm of his father, Joseph Graff, in Blakely township, three miles west of Beatrice, and the date of his nativity was March 3, 1862, due record concerning the family history being given on other pages of this volume. Mr. Graff is a son of Joseph and Teresa (Meyers) Graff, and in his boyhood days he gained a full quota of experience in connection with the conditions and influences of the pioneer era in the history of this now opulent section of Nebraska. He herded cattle on the widestretching prairie, had experience in the fighting of prairie fires, and made his share of youthful inroads on the wild strawberries, plums, and gooseberries that were then plentiful in this locality. He assisted in the work of the home farm and in the meanwhile made good use of the advantages of the schools established in Blakely township by the ambitious and progressive pioneers. He remained at the parental home until he had attained to the age of twenty-six years, and he then entered the employ of his older brothers, who were engaged in the agricultural-implement business at Wymore, this county. In 1889 he purchased an interest in a well established lumber yard in the city of Beatrice, and later he became sole owner of the business, which he has since successfully continued in the original location, at 413 West Court street, where he also controls a substantial trade in the handling of coal, paints, builders' hardware, etc. He has secure vantage-place as one of the most substantial and progressive business men of the capital and metropolis of his native county and is equally well entrenched in popular confidence and esteem, as attested by the success that has attended his business activities. He is financially interested also in important cement manufacturing plants in Dallas, Texas; near Kansas City, Missouri, and at Mason City, Iowa; and he handles the products of the same in connection with his extensive business at Beatrice. Mr. Graff is the owner of fifty acres of valuable land on the Rio Grande river, in Hildridge county, Texas, and twenty acres near Lake View, Oregon. He is liberal and public-spirited in his civic attitude, is a Republican in politics, is affiliated with the Beatrice organizations of the Modern Woodmen of America, the Benevolent & Protective Order of Elks, and the Woodmen of the World, and he and his wife are communicants of the Catholic church in their home city.

February 8, 1888, recorded the marriage of Mr. Graff to Miss Elizabeth Buckley, who was born in Canada and who was a daughter of John and Mary Buckley. Her father was born in Ireland and was a young man when he came to America and established his home in

Canada, where he married and where he remained until after the death of his wife. Finally he came with his six children to Gage county, Nebraska, where he engaged in farming and where he passed the remainder of his life, his remains being interred in the Catholic cemetery, at Beatrice. Mrs. Graff passed to the life eternal on the 8th of March, 1908, and is survived by three children: Irene T. is the wife of Leo who is associated with Mr. Graff in the conducting of the lumber business at Beatrice; Joseph J. is a member of the United States aviation corps that is preparing for service in the great European war, and at the time of this writing, in the winter of 1917-1918, he is stationed at San Antonio, Texas; and Carl H., in January, 1918, passed the examination in the training camp for officers in the United States aviation service in the European war. In 1910 Mr. Graff wedded Miss Mary Buckley, a sister of his first wife, and she is the gracious chatelaine of their pleasant and hospitable home. No children have been born of this union.

JESSE L. SCHLOSSER.—At this point it is possible to accord merited recognition to another of the venerable and honored pioneer citizens of Gage county, Mr. Schlosser having been a resident of Nebraska for the past forty years and now maintaining his home in the city of Beatrice.

Jesse L. Schlosser was born in Greene county, Ohio, on the 13th of October, 1842, and in the old Buckeye state he was reared to the sturdy discipline of the farm, the while he made good use of the advantages offered by the common schools of the locality. He was still a youth at the time of the family removal to Michigan, where he continued his active association with agricultural industry, and in that state was solemnized his marriage to Miss Polly Schock, who was born at Tiffin, Seneca county, Ohio. In 1877 Mr. Schlosser came with his family to Nebraska, and, prior to the construction of a railroad, they made the overland trip with team and wagon from Falls City to Gage county. Mrs. Schlosser had received as a heritage from the estate of her father a tract of eighty acres of land in Blue Springs township, this county, and on this embryonic farm Mr. Schlosser erected as a domicile for his family a pioneer shanty, twelve by fourteen feet in lateral dimensions and provided with a "lean-to" about ten feet square. With the passing years he developed his farm and made good improvements on the same, and there he continued his active alliance with agricultural industry for twenty-two years. In the early days he hauled his wheat to Marysville, Marshall county, Kansas, two days being required to compass this overland trip, and he sold wheat at times for a price as low as thirty-five cents a bushel—a statement that is specially significant in comparison with prices demanded at the present time, when the government is putting forth every effort for food conservation, incidental to the nation's entrance into the great European war. It may further be noted that the first hogs which Mr. Schlosser raised on his farm were sold at the rate of three and one-half dollars a hundredweight.

Mr. Schlosser remained on his farm, to the area of which he had added by degrees, until about the year 1898, when he sold the property and removed with his family to Beatrice, the county seat. For three or more years thereafter he was employed in connection with the grain business conducted by William N. Spellman, and later he was similarly associated with Henry H. Norcross, whose business finally was developed into that now controlled by the Dobbs Grain Company, with which Mr. Schlosser is connected. He is a recognized authority in the grain trade, as his experience has been long and varied, and though he is now venerable in years he preserves marked vigor of mind and physical powers, so that the thought of retiring from active association with business is repugnant to him.

Mr. Schlosser is a stalwart in the camp of the Republican party and while residing on his farm he served for a number of years in the office of treasurer of Blue Springs, township. He is affiliated with the Masonic fraternity and both he and his wife hold membership in the Presbyterian church. They became the parents of one child, Carrie M., who is the wife of Dr. Clemens A. Spellman, a leading dentist of Beatrice and individually mentioned on other pages of this work.

ALBERT T. MILBURN.—He whose name initiates this paragraph is the senior partner of the Milburn & Scott Company, printers and bookbinders, and the well established business with which he is thus connected is one of the important enterprises of Beatrice. This company has an establishment of most modern facilities for the handling of all kinds of job printing and book binding, a specialty being made of the manufacturing of high-grade blank books and the handling of a general line of supplies for county offices, banks, etc., while the concern keeps in stock also a full assortment of office stationery and supplies, so that the enterprise has been extended far outside the boundaries of Gage county. Mr. Milburn has been a resident of Gage county since he was about twelve years of age and in his independent career has here found ample opportunity for the achieving of substantial success and established place as one of the representative business men of the metropolis and judicial center of the county.

Mr. Milburn was born on a farm near Chebanse, Iroquois county, Illinois, on the 22d of March, 1874, and is a son of Thomas H. and Sarah E. (Fanning) Milburn, who were born in the province of Ontario, Canada, and whose marriage was solemnized in the state of Illinois. The paternal grandfather, John Milburn was born and reared in England, whence he finally immigrated to America and established his residence in the Dominion of Canada. Later he removed with his family to the state of Illinois, where he passed the remainder of his life, his vocation having been that of farming during the greater part of his active career. George Fanning, the maternal grandfather of the subject of this review, came to America from Ireland and after having lived for a term of years in Canada he removed to Illinois, where he became a prosperous farmer and where he died at the venerable age of eighty-four years.

Thomas H. Milburn established his residence in Illinois prior to the Civil war and he was one of the early employes of the celebrated McCormick Harvester Company. Later he engaged in farming near Chebanse, that state, and through this medium he laid the foundation for his substantial success. In 1886 Mr. Milburn came with his family to Gage county, Nebraska, and established his residence at Beatrice. He purchased farm land in the county, having owned two or three different farms, and he gave his personal supervision to his farm properties in a general way, though he continued to reside in Beatrice until his death, in 1901, at the age of sixty-two years. His political support was given to the Republican party and his religious faith was that of the Methodist

Episcopal church, of which his venerable widow likewise is a devoted member, she still maintaining her home at Beatrice and the year 1918 recording the seventy-eighth anniversary of her birth. Of their three children the subject of this sketch is the younger of the two surviving, and George H. is actively identified with mercantile enterprise at Beatrice.

To the public schools of Illinois Albert T. Milburn is indebted for his preliminary educational discipline and after the family removal to Beatrice he here continued his studies until he had profited by the advantages of the high school. At the age of seventeen years he initiated his apprenticeship to the trade of book-binding, and also that of printer. He became skilled in all technical details of these lines of business and finally engaged independently in business by associating himself with others in founding the enterprise with which he is now connected and to the upbuilding of which he has given his best energies, his associates in Milburn & Scott Company being John C. Scott and Albert H. Buckman.

While unremitting in his application to business, Mr. Milburn has simultaneously stood exponent of loyal and progressive citizenship and has taken deep interest in the social and material advancement of his home city. His political views are indicated by the unwavering support which he gives to the cause of the Republican party, and as a representative of the same he was elected a member of the city council when he was but twenty-eight years of age. He held this office four years, during which he was the youngest member of the municipal body, and he did all in his power to further wise and economical administration of the city government and to promote needed public improvements. He is one of the appreciative and popular members of the local lodge of the Benevolent & Protective Order of Elks, his religious faith is that of the Methodist Episcopal church and his wife is an active member of the Presbyterian church.

In June, 1909, was solemnized the marriage of Mr. Milburn to Miss Martha McClellan, who was born and reared at Holmesville, this county, and whose father, the late Robert H. McClellan, was one of the early pioneer settlers of Gage county, where he reclaimed and improved a valuable farm and where he served for a long period in the office of justice of the peace. Mr. and Mrs. Milburn have three children—Robert, William, and Martha Virginia.

JOHN T. YULE.—In the spring of 1879 John T. Yule became associated with his honored father in the preparation of the first set of abstracts of real-estate titles for Gage county, and these initial records, as supplemented by the careful additions made in the intervening years, continue to be recognized as the ultimate abstract authorities in this county, the while John T. Yule continues actively to conduct the important abstract business in which he was the coadjutor of his father until the latter's death, on the 2d of June, 1907. He is not only one of the best known and most essentially representative citizens of Gage county but takes deep pride in the position of influence gained by his father, who was long numbered among the foremost and most honored citizens of this county, a special tribute to his memory being entered on other pages of this work, so that in the present connection is not demanded further review of the family history.

John T. Yule was born in Columbia county, Wisconsin, on the 3d of June, 1856, and is one of the two surviving children of Thomas and Mary (Todd) Yule. In his native county John T. Yule was reared to adult age and after having there availed himself of the advantages of the high school at Portage, the county seat, he followed the course of his ambition by entering the law department of the University of Wisconsin, in which he was graduated as a member of the class of 1877, his admission to the bar of his native state having been virtually coincident with his reception of the degree of Bachelor of Laws. He served a brief professional novitiate by engaging in the practice of law at Portage, but within a year after his graduation he accompanied his parents on their removal to Beatrice, Nebraska, where the family home was established in May, 1879. Here Mr. Yule did not find it expedient to engage in the work of his profession, but he became closely associated with his father in the extending of financial loans on real-estate security and also in the important work of compiling from the county records the first complete set of books containing concise and authoritative abstracts of title to all realty in the county. Later they expanded their abstract business into other counties in this section of the state, as well as into adjoining sections of Kansas, and the business became one of extensive and important order, its cumulative ramifications having continued to the present time and the subject of this sketch having continued in full control of the enterprise since the death of his father. He maintains his well appointed offices in the Drake building, and so admirably has all work been systematized that the most absolute efficiency of service is given by this pioneer abstract institution, the records being kept constantly up to date, by the proper entrance of data concerning every real-estate transaction in the county. In connection with his long and active association with this line of enterprise Mr. Yule has found his knowledge of the law of inestimable value, though he has not engaged actively in the practice of the profession for which he so carefully prepared himself. By virtue of his intellectual and business ability he is well fortified for leadership in popular sentiment and action and he has been active and influential in the local councils of the Republican party, though never manifesting any ambition for political preferment in an official sense. His civic loyalty has been of insistent and helpful order and he has given effective service both as city clerk and city treasurer of Beatrice. Through his business activities he has contributed his quota to the civic and industrial progress of his home city and county and he commands the unqualified esteem of all who know him. He and his family are active members of the Presbyterian church.

On the 24th of October, 1877, was solemnized the marriage of Mr. Yule to Miss Emma Shattuck, who was born at Moundsville, Marshall county, West Virginia, and who was a girl at the time of the family removal to where she was reared and educated. Mr. and Mrs. Yule became the parents of eleven children, and concerning the nine now living the following brief record is given in conclusion of this review: Alice is the wife of James R. Robinson, who is engaged in the automobile business at Ennis, Texas; Lucille is the wife of C. R. Taylor, of Beatrice; Laura is the wife of Dale Chapman, of this city; Thomas K. is successfully and extensively engaged in the sheep-growing business in Colorado, with residence at Fort Collins, and it may be noted that in the season of 1917 he fed on his ranch twenty-one thousand head of sheep and lambs; Mary is employed as cashier in a leading meat market in Beatrice; Miriam and Mildred hold responsible positions in business offices in their home city; Hattie holds a clerkship in a local mercantile establishment; and Arlene is the youngest of the number, she being at the parental home, as are also the other unmarried daughters, the family being one of marked popularity in the representative social activities of Beatrice.

JOHN B. FULTON, M. D.—To no man should be accorded a higher degree of honor than to the skilled and loyal physician and surgeon who has given years of earnest and effective service in the alleviation of human suffering and distress, and to Dr. Fulton is uniformly accorded this honor in Gage county, where he has lived and labored unselfishly and devotedly in the work of his humane profession and where, as a pioneer physician and surgeon, he lived up to the full tension of exacting service demanded of him in the early days, when he traversed the country over a radius of many miles, in summer's heat and winter's rigorous blasts, often finding his way on horseback over almost impassable roads and even across the prairie where no roads were defined—and all this in his zeal to aid those who made call for his ministrations. Though he has now passed the eightieth mile-stone on the journey of life, he retains splendid mental and physical vigor, keeps in touch with the advances in his profession and responds frequently to the calls made for his ministrations on the part of families to which he has given such service during the course of many years. A man of strength and honor, he has been the friend and benefactor of humanity, and it may well be understood that he is held in reverent affection in the county that has so long represented his home and been the stage of his able and sympathetic services. Thus historic consistency is conserved in according to him a tribute in this publication, and even this brief record must bear its measure of lesson and inspiration.

Dr. John Blythe Fulton was born in Highland county, Ohio, on the 9th of June, 1833, and is a son of William and Catherine (Baskin) Fulton, the former a native of Pennsylvania and the latter of Ireland. The paternal grandparents of Dr. Fulton were born in Ireland and were numbered among the sterling pioneers of Pennsylvania. William Fulton, father of the Doctor, was reared and educated in the old Keystone state and thence went to Ohio, where he became a pioneer farmer in Highland county, both he and his wife there continuing their residence until they were summoned from the stage of their mortal endeavors—secure in the respect and esteem of all who knew them.

Under the sturdy and invigorating discipline of the home farm Dr. Fulton waxed strong of brain and brawn during the period of his childhood and youth, and his alert and receptive mind caused him to profit fully by the advantages afforded in the common schools of the locality and period. He supplemented this training by a course of higher study in Hillsboro Academy, a well ordered institution in his native county, and in preparation for the work of his profession he went to the state of Pennsylvania, where he prosecuted his technical studies under effective preceptorship and earnestly fortified himself for his exacting and responsible vocation. He began his professional novitiate in Pennsylvania, later removing to Fairbury, Livingston county, Illinois, and there he continued in active and successful general practice for the long period of twenty-one years. Gracious were the environment and associations which he there forsook to number himself among the pioneer representative of his profession in Nebraska, to which state he came in 1879, somewhat more than a decade after its admission to the Union. He established his home at Beatrice, the judicial center of Gage county, the now beautiful little city having then been a straggling frontier village, and in those days he was one of only three physicians in the county, the other two who were his contemporaries in this pioneer prestige having been Dr. Webb and Dr. Huff, both of whom have passed to the life eternal.

Dr. Fulton was earnest and indefatigable in his professional ministration during the pioneer epoch and in the latter years of opulent prosperity and progress, and in the early days he made a remarkably successful record in the treatment of the all prevalent fever from which the settlers suffered. The Doctor is an optimist by very nature and his altruism has always been on a parity with his abiding human sympathy, so that it may well be understood that his ministrations have been beneficent in the bringing of cheer as well as in relieving physical ailments. Aside from slight lameness, due to the improper adjustment of a broken hip when he was a youth, Dr. Fulton is still active and vigorous, the years resting lightly upon him and his lines being cast in pleasant places, as he lives and moves among a people who accord to him affectionate regard and hold him always as *persona grata*.

Dr. Fulton has been a leader in popular sentiment and action in Gage county during the many years of his residence within its borders and has been found aligned as a stalwart advocate of the principles and policies for which the Democratic party has ever stood sponsor in a basic way. He has for many years maintained affiliation with the Masonic fraternity, and while he was reared in the faith of the Presbyterian church, of which his father was an elder for forty years, his personal study and research have in later years led him to endorse many of the tenets of the spiritualistic faith.

In 1882 Dr. Fulton purchased two blood hounds and for thirty-six years he has maintained the "Beatrice Bloodhound Kennels," widely known for their effectiveness in breeding, raising, and training bloodhounds for use in tracing and locating criminals. The dogs are trained and managed by the Doctor's son, Richard, familiarly known as "Dick," who has a wide reputation as a detective. In the kennels are, in the spring of 1918, twenty or more animals, and at various times the number of hounds in these celebrated kennels has been as high as forty. A market for these animals is found all over the United States and in foreign countries, and high prices are paid for the animals.

As a young man of about twenty-nine years Dr. Fulton wedded Miss Sarah Phipps, who was born in Pennsylvania, a daughter of Judge David Phipps, and she passed to the life eternal in the year 1903. Of this union were born nine children, of whom eight are living, and concerning them the following brief data are available; Mary Maggie is the wife of W. W. Johnston, of Omaha, Nebraska; Oliver P. is engaged in the real-estate business in Beatrice; Belle is the widow of A. D. Butt, of Los Angeles, California; Thos. B. is associated with the Beatrice *Sun* and has been engaged in the newspaper business for thirty years; William S. is a successful sign painter in Beatrice; Hattie is the wife of J. H. Simon, of Boston, Massachusetts; Richard maintains his residence in Beatrice; Jesse E. died at the age of about thirty-five years; and Fitch B. is a talented artist, now a resident of the state of California.

In contracting a second marriage, Dr. Fulton wedded Miss Emily May, a daughter of one of the early clergymen of the Methodist church in Nebraska. No children have been born of this marriage.

FRANK E. LEFFERDINK.—Banking enterprise in Gage county numbers among its successful and popular exponents of the younger generation Frank E. Lefferdink, who is giving effective service in the position of cashier of the Farmers & Merchants' Bank of Wymore.

Mr. Lefferdink was born in Lancaster county, Nebraska, on the 16th of September, 1885, and his parents now maintain their residence at Hickman, that county, where his father is living virtually retired. William Lefferdink was born near the city of Amsterdam, Holland, in the year 1847, and was reared and educated in his native land. In 1868, about the time of attaining to his legal majority, he came to the United States. He passed the ensuing year in Wisconsin and then, in 1869, came to Nebraska, a state that had been admitted to the Union only two years previously. In Lancaster county he obtained a homestead claim of eighty acres, and he was so deeply impressed with the advantages and attractions of the new commonwealth that he soon returned to his native land and induced eighty of his fellow countrymen to come likewise to America and acquire for themselves government land in Nebraska. Later he made a second trip to Holland, and on his return he was accompanied by one hundred and thirty-two earnest and industrious Hollanders, who became colonists in the vicinity of Hickman, Nebraska. He was thus primarily instrumental in gaining to Lancaster county a goodly contingent of most valuable citizens, as the Hollanders are known for their frugality, industry, and effective methods of intensive farming—not an inch of ground being by them permitted to go to waste in the matter of productiveness. William Lefferdink merits from Nebraska enduring gratitude for his efforts in bringing to the state in the early period of its history a valuable element that has been conspicuous in the development and advancing of the agricultural interests of this now opulent commonwealth. Mr. Lefferdink was a carpenter by trade, and as an able contractor and builder he assisted in the erection of many buildings in the city of Lincoln in the early days when the fine capital city contained not more than twelve or thirteen buildings. With the passing years he added to his landed estate and gained substantial prosperity, so that, as the shadows of his earnest and useful life begin to lengthen from the golden west, he is enjoying well earned peace and comfort in the attractive home which he has provided in the village of Hickman.

While residing in Wisconsin William Lefferdink wedded Miss Anna Port, who was born in that state, in 1850, her parents having been pioneers of Wisconsin, where they continued to reside until their death and where the father was a farmer by vocation. William and Anna (Port) Lefferdink became the parents of seven children, concerning whom brief mention may be consistently made at this point: Dena is the wife of William Smith, a prosperous farmer in western Nebraska; Nellie is the wife of Richard Schutte, who has charge of one of her father's farms near Hickman, Lancaster county; Henry is a retired banker and resides in the city of Lincoln; Emma is the wife of Alfred Christopher, a farmer near Ashton, South Dakota; Frank E., of this review, was the next in order of birth; William is cashier of the State Bank of Hadar, Pierce county, Nebraska; and Cornelius is cashier of the State Bank of Calumet, Iowa.

Frank E. Lefferdink acquired his early education in the public schools of his native county, and this discipline included a course in the high school in the city of Lincoln. He was graduated in the high school as a member of the class of 1904, and thereafter he completed a course in a business college in the capital city, with special attention given to the theory and practical work of banking. In his initial experience in connection with the banking business he was employed two and one half years at Platte, South Dakota, and thereafter he held for a short period the office of president of the State Bank of Denton, Lancaster county, Nebraska. Prior to coming to Wymore, Gage county, he had been employed two years in the Farmers' Savings Bank of Gaza, Iowa, a position from which he retired to assume that of cashier of the Farmers' & Merchants' Bank of Wymore. Of this office he has been the incumbent since November 20, 1916, and within his tenure of this executive position the deposits of the bank have increased from one hundred and thirty thousand to two hundred and thirty-six thousand dollars—a definite testimonial to his ability and effective executive policies.

In politics Mr. Lefferdink gives his allegiance to the Republican party, he was reared in the faith of the Dutch Reformed church, and his wife holds membership in the Lutheran church. After establishing his residence in Wymore he here erected the attractive modern house which is the family home and which is one of the beautiful and hospitable domiciles of the thriving little city. While he gives close attention to the banking business, Mr. Lefferdink has made judicious investment in valuable land in Lancaster county, this property having been purchased by him from his father.

In June, 1916, was solemnized the marriage of Mr. Lefferdink to Miss Maude Martin, who was born at Hickman, Lancaster county, her parents having been pioneer settlers in that county. Mr. and Mrs. Lefferdink have a winsome little daughter, Dorothy.

JOHN L. HERSHEY is the efficient and popular incumbent of the position of official engineer for Gage county and also the city of Beatrice, and in his chosen profession he has won a station of substantial success

Mr. Hershey was born in Monmouth, Illinois, on the 19th of September, 1881, and is a son of Samuel and Barbara Ella (Swiler) Hershey, both natives of the state of Pennsylvania, where the former was born December 6, 1843, and the latter on the 22d of September, 1850, she being a daughter of David Swiler, who removed with his family to Kansas in an early day. Samuel Hershey was reared and educated in the old Keystone state and he was a young man when he accompanied his parents on their removal to Illinois. He is a son of Jacob Hershey, who was a farmer and miller in Pennsylvania and who became a successful exponent of agricultural enterprise after his removal to Illinois, where he and his wife passed the residue of their lives.

Samuel Hershey learned in his youth the trade of carpenter and he became a successful contractor and builder in Illinois. In 1884 he came with his family to Gage county, Nebraska, and established his residence in Beatrice, where he continued his activities as a contractor and builder and had the supervision of the erection of a number of important public and business buildings, including the Gage county court house, the Beatrice postoffice and many of the attractive business blocks of the city of Beatrice. He and his wife still maintain their home in the county's metropolis and he is now in the employ of the Dempster Mill Manufacturing Company. Mr and Mrs. Hershey became the parents of five children, of whom four are living: Frances R. is the widow of Charles F. Rogers and is now a popular teacher in the public schools of Beatrice; Charles W. is in the employ of the Pacific Electric Company, in the city of Los Angeles, California; Archibald C. is engaged in the real-estate business in Los Angeles; and John L., of this review, is the youngest of the number. The children received excellent educational advantages, all attending the University of Nebraska except Charles W., who finished his education at Knox College, Galesburg, Illinois. Samuel Hershey is a Republican in politics, is affiliated with the Independent Order of Odd Fellows, and both he and his wife hold membership in the Methodist Episcopal church.

John L. Hershey, the immediate subject of this review, was about three years of age when the family home was established in Beatrice. Here he attended the public schools until he had completed the curriculum of the high school, in which he was graduated as a member of the class of 1900. In 1906 he graduated from the Engineering College of the University of Nebraska, and for two years thereafter he was employed in the construction of reinforced concrete buildings in the state, for a Lincoln firm. The next five years found him in charge of important irrigation work in Colorado and Idaho, and this experience added greatly to his practical skill in his profession. In 1913 Mr. Hershey returned to Beatrice and, as an able and experienced civil engineer, was given appointment to his present responsible position as special engineer for the city and as county engineer, in which connection he had done a large amount of important work, especially for the city of Beatrice.

In politics Mr. Hershey is a Republican, and he takes loyal interest in all things pertaining to the welfare and progress of his home city and county. He is a member of the American Society of Civil Engineers and both he and his wife hold membership in the Methodist Episcopal church.

In March, 1907, was solemnized the marriage of Mr. Hershey to Miss Mae E. Brubaker, a daughter of the late I. H. Brubaker, who was a successful farmer and grain dealer in Gage county. Mr. and Mrs. Hershey have a winsome little daughter, Martha E.

PHILIP GRAFF.—The man who can to-day qualify as a progressive and successful exponent of the great basic industries of agriculture and stock-growing as carried forward under the admirable conditions and influences provided in the state of Nebraska, may well consider himself fortunate and have full confidence that his "lines are cast in pleasant places." Gage county is favored beyond measure in the personnel of its representative farmers and stock-raisers, and as one of the specially vigorous and resourceful exemplifiers of these all-important branches of productive enterprise Mr. Graff is eminently entitled to recognition in this history. He is the owner of one of the finely improved and distinctly model landed estates of Gage county, the same comprising six hundred and eighty acres, situated in Blakely township, with service on rural mail route No. 1, from the city of Beatrice.

Mr. Graff was born in the city of Milwaukee, Wisconsin, on the 21st of May, 1857, and is a scion of one of those sterling German families that were destined to play so large and benignant a part in the development and progress of the Badger state. Mr. Graff is a son of Joseph and Theresa (Meyer) Graff, both of whom were born in Baden, Germany, where they were reared and educated, and who were married in Wisconsin. In 1854 Joseph Graff severed the ties that bound him to the German fatherland and came to America. For a few years after his marriage the family home was maintained in the city of Milwaukee, and eventually he removed to Iowa, where he worked on the river. Soon, however, he determined to cast in his lot with the Territory of Nebraska, which was then aspiring to statehood. On the 15th of April, 1860, he arrived with his family in Gage county, which at that time was little more than an unbroken prairie wilderness, Indians and all manner of wild game being still plentiful in this section of the territory. He purchased a tract of wild land in what is now Blakely township and the same constitutes an integral part of the present highly improved farm property of his son Philip, the immediate subject of this review. Joseph Graff began the breaking of his land and making it available for cultivation. This work was done with ox teams and afforded no sybaritic indulgence, as may well be imagined. Nebraska City, about sixty miles distant, was at that time the nearest trading point and many deprivations and hardships were necessarily borne by these early settlers who laid the foundation for future opulence and progress in this section of Nebraska. After Nebraska had gained the dignity of statehood he was still found vigorously employed in the improvement and cultivation of his farm, and with the passing years he made the same one of the best in the county. As prosperity attended his efforts, he erected good buildings and made other modern provisions on the homestead, and here he remained, respected by all who knew him, until his death, on the 10th of October, 1897, at the age of sixty-seven years, his devoted wife, who had been a true helpmeet, having passed to the life eternal on the 2d of June, 1894, at the age of fifty-six years. Both were devout communicants of the Catholic church and the first Catholic services to be noted in the history of the county were held in the modest log-cabin home of these honored pioneers, besides which they assisted materially in the organization of the first Catholic church in the county and in the erection of the first church edifice. They became the parents of nine children, concerning whom the following brief data are accessible: Henry died at the age of fifty-five years; Philip, of this review, was the next in order of birth; Gustav is now a resident of Pasadena, California; Caroline died in infancy; Louis is successfully established in the lumber business at Beatrice; George, John, Otto, and Frederick are deceased. Of the immediate family only two continue as residents of Gage county, as the above record indicates.

Philip Graff was three years of age at the time of the family removal to the frontier wilds of Nebraska Territory, and on the old homestead farm in Gage county he was reared under the conditions and influences of the pioneer era, so that his memory compasses the entire period in which have been wrought the marvelous progress and development in this now favored section of the state. As soon as possible the pioneers established primitive schools for their children, and in these early "institutions of learning" the subject of this sketch acquired his youthful education. From his boyhood to the present day he has continued to be closely and actively associated with the agricultural and live-stock enterprise in Gage county, and in 1898, shortly after the death of his father, he purchased the interests of the other heirs and assumed full ownership of the old home place.

PHILIP GRAFF

When but seventeen years of age Mr. Graff initiated independent enterprise in the operation of a threshing machine, incidental to the garnering of the generous harvests in this section of the state, and he has continued his active alliance with this important industrial accessory during the long intervening years. From his youth he has done all of the threshing on the old homestead, as well as on many neighboring farms, and he has owned and operated several threshing outfits, in which connection he has kept his equipment up to the best standard, his present threshing outfit being of the most modern type. In addition to giving attention to well ordered agricultural exploitation Mr. Graff has been an extensive grower and feeder of cattle and has made this an important and successful feature of his farm enterprise. His progressiveness is further shown in his being a stockholder and vice-president and treasurer of a well ordered cement manufacturing company at Bonner Springs, Kansas; the New Monarch Mining Company, of Leadville, Colorado; and also of the company operating a modern smelter at Salida, Colorado. In a local way he has extended his business and capitalistic interests by becoming one of the principal stockholders of the German Savings & Loan Company, of Beatrice, of which important financial and fiduciary organization he is now the president, his well ordered executive policies having added much to the success of the business.

Mr. Graff has not been troubled with political ambition and though he has not consented to appear as a candidate for public office and is independent of strict partisan lines in politics, his influence and cooperation may always be counted upon in support of those things that conserve the best interests of the community, the state and the nation. He and his family are communicants of the Catholic church, as members of the parish of St. Joseph's church in the city of Beatrice, where he also maintains affiliation with the Knights of Columbus.

On the 24th of November, 1886, was solemnized the marriage of Mr. Graff to Miss Mary Meyer, who was born February 2, 1867, in Effingham county, Illinois, and who is a daughter of Joseph and Crecentia (Hiebler) Meyer, natives of Germany. The parents of Mrs. Graff came from Germany and settled in Illinois about the year 1853, and there they remained until 1870, when they came to Gage county, Nebraska, and settled on a farm in Blakely township, where they passed the remainder of their lives. In the concluding paragraph of this review is given brief record concerning the children of Mr. and Mrs. Graff:

Josephine is the wife of George H. Sullivan, a successful carpenter and contractor at Beatrice; Edwin is actively associated with his father in the work and management of the home farm; and the younger children of the ideal family home circle are Theresa, Linda, Hugo, and Harold.

JAMES E. BEDNAR.—It is gratifying to the publishers of this history to offer with in its pages recognition of James E. Bednar, a native son of Gage county, who is honoring the county in his effective services as a member of the Nebraska bar. He is now successfully engaged in the practice of his profession in the city of Omaha, as junior member of the firm of Ringer & Bednar, with offices in the First National Bank Building. Mr. Bednar is a son of the late Albert Bednar, an honored Gage county pioneer to whom a memoir is dedicated on other pages of this volume.

James E. Bednar was born on the family homestead in Sicily township, Gage county, September 28, 1882. As a boy and youth Mr. Bednar contributed his due quota to the work on the home farm, and after having availed himself of the advantages of the district schools, he continued his studies in the high school at Wymore. He defrayed the expenses incidental to acquiring his higher academic training and his professional education largely through his own resources. He taught the Sunny Side district school in Lancaster county prior to entering the University of Nebraska, was graduated from the University of Nebraska, in 1907, with the degree of Bachelor of Arts, but continued his service in the pedagogic profession for a short time as instructor in rhetoric and debating in the high school at Beatrice, Nebraska. In the meanwhile he was but working definitely along the course of his ambitious purpose, which was to prepare himself for the legal profession. Finally he was matriculated in the law department of his alma mater, the University of Nebraska, and from this department he was graduated in June, 1910, with the degree of Bachelor of Laws and with virtually coincident admission to the bar of his native state. Shortly afterward he formed a professional partnership with J. Dean Ringer, with whom he has since continued to be associated in the practice of law in the city of Omaha, under the firm title of Ringer & Bednar. He has proved resourceful and successful both as a trial lawyer and well fortified counselor and is now serving his second year as deputy county attorney of Douglas county.

In politics Mr. Bednar accords staunch allegiance to the Democratic party. In the time honored Masonic fraternity he has completed the circle of the Scottish Rite to the thirty second degree, besides being affiliated also with the Ancient Arabic Order of the Nobles of the Mystic Shrine. Both he and his wife hold membership in the Presbyterian church. On the 16th of June, 1910, the same day he received his long coveted sheepskin from the college of law, was solemnized the marriage of Mr. Bednar to Britania Daughters, who was born at Mooreshill, Indiana, but who at the time was a student in the graduate college of the University of Nebraska. Mr. and Mrs. Bednar have two children—James E., Jr., born October 13, 1911, and Bryce Renwick, born August 3, 1916.

ELBERT J. DOLE, who is a leading photographer in Nebraska's capital city, is a of a family that has been specially prominent and honored in Gage county, as is shown by reference to the review of the life of his mother, Mrs. Sophia H. Dole, of Beatrice, the founder of the Dole Floral Company, of which also is given specific record in this volume.

Elbert J. Dole was reared and educated in Gage county and thus is fully entitled to personal recognition in this history. He was born in Seward county Nebraska, December 3, 1877, and he was about nine years old when the family home was established in the city of Beatrice, judicial center of Gage county. Here he continued his studies in the public schools until he had completed a course in the high school, in which he was graduated as a member of the class of 1898. Soon afterward he took up the study of the photographic art, and in the same he has become a recognized expert and successful professional exponent of the photographic business. He has in the past been employed in some of the best studios both in Beatrice and Lincoln, as well as by the State Journal Company, and his experience in his chosen profession has been wide and varied. Since 1912 he has conducted in the capital city of Nebraska his present handsomely appointed and thoroughly modern photographic studio, at 1125 O street, and his large and representative patronage denotes alike his professional skill and his personal popularity. Mr. Dole is affiliated with the Knights of Pythias and he and his wife hold membership in the Christian church.

In 1904 was solemnized the marriage of Mr. Dole to Mrs. Sadie Crumpton, who was born in the state of Ohio and who was a resident of Lincoln, Nebraska, at the time of their marriage. They have no children.

ELWOOD BIGLER.—Prominent among those whose successful activities are potent in upholding the commercial prestige of the city of Beatrice is Elwood Bigler, who here conducts a substantial and prosperous general hardware and implement business, the same having been established in 1896, under the firm title of Jacob Bigler & Son. He has conducted the enterprise in an individual way, under his own name, since 1907. His honored father, who was senior member of the original firm, was a resident of the city of Lincoln, this state, at the time of his death, in 1898.

Mr. Bigler was born in Hardin county, Ohio, on the 23d of November, 1865, and is a son of Jacob and Margaret (Runyan) Bigler, the former of whom was born in the fair little republic of Switzerland, in 1838, and the latter of whom was born in the state of Ohio, in 1842. Jacob Bigler was reared and educated in his native land and was a young man when he came to the United States. He found employment in connection with navigation activities on the Mississippi river, with headquarters in the city of New Orleans, and he was on the last packet boat that passed up the river prior to the outbreak of the Civil war. His loyalty to the Union was marked by decisive action, as he enlisted in a regiment of volunteers that was organized in the city of St. Louis, and was with his command in numerous engagements, including the battle of Wilson's Creek, Missouri, in 1861—an engagement in which the gallant General Lyons met his death. After the war Mr. Bigler turned his attention to agricultural pursuits, and he was engaged in farming in Hardin county, Ohio, for some time prior to 1869, the year that was marked by his removal with his family to the new state of Nebraska. He settled on a pioneer farm near Crete, Saline county, in 1869, and there he continued his successful activities as an agriculturist and stock-grower until the Centennial year, 1876, when he was elected sheriff of Saline county. At that period the office of sheriff was no sinecure in Nebraska, for the state had an undue quota of lawless and incorrigible men within its borders, but Mr. Bigler gave so effective an administration in his county that he was continued as the incumbent of the shrievalty for six consecutive years, the ensuing two years finding him giving equally effective administration in the office of county clerk. After his retirement from this position he engaged in the hardware business at Crete, that county, where he remained until 1887, when he removed to Imperial, the judicial center of Chase county, where he established himself in the hardware and lumber business. He developed a large and prosperous enterprise in these lines and continued his residence at Imperial until 1895, when he removed to Lincoln, the capital city of the state, where he thereafter lived virtually retired until his death, which occurred in 1898. He was one of the sterling pioneers who contributed a generous quota to civic and material progress and prosperity in Nebraska and he commanded the high regard of all who knew him. His venerable widow now resides in the home of her son Elwood, subject of this review, and in addition to receiving the utmost filial solicitude she is graciously compassed by many friends who pay to her tribute as one of the noble pioneer women of this now favored commonwealth. Three children survive the honored father and of the number the subject of this sketch is the youngest; William T. is a resident of Casper, Wyoming, and Mrs. Rosa B. Reed resides in Aurora, Illinois.

Elwood Bigler was a lad of about three years at the time of the family removal to Nebraska. He was reared to adult age in Saline county, and was one of a few scholars in the first school established in that county. He profited by the advantages of the pioneer schools and early began to assist his father in the latter's varied business operations. In 1896 he became associated with his father in the establishing of a well ordered hardware business at Beatrice, and of the enterprise he assumed full charge, his father having been at the time a resident of Lincoln, as previously noted. He is now one of the leading exponents of the general hardware trade in Gage county, his well equipped store being situated at 400 Court street and each department of the same being well stocked at all times, so that the most efficient service is always given to the large and appreciative patronage.

Mr. Bigler takes loyal interest in all things touching the civic and material welfare and progress of his home city. He accords staunch allegiance to the Democratic party and does his part in the furtherance of its cause. In the time-honored Masonic fraternity he has received the thirty-second degree of the Ancient Accepted Scottish Rite, his maximum York Rite affiliation being with Mount Herman Commandery of Knights Templar, besides which he is a member of the Ancient Arabic Order of the Nobles of the Mystic Shrine. In his home city he is likewise a popular member of the lodge of the Benevolent & Protective Order of Elks and the aerie of the Fraternal Order of Eagles.

In 1909 was solemnized the marriage of Mr. Bigler to Miss Nellie B. Swartz, who was born in Brown county, Kansas, and who was a resident of Beatrice at the time of her marriage. Mr. and Mrs. Bigler have no children.

JAMES G. LAWRENCE.—In Gage county, Nebraska, not to know James G. Lawrence is virtually to argue oneself unknown, for this sterling pioneer citizen of Nebraska has served as assistant postmaster at Beatrice for fully thirty years, his incumbency having continued under the administrations of eight different postmasters, including John R. McCann, who is now in tenure of this office and who is individually mentioned on other pages of this publication. Mr. Lawrence came to Nebraska shortly after attaining to his legal majority, and that he gained his quota of pioneer experience is assured by the fact that he here established his residence in 1871, about four years after the territory had gained the dignity of statehood. He has done specially efficient service as an educator and was one of the efficient and popular representatives of the pedagogic profession in Nebraska in the early days, as well as in later years. Known and honored for his character and service, his circle of friends is coincident with that of his acquaintances and it is gratifying to be able to accord him recognition in this history.

A scion of sterling New England colonial stock, Mr. Lawrence was born in the city of Clinton, Worcester county, Massachusetts, on the 3d of February, 1850, and is a son of James S. and Caroline (Lowe)

Lawrence, the former of whom was born at Harvard and the latter at Clinton, both in Worcester county, Massachusetts. James S. Lawrence learned in his youth the trade of comb-maker, and for many years he was employed as shipping clerk in the Foster & Lawrence wholesale furniture house in the city of Boston. He later engaged independently in comb manufacturing at Clinton, Massachusetts, and through this medium he achieved definite success and prestige, both he and his wife having continued their residence at Clinton until their death and both having been zealous members of the Congregational church, in which connection it may be noted that during the period of his residence in the city of Boston Mr. Lawrence maintained membership in the historic old Winthrop church of this denomination. The subject of this review was the third in order of birth in a family of six children, and concerning the others the following brief data are available: Oscar is in the service of the municipal government of Worcester, Massachusetts; John is a prosperous farmer near Northboro, Worcester county, Massachusetts; Charles and Caroline are twins, the former being a resident of Northboro, Massachusetts, and the latter the widow of Harrison P. Fay, maintaining her home at Nanuet, New York, where her husband had been principal in the public schools; and the sixth child, a son, died in infancy. From the above record it will be discerned that of the immediate family James G. Lawrence is the only representative in the west, and his loyalty to Nebraska is on a parity with his appreciation of the historic old commonwealth of which he is a native son.

Mr. Lawrence is indebted to the public schools of his native city for his early educational discipline, and there he was graduated in the high school as a member of the class of 1868. Soon afterward he became a clerk in the postoffice at Clinton, and there he served as assistant postmaster for two years. In 1871, at the age of twenty-one years, he came to the new state of Nebraska and after visiting Beatrice, which was then a mere village, he made his way to Thayer county, where he entered claim to a homestead of one hundred and sixty acres of virgin land. He remained on the place until he had perfected his title thereto and later he disposed of the property. Mr. Lawrence soon found opportunity for making effective use of his ability as a teacher, and for a number of years he taught in the public schools of Thayer and Gage counties. After his marriage Mr. Lawrence returned to the east and engaged in comb manufacturing at Clinton, Massachusetts, but after an experience of two years he was unable to resist the lure of the vital and progressive west and accordingly returned to Beatrice, where he gave his attention to teaching in the county schools until he was appointed assistant postmaster, in 1887, under the administration of President Cleveland. He has held this position during the long intervening years, his original appointment having been made under the regime of Samuel E. Rigg as postmaster, and it may well be understood that each successive incumbent has placed high and fully justified estimate upon the value of his services, for no man in Gage county has a wider acquaintance with its people and none has so comprehensive a grasp upon all details pertaining to the administration of the postoffice business in Beatrice, where his service has kept pace with the march of civic and material development and progress that has made Beatrice one of the vital and prosperous cities of the state. A man of broad mental ken, strong in his convictions and unequivocally loyal and public-spirited as a citizen, Mr. Lawrence is unfaltering in his allegiance to the Democratic party and has been prominent in its local councils in Gage county. He is affiliated with the Modern Woodmen of America and attends and supports the Christian church, of which his wife was an active member.

On the 25th of December, 1878, Mr. Lawrence wedded Miss Laura E. Pheasant, whose father, the late Edward Pheasant, was one of the representative pioneers of Gage county, where he became the owner of a large tract of land and developed the same into a well improved and valuable property. In conclusion is entered brief record concerning the children of Mr. and Mrs. Lawrence: Harold E. is assistant superintendent of the Dempster Mill Manufacturing Company, of Beatrice; Clifford J. remains at the parental home; James E. is city editor of the Lincoln *Daily Star*, in the capital city of Nebraska, and he has been very successful as a representative of newspaper work, even as he showed his ambition and resourcefulness by defraying almost entirely through his own efforts the expenses incidental to his course in the University of Nebraska, in which he was graduated; he married Miss

Helen Graves, of Lincoln, and they have one child, Helen E.; Esther, the only daughter now living, was graduated in the Beatrice high school and since the death of her mother, which occurred November 23, 1917, she has taken the latter's place in the family home; Ruth, the youngest child, died at the age of eleven years.

JOSEPH HEBEL, who owns and resides upon a fine farm estate of two hundred and forty acres in Section 6, Paddock township, is a representative of one of the sterling pioneer families of Nebraska, and in his independent career he has well maintained the honors of the family name, both in the matter of loyal citizenship and also through his productive activities in connection with agricultural industry.

Mr. Hebel was born in Bohemia, Austria-Hungary, and the date of his nativity was January 3, 1858. He is a son of Joseph and Mary (Machova) Hebel, who likewise were born and reared in Bohemia, the former having been born in 1833 and the latter in 1840. In 1869 Joseph Hebel, Sr., immigrated with his family to America and in the same year he numbered himself among the pioneers of the new state of Nebraska. Prior to coming to the United States Mr. Hebel had served eleven years in one of the governmental military organizations of his native land. Upon coming to Nebraska he obtained a homestead claim in Saline county, and upon this wild prairie tract he built as a home for his family a primitive dug-out of the type common to the early pioneer days. This rudimentary building had a roof that was thatched with hay, and the only floor was the earth. On this pioneer farm Mr. Hebel continued his sturdy activities for ten years, at the expiration of which, in 1879, he came to Gage county and established a home on a tract of one hundred and sixty acres that is now in Section 7, Paddock township, the land having originally been a part of the Otoe Indian reservation, which had but shortly before been opened to settlement. Here Mr. Hebel continued his farm operations with vigor and success until he was called from the stage of his mortal endeavors, his death having occurred in 1889. His widow subsequently contracted a second marriage and she now resides at Wilber, Saline county, she being a devout communicant of the Catholic church, as was also Joseph Hebel, her first husband. Mr. and Mrs. Hebel became the parents of twelve children: Joseph is the immediate subject of this review; James was a resident of Rawlins county, Kansas, at the time of his death; Annie is the wife of Lewis Rathbun, of Glenwood township, Gage county; Charles likewise is a resident of this county; Mary is the wife of John Cacek, of Paddock township; Nettie is the wife of Joseph Synovec, of Paddock township; Robert is a resident of Fairbury, Jefferson county; Mary is the wife of Joseph Turhlicka, of Glenwood township, Gage county; and the other four children died when young.

He whose name introduces this review was a lad of ten years at the time of the family immigration to the United States and he was reared under the conditions and influences that marked the pioneer period of Nebraska history. As a boy and youth he herded cattle and worked on his father's farm in Saline county, and in the meanwhile he attended school when opportunity afforded. He was a sturdy youth of about twenty years when he accompanied his parents on their removal to Gage county, and before he had attained to his legal majority he purchased one hundred and twenty acres of land in Paddock township, this being the homestead place on which he has resided during the long intervening years. When he came into possession of this embryonic farm not a furrow had been turned on the land and no improvement had been made in any way, as the tract had but recently been placed on the market, as a part of the former Otoe Indian reservation. Within the forty years of his residence on this farm Mr. Hebel has made excellent improvements upon the place, as he has erected good farm buildings and given other distinct evidences of his progressiveness and good judgment. The passing years have brought to him a generous measure of prosperity, as attested by the fact that he has gradually added to his holdings until he now owns a valuable farm property of two hundred and forty acres. This achievement and success represent the tangible results of his own well directed efforts and unflagging industry.

As his wife and helpmeet Mr. Hebel chose Miss Mary Fitte, who was born in Bohemia, March 8, 1862, and who was twelve years of age when she came with her parents to the United States. She was a daughter of Michael and Anna Fitte, who were numbered among the early settlers of Saline county, Nebraska, and who now reside in the village of Swanton, that county. Mrs. Hebel was called to the life eternal on the 12th of September, 1908, and concerning the children the following brief record is consistently entered: Emma is the wife of Frank Vanosek, of Glenwood township; Minnie is the wife of Emil Novotny, of the same township; Kate is the wife of Frank Fleisleber, likewise of Glenwood township; Nellie is the wife of Philip Graff, of Sicily township; and Annie, Mattie, and Augusta remain at the paternal home.

Joseph Hebel is one of the highly respected pioneer citizens of his community, and he is always ready to give his influence and support to any cause tending to advance the best interests of the county in which he has maintained his home for more than forty years. In politics he maintains an independent attitude and votes for men and measures that meet the approval of his judgment. He has for eighteen years given efficient and valued service as treasurer of his school district, and has been influential in bringing the educational work of the district up to its present high standard.

Reverting to his many youthful experiences in connection with pioneer life in Nebraska, Mr. Hebel relates that on one occasion he accompanied his father on foot from the home in Saline county to Nebraska City. When night came they asked for lodging at a farm house, but no place could be found to accommodate them. They then attempted to sleep on a pile of straw in the barnyard, but they became so cold that they had to arise and travel on. They covered on foot the entire distance of eighty-five miles between their home and Nebraska City, and on their return trip they were more fortunate in obtaining a night's lodging, as they were given a place on the floor of a pioneer farm house and provided with a covering of sheep pelts. This is but one of many incidents which Mr. Hebel recalls concerning the conditions of the early days.

HENRY WILLIAMSON.—A resident of Gage county for nearly forty years, Mr. Williamson proved himself specially energetic and resourceful in his productive activities as an exponent of farm industry in this section of the state, and he developed one of the valuable farm properties of Glenwood township. He finally retired from the old homestead to establish his residence in the city of Beatrice, but a life of ease had no allurement for him and he has here proved again his success-proclivities by engaging in the coal business, in which line of enterprise he controls a large and representative trade—based alike on fair and honorable dealings and upon his unqualified personal popularity in the community. A share of pioneer honors attaches to his name and achievement and consistency is observed when he is here accorded recognition as one of the representative citizens of Gage county.

Mr. Williamson was born at Dixon, Lee county, Illinois, on the 6th of December, 1855, and is a son of John and Margaret (Uhl) Williamson, the former a native of Ireland and the latter of the state of Maryland, where their marriage was solemnized. In the early '50s John Williamson and his wife enrolled themselves as pioneers of Lee county, Illinois, to which section of the state they made their way from Chicago by means of team and wagon. In that county Mr. Williamson purchased, at the rate of one dollar and twenty-five cents an acre, a tract of land that is now worth more than two hundred dollars on acre. He continued to give his close attention to the reclamation and development of his farm until the outbreak of the Civil war brought to him the call of higher duty. In response to President Lincoln's first call, he enlisted, early in 1861, as a private in Company A, Seventy-fifth Illinois Volunteer Infantry. He proceeded with his command to the front, took part in the various engagements in which it was involved up to and including the battle of Missionary Ridge, in which engagement he was captured by the enemy. He was incarcerated as a prisoner of war in the famous Libby Prison of odious memory, and there it was his to endure the horrors and privations that made the name of that Confederate prison-pen infamous in the annals of history, besides which he made the supreme sacrifice in behalf of the cause for which he had enlisted, as he died while in Libby Prison, in November, 1863. His widow survived him by more than twenty years and was a resident of Carroll, Carroll county, Iowa, at the time of her death, on the 31st of January, 1887. They became the parents of six children, of whom four are living: George, a painter by trade and vocation, resides at Odell, Gage county, Nebraska; Lydia is the widow of E. L. Burkett, and maintains her home at Beaver Crossing, Seward county, this state; Henry, of this review, was the next in order of birth;

and Anna is the wife of C. C. Collins, who is engaged in the lumber business at Oak Park, Illinois. The honored father espoused the cause of the Republican party at the time of its organization and as a man and citizen he commanded the high regard of all who knew him. His father, George Williamson, likewise came from Ireland and became an early settler and prosperous farmer of Illinois, where he passed the remainder of his life. Peter Uhl, maternal grandfather of the subject of this review, likewise became one of the pioneer farmers of Illinois, where he remained until the close of his life. Mrs. Margaret (Uhl) Williamson bravely and unselfishly devoted herself to the care and rearing of her children after the untimely death of her husband, and she exemplified the truest and noblest traits of gracious womanhood, her religious faith having been that of the Methodist Episcopal church.

Henry Williamson was a lad of about eight years at the time of his father's death and soon afterward he became a member of the family circle of his uncle, Henry Uhl, a farmer near Dixon, Illinois. He remained with his uncle until he had attained to his legal majority and in the meanwhile profited by the advantages afforded in the schools of the locality. Soon after attaining to his legal majority Mr. Williamson went to the city of Keokuk, Iowa, where he completed a course in the Baylies Business College. For two years thereafter he was engaged in the grain and coal business at Carroll, Iowa, and in the spring of 1880, shortly before his marriage, he came to Gage county, Nebraska. He had first come to this county in 1872 and had purchased a tract of land in the southern part of the county—at the rate of three dollars an acre. At that time the railroad came only to Beatrice and from this point he had to go twenty-five miles on horseback to look over the land which he purchased.

On this embryonic farm of one hundred and sixty acres, in Section 30, Glenwood township, Mr. Williamson instituted improvements and he had provided a comfortable house before bringing his bride to the new home. Mr. Williamson developed his original farm into one of the valuable properties of the county and became specially successful in his well ordered activities as an agriculturist and stock-grower. While on the farm he was prominent in community affairs, served as justice of the peace and also as school director, and he continued his active association with farm industry until 1910, when he removed to the city of Beatrice. Here he lived retired for one year and he then engaged in the coal business, with which he has since continued his active and successful association. He handles also wood, tankage, and oil meal, and his business is of substantial order in all departments. Mr. Williamson is still the owner of a well improved landed estate in Gage county, his farm being in Midland township, near Beatrice, and comprising eighty acres. He is the owner also of a farm of one hundred and sixty acres in southeastern Kansas, and of another tract, of four hundred and eighty acres, in Washington county, that state. He has been in the most significant sense the founder and builder of his prosperity, as he had neither financial reinforcement or influential friends to aid him when he set forth as a youth to gain for himself independence and advancement. As a representative of livestock industry in this section of Nebraska Mr. Williamson did much to improve the type of cattle raised, and he exhibited on more than one occasion fine cattle at the international stock shows in the city of Chicago. In this connection it should be noted that the handsome silver cups which he was awarded on his exhibits of fine cattle are the only trophies of the sort held by a citizen of Nebraska. He specialized in the breeding and growing of fine Hereford cattle and of this stock he shipped a load to Chicago in December, 1907 where his exhibit gained not only a large silver cup but also a prize of three hundred dollars in cash. Later he received a silver cup on the exhibit which he made in the city of Denver, where further recognition was given in his being awarded a cash prize of seven hundred dollars. On his farms Mr. Williamson is now giving special attention to the raising of Hampshire swine, and he has more than four hundred head of these hogs yearly on his Gage county farm. Mr. Williamson is found staunchly aligned as a supporter of the cause of the Republican party, he is affiliated with the Masonic fraternity, and both he and his wife are active members of the Christian church in their home city.

On the 1st of April, 1880, was solemnized the marriage of Mr. Williamson to Miss Nellie A. Faxon, who was born in Whiteside county, Illinois, on the 21st of February, 1859, a daughter of John W. and

Asenath (Olds) Faxon, who established their home in Gage county in 1880, and who here passed the residue of their lives, the father having become one of the substantial farmers of the county. Mr. and Mrs. Williamson have four children: George F. is now employed by a concern engaged in the handling of school supplies in the city of Lincoln, he having been graduated not only in the University of Nebraska, but also in historic old Columbia University, in New York city; John H. has the active management of his father's fine farm near Beatrice; Rhetta is the wife of R. O. Parks, of Beatrice; and Nellie remains at the parental home.

THOMAS E. HIBBERT.—As a sterling pioneer citizen, a veteran of the Civil war, and as a member of the Nebraska legislature, the late Hon. Thomas E. Hibbert left a deep and benignant impress upon the history of the state in which he established his residence prior to its admission as one of the sovereign commonwealths of the Union, and this history of Gage county exercises a consistent function when it accords a tribute to his memory.

Mr. Hibbert was born in the city of Philadelphia, Pennsylvania, in the year 1846, and he was one of the honored pioneer citizens of Gage county, Nebraska, at the time of his death, which here occurred on the 3d of March, 1905. The paternal grandparents of Mr. Hibbert were born and reared in England and upon coming to America they settled in Wayne county, Pennsylvania, the father of the subject of this memoir having been a lad of nine years at the time.

Thomas E. Hibbert was reared and educated in the old Keystone state, and was but fifteen years of age at the outbreak of the Civil war. His youthful patriotism was roused to responsive protest and action, for at the age noted he gallantly tendered his services in defense of the Union. He weighed at the time only one hundred and five pounds but his loyal enthusiasm was unbounded. He enlisted from Wayne county, at Salem, in Company A, One Hundred and Thirty-seventh Pennsylvania Volunteer Infantry, under Captain J. M. Buckingham and Colonel Bassert. His regiment was assigned to the Third Brigade of the Second Division of the Sixth Army Corps, General Hancock having command of the brigade, in Franklin's corps of Smith's division. Mr. Hibbert took part in the battle of Poolsville, Maryland, September 10,

1862, and engagements in which he thereafter participated may be here noted: South Mountain, September 14, 1862; Antietam, September 17, 1862, his regiment having buried almost two thousand Confederate soldiers after the battle and on the field of Antietam. From his original brigade Mr. Hibbert was transferred to the Third Brigade (Paul's), First Division (Wadsworth's), First Army Corps (Reynolds'), and with this command he took part in the battles of Fredericksburg, December 13, 1862, and Chancellorsville, April 28 to May 12, 1863, having incidentally participated in the historic "mud march" of General Burnside's command. His term of enlistment had been for ninety days, and after the expiration of the same he was mustered out, on the 6th of June, 1863. He at once re-enlisted, and was assigned to Battery C. Second Pennsylvania Veteran Artillery. Thereafter he served with the Twenty-second Army Corps in the defences around Washington until May, 1864, when he again went to the front, in the Eighteenth Army Corps. He took part in the battle of Cold Harbor, in June, 1864, and on the 12th of that month he embarked on a transport, at Whitehouse Landing and sailed down the York river to Chesapeake Bay, past old Fortress Monroe. He thence proceeded up the James river to City Point, Virginia, and on the 15th of June he was in the movement against Petersburg. His regiment made the first attack on that city and he took part in all of the engagements in which the Eighteenth Army Corps was thereafter involved, up to the time when the Twenty-fourth Army Corps was organized, when the Second Pennsylvania Veteran Artillery became a part thereof and was assigned to its Third Division. Under these conditions Mr. Hibbert continued in active service until the surrender of General Lee, after which he was engaged in provost guard duty until he was mustered out, on the 6th of February, 1866. Further details concerning the gallant military career of Mr. Hibbert have been given and the record is worthy of perpetuation in this connection, as follows: "Despite his youth, Mr. Hibbert carried the heavy musket of the Civil war days and performed in the camp and field the same service that was expected of his older comrades. At the battle of Chapin's Farm he was reported killed, but he wrote to his father to announce the fact that he was alive and well, he having been reported among the dead by reason of the fact that a shell from a gunboat had exploded so close to him that he was knocked senseless for a few moments. Within the course of his service Mr. Hibbert was tendered a commission in a regiment of colored troops. He had been color guard in his command and upon the return of the regiment to Pennsylvania he carried back its state flag, which, on July 4, 1866, he in person handed to Governor A. G. Curtis, the famous war governor of the Keystone state. This stand of colors went out in 1861 and came back in 1866. Within this long interval Confederate hands never touched these colors. In general orders Mr. Hibbert was mentioned for making the three best shots at a target with a twenty-four-pound howitzer, while serving in the defences of Washington, he having been the gunner and having sighted the piece. When the Confederates made an attack on Redoubt Carpenter, below Dutch Gap, January 25, 1865, his services were loaned to a battery of the Thirteenth New York Artillery, and he was complimented for the assistance rendered by his howitzer in repulsing the enemy."

In 1866, after the close of his war service. Mr. Hibbert came to the Territory of Nebraska and entered claim to a homestead in Gage county, this place being in Section 13, Hooker township, and having been by him reclaimed and improved into one of the valuable farm properties of the county. On this homestead he passed the remainder of his long and useful life, and here his death occurred March 3, 1905, his widow still remaining on the old homestead, which is endeared to her by many hallowed memories and associations.

In politics Mr. Hibbert was a stalwart Republican and he gave yeoman service in the advancement of the party cause. He was influential in public affairs in Gage county and represented the same several terms in the lower house of the Nebraska legislature. He retained vital interest in his old comrades and manifested the same through his active affiliation with the Grand Army of the Republic.

On the 19th of March, 1874, was solemnized the marriage of Mr. Hibbert to Miss Nannie E. Fuller, of Adams, this county, her father having been an honored pioneer of Gage county, where both he and his wife passed the closing period of their lives. Mr. Fuller was of English lineage and birth, and was a child when he accompanied his parents to the United States. The parents were residents of Wayne county, Pennsylvania, for many years and there their death occurred. In the concluding paragraph of this memoir is given brief record concerning the children of Mr. and Mrs. Hibbert:

THOMAS E. HIBBERT

Guy is now a resident of Spearville; Kansas; Ila E. likewise lives at Spearville; Roscoe C. continues his residence in Gage county and lives in the village of Adams; Thomas E. resides at Crab Orchard, Johnson county, and Benjamin H. at Alliance, Box Butte county; Martha C. is the wife of Melvin Liggett, of Alliance, this state; James G. is perpetuating the patriotic spirit of his honored father, as he has become a member of the great national army that is being prepared for participation in the European war, he being, in the spring of 1918, a member of Company A, Three Hundred and Fifty-fifth Regiment, stationed at Camp Funston, Kansas; George D. remains with his widowed mother on the old home farm; Anna Josephine died April 6, 1877; Charles Edward passed away January 30, 1880; and Mary Pearl died February 17, 1880.

JACOB W. WIEBE.—This substantial farmer and honored citizen of Blakely township is a representative of the fine element of German citizenship that has exercised such beneficent influence in connection with the civic and industrial development of Gage county, and he is the owner of a well improved farm of one hundred and sixty acres, in Section 15 of the township mentioned.

Mr. Wiebe was born in Prussia, Germany, on the 29th of August, 1864, and is a son of Jacob and Emeline (Penner) Wiebe, his father having been a farmer by vocation and having been a comparatively young man at the time of his death. The subject of this sketch attended school in his native land until he was fourteen years of age, when he came with his widowed mother, his elder brother and his only sister to the United States, the family home being established in Gage county, where the two young sons found employment at farm work. The little family thus came to the county in 1878 and here the devoted mother remained until the summer of 1883, when she returned to her native land for a visit. Her health was impaired at the time and she did not live to rejoin her children, as her death occurred in 1884, while she was still in Prussia, she having been nearly fifty years of age at the time. Mrs. Wiebe was one of the pioneer representatives of the Mennonite faith in Gage county and was most earnest and zealous in church work.

After having been employed six years at farm work in this county Jacob W. Wiebe became associated with his brother, Henry J., of whom mention is made on other pages, in the renting of a farm, and his energy and ability brought to him success in these independent activities as an agriculturist and stock-grower. In 1896 he purchased his present homestead farm, upon which he has made excellent improvements of a permanent order and which he has brought up to a high state of productiveness. He remodeled the house and has also brought other buildings on the farm into good order, and he planted a goodly number of trees on the place, many of the same being now of large size and adding materially to the attractions of the homestead. Mr. Wiebe has not neglected his civic responsibilities while furthering his individual prosperity, but has given his influence in support of legitimate measures and enterprises tending to advance the general welfare of the community. He is a stockholder in the grain elevator at Hoag and is a substantial citizen who commands unqualified popular esteem. He is an independent Republican in politics and he and his family are zealous adherents of the Mennonite church, in the affairs of which they are actively interested.

The marriage of Mr. Wiebe to Miss Agatha Penner was solemnized November 16, 1899. She was born in Prussia and is a daughter of Johannes and Magdalena (Penner) Penner, who established their home in Gage county in 1877. Mrs. Penner passed to the life eternal in 1911, at the age of sixty-three years, and her venerable husband, who celebrated in 1917 his seventy-seventh birthday anniversary, now resides in the village of Hoag, this county. Of their five children who attained to maturity Mrs. Wiebe is the eldest. The pleasant home of Mr. and Mrs. Wiebe still claims as members of the family circle all of their children, namely: Harry, Edwin, John, Louis, and Richard, but one child, Anna, died when young.

JOHN RIECHERS. — Through enterprise and excellent management Mr. Riechers has gained distinctive success in connection with business affairs and is now established in the general merchandise business in the village of Clatonia, his ample and well appointed store receiving a representative supporting patronage and the stock in each department, including that devoted to furniture, being kept up to the standard of the trade requirements. Mr. Riechers has been a resident of Nebraska since boyhood and prior to entering the mercantile business he had been actively identified with agricultural industry in Gage county.

Mr. Riechers was born in Lafayette county, Wisconsin, on the 30th of May, 1873, and is the only child of Herman and Margaret (Helms) Riechers, he having been an infant at the time of his mother's death.

Herman Riechers was born in the province of Hanover, Germany, September 29, 1844, and was one of the honored citizens of Gage county,

Nebraska, for many years prior to his death, which here occurred in 1909. He was reared and educated in his native land and in 1865 he came to America in company with his brother Justus. Both established residence in Wisconsin, where their parents joined them two years later, to pass the remainder of their lives as sterling pioneer citizens of the Badger state. In Wisconsin Herman Riechers continued his productive activities as a farmer until 1883, when he came with his family to Nebraska and settled on a farm three miles west of Clatonia, Gage county. He purchased a half-section of land in Saline county and became one of the progressive and successful agriculturists and stock-growers of the county, besides which he added to his landed estate by purchasing three hundred and twenty acres just across the line in Gage county, in 1892. He was a man of strong and upright character and at all times commanded the high regard of his fellow men, his religious faith having been that of the Lutheran church. About the year 1875 Mr. Riechers contracted a second marriage, when Miss Sophia Hillman became his wife, she likewise being a native of Hanover, Germany, and having become a resident of Wisconsin about two years prior to her marriage. She now resides in the village of Clatonia, where she celebrated in 1917 the seventieth anniversary of her birth. Of this second marriage were born three sons and three daughters, all of whom survive the honored father: Diedrich owns and resides upon a part of his father's old homestead farm, three miles west of Clatonia; Herman is engaged in the hardware business at Clatonia; Grover is conducting a prosperous business as a dealer in agricultural implements, in the same village; Mrs. Emma Hunecke likewise resides in Clatonia; Mrs. Louisa Kock is a resident of Clay Center, Kansas; and Mrs. Nora Kracke and her husband maintain their home on an excellent farm five miles southwest of Clatonia.

John Riechers gained his rudimentary education in the district schools of his native county and was a lad of ten years at the time of the family removal to Nebraska. Here he found ample demands upon his youthful attention in connection with the work of the home farm, the while he made good use of the advantages of the public schools of the locality. In 1896 he rented land from his father and began independent operations as an agriculturist and stock-grower, but in 1899 he removed to Clatonia, where for the ensuing ten years he was engaged in the farm implement business. In 1909 he sold his well established business to his brother Grover, after which he here conducted a prosperous furniture business until 1914, when he amplified the scope of the enterprise by installing a stock of general merchandise, the efficient service given in his establishment combining with his personal popularity to make the business one of substantial and representative order. In politics he gives loyal support to the cause of the Democratic party and he served four or five terms as treasurer of Clatonia township. Both he and his wife are earnest communicants of the German Lutheran church in their home village.

December 26, 1895, recorded the marriage of Mr. Riechers to Miss Margaret Hereth, who was born in Bavaria, Germany, daughter of John and Anna Hereth, who established their home in Gage county in 1883, the father being now deceased and the widowed mother being a resident of the state of Washington. Mr. and Mrs. Riechers have four children— Rosa, Amelia, Herbert, and Anita.

WILLIAM A. MULLIGAN, B. D., the honored rector of Christ church, Protestant Episcopal, in the city of Beatrice, was born in Ontario, Canada, on the 10th of March, 1863, and is a son of William and Lucy (Montgomery) Mulligan, the former a native of the Province of Ontario, Canada, and the latter of Ireland. The parents of William Mulligan came to America from the north of Ireland and settled at Port Hope, Ontario, Canada the father becoming a prosperous farmer of that province and he and his wife having there passed the residue of their lives. William Mulligan long held precedence as one of the substantial exponents of agricultural industry in Victoria county, Ontario, and was a citizen of no little prominence and influence in his community. Both he and his wife were devout communicants of the Church of England. Of the five children the subject of this review is the eldest: John H. is a retired farmer residing in Ontario, Canada; Thomas lives on his father's old homestead farm, in Victoria county, Ontario; Alexander, a resident of Superior, Wisconsin, is in the government service, having been for fifteen years an attache of the customs service; Mary is the wife of William Carty, of Bobcaygeon, Canada.

Rev. William H. Mulligan acquired his early education in the public schools of his native province and his higher academic training through Trinity College, Toronto, and has a Bachelor of Divinity degree from Seabury Divinity School, of Minnesota. Father Mulligan was ordained to the priesthood at Detroit, Michigan, by Rt. Rev. Thos. F. Davies, D.D., bishop of the diocese of Michigan, and his first pastoral incumbency was that of assistant rector of St. James church at Sault de Ste. Marie, Michigan, where he remained six years. He then assumed the charge of Ascension church at Ontonagan, Michigan, and in the following year the entire town was virtually destroyed by fire, the Episcopal church edifice having been reduced to ashes in this conflagration. In the same year, 1896, Father Mulligan came to Beatrice, where he has since labored with all of consecrated zeal and devotion as rector of Christ church, the spiritual and temporal work of the parish having been vitalized and prospered under his earnest regime, and his status being that of one of the able and representative clergymen of the Protestant Episcopal church in the Nebraska diocese.

Father Mulligan has the vigor and civic loyalty that make him a leader in community thought and action and he is one of the honored and valued citizens of the Gage county metropolis. The church of which he is rector has a membership of two hundred and fifty and all departments of parish work are in excellent order. In connection with the affairs of the parish Father Mulligan issued a monthly church paper, the *Message*. He is a Republican in his political allegiance and is affiliated with the Masonic fraternity.

In 1889 was solemnized the marriage of Father Mulligan to Miss Mary Williams, who likewise was born and reared in the Province of Ontario, Canada, and whose father, Thomas Williams, was a prosperous farmer in the state of Michigan at the time of his death. In conclusion is given brief record concerning the children of Father and Mrs. Mulligan: Harold R. is an efficient and popular teacher in the high school in the city of Omaha, besides being athletic director of the school, and incidentally he is pursuing a course of study in the medical department of the University of Nebraska; Stella is a teacher in the public schools of Beatrice; Allan is a member of the class of 1920 in the medical department of the University of Nebraska; Edna K. is attending the school for trained nurses that is connected with the Clarkson hospital in the city of Omaha; Frederick A. is a member of the class of 1918 in the Beatrice high school; and Ernest A. and Arthur M. are likewise students in the high school.

FREDERICK O. McGIRR is one of the youngest men that has thus far been called upon to serve as a commissioner of the supreme court of Nebraska, and his appointment to this high office not only gave significant recognition of his fine professional attainments but also reflected distinction upon Gage county, where he was reared to manhood and where he had gained secure vantage-ground as a representative member of the bar of this part of the state. Prior to his elevation to his present office, involving his removal to Lincoln, the capital city of Nebraska, he had been for more than twenty years engaged in the successful practice of his profession in the city of Beatrice, and on this score alone he is entitled to special recognition in this history, as is he likewise by reason of his being a scion of one of the sterling pioneer families of Gage county. Of the McGirr family a further record is given on other pages of this work, in the sketch dedicated to Dr. John I. McGirr, brother of him whose name initiates this paragraph.

Judge Frederick O. McGirr was born in Kankakee county, Illinois, on the 11th of December, 1870, and there received his earlier educational discipline in the public schools and was fifteen years of age at the time of the family removal to Nebraska. Here be continued to attend the public schools until he had completed the curriculum of the high school, and in preparation for the work of his chosen profession he began reading law under the able preceptorship of Robert W. Sabin, a leading member of the bar of Gage county and its capital city. Through close application he made rapid progress in the absorption and assimilation of the science of jurisprudence, and he was admitted to the bar on the 20th of June, 1893. He served his professional novitiate in Beatrice and his character and ability soon enabled him to build up a substantial practice. In 1907 he formed a professional partnership with Menzo W. Terry, under the firm name of McGirr & Terry, and this alliance continued until December, 1912. In 1908 Judge McGirr was elected prosecuting attorney of Gage county, and of this office he continued the incumbent four years, retiring therefrom in January, 1913, after a forceful and able administration that inured greatly to the advancing of his professional prestige. He then resumed the practice of his profession, with a substantial and representative clientage, and continued as one of the leading members of the Gage county bar until June, 1915, when he was appointed a member of the supreme court commission of the state, for a term of two years. He assumed the duties of this office September 20, 1915, and at the expiration of his first term he was re-appointed, for another term of two years, on the 20th of September 1917. It is needless to say more than that on the bench he has fully justified the wisdom of his appointment and that he has shown the true judicial temperament, as well as a broad and accurate knowledge of law and precedent.

Judge McGirr is one of the honored members of the Nebraska State Bar Association, is a vigorous and effective advocate of the principles and policies of the Democratic party, for which he has done yeoman service in various campaigns, and he is affiliated with the Independent Order of Odd Fellows and the Benevolent & Protective Order of Elks, in each of which he has held various official chairs.

On the 20th of December, 1899, Judge McGirr wedded Miss Mary Moody, daughter of Samuel S. Moody, a pioneer merchant of Beatrice, where he was successfully established in business for many years. He had also conducted a mercantile business at Peru, Nemaha county, and it was while the family home was there maintained that Mrs. McGirr was born, she being one of the gracious and popular native daughters of Nebraska. Judge and Mrs. McGirr have no children.

HOMER B. AUSTIN, who died at his home, in the city of Beatrice, on the 12th of April, 1906, was an honored pioneer of the Territory of Nebraska and of Gage county, his character and his work having been such that a tribute to his memory properly finds place in this publication. In offering such a memoir it is but fitting that liberal and slightly modified quotation be taken from an appreciative estimate that appeared in a Beatrice newspaper at the time of his demise.

Mr. Austin was born at Austinburg, Ashtabula county, Ohio, in 1830, and there he was reared to manhood on his father's farm, in the meanwhile attending the common schools when opportunity afforded. In 1853 he wedded Miss Mary A. Dunbar, of Camden, Oneida county, New York, and in 1857 he joined the initial tide of immigration moving toward Nebraska Territory, his wife and infant son joining him in the following year. From the article that appeared in a local paper at the time of his death are made the following extracts: "He chose Gage county as his place of residence and selected a claim on Town creek, east of the present village of Pickrell and in the neighborhood of the Pethouds, the Joneses, the Wilsons, Judge Hiram W. Parker and other old friends from Ohio who were pioneers in the new territory. His claim joined the one occupied by Judge Parker, and a warm intimacy, cemented by trials, privations and dangers of pioneer life and destined to be broken only by death, sprang up between the two families. After spending a few years on his claim Mr. Austin returned with his family to Ohio, but in 1884 he returned to the west and established his residence in Washington county, Kansas, where he remained until 1895, when he returned to Gage county and established his home in Beatrice, where he passed the remainder of his life, the death of his devoted wife having here occurred in 1897, and the remains of both rest in the beautiful cemetery at Beatrice. He was survived by one son, Charles N., of whom mention is made on other pages, and by a cousin, L. E. Austin, who was a resident of Beatrice at the time of his death, in 1909, and who is survived by two sons—Lewis Benjamin, a resident of Kansas City, Missouri, and Edward, who is in the aviation service of the United States. Edward S. Austin, another cousin of Homer B., likewise became one of the very early settlers of Gage county, and he erected one of the first grist mills in the county. At a point eight miles north of Beatrice he laid out a little village, to which was given the name of Austin, and here he had charge of the pioneer postoffice which depended for mail service on the facilities afforded by the overland pony express. Edward S. Austin passed the remainder of his life in Gage county and here developed a valuable farm estate. The subject of this memoir assisted in the erection of the first saw mill in the little village of Beatrice.

"Though never taking an active part in public affairs Homer B. Austin was a public-spirited citizen, and up to the hour of his death was a useful and exemplary member of society. He was sober and industrious and in all of the relations of life was scrupulously honest. He was a man of strong feeling and deep emotion and although a good friend, when once his anger or resentment was aroused he was apt to be as implacable in his hatred as he was true and loyal in his friendships. By nature he was deeply religious. He believed, with a constancy and devotion that nothing could disturb, in the existence of a spiritual world, and that this is a higher and holier world than that which our poor senses apprehend. For many years this good man has been a familiar figure upon the streets of Beatrice, and it is no exaggeration to say that many in this community will learn of his demise with genuine sorrow."

It may well be said that in all of the relations of life Mr. Austin exemplified the faith that makes faithful, and as he was true to himself, so was he true to those who came within the circle of his kindly and generous influence.

WILLIAM F. ALBERT.—He whose name initiates this paragraph merits recognition as one of the representative agriculturists and stock-growers of his native county and also as a scion of one of the honored pioneer families of this favored section of the state. His well improved farm of one hundred and fifty-six acres, in Section 22 Clatonia township, is that on which he was born and reared, and his progressiveness and enterprise are further signalized in his ownership of three hundred and twenty acres of valuable land in South Dakota. A tribute to his honored father, Henry Albert, appears on other pages of this work, so that further review of the family history is not demanded in the present connection.

On the fine homestead farm which he now occupies William Frank Albert was born January 25, 1874, and in addition to receiving in his youth the advantages of the public schools of Clatonia township he also completed an effective course in a business college in the city of Lincoln. He has never wavered in his allegiance to the great fundamental industries of agriculture and stock-raising and he purchased his father's old homestead farm in 1906. He has here made excellent improvements of a permanent order, including the erection of his present modern and attractive residence. Prior to buying the old home farm he had successfully conducted a horse ranch for a period of about five years, and at the present time he amplifies his farm enterprise by doing a prosperous business as a buyer and shipper of live stock. He stands exponent of loyal and liberal citizenship and though he has had no ambition for political preferment of any kind he accords staunch allegiance to the Republican party.

On the 26th of February, 1902, Mr. Albert wedded Anna Carstens, who likewise was born and reared in this county, where her parents established their home more than forty years ago. Mrs. Albert is a daughter of Tebbe G. and Scente (Gerdes) Carstens, whose marriage was solemnized at Rushville, Illinois, March 2, 1870, and who became residents of Gage county in 1876. Mr. Carstens was born in Hanover, Germany, March 4, 1846, a son of John and Gesche (Aschen) Carstens, the latter of whom died in Germany and the former of whom passed the closing years of his life in Gage county, where two of his sons established homes in the pioneer days. Upon immigrating from his native land to America, in 1867, Tebbe G. Carstens settled in Illinois, and there he continued his active association with agricultural pursuits until 1876, when he came with his family to Gage county. Here he farmed on rented land for the first four years, and he then purchased eighty acres in Section 10, Clatonia township. Later he added eighty acres to his landed estate and he continued as one of the energetic and successful farmers of Clatonia township until 1904, when he and his wife established their residence in the village of Clatonia, where he has since lived virtually retired. Mrs. Carstens was born at Scheindorff, Germany, April 24, 1847, a daughter of Joachim A. and Steinten W. (Rademacher) Gerdes, who passed their entire lives in Germany. Mrs. Carstens came to America in 1869 and her marriage occurred the following year, as previously noted in this sketch. Mr. and Mrs. Carstens became the parents of five children, concerning whom the following brief data are available: Gesiene, who became the wife of Edward Krauter, is deceased; Joachim and John M. are residents of Fairbury, Jefferson county, Nebraska; Mrs. Anna Albert was the next in order of birth; and William G. has the active management of his father's old homestead farm. Mr and Mrs. Albert have three children—Melvin, Verneita, and Kermit.

www.ingramcontent.com/pod-product-compliance
Lightning Source LLC
Chambersburg PA
CBHW020414010526
44118CB00010B/253